THE BLACKWELL ENCYCLOPEDIA OF MANAGEMENT

HUMAN RESOURCE MANAGEMENT

THE BLACKWELL ENCYCLOPEDIA OF MANAGEMENT

SECOND EDITION

Encyclopedia Editor: Cary L. Cooper
Advisory Editors: Chris Argyris and William H. Starbuck

Volume I: *Accounting*
Edited by Colin Clubb (and A. Rashad Abdel-Khalik)

Volume II: *Business Ethics*
Edited by Patricia H. Werhane and R. Edward Freeman

Volume III: *Entrepreneurship*
Edited by Michael A. Hitt and R. Duane Ireland

Volume IV: *Finance*
Edited by Ian Garrett (and Dean Paxon and Douglas Wood)

Volume V: *Human Resource Management*
Edited by Susan Cartwright (and Lawrence H. Peters, Charles R. Greer, and Stuart A. Youngblood)

Volume VI: *International Management*
Edited by Jeanne McNett, Henry W. Lane, Martha L. Maznevski, Mark E. Mendenhall, and John O'Connell

Volume VII: *Management Information Systems*
Edited by Gordon B. Davis

Volume VIII: *Managerial Economics*
Edited by Robert E. McAuliffe

Volume IX: *Marketing*
Edited by Dale Littler

Volume X: *Operations Management*
Edited by Nigel Slack and Michael Lewis

Volume XI: *Organizational Behavior*
Edited by Nigel Nicholson, Pino G. Audia, and Madan M. Pillutla

Volume XII: *Strategic Management*
Edited by John McGee (and Derek F. Channon)

Index

THE BLACKWELL ENCYCLOPEDIA OF MANAGEMENT

SECOND EDITION

HUMAN RESOURCE MANAGEMENT

Edited by
Susan Cartwright
*Manchester Business School,
University of Manchester*

First edition edited by
Lawrence H. Peters, Charles R. Greer,
and Stuart A. Youngblood

© 1997, 1999, 2005 by Blackwell Publishing Ltd
except for editorial material and organization © 2005 by Susan Cartwright

BLACKWELL PUBLISHING
350 Main Street, Malden, MA 02148-5020, USA
9600 Garsington Road, Oxford OX4 2DQ, UK
550 Swanston Street, Carlton, Victoria 3053, Australia

The right of Susan Cartwright to be identified as the Author of the Editorial Material in this Work has been asserted in accordance with the UK Copyright, Designs, and Patents Act 1988.

All rights reserved. No part of this publication may be reproduced, stored in a retrieval system, or transmitted, in any form or by any means, electronic, mechanical, photocopying, recording or otherwise, except as permitted by theUKCopyright, Designs, and Patents Act 1988, without the prior permission of the publisher.

First published 1997 by Blackwell Publishers Ltd
Published in paperback in 1999 by Blackwell Publishers Ltd
This volume published with the Second Edition in 2005 by Blackwell Publishing Ltd

2   2006

Library of Congress Cataloging-in-Publication Data

The Blackwell encyclopedia of management. Human resource management.—2nd ed. / edited by Susan Cartwright.
   p. cm.— (The Blackwell encyclopedia of management ; v. 5)
Rev. ed. Of: The Blackwell encyclopedic dictionary of human resource management. 1997.
   Includes bibliographical references and indexes.
   ISBN 1-4051-1697-8 (hardcover : alk. paper)
1. Personnel management—Dictionaries. 2. Management—Dictionaries. I. Title: Human resource management. II. Cartwright, Susan, 1951–. III. Blackwell Publishing Ltd. IV. Blackwell encyclopedic dictionary of human resource management. V. Series.
   HD30.15.B455 2005 vol. 5

[HF5549.A23]
658′.003 s—dc22
[658.3/0
2004004338

ISBN 13: 978-1-4051-1697-8 (hardcover : alk. paper)

ISBN for the 12-volume set 0-631-23317-2

A catalogue record for this title is available from the British Library.

Set in 9.5 on 11pt Ehrhardt
by Kolam Information Services Pvt. Ltd, Pondicherry, India
Printed and bound in the United Kingdom
by TJ International Ltd, Padstow, Cornwall

The publisher's policy is to use permanent paper from mills that operate a sustainable forestry policy, and which has been manufactured from pulp processed using acid-free and elementary chlorine-free practices. Furthermore, the publisher ensures that the text paper and cover board used have met acceptable environmental accreditation standards.

For further information on
Blackwell Publishing, visit our website:
www.blackwellpublishing.com

Contents

Preface	vi
About the Editors	vii
List of Contributors	viii
Dictionary Entries A–Z	1
Index	441

Preface

When the original volume of the *Blackwell Encyclopedia of Management: Human Resource Management* was published in 1996, it provided a credible and comprehensive compilation of the important topics and terms in human resource management (HRM). The original editors, Larry Peters, Bob Greer, and Stuart Youngblood, are to be congratulated on their enormous efforts in achieving such a well-respected and authoritative publication and for securing the contributions of so many world-class scholars in the field. Their work has provided a strong foundation for this new revised volume. As well as a print edition, this second edition will be available online, hosted by EBSCO Publishing alongside their Business Source Premier Database.

The revised volume incorporates an increased number of entries, with approximately 150 new or significantly revised contributions. These new entries have been chosen to reflect emergent topics and terms during the intervening years and include entries relating to workplace bullying, emotional intelligence, virtual organization, balanced scorecard, and generation X. A significant number of country entries have been revised in light of recent social, economic, and political developments and include an extensive new entry for China. In total there are now in excess of 600 entries involving more than 240 contributors. To reflect the continued international nature of the field, most of the new contributors to this volume have come from Europe.

Editing this volume has been an interesting and challenging task and could not have been achieved without the efforts and support of others. Firstly, I would like to thank my long-time colleague, Cary Cooper, co-editor of the Blackwell Encyclopedia of Management, for providing me with this challenge. The staff at Blackwell, Rosemary Nixon, Bridget Jennings, and Karen Wilson, are to be thanked for their expertise and support, as well as Brigitte Lee for seeing the book through its copy-editing and proofing stages with such patience.

I am also extremely grateful to Susannah Robertson who worked on this project for many months as my editorial assistant. Her organizational skill and attention to detail were invaluable in managing the enormous amount of information this project entailed. My thanks also go to my secretary, Cath Hearne. Finally, I am very grateful to all the contributors for providing their expertise and responding so positively to my requests, and often short time scales.

Susan Cartwright

About the Editors

Editor in Chief
Cary L. Cooper is based at Lancaster University as Professor of Organizational Psychology. He is the author of over 80 books, past editor of the *Journal of Organizational Behavior*, and Founding President of the British Academy of Management.

Advisory Editors
Chris Argyris is James Bryant Conant Professor of Education and Organizational Behavior at Harvard Business School.
William Haynes Starbuck is Professor of Management and Organizational Behavior at the Stern School of Business, New York University.

Volume Editor
Susan Cartwright is Professor of Organizational Psychology at the Manchester Business School, the University of Manchester. She is currently an Associate Editor of the *British Journal of Management*, Chair of the British Academy of Management and past editor of *Leadership & Organization Development Journal*. She is the author of over 40 scholarly articles and 13 books and has an international reputation for her work in the area of human aspects of mergers and acquisitions.

Contributors

Roy J. Adams
McMaster University

George M. Alliger
State University of New York, Albany

Richard D. Arvey
University of Minnesota

Ronald A. Ash
University of Kansas

James T. Austin
Ohio State University

Timothy T. Baldwin
Indiana University

David B. Balkin
University of Colorado

Greg J. Bamber
Griffith Business School

Steve H. Barr
North Carolina State University

Richard W. Beatty
Rutgers University

P. B. Beaumont
University of Glasgow

Hadyn Bennett
University of Ulster

Nancy A. Bereman
Wichita State University

H. John Bernardin
Florida Atlantic University

Leonard Bierman
Texas A&M University

Stewart Black
University of Michigan

Richard S. Blackburn
University of North Carolina

R. Ivan Blanco
Barry University

Matthew C. Bloom
University of Notre Dame

Walter C. Borman
University of South Florida

John W. Boudreau
Cornell University

David E. Bowen
Arizona State University

Brian K. Boyd
Arizona State University

David W. Bracken
University of South Florida

Michael T. Brannick
University of South Florida

James A. Breaugh
University of Missouri

List of Contributors

J. William Breslin
Harvard University

Robert D. Bretz, Jr.
University of Iowa

Elmer H. Burack
University of Illinois at Chicago

Michael J. Burke
Tulane University

John F. Burton, Jr.
Rutgers University

Mark C. Butler
San Diego State University

Donald J. Campbell
National University of Singapore

Robert L. Cardy
Arizona State University

Susan Cartwright
Manchester Business School, University of Manchester

Wayne F. Cascio
University of Colorado at Denver

Georgia T. Chao
Michigan State University

James R. Chelius
Deceased

David J. Cherrington
Brigham Young University

Jeanette N. Cleveland
Pennsylvania State University

Gwen Coats
State University of New York, Albany

Adrienne Colella
Texas A&M University

Lisa M. Collings
Harris Methodist Health Services

Fang Lee Cooke
Manchester Business School, University of Manchester

William N. Cooke
Wayne State University

Annette Cox
Manchester Business School, University of Manchester

James A. Craft
University of Pittsburgh

David W. Cravens
Texas Christian University

Joel E. Cutcher-Gershenfeld
Michigan State University

Robert C. Dauffenbach
University of Oklahoma

Jannifer David
University of Minnesota Duluth

Helen L. De Cieri
Monash University

John T. Delaney
University of Iowa

John E. Delery
University of Arkansas

Beverly DeMarr
Michigan State University

Angelo S. DeNisi
Texas A&M University

Robert L. Dipboye
Rice University

Gregory H. Dobbins
Deceased

List of Contributors

Peter J. Dowling
University of Tasmania

George F. Dreher
University of Indiana

Randall B. Dunham
University of Wisconsin-Madison

James B. Dworkin
Purdue University

Ståle Einarsen
University of Bergen

Ellen A. Fagenson-Eland
George Mason University

Charles H. Fay
Rutgers University

Daniel C. Feldman
University of South Carolina

Jack Feldman
Georgia Institute of Technology

Gerald R. Ferris
University of Illinois

Peter Feuille
University of Illinois

Sandra Fielden
Manchester Business School, University of Manchester

Jack Fiorito
Florida State University

Cynthia D. Fisher
Bond University

Robert Folger
Tulane University

J. Kevin Ford
Michigan State University

John A. Fossum
University of Minnesota

Colette A. Frayne
Seattle University

Dwight D. Frink
University of Mississippi

Daniel G. Gallagher
James Madison University

Robert D. Gatewood
University of Georgia

Eduard Gaugler
University of Mannheim

Jennifer M. George
Rice University

J. Michael Geringer
California Poly State

Robert A. Giacalone
University of Richmond

William H. Glick
Arizona State University

Irwin L. Goldstein
University system of Maryland

Luis R. Gomez-Mejia
Arizona State University and Universidad Carlos III

Michael E. Gordon
Rutgers University

Linda S. Gottfredson
University of Delaware

Cynthia L. Gramm
University of Alabama, Hurstville

David A. Gray
University of Texas

Jeffrey H. Greenhaus
Drexel University

Charles R. Greer
Texas Christian University

List of Contributors   xi

Hal B. Gregersen
Brigham Young University

Martin M. Greller
New School University

Ricky W. Griffin
Texas A&M University

Robert M. Guion
Bowling Green State University

Robert J. Harvey
Virginia Tech

I. B. Helburn
Retired from University of Texas at Austin

Robert L. Heneman
Ohio State University

Helge Hoel
Manchester Business School, University of Manchester

William H. Holley, Jr.
Auburn University

William C. Howell
Arizona State and Rice Universities

Mark A. Huselid
Rutgers University Institute of Management and Labor Relations

Ellen F. Jackofsky
Southern Methodist University

Susan E. Jackson
New York University

Rick Jacobs
Penn State University

Vinod K. Jain
University of Maryland College

Larry James
University of Tennessee

Paul Jarley
Louisiana State University

Donald W. Jarrell
Drexel University

Gary Johns
Concordia University

Nancy Brown Johnson
University of Kentucky

Timothy A. Judge
University of Florida

Timothy J. Keaveny
Marquette University

John D. Keiser
State University of New York Brockport

Ian Kessler
University of Oxford

Peter H. Kim
University of South Carolina

Katherine J. Klein
University of Maryland

Richard Klimoski
George Mason University

Marianne J. Koch
University of Oregon

Deborah M. Kolb
Simmons College

Ellen Ernst Kossek
Michigan State University

Kathy E. Kram
Boston University

Charles E. Krider
University of Kansas

Gary P. Latham
University of Toronto

List of Contributors

Chung-Ming Lau
Chinese University of Hong Kong

Carrie R. Leana
University of Pittsburgh

Terry L. Leap
Clemson University

Gerald E. Ledford, Jr.
University of Southern California

Donna E. Ledgerwood
University of North Texas

Barbara A. Lee
Rutgers University

Thomas W. Lee
University of Washington

David Lei
Southern Methodist University

Mark L. Lengnick-Hall
University of Texas at San Antonio

Edward L. Levine
University of South Florida

David Lewin
University of California,
Los Angeles

Steffen Lichtenberger
University of Mannheim

Oliver London
London and Associates

Clinton O. Longenecker
University of Toledo

Douglas M. McCabe
Georgetown University

Robert M. McCaffery
Rutgers University

Michael A. McDaniel
University of Akron

Marilyn Macik-Frey
University of Texas

Fiona A. E. McQuarrie
University College of the Fraser Valley and
University of Prince Edward Island

Lisa Mainiero
Fairfield School of Business

Michael R. Manning
New Mexico State University

Charles C. Manz
University of Massachusetts

Cornelia Martin
University of Mannheim

James E. Martin
Wayne State University

Marick F. Masters
University of Pittsburgh

Nicholas J. Mathys
DePaul University

Bruce M. Meglino
University of South Carolina

Mark E. Mendenhall
University of Tennessee, Chattanooga

Marcia P. Miceli
Ohio State University

Susan Albers Mohrman
University of Southern California

Lucie Morin
University of Toronto

Shad S. Morris
Cornell University

Kevin W. Mossholder
Louisiana State University

Michael K. Mount
University of Iowa

Paul M. Muchinsky
University of North Carolina

Kevin R. Murphy
Colorado State University

Raoul C. D. Nacamulli
CRORA, Università L. Bocconi

Christopher P. Neck
Virginia Polytechnic Institute and State University

Debra L. Nelson
Oklahoma State University

Jerry M. Newman
State University of New York, Buffalo

Nigel Nicholson
London Business School

Stella M. Nkomo
University of North Carolina

Raymond A. Noe
Ohio State University

Stanley Nollen
Georgetown University

Christine Neylon O'Brien
Boston College

Judy D. Olian
University of Maryland

Colleen O'Malley
Transition Works

Paul Osterman
Massachusetts Institute of Technology

Catherine A. Ouellette
Moorehouse College

Benjamin M. Oviatt
Georgia State University

Ramona L. Paetzold
Texas A&M University

Lawrence H. Peters
Texas Christian University

Richard B. Peterson
University of Washington

James S. Phillips
University of Houston

Jon L. Pierce
University of Minnesota Duluth

Stephen Poelmans
Instituto Superior de Estudios Empresariales, University of Navarra

Jeffrey T. Polzer
Harvard Business School

Sheila M. Puffer
Northeastern University

Elaine D. Pulakos
Personnel Decisions Research Institute

James Campbell Quick
University of Texas

Jonathan D. Quick
Management Sciences for Health

David A. Ralston
University of Oklahoma

Jacques R. Rojot
University of Paris

Joseph G. Rosse
University of Colorado at Boulder

Hannah R. Rothstein
Baruch College

Denise M. Rousseau
Carnegie Mellon

List of Contributors

Richard L. Rowan
University of Pennsylvania

Jill Rubery
Manchester Business School, University of Manchester

Craig J. Russell
University of Oklahoma

Paul R. Sackett
University of Minnesota

Marcus Hart Sandver
Ohio State University

Vida Scarpello
Georgia State University

Edgar H. Schein
Massachusetts Institute of Technology

Frank Schmidt
University of Iowa

Neal Schmitt
Michigan State University

Benjamin Schneider
University of Maryland

Lyle F. Schoenfeldt
Texas A&M University

Chester A. Schriesheim
University of Miami

Randall S. Schuler
Rutgers University

Manuel G. Serapio, Jr.
University of Colorado at Denver

James B. Shaw
Bond University

John C. Shearer
Oklahoma State University

Mark R. Sherman
University of Houston

Anthony V. Sinicropi
University of Iowa

D. Brent Smith
University of Maryland

Scott A. Snell
Cornell University

David J. Snyder
University of Akron

Paul E. Spector
University of South Florida

Yvonne Stedham
University of Nevada at Reno

Richard M. Steers
University of Oregon

Dianna L. Stone
University of Central Florida

Thomas H. Stone
Oklahoma State University

Eugene F. Stone-Romero
University of Central Florida

John Storey
University of Loughborough

Stephen A. Stumpf
University of Tampa

Lorne Sulsky
Calgary University

Koji Taira
University of Illinois at Urbana Champaign

Scott I. Tannenbaum
State University of New York, Albany

M. Susan Taylor
University of Maryland

Mary B. Teagarden
American Graduate School of International Management

List of Contributors

James R. Terborg
University of Oregon

Rebecca A. Thacker
Ohio University

R. Roosevelt Thomas, Jr.
American Institute for Managing Diversity

Steven L. Thomas
Southwest Missouri State University

Darren C. Treadway
University of Mississippi

Linda Klebe Treviño
Pennsylvania State University

Leo Troy
Rutgers University

David P. Twomey
Fairleigh Dickinson University

Dave Ulrich
University of Michigan

Kelly A. Vaverek
The Mescon Group

Anil Verma
University of Toronto

Peter Villanova
Appalachian State University

Mary Ann Von Glinow
Florida International University

James W. Walker
The Walker Group

John P. Wanous
Ohio State University

Deidre Wasson
Michigan State University

Liqun Wei
Chinese University of Hong Kong

Theresa M. Welbourne
Cornell University

Hoyt N. Wheeler
University of South Carolina

Charles R. Williams
Texas Christian University

Kevin J. Williams
State University of New York, Albany

Larry J. Williams
Purdue University

James P. Womack
Massachusetts Institute of Technology

Richard W. Woodman
Texas A&M University

Patrick W. Wright
Texas A&M University

Thomas A. Wright
University of Nevada at Reno

Jixia Yang
Louisiana State University

Arthur K. Yeung
University of Michigan

Stuart A. Youngblood
Texas Christian University

William E. Youngdahl
Arizona State University

A

absenteeism

Gary Johns

Absenteeism is the failure to report for scheduled work. It can be distinguished from lateness, which indicates a failure to show up for work on time, and from turnover, which indicates a permanent break in the employment relationship (*see* EMPLOYEE TURNOVER). Traditionally, managers have been interested in absenteeism because of its cost to organizations, while academics have been interested in absenteeism on the assumption that it indicates something about employees' social or psychological attachment to the organization.

THE MEASUREMENT OF ABSENTEEISM

Organizations often codify absence instances with attributions as to cause, which are of suspect accuracy. Consequently, researchers most often simply divide absenteeism into *time lost*, the number of days missed over some period, and *frequency*, the number of inceptions of absence over some period irrespective of the duration of each incident. To permit comparisons of employees with a different number of scheduled days or to characterize absenteeism at the group level, these figures can also be expressed as rates. Since absence is missing *scheduled* work, jury duty, vacation time, and maternity leave are not generally counted as absence.

Absence is a low base-rate behavior, in that most employees exhibit relatively low absence levels while a few exhibit higher levels. Thus, a frequency distribution for absenteeism is truncated on the low end and positively skewed. Because it is a low base-rate behavior, absence measures for individuals must be aggregated over a reasonably long period (3 to 12 months) to achieve adequate reliability of measurement. Even then, the reliability of absence measures (indexed by interperiod stability or internal consistency) is variable. Some validity evidence suggests that frequency of absence is more likely than time lost to reflect a voluntary component (Chadwick-Jones, Nicholson, and Brown, 1982; Hackett and Guion, 1985). Because of its non-normal distribution, managers should be aware that a few extreme absentees can have a disproportionate effect on means calculated from absence distributions.

CORRELATES AND CAUSES OF ABSENTEEISM

A longstanding tradition concerns the correlation between demographic variables and absenteeism. This research reveals reliable associations between age and absence among men (younger workers exhibit more absence) and gender and absence (women are absent more than men). However, little theory has emerged to explain these associations. There is no dominant theory of absenteeism. Johns (1997) presents several "models" of absenteeism reflecting the fact that absence is the product of diverse causes and has been studied with a diversity of methodologies uncommon in the organizational sciences (Johns, 2003).

Concerning the *medical model*, health-related behaviors such as smoking and problem drinking are associated with absence, as are migraine pain, back pain, and depression. Self-reported health status is correlated with absence, and people attribute the majority of their own absence to minor medical problems. The ultimate accuracy of such attributions is questionable, since "sickness" has motivational correlates, medical diagnoses often reflect prevailing community standards, and people sometimes adopt sick roles that manifest themselves in absence.

The *withdrawal model* suggests that absenteeism is an attempt to remove oneself temporarily from aversive working conditions. The literature on the relationship between JOB SATISFACTION and absenteeism reveals a modest association, with dissatisfaction with the work itself being the facet most associated with absenteeism (Hackett and Guion, 1985). Feelings of inequity and weak organizational support are especially likely to prompt absence. The progression-of-withdrawal hypothesis, for which there is fairly convincing evidence, posits a movement from lateness to absence to turnover.

The *deviance model* derives from the negative consequences of absence for organizations. In one form, it suggests that absentees harbor negative dispositional traits that render them unreliable. People tend to make negative attributions about the causes of others' absenteeism, and absenteeism is a frequent cause of employee/management conflict. People also have a tendency to underreport their own absenteeism and to see their own behavior as exemplary compared to that of their coworkers and occupational peers. Evidence for a likely connection between negative traits and absenteeism includes the temporal and cross-situational stability of absence, its negative association with conscientiousness and personality-based measures of integrity, and its positive correlation with other negative work behaviors such as poor performance (Bycio, 1992).

The *economic model* of absence suggests that attendance behavior is influenced by economic and quasi-economic constraints and opportunities. Those who value highly their nonwork time are more likely to be absent, and looser contractual provisions regarding attendance result in more absence. Absenteeism is negatively associated with wages and the unemployment rate and positively associated with unionized status. Some INDUSTRIAL RELATIONS scholars have argued that absence is a form of unorganized conflict that substitutes for some of the functions of collective action.

The *cultural model* of absence begins with the observation that there is often more variance between aggregates of individuals (such as work groups, departments, organizations, occupations, industries, and nations) than within these aggregates. Mechanisms of social influence and control subsumed under the label *absence culture* have been advanced to account for these differences between groups (Chadwick-Jones et al., 1982; Johns and Nicholson, 1982). Work unit absence has been shown to account for individual absence over and above individual-level predictors, and some rich case studies of absence cultures exist. The content of such cultures implicates absence norms, cohesiveness, management expectations, and shared views about the consequences of the behavior.

MANAGING ABSENTEEISM

The deviance model has dominated management approaches to absence. As a result, punishment and discipline systems are the most common methods of controlling absence. Used alone, they are not especially effective because of negative side-effects and because few employees are actually punished. More effective are mixed consequence systems that punish extreme offenders but reward good attenders with money or time off (Rhodes and Steers, 1990). Job enrichment and flextime have both been associated with reduced absence, as have self-management programs that teach employees to regulate their own attendance behavior (*see* SELF-MANAGEMENT TRAINING). Badly needed are theories that translate the likely causes of absenteeism into credible interventions and organizations with the foresight to experiment with these interventions. Obsession with extreme offenders has distracted managers from giving attention to the attendance behavior of all employees.

Bibliography

Bycio, P. (1992). Job performance and absenteeism: A review and meta-analysis. *Human Relations*, **45**, 193–220.

Chadwick-Jones, J. K., Nicholson, N., and Brown, C. (1982). *Social Psychology of Absenteeism*. New York: Praeger.

Goodman, P. S. and Atkin, R. S. (eds.) (1984). *Absenteeism*. San Francisco: Jossey-Bass.

Hackett, R. D. and Guion, R. M. (1985). A reevaluation of the absenteeism–job satisfaction relationship. *Organizational Behavior and Human Decision Processes*, **35**, 340–81.

Harrison, D. A., Johns, G., and Martocchio, J. J. (2000). Changes in technology, teamwork, and diversity: New directions for a new century of absenteeism research. *Research in Personnel and Human Resources Management*, **18**, 43–91.

Harrison, D. A. and Martocchio, J. J. (1998). Time for absenteeism: A 20-year review of origins, offshoots, and outcomes. *Journal of Management*, **24**, 305–30.

Johns, G. (1997). Contemporary research on absence from work: Correlates, causes and consequences. *International Review of Industrial and Organizational Psychology*, **12**, 115–73.

Johns, G. (2003). How methodological diversity has improved our understanding of absenteeism from work. *Human Resource Management Review*, **13**, 157–84.

Johns, G. and Nicholson, N. (1982). The meanings of absence: New strategies for theory and research. *Research in Organizational Behavior*, **4**, 127–73.

Rhodes, S. R. and Steers, R. M. (1990). *Managing Employee Absenteeism*. Reading, MA: Addison-Wesley.

action learning

Sandra Fielden

The principal tenet of action learning is a form of learning through experience, where understanding and knowledge arise from the undertaking of a task. However, action learning does appear in numerous variants depending on the goal or purpose of the learning. Action-learning programs typically incorporate the following features:

- participants meet in small, stable groups called "sets" which share a common purpose or goal;
- each set holds meetings over a fixed program cycle which may or may not be facilitated;
- participants tackle real problems in real time with no "right" answers;
- problems are relevant to participants' own realities;
- the process is based on reflection, questioning, conjecture, and refutation in a collaborative and supportive environment.

Action learning has a flexible "elective" framework designed to draw out, capture, and build on what is, rather than operate in a pure, detached, analytical, and rational world of what should be (Smith and O'Neil, 2003). This approach, by promoting insightful inquiry, provides a unique environment in which individuals can explore different and innovative solutions to their problems. In this way, an individual can conceptualize, shape, and reshape his or her mental models in a "safe practice field," while retaining responsibility for the implementation of solutions.

Bibliography

Smith, P. A. C. and O'Neil, J. (2003). A review of action learning literature 1994–2000. *Journal of Workplace Learning*, **15** (2), 63–9.

affirmative action

Barbara A. Lee

Affirmative action is the practice of giving explicit consideration to race, gender, national origin, or some other protected characteristic in making an employment decision. It is designed to counter the lingering effects of prior discrimination, whether intentional or not, by employers individually and collectively, as well as to provide a workforce more representative of the gender and ethnic makeup of the qualified labor market for the positions within an organization.

Affirmative action is required by federal law for recipients of federal contracts, may be ordered by a court as part of the settlement or remedy in a lawsuit charging an employer with discrimination, or may be voluntary.

REQUIRED AFFIRMATIVE ACTION

Executive orders 11246 and 11375 (*see* EXECUTIVE ORDERS) require federal contractors and subcontractors to practice affirmative action in hiring and in other employment decisions (such as promotions, job assignments). The OFFICE OF FEDERAL CONTRACT COMPLIANCE PROGRAMS, part of the US Department of Labor, may conduct compliance reviews, either before or after the contract is awarded, may receive and investigate complaints from current employees or from applicants, and may commence administrative proceedings or judicial action. Remedies for violations of the executive orders include termination of the contract, debarment from future federal contracts, or injunctions.

Affirmative Action as a Remedy

Federal courts have ordered employers or trade unions to engage in race- or gender-conscious affirmative action as a remedy for prior intentional discrimination. For example, in *Local 28 of the Sheet Metal Workers' International Assn* v. *EEOC*, 478 US 421 (1986), the Supreme Court approved explicit quotas for admission to union membership to remedy prior intentional race discrimination that was "persistent" and "egregious." A similar outcome for gender discrimination occurred in *EEOC* v. *AT & T*, 365 F. Supp. 1105 (E.D. Pa. 1973) (see Kirp, Yudof, and Franks, 1986: 161–6 for a critical analysis of this case and other court-ordered affirmative action settlements related to gender).

Voluntary Affirmative Action

Voluntary affirmative action differs from court-ordered affirmative action in that the employer need not admit to prior discriminatory employment practices. The employer must first develop an affirmative action plan that meets the criteria listed in *United Steelworkers of America* v. *Weber*, 443 US 193 (1979):

1. the plan cannot "unnecessarily trammel" the interests of majority employees by requiring their discharge;
2. the plan cannot create an absolute bar to the advancement of majority employees, but a delay in advancement, in order to give minority employees an earlier opportunity at advancement, is permissible; and
3. the plan must be temporary in that it must be designed to eliminate a "manifest racial imbalance," but not operate to maintain that balance once it is attained. Preferences must cease when balance is attained.

The court approved a voluntary affirmative action plan in *Johnson* v. *Transportation Agency*, 480 US 616 (1987), in which the agency used gender as one criterion among several to select a woman for promotion to the position of road dispatcher. When, however, a layoff or other job loss is at stake, the outcome has been quite different. In *Wygant* v. *Jackson Board of Education*, 476 US 267 (1986), the Supreme Court ruled that a layoff plan that sought to maintain the same proportion of minority teachers after the layoff as previously violated the US Constitution's Equal Protection Clause. The court denied that affirmative action could be a remedy for "societal discrimination" if there was no evidence of past intentional discrimination by the School Board.

See also *affirmative action for non-victims; discrimination*

Bibliography

Kirp, D. L., Yudof, M. G., and Franks, M. S. (1986). *Gender Justice*. Chicago: University of Chicago Press.

affirmative action for non-victims

Barbara A. Lee

When an employer is found to have engaged in unlawful discrimination against a class of employees or applicants, the court may order the employer to engage in affirmative race- or gender-conscious employment practices as a remedy for the prior discrimination, including hiring or promotion quotas. If the actual victims of the prior discrimination cannot be found or are not interested in working for the employer, the court may require the employer to offer employment, promotions, salary increases, or whatever practice was attacked in the lawsuit to individuals in the same minority group as those against whom the discrimination was practiced, but who were not the actual victims of the employer's discrimination (see *United States* v. *Paradise*, 480 US 149, 1987).

See also *affirmative action; discrimination*

AFL-CIO

Stuart A. Youngblood

The American Federation of Labor and Congress of Industrial Organizations (AFL-CIO) is a federation of 78 labor unions representing nearly 13.6 million working women and men. The merger of the AFL (a craft union) with the CIO (an industrial union) in 1955 also coincided with the peak of trade union membership in the US, membership that reached 35 percent of the nonagricultural workforce. Today, membership in private nonagricultural industries is nearly 10 percent. The federation does not engage in COLLECTIVE BARGAINING, but instead advises and supports the international unions by providing information and technical services to assist UNION ORGANIZING, collective bargaining, and legislative and political action by the unions of the AFL-CIO. The federation is supported by a per capita tax from its member internationals.

The AFL-CIO has elected officers, who currently are: John J. Sweeney, president; Linda Chavez-Thompson, executive vice president; and Richard L. Trumpka, secretary treasurer. The AFL-CIO supports an Executive Council made up of 33 vice presidents who also serve as presidents of their respective national unions. Sweeney, elected president at the biennial convention in October of 1995, has vowed to increase efforts at organizing to attract younger workers and to reach out especially to women and minorities. A US$35 million political education campaign has been proposed and will be funded in part by the approval of a one-year assessment on national unions of 15 cents per member per month, as well as $10 million which has been earmarked for new organizing activity. President Sweeney announced a major reorganization of the federation, including the appointment as head of the Field Services Department of Marilyn Sneiderman, who previously served as education director at the Teamsters, and the creation of a new department, the Working Women's Department, to be headed by Karen Nussbaum, previously director of the Labor Department's Women's Bureau. The AFL-CIO has created a homepage on the Internet and can be reached at: www.aflcio.org.

Bibliography

Begin, J. P. and Beal, E. F. (1985). *The Practice of Collective Bargaining*. Homewood, IL: Richard D. Irwin.

Age Discrimination in Employment Act of 1967

Ramona L. Paetzold

The Age Discrimination in Employment Act of 1967 (ADEA) extends antidiscrimination protection to workers who are at least 40 years old. Originally, the Act included upper age limits as well, but in 1986 upper age limits were eliminated (with a few exceptions). The employment practices that are covered by the Act mimic those of Title VII of the CIVIL RIGHTS ACT OF 1964, but the entities that are covered are not as extensive. Only employers having 20 or more employees are covered under the ADEA.

The ADEA creates both protected and unprotected age categories – those 40 and over, and those under 40, respectively. Other federal antidiscrimination laws do not generally create unprotected categories within the class of protection (e.g., "race" protection extends to *all* races; "sex" protection extends to both men and women). This distinction introduces complexities into the meaning of age discrimination. Additionally, because age is measured continuously and changes over a person's lifetime, problems of proof in regard to age tend to be more complex in nature than other proof issues arising under protected class statuses. For example, differential treatment among members *within* the protected age category may be evidence of illegal discrimination; violations of the Act need not rest on comparisons of treatment *between* protected and unprotected categories.

In *Hazen Paper Co.* v. *Biggins* (1993), the US Supreme Court ruled that an employer's use of a factor that is correlated with age, but distinct from age, may not be illegal age discrimination. The court held that age itself must motivate the employer's decision and be a determining influence on the employment outcome in order for a finding of age discrimination to be obtained. This language makes unclear the future of the "mixed motive" model of disparate treatment under the ADEA. Also unclear is whether the ADEA accommodates DISPARATE IMPACT claims; to date the Supreme Court has not ruled on that issue and the Federal Courts of Appeal are split on the subject.

See also *discrimination*

agency shop

David A. Gray

The agency shop is a form of union security found in some labor agreements, whereby an employee is not required to join the union, but he or she must pay to the union an amount, known as an agency fee, which is usually equivalent to regular union dues. This fee is used to cover the costs of union representation for bargaining and grievance handling purposes. The Supreme Court ruled in *Beck* v. *Communication Workers* (1988) that the union can assess the fee, but if the costs of COLLECTIVE BARGAINING are less than regular union dues, the nonunion agency-fee-paying employee can obtain a refund for the difference. In most right-to-work states, which make union shop agreements illegal, the agency shop is also prohibited.

AIDS/AIDS-related complex

Jennifer M. George

Acquired Immune Deficiency Syndrome (AIDS) is a disease that impairs people's immune systems, leaving them unable to fight infections and cancers. AIDS is caused by the Human Immunodeficiency Virus (HIV). Individuals infected with HIV may show no AIDS symptoms, may not develop AIDS in the near future, can transmit the virus to others, are referred to as HIV-positive, and are often able to effectively perform their jobs. HIV-infected individuals who show signs that AIDS might develop, such as swollen lymph nodes, excessive fatigue, fever, weight loss, and diarrhea, have AIDS-related complex (ARC) and may or may not be able to effectively perform their jobs. HIV-infected individuals who have multiple infections, often requiring hospitalization, have full-blown AIDS and often are unable to perform their jobs. HIV is most commonly transmitted through sexual contact and the sharing of infected needles by intravenous drug users. AIDS also can be transmitted through contact with contaminated blood products. AIDS does not spread through casual, nonsexual contact. While progress has been made in the treatment of HIV/AIDS, there currently is no cure or vaccine for the disease. In the US, employees who are HIV-positive or have ARC or AIDS are protected by the AMERICANS WITH DISABILITIES ACT OF 1990.

See also *AIDS awareness training*

Bibliography

Esposito, M. D. and Myers, J. E. (1993). Managing AIDS in the workplace. *Employee Relations*, 19, 53–75.
Franklin, G. M., Gresham, A. B., and Fontenot, G. F. (1992). AIDS in the workplace: Current practices and critical issues. *Journal of Small Business Management*, April, 61–73.
Froiland, P. (1993). Managing the walking wounded. *Training*, August, 36–40.

AIDS awareness training

Jennifer M. George

Acquired Immune Deficiency Syndrome (AIDS) awareness training entails educating members of an organization about Human Immunodeficiency Virus (HIV) infection, how it is spread, and new developments in HIV/AIDS research and treatment. Training also focuses on insuring that HIV-positive employees are treated appropriately by their supervisors, coworkers, and the organization as a whole, have their rights to privacy respected, and are able to remain productive as long as they can. Dispelling myths about HIV and AIDS, educating employees in prevention, and communicating an organization's policies are important elements. Training can include the use of videos, group discussions, seminars, workshops, forums, and presentations as well as written educational materials.

See also *AIDS/AIDS-related complex*

Bibliography

Esposito, M. D. and Myers, J. E. (1993). Managing AIDS in the workplace. *Employee Relations*, 19, 53–75.
Pincus, L. B. and Trivedi, S. M. (1994). A time for action: Responding to AIDS. *Training and Development*, January, 45–51.
Stodghill, R., II, Mitchell, R., Thruston, K., and Del Valle, C. (1993). Why AIDS policy must be a special policy. *Business Week*, February 1, 53–4.

Albemarle Paper Company v. *Moody*, 422 US 405 (1975)

Leonard Bierman

To defend against a DISPARATE IMPACT charge, an employer must show that the hiring procedures it uses are clearly job-related (*see* JOB-RELATEDNESS). In *Albemarle* the company used test scores of verbal and nonverbal intelligence to evaluate applicants. To determine whether the tests were job-related, the company hired an industrial psychologist who found a correlation between test scores and supervisor ratings of employee performance. The Supreme Court held, however, that this *validation study* did not meet EQUAL EMPLOYMENT OPPORTUNITY COMMISSION guidelines and that the tests used were not sufficiently proven to be job-related.

alternative dispute resolution

Charles R. Greer

The term alternative dispute resolution (ADR) refers to procedures that are used to resolve employee relations disputes as opposed to reliance on litigation. ADR procedures include GRIEVANCE PROCEDURES (both union and nonunion), ARBITRATION, MEDIATION, fact finding, the use of ombudspersons, and combined approaches. As compared to litigation, ADR procedures are generally thought to provide a number of advantages, including more timely resolution of issues, reduced expense, more flexible remedies tailored to the unique circumstances of the parties involved, and less adversarial interaction (Zack, 1992; Lewicki et al., 1994). ADR procedures vary in the extent to which neutral third parties have formal authority. Arbitration is at one end of the spectrum, with arbitrators having the authority to formulate remedies which the parties must follow. Mediation is at the other end of the spectrum, with mediators having no formal authority and only their skills to work through the conflict to enable the parties to arrive at their own solution to the dispute. While there is no authority with mediation, the conventional wisdom of conflict resolution is that superior outcomes are more likely because the parties themselves decide the solution and therefore are more committed.

Bibliography

Lewicki, R. J., Litterer, J. A., Minton, J. W., and Saunders, D. M. (1994). *Negotiation*, 2nd edn. Burr Ridge, IL: Richard D. Irwin.

Zack, A. M. (1992). *A Handbook for Grievance Arbitration: Procedural and Ethical Issues*. New York: Lexington Books.

American Society for Training and Development

Scott I. Tannenbaum

Founded in 1944, the American Society for Training and Development (ASTD) is the world's premier professional association in the field of workplace learning and performance. ASTD provides information, research, and analysis on a wide range of topics; offers various conferences, expositions, seminars, and publications; and forms coalitions and partnerships through its research and policy work. ASTD membership includes more than 70,000 people working in 100 countries worldwide including managers, human resource specialists, designers, technical trainers, instructors, evaluators, front-line supervisors, consultants, researchers, and educators. Its members work in more than 15,000 multinational corporations, small and medium-sized businesses, government agencies, colleges and universities.

For further information, contact the American Society for Training and Development (ASTD), 1640 King Street, Box 1443, Alexandria, Virginia 22313-2043, USA. Telephone 703-683-8100. Fax 703-683-8103. Website: www.astd.org.

Americans with Disabilities Act of 1990

Stuart A. Youngblood

The Americans with Disabilities Act of 1990 (ADA) is similar to the REHABILITATION ACT OF 1973 in providing job protection for handicapped individuals, but ADA is designed to cover private sector employers with 15 or more employees. ADA went into full effect on July 26, 1994 after a gradual phase-in to allow employers time to make building accommodations and to allow small employers (fewer than 25 employees) time to adjust to new legislative requirements. ADA contains five titles or sections that:

1. make it illegal to discriminate against qualified individuals with a disability in employment;
2. make it illegal for state or local governments to discriminate against the handicapped in the provision of public services;
3. make it illegal for public accommodations to discriminate against the handicapped in the provision of goods, benefits, services, facilities, privileges, advantages, or accommodations and require public accommodations to be made accessible;
4. require common carriers engaged in interstate communication to insure that telecommunications systems are available to individuals with hearing and/or speech impediments and to provide accommodation; and
5. include a catch-all title that, among other things, makes it illegal to retaliate against individuals who exercise their rights under ADA.

A disabled or handicapped individual is any person who: (1) has a physical or mental impairment that limits one or more major life activities; (2) has a record of such an impairment; or (3) is regarded as having such an impairment.

The Act, in effect, covers any qualified person who with or without reasonable accommodation can perform the "essential functions" of the job. JOB ANALYSIS has become even more critical to employers for defining what the "essential functions" of the job are. Although employers are prohibited from making preemployment inquiries regarding a person's handicapped status, they are permitted to ask if the applicant can perform particular job functions. Although the ADA prohibits preemployment medical examinations, job offers may be conditioned on the results of a medical examination provided that all entering employees in the job category are subject to the same conditions. Preemployment drug screening is not considered a medical examination under ADA and is therefore permissible. Current users of illegal drugs are not considered disabled under ADA, but should such a person seek treatment or complete a rehabilitation program, then that person, whether an applicant or current employee, would meet the disabled definition and thus be protected by the ADA. Enforcement of the ADA is the responsibility of the EQUAL EMPLOYMENT OPPORTUNITY COMMISSION or designated state human rights agencies.

Bibliography

Meisinger, S. R. (1990). The Americans with Disabilities Act of 1990: A new challenge for human resource managers. *Legal Reports* (Winter).

Technical Assistance Manual (1992). *Americans with Disabilities Act, Equal Employment Opportunity Commission Office of Communications and Legislative Affairs*. Washington, DC: US Government Printing Office.

annual hours

Fang Lee Cooke

Annual hours, also known as annualized hours, is a form of working-time flexibility that became popular in the 1980s as a labor strategy. This strategy is often adopted by firms that are subject to seasonal or cyclical variations in market demand, such as the hotel and catering industry. The basic principle of annual hours is that instead of defining working time on the basis of the standard working week, working hours are distributed out over the whole year to match the fluctuation of work demand. The use of annual hours allows employers to vary the actual length of the working week within upper and lower limits and subject to an annual total of hours worked.

appraisal feedback

M. Susan Taylor

Appraisal feedback is the information an employee receives concerning the way his or her performance has been evaluated by a rater or group of raters. Traditionally, the primary rater has been the employee's immediate supervisor, but increasingly, a broader group of individuals who have observed the employee's performance from different vantage points (e.g., customers, peers, direct-report employees) are being called on to provide input to the appraisal (Antonioni, 1994). Prior research has found that appraisal feedback tends to be more readily accepted as fair by recipients and to lead to more positive affective reactions when it:

1 is preceded by a discussion of performance expectations at the beginning of the performance period and by the provision of interim feedback;
2 allows the recipient to input his or her views about performance;
3 discusses the rater's rationale for the performance evaluation; and
4 is given by a rater who strives to be unbiased and considerate of the employee's feelings (Folger, Konovsky, and Cropzano, 1992; Taylor et al., 1995).

Performance improvement in response to appraisal feedback appears to be a function of whether goals for improvement are set and monitored, the rater is supportive of the employee's capacity for improvement, and attractive organizational rewards are made contingent on high performance (Meyer, Kay, and French, 1965; Cedarblom, 1982; Prince and Lawler, 1986).

See also *performance appraisal; 360-degree appraisals*

Bibliography

Antonioni, D. (1994). The effects of feedback accountability on upward appraisal ratings. *Personnel Psychology* (Summer), 349–56.
Cedarblom, D. B. (1982). The performance appraisal interview: A review, implications, and suggestions. *Academy of Management Review*, 7, 219–27.
Folger, R., Konovsky, M. A., and Cropzano, R. (1992). A due process metaphor for performance appraisal. In L. L. Cummings and B. Staw (eds.), *Research in Organizational Behavior*. Greenwich, CT: JAI Press.
Meyer, H. H., Kay, E., and French, J. R. P. (1965). Split roles in performance appraisal. *Harvard Business Review*, 43, 123–9.
Prince, J. B. and Lawler, E. E. (1986). Does salary discussion hurt the developmental performance appraisal? *Organizational Behavior and Human Decision Processes*, 37, 357–75.
Taylor, S. M., Tracy, K. B., Renard, M. K., Harrison, J. K., and Carroll, S. J. (1995). Due process in performance appraisal: A quasi-experiment in procedural justice. *Administrative Science Quarterly*, 40, 495–523.

arbitration

Anthony V. Sinicropi

Arbitration can be broadly defined as a dispute resolution process in which two parties voluntarily agree to accept an impartial arbitrator's final and binding decision on the merits of the parties' dispute. An arbitrator sits as a judge over the parties' dispute, his or her decision is legally binding on the parties, and an arbitration proceeding is less formal than a court trial.

In the area of labor relations, arbitration can be further defined to mean either grievance arbitration (*see* RIGHTS ARBITRATION) or INTEREST ARBITRATION. Disputes between employers and unions over the meaning or application of the language in an existing COLLECTIVE BARGAINING agreement are called GRIEVANCES. Nearly all collective bargaining agreements include a GRIEVANCE PROCEDURE that culminates in final and binding arbitration. The grievance procedure generally identifies the type of dispute that constitutes a grievance, establishes an appeal process that the employee, grievant, or the union and the employer must follow, determines how an arbitrator will be selected, and defines the arbitrator's authority to resolve and remedy the parties' dispute. Management's agreement to be bound by the contractual grievance or arbitration procedure is generally considered to be a trade-off for the union's agreement not to STRIKE over grievances during the term of the collective bargaining agreement.

Disputes between employers and unions over the terms to be included in their collective bargaining agreements are called interest disputes. In the private sector, unionized employees usually have the legal right to strike once their collective bargaining agreement expires. The threat of a strike by the employees (or LOCKOUT by management) provides the parties with an economic incentive to reach an agreement on the terms to be included in their new collective bargaining agreement. In some private sector industries the right to strike over new contract terms is sometimes replaced by interest arbitration. Because most states ban economic strikes by police officers, firefighters, school teachers, and other public sector employees, these states often require that negotiation disputes over wage increases and contract language be decided by an impartial interest arbitrator. One form of interest arbitration that has captured the attention of public services where safety is involved is called FINAL OFFER ARBITRATION. In those cases each party will submit its final offer to the arbitrator and the criteria that the arbitrator must follow in selecting the parties' final offers are usually established by state law. As an aside, baseball salary arbitration follows this format.

Arbitration is favored by state and federal labor law as a less expensive and more expeditious alternative to litigation in the courts. Since arbitration is a product of voluntary collective bargaining, provides both management and unions with an effective means of industrial self-government, and is favored by state and federal labor law, the role of the courts in reviewing an arbitrator's decision is extremely limited. Guided by legal principles announced by the US Supreme Court in a series of cases known as the "Steelworkers' Trilogy" (*United Steelworkers of America* v. *American Manufacturing Company*, 363 US 564, 4 L. Ed. 2d 1403, 80 S. Ct 1343, 1960; *United Steelworkers of America* v. *Warrior and Gulf Navigation Company*, 363 US 574, 4 L. Ed. 2d 1409, 80 S. Ct 1347, 1960; *United Steelworkers of America* v. *Enterprise Wheel and Car Company*, 363 US 593, 4 L. Ed. 2d 1424, 80 S. Ct 1358, 1960), federal and state courts will overturn an arbitrator's decision only in the event that it fails to draw its essence from the parties' collective bargaining agreement or violates state and/or federal law.

See also *alternative dispute resolution; mediation*

Bibliography

Elkouri, F. and Elkouri, E. (1985). *How Arbitration Works*, 4th edn. Washington, DC: Bureau of National Affairs.

Shulman, H. (1955). Reason, contract and law in labor relations. *Harvard Law Review*, **68**, 999.

assessment centers

Richard Klimoski

Assessment centers (also referred to as the assessment center method) represent a structured and comprehensive approach to the measurement of individual differences regarding knowledge, skills, abilities, and other dispositions (*see* KSAOS) that have been found to be relevant to the work environment. Traditionally, assessment centers were designed to assess the potential of people for managerial assignments in large organizations (Thornton and Byham, 1982). More recently, they are seen as useful whenever the need for extensive individual assessments can justify the effort and expense.

The noteworthy features of an assessment center include job-related assessment dimensions, groups of ratees assessed by multiple raters, multiple and complementary methods for assessment, the separation of observations and evaluations, and flexibility of purpose.

In the assessment center literature, the word dimension is used to denote a set of job-relevant tasks, BEHAVIORS, performance domains, or specific abilities needed to perform well on a job (Zedeck, 1986; Klimoski, 1993). Examples of assessment dimensions are "delegation," "interpersonal skills," and "organizing and planning." The number of actual dimensions used has varied from 10 to 25 (Zedeck, 1986) and would depend on such things as the purpose of the center, the nature of the job to which the center is linked, and the need for comprehensiveness.

Candidates are assessed in cohorts of from 10 to 15, and many of the assessments themselves are based on observations of individuals performing as a member of a six- to eight-person group. Further, teams of assessors, rather than one individual, are used to observe and produce written evaluations of candidates.

The staff of a center are usually trained human resource professionals, but occasionally psychologists and line managers are involved in assessments. The assessments themselves can be based on paper-and-pencil tests (including INTELLIGENCE TESTS, PERSONALITY TESTS, and interest measures), work-task SIMULATIONS (e.g., the in-basket test), individual interviews, and situational exercises with groups of candidates. Such exercises can be leaderless group discussions or ROLE PLAYING in job areas like budget planning, negotiations, or personnel decision-making. In their review of the reports of 50 centers, Gaugler et al. (1987) found that the number of assessment devices used ranged from one to 11 (mean of seven), with observations of candidates taken over a one- to three-day period. To accomplish this, most centers had a 2:1 ratio of candidates to staff.

Procedurally, each candidate follows a schedule designed to insure that all tests and exercises can be administered given the time and staff available. For example, while some individuals are completing a test or an interview, others would be participating in group exercises. In the group exercises staff are trained to observe and record candidate behaviors and make preliminary evaluations. However, final assessments are formulated in an "integration session." This occurs at the end of the assessment phase and serves as the vehicle for discussing and integrating what has been learned and for generating reports.

The behavior and performance of each candidate is reviewed and summarized at the integration session. Depending on the purpose of the center, the staff will discuss and reach consensus on each candidate's performance on one or more of the following: the assessment tasks or exercises, behavioral and/or performance dimensions, and the assessment exercises as a whole (Harris, Becker, and Smith, 1993). In some instances, the staff might also be asked to make a rating or recommendation (for hiring or PROMOTION) or a prediction of the candidate's likely future success in the company (Zedeck, 1986).

As of the time of their review, Gaugler et al. (1987: 493) estimated that over 2,000 organizations were using assessment centers and doing so for a wide variety of purposes. These include PERSONNEL SELECTION, placement, the EARLY IDENTIFICATION OF MANAGEMENT TALENT, promotion, management development, and TRAINING. For some of these purposes, staff members not only prepare reports, but also provide personal (even face-to-face) feedback to the candidates themselves. Although assessment centers are most frequently used to get at management potential, they have also been used to assess college students, engineers, salespeople, military personnel, rehabilitation counselors, school administrators, and others (Gaugler et al., 1987).

There is now fairly convincing evidence that assessment center judgments or ratings are statistically related to important job outcomes. The meta-analysis of Gaugler et al. (1987) revealed a corrected correlation of 0.37 against a set of criteria. The highest correlations were obtained, however, when center data were used to predict advancement criteria; somewhat lower validities are usually found in attempts to predict future JOB PERFORMANCE.

Current writing and research on assessment centers has gone beyond questioning the potential usefulness of such centers. Instead the emphasis is now on why and how they work, when they should be used (relative to alternatives), and with whom (Klimoski and Brickner, 1987). Thus, scholars and practitioners seem less interested in concerns over PREDICTIVE VALIDITY and are trying to address issues of assessment center CONSTRUCT VALIDITY (e.g., Russell and Domm, 1995).

Bibliography

Gaugler, B. B., Rosenthal, D. B., Thornton, G. C., and Bentson, C. (1987). Meta-analysis of assessment center validity. *Journal of Applied Psychology Monograph*, 72, 493–511.

Harris, M. M., Becker, A. S., and Smith, D. E. (1993). Does the assessment center scoring method affect the cross-situational consistency of ratings? *Journal of Applied Psychology*, 78, 675–8.

Klimoski, R. J. (1993). Predictor constructs and their measurement. In N. Schmitt and W. Borman (eds.), *Personnel Selection in Organizations*. San Francisco: Jossey-Bass.

Klimoski, R. J. and Brickner, M. (1987). Why do assessment centers work? The puzzle of assessment center validity. *Personnel Psychology* 40, 243–60.

Russell, C. J. and Domm, D. R. (1995). Two field tests of an explanation for assessment centre validity. *Journal of Occupational and Organizational Psychology*, **68**, 25–47.

Thornton, G. C. and Byham, W. C. (1982). *Assessment Centers and Managerial Performance*. San Diego, CA: Academic Press.

Zedeck, S. A. (1986). A process analysis of the assessment center method. *Research in Organizational Behavior*, **8**, 259–96.

at-risk pay

Gerald E. Ledford, Jr.

At-risk pay is COMPENSATION that is not guaranteed, such as VARIABLE COMPENSATION. Schuster and Zingheim (1992) distinguish three types. "Add-on pay" is in addition to normal base pay. "Potential base pay at risk" funds a variable pay plan by deferring part of the market-based increases that otherwise would flow into base pay. Pure "at-risk pay" reduces base pay, providing an employee an "ante" for variable pay opportunities. Lawler (1990) argues that at least 5 percent of cash compensation must be at risk to motivate employee performance through variable pay. Variables affecting the motivational effectiveness of at-risk pay include percentage at risk, individual preferences, the employee's organizational level, and organizational culture.

Bibliography

Lawler, E. E., III (1990). *Strategic Pay: Aligning Organizational Strategies and Pay Systems*. San Francisco: Jossey-Bass.

Schuster, J. R. and Zingheim, P. K. (1992). *The New Pay: Linking Employee and Organizational Performance*. New York: Lexington Books/Macmillan.

attitude surveys

Bruce M. Meglino

Organizations often appraise employees' reactions to various aspects of their job at regular intervals using attitude surveys. When the object being assessed is some facet of the job (e.g., work, pay, supervision) or the job itself, the attitude is normally referred to as satisfaction (Locke, 1976).

Attitudes have traditionally been thought of as having three components: cognitions (what an individual believes), affect (how an individual feels), and behavioral intentions (how an individual intends to act) (Tesser and Shaffer, 1990). Some researchers maintain that a person's values should also be considered (Locke, 1976). Any or all of these components may be assessed in an attitude survey using open-ended or structured questions (Schmitt and Klimoski, 1991). Examples of structured questions assessing each component would be: "How much travel does your job require?" (cognition), "How much do you want to travel?" (value), "How satisfied are you with your job?" (affect), and "How likely are you to leave your job?" (behavioral intention).

The amount of detail and the number of attitude components that one should include in an attitude survey depend upon the objectives of the survey (Schmitt and Klimoski, 1991). A single question assessing job affect can provide an overall index of employee JOB SATISFACTION, but it will probably be insufficient to adequately capture the source of dissatisfaction or to provide guidance in enhancing employee attitudes. Expanding the survey to include a larger number of cognitions, relevant values, affect toward a greater number of objects, and more behavioral intentions will provide more diagnostic information for the purposes of assessment and intervention.

Bibliography

Locke, E. A. (1976). The nature and consequences of job satisfaction. In M. D. Dunnette (ed.), *Handbook of Industrial and Organizational Psychology*. Chicago: Rand McNally.

Schmitt, N. W. and Klimoski, R. J. (1991). *Research Methods in Human Resources Management*. Cincinnati, OH: South-Western Publishing.

Tesser, A. and Shaffer, D. R. (1990). Attitudes and attitude change. In M. R. Rosenzweig and L. W. Porter (eds.), *Annual Review of Psychology*. Palo Alto, CA: Annual Reviews.

attitudinal structuring

Paul Jarley

Attitudinal structuring refers to efforts by negotiators to shape their opponents' perceptions about the nature of the issues to be negotiated. Attitudinal structuring is one of four bargaining subprocesses identified by Walton and McKersie (1965). (For the others, *see* DISTRIBUTIVE BARGAINING; INTEGRATIVE BARGAINING; INTRA-ORGANIZATIONAL BARGAINING.)

The Nature of Attitudinal Structuring

Attitudinal structuring is typically viewed as the result of a conscious, carefully planned effort by negotiators to influence their opponents' perceptions about the nature of bargaining issues and the character of bargaining team members. However, perceptions of the entire negotiation process may also be influenced by the largely spontaneous actions and deeds of parties. Because labor–management negotiation occurs at regular intervals and agreements must be administered on a daily basis, the past actions of the parties both at and away from the bargaining table can influence how each party approaches the next bargaining round.

The Importance of Attitudinal Structuring

Because bargaining issues have both distributive and integrative elements, perceptions play a large role in determining how the parties approach negotiations. By cultivating an atmosphere of friendliness, mutual respect, trust, and cooperation, negotiators can encourage their opponents to view issues largely in integrative terms and participate in joint problem solving. In contrast, hostile language, shouting, threats, deception, and refusal to acknowledge a party's legitimate interests encourages the opponent to take a more distributive approach to negotiations. Such words and deeds can have long-term effects, hampering subsequent efforts to switch from distributive to integrative bargaining.

Bibliography

Fisher, R. and Ury, W. (1981). *Getting to Yes: Negotiating Agreement Without Giving In*. New York: Penguin.

Lewicki, R. J. and Litterer, J. A. (1985). *Negotiation*. Homewood, IL: Richard D Irwin.

Walton, R. E. and McKersie, R. B. (1965). *A Behavioral Theory of Labor Negotiations: An Analysis of a Social Interaction System*. New York: McGraw-Hill.

attraction–selection–attrition

Benjamin Schneider and D. Brent Smith

Responding to the predominant situationist trend in the organizational sciences to attribute the behavior in and of organizations to organizational attributes, Schneider (1987) proposed an alternative framework for understanding organizational behavior, the attraction–selection–attrition (ASA) model. The ASA model places primary causation for behavior in and of organizations on the collective characteristics (personality, attitudes, and values) of the people in the organization. At the crux of the ASA model are the goals of the organization originally articulated by the founder. The goals and the processes, structures, and culture that emerge to facilitate goal achievement are said to be the outcomes of the choices the founder and his or her early colleagues make in pursuit of goal achievement. Over time, these goals, processes, structures, and culture are thought to determine the kinds of people who are attracted to, selected by, and stay in the organization.

Each component of the ASA model operates on the principle of fit (between person and organization). The attraction process refers to the idea that people's preferences for particular organizations are based upon an implicit estimate of the congruence between their own personal characteristics and the attributes of potential work organizations. That is, people find organizations differentially attractive as a function of their tacit judgment of the congruence between those organizations' goals (and structures, processes, and culture) and their own personality. For example, a doctor may choose to affiliate with hospital A versus hospital B based on her estimate of the fit or congruence between her own personality and the values she believes characterize the two hospitals.

The next component of the ASA cycle refers to the formal and informal PERSONNEL

SELECTION procedures organizations use to recruit and hire people, these being procedures that increase the fit of people to the prevailing organization culture. Lastly, the attrition process refers to the idea that people will leave an organization they do not fit. The turnover literature is quite clear about the fact that people who do not fit an organization will tend to leave it (see EMPLOYEE TURNOVER).

In summary, ASA proposes that three processes – attraction, selection, and attrition – result in different organizations containing people with different kinds of personalities and that these different types of people are responsible for the goals, processes, structures, and cultures that characterize their organization. It should be clear that the natural outcome of the ASA cycle is to restrict the range of people in an organization or, alternatively, to yield homogeneity. Schneider, Goldstein, and Smith (1996) review the evidence for this proposition and find general support for the contention that organizations, over time, become increasingly homogeneous with regard to the type of people there.

Regarding organizational effectiveness, the ASA model suggests that homogeneity implies a trade-off. While homogeneity may facilitate internal integration through the reduction of conflict and the encouragement of cooperation, it may also inhibit an organization's ability to sense and adapt to changes in its environment. This happens when people of similar personality and value systems see the world through similar lenses, obscuring from their view issues that might require their attention.

Bibliography

Schneider, B. (1987). The people make the place. *Personnel Psychology*, **40**, 437–54.
Schneider, B., Goldstein, H. W., and Smith, D. B. (1996). The ASA framework: An update. *Personnel Psychology*, **48**, 747–73.

audiovisual training techniques

Raymond A. Noe

Audiovisual training techniques use sight and/or sound. They include video, films, laser discs, overheads, compact discs, and any other technique that provides visual or auditory stimulation to trainees.

See also *training*

Australia

Greg J. Bamber

With a population of 20 million, Australia is a medium-sized, developed market economy. It has a strong primary sector (including mining, agriculture, and forestry), but the tertiary (service) sector is much the largest employer, with a growing education and tourism industry. Australia's secondary (manufacturing) sector has declined in importance in terms of employment, as tariff protection has been reduced significantly since the 1970s. Nevertheless, it has developed strengths in some industries; its output of elaborately transformed manufactured products (e.g., automotive, other metal products, and information technology) has increased since the 1980s.

Australia hosts many subsidiaries of international businesses whose head offices are mainly in Europe, North America, Korea, or Japan. More than half of its private sector workplaces with 500 or more employees are partly or wholly foreign-owned. Therefore, to a considerable extent, Australia has adapted human resource management (HRM) techniques from overseas. Nonetheless, the Australian INDUSTRIAL RELATIONS (IR) context is distinct from that in most other countries. Hence, this entry focuses on IR.

In many larger enterprises, a demarcation used to exist between IR and personnel management. Few Australian enterprises still observe such a demarcation. By the 1990s, they generally treated IR as one aspect of the broader field of HRM. Increasingly, line managers are expected to take responsibility for HRM issues.

Compared with the UK and other "unitary" countries, *political power* is more devolved in Australia, which is a federation of states (as is the US). Despite constitutional constraints on the powers of federal governments, most *IR arrangements* have been more centralized in Australia than in the UK or US. In the 1983–96 period, in particular, the Australian Council of Trade Unions (ACTU) was much more influential in the Australian polity and economy than its British equivalent, the Trades Union Congress (TUC). Unlike the TUC, then, the ACTU was dealing with a national government that was generally sympathetic to employees' and unions' interests. The national political spectrum is broadly similar to the UK; governments alternate periodically between the Australian Labor Party (ALP) and a conservative coalition. Between 1983 and 1996 the federal government was led by the ALP, whose initial prime minister, Bob Hawke, had been the full-time ACTU president until 1980. In 1996 the social democratic-style Australian Labor Party was voted out of office at the federal level and replaced by the Liberal and National Conservative Party coalition. For the incoming prime minister, John Howard, IR reform was a priority.

Perhaps to a greater extent than in the UK and US, in most large enterprises executives generally see IR issues as important. This perception has been reinforced because IR reform has remained high on most public policy agendas. In contrast with earlier British traditions of voluntary COLLECTIVE BARGAINING, Australian employment relationships have long been regulated by legally binding arbitrated IR *awards* (*see* ARBITRATION). An award determines terms and conditions of employment in an enterprise or industry; awards are arbitrated or certified by an IR commission (for brief explanations of such Australian terms and institutions, see Bamber, Lansbury, and Wailes, 2004: ch. 5). They may apply at a national, state, industry, enterprise, workplace, and/or occupational level. Many awards are, in effect, voluntary collective agreements (or, in US terms, labor–management contracts), but are subsequently endorsed either by the Australian Industrial Relations Commission (AIRC), a state arbitration commission, or the equivalent.

Despite such contrasts, compared with most other countries, Australian HRM shows more similarities to than differences from that of the UK. Australia inherited a British legacy of craft unions with laborist ideologies. However, following a series of mergers, by the mid-1990s most unions had been rationalized into about 20 broad industry groups.

There is much rhetoric among employers about improving management development (cf. Karpin, 1995); for example, in terms of internationalization and improving people management skills. However, the realities of most enterprises' management development do not yet match up to the rhetoric. Much management is characterized by short-termism and there is fragmentation among the employers' organizations. There are more traditions of adversarialism than of social partnership.

In Australia (as in the UK), there are occasional and much publicized examples of confrontational unionism and employerism, including major strikes and legal action, much media coverage and threats of dismissals. Nevertheless, such examples are far from typical: 72 percent of Australian workplaces (with at least five employees) have never experienced any industrial action (Callus et al., 1991). Moreover, the number of working days lost in industrial disputes declined dramatically after the early 1980s.

Some influential leaders of the Australian labor movement have focused particularly at a macro level of HR policy, though they generally would not use the term HR. There have been more signs of such explicit macro-level HR strategies than in the US, but fewer than in Scandinavia and many other western European countries.

The close connection between the ACTU and the ALP allowed them to attempt to introduce a more consensual approach to national policy-making by forging the 1983–96 ALP–ACTU *Accord*. Its advent marked a change of direction from the confrontational approaches of earlier governments. The Accord was inspired by examples from Scandinavia and Austria. It had some similarities with the post-1974 UK Social Contract between the Labour government and the TUC, but the Accord lasted much longer than the Social Contract and appeared to have been more successful.

During the Accord, to a greater extent than in the UK, US, and Japan, unions exerted considerable influence at the national policy-making level in Australia. This influence remained despite a continuing decline in union density in Australia from 56 percent of employees in 1979 to around 35 percent in 1996, which paralleled the decline in unionization in most other industrialized market economies (*see* TRENDS IN UNIONISM).

The Accord did not formally embrace employers, who were less united and appeared to have had less explicit influence on the ALP government than the ACTU. However, the ALP government also listened to and took heed of employers' views, particularly those of the larger enterprises, most of which belong to the Business Council of Australia (BCA), and those of the engineering employers represented by the Australian Industry Group (AIG).

Following the change of federal government in 1996, the conservative coalition abandoned the Accord. This government has promoted a continuing decentralization of the industrial relations system, with further moves toward enterprise-level bargaining and more deregulation of Australia's markets, including its labor market. Nonetheless, it has introduced more constraints on unions and on strikes. Union rights to organize have been diminished and this government is aiming to reduce protection against unfair dismissal, but this aim has been frustrated by Australia's Senate (its federal upper house), where the government does not enjoy a majority. The aim has also been further constrained because, in the early years of the twenty-first century, the states' and territories' governments were controlled by the ALP rather than by the coalition.

Strong unions and those in growth industries tend to pursue larger wage increases, whereas weaker unions will be less able to bargain for even basic wage increases for their members. In general, unions have a decreasing influence at the national level. They are weak in most private sector small and medium-sized enterprises, especially those in the service sector. Despite unions' opposition, there is an increasing casualization of the labor force, as employers are seeking more labor market flexibility. There is a higher degree of casual (short-term) employment in Australia than in most comparable countries.

Bibliography

Australian Centre for Industrial Relations Research and Training (ACIRRT) (1999). *Australia at Work: Just Managing?* Sydney: Prentice-Hall.
Bamber, G. J., Lansbury, R. D., and Wailes, N. (eds.) (2004). *International and Comparative Employment Relations: Globalisation and the Developed Market Economies*, 4th edn. Sydney: Allen and Unwin.
Bamber, G. J., Park, F., Lee, C., Ross, K. P., and Broadbent, K. (eds.) (2000). *Employment Relations in the Asia-Pacific.* Sydney: Allen and Unwin.

Bell, S. (1997). *Ungoverning the Economy: The Political Economy of Australian Economic Policy.* Melbourne: Oxford University Press.
Callus, R., Morehead, A., Cully, M., and Buchanan, J. (1991). *Industrial Relations at Work: The Australian Workplace Industrial Relations Survey.* Canberra: Australian Government Publishing Service.
De Cieri, H. and Kramar, R. (2003). *Human Resource Management in Australia: Strategy, People, Performance.* Sydney: McGraw-Hill.
Dunphy, D. and Stace, D. (2001). *Beyond the Boundaries: Leading and Re-creating the Successful Enterprise.* Sydney: McGraw-Hill.
Gardner, M. and Palmer, G. (1997). *Employment Relations: Industrial Relations and Human Resource Management in Australia*, 2nd edn. Melbourne: Macmillan.
Karpin, D. S. (1995). *Enterprising Nation: Renewing Australia's Managers to Meet the Challenges of the Asia-Pacific Century.* Canberra: Australian Government Publishing Service.
Lansbury, R. D. (2003). Management in Australia. In M. Warner (ed.), *International Encyclopedia of Business and Management*, 2nd edn, vol. 1. London: Thomson, pp. 314–24.
Moorehead, A., Steele, M., Alexander, M., Stephen, K., and Duffin, L. (1997). *Changes at Work: The 1995 Australian Industrial Relations Survey.* Melbourne: Longman.
Patrickson, M. G., Bamber, V. M., and Bamber, G. J. (1995). *Organisational Change Strategies: Case Studies of Human Resource and Industrial Relations Issues.* Melbourne: Longman.
Peetz, D. (1998). *Unions in a Contrary World: The Future of the Australian Trade Union Movement.* Melbourne: Cambridge University Press.
Sutcliffe, P. and Callus, R. (1994). *Glossary of Australian Industrial Relations Terms.* Sydney: University of Sydney Australian Centre for Industrial Relations Research and Teaching/Queensland University of Technology.

Australian Human Resources Institute

Greg J. Bamber

The Australian Human Resources Institute (AHRI) was formed in 1992. It is Australia's professional society for specialists in people management. Its forerunner, the Institute of Personnel Management Australia, was developed from the Personnel and Industrial Welfare Officers' Association, which had been established in 1943 in the State of Victoria.

AHRI's mission is to promote and support the professional development of members and others involved in people management, and to uphold the standards of the profession.

AHRI's aims are:

1 To promote through human resource management the notion that people, individually and collectively, contribute directly to business and organizational achievement, while at the same time encouraging and improving the effectiveness and wellbeing of people in the workplace.
2 To provide professional development and other support services to human resource professionals and others with an interest in human resource management.
3 To reinforce the role of human resource professionals as being key contributors in developing organizational strategy and capability.
4 To encourage the development and dissemination of the evolving body of professional knowledge in human resource management.
5 To promote professional standards of competence and conduct.
6 To be recognized as the leading authority and influence on human resource issues.

AHRI organizes conferences and courses and accredits various human resource education courses. Its membership currently includes about 10,500 human resource practitioners, academics, consultants, senior managers, line managers in non-human resource areas, students, unionists, and others. AHRI is affiliated with the Asia Pacific Federation of Personnel Management Associations and the World Federation of Personnel Management Associations. AHRI circulates an electronic newsletter, magazine, and refereed journal: *Asia-Pacific Journal of Human Resources* (published by Sage). For more information consult the website: www.ahri.com.au.

AHRI has a governance structure which includes elected State Councils and a Council of State Presidents, supported by a National Office and Board. For most of its life AHRI was a professional member association, but, after experiencing financial difficulties, in 2000 it became a company wholly owned by Deakin University. AHRI is less comprehensive and less influential than its UK analogue, the CHARTERED INSTITUTE OF PERSONNEL AND DEVELOPMENT. Nonetheless, AHRI's leaders have ideas and aspirations to develop it further.

availability analysis

James A. Breaugh

An availability analysis, which is generally undertaken as part of an AFFIRMATIVE ACTION plan, involves determining the procurable labor supply of members of protected groups for a given job (Gutman, 1993). In order to estimate availability, an employer first needs to specify the requisite skills needed for doing the job. An employer next needs to specify the geographic area from which it can be expected to recruit (Breaugh, 1992). Typically, an employer will recruit hourly workers from a smaller geographic area than it will recruit managers and professionals. Next, the employer attempts to determine the size of the available workforce separately for each protected group. In some cases, the OFFICE OF FEDERAL CONTRACT COMPLIANCE PROGRAMS can supply an employer with needed availability figures. Frequently, however, the employer will have to do research to come up with such data. Among the sources that can be used for estimating availability are: the US Census Bureau, the Bureau of Labor Statistics, various professional groups, and educational associations.

Once an employer has determined both the total number of persons and the total number of persons from each protected group who are available for employment, availability percentages can be computed (e.g., the percentage of available mechanics who are women). By comparing this availability percentage (for a specific protected group) with the percentage of the company's current workforce in the same job (for the same protected group), an employer can determine if that protected group is underutilized.

Bibliography

Breaugh, J. A. (1992). *Recruitment: Science and Practice*. Boston: PWS-Kent.

Gutman, A. (1993). *EEO Law and Personnel Practices.* Newbury Park, CA: Sage.

award of attorney's fees

Barbara A. Lee

Title VII of the CIVIL RIGHTS ACT OF 1964 permits a court to award a prevailing plaintiff attorney's fees, to be paid by the defendant-employer. Although it is rare, courts have ordered plaintiffs to pay the attorneys for the defendants when the defendant prevails, but only in such cases where the judge believed the lawsuit to be frivolous and completely without merit.

B

background checking (generic)

Craig J. Russell

Background checking gathers information from people familiar with an applicant in previous situations (e.g., creditors, prior employers, neighbors). Information is typically obtained from archival records (court documents, credit checks, motor vehicle departments, health insurance records, etc.), written letters of recommendation, and telephone or in-person conversations. References are typically provided by the applicant (*see* REFERENCE CHECKS). Background checking can be used to verify information obtained from WEIGHTED APPLICATION BLANKS and BIOGRAPHICAL HISTORY INVENTORIES, though typically it targets dimensions of character or ethics not captured elsewhere. Information varies widely in reliability, causing further decline in its moderate ability to predict criteria of interest (Muchinsky, 1979). Background checks are required for employment in occupations requiring certain types of insurance (e.g., "bonded" couriers).

Lack of standardized reference forms causes major problems in comparing applicants, though forms with scoring procedures have been developed (see, e.g., Aumodt, Bryan, and Whitcomb, 1993). Further, all but the worst applicants can find someone to say positive things about them, permitting weak differentiation of candidates' qualifications. Fear of litigation – both US federal discrimination law (*see* DISCRIMINATION) and civil laws – prevents many sources from sharing negative information (White and Kleiman, 1991). Most prior employers strictly limit information to simple verifications of employment dates. Little evidence exists regarding how well information gathered from background checks of historical evidence of personal integrity exhibits CRITERION-RELATED VALIDITY with future performance outcomes.

Bibliography

Aumodt, M. G., Bryan, D. A., and Whitcomb, A. J. (1993). Predicting performance with letters of recommendation. *Public Personnel Management*, 22, 81–90.

Muchinsky, P. M. (1979). The use of reference reports in personnel selection: A review and evaluation of value. *Journal of Occupational Psychology*, 52, 287–97.

White, C. S. and Kleiman, L S. (1991). The cost of candid comments. *HR Magazine*, August, 54–6.

balanced scorecard

Hadyn Bennett

Originally developed by Kaplan (1994) and Kaplan and Norton (1992, 1993, 1996a) as an innovative performance measurement technique, the balanced scorecard "translates an organization's mission and strategy into a comprehensive set of performance measures and provides the framework for strategic measurement and management" (Kaplan and Norton, 1996b). It provides a framework for defining and assessing the critical success factors necessary for the achievement of organizational goals within four key business areas: financial, internal business processes, customer, and learning and growth. To these can be added additional areas as appropriate; for example, Kaplan and Norton (1996b) include EMPLOYEE EMPOWERMENT as an additional factor.

Bibliography

Kaplan, R. S. (1994). Devising a balanced scorecard matched to business strategy. *Planning Review*, September/October, 15–19, 48.

Kaplan, R. S. and Norton, D. P. (1992). The balanced scorecard: Measures that drive performance. *Harvard Business Review*, January/February, 71–9.
Kaplan, R. S. and Norton, D. P. (1993). Putting the balanced scorecard to work. *Harvard Business Review*, September/October, 134–47.
Kaplan, R. S. and Norton, D. P. (1996a). Using the balanced scorecard as a strategic management system. *Harvard Business Review*, January/February, 75–85.
Kaplan, R. S. and Norton, D. P. (1996b). *The Balanced Scorecard: Translating Strategy into Action*. Cambridge, MA: Harvard Business School Press.

bargaining unit

David A. Gray

A bargaining unit is a group of employees, union and nonunion, who are designated (by election outcome or by employer voluntary recognition) as appropriate for union representation. If a union representation election is held, these employees are eligible voters. Following a union election victory, these employees become the unit for which a COLLECTIVE BARGAINING agreement is negotiated. Most bargaining units are relatively small (200 employees or fewer), but some are very large, including several thousand workers employed at different locations of the same employer. One employer may also negotiate with several different unions, each representing a different group of employees in a different bargaining unit, at the same location.

Barnes v. *Costle*, 1977

Kelly A. Vaverek

The US Court of Appeals (DC Circuit) held that SEXUAL HARASSMENT violated Title VII (*Barnes* v. *Costle*, 561 F.2d 983, DC Circuit, 1977). Barnes's job was abolished when she resisted her supervisor's sexual advances. The Court of Appeals reasoned that the supervisor would not have made sexual advances "but for her womanhood." Thus, there was a prima facie case that Title VII had been violated (*see* CIVIL RIGHTS ACT OF 1964).

Bibliography

Fager, C. B. (1981). Sexual harassment on the job: The new reach of Title VII. *National Law Journal*, 4, 26.

base rate of success

Michael J. Burke

The base rate of success is the percentage of employees who are successful prior to the use of a new selection procedure. This index is often referred to as the success rate.

behavior

Jeanette N. Cleveland

A behavior is any observable act by an individual (e.g., talking, walking). Clusters of similarly related behaviors are often referred to as habits or traits (*see* TRAIT). Behavior represents the lowest observable level of this hierarchy; work behaviors might include either purposeful or reflexive acts. Purposeful behaviors are goal-directed. They are usually directed toward achieving some PERFORMANCE OUTCOME. Job behavior is believed to be a function of ability, motivation, and the opportunity afforded in a specific organizational setting (Campbell et al., 1970). Abilities include intelligence, skills and aptitudes, interests, and temperament factors (*see* KSAOs). Motivational factors include individual incentives, as well as temperament and preference predispositions to exert effort in performing one's job. Opportunity variables refer to situational and organizational factors, including nature of work, organizational climate, and group influences (see Campbell et al., 1970; Peters and O'Connor, 1980).

Bibliography

Campbell, J. P., Dunnette, M. D., Lawler, E. E., and Weick, K. E. (1970). *Managerial Behavior, Performance, and Effectiveness*. New York: McGraw-Hill.
Mischel, W. and Peake, P. K. (1982). Beyond *déjà vu* in the search for cross-situational consistency. *Psychological Review*, 89, 730–55.

Peters, L. H. and O'Connor, E. J. (1980). Situational constraints and work outcomes: The influences of a frequently overlooked construct. *Academy of Management Review*, 5, 391–7.

behavior modeling

Colette A. Frayne

Behavior modeling is one key aspect of social cognitive theory (Bandura, 1986) that has been investigated extensively in organizational settings. Through the process of observing others, an individual learns how behaviors are performed and the consequences they produce. As a result, observational learning enables individuals to reduce time-consuming trial-and-error behaviors. A meta-analysis of 70 studies on the effectiveness of management training showed that behavior modeling was effective in a variety of training situations (Burke and Day, 1986).

Behavior-modeling training is a process in which a live or videotaped model demonstrates the behavior(s) required for performance. Individuals then imitate the model's behavior in simulated (e.g., ROLE PLAYING) or actual work situations. Typically, learning points are generated by the trainers and are used as a basis for providing feedback to the trainees regarding what was done effectively and what should be done differently.

Bibliography

Bandura, A. (1986). *Social Foundations of Thought and Action*. Englewood Cliffs, NJ: Prentice-Hall.

Burke, M. J. and Day, R. R. (1986). A cumulative study of the effectiveness of managerial training. *Journal of Applied Psychology*, 71, 232–46.

behavioral consistency principle

Richard Klimoski

In PERSONNEL SELECTION theory it has been argued that the best predictor of future behavior or performance is present or past behavior or performance of the same type (Wernimont and Campbell, 1968). This is because of the similarity in demands on behaviors and capabilities that exists in both the assessment and the job contexts. This consistency principle is embedded in the behavioral sampling approach to measurement and is the basis for the development and use of such assessment/selection tools as WORK SAMPLES, ASSESSMENT CENTERS, structured interviews (*see* EMPLOYMENT INTERVIEW), SIMULATIONS, REFERENCE CHECKS, and BIOGRAPHICAL HISTORY INVENTORIES.

Bibliography

Wernimont, P. R. and Campbell, J. P. (1968). Signs, samples and criteria. *Journal of Applied Psychology*, 52, 372–6.

behavioral observation scales

H. John Bernardin

Behavioral observation scales (BOS) are summated rating scales, one of the oldest and most popular formats for the appraisal of performance (Kirchner and Dunnette, 1957; Latham and Wexley, 1977, 1994; *see* PERFORMANCE APPRAISAL). This popularity may be at least partially a result of the relatively simple process required for developing and using the scales.

The first step in the development of summated scales is to generate declarative statements that are related to work behavior and are either desirable or undesirable in nature. Latham, Fay, and Saari (1979) first gathered reports of CRITICAL INCIDENTS TECHNIQUE from persons familiar with the job of foreman and then wrote declarative statements based on those incidents. For example, all incidents that concerned a foreman rewarding an employee for doing a good job served as the basis for the declarative statement, "Praise and/or reward subordinates for specific things they do well." The same procedure was followed for all critical incidents. In this initial step of scale development, the idea is to err on the side of collecting too many items. Statistical analysis of the responses through an item analysis procedure can reduce the set of statements to a manageable number for practical use. However, the set of declarative statements should represent the entire domain of JOB PERFORMANCE.

Next, a format for scoring rater responses is selected. Numerous options are available, the most common of which are words of frequency (e.g., a continuum from "always" to "never") and of intensity (e.g., a continuum from "strongly agree" to "strongly disagree"). Although the response format is often arbitrarily selected, some studies indicate that there may be an optimal type and number of response categories for summated scales. Bass, Cascio, and O'Connor (1974), for example, derived statistically optimal 4- to 9-point scales with adverbs for frequency and amount, while Spector (1976) identified optimal categories of agreement, evaluation, and frequency. In terms of the optimal number of scale points for summated scales, the research results are mixed (e.g., Komorita and Graham, 1965; Matell and Jacoby, 1971). Lissitz and Green (1975), however, found that reliability increases only up to 5 scale points, and levels off thereafter.

Once the declarative statements have been written and the response format and number of scale points selected, the next step is to organize the sequence of declarative statements on the rating format. Most summated scales are set up with a series of items, each followed by a format such as "strongly agree, agree, undecided, disagree, and strongly disagree." It is, however, advisable to change the order for the response format so that the responses are not always in the same position. This procedure is designed to preclude a response-set bias whereby the rater merely checks all responses on the far left (e.g., "strongly agree") or far right ("strongly disagree") without even reading the items. If the sequence of the response format is varied, the rater may have to pay greater attention to what and how to rate (*see* RATING ERRORS).

There should be a number of declarative statements representing each dimension. It is advisable to randomize all items on the appraisal instrument across dimensions. With the completion of these procedures, the summated scale is ready for an initial run. It is important to conduct an item analysis on the summated responses, but the item analysis can be done on data that are administratively useful. Thus, after the summated scales have been adjusted to reflect the item analysis information, the resultant scores can be used for personnel decisions.

Research with BOS compared to other rating formats such as BEHAVIORALLY ANCHORED RATING SCALES shows little difference in psychometric characteristics, but raters prefer BOS to most other formats. There is no evidence of less (or more) bias as a function of this format (Bernardin, Hennessey, and Peyrefitte, 1995).

Bibliography

Bass, B. M., Cascio, W. F., and O'Connor, E. J. (1974). Magnitude estimations of expressions of frequency and amount. *Journal of Applied Psychology*, **59**, 313–20.

Bernardin, H. J., Hennessey, H. W., and Peyrefitte, J. (1995). Age, racial, and gender bias as a function of criterion specificity: A test of expert testimony. *Human Resource Management Review*, **5**, 63–77.

Kirchner, W. K. and Dunnette, M. D. (1957). Identifying the critical factors in successful salesmanship. *Personnel*, **34**, 54–9.

Komorita, S. S. and Graham, W. K. (1965). Number of scale points and the reliability of scales. *Educational and Psychological Measurement*, **4**, 987–95.

Latham, G. P., Fay, C. H., and Saari, L. M. (1979). The development of behavioral observation scales for appraising the performance of foremen. *Personnel Psychology*, **32**, 299–311.

Latham, G. P. and Wexley, K. N. (1977). Behavioral observation scales for performance appraisal purposes. *Personnel Psychology*, **30**, 255–68.

Latham, G. P. and Wexley, K. N. (1994). *Increasing Productivity through Performance Appraisal*, 2nd edn. Reading, MA: Addison-Wesley.

Lissitz, R. W. and Green, S. B. (1975). Effect of the number of scale points on reliability: A Monte Carlo approach. *Journal of Applied Psychology*, **60**, 10–13.

Matell, M. S. and Jacoby, J. (1971). Is there an optimal number of alternatives for Likert scale items? Study I: Reliability and validity. *Educational and Psychological Measurement*, **31**, 657–74.

Spector, P. E. (1976). Choosing response categories for summated rating scales. *Journal of Applied Psychology*, **61**, 374–5H.

behaviorally anchored rating scales

H. John Bernardin

Behaviorally anchored rating scales (BARS) are graphic performance rating scales with specific behavioral descriptions defining various points along each scale (Smith and Kendall, 1963). Each scale represents a dimension, factor, or work function considered important for work performance. Typically, both raters and ratees are involved in the development of the dimensions and the generation of behavioral descriptions.

The original BARS procedure was basically an iterative process whereby a sample from the rater population began development of the scales. Their work was then scrutinized by additional samples of raters. In the original conceptualization of the BARS method, raters were instructed to record the behaviors observed on each applicable job dimension throughout the appraisal period. They were then to decide to which dimension each behavior belonged, and to indicate, on the rating scale, the date of and details associated with each incident. Each entry was to be made on the rating scale at the effectiveness level that was considered most appropriate for that incident. The scaling of the effectiveness level of the observation (i.e., the place on the page at which the observer recorded the incident) was to be guided by a comparison with the series of illustrative "behavioral anchors" and generic performance-level descriptors. The illustrative behaviors would have been identified from prior research as belonging to a particular job dimension and as representing a specific effectiveness level for that dimension.

It was not necessary that the notation of observed behavior be made at the exact point on the graphic scale at which some illustrative behavior had been previously scaled. Rather, the observer was to *infer* the behavioral dimension involved and to decide what had been observed in relation to the specific behavioral and more generic examples. The rater, thus, would interpolate between the illustrative examples when recording a brief notation of the behavior that had been observed.

The behavioral anchoring illustrations were to be concrete and specific, and located at irregular intervals along the relevant scale according to effectiveness. The dimensions themselves would have been chosen only after considerable discussion of organizational goals and objectives. After a period of observation and incident-recording, the rater could, if necessary, make a summary rating. This summary, plus the notes, could serve as a basis for discussion with the ratee and/or as a criterion measure.

Numerous variants of the BARS procedure have been introduced since the approach was first proposed. A complete discussion of the various appraisal formats that have been introduced under the guise of BARS can be found in Bernardin and Smith (1981). Several comparisons of the BARS approach to other rating methods, such as BEHAVIORAL OBSERVATION SCALES, have found no reliable advantage to any rating method, including BARS.

Bibliography

Bernardin, H. J. and Smith, P. C. (1981). A clarification of some issues regarding the development and use of behaviorally anchored rating scales. *Journal of Applied Psychology*, **66**, 458–63.

Smith, P. C. and Kendall, L. M. (1963). Retranslation of expectations: An approach to the construction of unambiguous anchors for rating scales. *Journal of Applied Psychology*, **47**, 149–55H.

Belbin teams

Hadyn Bennett

Belbin (1983, 1991, 1993) argues that in a team situation particular individuals will adopt specific "team" roles, distinct from their task responsibilities; the blend of these roles, it is argued, has a crucial impact on the efficiency and effectiveness of the team. An individual's preferred team role is a function of personality type, and using Cattell's 16PF test (Cattell and Kline, 1977) Belbin identifies eight team roles essential for team success (1983), to which he later added a ninth (1993).

The nine roles are: the Chairman/Coordinator (calm, self-confident, controlled – presides over the efforts of the team); the Plant (individualistic, imaginative, unorthodox – the source of original ideas); the Shaper (high levels of drive, dynamic – drives the practical application of the team's efforts); the Resource Investigator (extraverted, enthusiastic, communicative – develops external contacts and sources resources required); the Monitor Evaluator (sober, unemotional, prudent – contributes measured and dispassionate analysis); the Teamworker (socially oriented, cooperative, and perceptive – perceives emotional undercurrents within the team and tries to promote harmony); the Company Worker/Implementor (conservative, dutiful, predictable – the practical organizer); the Finisher/Completer (conscientious and anxious – tries to insure tasks are completed accurately and on time); and the Specialist (single-minded and dedicated – provides specialist knowledge and skills).

While there has been some criticism that Belbin's team-role inventory has limited validity and reliability (Furnham, Steele, and Pendleton, 1993; Dulewicz, 1995), other authors have refuted these claims (Swailes and McIntyre-Bhatty, 2002), with Lessem and Baruch (2000: 77) arguing that in the UK and western Europe generally, Belbin's approach to team building "has become perhaps the most often used amongst managers."

Bibliography

Belbin, R. M. (1983). *Team Roles at Work*. Oxford: Butterworth.
Belbin, R. M. (1991). *Management Teams: Why They Succeed or Fail*. Oxford: Butterworth.
Belbin, R. M. (1993). *Team Roles at Work*. Oxford: Butterworth-Heinemann.
Cattell, R. B. and Kline, P. (1977). *The Scientific Analysis of Personality and Motivation*. New York: Academic Press.
Dulewicz, V. (1995). A validation of Belbin's team roles from 16PF and OPQ using bosses' ratings of competence. *Journal of Occupational and Organizational Psychology*, **68**, 1–99.
Furnham, A., Steele, H., and Pendleton, D. (1993). A psychometric assessment of the Belbin team-role self-perception inventory. *Journal of Occupational and Organizational Psychology*, **66**, 45–57.
Lessem, R. and Baruch, Y. (2000). Testing the SMT and Belbin inventories in top management teams. *Leadership and Organization Development Journal*, **21** (2), 75–83.
Swailes, S. and McIntyre-Bhatty, T. (2002). The "Belbin" team role inventory: Reinterpreting reliability estimates. *Journal of Managerial Psychology*, **17** (6), 529–36.

benchmarking and competitor analysis

Dave Ulrich

Human resource (HR) benchmarking is the process of learning how other firms perform HR practices. Learning how other firms do their HR work helps firms to compare and improve their methods. Competitor analysis is the process of comparing one's HR practices with another firm as a way to outperform the competitor.

WHY DO BENCHMARKING?

In the business world, benchmarking HR practice serves three purposes (Fitz-enz, 1992; Glanz and Dailey, 1993):

1 It enables a company to calibrate how it is doing compared to well-respected companies. This calibration enables HR professionals to gauge, compare, or audit their HR work. For example, if Motorola is respected as a leader and innovator in training activities and Motorola is investing 2.5 percent of payroll in training, this number can serve as a standard for training investments.

2 It enables a company to learn from others. Benchmarking forces an external perspective on HR practices and is done by visiting other companies. Since Florida Power and Light won the coveted Deming Award in 1989, over 1,000 companies have visited their operations to learn how to better engage in quality processes.

3 It enables a company to set priorities and allocate resources for an HR department. By comparing against others and learning from what others are doing, HR professionals may invest in some activities more than others. Lessons from benchmarking quality programs at Motorola have helped Philips Electronics to introduce and improve its quality initiatives.

In the academic world, benchmarking creates the institutionalization of knowledge within the HR function. Institutionalization theory suggests that as ideas shift from firm to firm, some ideas become more legitimate and therefore accepted as standard practice (Scott, 1987). HR benchmarking creates the body of knowledge on which HR practices are created.

WHAT IS BENCHMARKED?

Three types of HR benchmarks may be done:

1   broad organizational issues, such as PRODUCTIVITY, labor ratios, or other administrative costs;
2   HR practices (e.g., TRAINING, COMPENSATION, STAFFING, organization design);
3   competencies of HR professionals.

How to Benchmark

HR benchmarking generally follows four steps:

1   creating a framework of practices or issues to benchmark;
2   collecting data from targeted companies;
3   integrating and analyzing the data; and
4   acting on the information collected.

Data collected may be qualitative or quantitative, collected by HR professionals or line managers, focused within an industry or across an industry.

Benchmarking fails to deliver on its promises when data collected are not acted on, when firms try to copy what other firms are doing without adapting to firm-specific conditions, when relationships between HR practices are not taken into account, when line managers are not involved in collecting or using the information collected, and when ideas learned from benchmarking are not integrated or implemented into a firm.

Bibliography

Fitz-enz, J. (1992). Benchmarking: HR's new improvement tool. *HR Horizons*, **107**, 7–13.
Glanz, E. and Dailey, L. (1993). Benchmarking. *Human Resource Management Journal*, **31**, 9–20.
Liefried, K. and McNair, C. J. (1992). *Benchmarking: A Tool for Continuous Improvement*. New York: Harper Business.
Scott, R. (1987). The adolescence of institutional theory. *Administrative Science Quarterly*, **32**, 493–511.

benefit programs: evolution

Charles H. Fay

Benefit programs have grown for a number of reasons. Initially, wartime controls on wage increases made the addition of BENEFITS the only way to increase employee COMPENSATION. The US federal government has encouraged the growth of benefits by providing favorable tax treatment to income received in the form of benefits by employees and to benefits expenditures by employers. Group coverage for a benefit by an employer is cheaper than the benefit would cost the employee. Unions and non-represented employees like receiving benefits since they are entitlements under organizational membership rather than earned through individual performance or increased PRODUCTIVITY. Many benefits are government-mandated, and benefit levels have been increased by law. Finally, employers have found they can attract and retain employees by offering benefit packages that employees want.

This has resulted in a growth in benefits costs to employers far greater than the increase in wages. In 1960, benefits (then called "fringe" benefits) accounted for about 8 percent of total compensation costs for private sector US employers; in 1993 benefits accounted for about 29 percent of total compensation costs, and 27.4 percent in 2000 (Employee Benefit Research Institute, 1995: 15; Employee Benefit Research Institute, 1997, updated to 2002). This increase has led employers to take a number of actions to reduce or at least stabilize costs. Copayment techniques require employees to help pay for the benefit offered. Coinsurance approaches require employees to bear part of the risk. Cafeteria plans have been introduced to allow employees to select only those benefits which they want. Administrative techniques have been introduced which reduce costs, especially in healthcare, using MANAGED CARE approaches.

Bibliography

Allen, D. (1969). *Fringe Benefits: Wages or Social Obligation?* Ithaca, NY: Cornell University Press.
Employee Benefit Research Institute (1995). *EBRI Databook on Employee Benefits*, 3rd edn. Washington, DC: Employee Benefit Research Institute.
Employee Benefit Research Institute (1997). *EBRI Databook on Employee Benefits*, 4th edn. Washington, DC: Employee Benefit Research Institute. (Data updated to 2002 on EBRI website: www.ebri.org.)

benefits

Steven L. Thomas

Employee benefits are the indirect components of the total COMPENSATION package including all tangible returns for an employee's labor except for direct pay (Milkovich and Newman, 1993).

Benefit growth has been rapid over the latter half of the twentieth century (*see* BENEFIT PROGRAMS: EVOLUTION) as the result of changing federal regulations, tax codes, union influence, and even employer initiatives (McCaffery, 1992). Benefits, in the past referred to as "fringe benefits," are an important and expensive portion of the total compensation package, accounting for more than one-third of the cost of employee compensation, with more than US$1,000 billion spent in benefits each year (Henderson, 1994).

There is no standard benefit classification scheme (McCaffery, 1992), but it is common to distinguish among several different benefit dimensions. Legally required or mandatory benefits include SOCIAL SECURITY BENEFITS, UNEMPLOYMENT COMPENSATION, and WORKERS' COMPENSATION BENEFITS. Most employers are required to offer these benefits to employees and the cost of each is borne totally (or at least partially) by the employer.

Discretionary benefits are not required of employers, although they may be regulated if offered, and may include: (1) PAID TIME OFF (vacations and sick leave); (2) healthcare expense plans (MANAGED CARE networks, HEALTH MAINTENANCE ORGANIZATIONS, preferred provider organizations); (3) deferred income and income continuation plans (PENSION PLANS, life insurance, and GROUP DISABILITY BENEFITS); and (4) income equivalents such as CHILDCARE BENEFIT, FINANCIAL ASSISTANCE PLANS, employee discounts, and club memberships (Henderson, 1994).

The designing of benefit programs requires employers to make several decisions that balance the company's objectives of offering an adequate, competitive, yet cost-contained benefit package. Employers must decide which groups to provide with benefit coverage, how much choice to offer employees in the selection of benefits (*see* FLEXIBLE BENEFIT PLANS), and the extent to which employees should pay none (noncontributory), some (contributory), or all of the cost of a benefit option (Milkovich and Newman, 1993). Finally, communication of the benefits program (*see* BENEFITS COMMUNICATION) is important to enable employees to understand and value the benefits package.

Bibliography

Henderson, R. I. (1994). *Compensation Management: Rewarding Performance.* Englewood Cliffs, NJ: Prentice-Hall.

McCaffery, R. M. (1992). *Employee Benefit Programs: A Total Compensation Perspective*, 2nd edn. Boston: PWS-Kent.

Milkovich, G. T. and Newman, J. M. (1993). *Compensation*, 4th edn. Homewood, IL: Richard D. Irwin.

benefits administration

Charles H. Fay

Benefits administration consists of developing and integrating the components of the benefits package and then managing the various programs as a unified system. Key activities of benefits administration include enrolling employees, communicating with employees, handling changes in employee contributions and program status, and dealing with benefits vendors. Major trends in benefits administration include increased use of cafeteria or flexible benefit programs (*see* FLEXIBLE BENEFIT PLANS), cost control and/or reduction, and outsourcing of all aspects of benefits administration.

Flexible benefit programs have increased in use because they provide a means of insuring that employees do not receive benefits that they do not value, and because they provide a mechanism for introducing cost controls. Many employers have provided full benefits coverage to employees in terms of defined levels of service. As costs increase, any cost-shifting to employees is viewed as a reduction in service. With flexible plans, a menu of benefits is offered to employees, and choice up to some level of employer cost is allowed. Additional benefits may be purchased, introducing the notion of employee contributions, or copayments. When benefits costs increase, it becomes much easier to shift part of the increase to the employee. Outsourcing of all aspects of benefits administration is increasing. In many organizations, an employee can call a toll-free number, and the outside vendor will provide any information about the employee's status, can make changes in plan selection, and provide benefits counseling. Organizations adopting benefits administration outsourcing have been able to reduce internal benefits staff to a few benefits planners and vendor relations managers.

Bibliography

Beam, B. T. and McFadden, J. J. (2001). *Employee Benefits*, 6th edn. Chicago: Dearborn Financial Publishing, pp. 13–42.

Mahoney, D. F. (2001). Managing employee benefit plans. In J. S. Rosenbloom (ed.), *The Handbook of Employee Benefits: Design, Funding and Administration*, 5th edn. New York: McGraw-Hill, pp. 859–89.

benefits communication

Robert M. McCaffery

Compared with pay (direct COMPENSATION), the communication of BENEFITS (indirect compensation) is a much greater challenge for employers. Although benefits typically comprise at least a third of total compensation costs, many benefit plans are not clearly apparent to employees. For example, vacations, holidays, and other forms of PAID TIME OFF are part of employees' paychecks and not always recognized as benefits even though they represent an expense to employers. Also some benefits (e.g., PENSION PLANS and FLEXIBLE BENEFIT PLANS) can be especially difficult for employees to understand.

To insure that employees receive essential information about pension and other benefit plans, the EMPLOYEE RETIREMENT INCOME SECURITY ACT OF 1974 (ERISA) mandates certain written communication. These include requirements that participants receive the following documents, written in clear and appropriate language:

1 a summary plan description (SPD) for all applicable plans with information about eligibility and plan features;

2 a statement of ERISA rights with plan identification information and an explanation of inquiry and appeal processes; and

3 a summary annual report (SAR) containing relevant financial information for all applicable plans.

Beyond meeting mandatory requirements, most employers now realize that a proactive communications program is needed to build awareness, understanding, and appreciation among employees with respect to benefits.

An increasingly popular method of communication is the personalized annual benefit report, which combines computer-produced individual information with standard text. Other techniques now utilized by employers to achieve communications goals include: (1) paycheck inserts; (2) articles in company publications; (3) contests; (4) interactive computer programs; (5) video cassettes; (6) employee meetings and focus groups; or (7) letters to the home and internal memoranda.

Bibliography

Kumata, H. (1979). *Communication Dynamics for Employee Benefit Programs*. Brookfield, WI: International Foundation of Employee Benefit Plans.

McCaffery, R. M. (1992). *Employee Benefit Programs: A Total Compensation Perspective*, 2nd edn. Boston: PWS-Kent.

Big Five personality tests

Michael K. Mount

The views of many personality psychologists have converged regarding the structure and concepts of personality. It is generally now agreed that there are *five* robust factors, known as the Big Five or the Five Factor Model (FFM) of personality, that can serve as a meaningful taxonomy for classifying personality attributes. This taxonomy has consistently emerged in longitudinal studies, across different sources of raters, with numerous specific personality inventories and theoretical systems, and in different age, sex, race, and language groups (Digman, 1990). Although the specific names applied to the five factors vary somewhat across researchers, they are commonly labeled and defined in the following way: conscientiousness (dependable, achievement-oriented, efficient), extraversion (sociable, ambitious, dominant), emotional stability (secure, steady, well adjusted), agreeableness (cooperative, trusting, considerate), and openness to experience (imaginative, artistically sensitive, intellectual). Big Five personality inventories measure these personality dimensions using paper-and-pencil, self-report formats. Some use observers' ratings rather than self-ratings. Commonly used Big Five personality inventories are the Hogan Personality Inventory (HPI), the NEO-PI, and the Personal Characteristics Inventory (PCI).

See also *personality tests*

Bibliography

Buros, O. K. (1992). *The Mental Measurements Yearbook*. Highland Park, NJ: Grython Press.

Digman, J. M. (1990). Personality structure: Emergence of the five factor model. *Annual Review of Psychology*, 41, 417–40.

Gatewood, R. D. and Field, H. S. (1992). *Human Resource Selection*, 2nd edn. Hinsdale, IL: Dryden Press.

biographical history inventories

Craig J. Russell

Biographical history (biodata) inventories were developed around a century ago for PERSONNEL SELECTION (Owens, 1976). Biodata inventories typically contain questions about prior events in the lives of job applicants. Scores from biodata inventories have been found to predict subsequent JOB PERFORMANCE as accurately as paper-and-pencil mental ability tests and WORK SAMPLES (uncorrected criterion-related validity of approximately 0.30 to 0.40; Hunter and Hunter, 1984).

Various conceptual models try to explain why past experiences should predict individuals' future work and career outcomes (Mumford, Stokes, and Owens, 1990; Mael, 1991), although none has particularly strong support. Mumford et al.'s ecology model has perhaps the best support, suggesting that biodata items tap past sequences of knowledge acquisition, skill development, motivation, needs, desires, and choices. Individual differences in these sequences then influence development outcomes, including job performance.

ITEM CONTENT

Many "types" of biodata item content have been described, though most categorization systems are not accompanied by strong theoretical rationales and must be considered arbitrary (see Asher, 1972). Perhaps the simplest biodata item description is "any question aimed at life experiences phrased in the past tense." Typical items might include: "How much life insurance did you sell last year?" and "How often did you break off steady dating relationships in high school" (Russell, 1994). The former might predict applicants' subsequent life insurance sales volume, while the latter predicts subsequent performance of freshmen at the US Naval Academy (Russell et al., 1990). However, the former has an intuitive correspondence with a criterion (*see* BEHAVIORAL CONSISTENCY PRINCIPLE), while the latter seems to have no overlap with 18-year-olds' future performance as officers in the Navy. A strong theory of biodata should indicate how to sample prior examples of the criteria (e.g., life insurance sales) *and* prior events bearing no obvious relationship to the criteria. Strong theory is not currently available.

Multiple aspects of life events can be captured by biodata items. The development of item content can follow almost any procedure, though items developed in concert with some a priori rationale predict best (Williams, 1961; Russell, 1990). See Russell (1994) for a review of item development methods, to include incumbents' narrative answers to life history questions, biographies, interviews, focus groups, and "best" psychological judgment of investigator(s).

KEYING PROCEDURES

Biodata inventories are distinctive in their scoring. *Rationale keys* use experts' judgments of the "expected" relationship between item responses and the criterion. For example, one would expect high levels of past life insurance sales to predict future life insurance sales. Response options to a question about past life insurance sales would be scored to give more "points" to applicants who sold large amounts of insurance in the past. Biodata items with no obvious relationship to performance cannot enter rationale keys.

Empirical keys are used most often in selection venues, optimally allocating "biodata points" to response options to predict performance. Methods are complex, though the "vertical percent difference method" seems most powerful (Devlin, Abrahams, and Edwards, 1992; Brown, 1994). To exemplify this method, assume that the "dating item" above was part of an inventory given to 1,000 new undergraduate management majors as part of a study designed to predict career success (measured ten years later in terms of career performance measures such as income and number of promotions). The 1,000 participants are randomly assigned to groups of 750 (validation sample) and 250 (cross-validation sample). Statistical associations between response alternatives on the biodata items and income are examined in the validation sample and verified in the cross-validation sample (*see* CRITERION-RELATED VALIDITY; PREDICTIVE VALIDITY). The 750 students are sorted into three equal-sized groups ($n = 250$ each) on some performance measure (say, income). For each biodata item, response alternative frequencies are then compared for high- versus low-income groupings for each of the response options (e.g., response options of 1 to 5, corresponding to rating scale anchors ranging from 1 = "not very often" to 5 = "very often"). If high-income students selected response alternative 3 much more frequently than low-income students, the empirical key would award more biodata points to students selecting this response option. The greater the percentage of persons in the high-income group choosing this option relative to those in the low-income group, the more the biodata points that would be awarded. This procedure would be completed for each response alternative. If the high- and low-income groups endorsed a particular response alternative with similar frequency, it would *not* be scored, since it does not differentiate high- versus low-income groups. Thus, high- and low-income groups are compared for each response alternative for each item. Those which differentiate these groups receive biodata points that reflect that degree of predictability. The sum of points assigned by the key yields its "biodata score."

The VALIDITY of the biodata scoring key is examined by using the empirical scoring key within the cross-validation sample. Responses from the 250 students initially held back are scored and these scores are then correlated with the actual income earned by these persons ten years after graduation. Valid empirical keys should predict the income criterion in this sample. If found valid in the hold-out sample, the key would be used in future samples to predict standing on the outcome of interest (in this example, income).

Bibliography

Asher, E. J. (1972). The biographical item: Can it be improved? *Personnel Psychology*, **25**, 251–69.

Brown, S. H. (1994). Validating biodata. In G. Stokes, M. Mumford, and W. C. Owens (eds.), *Biodata Handbook: Theory, Research and Use of Biographical Information for Selection and Performance Prediction*. Orlando, FL: Consulting Psychologists Press, pp. 199–236.

Devlin, S. E., Abrahams, N. M., and Edwards, J. E. (1992). Empirical keying of biographical data: Cross-validity as a function of scaling procedure and sample size. *Military Psychology*, **4**, 119–36.

Hunter, J. E. and Hunter, R. F. (1984). Validity and utility of alternate predictors of job performance. *Psychological Bulletin*, **96**, 72–98.

Mael, F. A. (1991). A conceptual rationale for the domain and attributes of biodata items. *Personnel Psychology*, **44**, 763–92.

Mumford, M. D. and Owens, W. C. (1987). Methodology review: Principles, procedures, and findings in the application of background data measures. *Applied Psychological Measurement*, **11**, 1–31.

Mumford, M. D., Stokes, G. S., and Owens, W. C. (1990). *Patterns of Life History: The Ecology of Human Individuality*. Hillsdale, NJ: Erlbaum.

Owens, W. C. (1968). Toward one discipline of psychology. *American Psychologist*, **23**, 782–5.

Owens, W. C. (1976). Background data. In M. D. Dunnette (ed.), *The Handbook of Industrial and Organizational Psychology*. Chicago: Rand McNally, pp. 609–44.

Owens, W. C. and Schoenfeldt, L. F. (1979). Toward a classification of persons. *Journal of Applied Psychology*, **64**, 569–607.

Russell, C. J. (1990). Selecting top corporate leaders: An example of biographical information. *Journal of Management*, **16**, 71–84.

Russell, C. J. (1994). Biodata item generation procedures: A point of departure. In G. Stokes, M. Mumford, and

W. C. Owens (eds.), *Biodata Handbook: Theory, Research and Use of Biographical Information for Selection and Performance Prediction*. Orlando, FL: Consulting Psychologists Press, pp. 18–38.

Russell, C. J., Mattson, J., Devlin, S. E., and Atwater, D. (1990). Predictive validity of biodata items generated from retrospective life experience essays. *Journal of Applied Psychology*, 75, 511–20.

Williams, W. E. (1961). Life history antecedents of volunteers versus nonvolunteers for an AFROTC program. Paper read at the Midwestern Psychological Association, Chicago.

bona fide occupational qualification

Barbara A. Lee

Employers may discriminate on the basis of religion, age, national origin, or sex if one of these characteristics is a bona fide occupational qualification (BFOQ) for the position. To qualify as a BFOQ, the characteristic must be "reasonably necessary to the normal operation of that particular business" (29 USC section 2000e-2(e)(1)), or serve as a proxy for a characteristic that is impossible or impracticable to ascertain in some other way. For example, age was considered to be a BFOQ for cardiac fitness in *Western Airlines* v. *Criswell* (472 US 400, 1985) because it was impracticable for the airline to make individualized determinations of cardiac fitness. Religion may be a BFOQ for a job in a religious organization (29 USC section 2000e-2(e)(2)), but race is never a permissible BFOQ.

See also *discrimination*

bona fide seniority system

Barbara A. Lee

A bona fide seniority system is one that recognizes job tenure and allocates employment rights on that basis, but which was not created with the intent to discriminate. For example, a seniority system that added a segregated seniority list of African-American workers to the bottom of the white seniority list would not be a bona fide seniority system. However, a seniority system that resulted in recently hired minority workers having less seniority than long-tenured white workers would, absent other evidence of discriminatory treatment of the minority workers, qualify as a bona fide seniority system.

See also *discrimination*

bonuses

David B. Balkin

Bonuses are cash payments for employees who achieve a goal or level of performance that is desired by management. Bonuses are a type of VARIABLE COMPENSATION that is given out on a one-time-only basis and is not built into the salary (Belcher and Atchison, 1989). Bonuses are very flexible and can be used to reward employees for achieving goals that represent individual, team, unit, or organization performance (Gomez-Mejia and Balkin, 1992). For example, GAINSHARING plans will provide a bonus to all employees in a work unit if they are able to exceed expected unit performance standards within a specified period of time.

Bibliography

Belcher, D. W. and Atchison, T. J. (1989). *Compensation Administration*, 2nd edn. Englewood Cliffs, NJ: Prentice-Hall.

Gomez-Mejia, L. R. and Balkin, D. B. (1992). *Compensation Organizational Strategy and Firm Performance*. Cincinnati, OH: South-Western Publishing.

broadbanding

David B. Balkin

Broadbanding is a pay innovation that collapses a pay structure with many pay grades (*see* PAY GRADE) into a structure with a few larger pay ranges called bands (Caudron, 1993). Each band covers a pay range that formerly represented several pay grades. Broadbanding gives managers greater flexibility to encourage employees to move in a horizontal direction in their careers by broadening their skills and competencies. Firms that have delayered their hierarchies and reduced the number of job titles and PROMOTION opportunities for employees may benefit from the increased flexibility in the pay structure that can be provided by broadbanding (Abosch, 1995). Broadbanding places a decreased emphasis on remuneration based on job evaluation (*see* JOB EVALUATION METHODS) and use of control points such as a midpoint or a maximum of pay range. It places an increased emphasis on encouraging employees to develop new skills and paying for the skills according to their market value.

Broadbanding can be used to reinforce teamwork and collaboration since it reduces hierarchy and status differences between employees in the pay structure. Firms that use the pay and promotion systems to recognize status and hierarchical differences between employees may not have a culture that is supportive of a broadbanding pay policy (Hofrichter, 1993).

Bibliography

Abosch, K. S. (1995). The promise of broadbanding. *Compensation and Benefits Review*, 27, 54–8.

Caudron, S. (1993). Master the compensation maze. *Personnel Journal*, 72, 64B–64O.

Hofrichter, D. (1993). Broadbanding: A "second generation" approach. *Compensation and Benefits Review*, 25, 53–8.

bullying

Helge Hoel and Ståle Einarsen

Bullying in the workplace has been acknowledged as a major occupational stressor, with severe consequences for the individuals involved, and financial impact on organizations (Hoel, Zapf, and Cooper, 2002). Influenced by the debate on "bullying in schools," the phenomenon was first studied in Scandinavia (Einarsen, 2000). The terminology for this phenomenon has been varied, with different labels attributed to the problem in different parts of the world (Hoel, Rayner, and Cooper, 1999). Thus, whilst "mobbing" is the preferred term in Scandinavia and German-speaking countries, the favored term in the UK, Ireland, and Australia is "bullying," whilst in the US and Canada the problem has been variously referred to as "emotional abuse," "employee abuse," and "mistreatment at work" (Einarsen et al., 2003).

Despite a number of definitions in use, the following incorporates the key features of the phenomenon:

> Bullying at work means harassing, offending, socially excluding someone or negatively affecting someone's work tasks. In order for the label bullying (or mobbing) to be applied to a particular activity, interaction or process it has to occur repeatedly and regularly (e.g. weekly) and over a period of time (e.g. about six months). Bullying is an escalating process in the course of which the person confronted ends up in an inferior position and becomes the target of systematic negative social acts. A conflict cannot be called bullying if the incident is an isolated event or if two parties of approximately equal "strength" are in conflict. (Einarsen et al., 2003)

The negative behaviors involved are used with the aim, or at least the effect, of persistently humiliating, intimidating, frightening, or punishing the victim. Many of these acts may be relatively common in interaction between employees in the workplace and may not be so serious in isolation. But when they are frequent and, over a longer period of time, persistently directed toward the same individual, they may be considered an extreme source of social stress, capable of causing severe harm and damage (Zapf, 1999).

The bullying process tends to evolve through a series of distinct phases or stages which may often be referred to as *aggressive behaviors*, *bullying*, *stigmatization*, and *severe trauma* (Einarsen, 1999). The initial phase, where indirect and subtle forms of aggression prevail, tends to be followed by a stage of more direct negative behaviors, often leaving the target humiliated, ridiculed, and increasingly isolated. As a result the targets become stigmatized and find it more and more difficult to defend themselves. The frequency and intensity of the exposure also have the function of changing the meaning of the behavior (Leymann, 1996). Thus, the target would tend to feel hounded or at the mercy of someone whose aim is to "get you." Unsurprisingly, exposure to such treatment has a significant impact on the target. The stigmatizing effects of these activities, and their escalating frequency and intensity, make the victims constantly less able to cope with their daily tasks and cooperation with colleagues, thus making them continually more vulnerable and "a deserving target" (Einarsen, 2000).

A number of studies have explored the relationship between bullying and negative health outcomes. Typically, targets of bullying have been found to suffer from psychosomatic stress symptoms, anxiety, and depression (Björkqvist, Österman, and Hjelt-Bäck, 1994; Leymann, 1996; Vartia, 2001). Many of the more severely affected bullying victims reported similar symptoms to those identified with post-traumatic stress disorder (PTSD) (Einarsen et al., 2003). The erratic and obsessive behavior observed in many victims frequently cut them off from support, exacerbating their isolation and the victimization process. Recent studies have confirmed that bullying appears to manifest itself behaviorally by affecting levels of ABSENTEEISM and EMPLOYEE TURNOVER as well as PRODUCTIVITY (Rayner, 1999; Einarsen et al., 2003) along with other organizational consequences, which together may represent a considerable cost to the organization. The fact that third parties or witnesses also appear to be affected by bullying, possibly due to fear of becoming a target themselves, further exacerbates the impact of the problem (Rayner, 1999). Depending upon the definition and measurement used, the results of a number of prevalence studies across Europe, the US, and Australia suggest that 1–4 percent of employees may experience a severe degree of bullying, a figure rising to 10–20 percent or above when occasional exposure to bullying behavior is considered (see Einarsen et al., 2003, for a review).

A work situation characterized by role conflict and a lack of interesting and challenging work tasks, combined with a negative interpersonal climate in the work group, seems to be a high-risk situation for bullying (Einarsen, 1999). Low satisfaction with the leadership is also typical of workplaces where bullying prevails. In fact, as many as 50–80 percent of the victims of bullying claim to be bullied by a superior, again linking bullying closely to leadership. Theoretically, five factors are claimed to be risk factors of bullying at work: (1) deficiencies in work design; (2) deficiencies in leadership behavior; (3) the victim's vulnerability; (4) a negative social climate in the unit; and (5) an organizational culture permissive or supportive of aggressive behavior (Leymann, 1993; Einarsen, 1999). However, the causes of bullying at work have also been related to concepts such as personality, interpersonal conflicts, aggression, and human resource management (HRM) practices (see Einarsen et al., 2003, for a review).

During the late 1990s, the concept of workplace bullying found a resonance within the European working population as well as in the academic community (Einarsen et al., 2003). As a psychosocial hazard the issue has obvious relevance to the stress discipline. Moreover, bullying research has benefited from progress in the more mature academic field of SEXUAL HARASSMENT, and, to some extent, from research into aggression and work-related violence. In both cases the opportunity for cross-fertilization between the fields is evident. Recent years have also seen a growing interest among human resource specialists, with many organizations adopting antibullying policies and exploring proactive approaches such as a risk-assessment strategy (Einarsen et al., 2003). However, future research needs to establish the effectiveness of various interventions.

See also *workplace violence*

Bibliography

Björkqvist, K., Österman, K., and Hjelt-Bäck, M. (1994). Aggression among university employees. *Aggressive Behavior*, 20, 173–84.

Einarsen, S. (1999). The nature and causes of bullying at work. *International Journal of Manpower*, 20, 16–27.

Einarsen, S. (2000). Bullying and harassment at work: A review of the Scandinavian approach. *Aggression and Violent Behavior*, 5, 379–401.

Einarsen, S., Hoel, H., Zapf, D., and Cooper, C. L. (2003). Bullying and emotional abuse in the workplace. In S. Einarsen, H. Hoel, D. Zapf, and C. L. Cooper (eds.), *International Perspectives in Research and Practice*. London/New York: Taylor and Francis.

Hoel, H., Rayner, C., and Cooper, C. L. (1999). Workplace bullying. In C. L. Cooper and I. T. Robertson (eds.), *International Review of Industrial and Organizational Psychology*. Chichester: John Wiley, pp. 195–230.

Hoel, H., Zapf, D., and Cooper, C. L. (2002). Bullying and stress. In D. Ganster and P. Perrewe (eds.), *Research in Occupational Stress and Well-Being*, vol. 2. London: JAI/Elsevier Science, pp. 293–333.

Leymann, H. (1996). The content and development of mobbing at work. *European Journal of Work and Organizational Psychology*, 5, 165–84.

Rayner, C. (1999). From research to implementation: Finding leverage for prevention. *International Journal of Manpower*, 20, 28–38.

Vartia, M. (2001). Consequences of workplace bullying with respect to well-being of its targets and the observers of bullying. *Scandinavian Journal of Work Environment and Health*, 27, 63–9.

Zapf, D. (1999). Organizational, work group related and personal causes of mobbing/bullying at work. *International Journal of Manpower*, 20, 70–85.

burden of proof

Ramona L. Paetzold

The term "burden of proof" refers to the elements that must be proven at various stages of a trial, and to the party that must establish them. Thus, "burden of proof" signifies a formal scheme by which both sides to a lawsuit present their evidence. In employment DISCRIMINATION cases, the burden of proof depends on the model(s) of discrimination that the plaintiff has invoked, as well as the stage of consideration of evidence within the model(s).

In general, the law recognizes two different "proof" burdens – the burden of production and the burden of persuasion. The burden of production typically means a burden to articulate credible evidence that puts forth disputed facts and/or addresses the opposing party's evidence (*see* DISPARATE TREATMENT). The burden of persuasion means that the burden is to convince the factfinder of the validity of the claim, according to the prevailing legal standard (such as preponderance of the evidence). Although it is common to associate the burden of persuasion with the plaintiff (i.e., the person bringing the suit has the burden to convince the factfinder), defendants may also at times bear the burden of persuasion (*see* DISPARATE IMPACT).

business necessity

Barbara A. Lee

Business necessity must be demonstrated by an employer-defendant to rebut a presumption that an employment practice that has a DISPARATE IMPACT on a protected class is discriminatory. Employers must show that the practice is necessary to the conduct of their business and that an alternative with a less discriminatory effect on the protected class is less effective. One method of proving business necessity is to show that the challenged practice is job-related. Other methods include showing that the practice affords a strong benefit to the business, and that its cessation would impose a heavy burden on the employer (Schlei and Grossman, 1983: 1329).

See also *discrimination; job-relatedness*

Bibliography

Schlei, B. L. and Grossman, P. (1983). *Employment Discrimination Law*, 2nd edn. Washington, DC: Bureau of National Affairs.

business process reengineering

Willam H. Glick

Definitions of "reengineering" have proliferated since Hammer's popularization of the term (Hammer, 1990; Hammer and Champy, 1993). Hammer and Stanton's (1995) self-proclaimed "official definition" of reengineering is "the fundamental rethinking and radical redesign of business processes to bring about dramatic improvement in performance." Most variations on this definition have focused on the methodology of reengineering, rather than the outcomes. Each change agent or researcher with a slightly different methodology has crafted a new definition of business process reengineering, or coined his or her own terms, such as business process improvement (Harrington, 1991), process innovation (Davenport, 1993), or business process redesign.

METHODOLOGY FOR CHANGE

Sorting through the plethora of definitions, there are several common elements. A more generic definition is that business process reengineering is a systematic methodology for fundamentally rethinking and changing an entire business system to realign the strategy, business processes, jobs, organizational structures, management and measurement systems, information systems, and values and beliefs. It is a methodology for focusing the organization on the process of delivering measurable value to the customer.

The most important defining characteristics of business process reengineering are:

1. *Change*: All variants of reengineering are focused on creating organizational change.
2. *Systematic methodology*: It involves a common set of techniques and steps for leading CHANGE MANAGEMENT.
3. *Processes and systems*: Rather than pointing fingers, creating scapegoats, and raising resistance to change, reengineering involves changes in both processes *and* systems (the systems perspective involves processes, jobs, structures, measurement, reward systems, beliefs, values, information flows, strategic analysis, and so forth).
4. *Strategic focus on the customer*: It requires a vision of what is needed to deliver value to the customer.
5. *Realignment*: Changes are intended to improve the fit of processes and systems with the overall strategy.
6. *Cognitive approach*: Proponents talk about "rethinking the organization" and "challenging assumptions" to change behaviors through changes in beliefs and attitudes.
7. *Measurable results*: Reengineering is results-oriented, with a clear focus on providing measurable benefits to the organization.

Although Hammer (1990; Hammer and Champy, 1993; Hammer and Stanton, 1995) argues that reengineering must be radical, high risk, and driven from the top of the organization, most reengineering efforts do not fit all of these requirements (Davenport and Stoddard, 1994). Business process reengineering has also been inappropriately "equated to downsizing [*see* DOWNSIZING], client/server computing, quality, activity-based costing, and several other management nostrums" (Davenport and Stoddard, 1994). Further, although INFORMATION TECHNOLOGY ENABLERS are often critical in the redesigned organization, reengineering does not necessarily involve changes in information systems (Davenport and Stoddard, 1994).

PROCESS OF REENGINEERING

Reengineering frequently includes the following steps: clarifying the firm's strategy, enlisting executive leadership, selecting processes for reengineering, creating frame-breaking visions, mapping and assessing existing processes and systems, developing a case for action, designing the new processes and systems, developing an implementation plan, prototyping the new process, implementation, and continuous process improvement (Davenport, 1993; Andrews and Stalick, 1994; Hammer and Stanton, 1995).

By challenging assumptions, developing a case for action that conveys a sense of urgency for change, and creating a vision of the future identity of the organization, reengineering can provide a cognitive approach to organizational change (Reger et al., 1994). At these steps in the reengineering process, it is sometimes possible to involve a broad spectrum of individuals to develop a collaborative approach to change.

REALIGNING PROCESSES AND SYSTEMS

Assessing existing and designing new processes and systems relies most heavily on broad human resource management (HRM) skills. The objective of reengineering is to realign the strategy, business processes, jobs, organizational structures, management and measurement systems, information systems, and values and beliefs. Assessing the level of alignment among systems and processes is a complex problem, requiring knowledge of a variety of alternative organizational forms that might be adopted. New organizational forms that are particularly popular in this context include learning organizations (*see* LEARNING ORGANIZATION), LEAN PRODUCTION systems, and HORIZONTAL MANAGEMENT.

Hammer (1990; Hammer and Champy, 1993) and other leading authors on reengineering (Harrington, 1991; Davenport, 1993; Andrews and Stalick, 1994) have also articulated a set of internally consistent design principles for re-aligning systems and processes. These principles include: organize around outcomes, assign ownership of processes and process performance, link performance objectives and evaluation to customer satisfaction, subsume information-processing work in real work, build in feedback channels, combine several jobs into one, and empower workers. Many of these design principles can be traced to sociotechnical systems (Pasmore, 1988) and Hackman and Oldham's (1980) model of work redesign.

See also *business processes*

Bibliography

Andrews, D. C. and Stalick, S. K. (1994). *Business Reengineering: The Survival Guide*. Englewood Cliffs, NJ: Yourdon Press.

Davenport, T. H. (1993). *Process Innovation: Reengineering Work through Information Technology*. Boston: Harvard Business School Press.

Davenport, T. H. and Stoddard, D. B. (1994). Reengineering: Business change of mythic proportions? *MIS Quarterly*, 18, 121–7.

Hackman, J. R. and Oldham, G. R. (1980). *Work Redesign*. Reading, MA: Addison-Wesley.

Hammer, M. (1990). Reengineering work: Don't automate, obliterate. *Harvard Business Review*, 68, 104–12.

Hammer, M. and Champy, J. (1993). *Reengineering the Corporation*. New York: HarperCollins.

Hammer, M. and Stanton, S. A. (1995). *The Reengineering Revolution*. New York: HarperCollins.

Harrington, H. J. (1991). *Business Process Improvement*. New York: McGraw-Hill.

Pasmore, W. A. (1988). *Designing Effective Organizations: The Sociotechnical Systems Perspective*. New York: John Wiley.

Reger, R. K., Mullane, J. V., Gustafson, L. T., and DeMarie, S. M. (1994). Creating earthquakes to change organizational mindsets. *Academy of Management Executives*, 8 (4), 31–46.

business processes

William H. Glick

A process is the transformation of inputs into outputs through some sequencing of activities. A business process carries the additional distinction of creating outputs that are valued by a customer external to the organization. Although a series of accounting procedures may produce financial records for a restaurant, accounting is a function, not a business process. The financial records are not valued by the customer; good food and good service are the valued outcomes. Note, however, that the accounting may be necessary for the long-term survival of the organization. Further, accounting activities may be included as part of the overall business process of delivering good food and service. In the context of BUSINESS PROCESS REENGINEERING, the accounting activities would not be considered in isolation, but might be reengineered in conjunction with the overall business process.

Alternative definitions of business process also appear (Keen and Knapp, 1996). For example, Harrington (1991) excludes production processes, while Davenport (1993) excludes unstructured, unmeasured processes, and/or processes with nonspecific outputs. Keen and Knapp (1996) explicitly include coordination processes as key business processes that create competitive advantage.

Bibliography

Davenport, T. H. (1993). *Process Innovation: Reengineering Work through Information Technology*. Boston: Harvard Business School Press.

Harrington, H. J. (1991). *Business Process Improvement*. New York: McGraw-Hill.

Keen, P. and Knapp, E. (1996). *Every Manager's Guide to Business Processes*. Boston: Harvard Business School Press.

Canada

Roy J. Adams

Canada is composed of ten provinces and three territories, each of which has separate responsibility for employment and labor legislation. The federal government has responsibility for trans-provincial industries such as transport, communications, and banking. Like the US, the Canadian labor market is demarcated into two segments. Employees are either represented by trade unions and covered by collective agreements or are dependent on a combination of legislation, individual bargaining, and unilateral employer policy.

The Collective Bargaining Sector

Trade unions. Craft, industrial, and general unions all operate in Canada. About 30 percent of Canadian unionists belong to international unions who have their headquarters in the US International unionism, which has been a major factor in Canada throughout the twentieth century, although it has been declining in significance during the past two decades. The major trade union federation today is the Canadian Labor Congress, to which unions representing about 67 percent of union members affiliate. The remaining trade union members belong primarily to unaffiliated national unions. The Confederation of National Trade Unions, which is based almost exclusively in Quebec, is the current-day successor to an early Christian trade union federation. It is entirely independent.

The dominant ideology of Canadian unions is a mix of business unionism focused on COLLECTIVE BARGAINING and a broader concern for social development. The Canadian Labor Congress is closely aligned with the social democratic New Democratic Party.

Employers. Labor and human resources policy in Canada is largely controlled by individual enterprises. Although one finds employer associations in some industries (e.g., construction, shipping), they play a much smaller role in Canada than they do in many European countries. Perhaps the most important voice of Canadian business on national employment and labor issues is the Canadian Council of Chief Executives (CCCE), composed primarily of the chief executive officers of major corporations.

In the private sector about 20 percent of the labor force is covered by collective agreements, but collective agreement coverage has fallen substantially in recent decades, whereas the rate in the public sector is well over 70 percent and has been relatively stable.

Government. Although each jurisdiction is responsible for its own legislation, each has adopted the basic framework of the US National Labor Relations Act. Under this model employers are legally compelled to recognize and negotiate with certified unions periodically over a wide range of terms and conditions of employment with a view toward signing written collective agreements. Strikes are permitted over interests disputes but disputes over the interpretation of collective agreements generally must be submitted to binding ARBITRATION. Certification, which requires majority support of the relevant employees, generally takes place at the enterprise level and it is at that level that most bargaining takes place. Uncertified unions have generally been considered to have no right to be recognized, although recent court decisions have placed that norm in question.

The Individual Contract Sector

There is a wide range of employment legislation that has its primary effect on employees outside of collective bargaining, including minimum wages, maximum hours of work, paid vacations and holidays, pensions and long-term disability, health and safety regulation, and workers' COMPENSATION as well as employment and pay equity. Within legal requirements the employer and the individual employee may negotiate any other legal condition of work. Like European practice, but unlike the US, employers must provide reasonable notice to employees dismissed without cause. The employee's recourse is the regular court system, where cases over the allegation of wrongful dismissal grew substantially in recent decades as a result of restructuring and DOWNSIZING.

Private sector employers in the individual contract sector generally oppose unionization and collective bargaining but within legal constraints that preclude DISCRIMINATION against union sympathizers.

Beyond the Enterprise

The Canadian system is commonly characterized as adversarial and levels of industrial conflict are high by international standards. Unlike many European countries, Canada is without legally required works councils, although many jurisdictions do require occupational health and safety committees in both unionized and non-unionized enterprises. At the national level there is a tripartite Canadian Labor and Business Center, which attempts to achieve consensus on a range of relatively noncontroversial issues, and similar agencies in some of the provinces. In international comparison, however, tripartism is underdeveloped in Canada.

career

Daniel C. Feldman

Career refers to the series of occupations and jobs which individuals hold over their work lives. The study of careers in organizations has focused on six issues in particular:

1. how individuals' aptitudes, interests, and skills change over the course of their working lives;
2. how individuals make decisions about which jobs to pursue and which organizational positions to accept (or leave);
3. how individuals adjust to new job situations;
4. how organizations plan for and manage these transition processes;
5. the impact of short-run career decisions on longer-term career options; and
6. the integration (or conflict) between career demands and personal life demands (Feldman, 1988).

While the term career generally applies to all occupations and jobs, over time the term has also developed some frequently used connotations. In some cases, the term career has been used to connote an occupation or profession requiring high levels of education and training. For example, it is not uncommon for law and medicine to be labeled as careers, but plumbing and construction not to be so labeled. In other cases, the term career has been used to connote either long-term commitment to or heavy psychological investment in an occupation or an organization. For instance, the term career diplomat refers to an individual who has made a long-term commitment to public service, while the term career employee refers to an individual who has spent most of his or her life working for one company.

See also *career anchors; career choice; career models; career pathing; career patterns of scientists and engineers; career plateau; career stages; career success*

Bibliography

Feldman, D. C. (1988). *Managing Careers in Organizations.* Glenview, IL: Scott Foresman.

career anchors

Edgar H. Schein

Career anchors are the self-perceived sources of stability in the individual's internal CAREER.

When people enter a field or occupation they typically are anchored only in the externally defined criteria of progress: grades in school, encouragement from counselors, test scores on talents or interests, and feedback if they are in an apprenticeship or other kind of work situation. As the individual progresses through school and early occupational experiences, he or she begins to form a self-image based on the matching of external feedback and internal feelings of accomplishment and satisfaction. In other words, individuals begin to define themselves in terms of a matching of what they feel they are good at and enjoy doing with external feedback that they are good at it and that their efforts are considered worthwhile by others. If mismatches occur, because either they find they do not have the talent for a certain kind of work or they discover that they do not like a certain kind of work, they seek a change in career until there is some matching of talents and motives with external rewards and feedback.

As we progress into our careers we also find that our values have to match those of our chosen occupation or organization. The emerging self-image, what I am defining as the career anchor, then consists of three components:

1 my self-perceived talents;
2 my motivation toward certain kinds of work; and
3 my values as they are articulated in my work.

The career anchor is a product of work experience and is therefore not likely to be very firm until we are at least five to ten years into our career. But once we have stabilized our self-image we tend to want to hold on to that image even if our external work situation begins not to match it. The career anchor, then, can be defined as that element of ourselves that we would not give up if forced to make a choice. What we do in our occupations is not necessarily correlated with our anchors and most occupations have in them people with different career anchors.

Research has so far revealed at least eight kinds of career anchors.

1 *Technical or functional competence*: These people define themselves by competence in a certain craft and continue to look for ever more challenge in that area of competence. This kind of person wants to become the world's best salesperson, engineer, auto mechanic, surgeon, or whatever.
2 *Managerial competence*: These people define themselves by the ability to manage others and measure progress by climbing to ever higher positions of responsibility in organizations. This person wants to be able to attribute the success of an organization or project to his or her own managerial capabilities based on analytical skills, interpersonal and group skills, and the emotional capacity to deal with high levels of responsibility.
3 *Security or stability*: These people define themselves by having achieved a position of career success and stability that allows them to relax and to experience a feeling of having made it. This sort of person is less concerned with type of work and more concerned with a feeling of security.
4 *Autonomy or independence*: These people define themselves by their need to be free of organizational constraints and rules in terms of what they do in their career. Freelance consultants, teachers, some independent business people, field salespersons, and so forth would exemplify this anchor.
5 *Entrepreneurial creativity*: These people define themselves by their ability to create their own enterprise. They measure themselves by the size of the enterprise and its success.
6 *Service or dedication to a cause*: These people define themselves by their commitment to some deep value that the occupation permits them to express, e.g., teaching, environmentalism, human resource management, some aspects of medicine and the ministry.
7 *Pure challenge*: These people define themselves less by the type of work they do and more by the sheer joy of competing or winning out over impossible obstacles.
8 *Lifestyle*: These people define themselves by the ability to integrate the demands of work, family, and self-oriented growth concerns. The career is not perceived as the dominant element, but only one element to be integrated into the whole of life.

Career anchors serve to stabilize and give meaning to the internal career and thus must be identified by the career occupant at those points when career or life choices have to be made, so that those choices maximize the opportunities to match the needs of the individual with the requirements of the organization or occupation.

See also *career choice*

Bibliography

Schein, E. H. (1971). The individual, the organization, and the career: A conceptual scheme. *Journal of Applied Behavioral Science*, 7, 401–26.
Schein, E. H. (1978). *Career Dynamics: Matching Individual and Organizational Needs*. Reading, MA: Addison-Wesley.
Schein, E. H. (1984). Culture as an environmental context for careers. *Journal of Occupational Behavior*, 5, 71–81.
Schein, E. H. (1985). *Career Anchor: Discovering Your Real Values*. San Diego, CA: Pfeffer.
Schein, E. H. (1990). Career stress in changing times: Some final observations. *Prevention in Human Services*, 8, 251–61.
Schein, E. H. (1993a). *Career Anchors*, rev. edn. San Francisco: Jossey-Bass.
Schein, E. H. (1993b). *Career Anchors*, rev. edn. *Trainer's Manual*. San Francisco: Jossey-Bass.
Schein, E. H. (1993c). *Career Survival: Strategic Job/Role Planning*. San Francisco: Jossey-Bass.
Schein, E. H. (1996). Career anchors revisited: Implications for career development in the 21st century. *Academy of Management Executive*, 10, 80–8.

career choice

Stephen A. Stumpf

Career choice, defined as a decision about which CAREER to pursue, is one of many work–leisure decisions made by people throughout their lives. Related, but somewhat more focused, decisions are OCCUPATIONAL CHOICE and job choice. A career is "a sequence of work-related positions occupied throughout a person's life" (London and Stumpf, 1982: 4). Career choice encompasses those CAREER STAGES and transitions over time that reflect personal needs, motives, and aspirations, as well as societal and organizational expectations and constraints.

In practice, career choice is not a singular decision. People make many choices within their broader, often unarticulated, decisions about their work life. Decisions to change positions within an organization, change jobs, change organizations, change work locations, or change occupations are all part of a broader choice regarding one's career. As such, each of these decisions is a career decision, or at least part of the collection of activities that is viewed as one's career choice.

Bibliography

London, M. and Stumpf, S. A. (1982). *Managing Careers*. Reading, MA: Addison-Wesley.

career models

Timothy A. Judge

Career models describe the process by which individuals can best manage their careers in organizations. Three of the most prominent career models are reviewed below. Because most of these models lack support, however, they must be viewed cautiously.

CAREER LIFE CYCLES

If inclusion in textbooks and practitioner publications is any indication, the most popular career model is the career life cycle. This model is reviewed elsewhere in this dictionary (*see* CAREER STAGES) and therefore only a brief evaluation is provided here. The life-cycle approach proposes that individuals progress through four career stages (e.g., exploration for individuals under age 30, establishment for individuals aged 30–45, maintenance for individuals aged 45–60, and disengagement for those over age 60).

There are many problems with the life-cycle model. Not all employees progress through these stages in the specified order (e.g., plateaued individuals often develop new careers). Also, workers begin second careers at any age, so age-normed models are not particularly appropriate. Thus, while biological metaphors such as the life-cycle model are popular, their utter lack of empirical support suggests they are somewhat simple-minded.

Career Concepts

Career concepts are the assumptions people hold about their careers. The career concepts model assumes that most individuals possess one of four career concepts (Driver, 1989). The *linear concept* emphasizes upward mobility, defining CAREER SUCCESS in terms of extrinsic outcomes. The *expert concept* considers the initial career choice a lifelong commitment to a single area of expertise. The *spiral concept* consists of major changes into related career fields every 5–10 years. Finally, the *transitory concept* is characterized by a great deal of change in jobs and career fields – in other words, a "consistent pattern of inconsistency."

One of the implications of the career concepts model is that individuals' concepts sometimes do not match the organization's career system. Dissatisfaction and withdrawal may result. Two means of remedying the mismatch are to attempt to develop individuals away from their dominant concept, or to change the career system. Neither of these changes is likely to be easy.

Career Anchors

As noted in a separate entry in this dictionary (*see* CAREER ANCHORS), a career anchor is an occupational self-concept that evolves from self-knowledge acquired during early work experiences. The discovery and evolution of one's career anchor is based on one's needs, values, and abilities. Schein's (1978) conceptualization of career anchors considers five anchors:

1   *Managerial competence* emphasizes the use of interpersonal and analytical competence.
2   *Technical/functional competence* emphasizes development of technical expertise (this anchor is quite similar to the expert career concept).
3   *Security* characterizes individuals who seek security and stability.
4   *Creativity* describes individuals who are innovative and entrepreneurial.
5   *Autonomy and independence* characterizes individuals who value personal control and freedom.

Research has suggested that individuals in different occupations possess very different career anchors. By identifying employee career preferences, the career anchors approach seeks to match individuals' career preferences to their occupational choices or to job assignments within organizations. As such, the career anchors model fits well with conceptualizations of person–organization fit (*see* PERSON–JOB FIT).

See also *career*

Bibliography

Driver, M. J. (1989). Careers: A review of personnel and organizational research. *International Review of Industrial and Organizational Psychology*, 3, 245–77.
Schein, E. H. (1978). *Career Dynamics: Matching Individual and Organizational Needs*. Reading, MA: Addison-Wesley.

career pathing

Elmer H. Burack

Career pathing (CP) is a basic planning tool linked to career planning and career development. It is used by both individuals and organizations, although for substantially different purposes. The essence of CP is a coherent series of steps to achieve a particular job or career objective. It combines developmental goals, activities to achieve these goals, and timing. The format of CP varies widely; common forms range from listings of steps to sophisticated charts and diagrams generated by computers. Since its introduction in the 1970s and fast growth subsequently, the basic concepts and applications of CP have undergone remarkable transformation.

The rationalization of career planning and development methods, mostly in large or high-tech organizations, led to the design of sophisticated CP tools (Burack and Mathys, 1996). A number of factors nurtured this growth and included: relatively stable economic and competitive conditions; rapid advances in software packages and computer technology, including the personal computer; the need for more powerful succession and management development tools; and rapid access to career planning information. The process of planning the organization's future STAFFING defines future human resource needs, timing, positional capabilities, and the availability of current personnel to meet these requirements. CP became the road map that translated general staffing planning into individualized time–activity paths. Where job structures were relatively stable, general CP documents and matrices were generated which defined standard "career ladders" and job relationships. Thus, within organizations, two quite different forms of CP emerged. One was driven primarily by internal organization needs and the other by individual enterprise members interested in internal opportunities.

CP for people outside organizations was driven by both short- and long-range individual needs (Burack and Mathys, 1996). This CP reflected work–family matters, focused on formal and informal learning, and emphasized individual growth. It was driven by personal and job-related needs, values, and goals. This CP model encouraged broad, flexible, and contingent thinking.

Recent economic and competitive developments, however, greatly changed the focus of CP for the organization, its members, and individuals generally. The reinvention of organizations, driven by turbulent economic and global competitive conditions, transformed CP for individuals and organizations alike. Change drivers included: global competition; the replacement of job security by job or skill mobility; newly emerging technologies, job families (see JOB FAMILY), and work procedures; shifts to process flow from a hierarchical orientation; dual careers (see DUAL-EARNER AND DUAL-CAREER COUPLES); and workforce DIVERSITY.

New models of CP are emerging that are developmental for the person and organization. They combine a long-term view with short-term needs for flexibility and possible career changes for individuals. CP also includes spiritual and emotional dimensions (Otte and Kahnweiler, 1995). Job, positional, and employer changes, along with concurrent learning and reflective processes, are to nurture an inner voice or vision of future possibilities and valued directions and goals. New career planning approaches include analyzing past and future needed competencies, exploring and executing plans, and learning from these experiences to guide "next steps." CP provides the specific steps and experiences to achieve the plans. Short-term survival dictates the development of contingency CP models, much flexibility, and frequent reviews for possible changes.

The new organizational CP models *consciously* link enterprise staffing needs and learning strategies with people's career plans (Gutteridge, Leibowitz, and Shore, 1993; Stewart, 1995; Burack and Mathys, 1996) and are often enacted on a global stage. Short- and long-term strategic business needs drive individual development while CP structures incorporate self-development and optional paths based on individual progress and needs and shifting competitive circumstances. Ford's Leadership and Development Program, Motorola's Globally Oriented Development Programs, and Nationwide Insurance's Technical Excellence Program for Information Service Employees provide examples of CP models.

See also *career; career choice*

Bibliography

Burack, E. H. and Mathys, N. (1980). *Career Management in Organizations.* Lake Forest, IL: Brace-Park Press.

Burack, E. H. and Mathys, N. (1996). *Human Resource Planning*, 3rd edn. Northbrook, IL: Brace-Park Press.

Gutteridge, T. G., Leibowitz, Z. B., and Shore, J. E. (1993). *Organizational Career Development.* San Francisco: Jossey-Bass.

Otte, F. L. and Kahnweiler, W. M. (1995). Long-range career planning during turbulent times. *Business Horizons*, January/February, 2–7.

Stewart, T. A. (1995). Planning a career in a world without managers. *Fortune*, March 20, 72–80.

career patterns of scientists and engineers

Robert C. Dauffenbach

Rarely does an individual hold just one type of job in his or her CAREER. Instead, a variety of jobs typifies experience. These are jobs that differ in content, requirements, and TRAINING needed; that are geographically dispersed; that involve, potentially, changes in employer or industry; and that make varying use of one's specific educational endowments. With jobs that are high in formal educational requirements, mobility in many forms would be expected to be lower. But evidence suggests that even among highly educated scientists and engineering-trained personnel, mobility is substantial. For example, fewer than one-half of the US population who hold a bachelor's degree or higher in engineering are working in a science or engineering occupation, including the computer sciences. Only one-fourth of the math and statistics degree holders and only one-fifth of the holders of biology degrees work in any science or engineering occupation (Committee on National Statistics, National Research Council, 1989). Even among those educated in science and engineering who are working in a science and engineering occupation, mobility is considerable. One-fourth of those working in an engineering occupation do not have a degree in engineering. Over one-half who work in a math/computer occupation do not have a degree in mathematics or computer science. Some of these individuals have less than a bachelor's degree, but most of them are holders of degrees from other fields of science. The biological and physical science fields are more educationally pure, but even in these occupations many job incumbents have degrees in fields that do not have an exact match with their detailed science or engineering specialty (Dauffenbach, 1989).

The above discussion relates to field mobility because it compares field of degree with occupational employment. It is apparent that this type of mobility, even among high-education-content jobs, is high. Switching occupations is also prevalent for scientists and engineers. Studies reveal that over a five-year period, about 10 to 17 percent of such individuals are occupationally mobile. Many who are trained in science and engineering move into management occupations, including management of research and development facilities. This is a very positive career move, averaging a pay differential of 10 to 15 percent. The wide extent and broad character of mobility that typifies the careers of even specifically trained personnel provides flexibility in society's utilization of human resources. It also underscores the importance of the educational experience as a facilitator of mobility by producing both trained and retrainable people who are capable of responding to differential opportunities.

Bibliography

Committee on National Statistics, National Research Council (1989). *Surveying the Nation's Scientists and Engineers: A Data System for the 1990s*. Washington, DC: National Academy Press.

Dauffenbach, R. C. (1989). *Quality and Qualifications in the Market for Scientists and Engineers: A Report to the Division of Science Resource Studies*. Washington, DC: National Science Foundation.

career plateau

Nigel Nicholson

The phenomenon of career plateauing in organizations presents an important and perplexing challenge to human resource management (HRM) and an array of conceptual and empirical problems to organizational behavior scholars. The first problem is definitional. How do we decide when an employee is plateaued? Three types of criteria can be found applied in the literature. First, many researchers have taken time in current position as a measurable and objective benchmark. Employees in post for more than five years would typically be counted as immobile or "plateaued" by this standard, though this or alternative cutoffs have the drawback of looking worryingly arbitrary, and, at the same time, liable to mischaracterize the experience and career positions of many groups, such as professionals. A second alternative is to use a subjective criterion – individuals' expectations of future advancement – defining as plateaued those who expect no or minimal further status increase. The problem with this approach is the questionable accuracy of people's reading of future opportunities and their own capabilities. A less common third alternative, of increasing interest, is the concept of implicit age–grade timetables. These may be assessed subjectively – whether employees believe themselves to be on track relative to peers, or ahead of or behind schedule. Individuals' positions relative to company norms may also be assessed objectively.

Plateauing by any of these definitions is an organizational problem to the degree that the people to whom it applies have desires or expectations which have not been or are not being fulfilled. This is regarded as especially problematic for managerial ranks, whose career expectations are more deeply socialized and hierarchical than other workers', and whose motivation and commitment organizations are most concerned to maintain.

Research has shed light on several aspects of the phenomenon. First, CAREER SUCCESS is often foretold by rapid early upward movements in a person's history, and conversely, people who get off-track early typically fail to recover momentum. Second, it is mistaken to assume that plateauing is necessarily associated with loss of motivation and effectiveness. The distinction needs to be drawn between mere immobility and frustrated feelings of being "stuck." Some people are contentedly plateaued, often called "solid citizens," as distinct from "high fliers" and "deadwood." Third, people's aspirations and interests change over the career cycle. Early career ambition may, as the person matures and the realities of limited horizons sink in, become deflected into other life spheres. Not all forms of this displacement need detract from the individual's organizational contribution, though in some cases "insurgent" and "alienated" orientations may develop if there is resentment and frustration at perceived unfairness of career opportunities.

Finally, the phenomenon of plateauing is becoming more common as organizations restructure toward "delayered" or "flattened" structures. One recent survey estimated that 25 percent of the US workforce was plateaued. Plateauing presents a challenge to HRM to the degree that employees maintain hierarchical views of career fulfillment – the view that "up is the only way." One solution is increased lateral mobility, sabbaticals, and alternative developmental paths. To date, organizations have been slow to seek these remedies, often being more aware of the short-term costs than of the long-term benefits to the organizational culture.

Bibliography

Chao, G. T. (1990). Exploration of the conceptualization and measurement of career plateau: A comparative analysis. *Journal of Management*, 16, 181–93.

Feldman, D. C. and Weitz, B. A. (1988). Career plateaus reconsidered. *Journal of Management*, 14, 69–90.

Lawrence, B. S. (1988). New wrinkles in the theory of age: Demography, norms, and performance ratings. *Academy of Management Journal*, 31, 309–37.

Nicholson, N. (1993). Purgatory or place of safety? The managerial career plateau and organizational age grading. *Human Relations*, 46, 1369–89.

Veiga, J. F. (1981). Plateaued versus nonplateaued managers: Career patterns, attitudes, and path potential. *Academy of Management Journal*, 24, 566–78.

career stages

Edgar H. Schein

The word CAREER has both an internal and an external meaning. From an external, societal point of view the concept of career refers to the sequence of formal roles that are associated with a given occupation. In academia, for example, the external career consists of being a graduate student, instructor, assistant professor, and associate professor, the granting of tenure, and then being made full professor. Most occupations have formal or informal status progressions of this sort. From an internal point of view, the concept of career refers to the sequence of life roles that an individual envisions as he or she progresses through one or more external careers. Thus, in the internal career of an academic there may be a progression from student to graduate student in a specific field of interest, to researcher, teacher, scholar, and ultimately revered and successful scholar, measured by peer acceptance, publications, references, and so forth. There will usually be some correspondence between the formal occupationally designated sequence of roles and the internal experienced sequence, but not necessarily. In defining career *stages*, therefore, it is necessary to specify whether we mean in the internal or in the external career.

Externally defined career stages are usually well defined by formal occupational criteria and by organizations if the career is embedded in an organization. Thus a young engineer can pretty well see his or her external career in terms of the amount of schooling necessary, entry into an organization as a technical person or management trainee, followed by that organization's specification of how it defines career development. Most organizations have some career paths that are based on historical data of what previous entrants have experienced and can tell the young engineer or manager-to-be what steps to expect (*see* CAREER PATHING).

When one analyzes a large number of occupations certain generic career stages seem to characterize most of them:

1 a period of pre-career choosing of a field and educational preparation for entry into that field;
2 formal training in the chosen field or occupation;
3 entry into the occupation or organization;
4 a period of learning, apprenticeship, and socialization;
5 a period of full use of one's talent, leading to some form of granting of tenure through being given permanent membership, a professional license, or some other form of certification;
6 a period of productive employment;
7 a branching into administrative, managerial, and other forms of becoming a leader; and
8 gradual disengagement, part-time work, and eventual retirement.

At any point in the external career the person may discover that his or her internal career and CAREER ANCHORS are out of line with what the external career offers in terms of challenge, opportunities, and rewards. At that point the person may switch to another career and start going through the stages over again, but usually in a more truncated form because the experience acquired in one career is often transferable to another career. The engineer employed in a technical organization may discover a talent and desire for entrepreneurial work or for management, and may decide to start a company or switch to an organization that provides more managerial opportunities. Some training in management may then be required and the person may have to start at the bottom of the new career ladder.

Career stages in the external career can be thought of as a series of movements along three different dimensions:

1 *moving up* in the hierarchical structure of the occupation or organization;
2 *moving laterally* across the various subfields of an occupation or functional groups of an organization; and
3 *moving in* toward the centers of influence and leadership in the occupation or organization.

Depending on what the person is looking for in his or her internal career, movement along each of these dimensions will have different meanings. For some, like managers, it is moving up that is important; for some, like the technical person, it is job challenge and lateral movement to new and challenging work that is most important; and for some, like the power- or socially motivated person, it is moving toward the inner circle and positions of influence that is most important.

Each dimension has its own stages associated with it, but these are usually idiosyncratic in particular occupations or organizations. In summary, career stages in the externally defined career are the sequence of roles and statuses defined by a particular occupation or organization as the way to progress through the career. They may or may not correspond to the individual's own sense of his or her internal career stages.

Bibliography

Schein, E. H. (1971). The individual, the organization, and the career: A conceptual scheme. *Journal of Applied Behavioral Science*, 7, 401–26.
Schein, E. H. (1978). *Career Dynamics: Matching Individual and Organizational Needs*. Reading, MA: Addison-Wesley.
Schein, E. H. (1984). Culture as an environmental context for careers. *Journal of Occupational Behavior*, 5, 71–81.
Schein, E. H. (1985). *Career Anchor: Discovering Your Real Values*. San Diego, CA: Pfeffer.
Schein, E. H. (1990). Career stress in changing times: Some final observations. *Prevention in Human Services*, 8, 251–61.
Schein, E. H. (1993a). *Career Anchors*, rev. edn. San Francisco: Jossey-Bass.
Schein, E. H. (1993b). *Career Anchors*, rev. edn. *Trainer's Manual*. San Francisco: Jossey-Bass.
Schein, E. H. (1993c). *Career Survival: Strategic Job/Role Planning*. San Francisco: Jossey-Bass.
Schein, E. H. (1996). Career anchors revisited: Implications for career development in the 21st century. *Academy of Management Executive*, 10, 80–8.

career success

Timothy A. Judge

Career success is defined as the outcomes or achievements accumulated as a result of work experiences. It is important to understand the multiple definitions of career success as well as what determines it.

Definitions of Career Success

Career success is an evaluative concept, since how success is defined depends on who does the judging. Career success as judged by others generally is determined by objective criteria. This type of success has often been referred to as *extrinsic career success*, and can be indexed by pay and ascendancy (e.g., job level, promotions). Most research implicitly has equated career success with extrinsic success.

However, *intrinsic career success* – how individuals feel about their careers or their accomplishments (i.e., career satisfaction) – is also important. Korman (1980) found that many objectively successful managers felt dissatisfied with their jobs and lives. This finding has been replicated in many studies (e.g., Bray and Howard, 1988). Thus, intrinsic and extrinsic career success are not the same, and it is important to consider each when thinking of career success.

On the other hand, this does not mean that extrinsic and intrinsic career success are unrelated. Past research suggests that intrinsic and extrinsic success are positively but moderately correlated. Data from a sample of 1,294 high-level managers (Judge et al., 1995) demonstrates this. Splitting the managers into four groups based on their career satisfaction and pay relative to the median reveals that managers with below-average salaries are more likely to be less satisfied with their careers (see table 1). Similarly, managers with high salaries are more likely to have above-average career satisfaction. But there are many highly paid managers who are dissatisfied with their careers and just as many (relatively) poorly paid managers who are satisfied. These results go to show that while extrinsic and intrinsic success are related, the relationship is far from perfect.

Table 1 Average pay in relation to career satisfaction

	Below-average pay (below $100,000)	Above-average pay (above $100,000)
Below-average career satisfaction	352 managers (27%)	251 managers (19%)
Above-average career satisfaction	259 managers (20%)	432 managers (34%)

Influences on Career Success

Past research from the careers literature has identified both individual-level and organizational influences on career success. Individual-level influences consist of ability, motivation, and demographics. Ability variables, such as intelligence, have been found to predict extrinsic career success. Similarly, motivational variables, such as hours worked, ambition, and work centrality, have been found to positively predict extrinsic career success but, in the case of hours worked and ambition, negatively predict intrinsic success. Some variables that influence career success, such as education and family demands, are a mix of ability and motivation. Finally, demographic variables, such as race, gender, marital and socioeconomic status, predict career success although in many cases it is not clear why.

Many organizational characteristics have been found to affect career success. Some of the more prominent organizational determinants of career success identified by past research include socialization, mentoring (*see* MENTORING PROGRAMS), early career challenge, and career systems.

Bibliography

Bray, D. W. and Howard, A. (1988). Career success and life satisfactions of middle-aged managers. In L. A. Bond and J. C. Rosen (eds.), *Competence and Coping During Adulthood*. Hanover, NH: University Press of New England.

Judge, T. A., Cable, D. M., Boudreau, J. W., and Bretz, R. D. (1995). An empirical investigation of the predictors of executive career success. *Personnel Psychology*, 48, 485–519.

Korman, A. K. (1980). *Career Success/Personal Failure*. Englewood Cliffs, NJ: Prentice-Hall.

case study/discussion method

J. Kevin Ford and Deidre Wasson

The case study/discussion training method is one in which trainees are given a written report of either an actual or a fictitious organization problem that they analyze individually or in small groups, devise a solution based on assumptions about resource, economic, and legal restraints, and develop an implementation plan (Camp, Blanchard, and Huszczo, 1986). After the final solutions have been made, the large group reconvenes to a discussion led by the trainer about their solutions, the decision-making process, and the effects of their interventions. Most importantly, trainees must receive feedback on their solution development to insure successful transfer of training (Saal and Knight, 1988). Case studies offer a less costly alternative to SIMULATIONS with often equal learning benefits (Simmons, 1975).

See also *training; training evaluation*

Bibliography

Camp, R. R., Blanchard, P. N., and Huszczo, G. E. (1986). *Toward a More Organizationally Effective Training Strategy and Practice*. Englewood Cliffs, NJ: Prentice-Hall.

Saal, F. E. and Knight, P. A. (1988). *Industrial/Organizational Psychology*. Pacific Grove, CA: Brooks/Cole.

Simmons, D. D. (1975). The case method in management training. In B. Taylors and G. L. Lippitt (eds.), *Management Development and Training Handbook*. London: McGraw-Hill.

central tendency effects

Angelo S. DeNisi

Central tendency effects refer to a type of distributional effect (*see* DISTRIBUTIONAL EFFECTS IN PERFORMANCE APPRAISAL). Here, we are concerned with ratings that exhibit little variance and cluster around the midpoint of the scale. As with other similar effects, this has been assumed to reflect RATING ERRORS or an unwillingness by the rater to provide ratings that discriminate among ratees. In addition, since the ratings cluster around the scale midpoint, ratings that display central tendency are not particularly useful, since everyone is essentially rated as "average." But, again, unless we know the "true" underlying distribution of performance in a work group, it is impossible to state whether central tendency reflects an error, a lack of rater motivation to make discriminations among ratees, or a true restriction of range on ratee performance. Although there has been some disagreement over the best way to assess central tendency effects (see Saal, Downey, and Lahey, 1980), they have received relatively little attention in the literature, and proposed solutions in the popular business press have even included using only scales with an even number of scale anchor points, so that there is no "midpoint."

Bibliography

Saal, F. E., Downey, R. G., and Lahey, M. A. (1980). Rating the ratings: Assessing the quality of ratings data. *Psychological Bulletin*, 88, 413–28.

change management

Sandra Fielden

Change management is not a distinct discipline; it draws on a wide variety of social science and management theories. This integration of different but complementary concepts is an essential aspect of effective approaches to change management. The practice of change management is dependent on a number of factors, not least the particular school of thought involved (Burnes, 2000). The *individual perspective*, *group dynamics*, and *open systems* schools form the basis of modern change management models, with variations arising depending on the context in which change is taking place. Currently, the two main approaches to organizational change are *planned* (the conscious decision to move an organization from one state to another) and *emergent* (a process that unfolds through the interplay of multiple variables within an organization).

Organization development (OD) has been a key in the growth of planned change, with OD defined as "a systemwide application of behavioral science knowledge to the planned development and reinforcement of organizational strategies" (Cummings and Huse, 1989: 1). However, it is argued that most attempts to implement change in organizations are less successful than intended because the principles and knowledge about the psychology of change are violated or ignored (Winum, Ryterband, and Stephenson, 1997). Those attempts that do find success tend to be small-scale changes, occurring in stable environments, with localized change and a technical or structured focus. It is asserted that in order to manage greater, organization-wide changes a processual approach, which is less prescriptive and more analytical, is better able to achieve a broader understanding of the problems and practice of change management in a complex environment. Change is viewed as a continuous process which is dependent on the context of the change, organizations' structure, organizational culture, political processes, and managerial behavior.

It is commonly acknowledged that organizational change has become the norm, being both persistent and pervasive. However, successful organizational change is difficult to achieve. Change management initiatives take many forms, e.g., BUSINESS PROCESS REENGINEERING and TOTAL QUALITY MANAGEMENT, but typically they achieve much less than they promised (Burnes, 2003). Trompenaars and Wooliams (2003) argue that, because organizations seek to preserve the company, profitability, market share, and core competencies, the reason for one change is often to prevent change in other respects. They view such compromises as undermining the change process and inhibiting the successful management of change, advocating that organizations must reconcile change with continuity in order to preserve an evolving identity. Burnes (2003) proposes that organizations need to recognize and exploit the links between management development and the management of organizational change. Change management projects provide significant management development opportunities, which organizations are failing to capitalize on and thereby missing genuine opportunities for organizational and managerial improvement.

In order for organizations to manage change successfully, they need to understand the change process, be conscious of their approach to change, proactively utilize the change process as a developmental tool, and most of all be prepared to change.

See also *organization development and change*

Bibliography

Burnes, B. (2000). *Managing Change: A Strategic Approach to Organizational Dynamics*. Harlow: Financial Times Management.

Burnes, B. (2003). Managing change and changing managers from ABC to XYZ. *Journal of Management Development*, 22 (7), 627–42.

Cummings, T. G. and Huse, E. F. (1989). *Organizational Development and Change*. St. Paul, MN: West Publishing.

Trompenaars, F. and Wooliams, P. (2003). A new framework for managing change across cultures. *Journal of Change Management*, 3 (4), 361–75.

Winum, P., Ryterband, E., and Stephenson, P. (1997). Helping organizations change: A model for guiding consultation. *Consulting Psychology Journal: Practice and Research*, 49 (1), 6–16.

Chartered Institute of Personnel and Development

Susan Cartwright

The Chartered Institute of Personnel and Development (CIPD) is the leading professional body for human resource and development professionals and practitioners in the UK. It was formed in 1994 as a result of the merger between the Institute of Personnel Management (representing HRM specialists) and the Institute of Training and Development (representing training and development specialists). In July 2000 it gained chartered status. The CIPD, through its grades of membership, offers accreditation to professionals and sets standards of qualification and attained experience that are widely accepted by employers as requirements for practice.

The origins of the CIPD can be traced back to the establishment in 1913 of the Welfare Workers Association (WWA), which in 1946 became the Institute of Personnel Development. The Institute of Training Development was formed in 1979 and has a history going back to the formation of the British Institute of Training Officers in 1964.

The primary objectives of the CIPD are to provide professional education and development of its members and to research and provide appropriate information to support practitioners in their professional roles. In 2001 the CIPD had 105,000 members, which included 25,000 affiliate members undertaking formal programs of professionally recognized studies. The CIPD publishes a practitioner journal, *People Management*, as well as research reports and books. It also offers short training courses and consultancy services and runs a number of conferences each year.

For further information contact The Chartered Institute of Personnel Development, CIPD House, Camp Road, London, SW19 4UX, UK.

checklist method of performance evaluation

Rick Jacobs

The checklist method is a behaviorally based approach to PERFORMANCE APPRAISAL that requires raters to observe ratees' behavior and record performance-related judgments about these behaviors. In this approach to performance appraisal, a list of job-relevant behaviors is developed. Raters are asked to record (a) whether or not each behavior has been performed by the ratee or (b) the degree to which each item describes the person being evaluated.

Several important characteristics of the checklist can help us to appreciate this method. Determining the items to appear on the checklist is driven by a JOB ANALYSIS that identifies the key tasks of the job and/or critical incidents. The resulting checklist reflects the complexity of the job being evaluated. Next, the number of items that will appear on the checklist must be determined. Here the issue is balance, as the developer tries to maximize the comprehensiveness of the checklist without overburdening the rater with too many items to evaluate. Related to these first two issues is the presentation of items. Checklists can arrange items by groups of homogeneous tasks, or the items can be placed throughout the checklist in random order. Organizing the list by groups eases the burden of the rater, but may introduce spurious correlation among checklist items. Finally, the issue of scoring must be addressed. In many instances, a score is generated based on summing across all ratings. These summated scores can be the result of adding all items, creating a total score, and/or of summing particular items to create subscale scores.

Performance evaluation conducted using a checklist format has several distinct advantages. First, the rater only needs to make simple judgments about whether or not a specific event or behavior has occurred or the degree to which an item describes an individual. Next, checklists, when generated from good job analytic data, are behaviorally based, with a high degree of JOB-RELATEDNESS. Finally, because checklists generally deal with specific and observable events, a great deal of information for purposes of APPRAISAL FEEDBACK and PERFORMANCE COACHING is available for the rater to discuss with the ratee.

On the problematic side, checklist ratings require a substantial amount of work to develop. They tend to be customized to specific jobs and an organization wishing to develop a performance evaluation system for many jobs will find it necessary to conduct job analyses for each job title. While this is not a negative, it does mean the organization is not likely to simply adapt a single checklist for multiple jobs. Next, raters do not make direct evaluations of their subordinates. Rather, they rate numerous items, and these ratings are then summed to create a total score. This can result in rating surprises when the summary measure is not what the rater expected. Finally, ratings tend to take longer with this method of evaluation, and as a result, raters can experience reduced interest in carefully evaluating each checklist item.

Bibliography

Cascio, W. F. (1991). *Applied Psychology in Personnel Management*, 4th edn. Englewood Cliffs, NJ: Prentice-Hall, pp. 85–6.

Flanagan, J. C. (1954). The critical incident technique. *Psychological Bulletin*, **51**, 327–58.
Landy, F. J. (1989). *Psychology of Work Behavior*. Pacific Grove, CA: Brooks/Cole.
Muchinsky, P. M. (1995). *Psychology Applied to Work*. Pacific Grove, CA: Brooks/Cole.
Saal, F. E. and Knight, P. A. (1995). *Industrial/Organizational Psychology: Science and Practice*. Pacific Grove, CA: Brooks/Cole.

childcare benefit

Ellen Ernst Kossek

Childcare, defined as assisting employees with caring for children, is a type of dependant care benefit and family supportive policy. Childcare benefits can reduce employees' financial burden and level of WORK–FAMILY CONFLICT. Work–family conflict can negatively influence employee behaviors, including tardiness, intention to turnover (Youngblood and Chambers-Cook, 1984; *see* EMPLOYEE TURNOVER), performance, ABSENTEEISM, JOB SATISFACTION, recruitment (Kossek and Nichol, 1992), and organizational commitment (Grover and Crocker, 1995).

Although large employers (over 100 employees) are more likely to offer at least several types of childcare benefits, under the US FAMILY AND MEDICAL LEAVE ACT OF 1993 (FMLA), all employers with 50 or more employees located within a 75-mile radius must provide an unpaid leave of absence of up to 3 months for the birth or adoption of a child, and/or to take care of serious health problems for a child and other family members (including oneself). Beside leaves, the most popular forms of assistance relate to:

1. time (flextime, JOB SHARING, part-time work, and flexplace; *see* FLEXIBLE WORKING HOURS; FLEXIBLE WORKPLACE/TELECOMMUTING; PART-TIME EMPLOYMENT);
2. information (resource and referral, work–family seminars);
3. financial (flexible benefits or spending accounts, discounts, vouchers, adoption; *see* FLEXIBLE BENEFIT PLANS); and
4. direct services (on or near site care center, sick care, consortiums, and summer camps) (Galinsky, Friedman, and Hernandez, 1991).

As employers become more experienced with childcare, they usually develop policies to manage broader issues of work–family and work–life integration. Such policies include those related to elder care, organizational culture change (training supervisors to be aware of work–family issues, assessment of cultural barriers impeding policy use); work–family stress management (seminars and coordination with EMPLOYEE ASSISTANCE PROGRAMS (EAPS)), and corporate giving (both financial and through donation of employee time) to community and national work–family initiatives (Galinsky et al., 1991).

Bibliography

Galinsky, E., Friedman, D. E., and Hernandez, C. A. (1991). *The Corporate Reference Guide to Work–Family Programs*. New York: Families and Work Institute.
Grover, S. L. and Crocker, K. (1995). Who appreciates family-responsive human resource policies? The impact of family-friendly policies on the organizational attachment of parents and non-parents. *Personnel Psychology*, **48**, 271–88.
Kossek, E. E. and Nichol, V. (1992). The effects of on-site child care on employee attitudes and performance. *Personnel Psychology*, **45**, 485–509.
Youngblood, S. A. and Chambers-Cook, K. (1984). Child care assistance can improve employee attitudes and behavior. *Personnel Administrator*, **29**, 45–7.

China

Chung-Ming Lau and Liqun Wei

China has a land area of 9.6 million km^2 and is the third-largest country in the world. With a population of 1.295 billion people at the end of 2000, about 22 percent of the world's total, China is the world's most populous country. China's gross domestic product (GDP) was US$860 per capita in 2000, with a growth rate of around 7 percent per year.

People in cities and towns make up 30.4 percent of the population, and those in rural areas make up 69.6 percent. At the end of 2001, the total number of those in employment was 737.4 million, with 247.8 million people employed in urban cities. Of all those employed, 7.16 million people are in state-owned enterprises (SOEs), 1.12 million in collective firms, 3.91 million in foreign-invested firms, and 3.67 million in Hong Kong-, Macao-, and Taiwan-invested firms. The remaining labor is in private-owned firms.

Before the introduction of economic reform in late 1978, China followed a centrally planned economy and adopted the mode of public ownership in all kinds of operations. Since the reform, the Chinese central government has encouraged diversified ownership, but still insists on the primacy of public ownership. As a result, individual small businesses and private firms have grown rapidly. By the end of 2001, the number of individually and privately owned registered industrial and commercial enterprises amounted to 13.2 million, covering 43.7 percent of the total number of enterprises and representing 20 percent of total employment. The development of foreign-invested firms, including Chinese–foreign joint ventures, Chinese–foreign cooperative enterprises, and foreign direct investments, contributes much to Chinese employment. Although the number of foreign-invested firms is only 1.9 percent of the total number of firms in China, they nevertheless represented 3.9 percent of total employment.

Human resource management (HRM) of Chinese businesses has gone through several stages of reform. The changes closely reflect the political and economic requirements of a transition from a planned economy to a "socialist market" economy. With the alleviation of tight control by government on firms' daily operation and development, more autonomy is given to businesses for the responsibility of profits and losses through more independent operation and management. Hence, more effective utilization of human resources for improved performance and market competitiveness is on the reform agenda. As a result, performance-based compensation is increasingly popular (*see* PAY FOR PERFORMANCE), and the relatively fixed, rank-based reward system has had to be changed.

Recent studies on the development of HRM in China show that there are trends toward a higher adoption of HR planning, PERFORMANCE APPRAISAL, and training and development programs (*see* TRAINING), and more discretion on COMPENSATION. Also, the role of HR practitioners has started to change from that of routine administrator to someone who is in charge of formal HRM functions. It is suggested in a recent study that the role of HRM is critical in determining firm performance (Law, Tse, and Zhou, 2003).

However, as China is a vast country with different ownership forms and is in a transitional stage, there are great differences in the degree of adoption of HRM practices. The development of HRM systems in Chinese businesses is significantly influenced by the unique sociocultural and political environment of China (Warner, 1993, 1999). Wong et al. (2001) examined the effect of culture on employee attitudes in China. They found that organizational commitment is important in Chinese firms which have strong effects on JOB SATISFACTION and turnover intention (*see* EMPLOYEE TURNOVER). They suggested that some Chinese values, for example, relationships (*guanxi*) and reciprocity (*pao*), still prevail in modernized Chinese firms. Tata, Fu, and Wu (2003) further found that culture affected the perception of justice in Chinese organizations.

In addition, institutional forces also have influences on the development of HRM in China. These institutional forces are embodied in social, cultural, and organizational practices. Warner (1996) suggested that China's HRM system has evolved into a more "marketized" hybrid from one "with Chinese characteristics." Given the above, it is not surprising to find differences among businesses of different ownership and in different geographic locations. Even within the state sector, there are varied degrees of reform and hence great variations in HRM practices adopted. For example, the Haier Group, which has been transformed from a collective to a global brand, has a mix of both western and Chinese HRM practices (Yi and Ye, 2003). The issue of convergence and divergence in HRM in a transitional economy is therefore a needed area for further research (Tsui and Lau, 2002).

At any rate, when compared with the foreign firms, Chinese businesses are highly unionized with workers' participation in the form of Workers' Congresses (an organized committee with worker representatives). Only recently has COLLECTIVE BARGAINING emerged in some sectors, owing to the economic and enterprise reforms. Labor contracts have also been introduced, and a free labor market has emerged in some sectors (Warner, 1995; Benson, 1996). Zhu and Dowling (1994) and Ding and Warner (1999) contrasted the slow pace of reform in SOEs with the rapid development of other business types, which are often called *Laoban* (private firms), *Laoxiang* (township enterprises), and *Laowai* (foreign-invested enterprises). It was found that SOEs were still behind joint ventures in almost all HRM practices. For example, the complex compensation system of SOEs is only partially performance-based, and very often employees in SOEs are paid less than those in most joint ventures. HR personnel in most SOEs can be involved in decisions of HR recruitment, selection, and appraisal, but few have more decision-making power in PROMOTION and demotion of employees. Furthermore, most Chinese firms do not have formal, long-term HR planning. Training and development and career management are also quite limited in Chinese businesses.

Bjorkman and Lu (2001) found that the international joint ventures in China have a different set of HR practices. Their HRM practices more closely resemble those of foreign parent companies. In another study of joint ventures in China, Wong, Ngo, and Wong (2002) discovered that trust in organizations mediates the relationship between DISTRIBUTIVE JUSTICE, PROCEDURAL JUSTICE, job security, and affective commitment among the workers. However, Giacobbe-Miller et al. (2003) confirmed that there are divergent values of procedural justice, regardless of SOEs or joint ventures.

In 1995 the Labor Law was promulgated, which combined features of the old command economy and a market economy. The law covers all forms of business organization, encompasses both blue-collar and white-collar occupations, and applies equally to domestic and foreign firms. This represents a significant achievement in labor protection. According to the Labor Law, a written contract is required for all employment relationships. Other major provisions include: normal working hours, mandatory rest periods, limitations on overtime and overtime pay, guaranteed minimum wage, and legal liabilities. Gender DISCRIMINATION issues are highlighted in the law as well.

HONG KONG SPECIAL ADMINISTRATIVE REGION

After the return of sovereignty to China in 1997, Hong Kong is now a special administrative region of China. Hong Kong still retains its free-market economic system, under China's "one country, two systems" scheme. Its population as of the 2001 census was 6.7 million, with a per capita GDP of US$25,100 in 2002, the second highest in Asia.

HRM practices and systems in Hong Kong are greatly influenced by social, political, and economic factors. After China adopted an open economy policy in the late 1970s, more and more manufacturing establishments have moved to China to take advantage of its low land and labor costs. Because the infrastructure and communication facilities are among the best in the region, Hong Kong's economy is gradually shifting to a service-oriented economy. The services sector contributed 86.5 percent to the GDP of Hong Kong in 2001. With a labor force of around 3.2 million in 2002, no more than 7 percent were engaged in the manufacturing sector, whereas the proportion of the labor force in personal services was 25 percent. The financial industry attracts 15 percent of the working population, and the wholesale, retailing, and other hospitality industries comprise 32 percent of the workforce.

This structural change has given rise to a number of issues. People previously in the manufacturing sector have to have retraining in order to move into the service industries. However, the move is not always possible. This structural change has led to an unbalanced labor market. Some service industries have huge numbers of vacancies, and some skilled workers are not able to find jobs. However, due to the Asian currency crisis in late 1997 and a slow recovery of the Hong Kong economy, Hong Kong has suffered from deflation. The unemployment rate was 4.9 percent in 2000, worsened to 5.1 percent in 2001, and deteriorated to 7.3 percent in 2002. The first quarter and third quarter unemployment rate in 2003 were at 8.3 percent and 8.6 percent, respectively. Further, the government launched a labor importation scheme to ease the labor shortage in some sectors before unemployment skyrocketed. These people include craftspersons, technicians, experienced operatives, and construction workers for the new airport project. The scheme has now been revised to import highly skilled personnel only. Retraining programs for unskilled workers and training programs for school leavers and young people are also launched.

Labor relations in Hong Kong are generally peaceful, and only very few major disputes that resulted in strikes have occurred in the past decade. Labor legislation is also sound and employment regulations are well observed. New legislation about mandatory retirement schemes and discrimination at work are in place. However, due to the poor economy, more large-scale layoffs have been experienced.

HRM practices vary in Hong Kong, mainly due to firm size and the owner's culture (Shaw et al., 1993). Performance appraisals and welfare/fringe benefits packages are related to the owner's culture. Anglo-American firms are more active in these programs than Chinese firms. Large-size firms have more formalized RECRUITING, selection, training, and incentive programs. The study of Lau and Ngo (2001) also found that local Chinese firms used less HR planning and organization development activities than American and European firms.

Nyaw (1993) surveyed some services firms in Hong Kong and found that the average turnover rate was 21 percent in 1991. Around 40 percent of the responding firms claimed that turnover is a serious problem. Because Hong Kong is a small economy with high mobility, coupled with the brain-drain problem associated with 1997, such a high turnover rate is understandable.

In general, issues facing HRM in Hong Kong are greatly influenced by macro social, economic, and political factors. Popular western concepts of managing human resources are receiving increasing attention (such as employee participation, EMPLOYEE EMPOWERMENT, and organization culture). A basic challenge in HRM is to blend western practices with Chinese values and implement them in the context of a highly developed, international metropolitan city. The issue of convergence of HR practice was, however, not substantiated in a recent study (Lui, Lau, and Ngo, 2004). Hence, there is a need to explore the HR strategies of modernized firms in an international context, and not just those in transitional economies.

Bibliography

Benson, J. (1996). The sleeping giant slumbers no more. *People Management*, 2 (12), 22–6.

Bjorkman, I. and Lu, Y. (2001). Institutionalization and bargaining power explanation of HRM practices in international joint ventures: The case of Chinese–western joint ventures. *Organization Studies*, 22 (3), 491–512.

Ding, D. Z. and Warner, M. (1999). Re-investing Chinese industrial relations at enterprise-level: An empirical field-study in four major cities. *Industrial Relations Journal*, 30 (3), 243–60.

Giacobbe-Miller, J. K., Miller, D. J., Zhang, W., and Victorov, V. I. (2003). Country and organizational-level adaptation to foreign workplace ideologies: A comparative study of distributive justice values in China, Russia and the United States. *Journal of International Business Studies*, 34 (4), 389–406.

Josephs, H. K. (1995). Labor law in a "socialist Marxist economy": The case of China. *Columbia Journal of Transnational Law*, 33 (3), 561–81.

Lau, C. M. and Ngo, H. Y. (2001). Organization development and firm performance: A comparison of multinational and local firms. *Journal of International Business Studies*, 32 (1), 95–114.

Law, K. S., Tse, D. K., and Zhou, N. (2003). Does human resource management matter in a transitional economy? China as an example. *Journal of International Business Studies*, 34 (3), 255–65.

Lui, S., Lau, C. M., and Ngo, H. Y. (2004). Global convergence, human resource best practice, and firm performance: A paradox. *Management International Review*.

Nyaw, M. K. (1993). Perspectives of human resource management in Hong Kong. In M. K. Nyaw and S. S. M. Ho (eds.), *Hong Kong Business Management in Transition*. Hong Kong: Joint Publishing (in Chinese).

Shaw, J. B., Tang, S. W. Y., Fisher, C. D., and Kirkbride, P. S. (1993). Organizational and environmental factors related to HRIv1 practices in Hong Kong: A cross-cultural expanded replication. *International Journal of Human Resource Management*, 4, 785–815.

Tata, J., Fu, P. P., and Wu, R. (2003). An examination of procedural justice principles in China and the U.S. *Asia Pacific Journal of Management*, 20 (2), 205–16.

Tsui, A. S. and Lau, C. M. (2002). Research on the management of enterprises in the People's Republic of China: Current status and future directions. In A. S. Tsui and C. M. Lau (eds.), *The Management of Enterprises in the People's Republic of China*. Boston: Kluwer.

Warner, M. (1993). Human resource management "with Chinese characteristics." *International Journal of Human Resource Management*, **4** (1), 45–65.

Warner, M. (1995). Managing China's human resources. *Human Systems Management*, **14** (3), 239–49.

Warner, M. (1996). Economic reforms, industrial relations, and human resources in the People's Republic of China. *Industrial Relations Journal*, **27** (3), 195–210.

Warner, M. (1999). Human resources and management in China's "hi-tech" revolution: A study of selected computer hardware, software and related firms in the PRC. *International Journal of Human Resource Management*, **10** (1), 1–20.

Wong, C. S., Wong, Y. T., Hui, C., and Law, K. S. (2001). The significant role of Chinese employees' organizational commitment: Implications for managing employees in Chinese societies. *Journal of World Business*, **36** (3), 326–40.

Wong, Y. T., Ngo, H. Y., and Wong, C. S. (2002). Affective organizational commitment of workers in Chinese joint ventures. *Journal of Managerial Psychology*, **17** (7), 580–98.

Yi, J. J. and Ye, S. X. (2003). *The Haier Way*. Dumont, NJ: Homa and Sekey.

Zhu, C. J. and Dowling, P. J. (1994). The impact of the economic system upon human resource management. *Human Resource Planning*, **17** (4), 1–21.

Civil Rights Act of 1866

Christine Neylon O'Brien

In the aftermath of the American Civil War, the Civil Rights Act of 1866 was enacted pursuant to the congressional power to eradicate slavery provided by the THIRTEENTH CONSTITUTIONAL AMENDMENT. The statute was reenacted in 1870 following ratification of the FOURTEENTH CONSTITUTIONAL AMENDMENT. Lawsuits brought under the Civil Rights Act of 1866 are often referred to as section 1981 and section 1982 cases because of the codification of this statute at those section numbers within Title 42 of the United States Code. Section 1981 provides a remedy for all forms of racial DISCRIMINATION in private sector employment in addition to that afforded by Title VII of the CIVIL RIGHTS ACT OF 1964. Unlike a Title VII plaintiff, those pursuing a section 1981 claim need not exhaust the EQUAL EMPLOYMENT OPPORTUNITY COMMISSION administrative agency route. Also, the period for filing a section 1981 claim is longer than the time allowed for filing claims under Title VII. Only purposeful or intentional DISCRIMINATION is actionable under section 1981, whereas Title VII provides for discrimination claims based both upon DISPARATE IMPACT or DISPARATE TREATMENT (Twomey, 1994).

Bibliography

Twomey, D. P. (1994). *Labor and Employment Law*. Cincinnati, OH: South-Western Publishing.

Civil Rights Act of 1871

Christine Neylon O'Brien

This Reconstruction-era law (Sedmak and Vidas, 1994) provides relief for individuals who have been deprived of constitutional or federal statutory rights by a state or local government official (Estreicher and Harper, 1990). Such lawsuits are often referred to as section 1983 cases because section 1 of the 1871 statute is codified as section 1983 of Title 42 of the United States Code. Passage of the statute followed ratification of the FOURTEENTH CONSTITUTIONAL AMENDMENT in 1868, and state action or involvement in the challenged practices is required (Schlei and Grossman, 1983). The bases for DISCRIMINATION that are actionable under section 1983 are broader than those prohibited under section 1981, the CIVIL RIGHTS ACT OF 1866.

Bibliography

Estreicher, S. and Harper, M. (1990). *The Law Governing the Employment Relationship*. St. Paul, MN: West Publishing.

Schlei, B. L. and Grossman, P. (1983). *Employment Discrimination Law*. Washington, DC: Bureau of National Affairs.

Sedmak, N. J. and Vidas, C. (1994). *Primer on Equal Employment Opportunity*. Washington, DC: Bureau of National Affairs.

Civil Rights Act of 1964

David P. Twomey

Title VII of the Civil Rights Act of 1964, as amended by the Equal Employment Opportunities Act of 1972 and the CIVIL RIGHTS ACT OF 1991, forbids employer and union DISCRIMINATION based on race, color, religion, sex, or national origin. Title VII specifically forbids any employer to fail to hire, to discharge, to classify employees, or to discriminate with respect to compensation, terms, conditions, or privileges of employment opportunity due to race, color, religion, sex, or national origin. Title VII also prohibits retaliation against persons who file charges or participate in EQUAL EMPLOYMENT OPPORTUNITY COMMISSION (EEOC) investigations.

Title VII covers private employers, state and local governments, and educational institutions that have 15 or more employees. The federal government, private and public employment agencies, labor organizations, and joint labor–management committees for apprenticeship and training must also abide by the law.

THEORIES OF DISCRIMINATION

There are two primary legal theories under which a plaintiff may prove a case of unlawful discrimination: DISPARATE TREATMENT and DISPARATE IMPACT. A disparate treatment claim exists where an employer treats some individuals less favorably than others because of their race, color, religion, sex, or national origin. Proof of the employer's discriminatory motive is critical in a disparate treatment case.

A disparate impact claim exists where an employer's facially neutral employment practices, such as hiring or PROMOTION examinations, though neutrally applied and making no adverse reference to race, color, religion, sex, or national origin, have a significantly adverse disparate impact on a protected group, and the employment practice in question is not shown to be job-related (*see* JOB-RELATEDNESS) and consistent with BUSINESS NECESSITY by the employer. Under the disparate impact theory it is not a defense for an employer to demonstrate that the employer did not intend to discriminate. The EEOC itself in unusual situations may bring a "pattern or practice" case on behalf of a class of affected employees in disparate treatment cases.

FILING PROCEDURES

The EEOC is a five-member commission appointed by the president to establish equal employment opportunity policy under the law it administers. The EEOC supervises the conciliation and enforcement efforts of the agency.

The time limitation for filing charges with the EEOC is 180 days after the occurrence of the discriminatory act. After the conclusion of the proceedings before the EEOC, an individual claiming a violation of Title VII has 90 days after receipt of a right-to-sue letter from the EEOC to file a civil lawsuit in a federal district court. If an aggrieved individual does not meet the time limit of Title VII, the individual may well lose the right to seek relief under the Act.

PROTECTED CLASSES

The legislative history of Title VII of the Civil Rights Act demonstrates that a primary purpose of the Act is to provide fair employment opportunities for black Americans. The protections of the Act are applied to blacks based on race or color. The word race, as used in the Act, is applied to all members of the four major racial groupings: white, black, native American, and Asian-Pacific. Native Americans can file charges and receive the protection of the Act on the basis of national origin, race, or in some instances color. Individuals of Asian-Pacific origin may file discrimination charges based on race, color, or in some instances national origin. Whites are also protected against discrimination because of race and color.

Title VII requires employers to accommodate their employees' or prospective employees' religious practices. Most cases involving allegations of religious discrimination revolve around the determination of whether an employer has made reasonable efforts to accommodate religious beliefs (see *Trans World Airlines* v. *Hardison*, 432 US 63, 1977).

Title VII permits religious societies to grant hiring preferences in favor of members of their religion. It also provides an exemption for educational institutions to hire employees of a particular religion if the institution is owned, controlled, or managed by a particular religious society. The exemption is a broad one and is not restricted to the religious activities of the institution.

Employers that discriminate against female or male employees because of their sex are held to be in violation of Title VII. The EEOC and the courts have determined that the word sex, as used in Title VII, means a person's gender and not the person's SEXUAL ORIENTATION. State and local legislation, however, may provide specific protection against discrimination based on sexual orientation. An employer must be able to show that criteria used to make an employment decision that has a disparate impact on women, such as minimum height and weight requirements, are in fact job-related. All candidates for a position requiring physical strength must be given an opportunity to demonstrate their capability to perform the work. Title VII was amended by the PREGNANCY DISCRIMINATION ACT OF 1978 (section 701 (k)). The amendment prevents employers from treating pregnancy, childbirth, or other related medical conditions in a manner different than the treatment of other disabilities. Thus, women disabled due to pregnancy, childbirth, or other related medical conditions must be provided with the same BENEFITS as other disabled workers. An employer who does not provide disability benefits or paid sick leave to other employees is not required to provide them for pregnant workers.

Quid pro quo tangible employment action SEXUAL HARASSMENT involves supervisors seeking sexual favors from their subordinates in return for job benefits such as continued employment, promotion, a raise, or a favorable performance evaluation. In such a case, where a supervisor's actions affect job benefits, the employer is liable to the employee for the loss of benefits plus punitive damages because of the supervisor's misconduct. A second form of sexual harassment is hostile working environment harassment. With this type of harassment, an employee's economic benefits have not been affected by the supervisor's misconduct, but the supervisor's sexually harassing conduct has nevertheless caused anxiety and "poisoned" the work environment. An injunction against such conduct can be obtained and attorneys' fees awarded. Where no tangible employment action is taken, the employer may raise an affirmative defense to liability for damages by proving (1) it exercised reasonable care to prevent and promptly correct any sexually harassing behavior at its workplace and (2) the plaintiff employee unreasonably failed to take advantage of corrective opportunities provided by the employer (see *Burlington Industries, Inc. v. Ellerth*, 524 US 742, 1998).

Title VII protects members of all nationalities from discrimination. The judicial principles that have emerged from cases involving race, color, and gender employment discrimination are generally applicable to cases involving allegations of national origin discrimination. Thus, physical standards such as minimum height requirements, which tend to exclude persons of a particular national origin because of the physical stature of the group, have been unlawful when these standards cannot be justified by business necessity.

Adverse employment based on an individual's lack of English-language skills violates Title VII when the language requirement bears no demonstrable relationship to the successful performance of the job to which it is applied.

TITLE VII EXCEPTIONS

Section 703 of Title VII exempts several key practices from the scope of Title VII enforcement. It is not an unlawful employment practice for an employer to hire employees on the basis of religion, sex, or national origin in those certain instances where religion, sex, or national origin is a BONA FIDE OCCUPATIONAL QUALIFICATION (BFOQ) reasonably necessary to the normal operation of a particular enterprise. Section 703 (h) of the Act authorizes the use of "any professionally-developed ability test [that is not] designed, intended, or used to discriminate."

Employment testing and educational requirements must be "job-related"; that is, the employers must prove that the tests and educational requirements bear a relationship to JOB PERFORMANCE.

Section 703 (h) provides that differences in employment terms based on a BONA FIDE SENIORITY SYSTEM are sanctioned as long as the differences do not stem from an intention to discriminate.

AFFIRMATIVE ACTION

Employers, under AFFIRMATIVE ACTION plans (AAPs), may undertake special RECRUITING and other efforts to hire and train minorities and women and help them advance within the company. Such plans have resulted in numerous lawsuits contending that Title VII, the Fourteenth Amendment, or COLLECTIVE BARGAINING contracts have been violated.

Following the US Supreme Court's *Adarand Constructors, Inc.* v. *Pena* decision, 515 US 200 (1995), the EEOC issued a statement of guidance on affirmative action plans as follows:

> Affirmative action is lawful only when it is designed to respond to a demonstrated and serious imbalance in the work force, is flexible, time-limited, applies only to qualified workers, and respects the rights of nonminorities and men.

When an employer's AAP is not shown to be justified, or "unnecessarily trammels" the interest of nonminority employees, it is often called REVERSE DISCRIMINATION. For example, a city's decision to rescore police promotional tests in order to achieve specific racial and gender percentages unnecessarily trammeled the interests of nonminority police officers (see *San Francisco Police Officers' Association* v. *San Francisco*, 812 F2d 1125, CA 9, 1987).

Civil Rights Act of 1991

David P. Twomey

Between 1989 and 1991 the US Supreme Court reoriented Title VII jurisprudence to favor employers. The Civil Rights Act of 1991 (CRA 1991) modified or reversed these decisions, augmented the types of damages available to plaintiffs, and provided for jury trials in cases of intentional DISCRIMINATION.

In a DISPARATE TREATMENT (intentional discrimination) case, the plaintiff must prove discriminatory intent. Section 105 of CRA 1991 set forth the burden of proof for DISPARATE IMPACT (facially neutral employment practices that have an adverse impact on a protected group) cases, codifying the concepts of BUSINESS NECESSITY and JOB-RELATEDNESS enunciated in GRIGGS V. DUKE POWER, 401 US 424 (1971). A new shifting BURDEN OF PROOF scheme resulted:

1 the plaintiff must demonstrate through relevant statistical comparisons that a particular employment practice used in selecting or promoting employees causes a disparate impact;
2 the defending employer may then proceed to demonstrate that a particular employment practice does not cause the disparate impact; or
3 the defending employer must demonstrate (with the burden of persuasion, not just production of evidence) that the challenged practice is job-related for the position in question and consistent with business necessity.

Victims of discrimination are entitled to be made whole, including backpay and BENEFITS, less their interim earnings. In addition to these remedies, under the Civil Rights Act of 1991, victims of intentional discrimination can now receive compensatory and punitive damages capped for sex and religious discrimination, depending on the size of the employer.

The Civil Rights Act of 1991 makes it an unlawful employment practice for an employer to adjust scores, use different cutoff scores (*see* CUTOFF SCORE), or otherwise alter the results of employment tests on the basis of race, color, religion, sex, or national origin. This provision addresses the so-called "race norming" issues, whereby the results of hiring and PROMOTION tests are adjusted to assure that a minimum number of minorities are included in application pools.

classification

Michael A. McDaniel and David J. Snyder

Classification is concerned with maximizing institutional outcomes by placing individuals who are already hired into one of two or more treatments (i.e., jobs) on the basis of multiple criteria. In classification, one has many predictors in which one or more corresponds to at least one treatment and the goal is to obtain an optimal match of persons to treatments based on individual differences on the criteria. Classification can be contrasted with PLACEMENT, in which a single criterion scale is divided into two or more sections and individuals falling into different sections are assigned to different treatments.

classification job evaluation method

Matthew C. Bloom

The classification method of job evaluation involves positioning job descriptions into a series of categories or classes. Milkovich and Newman (1993: 121) characterize these classes as "a series of carefully labeled shelves on a bookshelf." Each shelf or class is defined in such a way that critical job duties, responsibilities, and other work factors are described in enough detail to allow jobs to be slotted, yet retain enough generality to cover all jobs in the organization. These class descriptions serve as the standard against which job descriptions are compared and ultimately slotted into a specific job class. Benchmark jobs are often used to anchor a class and facilitate slotting by serving as a model of comparison for all jobs in that class. Classification systems are very adaptable because the vagueness of class descriptions permits reevaluation of jobs as situations dictate (e.g., introduction of new technology). However, this vagueness also may make justifying pay decisions more difficult, since they are open to multiple interpretations.

The job evaluation system used by the US government is a classification method. This system is the Office of Personnel Management's General Schedule (GS). It is most likely the job evaluation method applied to the greatest variety of jobs. The GS schedule uses level of difficulty to slot jobs into classes (Hays and Reeves, 1984). The GS system is used to classify jobs as varied as US Agriculture Department conservationist, immigration border patrol officer, and Internal Revenue Service account auditor (Milkovich and Newman, 1993).

See also *job evaluation methods*

Bibliography

Hays, S. W. and Reeves, T. Z. (1984). *Personnel Management in the Public Sector*. Boston: Allyn and Bacon.

Milkovich, G. T. and Newman, J. M. (1993). *Compensation*, 4th edn. Homewood, IL: Richard D. Irwin.

coaching

Gary P. Latham and Lucie Morin

Coaching is an on-site training method that can be used to increase the knowledge, skills, and abilities (*see* KSAOS) of trainees in entry level as well as in managerial positions. A coach or coaches (e.g., supervisor, trainer, peers) provides guidance by setting goals that are difficult, yet attainable (Locke and Latham, 1990), monitoring JOB PERFORMANCE, and providing feedback regarding ways to improve the trainee's performance. The coaching process usually encompasses ORGANIZATIONAL SOCIALIZATION regarding the informal "dos and don'ts" that can advance or hurt one's standing in the organization.

The benefits of coaching are that it:

1 gives employees feedback on how significant others view their work;
2 enables employees to learn ways to increase their performance;
3 improves communication and collaboration between newcomers and veteran employees; and
4 provides a framework for understanding of and commitment to the organization's goals (Wexley and Latham, 1991).

To maximize coaching effectiveness, coaches must learn ways to increase the newcomer's self-efficacy, namely the conviction that "I will do well" on this task. To do this, coaches must learn how to:

1 sequence tasks in such a way that newcomers experience early successes;
2 model the desired organizational behavior; and
3 persuade the person that he or she has the ability to do well (Latham and Wexley, 1994).

Finally, the coaching intervention should teach employees skills in self-management (*see* SELF-MANAGEMENT TRAINING). That is, employees learn to set goals and monitor their own performance in relation to these goals so that they are effective in the workplace.

See also *training; training evaluation*

Bibliography

Latham, G. L. and Wexley, K. N. (1994). *Increasing Productivity through Performance Appraisal*, 2nd edn. Reading, MA: Addison-Wesley.

Locke, E. A. and Latham, G. P. (1990). *A Theory of Goal Setting and Task Performance*. Englewood Cliffs, NJ: Prentice-Hall.

Wexley, K. N. and Latham, G. P. (1991). *Developing and Training Human Resources in Organizations*, 2nd edn. New York: HarperCollins.

cognitive process models of performance appraisal

Jack Feldman

Cognitive models of PERFORMANCE APPRAISAL assume that human judgment is necessary to the appraisal process; that JOB PERFORMANCE cannot be completely specified in terms of observable behaviors or countable products (*see* CRITERION PROBLEM). Judgment is necessary to assess the degree to which people's activities have contributed to organizational/professional goals (see Feldman, 1986, 1994). Performance appraisal judgments result from any of several alternative cognitive processes, carried out under particular circumstances by people of particular abilities, dispositions, and motives.

THE NATURE OF APPRAISAL MODELS

Appraisal models must explain how judgments may be accurate, as well as how specific kinds of inaccuracy, invalidity, and unreliability occur, using the same set of process assumptions (Feldman, 1981, 1994). The problem is like that of developing a conceptual model of an automobile: one must simultaneously consider *all* of the systems and functions as related to its intended purpose and real-world constraints. Models of subcomponents (e.g., engines, suspensions) are necessary but insufficient. Existing appraisal models approach this ideal to varying degrees.

MODEL COMPONENTS AND THEIR FUNCTIONS

Performance appraisal models are based on theories of six cognitive processes. These processes and their contribution to appraisal judgments must be understood in order to appreciate the unique contributions of each to an overall model.

Attention and search refer to processes which determine how information is obtained from the environment under different circumstances. Attention and search processes are governed by "cognitive structures" (e.g., value systems, implicit theories) containing categories of individuals and of behaviors, represented variously by abstract images (prototypes) or ideals (goal-relevant conceptions) based on experience. Categories differ in their "accessibility" at any given time. Accessibility may be either chronic, due to elaborated value systems and expert knowledge, or temporary, due to recent events, operative motives, moods, or the like. The features of the environment, including other people, that one attends to or searches for are governed by the representations of accessible categories. Attention may be drawn also to features of people or the environment that are vivid, novel, or otherwise salient. Salience of some feature of the environment or the ratee in turn influences the accessibility of relevant categories.

Encoding refers to those processes that determine the meaning assigned to information obtained by attention and search. In fact, encoding operates via the same system that directs attention. Thus, a person is categorized based on his or her resemblance to a category representation; likewise, a person's behavior has meaning in terms of a TRAIT or other category it exemplifies (see, e.g., Srull and Wyer, 1989). Any object, behavior, or person fitting multiple categories will be encoded in terms of the most accessible category that is sufficiently relevant to the characteristics or behavior observed (i.e., for which the stimulus information is diagnostic).

Encoding takes place via either of two interacting processes: "automatic" or "controlled." The automatic process is a default option; it functions to preserve limited cognitive capacity and is experienced as perception. Based on consistent stimulus–response associations, it uses little or no cognitive capacity, operates in parallel with conscious thought, does not require monitoring, is often nonvolitional, and takes effort and capacity to interrupt, once begun. Driving a familiar route or experiencing an optical illusion are examples. Categorizing people in terms of race or gender, or behavior in terms of trait-like categories (see Bargh, 1989), also exemplifies encoding processes.

Controlled processing, in contrast, must be intentionally initiated and monitored to completion. It requires capacity, and is experienced as active problem solving. Controlled processing may take the form of logical, systematic reasoning (e.g., attribution theory) or the use of any of several heuristic "shortcuts." The outcome of processing is the formation of a more or less elaborated person impression, ranging from a simple categorization (e.g., "extravert") to a unique, detailed "person concept" (Srull and Wyer, 1989; Fiske and Neuberg, 1990).

Controlled processing occurs when motivated by external contingencies (e.g., accountability), personal values, or discrepancies between prior expectation and salient behavior (see discussion in Feldman, 1994), *and* when sufficient capacity exists. Further, the specific motive for processing influences the degree and direction of thought. Thus, impressions and evaluations of coworkers, superiors, and subordinates may be formed in terms of *both* job-relevant categories and extraneous information; impressions may be formed and modified spontaneously, in the course of interaction, or later in the appraisal process.

Memory storage and organization refers to processes governing the information entering long-term memory and the patterns of association among memories. Storage and organization are strongly influenced by encoding (Srull and Wyer, 1989). Person memories are organized first around a spontaneously formed overall evaluation, which is linked to trait judgments. *Which* trait judgments are formed, if any, depends on the accessibility of concepts at the time information is encountered. Memories of specific behaviors are associated with general evaluation *and* with relevant trait concepts active during encoding. Behaviors may be associated with one another as well, especially if evaluative inconsistencies during encoding prompt extensive thought. Taken together, these evaluations, trait judgments, and behavioral memories constitute the person impression.

Memory retrieval refers to processes governing how information is brought from long- and short-term storage under various circumstances, and the form in which it is retrieved. Retrieval depends strongly on encoding and organization. The overall evaluation is most accessible, followed by trait-like judgments. Specific memories are differentially accessible: behaviors linked only to evaluation, and not to trait categories, are generally less accessible than those linked to trait categories or to one another via controlled processing. Thus, two types of specific memories are most accessible: those *descriptively consistent* with trait judgments, and those *evaluatively inconsistent* (because the latter receive more thought). At any given level of effort, more accessible judgments and behaviors will be retrieved before less accessible judgments and behaviors.

It should be noted that recognition memory measures (such as BEHAVIORAL OBSERVATION SCALES) do not depend on retrieval alone. Rather, recognition responses may depend either on retrieval or on a judgment of familiarity. Thus, if there is uncertainty in recognition, a respondent is likely to report having seen a category-consistent behavior that has not, in fact, occurred. Such "false alarms" are a consequence of categorization, but may be reduced by increased effort at retrieval and other strategies (see Lord, 1985; Feldman, 1994).

Judgment and inference processes determine how information is used to create summary expectations and evaluations about others and the reasoning (if any) by which this takes place. Of course, encoding may be considered a judgment process; thus, performance judgments might simply be retrieved from memory if such encodings have taken place. Performance judgments may also be based on earlier judgments (encodings), on memories of earlier behavior, or on immediately present information. *Which* occurs depends on two factors: diagnosticity of some earlier judgment for the judgment required at the moment; and the capacity available for memory retrieval and "online" judgment.

Motivation, both direction and intensity, influences both the sufficiency of prior judgments and capacity allocation. Thus, the content and format of a performance appraisal instrument may influence the nature of the judgment process; BEHAVIORALLY ANCHORED RATING SCALES, for instance, may be responded to based simply on one's overall evaluation, if relevant judgments do not already exist, or via more specific retrieved judgments, if these have already been formed. In neither case would behavioral memories be involved. If, however, the rater was motivated to recall behaviors prior to the rating task, these would be included in the judgment due to their increased accessibility and the implicit demand that they be included (see, e.g., Woehr and Feldman, 1993). Conversely, raters might be motivated to search for specific evidence to justify a previously made decision (Kunda, 1990), or to reintegrate specific memories in order to reach a new judgment (e.g., about work assignments or new responsibilities). Prior processing would strongly influence the nature and accessibility of memories, and thus, at any given level of motivation, the completeness of the information considered and the quality (reliability, validity, accuracy) of the judgment or decision.

Response generation occurs subsequent to judgment or inference, when subjective evaluations must be recorded. Strack (1994) discusses how question wording, order, and other contextual features may influence responding. For instance, requesting overall evaluations prior to specific judgments may change the basis for those judgments, as compared to the reverse order. Changing the range of a numerical response scale may change the conception of what is "average" or "expected." One of the major contributions of the behaviorally anchored rating scale is a shared definition of the response scale. Raters evaluating a highly variable sample of subordinates may use the response scale differently than those evaluating a narrower range (see Feldman, 1994), even if raters are relatively knowledgeable.

Another aspect of response generation is "motivated distortion," the deliberate use of ratings for some purpose other than valid evaluation (Longnecker, Sims, and Gioia, 1987). This common practice is not in the domain of cognitive appraisal models; it should be considered an aspect of organizational politics.

MAJOR APPRAISAL MODELS

DeNisi and Williams (1988) and Feldman (1994) review major appraisal models ranging from Wherry's (1952; presented in Landy and Farr, 1983) psychometric perspective to recent cognitive theories. They discuss two major approaches, differing in their emphasis on the processes above.

Categorization models. Represented by Feldman (1981, 1994) and Ilgen and Feldman (1983), as well as others (e.g., Lord, 1985), these models focus on the ordinary interactions among supervisors, peers, and subordinates and their consequences for performance judgments. They emphasize automatic processes of categorization and inference when attention is focused on work and social goals rather than on the judgment process. In these models, accuracy and various sources of bias and invalidity depend on the accessibility of job-relevant and irrelevant categories and other concepts, their use in forming person representations, and subsequent use of these representations in judgment. Categorization models have implications for such issues as the relationships among halo error (*see* HALO EFFECTS), racial, gender, and other biases, and judgment accuracy, as well as for the development of appraisal systems and appraisal training.

Active search models. Represented by DeNisi, Cafferty, and Meglino (1984), these models focus on active information search when raters are motivated to form particular types of judgments. They depend on attribution theory, as a model of rational judgment, to depict the thought process guiding the formation of person concepts. They also consider information search and presentation as influences on subsequent memory organization and judgment accuracy (see DeNisi and Williams, 1988).

Categorization and active search models are not competing theories; rather, each focuses on one or more component processes to deal with specific, problematic issues. Each offers useful insights and contributions to practice.

Bibliography

Bargh, J. A. (1989). Conditional automaticity: Varieties of automatic influence on social perception and cognition. In J. Uleman and J. Bargh (eds.), *Unintended Thought*. New York: Guilford Press.

DeNisi, A. S., Cafferty, T. P., and Meglino, B. M. (1984). A cognitive view of the performance appraisal process: A model and research propositions. *Organizational Behavior and Human Performance*, 33, 360–96.

DeNisi, A. S. and Williams, K. J. (1988). Cognitive approaches to performance appraisal. In G. R. Ferris and K. M. Rowland (eds.), *Research in Personnel and Human Resources Management*, vol. 6. Greenwich, CT: JAI Press.

Feldman, J. M. (1981). Beyond attribution theory: Cognitive processes in performance appraisal. *Journal of Applied Psychology*, 66, 127–48.

Feldman, J. M. (1986). Instrumentation and training for performance appraisal: A perceptual-cognitive viewpoint. In G. R. Ferris and K. M. Rowland (eds.), *Research in Personnel and Human Resources Management*, vol. 4. Greenwich, CT: JAI Press.

Feldman, J. M. (1994). On the synergy between theory and application: Social cognition and performance appraisal. In R. S. Wyer, Jr. and T. K. Srull (eds.), *Handbook of Social Cognition*, 2nd edn, vol. 2. Hillsdale, NJ: Erlbaum.

Fiske, S. T. and Neuberg, S. L. (1990). A continuum of impression formation, from category-based to individuating processes: Influence of information and motivation on attention and interpretation. In M. Zanna (ed.), *Advances in Experimental Social Psychology*, vol. 23. New York: Academic Press.

Ilgen, D. R. and Feldman, J. M. (1983). Performance appraisal: A process focus. In L. Cummings and B. Staw (eds.), *Research in Organizational Behavior*, vol. 5. Greenwich, CT: JAI Press.

Kunda, Z. (1990). The case for motivated reasoning. *Psychological Bulletin*, 108, 480–98.

Landy, F. J. and Farr, J. L. (1983). *The Measurement of Work Performance*. New York: Academic Press.

Longnecker, C. O., Sims, H. P., and Gioia, D. A. (1987). Behind the mask: The politics of employee appraisal. *Academy of Management Executive*, 1, 183–93.

Lord, R. G. (1985). An information-processing approach to social perceptions, leadership, and behavioral measurement in organizations. In L. Cummings and B. Staw (eds.), *Research in Organizational Behavior*, vol. 20. Greenwich, CT: JAI Press.

Srull, T. K. and Wyer, R. S., Jr. (1989). Person memory and judgment. *Psychological Review*, 96, 58–84.

Strack, F. (1994). Response processes in social judgment. In R. S. Wyer, Jr. and T. K. Srull (eds.), *Handbook of Social Cognition*, 2nd edn, vol. 1. Hillsdale, NJ: Erlbaum.

Woehr, D. J. and Feldman, J. M. (1993). Processing objective and question order effects on the causal relation between memory and judgment in performance appraisal: The tip of the iceberg. *Journal of Applied Psychology*, 78, 232–41.

collective bargaining

John T. Delaney

Collective bargaining is a term used to describe the process that unions and employers follow to jointly establish the terms and conditions of employment for workers represented by unions. Although nonunion employees cannot engage in collective bargaining, some individuals who do not belong to unions are covered by collective bargaining agreements because their coworkers are unionized. To accomplish the process of bargaining, representatives of labor and management must meet and confer about mandatory bargaining issues, such as wages, hours, grievance procedures (*see* GRIEVANCE PROCEDURE), and other terms and conditions of employment. Bargaining legislation determines the issues over which unions and employers must bargain, and differences in the scope of bargaining exist across nations and the private and public sectors. For example, in the US, public sector bargaining laws have created different mandatory bargaining issues across states.

There is no legal requirement that collective bargaining end in an agreement. If the negotiating parties reach an agreement, a contract or collective bargaining agreement covering a specific period of time is signed and the terms and conditions of employment are set out in that agreement. If the parties fail to reach agreement, a bargaining impasse occurs and several things can happen. The workers may continue to work without an agreement.

The employer may impose its final bargaining offer as the new agreement (unions may strike in response to this; *see* STRIKE). The parties may jointly agree to submit the dispute to a neutral third party, though this occurs rarely. Finally, the workers may decide to engage in a work stoppage or the employer may lock the workers out (which prevents them from working during the impasse; *see* LOCKOUT). Although private sector workers are permitted to conduct a strike, US public sector employees are generally forbidden by law from striking. Accordingly, public sector bargaining impasses are resolved by a variety of procedures (as determined by state law), including mandatory INTEREST ARBITRATION, fact finding, MEDIATION, or conciliation efforts by state officials or neutral third parties (for a review of public sector bargaining, see Lewin et al., 1988).

The extent of collective bargaining varies considerably across industries, occupations, and nations (see Curme, Hirsch, and Macpherson, 1990; Freeman and Rogers, 1993). In general, although employers have never completely approved of collective bargaining, it has been argued that firms have bargained more aggressively in recent years to obtain union concessions or break the union (see Freeman and Rogers, 1993). This is partly responsible for the decline in union coverage in the US from about 35 percent of the private, nonagricultural workforce in 1955 to less than 10 percent in 2002. Research has indicated that workers who are covered by collective bargaining agreements typically earn higher wages (by about 15 percent) and have better employment conditions than similar workers who are not unionized. Research also indicates that firms bargaining with their workers are somewhat less profitable than comparable nonbargaining firms. There is substantial debate in the academic literature regarding differences in the productivity rates of unionized and nonunion workers (for a review, see Freeman and Medoff, 1984).

Bibliography

Curme, M. A., Hirsch, B. T., and Macpherson, D. A. (1990). Union membership and contract coverage in the United States, 1983–1988. *Industrial and Labor Relations Review*, 44, 5–33.

Freeman, R. B. and Medoff, J. (1984). *What Do Unions Do?* New York: Basic Books.

Freeman, R. B. and Rogers, J. (1993). Who speaks for us? Employee representation in a nonunion labor market. In B. E. Kaufman and M. M. Kleiner (eds.), *Employee Representation: Alternatives and Future Directions*. Madison, WI: Industrial Relations Research Association, pp. 13–79.

Lewin, D., Feuille, P., Kochan, T. A., and Delaney, J. T. (1988). *Public Sector Labor Relations: Analysis and Readings*, 3rd edn. Lexington, MA: D. C. Heath.

color

Ramona L. Paetzold

Color is one of the protected categories under Title VII of the CIVIL RIGHTS ACT OF 1964. Few cases based on this category of protection have been litigated. However, the prototypical case has involved claims by a darker-skinned person that he or she was denied a privilege of employment in favor of a lighter-skinned person of the same race (or vice versa).

commission-based pay

Timothy J. Keaveny

A commission is INCENTIVE PAY based on a percentage of the selling price of a product or service. Sales jobs are commonly paid partially or totally on commission. There are various systems of commission-based pay. A straight commission is a plan in which the salesperson receives a fixed percentage of the sales price of the product or service. A graduated commission plan is one in which the percentage changes for higher sales volume, e.g., 5 percent commission for less than $500,000, 6 percent for $500,000 up to $750,000, and so forth. A salary plus commission plan is one in which the salesperson has a base salary to which a commission based on sales is added.

Factors to be considered in the design of commission plans include the emphasis on customer service, nature of the product, and sales potential of the sales territory. When there is high concern for customer service, or when the product is technical and time is required to understand it, or when the sales territory has low market potential, one should consider having a significant salary component in the compensation plan.

Bibliography

Milkovich, G. T. and Newman, J. M. (1993). *Compensation*, 4th edn. Homewood, IL: Richard D. Irwin.

Moynahan, J. K. (1991). *The Sales Compensation Handbook*. New York: AMACOM.

compa-ratios

Thomas H. Stone

A compa-ratio expresses the relationship of actual pay of an individual or a group of employees (average) to their rate range midpoint (*see* RATE RANGES). The formula is the actual individual or average pay rate(s) divided by the range midpoint. As a control index, it shows the correspondence of actual pay levels to intended pay levels. Therefore, a compa-ratio of 1.0 for a JOB FAMILY means that actual average pay is equal to the rate range midpoint; under 1.0 means actual pay averages below the midpoint, while over 1.0 means the opposite. If many employees are long-tenured and/or high performers, compa-ratios may exceed 1.0 because the employees have "topped out" of the pay range. In job families with many new and/or poor-performing employees, compa-ratios less than 1.0 will occur. Thus, compa-ratios are influenced by both employee flows within the organization and employee performance.

comparable worth

John A. Fossum

Comparable worth is the notion that pay should be based on the relative value of jobs within employing organizations without regard to gender-based differences in labor supply behavior and/or job segregation. Comparable worth was developed to address situations in which jobs held predominantly by women requiring substantial education and responsibility (e.g., registered nurses) are often paid less within employing organizations than jobs held predominantly by men that do not (e.g., carpenters and painters). The EQUAL PAY ACT OF 1963 requires men and women working in the *same* job or one with *substantially similar* requirements to be paid the same (unless there are bona fide differences in performance, experience, merit, and so forth). The Act lists factors to be compared in measuring similarity, including skill, effort, responsibility, and working conditions. Comparable worth argues that pay for *dissimilar* jobs should be equal if the relative requirements across the factors are similar (or comparable).

Comparability is determined by applying job evaluation to measure levels of skill, effort, responsibility, and working conditions (or other similar factors) across a set of jobs (*see* JOB EVALUATION METHODS). Each job's point total is the sum of the measures across these factors. Jobs with equal points are considered of comparable worth and would be expected to be paid equally. The evaluation would also be used to establish pay differences between jobs of different worth.

Comparable worth has been implemented in some US state and local public employment jurisdictions and across all employers in the Province of Ontario.

compensable factor

Jerry M. Newman

Compensable factors are job attributes that reflect the relative worth of jobs inside an organization and are chosen to reflect its values and strategic plan. A company concerned with costs might evaluate jobs for their accountability, defined in terms of fiscal responsibility. Jobs lower in accountability would receive lower ratings on this compensable factor. Jobs lower across all compensable factors would be of relatively less value than other jobs. A compensable factor must be work-related, business-related, and acceptable to the parties involved.

compensation

Steven L. Thomas

Compensation is the total package of tangible returns (financial rewards, services, and BENEFITS) provided by the organization to employees in return for their labor. The compensation package includes two basic components: (1) direct pay, and (2) indirect pay or benefits (Milkovich and Newman, 1993). The compensation system includes the process by which the total compensation package is designed and administered.

Direct pay includes (1) base pay (the fixed portion of pay that includes wages or salary), (2) base pay add-ons (such as overtime pay, cost-of-living adjustments, and shift premiums), and (3) pay for performance (BONUSES, MERIT PAY, and INCENTIVE PAY). Indirect pay consists of services or benefits provided to employees. Some benefits, such as SOCIAL SECURITY BENEFITS, are mandatory benefits and are legally required of all employers. Other benefits are offered at the discretion of employers and may include PAID TIME OFF (vacations), health insurance plans, deferred income and income continuation plans (PENSION PLANS), and income equivalents such as childcare benefits (see CHILDCARE BENEFIT) and employee discounts (Henderson, 1994).

Contemporary compensation administration frequently embraces a strategic approach where the mix and level of direct pay and benefits are chosen to reinforce the organization's overall strategic objectives (Gomez-Mejia and Balkin, 1992). Integration among four basic policy decisions is required in the design of a consistent compensation system (Milkovich and Newman, 1993). These decisions involve:

1 the comparison of jobs within an organization (see INTERNAL EQUITY/INTERNAL CONSISTENCY; JOB EVALUATION METHODS);
2 setting pay levels relative to competitors (see EXTERNAL EQUITY/EXTERNAL COMPETITIVENESS);
3 adjusting pay for individual employees (see PAY FOR PERFORMANCE; REWARD SYSTEMS; SKILL-BASED PAY DESIGN); and
4 the administration of the compensation function (see BENEFITS ADMINISTRATION; BENEFITS COMMUNICATION; JOB EVALUATION ADMINISTRATIVE ISSUES).

Bibliography

Gomez-Mejia, L. R. and Balkin, D. B. (1992). *Compensation, Organizational Strategy, and Firm Performance*. Cincinnati, OH: South-Western Publishing.
Henderson, R. I. (1994). *Compensation Management: Rewarding Performance*. Englewood Cliffs, NJ: Prentice-Hall.
Milkovich, G. T. and Newman, J. M. (1993). *Compensation*, 4th edn. Homewood, IL: Richard D. Irwin.

compensation strategy

Luis R. Gomez-Mejia

Compensation strategy is the deliberate utilization of the pay system as an essential integrating mechanism through which the efforts of various subunits and individuals are directed toward the achievement of an organization's strategic objectives, subject to internal and external constraints. Consistent with this definition, each firm faces a repertoire of pay choices. The degree of success associated with each of these depends on two factors. The first is how well the alternative(s) selected enable the organization to cope better with contingencies affecting it at a given point in time. The second is the extent to which the pay choices made are synchronized with the firm's overall strategic direction.

Bibliography

Gomez-Mejia, L. R. (1992). Structure and process of diversification, compensation strategy, and firm performance. *Strategic Management Journal*, 13, 381–97.
Gomez-Mejia, L. R. and Balkin, D. B. (1992). *Compensation, Organization Strategy, and Firm Performance*. Cincinnati, OH: South-Western Publishing.

composite and multiple criteria

James T. Austin

Composite and multiple criteria are choices concerning a set of criterion measures. Should a single weighted composite or the diverse set be utilized? Given an increasingly large domain of JOB PERFORMANCE measures, this subject has been widely considered (Brogden and Taylor,

1950; Sparks, 1970; Srinivasan, Shocker, and Weinstein, 1973). One practical implication is weighting, because a composite requires combination of the elements, whether statistically, monetarily, or judgmentally. Schmidt and Kaplan (1971) reviewed the controversy, identified test validation and validation research, and concluded that the choice depended upon the purposes of the investigator. Practical purposes require composites, whereas research purposes require multiple criteria. Nonetheless, counter-examples to this rule are possible, as in developmental counseling of subordinates, and thus there are good reasons to develop both systems simultaneously.

Bibliography

Brogden, H. E. and Taylor, E. K. (1950). The dollar criterion: Applying the cost accounting concept to criterion construction. *Personnel Psychology*, 3, 133–54.

Schmidt, F. L. and Kaplan, L. B. (1971). Composite versus multiple criteria: A review and resolution of the controversy. *Personnel Psychology*, 24, 419–34.

Sparks, C. P. (1970). Validity of psychological tests. *Personnel Psychology*, 23, 39–46.

Srinivasan, V., Shocker, A. D., and Weinstein, A. G. (1973). Measurement of a composite criterion of managerial success. *Organizational Behavior and Human Decision Processes*, 9, 147–67.

compressed work schedules

Randall B. Dunham and Jon L. Pierce

A compressed work schedule contains the same number of hours in the work week as a traditional schedule, but the number of hours worked in a given day increases. Perhaps the best known of the compressed schedules is the four-day, 40-hour work week, in which four consecutive 10-hour days are worked, followed by three days off. Variations on this model include:

1 the floating 4/40, in which four 10-hour days are worked followed by 4 days off, with a repeating cycle based on an 8-day week;
2 the 4.5/40, composed of four 9-hour days plus one 4-hour day, followed by 2.5 days off; and
3 the 5/45–4/36, which consists of 9-hour days and alternating 5-day and 4-day work weeks.

A variety of shift work compressed schedules also exist, the most common of which involve 9-hour and 12-hour shifts implemented with a variety of rotating schedules. Discussion of more alternatives can be found in Cunningham (1990) and Pierce et al. (1989).

The most significant advantage is perceived additional leisure time and reduced interference with personal activities (see Cunningham, 1990; Pierce and Dunham, 1992). Other potential advantages include fewer weekly commutes to work, fewer conflicts with personal needs during the work day, less impact of nonwork stress on work time, favorable employee attitudes (see Dunham, Pierce, and Castaneda, 1987; DeCarufel and Schaan, 1990), and decreased employee ABSENTEEISM.

The most significant disadvantage arising from compressed work schedules involves fatigue. Other potential disadvantages include the greater cost of absenteeism (a single day represents a larger percentage of the work week), and increased moonlighting and associated fatigue and stress.

It is likely that compressed schedules will continue to be used as a joint response to the needs of the organization and the personal needs of organizational members. A key to the success of compressed programs appears to be whether workers have a days-per-week leisure orientation or an hours-per-day orientation.

Bibliography

Cunningham, J. B. (1990). Twelve hour shift schedules in policing: A review of the evidence. *Canadian Police College Journal*, 14, 184–201.

DeCarufel, A. and Schaan, J. L. (1990). The impact of compressed work weeks on police job involvement. *Canadian Police College Journal*, 14, 81–97.

Dunham, R. B., Pierce, J. L., and Castaneda, M. B. (1987). Alternative work schedules: Two field quasi-experiments. *Personnel Psychology*, 40, 215–42.

Pierce, J. L. and Dunham, R. B. (1992). The 12-hour work day: A 48-hour, eight-day week. *Academy of Management Journal*, 35, 1086–98.

Pierce, J. L., Newstrom, J. W., Dunham, R. B., and Barber, A. E. (1989). *Alternative Work Schedules.* Boston: Allyn and Bacon.

Rosa, R. R. and Bonnet, M. H. (1993). Performance and alertness of 8 hour and 1 hour rotating shifts at a natural gas utility. *Ergonomics*, **36**, 1177–93.

Waddington, D. P. (1986). The Ansells Brewery dispute: A social-cognitive approach to the study of strikes. *Journal of Occupational Psychology*, **59**, 231–46.

computer-assisted instruction

Raymond A. Noe

Computer-assisted instruction (CAI) refers to an instructional system in which the student interacts directly with the computer which has stored informational and instructional materials related to the program. CAI permits individualized instruction: the student can choose content, level of difficulty, and practice opportunities. The trainee also receives direct feedback about his or her performance in the program. CAI permits the trainee to skip material or return to previously seen materials for remediation. Because training materials are self-contained on the computer, CAI gives the learner the flexibility to decide when he or she wants to be trained and how much content to cover in a session.

See also *training*

Computer Matching and Privacy Protection Act of 1988

Vida Scarpello

This Act's purpose is to regulate the use of computer matching by federal agencies and for use of federal records (subject to the provisions of the PRIVACY ACT OF 1974), for matching state and local government records. Matching refers to several different computer-assisted techniques used in identifying similarities and differences between records. It is primarily used to locate an individual, verify eligibility for federal benefit programs, and recoup payment or delinquent debts under such programs. Not covered are matches performed for statistical research, tax, law enforcement, and certain other purposes. Basically, matching is intended as a tool against fraud.

This law was passed because disclosure restrictions of the 1974 Privacy Act have been interpreted by the Office of Management and Budget (OMB) and other federal agencies as permitting disclosures necessary to support computer matching. Thus, the privacy law offered little protection to individual subjects of computer matching. Accordingly, the Computer Matching and Privacy Protection Act was passed to address due process, administrative controls, and cost-effectiveness issues. Section 2(D)(p) of the Act prohibits adverse action against individuals by matching programs, until the relevant agency has independently verified the accuracy of the information. Section 4(u)(1) establishes a data integrity board within each agency and charges the board with complete administrative responsibility for implementation and monitoring of all written agreements for receipt or disclosure of agency records and for all matching programs the agency participates in during the year. Section 4(6) instructs the director of the OMB to consolidate information contained from the data integrity boards and submit the consolidated report to Congress. The OMB director's report must include an analysis of the costs and benefits of matching programs for specified periods of time, and reasons for why a data integrity board may have granted a waiver from completion and submission of a cost-benefit analysis. This last requirement is based on the acknowledged benefit that matching is useful in identifying and limiting program losses. However, matching also raises concern about Fourth Amendment rights, privacy rights, and computer linkage. Consequently, matching should be restricted to the situations where there is a demonstrable benefit as well as clearly inadequate less intrusive alternatives.

Bibliography

Computer Matching and Privacy Protection Act of 1988, in Legislative History, Senate Report No. 100–446. 3107–53.

Computer Matching and Privacy Protection Act of 1988, Public Law 100–503[S.496], Laws of the 100th Congress – 2nd Session, 102 STAT. 2507–2515.

concurrent validity

Chester A. Schriesheim

Concurrent validity is one of two subdomains of CRITERION-RELATED VALIDITY, the other being PREDICTIVE VALIDITY. Concurrent validation procedures assess the degree to which scores on an instrument (the predictor) are statistically associated with values obtained by a theoretically appropriate outcome measure (the criterion), when both are measured at approximately the same point in time (i.e., concurrently).

Evidence of concurrent validity is particularly appropriate when the purpose of applying an instrument is to diagnose or determine an existing status or situation (rather than to predict future outcomes). For example, correlating an instrument measuring attitudes toward customers with observations of employee–customer interactions collected over a short time period (close to the administration of the instrument) provides concurrent validity evidence on that instrument (and may allow it to substitute for observing employee–customer interactions in certain circumstances). Another appropriate use of concurrent validation is when a network of concurrent relationships is required as evidence for the construct validation process (see the description of this process under CONSTRUCT VALIDITY).

A less appropriate use of concurrent validation is as a short-term substitute for predictive validation. For example, when a selection test is developed to predict the performance of job applicants one year after they have been hired, an early indication of the usefulness of the test may be sought. Thus, the test may be administered to current employees and their obtained scores correlated with concurrently obtained measures of JOB PERFORMANCE. Caution is needed in interpreting such results, however, due to such things as restriction in the range of criterion scores owing to earlier termination of poorly performing employees.

Bibliography

American Educational Research Association, American Psychological Association, and National Council on Measurement in Education (1999). *Standards for Educational and Psychological Testing*. Washington, DC: American Educational Research Association.

conference method

J. Kevin Ford and Deidre Wasson

The conference method is a carefully planned meeting with specific goals and purposes and is primarily used for the learning of conceptual information (e.g., new policies or procedures), and for attitudinal change and development (Wexley and Latham, 1991). The trainer plays an integral role in the development and execution of the conference by stressing two-way communication between trainee and trainer. Conferences are especially effective when the ratio of trainees to trainer is relatively small and the material to be taught requires elaboration or clarification (Muchinsky, 1990). More importantly, the trainer needs to maintain an interesting discussion that actively involves all trainees to facilitate learning.

See also *training*

Bibliography

Muchinsky, P. M. (1990). *Psychology Applied to Work: An Introduction to Industrial and Organizational Psychology*, 3rd edn. Pacific Grove, CA: Brooks/Cole.

Wexley, K. N. and Latham, G. P. (1991). *Developing and Training Human Resources in Organizations*, 2nd edn. New York: HarperCollins.

Connecticut v. *Teal*, 457 US 440 (1982)

Leonard Bierman

In *Teal*, black employees of the state claimed that the examination required for PROMOTION to supervisor and the set passing score of 65 resulted in DISPARATE IMPACT. These employees temporarily performed the supervisory jobs satisfactorily, applied for the jobs permanently, failed to meet the test cutoff, and were subsequently denied promotion into the supervisory positions. From the list of those who passed the exams, the state promoted a disproportionate number of minority group members by applying an AFFIRMATIVE ACTION program to insure significant minority representation. Indeed, the overall result of the process or the *bottom line* was more favorable to minorities than to whites. The court held, however, that the pass–fail barrier exam still resulted in disparate impact and therefore was discriminatory to *specific* individuals regardless of the employer's nondiscriminatory *bottom line*.

Consolidated Omnibus Budget Reconciliation Act of 1985

Ramona L. Paetzold

The Consolidated Omnibus Budget Reconciliation Act of 1985 (COBRA) amended Title I of the EMPLOYEE RETIREMENT INCOME SECURITY ACT OF 1974 (ERISA) to require group health plan providers to allow employees and certain beneficiaries to extend their current health coverage in circumstances that would ordinarily result in loss of coverage. Group health plans include not only medical plans, but also vision care plans, dental plans, and prescription drug plans, even if self-funded. Employers having fewer than 20 employees are exempt from COBRA's coverage.

The Act identifies "qualifying events" that would otherwise result in loss of coverage for the employee or the employee's spouse or dependant child. These qualifying events include the death of the covered employee, a reduction in the employee's hours making him or her ineligible for continued coverage, the termination of the employee (except for gross misconduct), the divorce or legal separation of the covered employee and his or her spouse, the employee's eligibility for Medicare, and a child no longer being considered an eligible dependant under the plan. The period of transitional coverage is either 18 or 36 months, depending on the nature of the qualifying event. Proof of insurability cannot be required as a condition of the transitional coverage.

COBRA coverage must be elected by the employee or qualified beneficiary; additionally, the employee or qualified beneficiary must be given notice of his or her COBRA rights at the start of plan coverage and when qualifying events occur. The cost of the COBRA continued coverage may be passed on to covered persons but may not exceed 102 percent of the applicable premium for active employees for the first 18 months and 150 percent thereafter.

construct validity

Linda S. Gottfredson

Many psychological assessments purport to measure particular hypothetical traits (*see* TRAIT) or constructs such as extraversion, intelligence, self-efficacy, anxiety, or morale. Construct validity is a judgment about the extent to which an assessment actually measures the proposed trait in the populations of interest, and thus what can be appropriately inferred from individuals' scores on it. Validity is never a blanket judgment, but is established for specified uses of the assessment.

CONSTRUCT VALIDATION AS THEORY TESTING

A construct is a tentative theory about an unobservable, underlying trait that is invoked to explain patterns of responses on an assessment. Construct validity requires evidence that individuals with different scores on the assessment actually behave as predicted by the theory. No single procedure or piece of evidence suffices to establish construct validity. The more evidence collected concerning the nature, causes, correlates, and effects of the attribute being measured, the clearer the inferences that may properly be drawn from scores for it.

Construct validation is a complex inferential process drawing on many sorts of evidence, i.e., a process of theory testing. Cronbach (1990: 183) distinguished between weak validation (an undirected, inductive process) and strong validation (a tough-minded testing of specific hypotheses). Positive evidence supports both the measure and the theory. Negative evidence means that the measure, the theory, or both may be faulty. Different procedures in this inferential process are often identified as different forms of validity. Although construct validity is sometimes treated as only one among various forms of validity, it is increasingly viewed as a concept unifying all of them (Messick, 1989).

KINDS OF EVIDENCE

Content-related evidence of validity (what used to be called CONTENT VALIDITY) refers to the care with which test items were chosen to represent the specific processes or content thought to instantiate the construct. For achievement tests, this means appropriate breadth and depth in sampling from the intended achievement domain, say, physics. For ability tests, it means sampling the mental processes thought to comprise the ability, such as visualizing objects in three-dimensional space for spatial ability. Content-related evidence is obtained by examining how the test items were developed or by having examinees report their thought processes while tackling items on the test. Such evidence increases the likelihood that an assessment will measure the intended construct, but it provides no proof it succeeds in doing so.

Criterion-related evidence of validity (CRITERION-RELATED VALIDITY) refers to the degree to which scores on the assessment correlate with other traits, behaviors, and outcomes (the criteria). We might ask, for example, how well students' IQ scores correlate with their current academic performance (CONCURRENT VALIDITY) or later JOB PERFORMANCE (PREDICTIVE VALIDITY).

Convergent and discriminant validity refer to the patterns of correlations predicted by the broader theory in which the construct is embedded. Two assessments that supposedly measure the same construct (e.g., intelligence) should correlate highly with each other and also with behaviors the theory says will be affected by the trait (e.g., performance in school or job training). Measures of the construct should correlate only weakly, however, with measures of different constructs (e.g., anxiety or creativity) or with supposedly unaffected outcomes (e.g., athletic prowess).

Evidence of DIFFERENTIAL VALIDITY and SINGLE-GROUP VALIDITY also affects the interpretation of test scores. For instance, there was once much concern that job aptitude tests predict job performance for white job applicants better than (or only) for ethnic minorities, and thus should not be used to infer the job qualifications of the latter. This issue was settled by meta-analyzing many small studies (Hunter, Schmidt, and Hunter, 1979).

Other research strategies are also useful in determining just what constructs different assessments are capturing, whatever the original intent. For example, the structure, relatedness, and homogeneity of the traits being measured can be clarified through factor analysis, both exploratory and confirmatory. If the construct is a developmental one, then longitudinal or cross-sectional studies should reveal predictable age differences. Scores should also differ, or not differ, for other subgroups or circumstances (e.g., gender, personality type, job tenure) in the manner predicted. Interventions to change traits can also test assumptions about them. For example, studies of adoption and compensatory education forced some rethinking about the malleability of intelligence and the consequent meaning of high versus low IQ scores.

Bibliography

Braun, H. I., Jackson, D. N., and Wiley, D. E. (2002). *The Role of Constructs in Psychological and Educational Measurement*. Mahwah, NJ: Erlbaum.

Cronbach, L. J. (1990). *Essentials of Psychological Testing*, 5th edn. New York: HarperCollins.

Cronbach, L. J. and Meehl, P. E. (1955). Construct validity in psychological tests. *Psychological Bulletin*, **52**, 281–302.

Hunter, J. E., Schmidt, F. L., and Hunter, R. (1979). Differential validity of employment tests by race: A comprehensive review and analysis. *Psychological Bulletin*, **86**, 721–35.

Messick, S. (1989). Validity of psychological measurement. In R. L. Linn (ed.), *Educational Measurement*, 3rd edn. New York: Macmillan, pp. 13–103.

content validity

Robert M. Guion

The term "content validity" was initially introduced in 1954 (American Psychological Association, 1954) to mean the adequacy of test content as a sample of a larger content domain. Claims of adequacy were to be based on the "representativeness of the test content in relation to the universe of items adopted for reference" (American Psychological Association, 1954: 13). Such claims evaluated test development without recognizing the difference between test development and drawing inferences from test scores (i.e., the basic concept of validity).

Three conferences on content validity held at Bowling Green State University concluded that "there is no such thing" (Cranny, 1987). The 1985 *Standards* referred not to content validity but to "content-related evidence of validity," showing that test content is "appropriate relative to its intended purpose" (see American Educational Research Association et al., 1985: 90). A test intended to measure a factor-analytically determined construct need not sample all kinds of test items defining the factor. There may be "appropriate" evidence of validity even with a single-item type among the many that have in the past served to define the factor. Valid inferences from scores require content appropriate for such inferences, regardless of the nature of the measurement or of the attribute (construct) being measured, but it is not the case that an entire universe of item content must be sampled to support intended inferences.

See also *content validity ratio*

Bibliography

American Educational Research Association, American Psychological Association, and National Council on Measurement in Education (1985). *Standards for Educational and Psychological Testing*. Washington, DC: American Psychological Association.
American Psychological Association (1954). Technical recommendations for psychological tests and diagnostic techniques. *Psychological Bulletin*, **51** (2), Part 2.
Cranny, C. J. (ed.) (1987). *Content Validity III: Proceedings*. Bowling Green, OH: Bowling Green State University Press.

content validity ratio

Robert M. Guion

CONTENT VALIDITY was introduced in an era when validity was mainly associated with validity coefficients in employment testing. Lawshe (1975) provided a quantitative index for assessing content validity, termed a content validity ratio (CVR), for individual test items. To compute it, job experts independently judge the item as measuring content that is essential, useful, or not necessary for JOB PERFORMANCE. With N judges, of whom n_e have judged the knowledge required for the item to be essential, CVR = $(n_e - N/2)/(N/2)$. Items with low or negative CVRs can be deleted; the mean CVR of items retained is the "content validity index" for the total test.

Bibliography

Lawshe, C. H. (1975). A quantitative approach to content validity. *Personnel Psychology*, **28**, 563–75.

contingency approach

Annette Cox

Contingency approach refers to a method of decision-making often applied in devising appropriate human resource (HR) strategies and termed the "best fit" approach in contrast to "best practice" approaches. It is based on the premise that picking the most effective HR policies and practices depends on matching them appropriately to the organization's environment. The contingent factors influencing HR strategy might include type of business strategy pursued, organization size, type of technology, geographic location and labor market, management skills and preferences, industry sector and economic conditions. One formulation of contingency theory to prescribe HR practices for different organizations is the business strategy model based on Michael Porter's threefold categorization of business strategies as focused on the pursuit of low costs, product innovation, or quality. Another variant is the business life-cycle model, which specifies different HR techniques according to organization age from start-up to decline.

Contingency models can be static and offer no help to dynamic organizations undergoing frequent change and neglect to recognize that organizations often need to satisfy multiple conflicting goals. They can be either too simplistic and fail to include every contingency or too complex for managers to apply in practice. Future contingency research should be refined to address these concerns.

Bibliography

Boxall, P. and Purcell, J. (2002). *Strategy and Human Resource Management*. Basingstoke: Palgrave.
Donaldson, L. (2001). *The Contingency Theory of Organizations*. London: Sage.

contingent employment

Stanley Nollen

Contingent employment, or atypical employment (the term more frequently used in Europe), is employment that depends on employers' changing and transitory needs for labor input (other terms are peripheral, precarious, or supplemental employment). It is demand-driven, "on-call" employment, determined by the employers' decisions about when, where, and how much work is to be done. It is the opposite of regular core employment.

Employers use contingent labor to achieve flexibility in the size of their workforces as the demand for labor fluctuates, to buffer core employees from JOB LOSS during business downturns, to reduce labor costs through lower wage or BENEFITS payments (sometimes this goal is not achieved), and to ease management tasks to the extent that contingent workers are not employees of the organization where they work.

In practice, the distinction between contingent and core employment is not always clear. Four characteristics help to identify who is a contingent worker (though no one trait by itself is a sufficient definition). Contingent workers have:

1. little job or employment security;
2. irregular work schedules;
3. lack of access to benefits; and
4. little attachment to the company at which they work (Polivka and Nardone, 1989).

JOB INSECURITY

Contingent workers have no explicit or implicit contract or commitment from the organization for which they work. They have no expectation of continuing employment. They may work for a day or a year or longer. Correspondingly, contingent workers usually change from one company's workplace to another's frequently. Regular core employees have decreasing employment security, especially in North America, but there is a mutual expectation between employer and employee of continuing service.

IRREGULAR WORK TIME

Contingent workers often have irregular and unpredictable work schedules. Both the total number of hours they work in a year and the days, weeks, or months when they work are unstable and dependent on management decisions rather than their preferences.

LACK OF ACCESS TO BENEFITS

Contingent workers usually do not get access to employer-provided benefits that are not required by law, ranging from vacation leave to health insurance to retirement plans, even though regular employees in the same workplace receive these benefits. The benefits gap between contingent and regular employees is larger in the US, where fewer benefits are mandated than in most other countries. Contingent workers usually do not participate in the full range of other privileges and opportunities that are often available to regular employees, such as membership in company clubs or eligibility for continuing education.

LACK OF ATTACHMENT TO THE COMPANY

Contingent workers do not belong to the company as regular employees do, even if they are on the payroll. They are not expected to be as committed to the company's mission, although they may be as fully committed to the work they do as regular employees are, especially among contingent, highly skilled professional and technical people.

Contingent employment occurs as one of several main STAFFING options. Contingent workers are supplied from staffing companies or agencies to companies where they work as needed or they are hired directly by the company into an in-house temporary labor pool. Some part-time employees (*see* PART-TIME WORK SCHEDULE) are hired on an hourly basis to work a variable number of hours according to the amount of work to be done (other part-timers are regular core employees). They are used by companies to perform specific projects or work for defined short-term periods on a contract basis; they are self-employed workers.

Bibliography

Nollen, S. D. and Axel, H. (1995). *Managing Contingent Workers*. New York: AMACOM.

Polivka, A. E. and Nardone, T. (1989). On the definition of contingent work. *Monthly Labor Review*, **112**, 9–16.

continuous improvement

Vinod K. Jain

Continuous improvement refers, in general, to systematic organizational efforts aimed at creating and sustaining a culture of constant improvement and change (Locke and Jain, 1995). A continuous improvement program (CIP), by definition, is a systematic and well-thought-out effort on the part of the organization to make ongoing improvements in one or more of its work systems. It is not at odds with meeting goals and specifications; it is just that improvement efforts never cease (*see* LEARNING ORGANIZATION). Practiced in Japan for over 40 years, CIPs became popular in the West during the 1990s as a result of the globalization of competition and programs such as ISO 9000 and the MALCOLM BALDRIGE NATIONAL QUALITY AWARD.

Researchers have equated continuous improvement with suggestion systems (Schroeder and Robinson, 1991), process improvement (Dewar, 1992), TOTAL QUALITY MANAGEMENT (Porter, 1993), and so on, depending upon their individual perspectives. Organizations adopt CIPs for a variety of reasons, such as survival, within the context of the global economy, because their competitors are already using CIP. CIPs are often operationalized in terms of such goals as improved customer satisfaction, PRODUCTIVITY, and quality, and reduced cycle times and costs.

Continuous improvement entails new, ongoing learning. New ideas are essential if organizational learning is to take place and these new ideas can trigger organizational improvement (Garvin, 1993). The implementation of a CIP requires the development of organizational policies, strategies, and structures needed for continuous learning (Senge, 1990). Most of all, it requires the building of a continuous improvement culture within the organization through means such as TRAINING, goal setting, performance measurement and feedback, open communication, EMPLOYEE EMPOWERMENT, experimentation, and benchmarking (Locke and Jain, 1995; *see* BENCHMARKING AND COMPETITOR ANALYSIS).

Bibliography

Dewar, D. L. (1992). The process flowchart and continuous improvement. *Journal of Quality and Participation*, 15, 56–7.

Garvin, D. A. (1993). Building a learning organization. *Harvard Business Review*, 71, 78–91.

Locke, E. A. and Jain, V. K. (1995). Organizational learning and continuous improvement. *International Journal of Organizational Analysis*, 3, 45–68.

Porter, A. M. (1993). Baldrige winners discuss continuous improvement path. *Purchasing*, January, 55–88.

Schroeder, D. M. and Robinson, A. G. (1991). America's most successful export to Japan: Continuous improvement programs. *Sloan Management Review*, 32, 67–81.

Senge, P. M. (1990). The leader's new work: Building learning organizations. *Sloan Management Review*, 31, 7–23.

contract administration

David Lewin

Contract administration is defined as the processes by which terms and conditions of employment contained in COLLECTIVE BARGAINING agreements between unionized workers and management are enforced. While the vast bulk of such enforcement occurs on a day-to-day basis in the workplace through supervisory and management directives and actions, most popular and scholarly attention has focused on those instances in which employees claim that contractual provisions governing terms and conditions of employment have been misapplied or unfairly applied. Consequently, GRIEVANCES, grievance procedures (*see* GRIEVANCE PROCEDURE), and RIGHTS ARBITRATION are widely considered to be at the heart of contract administration (Lewin, 1999; Lewin and Mitchell, 1995).

GRIEVANCES AND GRIEVANCE PROCEDURES

Grievance procedures are found in virtually all collective bargaining agreements, contain multiple hierarchical steps for the processing of written grievances, and provide for binding third-party ARBITRATION as the final settlement step (Delaney, Lewin, and Ichniowski,

1989). Grievance filing rates, measured by the number of written grievances filed annually per every 100 unionized employees, average about 10 percent in the US, with wide variation by industry, firm, occupation, and work location. Most grievances are settled at the lower steps of the procedure, with about 2 to 3 percent being settled at the arbitration step (Lewin and Peterson, 1988; Peterson and Lewin, 2000). There is evidence that grievance filers fare more poorly than nonfilers in terms of post-grievance settlement JOB PERFORMANCE, promotions (see PROMOTION), work attendance, and EMPLOYEE TURNOVER (Lewin, 1992; Lewin and Peterson, 1999).

MODELING THE GRIEVANCE PROCESS

Economists have used exit–voice–loyalty theory to model the grievance process in unionized settings. From this perspective, grievance filing is an expression of employee voice, and this exercise of voice is hypothesized to be inversely related to employee exit behavior, or quitting. Concomitantly, loyalty is hypothesized to be positively related to grievance filing (the exercise of voice) and negatively related to exit (quits) (Hirschman, 1970; Freeman and Medoff, 1984). While some evidence has been adduced to support these hypotheses, more recent research finds negative relationships between employee loyalty and grievance filing, and positive relationships between grievance filing and intent to exit the unionized firm (Boroff and Lewin, 1997; Lewin, 2004b).

Behavioral scientists have used procedural justice–distributive justice theory to model the grievance procedure (Sheppard, Lewicki, and Minton, 1992; see DISTRIBUTIVE JUSTICE; PROCEDURAL JUSTICE). From this perspective, employee perceptions of the fairness, equity, or justness of contract administration processes are as important, perhaps more important, than employee perceptions of the fairness, equity, or justness of the outcomes of contract administration processes in terms of employee decisions to file written grievances. Recent evidence tends to support this view, and also finds that the perceived fairness of the grievance procedure is inversely associated with employee grievance filing under the procedure (Lewin and Boroff, 1995).

CONTRACT ADMINISTRATION IN THE NONUNION SECTOR

Grievance procedures have grown markedly in the nonunion sector in recent years, and between one-third and one-half of nonunion companies in the US have a grievance or grievance-like ALTERNATIVE DISPUTE RESOLUTION (ADR) procedure in place for one or more (major) employee groups (Delaney et al., 1989; Ichniowski, Delaney, and Lewin, 1989). Grievance filing rates under these procedures are about one-half lower than grievance filing rates in unionized settings, and only about 20 percent of these procedures culminate in binding third-party arbitration (Lewin, 1987, 1992, 2004a; Delaney et al., 1989). However, recent court decisions strongly favoring deferral to arbitration under these procedures imply that they will become even more widely adopted. Such procedures are often criticized for their alleged one-sidedness, including that the employer picks and pays for the arbitrator and determines the scope of issues subject to arbitration (Stone, 1999). Also notable in recent years has been the growth of individual explicit employment contracting, including for executives, in which terms and conditions of employment between the individual employee and the employer are put in writing (Lewin, 1994). The extent to which these contracts contain grievance procedures or other dispute resolution mechanisms is unknown, and this is obviously an important area for future research on contract administration.

Bibliography

Boroff, K. E. and Lewin, D. (1997). Loyalty, voice, and intent to exit a union firm: A conceptual and empirical analysis. *Industrial and Labor Relations Review*, **51**, 50–63.

Delaney, J. T., Lewin, D., and Ichniowski, C. (1989). *Human Resource Policies and Practices of American Firms*. Washington, DC: US Department of Labor, Bureau of Labor–Management Relations and Cooperative Programs.

Freeman, R. B. and Medoff, J. L. (1984). *What Do Unions Do?* New York: Basic Books.

Hirschman, A. O. (1970). *Exit, Voice, and Loyalty.* Boston: Harvard University Press.

Ichniowski, C., Delaney, J. T., and Lewin, D. (1989). The new human resource management in US workplaces: Is it really new and is it only nonunion? *Relations Industrielles/ Industrial Relations*, **44**, 97–119.

Lewin, D. (1987). Dispute resolution in the nonunion firm: A theoretical and empirical analysis. *Journal of Conflict Resolution*, **31**, 467–502.

Lewin, D. (1992). Grievance procedures in nonunion workplaces: An empirical analysis of usage, dynamics, and outcomes. *Chicago-Kent Law Review*, **66**, 823–44.

Lewin, D. (1994). Individual explicit contracting in the labor market. In C. Kerr and P. D. Staudohar (eds.), *Labor Economics and Industrial Relations*. Boston: Harvard University Press, pp. 401–28.

Lewin, D. (1999). Theoretical and empirical research on the grievance procedure and arbitration. In A. E. Eaton and J. H. Keefe (eds.), *Employment Dispute Resolution and Worker Rights in the Changing Workplace*. Champaign, IL: Industrial Relations Research Association, pp. 137–86.

Lewin, D. (2004a). Dispute resolution in nonunion organizations: Key empirical findings. In S. Estreicher (ed.), *Alternative Dispute Resolution in the Employment Arena*. New York: Kluwer.

Lewin, D. (2004b). Unionism and organizational conflict resolution: Rethinking collective voice and its consequences. *Journal of Labor Research*, **25**.

Lewin, D. and Boroff, K. E. (1996). The role of loyalty in exit and voice: A conceptual and empirical analysis. *Advances in Industrial and Labor Relations*, **7**, 69–96.

Lewin, D. and Mitchell, D. J. B. (1995). *Human Resource Management: An Economic Approach*. Cincinnati, OH: South-Western Publishing.

Lewin, D. and Peterson, R. B. (1988). *The Modern Grievance Procedure in the United States*. Westport, CT: Quorum.

Lewin, D. and Peterson, R. B. (1999). Behavioral outcomes of grievance activity. *Industrial Relations*, **38**, 554–76.

Peterson, R. B. and Lewin, D. (2000). Research on unionized grievance procedures: Management issues and recommendations. *Human Resource Management*, **39**, 395–406.

Sheppard, B. H., Lewicki, R. J., and Minton, J. (1992). *Organizational Justice*. Lexington, MA: Lexington.

Stone, K. V. W. (1999). Employment arbitration under the Federal Arbitration Act. In A. E. Eaton and J. H. Keefe (eds.), *Employment Dispute Resolution and Worker Rights in the Changing Workplace*. Champaign, IL: Industrial Relations Research Association, pp. 27–65.

control issues in foreign holdings

J. Michael Geringer

As a result of disparate and changing competitive, market, and regulatory circumstances, many organizations have been pressured to adapt their resources and objectives. Such organizations have internationalized some or all of the activities comprising their value chains, often through full or partial ownership of foreign operations. Efforts to effectively manage foreign holdings may be complicated, however, by the increased strategic and operational complexity associated with coordinating and controlling activities across multiple national and competitive environments (Bartlett and Ghoshal, 1995).

Control is the process by which one entity uses mechanisms of a formal nature (e.g., ownership, organizational structure) or informal nature to influence the behavior and output of another entity (Geringer and Hebert, 1989). Control plays a critical role in determining an organization's capacity for achieving its strategic objectives, since it affects the organization's ability to monitor, coordinate, and integrate the activities of its various business operations in a manner consistent with critical organizational and environmental variables. To fully achieve their objectives, organizations must therefore design and implement appropriate and effective control systems within and among their foreign holdings.

Three complementary and interdependent dimensions comprise the foundation of an effective control system:

1. the *focus* of control (i.e., the scope of activities over which the organization seeks to exercise control);
2. the *extent* or degree of control sought over these focal activities; and
3. the *mechanisms* used to exercise control (Geringer and Hebert, 1989).

An organization must simultaneously consider all three of these dimensions in order to design and implement an effective control system; otherwise the organization's competitiveness and prospects for attainment of its objectives may be compromised.

Bibliography

Bartlett, C. A. and Ghoshal, S. (eds.) (1995). *Transnational Management: Text, Cases, and Readings*, 2nd edn. Burr Ridge, IL: Richard D. Irwin.

Geringer, J. M. and Hebert, L. (1989). Control and performance of international joint ventures. *Journal of International Business Studies*, 20, 234–54J.

coordination of benefits

Robert M. McCaffery

Coordination of benefits refers to methods for determining primary and secondary responsibility for healthcare expenses when an employee and spouse are both covered by a group benefit plan. Insured plans are governed by state regulations; self-insured plans are not.

In determining which plan is primary, two fundamental rules broadly apply:

1 coverage as an employee is primary to coverage as a dependant;
2 for dependent children the plan of the parent whose birth anniversary occurs first in the year is primary.

In determining the amount payable by the secondary plan, several alternative methods may be used. Depending on the method, secondary plan responsibility can range from zero to the entire remaining balance.

Bibliography

Beam, B. T. and McFadden, J. J. (2001). *Employee Benefits*, 6th edn. Chicago: Dearborn Financial Publishing, pp. 13–42.

McCaffery, R. M. (1992). *Employee Benefit Programs: A Total Compensation Perspective*, 2nd edn. Boston: PWS-Kent.

corrective discipline

Mark R. Sherman

The prevalence of the EMPLOYMENT-AT-WILL doctrine in the US has, until recently, resulted in only minimal emphasis on appropriate approaches to discipline for employees who were not covered by labor agreements. At-will employees could legally be discharged for any number of unfair reasons, so there was little practical or scholarly interest in the procedural and substantive fairness of their treatment. On the other hand, roughly half of all grievance arbitration (*see* RIGHTS ARBITRATION) in the US has traditionally involved determining whether management issued discipline for "just cause." As a consequence, the earliest authoritative pronouncements on the meaning of corrective discipline and PROGRESSIVE DISCIPLINE are found in the texts of ARBITRATION decisions.

In his early decision in the *International Harvester* case (Elkouri and Elkouri, 1985), Arbitrator Seward explained corrective discipline in the following manner: "corrective rather than retributive discipline... involves more than the mere matching of penalties with offenses... its purpose is not to 'get even' with the employee but to influence his future conduct." From these humble beginnings in the realm of arbitral jurisprudence, corrective discipline has since become a fundamental principle of human resource management. This is largely because it is consistent with the concept of employees as human resources who can be developed and enhanced like any other resources. While the corrective approach to discipline recognizes that most types of misconduct at work do not disqualify an employee from continued employment, it acknowledges that certain extreme types of misconduct render employees unworthy of corrective efforts. Typically these types of gross misconduct include assault, theft, and other types of criminal activity taking place on the employer's time or premises.

Bibliography

Elkouri, F. and Elkouri, E. (1985). *How Arbitration Works*, 4th edn. Washington, DC: BNA.

Fairweather, O. (1984). *Practice and Procedure in Labor Arbitration*, 2nd edn. Washington, DC: BNA.

Redeker, J. R. (1989). *Employee Discipline*. Washington, DC: BNA.

correspondence method

J. Kevin Ford and Deidre Wasson

A training technique that occurs primarily through the mail, correspondence is the exchange of learning materials and tests between a student and an instructor with little verbal communication (Salinger, 1973). Progress is monitored through assignments and exams returned to the instructor at the student's pace as course completion is dependent on the learner's speed in mastering the assigned material (Robinson, 1981). Several advantages are flexibility in time and location, reduced instructor and facility costs, and time and resource efficiency. However, long feedback lag times, low learning motivation, little or no interaction, limited subject matter, and high rates of incompleteness can occur.

See also *training; training evaluation*

Bibliography

Robinson, K. R. (1981). *Handbook of Training Management.* London: Kogan Page.

Salinger, R. D. (1973). *Disincentive to Effective Employee Training and Development.* Washington, DC: US Civil Service Commission, Bureau of Training.

counseling

Fang Lee Cooke

Counseling has been defined as a nondirective process by which a counselor helps an individual to overcome problems or come to terms with feelings, see what options are open, and choose between them by tapping into their own inner resources. Counseling has often been associated with the issue of sickness or problem resolution. Appropriate use of counseling in the workplace can be a sign of corporate health, encouraging people to confront and solve problems. In addition, by integrating counseling skills with other managerial techniques and ensuring they are used properly, organizations can improve effectiveness by encouraging the identification of problems before they escalate, and can facilitate better communications and promote a more open and honest culture where people are supported to make decisions.

Workplace counseling often has tangible and measurable benefits such as a reduction in ABSENTEEISM or EMPLOYEE TURNOVER, an increase in performance levels, and the avoidance of litigation or costly disciplinary procedures. A most common model of counseling provision is through EMPLOYEE ASSISTANCE PROGRAMS (EAPs). There are a number of issues that need to be taken into consideration when setting up an organizational counseling scheme. These are: confidentiality of information, accountability of counselors, supervision from professional bodies, workplace counseling skill training, monitoring and evaluation of the scheme.

Bibliography

Chartered Institute of Personnel and Development (1997). *The CIPD Guide on Counselling at Work.* London: CIPD.

countercyclical hiring

Charles R. Greer

Countercyclical hiring is a STAFFING strategy that is pursued to a limited extent by companies seeking to obtain bargains in key managerial and professional personnel by hiring during economic downturns. With conventional hiring, which occurs on a procyclical basis, companies hire during economic upturns. As such they attempt to hire employees at times when other companies are also competing for labor. Thus, there is higher demand for labor during economic upturns and it should be more difficult to obtain highly qualified key employees (Bright, 1976). As a result, companies that do not practice countercyclical hiring should find it more difficult to obtain the human resources needed to develop an advantage vis-à-vis their competitors.

The contrarian strategy of countercyclical hiring is based on the rationale that companies can invest in their stock of human resources by hiring key managerial and professional employees before there is a realized need, based on the knowledge that the services of such highly qualified individuals will be needed in the future. Thus companies that pursue countercyclical hiring strategies stockpile human resources for the future (Greer, 1984; Greer and Stedham, 1989; Greer and Ireland, 1992).

To date there have been two empirical studies of countercyclical hiring. The first found that companies that practice countercyclical hiring do so because of the quality of employees that can be hired. Unsurprisingly, organizations that conduct human resource forecasting (to avoid personnel shortages) are more likely to hire on a countercyclical basis (Greer and Stedham, 1989). A more recent study found the financial performance of companies to be positively related to countercyclical hiring, along with human resource planning (to avoid personnel shortages), the importance of having a regular managerial age distribution, emphasis on employee development and career development, and the perceived quality of applicants (Greer and Ireland, 1992). Because there are obvious economic costs and potential risks of creating perceptions of unfairness when new employees are hired concurrently with layoffs of present employees, countercyclical hiring strategies are envisioned to be implemented only on a limited basis. Nonetheless, countercyclical hiring can be an important contributor to the development of competencies which allow companies to differentiate themselves from their competitors.

Bibliography

Bright, W. E. (1976). How one company manages its human resources. *Harvard Business Review*, **54**, 81–93.
Greer, C. R. (1984). Countercyclical hiring as a staffing strategy for managerial and professional personnel: Some considerations and issues. *Academy of Management Review*, **9**, 324–30.
Greer, C. R. and Ireland, T. C. (1992). Organizational and financial correlates of a contrarian human resource investment strategy. *Academy of Management Journal*, **35**, 956–84.
Greer, C. R. and Stedham, Y. (1989). Countercyclical hiring as a staffing strategy for managerial and professional personnel: An empirical investigation. *Journal of Management*, **15**, 425–40.

craft unions

James B. Dworkin

A craft union represents workers who possess a specialized skill or perform a particular function. Examples include bricklayers, masons, plasterers, and electricians. Employees enter the craft as an apprentice and work their way up to the role of journeyman and through several years of ON-THE-JOB TRAINING. The union represents these employees in COLLECTIVE BARGAINING and also determines which individuals will have the opportunity to enter the trade. By restricting entry into the skilled trades, craft unions are able to keep wages high. Craft unions also control the hiring process through the mechanism of the hiring hall.

Bibliography

Kochan, T. A., Katz, H. C., and McKersie, R. B. (1986). *The Transformation of American Industrial Relations*. New York: Basic Books.
Slichter, S. H., Healy, J. J., and Livenash, E. R. (1960). *The Impact of Collective Bargaining on Management*. Washington, DC: Brookings Institution.

criterion contamination

Lorne Sulsky

Criterion contamination exists whenever nonperformance factors influence the JOB PERFORMANCE scores assigned to individuals (Borman, 1991). These nonperformance factors can take the form of a systematic bias such as LENIENCY EFFECTS, or can be random, such as measurement error (Muchinsky, 1995; *see* RELIABILITY). Because contamination lowers CONSTRUCT VALIDITY, criterion contamination and CRITERION RELEVANCE are inversely related, such that increasing contamination decreases relevance.

Bibliography

Borman, W. C. (1991). Job behavior, performance, and effectiveness. In M. D. Dunnette and L. M. Hough (eds.), *Handbook of Industrial and Organizational Psychology*, 2nd edn, vol. 2. Palo Alto, CA: Consulting Psychologists Press, pp. 271–326.

Muchinsky, P. M. (1995). *Psychology Applied to Work.* Pacific Grove, CA: Brooks/Cole.

criterion deficiency

Lorne Sulsky

Criterion deficiency implies that the measures used to assess JOB PERFORMANCE fail to assess one or more aspects of the criterion domain considered to be part of the conceptual criterion. For instance, deficiency would exist if a component of the job of secretary is word processing and there is no criterion measure which assesses competency in performing word-processing tasks. Thus, increases in deficiency imply decreases in CRITERION RELEVANCE (Borman, 1991). Examining for deficiency requires that the CONTENT VALIDITY of the criteria be considered.

Bibliography

Borman, W. C. (1991). Job behavior, performance, and effectiveness. In M. D. Dunnette and L. M. Hough (eds.), *Handbook of Industrial and Organizational Psychology,* 2nd edn, vol. 2. Palo Alto, CA: Consulting Psychologists Press, pp. 271–326.

criterion problem

James T. Austin and Peter Villanova

Patricia Cain Smith (1976) used the term criterion problem to characterize the dilemmas of measuring JOB PERFORMANCE for multiple purposes. This entry elaborates the problems of criteria using two facets: values and scientific understanding. The term also connotes the difficulty of understanding value-based constructs. Because criteria represent preferences, they cannot be understood independent of values that "guide" their selection (Austin and Villanova, 1992). This covariation of fact and value leads commentators to emphasize that the problems of criteria are conceptual, not methodological or statistical. Many advise that efforts would be better invested toward careful conceptual analysis to represent a job success construct.

Values define the interests and broad goals of different groups. Stakeholder models, with multiple interacting groups having interests in the measurement of performance, help to frame the influence of values. Traditional constituencies are management, employees, unions, and researchers. Viewed in this manner, criteria may serve to augment or weaken the interests of different constituencies. For example, a seniority criterion for PROMOTION decisions may be more consistent with advancement and security interests of organizational members with substantial tenure. Alternatively, a results-oriented criterion advantages productive members' interests.

Part of the "criterion problem" is choosing from the domain of work activities the samples that constitute formally recognized inputs for personnel decisions. Similarly, once identified for use, components must be combined to arrive at a score (*see* COMPOSITE AND MULTIPLE CRITERIA). Again, the weighting of elements reflects the value configurations of different constituencies.

Traditionally, management determines what behaviors reflect job success and how aspects are chosen and weighted to index success. However, the last two decades have witnessed an expansion of definitions of job performance and, consequently, what constitute the indicators of success (Borman, 1991; Borman and Motowidlo, 1993; Sackett, 2002; Motowidlo, 2003). The criterion problem is further compounded by the values of such external constituencies as customers and government agencies. Constituencies reflected in government regulations seem to be waning, while the influence of customers on criterion systems appears to be strengthening. This trend is strongest among service-providing organizations that now include customers as feedback sources concerning organizational effectiveness. Therefore, incorporating customer-based criteria measures is a challenge for criterion conceptualization. Representing and weighting the various dimensions that customers value remains largely uncharted (Villanova, 1992), but the increased opportunities to observe are worth the challenge. What's more, linking these customer preferences to actual work activities or service providers or product manufacturers will inevitably require judgments of relevance from constituents internal to the organization who have knowledge about how different work activities translate into such different product or service attributes as reliability, cost effectiveness, and product availability.

A second fundamental facet of the criterion problem involves scientific inquiry. The challenge here concerns a search for scientific understanding with an associated recognition of values. The issue is developing relevant, reliable, and practical measures of actual criteria to represent success. One component of the scientific facet is the relative neglect of criteria relative to predictors; another is the application of statistical combination methods to arrive at overall judgments of success. Historically, there has been a persistent failure to attend to criteria as measures. Validation of criteria is neglected and the reliability of criteria tends to be lower than that of predictors. Recent treatments of validity, however, include several inferences concerning the performance domain (Binning and Barrett, 1989). The inequality between predictors and criteria is being remedied in current research, motivated in part by calls for construct validation (Thayer, 1992; James, 1973). On the other hand, a researcher–practitioner gap is growing (Anderson, Heriot, and Hodgkinson, 2001).

In summary, the problems of criteria are unlikely to go away. They will always confront theory and practice because they are at the heart of the field. Although some progress is evident, the central problem of values will be tractable only to the extent that investigators are willing to address the values of multiple constituencies, including individual and organizational. Messick's (1989) reformulation of validity explicitly invokes values in terms of consequences. Recall that commentators have consistently advised that statistical legerdemain cannot finesse the criterion problem. Smith (1976), for example, advised that "all of the possible sources and measures of performance variation ... need to be given an opportunity to be studied within the nomological network of each ultimate criterion construct" (p. 768). Regrettably, three decades later, few criterion investigations or operational systems meet her standard!

Bibliography

Anderson, N., Heriot, P., and Hodgkinson, G. P. (2001). The practitioner–research divide in industrial, work, and organizational psychology: Where are we now and where do we go from here? *Journal of Occupational and Organizational Psychology*, **74**, 391–411.

Anderson, N., Ones, D., Sinangil, H., and Viswesvaran, C. (eds.) (2001). *Handbook of Industrial, Work, and Organizational Psychology*. London: Sage.

Austin, J. T. and Villanova, P. (1992). The criterion problem 1917–1992. *Journal of Applied Psychology*, **77**, 836–74.

Binning, J. and Barrett, G. V. (1989). Validity of personnel decisions: A review of the inferential and evidential bases. *Journal of Applied Psychology*, **74**, 478–94.

Borman, W. C. (1991). Job behavior, performance, and effectiveness. In M. D. Dunnette and L. M. Hough (eds.), *Handbook of Industrial and Organizational Psychology*, 2nd edn, vo.. 2. Palo Alto, CA: Consulting Psychologists Press, pp. 271–326.

Borman, W. C. and Motowidlo, S. J. (1993). Expanding the criterion domain to include elements of contextual performance. In N. Schmitt, W. C. Borman, et al. (eds.), *Personnel Selection in Organizations*. San Francisco: Jossey-Bass, pp. 71–98.

James, L. R. (1973). Criterion models and construct validity for criteria. *Psychological Bulletin*, **80**, 73–84.

Messick, S. (1989). Validity. In R. L. Linn (ed.), *Educational Measurement*, 3rd edn. New York: Macmillan/American Council on Education, pp. 13–113.

Motowidlo, S. J. (2003). Job performance. In W. C. Borman, D. R. Ilgen, and R. J. Klimoski (eds.), *Handbook of Psychology*, vol. 12, *Industrial/Organizational Psychology*. New York: John Wiley, pp. 39–53.

Sackett, P. R. (2002). The structure of counterproductive work behaviors: Dimensionality and relationships with facets of job performance. *International Journal of Selection and Assessment*, **10**, 5–11.

Smith, P. C. (1976). Behaviors, results, and effectiveness: The problem of criteria. In M. D. Dunnette (ed.), *Handbook of Industrial and Organizational Psychology*. Chicago: Rand-McNally, pp. 745–75.

Thayer, P. W. (1992). Construct validation: Do we understand our criteria? *Human Performance*, **5**, 97–108.

Villanova, P. (1992). A customer-based model for developing job performance criteria. *Human Resources Management Review*, **2**, 103–14.

Viswesvaran, C. and Ones, D. S. (2000). Perspectives on models of job performance. *International Journal of Selection and Assessment*, **8**, 216–26.

criterion relevance

Lorne Sulsky

Criterion relevance is the extent to which measures that are used to assess JOB PERFORMANCE overlap with the conceptual criterion (Muchinsky, 1995). The conceptual criterion is an abstract representation of the behaviors, skills, characteristics, and outcomes associated with a job. It has also been called the "ultimate criterion" (Dipboye, Smith, and Howell, 1994; *see* COMPOSITE AND MULTIPLE CRITERIA; CRITERION PROBLEM). For example, a salesperson must perform a series of job tasks, possess certain skills and characteristics, and produce (i.e., outcome) sales. Relevance increases as more of these tasks, skills, and so forth are validly assessed by the criteria. Thus, investigating criterion relevance is tantamount to examining the CONSTRUCT VALIDITY of criteria.

Bibliography

Dipboye, R. L., Smith, C. S., and Howell, W. C. (1994). *Understanding Industrial and Organizational Psychology: An Integrated Perspective*. Fort Worth, TX: Harcourt Brace.

Muchinsky, P. M. (1995). *Psychology Applied to Work*. Pacific Grove, CA: Brooks/Cole.

criterion-related validity

Chester A. Schriesheim

Criterion-related validity refers to empirical evidence which supports a particular interpretation about an instrument's (test, questionnaire, etc.) score. Criterion-related validity is one of three traditional lines of validity evidence, the other two being CONTENT VALIDITY and CONSTRUCT VALIDITY (American Educational Research Association et al., 1999).

Criterion-related validity is a judgment that is based upon quantitative data, and it has two subdomains, termed CONCURRENT VALIDITY and PREDICTIVE VALIDITY. The salience of concurrent and predictive validity for assessments of criterion-related validity depends upon the particular instrument and interpretation involved (see the entries under concurrent and predictive validity for further details). Criterion-related validation procedures assess the degree to which scores on an instrument (the predictor) are statistically associated with values obtained by a theoretically appropriate outcome measure (the criterion). Statistical procedures commonly employed in criterion-related validity studies include simple and multiple correlation and regression, although other data-analytic methods (such as canonical correlation) may be equally or more appropriate under some circumstances.

Judgments about an instrument's criterion-related validity hinge upon the quality and appropriateness of the criteria employed, as well as upon the diversity and quality of the evidence which is marshaled. All else equal, the use of multiple criteria is generally preferred to the use of a single criterion, but the quality of the evidence is the single most important concern in assessments of an instrument's criterion-related validity.

Bibliography

American Educational Research Association, American Psychological Association, and National Council on Measurement in Education (1999). *Standards for Educational and Psychological Testing*. Washington, DC: American Educational Research Association.

critical incidents technique

James B. Shaw

The critical incidents technique (CIT) was developed by Flanagan (1954) for assembling lists of behaviors that are critical to effective JOB PERFORMANCE. The procedure consists of four steps.

1 A panel of subject matter experts (SMEs), e.g., supervisors, job incumbents, or other knowledgeable persons, provides written examples of effective or ineffective job behaviors. These are called critical incidents. These examples indicate what led up to the behavior, what the employee actually did, the consequences of the behavior, and whether the consequences were under the control of the employee.

2 All the examples are put on index cards and then sorted into categories of similar behaviors (e.g., all cards that describe examples of how one would handle an emergency situation are grouped together).
3 The categories of behaviors identified in step 2 are given a name descriptive of the behaviors that comprise them (e.g., handling emergency situations).
4 These categories are then rated according to how critical or important they are for effective job performance.

A refinement of the original CIT approach is to use two groups of SMEs. The second group is used to verify the work of the first group. Once the incidents have been developed and categorized by the first group of SMEs, the second group is given the names and definitions of all categories and a separate listing of all incidents. The second group attempts to place each incident into one of the predefined categories. If a sufficient percentage of the second group of SMEs places an incident in its appropriate category, the incident is retained. If not, the incident is dropped. Another refinement has been to ask SMEs for examples of "routine" behaviors, in addition to examples of particularly effective and ineffective behaviors. This provides a broader overall view of job activities. The CIT is well suited for developing PERFORMANCE APPRAISAL systems and for determining the TRAINING needs of employees.

Bibliography

Flanagan, J. C. (1954). The critical incidents technique. *Psychological Bulletin*, **51**, 327–58.

cross-training

Daniel C. Feldman

Cross-training refers to teaching employees the knowledge, skills, and abilities (*see* KSAOS) necessary to successfully perform the work duties of other members of their work group. As distinguished from TRAINING, cross-training refers to the instruction of employees in knowledge, skills, and abilities outside those required by the positions for which they were explicitly or initially hired (Schneider, 1976; Cascio, 1986).

From the organization's perspective, cross-training is implemented to increase flexibility in staffing positions, to prevent workers' obsolescence or CAREER PLATEAU, and to make work teams more autonomous and self-sufficient. From the individual's perspective, cross-training is undertaken to acquire additional skills and abilities necessary for PROMOTION or pay raises, to enhance his or her contributions to current work groups, and to increase external marketability. Increasingly, cross-training is being utilized to create and sustain semi-autonomous or self-managing teams (Hackman and Oldham, 1980).

The introduction of cross-training usually takes place in three stages:

1 analysis of the job demands required by other positions and employees' current levels of abilities;
2 implementation of the training itself through a variety of methods (e.g., lectures, demonstrations, and vestibule training; *see* LECTURE METHOD; VESTIBULE TRAINING METHOD); and
3 evaluation of the effectiveness of the training (as measured by employee reactions to the training and measures of employee learning and performance) (Wexley and Latham, 1981).

Bibliography

Cascio, W. F. (1986). *Managing Human Resources*. New York: McGraw-Hill.
Hackman, J. R. and Oldham, G. R. (1980). *Work Redesign*. Reading, MA: Addison-Wesley.
Schneider, B. (1976). *Staffing Organizations*. Pacific Palisades, CA: Goodyear.
Wexley, K. and Latham, G. P. (1981). *Developing and Training Human Resources in Organizations*. Glenview, IL: Scott Foresman.

cross-validation

James S. Phillips

Cross-validation is the process of estimating the expected CRITERION-RELATED VALIDITY of a battery of selection tests in a sample other than the one in which the original validities were estimated. When regression analysis is used to estimate test validity, regression weights are calculated to represent the optimal relationship between the selection tests and some measure of JOB PERFORMANCE. Due to measurement error, however, their accuracy will generally be less when they are applied to a new sample. This reduction in accuracy is called "shrinkage," and it is important to know how much shrinkage to expect before using the tests in actual selection decisions (Gatewood and Feild, 1994: 232).

Two major approaches to cross-validation exist. One method splits the validation sample into two smaller subsamples. The first of these subsamples (called a derivation subsample) is used to calculate the validity coefficients. The second sample (called a holdout subsample) is then used to estimate shrinkage (Murphy, 1983).

An alternative strategy to cross-validation is to use the entire available sample for estimating predictors' validities, and then estimate the likely shrinkage by using formula estimation techniques. Such formulae provide mathematical estimates of expected validities if a prediction equation was cross-validated in an infinite number of new samples (Schneider and Schmitt, 1986: 205). In comparison to sample-splitting methods, these formula estimation techniques are generally well accepted as the preferred approach to cross-validation, since regression weights are based on larger sample sizes, and thus overcome many measurement error problems associated with smaller samples.

Bibliography

Gatewood, R. D. and Feild, H. S. (1994). *Human Resource Selection*, 3rd edn. Fort Worth, TX: Dryden Press.
Murphy, K. R. (1983). Fooling yourself with cross-validation: Single sample designs. *Personnel Psychology*, 36, 111–18.
Schneider, B. and Schmitt, N. (1986). *Staffing Organizations*, 2nd edn. Glenview, IL: Scott Foresman.

cultural literacy

Mark E. Mendenhall

Cultural literacy is the expert knowledge of both surface and core cultural values, norms, mores, traditions, and operating procedures of a culture. Empirical research in the field shows that expatriates serving in an EXPATRIATE ASSIGNMENT must increase their cultural literacy in order to be successful in these assignments.

Cultural literacy involves more than knowing, for example, when and how to bow in Japan when greeting a client. An expatriate who is culturally literate understands why that tradition exists, and understands the deeper core cultural values to which that tradition is linked. When expatriates do not possess high levels of cultural literacy they naturally operate from their personal views regarding what is and what is not appropriate behavior across various life situations in the foreign culture. One's personal views are obviously only workable as guides to behavior in one's culture of birth. Thus, applying personal views as guides to one's behavior while overseas invariably leads expatriates into troubling, embarrassing, and sometimes dangerous incidents in the foreign culture.

Cultural literacy enables an expatriate to understand the reasons behind the behavior he or she encounters overseas, and this understanding enables the expatriate to avoid stereotyping, racial prejudice, and other forms of inappropriate behavior while living and working in a foreign culture. Living and working in a foreign culture requires the expatriate to learn a new mental framework, one that can guide the expatriate in choosing culturally correct behaviors in the foreign culture. The acquisition of cultural literacy requires significant amounts of effort by the expatriate. Companies often try to assist in this task by offering cross-cultural training programs and other types of training (*see* TRAINING).

See also *preparation for an international work assignment*

Bibliography

Black, J. S., Gregersen, H. B., and Mendenhall, M. E. (1992). *Global Assignments: Successfully Expatriating and Repatriating International Managers*. San Francisco: Jossey-Bass.
Black, J. S. and Mendenhall, M. (1990). A practical but theory-based framework for selecting cross-cultural training methods. *Human Resource Management*, **28**, 511–39.

Black, J. S., Mendenhall, M., and Oddou, G. (1991). Toward a comprehensive model of international adjustment: An integration of multiple theoretical perspectives. *Academy of Management Review*, **16**, 291–317.

Mendenhall, M. and Oddou, G. (1985). The dimensions of expatriate acculturation: A review. *Academy of Management Review*, **10**, 39–47.

Oddou, G. and Mendenhall, M. (1984). Person perception in cross-cultural settings: A review of cross-cultural and related literature. *International Journal of Intercultural Relations*, **8**, 77–96.

custom and practice

Annette Cox

Custom and practice refers to norms of workplace behavior developed over time without explicit discussion or agreement which deviate from organizations' official (written) rules or procedures. Examples include leaving work early the day before a statutory public holiday or using shortcuts in making a product or delivering a service. Problems usually occur when managers try either to reinforce the original rules or change them completely, which can create employee perceptions that they are adversely affected and lead to hostility and resistance. Depending on national employment law, custom and practice can sometimes form part of an employee's implied contract terms.

customer-oriented human resource management

Dave Ulrich

Most human resource (HR) practices are created to affect the behavior of employees within a firm. For example, hiring practices are created to improve the competence of employees. Customer-oriented human resource management (HRM) goes a step beyond by shifting the focus from the firm to the value chain.

From Firm to Value chain

A value chain defines the supplier–firm–customer relationship. In a retail store, the value chain would be the producer, the retailer, and the buyer. For example, Whirlpool produces washing machines, Sears sells them, and customers buy them. Every firm may be conceived as a series of value-chain relationships. When HR practices focus on the value chain, they remove boundaries between the firm and its suppliers and customers (Ashkenas et al., 1995). The purpose of using HR practices across the value chain is to create a common mindset or culture between firms and customers. An industry culture creates commitment across firms and increases shared interests (Ulrich, 1989).

Two maxims capture the shift toward customer-oriented HR. First, HR is shifting from the assumption that people are our most important asset to the assumption that people are our customers' most important asset. The shift focuses on how customers think about and use people. Second, HR is shifting from believing that we want to be the employer of choice to believing that we want to be the employer of choice of employees our customers would choose. Again, through the focus on customers, HR practices are used across the value chain.

Examples of Customer-Oriented HRM

Many companies involve customers in HR practices. When Southwest Airlines hires flight attendants, it includes customers in the interviewing process. A customer panel screens and interviews potential candidates. At General Electric (GE), many training programs (*see* TRAINING) are focused on bridging boundaries between GE and customers and suppliers. Much of the GE training program is targeted to teams that work on projects requiring customer involvement. Frito-Lay has included customers in its job orientation, asking new employees to spend time in stores getting oriented to the job requirements. When Motorola reengineered its HR processes, it included customers and suppliers on the reengineering teams. Coopers and Lybrand has created a program called Nexus in which account teams and customers are trained to identify and share common interests.

In each of these cases, HR practices were used to build organizations that focused on and served external customers. When employee-focused HR practices shift to customer-focused HR practices, both employees and customers win. Employees win by seeing how their work adds value to customers, by being able to quickly change their work to meet customer needs, and by feeling more intimately tied to customer expectations. Customers win by having employees in supplier firms who become customer resources, by having suppliers who are dedicated to their needs, and by being able to reduce the cycle time to make changes in how work is done.

Bibliography

Ashkenas, R., Ulrich, D., Jick, T., and Kerr, S. (1995). *The Boundaryless Organization.* San Francisco: Jossey-Bass.

Ulrich, D. (1989). Tie the corporate knot: Gaining complete customer commitment. *Sloan Management Review* (Summer), 19–28.

customer service training

David E. Bowen

Firms that excel at delivering service quality (e.g., Disney, Federal Express, L. L. Bean) invest more time and money in TRAINING than their counterparts with lesser service reputations. The importance of training in achieving superior customer service is likely only to increase because of two trends:

1 customers' expectations of service continue to rise; and
2 demographics indicate that the numbers of new applicants who can provide high levels of service quality, particularly in the 18–25 years age bracket, will not meet expected demand.

Firms, therefore, will have to take the best available of these limited applicants and train them.

There are two approaches to customer service training (Schneider and Bowen, 1995). *Informal* training deals with learning about the organization and the culture more than about the job. Much of this learning takes place informally, primarily among coworkers. Therefore, it is important for firms to manage which coworkers spend time with new employees (*see* ON-THE-JOB TRAINING). *Formal* training has to do with learning important job skills and often happens in the classroom. Organization-sponsored training increases employees' *motivation* to serve (because they know the organization takes service seriously) and their *ability* to serve (because they learn service-relevant skills).

Bibliography

Schneider, B. and Bowen, D. E. (1995). *Winning the Service Game.* Boston: Harvard Business School Press.

cutoff score

George M. Alliger and Gwen Coats

Cutoff (or "critical" or "passing") scores represent minimum acceptable standards on employment, licensing, certification, or academic tests. Scores below the cutoff indicate unacceptable performance, except in the case of multiple cutoffs, when each cutoff represents a distinct level of performance.

Cutoff scores are typically calculated from both empirical data and some form of judgment. The fact that subjectivity plays a role does not represent a legal problem as long as the method used is rational, systematic, and documented (Society for Industrial and Organizational Psychology, 1987). While adverse impact for different gender, ethnic, and age groups generated by cutoff scores is a concern (Cascio, Alexander, and Barrett, 1988), court rulings indicate that the standard to be met is equal treatment, not equal results. The setting of separate cutoffs by race, color, religion, sex, or national origin is prohibited by the CIVIL RIGHTS ACT OF 1991.

TYPES

After Berk (1986), the procedures used to develop cutoff scores can be classified into three major categories: judgmental, judgmental-empirical, and empirical-judgmental. There are many variants within each category. Unfortunately, different methods may yield different cutoff scores. Recent research, however, has demonstrated some convergence among methods (see Woehr, Arthur, and Fehrmann, 1991).

Judgmental. Included here are the Angoff, the Nedelsky, and the Ebel methods and variants of these (see Cascio et al., 1988). In the Angoff method, subject matter experts (SMEs) are asked to rate each test item in terms of the probability that a minimally competent (but nonetheless competent) individual could answer the item correctly. The mean for all judges is computed for each item, and the cutoff score is then simply the mean of all item means. The other SME methods are more complicated, for the judges are also asked to either rate item importance (Nedelsky method) or identify incorrect item alternatives prior to providing probability ratings (Ebel method). These methods are popular and relatively easy, and can be completed prior to the collection of any test data. However, they are sensitive to method of implementation (e.g., whether test answers as well as questions are provided to SMEs; Hudson and Campion, 1994).

Judgmental-empirical. Here, expert judgments are augmented by empirical data. Very often, some kind of iterative rating is used (e.g., experts rate item probabilities, are shown actual item difficulties computed from pilot data, and are permitted to revise probability estimates). Under this heading we can also place norm-referenced models, where cutoff scores are based on an examination of the test score distribution alone or including other information. One may simply establish a cutoff score deemed to be appropriate given the distribution (e.g., one standard deviation above the mean). Thorndike's method of predictive yield also integrates projected personnel needs, proportion of offers accepted, and distribution of test scores to establish a cutoff score which will make available the required number of new hires. Or issues like adverse impact, selection ratio, and recruiting cost information can be combined to set a cutoff score which optimizes utility (Martin and Raju, 1992).

Empirical-judgmental. These methods include the contrasting groups method, where high and low performers are identified on some criterion (e.g., job ratings). Members in both groups take the test, and the score that best discriminates between the two groups becomes the cutoff score (unless either false positives or false negatives are undesirable, in which case the cutoff score is set to achieve one of these ends). The borderline method also fits under this category. In this method, minimally competent job performers are identified, and the mean or median score of these individuals on the test in question is the cutoff score. The judgmental element in these and similar methods lies in how the relevant individuals or groups are initially identified.

SELECTION ABOVE THE CUTOFF: RANKING VERSUS BANDING

The selection of individuals above a cutoff score can occur in a variety of ways. It may be a simple pass–fail decision. Individuals may also be rank ordered by their score on the examination with selection taking place in some form of top-down procedure. In band scoring, multiple cutoff scores are set and individuals within each band (bounded by the cutoff scores) can be selected at random. After all the candidates in the highest scoring band have been selected, the process then shifts to the next lowest band, so that all individuals in that band are eligible.

Bibliography

Berk, R. A. (1986). A consumer's guide to setting performance standards on criterion-referenced tests. *Review of Educational Research,* 56, 137–72.

Cascio, W. F., Alexander, R. A., and Barrett, G. V. (1988). Setting cutoff scores: Legal, psychometric, and professional issues and guidelines. *Personnel Psychology,* 41, 1–24.

Hudson, J. P. and Campion, J. E. (1994). Hindsight bias in an application of the Angoff method for setting cutoff scores. *Journal of Applied Psychology,* 79, 860–5.

Martin, S. L. and Raju, N. S. (1992). Determining cutoff scores that optimize utility: A recognition of recruiting costs. *Journal of Applied Psychology,* 77, 15–23.

Society for Industrial and Organizational Psychology (1987). *Principles for the Validation and Use of Personnel Selection Procedures.* 3rd College Park, MD: Society for Industrial and Organizational Psychology.

Woehr, D. J., Arthur, W., and Fehrmann, M. L. (1991). An empirical comparison of cutoff score methods for content-related and criterion-related validity settings. *Educational and Psychological Measurement,* 51, 1029–39.

Davis-Bacon Act of 1931

Charles H. Fay

Under this prevailing wage law, any employer with a federal government construction contract in excess of US$2,000 must pay wages to laborers and mechanics found to be prevailing locally (as determined by the Department of Labor). The employer must in any case pay at least minimum wages under the FAIR LABOR STANDARDS ACT OF 1938.

The impact of the Davis-Bacon Act (as is the case with the Services Contract Act and the WALSH-HEALY ACT OF 1936) is that employers pay local union rates. Davis-Bacon is estimated to add $4.245 billion to government construction costs over the FY2001–FY2005 (General Accounting Office, 2000: 278).

Bibliography

Dixon, R. B. (2002). *Federal Wage and Hour Laws*, 2nd edn. Washington, DC: SHRM Foundation.

General Accounting Office (2000). *Budget Issues: Budgetary Implications of Selected GAO Work for Fiscal Year 2001*. Washington, DC: General Accounting Office, pp. 277–9.

Shilling, D. (2001). *Human Resources and the Law: The Complete Guide with Supplement*. Englewood Cliffs, NJ: Prentice-Hall.

decertification elections

Charles R. Greer

Just as employees may vote in union representation elections to determine whether they will be represented by a union, they can also vote in decertification elections to determine whether a union shall continue to be their bargaining agent. As with REPRESENTATION ELECTIONS, the NATIONAL LABOR RELATIONS BOARD (NLRB) will order a decertification election if petitioned by at least 30 percent of employees eligible to participate in an election. In a manner similar to representation elections, the conduct of employers during the period prior to a decertification election is carefully regulated. Employers cannot petition the NLRB for a decertification election, except under unusual circumstances, and they are prohibited from conducting campaigns for the purpose of persuading employees to petition the NLRB for decertification elections (Cibon and Castagnera, 1993).

Bibliography

Cibon, P. J. and Castagnera, J. O. (1993). *Labor and Employment Law*, 2nd edn. Boston: PWS-Kent.

defamation waivers

Kelly A. Vaverek

Defamation waivers are a form of WAIVER that prevent an individual from suing an employer who provides a defamatory employment recommendation. A defamatory statement is one "sufficient to lower the (individual) in the estimation of the community or to deter third parties from associating or dealing with (him)" (American Law Institute, 1965: section 559). While the truth of the statement is a complete defense to defamation, some employers have adopted a "no comment" policy or merely confirm dates and location of employment for REFERENCE CHECKS rather than risk a lawsuit. Others use defamation waivers to insulate themselves from liability.

Bibliography

American Law Institute (1965). *Restatement of Torts*, 2nd edn. St. Paul, MN: American Law Institute.

Sarrazin, R. T. (1993). Defamation in the employment setting. *Tennessee Bar Journal*, 29, 18–24.

derailing

Thomas H. Stone

Derailing occurs when employees or managers are thrown off their expected CAREER PATHING by either their own behaviors or external events. Derailment may take the form of plateauing early (*see* CAREER PLATEAU), being demoted, or being terminated. Derailment does not refer to: persons who, having reached their career potential ("topping out"), "drop or opt out"; promotable employees with no place to go; or those who fail to win a PROMOTION every time one is available. Persons who are derailed have typically experienced at least moderate CAREER SUCCESS prior to derailment. McCall, Lombardo, and Morrison (1988: 168–9) have identified ten factors associated with derailing of successful executives:

1. insensitivity to others (abrasive or bullying style), the most frequent cause for derailment;
2. failing to meet organizational performance problems;
3. cold, aloof, and arrogant interpersonal style;
4. betrayal of trust;
5. overmanaging and failing to build a team;
6. too ambitious and playing politics;
7. failing to staff effectively, picking people who fail;
8. inability to think strategically;
9. failure to adapt to a boss with a different style; and
10. overdependence on a mentor or advocate.

Bibliography

McCall, M. W., Lombardo, M. M., and Morrison, A. M. (1988). *The Lessons of Experience*. Lexington, MA: Lexington Books.

deskilling

Hadyn Bennett

Deskilling refers to the process whereby jobs are reduced to narrowly defined and repetitive processes in pursuit of efficiency and PRODUCTIVITY gains. However, such specialization based on the principles of scientific management fails to meet the psychological needs of employees (Capelli and Rogovsky, 1994), and militates against employee satisfaction, organizational and labor force flexibility, and employee development, while creating both employee and customer alienation (Drummond, 1992). The business environment facing most industries in recent years has created increasing pressures for organizational flexibility and creativity, conditions in which the use of deskilling in pursuit of efficiency gains can be seen as being increasingly questionable.

Bibliography

Cappelli, P. and Rogovsky, N. (1994). New work systems and skill requirements. *International Labor Review*, 133 (2), 204–20.

Drummond, H. (1992). *The Quality Movement*. London: Kogan Page.

developing globally competent executives/managers

Helen L. De Cieri and Peter J. Dowling

The development of globally competent managers refers to organizational strategies and programs which equip managers with the flexibility on an organizational and sociocultural level to operate across national boundaries (*see* EXPATRIATE ASSIGNMENT).

Both formal and informal training and development programs to prepare expatriate managers for global competence may include: cross-cultural training, language training, discussions with managers with international experience, provision of audiovisual materials, preliminary site visits, MENTORING PROGRAMS, and SUCCESSION PLANNING (Feldman and Thomas, 1992). Many multinational enterprises have increased the scope and scale of their training and development programs, incorporating efforts to enhance communication skills and sharing of corporate values. These programs may be linked to the use of multicultural teams. The ability to work effectively in teams is often seen as vital for the development of organization-wide, cross-national effectiveness.

Several authors have proposed models of training and development for expatriate managers, focusing to some extent on cross-cultural training (see Mendenhall, Punnett, and Ricks, 1995). A common recommendation is that the level of rigor and time spent in training should be contingent upon factors such as the task, environment, individual, length of stay, level of integration into local culture, and cultural distance between home and host cultures (*see* CULTURAL LITERACY). Cross-cultural training has been suggested to have a positive relationship with the development of appropriate perceptions relative to members of another culture. Cross-cultural training has also been positively correlated with cross-cultural skills development, expatriate adjustment and performance (Black, Gregersen, and Mendenhall, 1992). In addition, when management development is integrated with business strategy and STAFFING approaches, it can become a tool for organizational development (Evans, 1992).

Transnational enterprises (those organizations able to achieve an effective balance of global integration and local responsiveness) rely to some degree on globally competent managers. Adler and Bartholomew (1992) discuss the management competencies required in transnational enterprises. These competencies include the need for managers to understand the business environment from a global, not parochial, perspective. This is facilitated by learning about foreign countries' cultures, norms, and approaches to business, often through undertaking training programs and by working in multicultural teams. Further, managers will be required to adapt to living in other cultures, using cross-cultural skills on a daily basis. Overall, the variety, frequency, and nature of cross-cultural interactions are quite complex. For globally competent managers to develop in a transnational organization, requirements of the human resource management (HRM) approach include the capacity to cover a worldwide scope, a multinational senior management team, and the ability to include representatives and ideas from many cultures in strategic planning and decision-making processes.

Overall, a key objective for many multinational enterprises is to develop a global cadre of expatriate managers (Welch, 1994). While the "universal manager" myth may have lost some credibility, the "universal management team" seems to have gained in popularity. Empirical research into the development of globally competent managers, although in its infancy, is exhibiting significant growth.

See also *preparation for an international work assignment*

Bibliography

Adler, N. J. and Bartholomew, S. (1992). Managing globally competent people. *Academy of Management Executive*, 6, 52–65.

Black, J. S., Gregersen, H. B., and Mendenhall, M. E. (1992). *Global Assignments: Successfully Expatriating and Repatriating International Managers*. San Francisco: Jossey-Bass.

Evans, P. A. L. (1992). Management development as glue technology. *Human Resource Planning*, 15, 85–106.

Feldman, D. C. and Thomas, D. C. (1992). Career management issues facing expatriates. *Journal of International Business Studies*, 23, 271–93.

Mendenhall, M. E., Punnett, B. J., and Ricks, D. (1995). *Global Management*. Oxford: Blackwell.

Welch, D. E. (1994). HRM implications of globalization. *Journal of General Management*, 19, 52–68.

Dictionary of Occupational Titles

Michael T. Brannick and Edward L. Levine

The Dictionary of Occupational Titles (DOT) is a comprehensive listing of brief job descriptions for thousands of jobs in the US economy, and is compiled by the US Department of Labor. The DOT contains not only narrative descriptions, but also a classification system based on the work performed and worker involvement with data, people, and things. Information derived from the DOT may be used for broad social purposes, such as job placement and vocational guidance (Droege, 1988). The DOT is currently under revision. The revised DOT is expected to depart from earlier versions in at least two ways:

1 the newer version will be published as an electronic database that can be searched several ways through computers; and
2 the taxonomic descriptions applied to job and worker attributes will be much more comprehensive.

Bibliography

Droege, R. C. (1988). Department of Labor job analysis methodology. In S. Gael, E. T. Cornelius, III, E. L. Levine, and G. Salvendy (eds.), *The Job Analysis Handbook for Business, Industry, and Government*, vol. 2. New York: John Wiley.

differential validity

Larry James

A very narrow definition of differential validity is that the validity coefficient for one group differs significantly from the validity coefficient for another group. A broader, and a more robust, definition of differential validity takes into account differences in the respective prediction equations. In this case, differential validity refers to the possibility that different prediction equations can be generated for different subgroups of a population, as defined by factors such as race, sex, ethnic group, or religion. Slopes of the regression lines, intercepts, and standard errors of estimate are all considered under the umbrella of different prediction equations.

To determine if differential validity exists between groups, one must initially generate separate prediction equations for each group (e.g., separate regression equations for black versus white applicants). Evidence for differential validity exists in the narrow case if the slopes of the regression lines differ significantly between the groups. In the broader case, tests of significance are also conducted on intercepts and standard errors of estimate. When significant differences are found for any of these factors, it suggests that information from the predictor should not be interpreted without considering subgroup membership.

When evidence of differential validity exists, a score on the predictor is related to a different score on the criterion, depending on group membership. In this case, the same desired criterion score will require a different predictor CUTOFF SCORE when selection is from different subgroups. For example, if a selection test displays evidence of differential validity between males and females, different test-score cutoff points would be needed to provide the same level of predicted criterion performance. A regression line derived from a combined sample of males and females using this test would systematically overpredict future performance for one group and underpredict performance for the other group (*see* TEST FAIRNESS).

Differential validity is often considered in examination for test bias. However, the bias or fairness of a test is often determined by more than a differential validity analysis. For example, different social and political circumstances may underlie a claim that a test is not fair even if there is no evidence of differential validity for the test.

Bibliography

American Educational Research Association, American Psychological Association, and National Council on Measurement in Education (1999). *Standards for Educational and Psychological Testing*. Washington, DC: American Educational Research Association.

disclaimer

Kelly A. Vaverek

A disclaimer is the "disavowal, denial, or renunciation of an interest, right, or property imputed to a person or alleged to be his" (Black's Law Dictionary, 1990: 464). Employers often use a disclaimer in employee handbooks to avoid interpretation of the handbook as an employment contract; for example, "This handbook does not constitute an express or implied contract" (*see* EMPLOYEE HANDBOOK). Courts differ in their enforcement of the disclaimer. Some courts have ruled that the disclaimer absolves the employer from fulfilling the promises made in a handbook. Others conclude that a general disclaimer is not enough to negate the specific promises.

Bibliography

Black's Law Dictionary (1990). *Black's Law Dictionary*, 6th edn. St. Paul, MN: West Publishing.

McWhirter, D. (1989). *Your Rights at Work*. New York: John Wiley.

Winters, R. H. (1985). Employee handbooks and employment-at-will contracts. *Duke Law Journal*, 196–220.

discrimination

Ramona L. Paetzold

As applied to employment situations, discrimination refers to behavior that has the purpose or effect of harming some individuals by virtue of their membership in a protected class. The term "discrimination" therefore legally encompasses a wide range of attitudes, conducts, and processes that produce differential results without appropriate justification. Prohibitions against employment discrimination can exist at all government levels; however, the major antidiscrimination legislation exists at the federal level and applies to both public and private employers. Examples include the CIVIL RIGHTS ACT OF 1964, the AGE DISCRIMINATION IN EMPLOYMENT ACT OF 1967, and the AMERICANS WITH DISABILITIES ACT OF 1990. Federal legislation allows state and local governments to expand protections against employment discrimination, so that some regions of the country have defined additional protected classes (e.g., marital status, appearance, SEXUAL ORIENTATION).

In general, antidiscrimination law identifies the four models of discrimination: the DISPARATE TREATMENT model, the DISPARATE IMPACT model, the reasonable accommodation model, and the hostile environment model. These models are not so much theories of discrimination as they are models of organizing evidence to prove discrimination – they identify what courts will recognize as illegal discrimination. The models can be used to prove discrimination in virtually any aspect of the employment relationship, such as hiring, firing, PROMOTION, TRAINING, COMPENSATION and BENEFITS, or working conditions. Although all prohibitions against employment-related discrimination protect the current employees of an employer, that particular employment relationship is not necessary to a finding of illegal employment-related discrimination. The prohibitions placed on employers have been found to flow to applicants, to former employees, and to other individuals (e.g., contract workers who are determined not to be employees) as well.

disparate impact

Ramona L. Paetzold

The disparate or adverse impact model of DISCRIMINATION describes situations in which an employer uses a criterion, mechanism, or practice that works to the disadvantage of members of a protected group and fails to further sufficiently important interests of the employer. The key inquiries or elements under the disparate impact model include: (a) is there a facially neutral criterion, mechanism, or practice that the employer uses, (b) that tends to disproportionately exclude members of a protected group from consideration for a particular job? If so, then (c) is an individual's ability to satisfy the criterion, mechanism, or practice closely related to that individual's ability to perform the job in question? Intent is not a required element of the disparate impact model.

The plaintiff bears the burden of proving elements (a) and (b) (*see* BURDEN OF PROOF). He or she must identify a specific neutral employment practice and demonstrate, typically through statistical evidence, that the practice has an adverse impact on his or her protected group. Once these elements are established, the defense will lose unless it can prove (burden of persuasion) the second element, that the employment practice is job-related or meets BUSINESS NECESSITY guidelines.

Statistical evidence is almost essential to the showing of a group-based impact. Traditionally, this evidence has taken the form of selection rates satisfying the four-fifths rule, but more recently, statistically significant differences in selection rates may be required. An employer may not refute statistical evidence by showing that there is no impact on the bottom line (i.e., over the whole process, such as over all of selection).

See also *Civil Rights Act of 1964; disparate treatment; job-relatedness*

disparate treatment

Ramona L. Paetzold

The disparate treatment model focuses on the intentions of employers in making employment-related decisions. Thus, DISCRIMINATION is proven under this model by showing that employers acted with discriminatory intent. The requisite intent can be overt or subtle, but it is not required to reach a level of animosity or ill will. Intent, for disparate treatment purposes, means that the employer took the plaintiff's protected class membership into account when making the employment decision that is being challenged. Thus, the plaintiff's initial BURDEN OF PROOF is to demonstrate that his or her protected class is a plausible reason for the differential treatment that occurred. Plaintiffs usually do this through anecdotal or comparative evidence (individual model of disparate treatment), or through statistical analysis of the employer's conduct (systemic model of disparate treatment; *see* PATTERN OR PRACTICE CASES). The defendant will lose at this point unless it can refute (burden of production) the plaintiff's showing. In the individual model, the defendant need only articulate a legitimate, non-discriminatory reason for the treatment. In the systemic model, the defendant often produces its own statistical evidence. The ultimate burden of persuasion remains with the plaintiff throughout the trial, so that it is the plaintiff who must ultimately convince the factfinder that illegal discrimination has occurred.

One additional variant of disparate treatment, the mixed motives model (*see* PRICE WATERHOUSE V. HOPKINS), arises when the issue of causation of the differential treatment is unclear. The central inquiry focuses on whether the employer's decision would have been different if it had not taken the plaintiff's group membership into account (*see* CIVIL RIGHTS ACT OF 1964).

distance learning

J. Kevin Ford and Deidre Wasson

To accommodate rapidly changing instructional needs, organizations are adopting distance learning as an affordable, low time-expense, learner-tailored, effective alternative to live instruction (Hannafin and Hannafin, 1995). Distance learning is characterized by a physical separation between learners themselves and facilitators, where communication between all parties can be made via television, telephone, computer, and/or radio. The majority of instruction is provided by prepackaged learning resources or courseware (Goodyear, 1995). The success of distance learning is due to high levels of interactions among peers and instructors. Peer support and instructor help is available to the learner either immediately, through the telephone, or with a slight delay, through fax or email systems.

See also *training*

Bibliography

Goodyear, P. (1995). Asynchronous peer interaction in distance education: The evolution of goals, practices, and technology. *Training Research Journal*, 1, 71–102.

Hannafin, K. M. and Hannafin, M. J. (1995). The ecology of distance learning environments. *Training Research Journal*, 1, 49–69.

distributional effects in performance appraisal

Angelo S. DeNisi

Distributional effects in PERFORMANCE APPRAISAL have traditionally referred to effects that influence the distribution of a set of ratings. Specifically, these effects, which include LENIENCY EFFECTS and CENTRAL TENDENCY EFFECTS, were viewed as causing distributions of ratings to deviate from a "true" underlying normal distribution. Distributional effects were often seen as proxies for rating accuracy, and were the focus of various interventions over the years, including the development of alternative ratings scale formats and rater training programs, though there was not even total agreement on how these effects should be assessed (see Saal, Downey, and Lahey, 1980).

It has become clear, however, that there is no basis for assuming that the true distribution of ratings in a group is normal, and so there is no basis for assuming that any deviations from a normal distribution reflect rating inaccuracy or even rating errors. This has led some scholars to suggest that we simply abandon any consideration of these indices as criterion variables in performance appraisal research since they are not reasonable proxies for rating accuracy. Others, while agreeing that these indices are not good proxies for accuracy, and should not, therefore, be considered as errors, have instead proposed a different use of distributional effects as criterion measures in appraisal research conducted in field settings.

Specifically, DeNisi and Peters (1991, 1992) have suggested that indices of these effects, as well as indices of HALO EFFECTS, all provide important information about the distribution of ratings, both within and between ratees. Although they should not be considered errors or proxies of accuracy, DeNisi and Peters argue that they can provide important information in field settings where measures of rating accuracy are usually not available. As such, they have suggested renaming these indices "elevation indices" (which would be similar to leniency effects), "within-ratee discriminability indices" (which would be similar to halo effects), and "between-ratee discriminability indices" (which would include information about central tendency as well as the overall distribution of ratings). These indices would then provide information about the extent to which raters could provide information about relative strengths and weaknesses for ratees (see Murphy, 1991, for a discussion of behavioral accuracy), as well as the extent to which raters could differentiate among ratees for allocating MERIT PAY and other rewards (see Kane et al., 1995).

Thus, distributional indices may provide information about the limitations to the usefulness of a set of ratings obtained in the field. Furthermore, these authors, and others (see Dickinson, 1993), have suggested that indices of rating distribution might be related to ratees' perceptions of the fairness of the appraisal system and the ability of the raters to defend their ratings and decisions. Such reactions may well be more important to organizations interested in using appraisals to improve performance on the job than are measures of rating accuracy (Ilgen, 1993), and information about distributions of ratings (and halo) may be quite important as determinants of these reactions. Although further research is clearly needed before this proposed role can be considered seriously, this does represent a new direction for research on distributional effects in performance appraisal.

Bibliography

DeNisi, A. S. and Peters, L. H. (1991). Memory reorganization and performance appraisal: A field experiment. Paper presented at the Annual Meeting of the Academy of Management, Miami, FL.

DeNisi, A. S. and Peters, L. H. (1992). Diary keeping and the organization of information in memory: A field extension. Paper presented at the Conference of the Society for Industrial and Organizational Psychology, Montreal.

Dickinson, T. L. (1993). Attitudes about performance appraisal. In H. Schuler, J. Farr, and M. Smith (eds.), *Personnel Selection and Assessment*. Hillsdale, NJ: Erlbaum.

Ilgen, D. R. (1993). Performance appraisal accuracy: An illusive or sometimes misguided goal? In H. Schuler, J. Farr, and M. Smith (eds.), *Personnel Selection and Assessment*. Hillsdale, NJ: Erlbaum.

Kane, J. S., Bernardin, H. J., Villanova, P., and Peyrefitte, J. (1995). The stability of rater leniency: Three studies. *Academy of Management Journal*, 38, 1036–51.

Murphy, K. R. (1991). Criterion issues in performance appraisal: Behavioral accuracy versus classification accuracy. *Organizational Behavior and Human Decision Processes*, 50, 45–50.

Saal, F. E., Downey, R. G., and Lahey, M. A. (1980). Rating the ratings: Assessing the quality of ratings data. *Psychological Bulletin*, 88, 413–28.

distributive bargaining

Paul Jarley

Distributive bargaining refers to situations where the parties view their interests as irreconcilable and see little opportunity for a settlement that will yield joint gain. Distributive bargaining is often contrasted with INTEGRATIVE BARGAINING, but elements of both may be present in any negotiation.

The Character of Distributive Bargaining

Distributive bargaining emphasizes bargaining positions, is adversarial, and creates winners and losers. Central to distributive bargaining is the notion of a contract zone. The size of the contract zone is defined by the parties' resistance points. A resistance point is the least desirable position a party is willing to accept to achieve an agreement. Where the parties' resistance points overlap, settlement is possible since each party can make an offer that exceeds the other's minimum acceptable position. The greater the overlap in the parties' resistance points, the greater the range of potential settlements. Agreement is achieved through a series of offers and counter-offers that lead to convergence in the parties' positions. The winner is the party that achieves a settlement that is closer to the opponent's resistance point than its own.

Distributive Bargaining Strategies

Negotiators attempt to discover their opponent's resistance point while concealing their own. Each negotiator applies a combination of persuasive and coercive tactics to induce movement in the opponent's position. Concessions must be made in a manner that gives the impression that the party's new position reflects its true resistance point. Common tactics include commitment, deception, information manipulation, and threats (see NEGOTIATION TACTICS).

Bibliography

Lax, D. A. and Sebenius, J. K. (1986). *The Manager as Negotiator: Bargaining for Cooperation and Competitive Gain.* New York: Free Press.

Lewicki, R. J. and Litterer, J. A. (1985). *Negotiation.* Homewood, IL: Richard D. Irwin.

Walton, R. E. and McKersie, R. B. (1965). *A Behavioral Theory of Labor Negotiations: An Analysis of a Social Interaction System.* New York: McGraw-Hill.

distributive justice

Robert Folger

Distributive justice refers to the *perceived fairness* of amounts received from resource allocation decisions (e.g., whether employees' salary increases are considered fair). Judgments of fairness vary depending on which norm of distributive justice is applied: equity, equality, need, or others.

Equity theory (Adams, 1965) applies readily to distributive justice in the workplace. Equity calls for correspondence between outcomes (e.g., wages) and the performance-related inputs of employees (e.g., PRODUCTIVITY). With equivalent outcome–input ratios across workers, pay, for example, would be considered equitable. Equity, however, is "in the eye of the beholder" – perceptions determine the assumed sizes of outcomes and inputs, which outcomes and inputs seem relevant, and the choice of which outcome–input ratio to use for comparison (e.g., one coworker versus another, or a national industry-wide average versus the average in all local businesses). The equality norm says that each person should be treated the same; therefore, each person would receive the same outcome. The need norm argues that each person is treated differently depending on need. Those with greater needs would receive greater outcomes.

Lack of distributive justice (e.g., perceived underpay) can provoke a number of responses, including poor work quantity or quality, ABSENTEEISM, EMPLOYEE TURNOVER, employee theft, and sabotage. In general, reactions to undesirable events, such as distributive injustice, produce numerous unpredictable coping responses.

People can rationalize being underpaid, for example, by exaggerating (cognitively distorting) perceived intrinsic benefits such as fun in performing a task (i.e., task-enhancement effects). These "bad pay, but enjoyable work!" effects tend to result from PROCEDURAL JUSTICE, i.e., when outcomes come from fair decision-making methods. When unfair outcomes come from *unfair* procedures, employees more often show resentment, retaliation, and lower quantity and/or quality of performance (see Folger, Rosenfield, and Hays, 1978).

Bibliography

Adams, J. S. (1965). Inequity in social exchange. In L. Berkowitz (ed.), *Advances in Experimental Social Psychology*, vol. 2. New York: Academic Press.

Cropanzano, R. and Folger, R. (1989). Referent cognitions and task decision autonomy: Beyond equity theory. *Journal of Applied Psychology*, **74**, 293–9.

Folger, R. and Cropanzano, R. (1996). *Organizational Justice and Human Resources Management*. San Francisco: Jossey-Bass.

Folger, R., Rosenfield, D., and Hays, R. P. (1978). Equity and intrinsic motivation: The role of choice. *Journal of Personality and Social Psychology*, **37**, 2243–61.

Greenberg, J. (1987). A taxonomy of organizational justice theories. *Academy of Management Review*, **12**, 9–22.

diversity

Susan E. Jackson

The term diversity is used to recognize the fact that any organization's workforce includes people from many different backgrounds. "Diversity" does not exist at the individual level; differences among the people who comprise a team, department, or organization create diversity (see Jackson, May, and Whitney, 1995, for an extended discussion).

TYPES OF DIVERSITY

Gender diversity is increasingly apparent throughout the world. Not only are more women working, but gender-based occupational segregation is declining in many countries, so within corporations men and women are more likely to be found working side by side. Age diversity is increasing too. Many industrialized countries are experiencing declining rates of population growth, which push employers to hire both more youth and more older employees. Furthermore, as organizations allow the higher education of younger employees to substitute for the job experiences that previous cohorts of employees had to accrue in order to be promoted, relatively young employees are found more often in higher-level jobs. Consequently, age diversity is replacing the homogeneity associated with traditional age-based stratification.

Throughout much of the world, ethnic and cultural diversity is increasingly important to businesses. For example, as the 1980s drew to a close, the US Department of Labor projected that 22 percent of new entrants into the labor force would be immigrants and that an additional 20 percent would be ethnic minorities (Johnston and Packer, 1987). In many European countries, ethnic and cultural diversity is increasing owing in part to the consolidation of economic markets and related changes in immigration and employment policies. Finally, the need to manage cultural diversity effectively becomes apparent to corporations as they expand their operations into foreign countries.

MANAGING DIVERSITY

The phrase managing diversity is used as a broad umbrella term to refer to management practices intended to improve the effectiveness with which organizations utilize the diverse range of available human resources. Programs designed to actively manage diversity recognize that diversity can have many consequences, including some that are positive and some that are negative. For example, knowledge-based diversity can improve the quality and creativity of a group's decision-making processes. On the other hand, demographic diversity appears to increase the amount of EMPLOYEE TURNOVER – presumably because it causes interpersonal conflict and interferes with communications (for reviews, see Cox, 1993; Triandis, Kurowski, and Gelfand, 1994; Jackson and Ruderman, 1996). The challenge is to manage diversity in ways that maximize the positive consequences and minimize the negative consequences.

Because there are many types of diversity and many possible consequences of diversity, no single program or set of practices can be used to manage diversity effectively. Reaping the benefits of diversity often requires investing substantial time and effort to create large-scale organizational change. The components of such a change effort can affect many aspects of human resource management, but the activities most likely to be affected are training and development (*see* TRAINING), career planning, performance measurement, COMPENSATION, and BENEFITS (for detailed descriptions of what US organizations are doing, see Morrison, 1992; Cox, 1993; Jackson, 1993; Cross et al., 1994).

Education and training may be offered in an effort to increase cultural sensitivity, reduce stereotyping, and develop interpersonal skills for working in multicultural environments. Among the many possible career-planning activities that may be changed, the introduction of

MENTORING PROGRAMS, which can help to insure that employees from all backgrounds have access to informal networks, may be one of the most beneficial. Sound performance measurement practices can improve an organization's ability to fully utilize a diverse workforce by reducing bias, insuring that all employees receive feedback and coaching, regardless of their personal backgrounds. In addition, 360-DEGREE APPRAISALS can be used to identify whether employees are perceived as equally effective, regardless of whether they are similar or different to the raters. To communicate how serious they are about the importance of managing diversity effectively, some organizations link pay raises and BONUSES to a manager's demonstrated effectiveness in this area. Regarding benefits, the area most affected is family-centered benefits, which may be expanded in recognition of the diversity of family situations faced by employees. Finally, nontraditional work arrangements such as FLEXIBLE WORKPLACE/TELECOMMUTING are additional practices that organizations use in their effort to effectively manage diversity.

Ultimately, the best approach to managing diversity will depend on the specific types of diversity present in an organization and the types of outcomes of most concern to the organization. Therefore, those who wish to improve the ability of an organization to manage diversity effectively must be willing to develop a comprehensive understanding of the issue, design interventions that fit the situation, carefully monitor the many potential consequences, and learn throughout the process.

See also *strategic issues in diversity; workforce demographics*

Bibliography

Cox, T., Jr. (1993). *Cultural Diversity in Organizations: Theory, Research, and Practice.* San Francisco: Berrett-Koehler.
Cross, E., Katz, J. H., Miller, F. A., and Seashore, E. (1994). *The Promise of Diversity.* Burr Ridge, IL: Richard D. Irwin.
Jackson, S. E. (ed.) (1993). *Diversity in the Workplace: Human Resources Initiatives.* New York: Guilford Press.
Jackson, S. E., May, K. A., and Whitney, K. (1995). Understanding the dynamics of diversity in decision-making teams. In R. A. Guzzo and E. Salas (eds.), *Team Decision-making Effectiveness in Organizations.* San Francisco: Jossey-Bass.
Jackson, S. E. and Ruderman, M. N. (1996). *Diversity in Work Teams: Research Paradigms for a Changing Workplace.* Washington, DC: American Psychological Association.
Johnston, W. B. and Packer, A. E. (1987). *Workforce 2000: Work and Workers for the 21st Century.* Washington, DC: US Department of Labor.
Morrison, A. M. (1992). *The New Leaders: Guidelines on Leadership Diversity in America.* San Francisco: Jossey-Bass.
Triandis, H. C., Kurowski, L., and Gelfand, M. (1994). Workplace diversity. In H. C. Triandis, M. Dunnette, and L. Hough (eds.), *Handbook of Industrial and Organizational Psychology,* vol. 4. Palo Alto, CA: Consulting Psychologists Press.

downsizing

Wayne F. Cascio

Downsizing refers to the planned elimination of positions or jobs. While there are as many positions as there are employees, jobs are groups of positions that are significant in their significant duties – such as nurses, computer programmers, or financial analysts. Downsizing may occur by the reduction of work (not just employees), as well as the elimination of functions, hierarchical levels, or units of an organization. It may also occur by the implementation of cost-containment strategies that streamline activities such as transaction processing, information systems, or authorization procedures.

Downsizing does not include the discharge of individuals for cause, or individual departures via normal retirement or resignations. The word "normal" is important in this context. Voluntary severance and early retirement packages are commonly used to reduce the size of the workforce, especially among firms with traditional "no layoff" policies. Even if targeted workers are considered "redundant," "excessed," or "transitioned," the result is the same – employees are shown the door – but it is called something else (Cascio, 1993, 2002a).

Downsizing is often a reactive response to organizational decline (Cameron, Sutton, and Whetten, 1988), although it may also be a proactive measure taken by organizations that perceive future competitive threats. For example, many banks are downsizing proactively because they perceive threats to their competitive position in the marketplace as a result of further deregulation of their industry and resulting competition from a host of other providers of financial services, including insurance companies and brokerage firms.

Regardless of cause, however, downsizing is less an analytical concept than a descriptive term that lacks a body of theory associated with it. It has been examined in hundreds of articles from a number of perspectives in academic journals, books, and the popular press. Some of these perspectives are: organizational symptoms and consequences (e.g., DeWitt, 1998); strategic management of downsizing processes (e.g., Kozlowski et al., 1993); impact of downsizing on organizational survivors (e.g., Noer, 1994; Mishra and Spreitzer, 1998), as well as on those who leave (e.g., Cappelli, 1992); legal issues in downsizing; downsizing issues in countries other than the US (e.g., Vollmann and Brazas, 1993; Winestock, 2002); and the financial and economic consequences of downsizing (e.g., Cascio and Young, 2003).

Conditions that precipitate downsizing, or related types of organizational changes, may be internal (excessive overhead costs, labor-displacing new technology) or external (economic recession, global competition, deregulation, industry consolidation). One or more of these conditions leads to a strategic decision to change the organization (e.g., by downsizing, delayering, restructuring, or reengineering). To implement the strategy, decision-makers initiate a set of processes. Depending on the strategy in question, such processes may include one or a combination of the following: reducing the number of employees, flattening the hierarchy of the organization, selling off assets, or eliminating activities that do not add value. Such actions lead to a series of outcomes: organizational, psychological, and financial.

- Organizational outcomes include, for example, changing spans of control, outsourcing activities or functions, redesigning management jobs, empowering lower-level employees (often forming self-managed work teams; *see* EMPLOYEE EMPOWERMENT), and changing REWARD SYSTEMS.
- Psychological outcomes include alterations in the PSYCHOLOGICAL CONTRACT that binds workers to their employers (Lester et al., 2003) and changes in commitment, motivation, and career orientation.
- Finally, financial outcomes include changes in the financial performance of the organization. Financial performance includes variables such as changes in cost structure, changes in sales, profits, earnings, and returns on common stock.

THE LURE OF DOWNSIZING

To achieve the organizational and financial outcomes described above, many executives see downsizing as a compelling strategy. It is compelling because only two ways exist for companies to become more profitable: either increase revenues or cut costs. Further, most observers would agree that future costs are more predictable than future revenues. Human resources represent costs, so, logically, to become more profitable, costs are lowered by decreasing the number of employees.

CONSEQUENCES OF DOWNSIZING

Many myths surround the practice of downsizing, but facts show a different picture. Mounting evidence suggests that, when it is used as a "quick fix" to reduce the costs of doing business, the cutting of large numbers of employees over a relatively short period of time will produce little long-term reduction. In fact, it may even *increase* costs. Here are some facts about downsizing practices (Cascio, 2002b):

1. profitability does not necessarily follow downsizing;
2. PRODUCTIVITY results after downsizing are mixed;
3. for most employers, downsizing employees does not lead to long-term improvements in the quality of products or services;
4. downsizing continues long after economic recession is over;
5. financially sound companies, some with record profits, are downsizing;

6 the best predictor of whether a company will downsize in a given year is whether it has downsized in the previous year;
7 in knowledge- or relationship-based businesses, the most serious cost is the loss of employee contacts, business forgone, and lack of innovation;
8 for the majority of companies, downsizing has had adverse effects on workload, morale, and employee commitment;
9 for those who lose their jobs, downward mobility is the rule rather than the exception; and
10 stress-related medical disorders are as likely for those laid off as they are for those who remain.

In light of these findings, a number of organizations are rethinking the basic philosophy of downsizing. Instead of asking, "What is the irreducible core number of people we need to run our business?" (a downsizing philosophy), some are raising a different question, namely, "How can we change the way we do business, so that we can use the people we do have most effectively?" This is a philosophy of responsible restructuring in which companies rely on their workers to provide sustained competitive advantage.

Bibliography

Cameron, K. S., Sutton, R., and Whetten, D. A. (1988). *Readings in Organizational Decline*. Cambridge, MA: Ballinger.
Cappelli, P. (1992). Examining managerial displacement. *Academy of Management Journal*, 35, 302–17.
Cascio, W. F. (1993). Downsizing: What do we know? What have we learned? *Academy of Management Executive*, 7, 95–104.
Cascio, W. F. (2002a). Strategies for responsible restructuring. *Academy of Management Executive*, 16 (3), 80–91.
Cascio, W. F. (2002b). *Responsible Restructuring: Creative and Profitable Alternatives to Layoffs*. San Francisco: Berrett-Kohler.
Cascio, W. F. and Young, C. (2003). Financial consequences of employment-change decisions in major U.S. corporations: 1982–2000. In K. P. De Meuse and M. L. Marks (eds.), *Resizing the Organization: Managing Layoffs, Divestitures, and Closings*. San Francisco: Jossey-Bass, pp. 131–56.
DeWitt, R. L. (1998). Firm, industry, and strategy influences on choice of downsizing approach. *Strategic Management Journal*, 19, 59–79.
Kozlowski, S., Chao, G., Smith, E., and Hedlund, V. (1993). Organizational downsizing: Strategies, interventions, and research implications. *International Review of Industrial and Organizational Psychology*, 8, 263–332.
Lester, S. W., Kickul, J. R., Bergmann, T. J., and De Meuse, K. P. (2003). The effects of organizational resizing on the nature of the psychological contract and employee perceptions of contract fulfillment. In K. P. De Meuse and M. L. Marks (eds.), *Resizing the Organization: Managing Layoffs, Divestitures, and Closings*. San Francisco: Jossey-Eass, pp. 78–107.
Mishra, A. K. and Spreitzer, G. M. (1998). Explaining how survivors respond to downsizing: The roles of trust, empowerment, justice, and work redesign. *Academy of Management Journal*, 23, 567–88.
Noer, D. (1994). *Healing the Wounds: Overcoming the Trauma of Layoffs and Revitalizing Downsized Organizations*. San Francisco: Jossey-Bass.
Vollmann, T. and Brazas, M. (1993). Downsizing. *European Management Journal*, 11, 18–29.
Winestock, G. (2002). A reticent European right balks on labor. *Wall Street Journal*, June 21, A6, A7.

drug testing

Joseph G. Rosse

Drug testing refers to a variety of techniques used to determine if employees or job applicants are likely to use drugs. Drug tests may be used to decide who is hired, terminated, or referred to EMPLOYEE ASSISTANCE PROGRAMS.

TYPES OF DRUG-TESTING PROCEDURES

Drugs are metabolized into byproducts that can be detected for a period of days to weeks, depending on the drug and the extent of its use. These metabolites form the basis for the most common type of drug test, a biochemical assay of urine (or, much less frequently, of blood or hair). Thin-layer chromatography and enzyme immunoassay or radioimmunoassay are inexpensive tests that can be used to quickly screen for metabolites from a number of drugs. However, because of their high error rates, these techniques should be confirmed by more expensive gas chromatography or mass spectrometry tests (Frings, Battaglia, and White, 1989).

A less common approach involves screening employees on the basis of their likelihood of *future* drug use. Many integrity tests (*see* INTEGRITY TESTING) include an assessment of substance use based on self-reports of attitudes toward, and prior involvement with, drugs or drug users. PERSONALITY TESTS can be used to assess more general tendencies toward drug use and other counterproductive behavior.

A third approach uses either psychomotor or cognitive tasks – usually presented via computer – to directly assess performance impairment. By testing employees daily and comparing their responses to baseline levels of performance, this approach has the potential to detect impairment caused by a number of factors in addition to drug use, while also reducing complaints of invasion of privacy.

BASIS FOR TESTING

In addition to screening job applicants, drug-testing programs may also target current employees. *Random* testing programs are designed to detect drug users who are not eliminated by pre-employment drug testing. Firms can also test "*for cause*," such as following an accident or when there is some other reason to suspect drug use. Employees who have undergone drug rehabilitation may be required to undergo periodic *fitness-for-duty* testing to insure they remain drug-free. Finally, some organizations test employees prior to their performing safety-sensitive tasks.

The different reasons for testing may call for different types of drug tests. Pre-employment screening can be based either on a history of drug use (the justification for biochemical methods) or a prediction of future drug or alcohol use (the justification for integrity-type tests). Biochemical drug tests are generally the best option in testing based on suspicion of drug use because they offer evidence of actual drug use. Their major limitation is that the presence of metabolites only establishes that drugs were used at some time in the past; they cannot determine if they were used at work or home or if they affected JOB PERFORMANCE. Only analyses of actual levels of drugs or alcohol can determine if an employee is currently under the influence of drugs. Impairment testing may be a suitable alternative for screening incumbents' readiness to perform.

EFFECTIVENESS

As Crown and Rosse (1991) note, most research on the VALIDITY of drug testing has been concerned with validity of measurement (e.g., whether urinalysis accurately detects drug use), rather than validity of prediction (e.g., whether drug test results predict relevant job outcomes). Urinalysis, with appropriate confirmatory testing, appears to have adequate validity of measurement, if proper procedures and a certified laboratory are used. Existing research evidence suggests that urinalysis testing is modestly related to subsequent ABSENTEEISM, accidents, and EMPLOYEE TURNOVER, but not necessarily to job performance (Normand, Salyards, and Mahoney, 1990). Reviews suggest that integrity tests are related to a variety of counterproductive behavior, as well as to job performance (Ones, Viswesvaran, and Schmidt, 1993). Too few data regarding impairment testing exist to allow generalizations about its validity.

The type of testing and the manner in which drug testing is conducted can substantially affect perceptions of PROCEDURAL JUSTICE, which can, in turn, affect employees' loyalty and motivation (Konovsky and Cropanzano, 1993). Testing programs are most likely to be seen as fair if they are not punitive, provide advance notice, or are based on credible suspicion of drug use. Employers need to weigh the benefits of drug testing against the potential costs of alienating applicants and employees who perceive such testing as unfair and invasive of privacy.

Bibliography

Crown, D. F. and Rosse, J. G. (1991). Critical issues in drug testing. In J. Jones, B. Steffy, and D. Bray (eds.), *Applying Psychology in Business: The Handbook for Managers and Human Resource Professionals*. Lexington, MA: Lexington Books.

Frings, C. S., Battaglia, D. J., and White, R. M. (1989). Status of drugs-of-abuse testing in urine under blind conditions: An AACC study. *Clinical Chemistry*, 35, 891–4.

Konovsky, M. and Cropanzano, R. (1993). Justice considerations in employee drug testing. In R. Cropanzano (ed.), *Justice in the Workplace: Approaching Fairness in Human Resource Management*. Hillsdale, NJ: Erlbaum, pp. 171–92.

Lehman, W. E. K. and Simpson, D. D. (1992). Employee substance use and on-the-job behaviors. *Journal of Applied Psychology*, 77, 309–21.

Normand, J., Salyards, S. D., and Mahoney, J. J. (1990). An evaluation of preemployment drug testing. *Journal of Applied Psychology*, 78, 629–39.

Ones, D. S., Viswesvaran, C., and Schmidt, F. L. (1993). Comprehensive meta-analysis of integrity test validities: Findings and implications for personnel selection and theories of job performance. *Journal of Applied Psychology*, 78, 679–703.

Rosse, J., Miller, J., and Ringer, R. (1996). The deterrent effect of drug and integrity testing. *Journal of Business and Psychology*.

Zwerling, C., Ryan, J., and Orav, E. J. (1990). The efficacy of preemployment drug screening for marijuana and cocaine in predicting employee outcomes. *Journal of the American Medical Association*, 264, 2639–43.

dual-earner and dual-career couples

Ellen A. Fagenson-Eland and Colleen O'Malley

Rapoport and Rapoport (1969) were the first to use the term dual-career couple to describe couples where both partners were committed to their careers, supported one another's career pursuits, and shared family responsibilities. Today, dual-career couples are more broadly defined as couples living together in a committed relationship, where both work outside of the home. Dual-career couples are also called dual-earner couples, two-income couples, and dual-wage earners.

According to Eby et al. (2002), the number of dual-career spouses is on the rise. Sixty-four percent of all married couples with children under 18 are working spouses, while the "traditional family" (unemployed wife, employed husband) comprises only 19.3 percent of all families (Eby et al., 2002). This rise in the number of nontraditional families has prompted many new human resource management (HRM) programs to be sponsored by organizations, e.g., flextime (*see* FLEXIBLE WORKING HOURS), JOB SHARING, TRAINING and COUNSELING, revisions of travel policies, antinepotism rules (*see* NEPOTISM POLICIES), and the redrafting of benefit packages (*see* BENEFITS) for employees (Eby et al., 2002).

There are many intellectual, financial, emotional, and psychological benefits associated with a dual-career lifestyle (Gilbert, 1994; Elloy and Smith, 2003). When compared to traditional couples, women in dual-career couples experience greater self-esteem, better physical and mental health, and greater economic independence. Men in dual-career families report increased emotional involvement with children, improved health, and lowered pressure to be financial providers.

While dual-career couples report many advantages to their lifestyle, they also experience stress while balancing work and family roles. Dual-career couples and earners experience greater work overload and WORK–FAMILY CONFLICT than single-career couples (Elloy and Smith, 2003). General work–family conflict, defined as conflict arising from competition between job and home responsibilities, is related to strain and decreased marital job and family satisfaction (Elloy and Smith, 2003; Greenhaus, Bedian, and Mossholder, 1987; Parasuraman, Greenhaus, and Granrose, 1992). Kossek and Ozeki (1998) found that job and life dissatisfaction was highest when work interfered with family life rather than when family interfered with work life. Despite the financial benefits women's income brings to the family, men's satisfaction in their marriage decreased when their wives' income relative to their own increased (Brennan, Barnett, and Gareis, 2001). In contrast, women's marital satisfaction increased when their husband's contribution to childcare increased (Brennan et al., 2001).

The term dual-career couple conjures up images of partners who have achieved true equality through supporting each other's career interests and equitably sharing home and family duties. Men's participation in the home has increased since 1970, primarily due to their increased involvement in childcare rather than in household work (Gilbert, 1994). However, studies consistently find that women in dual-career couples still shoulder most of the home and family responsibilities, experience greater role overload, and have less leisure time than dual-career men (see Duxbury and Higgins, 1994; Greenhaus and Parasuraman, 1999).

Both gender role and societal expectations contribute to differences between women and men in dual-career couples. For example, Duxbury and Higgins (1991) examined the sources of stress in dual-career couples when balancing work and family demands. They found that women who were highly dedicated to their jobs were more likely to experience stress at work than men who were similarly involved and committed to their jobs (see JOB STRESS). Duxbury and Higgins suggested that this occurs because employers see women, and women see themselves, as being primarily responsible for family and household tasks. Hence, these women may experience strain at work because they are behaving in nontraditional ways and are perceived as not attending to their family responsibilities.

Conversely, men who were highly committed and involved in their family roles were found to be more likely to experience stress at work than women who were similarly committed to their families. Duxbury and Higgins suggested that this occurs because men themselves and their employers see men's core role as that of breadwinner. Family-involved men may experience stress from work because they are seen by their employers as uncommitted to their jobs.

Although the number of dual-career couples in the US has increased dramatically since the 1960s, organization and government policies are lagging behind in their support of their unique needs. Many organizations still operate under the paradigm that employees are in traditional families with a working husband, homemaker wife, and children. Unfortunately, even when the organization's policies and programs are supportive of dual-career couples, the organizational culture, norms, and values often reinforce long hours and job commitment as the way to succeed and sanction employees who strive for more balance in their lives (Kofodimos, 1993). Moreover, women are treated inequitably by their organizations as compared to men when it comes to family support. Eby et al. (2002) found that the spouses of male employees received greater assistance from their supervisors than did the spouses of female employees. This is unfortunate since social support, particularly from supervisors and spouses, reduces perceived stress and directly improves wellbeing (Rudd and McKenry, 1986; Parasuraman et al., 1992; Gilbert, 1994).

The FAMILY AND MEDICAL LEAVE ACT OF 1993 has made it easier for couples to juggle home, career, and family responsibilities in times of critical need or illness; however, much debate exists between government decision-makers over how far the government should go to support working couples. The dual-career/dual-earner family will continue to be a major political and social issue in the future.

Bibliography

Brennan, R., Barnett, R., and Gareis, K. (2001). When she earns more than he does: A longitudinal study of dual-earner couples. *Journal of Marriage and Family*, 63, 168–83.

Duxbury, L. E. and Higgins, C. A. (1991). Gender differences in work–family conflict. *Journal of Applied Psychology*, 76, 60–74.

Duxbury, L. and Higgins, C. (1994). Interference between work and family: A status report on dual-career and dual-earner mothers and fathers. *Employee Assistance Quarterly*, 9, 55–80.

Eby, L., Douhitt, S., Perrin, T., Noble, C., Atchley, K., and Ladd, R. (2002). Managerial support for dual-career relocation dilemmas. *Journal of Vocational Behavior*, 60, 354–73.

Elloy, D. and Smith, C. (2003). Patterns of stress, work–family conflict, role conflict, role ambiguity and overload among dual-career and single-career couples: An Australian study. *Cross-Cultural Management*, 10 (1), 55–67.

Gilbert, L. A. (1994). Current perspectives on dual-career families. *Current Directions in Psychological Science*, 3, 101–5.

Greenhaus, J. H., Bedian, A. G., and Mossholder, K. W. (1987). Work experiences, job performance, and feelings of personal and family well-being. *Journal of Vocational Behavior*, 31, 200–15.

Greenhaus, J. H. and Parasuraman, S. (1999). Research on work, family and gender: Current status and future directions. In G. Powell (ed.), *Handbook of Gender and Work*. Newbury Park, CA: Sage.

Gutek, B. A., Searle, S., and Klepa, L. (1991). Rational versus gender role explanations for work–family conflict. *Journal of Applied Psychology*, 76, 560–8.

Hochschild, A. (1989). *The Second Shift*. New York: Viking Press.

Kofodimos, J. (1993). *Balancing Act: How Managers Can Integrate Successful Careers and Fulfilling Personal Lives*. San Francisco: Jossey-Bass.

Kossek, E. and Ozeki, C. (1998). Work–family conflict, policies and the job–life satisfaction relationship: A review and directions for organizational behavior-human resources research. *Journal of Applied Psychology*, 83, 139–49.
Parasuraman, S., Greenhaus, J. H., and Granrose, C. S. (1992). Role stressors, social support, and well-being among two-career couples. *Journal of Organizational Behavior*, 13, 339–56.
Rapoport, R. and Rapoport, R. N. (1969). The dual-career family: A variant pattern and social change. *Human Relations*, 22, 3–30.
Rudd, N. M. and McKenry, P. C. (1986). Family influences on the job satisfaction of employed mothers. *Psychology of Women Quarterly*, 10, 363–71.
Sekaran, U. (1986). *Dual-Career Families*. San Francisco: Jossey-Bass.

duty

Robert J. Harvey

A duty is a descriptor of work activity or responsibility that is composed of a number of related tasks. The fact that duties are written at a higher level of behavioral abstraction than tasks or elements makes them useful for personnel functions that require a more abstract view of a job (e.g., to identify the rating dimensions to be used in a PERFORMANCE APPRAISAL instrument, or to identify similarities between jobs that differ at the task level of analysis for VALIDITY GENERALIZATION purposes).

See also *job; task*

dynamic criteria

James T. Austin

Dynamic criteria, as an aspect of the CRITERION PROBLEM, refers at times to the stability of JOB PERFORMANCE measures and at times to shifting validity coefficients. Ghiselli's (1956) classic defined temporal, individual, and dimensional sources of variance. Theoretically and pragmatically, this issue is important. Debates have clarified issues (Barrett, Caldwell, and Alexander, 1985; Austin, Humphreys, and Hulin, 1989), innovative investigations have provided data (Hofmann, Jacobs, and Baratta, 1993; Deadrick, Bennett, and Russell, 1997), and quantitative reviews have substantiated the concept (Hulin, Henry, and Noon, 1990). Practically, recognition and use of shifting sources of variance in job performance, accurate estimation of validity and dollar utility, and the timing of PERFORMANCE APPRAISAL are some implications of dynamic criteria. Despite these efforts, a conceptual explanation of criterion dynamics was lacking. Steele-Johnson, Osburn, and Pieper (2000), however, recently integrated multiple constructs, namely JOB, TASK, organization, learning, and ability, to predict job performance.

Bibliography

Austin, J. T., Humphreys, L. G., and Hulin, C. L. (1989). Another view of dynamic criteria: A critical reanalysis of Barrett, Caldwell, and Alexander. *Personnel Psychology*, 42, 583–96.
Barrett, G. V., Caldwell, M., and Alexander, R. A. (1985). The concept of dynamic criteria: A critical reanalysis. *Personnel Psychology*, 38, 41–56.
Deadrick, D. L., Bennett, N., and Russell, C. J. (1997). Using hierarchical linear modeling to examine dynamic performance criteria over time. *Journal of Management*, 23, 745–57.
Deadrick, D. L. and Madigan, R. J. (1990). Dynamic criteria revisited: A longitudinal study of performance stability. *Personnel Psychology*, 44, 717–44.
Ghiselli, E. E. (1956). Dimensional problems of criteria. *Journal of Applied Psychology*, 40, 1–4.
Hofmann, D. A., Jacobs, R., and Baratta, J. E. (1993). Dynamic criteria and the measurement of change. *Journal of Applied Psychology*, 78, 194–204.
Hulin, C. L., Henry, R., and Noon, S. (1990). Adding a dimension: Time as a factor in the generalizability of predictive relations. *Psychological Bulletin*, 107, 328–40.
Ployhart, R. E. and Schneider, B. (2002). A multi-level perspective on personnel selection research and practice: Implications for selection system design, assessment, and construct validation. In F. J. Yammarino and F. Dansereau (eds.), *The Many Faces of Multi-Level Issues*, vol 1. London: JAI/Elsevier Science, pp. 95–140.
Steele-Johnson, D., Osburn, H. G., and Pieper, K. F. (2000). A review and extension of current models of dynamic criteria. *International Journal of Selection and Assessment*, 8, 110–36.

dysfunctional performance appraisals

Clinton O. Longenecker

A dysfunctional appraisal is the result of any intentional or unintentional rater, ratee, or organizational action that undermines the intended purpose of an organization's PERFORMANCE APPRAISAL process. Organizations typically develop, implement, and operate performance appraisal systems with the underlying assumption that the process provides the organization with a host of *potential benefits*. These benefits can include:

1. effective performance planning and goal setting;
2. a systematic basis for evaluating and documenting employee contributions to the organization;
3. increased emphasis on employee development and performance improvement; and
4. a systematic basis for making critical human resource management (HRM) decisions, including those such as COMPENSATION, PROMOTION, discharge, and TRAINING (Cardy and Dobbins, 1994).

Appraisals become dysfunctional when the potential benefits of the appraisal process fail to be realized.

CAUSES AND OUTCOMES OF DYSFUNCTIONAL APPRAISALS

Dysfunctional performance appraisals are caused by organizational, managerial, and/or employee factors that reduce or diminish the overall effectiveness of the process (Murphy and Cleveland, 1991). Organizational factors include poorly designed rating formats and procedures, lack of top management support, lack of effective rater training, insufficient resources to effectively reward performance, and a nonsupportive organizational culture (Mohrman, Resnick-West, and Lawler, 1989).

Managers, in their role as raters, are frequently viewed as the primary cause of dysfunctional appraisals when they lack the ability and/or motivation to conduct effective appraisals (Longenecker, Gioia, and Sims, 1987). When managers (raters) fail to establish unambiguous performance standards, fail to provide ongoing performance measurement and feedback, fail to take sufficient time to prepare and conduct the appraisal, and fail to interact with candor and honesty in their review of an employee's performance, the process can easily become dysfunctional (Longenecker and Goff, 1992). Employees (ratees) can cause the appraisal process to become dysfunctional when they possess unrealistic expectations, are defensive in responding to performance feedback, are cynical or contemptuous of the process, or take a passive role in reviewing and responding to their performance review.

The outcomes of dysfunctional appraisals are numerous. When appraisals are dysfunctional, organizations lose a valuable HRM tool, managers fail to utilize a potentially useful process for improving employee performance, and employee JOB SATISFACTION, motivation, commitment, and development typically suffer.

Bibliography

Cardy, P. L. and Dobbins, G. H. (1994). *Performance Appraisal: An Alternative Perspective*. Cincinnati, OH; South-Western Publishing.

Longenecker, C. O., Gioia, D. A., and Sims, H. P. (1987). Behind the mask: The politics of employee appraisal. *Academy of Management Executive*, 1, 183–93.

Longenecker, C. O. and Goff, S. (1992). Performance appraisal effectiveness: A matter of perspective. *SAM-Advanced Management Journal*, 57, 17–23.

Mohrman, A. M., Jr., Resnick-West, S. M., and Lawler, E. E. (1989). *Designing Performance Appraisal Systems*. San Francisco: Jossey-Bass.

Murphy, K. R. and Cleveland, J. N. (1991). *Performance Appraisal: An Organizational Perspective*. Boston: Allyn and Bacon.

early identification of management talent

Lyle F. Schoenfeldt

The early identification of management talent refers to the process whereby individuals are recognized early in their careers for their unique abilities to lead and direct others. They are then put in positions to use and further develop these capabilities. A manager is a person responsible for the control and direction of an organization. The key to identifying and developing individuals for managerial jobs is understanding the managerial role and what it takes to be effective in managerial positions.

What Managers Do

There has been a great deal of research to show that the managerial job is complex and varied (McCall, Morrison, and Hannan, 1978). Useful categorical and process models of what managers do have been developed.

The categorical conceptualizations of managerial behavior attempt to list the dimensions or areas of managerial activity. For example, the work of Mintzberg (1973) defined ten managerial roles organized into the following three categories:

1 interpersonal (figurehead, leader, liaison);
2 informational (monitor, disseminator, spokesperson); and
3 decisional (entrepreneur, disturbance handler, resource allocator, negotiator).

The process models seek to go beyond an explanation of what managers do by also specifying *how* these actions are accomplished. The two most comprehensive approaches are the six-cluster (human resource, leadership, goal and action management, directing subordinates, focus on others, and specialized knowledge) model of Boyatzis (1982) and the four-dimensional model (functions, roles, style, and targets) of Steger and his colleagues (Schoenfeldt and Steger, 1989).

The research on the managerial role is seen as the vehicle for understanding what managers do to achieve organizational goals. An understanding of the managerial role allows for the profiling of managerial job requirements, in terms of either clusters of competencies or the four dimensions of the managerial job.

Identifying Management Talent

The value of understanding what managers do is vital to the early identification of individuals for managerial positions or selecting novice managers for further challenge. An understanding of what managers do provides a road map for the selection and development of management talent.

There are numerous sources of information to assess individuals for managerial positions, and these vary considerably in terms of cost and utility. ASSESSMENT CENTERS, along with the SITUATIONAL TESTS (e.g., in-basket test, leaderless group discussion, problem-solving exercises) that characterize this procedure, are popular in identifying individuals for managerial jobs. Assessment centers tend to be expensive to establish and operate, and thus may not be as cost-effective as other approaches.

Performance measurement can also be valuable in identifying individuals for managerial jobs. The goal would be to look at the performance of those aspects of the current job that are most indicative of performance in managerial functions and roles, along with style compatibility of the individual with the managerial job. Measurement of current performance tends to be extremely cost-effective, but present JOB PERFORMANCE may not sufficiently *overlap* with the managerial role to allow accurate inferences about future managerial attainment.

SUMMARY

In summary, the challenge of the early identification of management talent is an understanding of what managers do, and then the identification of individuals who have the competencies to be effective in this role. Using available process models, it is possible to assess individuals against the requirements for effectiveness in the managerial job, and to do so on the basis of college accomplishments or early job performance.

Bibliography

Boyatzis, R. E. (1982). *The Competent Manager: A Model for Effective Performance*. New York: John Wiley.

McCall, M. W., Jr., Morrison, A. M., and Hannan, R. L. (1978). *Studies of Managerial Work: Results and Methods*. Greensboro, NC: Center for Creative Leadership.

Mintzberg, H. (1973). *The Nature of Managerial Work*. New York: Harper and Row.

Schoenfeldt, L. F. and Steger, J. A. (1989). Identification and development of management talent. In G. R. Ferris and K. M. Rowland (eds.), *Research in Personnel and Human Resources Management*, vol. 7. Greenwich, CT: JAI Press.

early retirement buyout

Charles H. Fay

Defined benefit PENSION PLANS typically have both age and service requirements for an employee to receive full pension benefits. Employees can retire early, but with reduced benefit levels. Employers seeking to reduce their headcount sometimes offer to "add" both years of age and years of service to records of employees aged 55 and over so they can retire with full benefits. One disadvantage to employees accepting a buyout is that defined benefit pension plans usually calculate payouts on "final average" income (the average of the past five years' income); early retirement means payouts are calculated against lower wages.

Bibliography

Damato, K. (1995). Retire with the biggest pension check you can get. *Wall Street Journal*, April 14, C1.

early retirement policy

Carrie R. Leana

Retirement has traditionally been defined as withdrawal from the workforce altogether or at the end of a person's active life. Feldman (1994) provides a modified definition of retirement as the exit from an organizational position or career path of considerable duration, taken by individuals after middle age, and taken with the intention of reduced psychological commitment to work thereafter. The concept of early retirement, however, is ambiguous and there is no precise reference point which is considered early. Generally, the usual age for retirement in most western countries is around age 65. Hence age 65 is generally considered as both a legal and a labor-force or behavioral reference point (Kohli and Rein, 1991). Job changes in a person's twenties and career changes in a person's thirties are transitions, but these are not thought of as retirement (Feldman, 1994).

There are several factors influencing an individual's decision to retire early. These include individual differences (especially demographic), opportunity structures in career paths, organizational variables, and macroeconomic and external environment variables (Feldman, 1994).

There are two reasons why employers and sometimes employees support early retirement. One is centered on PRODUCTIVITY. There is literature suggesting that the wages of some older workers exceed their marginal productivity. Second, due to reputational concerns, both employers and employees prefer early retirement to dismissal (Casey, 1992).

In many western economies, early retirement has been utilized to facilitate the elimination of redundancies and organizational DOWNSIZING (Casey, 1992). In addition, early retirement can help a company restructure its workforce and provide new career opportunities to younger workers.

Bibliography

Casey, B. (1992). Redundancy and early retirement: The interaction of public and private policy in Britain, Germany and the USA. *British Journal of Industrial Relations*, **30**, 426–43.

Feldman, D. C. (1994). The decision to retire early: A review and conceptualization. *Academy of Management Review*, **19**, 285–311.

Kohli, M. and Rein, M. (1991). The changing balance of work and retirement. In M. Kohli, M. Rein, A. Guillemard, and H. V. Gunsteren (eds.), *Time for Retirement: Comparative Studies of Early Exit from the Labor Force*. Cambridge: Cambridge University Press.

elder care benefit

Ellen Ernst Kossek and Beverly DeMarr

Elder care, defined as assisting an employee with care for an elderly relative (e.g., spouse, parent, in-laws, grandparents, siblings) is a type of dependant care benefit. It involves helping an elder with (1) activities of daily living (ADL), including eating, dressing, bathing, and toileting; and (2) instrumental activities of daily living (IADL), including housework, meals, transportation, and financial management. Being employed full-time does not reduce the odds of helping with IADLs (Dwyer and Coward, 1991). At least one-third of most companies' workforces currently provide elder care ranging from 6–10 hours weekly up to 4 hours daily (Kossek et al., 1993). Elder care can cause problems with ABSENTEEISM, tardiness, stress, interruptions, overtime, EMPLOYEE TURNOVER, health, quality, and accidents (Bureau of National Affairs, 1989).

Employers offer these forms of aid:

1. time (flextime, part-time work, leaves);
2. information (resource and referral, seminars);
3. financial (pre-tax dollar accounts for expenses, vouchers, discounts); and
4. direct services (care network, centers, sick care).

Elder care differs from childcare in its duration, complexity, life cycle, and psychological impact. Employees can assume the role of caregiver for several elders on multiple occasions throughout their lives. Care requirements can vary dramatically, ranging from a short-term illness to years for debilitating diseases. Care initially begins informally, such as "helping out" with household matters, and becomes more formal as the elder ages, is less able to perform ADLs, and becomes too much to handle alone (Kossek et al., 1993). Caring for an elder often has not been planned, and ultimately ends with the elder's death.

Bibliography

Bureau of National Affairs (1989). *Bulletin to Management*, **40**, 1–4.

Dwyer, J. W. and Coward, R. T. (1991). A multivariate comparison of the involvement of adult sons versus daughters in the care of impaired adults. *Journals of Gerontology: Social Sciences*, **46**, S259–69.

Kossek, E. E., DeMarr, B., Backman, K., and Kollar, M. (1993). Assessing employees' elder care needs and reactions to dependent care benefits. *Public Personnel Management Journal*, **22**, 617–38.

emotional intelligence

Susan Cartwright

Emotional intelligence (EI) gained popularity and organizational interest following the publication of Daniel Goleman's bestselling book (1998), although the concept has a longer history. There is still debate amongst academics as to whether EI is a true form of intelligence, a set of competencies, or a cluster of personality traits (Davies, Stankov, and Roberts, 1998; *see* TRAIT). However, it is accepted that the essence of EI is the ability of individuals to be aware of, recognize, and effectively integrate emotions with thoughts and behavior, both in themselves and in others. There are several psychometric tests of emotional intelligence which can be used to measure INDIVIDUAL DIFFERENCES (e.g., Bar-On, 1997) and are used in the context of selection and development. Unlike traditional intelligence quotient (IQ), EI can be developed through training and has been linked to improvements in leadership behavior (Barling, Slater, and Kelloway, 2000) and stress resilience (Slaski and Cartwright, 2003).

Bibliography

Bar-On, R. (1997). *Bar-On Emotional Quotient Inventory: A Measure of Emotional Intelligence*, Technical Manual. Toronto: Multi Health Systems.

Barling, J., Slater, F., and Kelloway, K. (2000). Transformational leadership and emotional intelligence. *Leadership and Organization Development Journal*, 21, 145–50.

Davies, M., Stankov, L., and Roberts, R. D. (1998). Emotional intelligence in search of an elusive contract. *Journal of Personality and Social Psychology*, 75, 989–1015.

Goleman, D. (1998). *Working with Emotional Intelligence*. London: Bloomsbury.

Slaski, M. and Cartwright, S. (2003). Emotional intelligence training and its implications for stress, health and performance. *Stress and Health*, 19, 223–39.

employability

Arthur K. Yeung

Employability, as opposed to employment security, is a new form of PSYCHOLOGICAL CONTRACT between employers and employees. It implies three elements in the employment relationship:

1. the employee is responsible for developing the right skills to be employable inside and outside the company;
2. the employer is responsible for providing employees information, time, resources, and opportunities to assess and develop skills that are needed; and
3. the employment relationship can be dissolved if the employee's contribution or aspiration does not match the employer's needs.

Employability emerged in the late 1980s because of two contributing forces. First, many companies like IBM cannot afford their traditional commitment to employment security in the midst of DOWNSIZING and restructuring. Second, new business realities mandate companies to be flexible to capture changing business opportunities. For example, one of Intel's strategic capabilities is to shift its resources (especially people) swiftly from declining businesses to emerging businesses.

Employability requires a supportive infrastructure in four areas (Waterman, Waterman, and Collard, 1994):

1. a change in attitudes and values – shifting loyalty from company to individual career;
2. open sharing of information – future business direction and required competencies;
3. resource allocation to offer employees self-assessment and continuous learning; and
4. clear and fair procedures to transfer and redeploy employees.

Researchers have different views on employability. While some believe that it may improve organizational PRODUCTIVITY and flexibility (Waterman et al., 1994), others are concerned about its impact on employee commitment and contribution to companies (Pfeffer, 1994).

Bibliography

Pfeffer, J. (1994). *Competitive Advantage through People*. Boston: Harvard Business School Press.

Waterman, R. H., Waterman, J. A., and Collard, B. A. (1994). Toward a career resilient workforce. *Harvard Business Review*, July/August, 87–95.

employee assistance programs

Stuart A. Youngblood

An employee assistance program (EAP) is an employer-sponsored intervention designed to identify and assist employees with personal problems that interfere with their work performance. Personal problems may include substance abuse (alcohol and other drugs), AIDS/AIDS-RELATED COMPLEX, psychiatric disorders, WORKPLACE VIOLENCE, marital and family problems, and financial and legal difficulties. EAPs serve the organization by:

1. assessing the nature of the employee's problem;
2. selecting appropriate community resources to assist the employee;

3 assisting the employee in acquiring such services;
4 follow-up of the employee at the workplace; and
5 training and consultation with supervisors and managers about related policies and procedures.

EAPs provide a means for both employee self-referral and supervisory referral. EAPs by definition are concerned with performance management and must also protect employee privacy. The growth and diffusion of EAPs is related to technological innovation in the workplace that places lower tolerance on substandard employee performance, increasing availability of health services for behavioral problems, and increasing legal liability (see AMERICANS WITH DISABILITIES ACT OF 1990) by employers for employee behavioral problems.

In the public sector EAPs grew out of a concern for alcohol abuse and a federal mandate to provide EAPs for all civilian employees. In the private sector EAPs grew out of the welfare tradition of early human resource management (HRM) and the human relations movement of the 1940s and 1950s. Estimates of EAP coverage vary. Smits and Pace (1992) estimated that only about 10 percent of the US workforce has access to EAP benefits, while Blum and Roman (1985) suggest higher estimates; between 25 and 33 percent of working adults are employed by organizations providing this benefit. Larger employers (more than 1,000 employees) are more likely to provide an internal EAP while smaller employers are more likely to contract with an external provider of EAP services. In the US four types of EAPs exist:

1 an internal program based within the organization staffed by an employee(s) of that organization;
2 an external program run by an agency that contracts with the client organization to provide services based on a contract fee which is a function of employees served and scope of services provided;
3 a labor union-sponsored program designed primarily for mobile craft workers employed in the building trades; and
4 professional association-sponsored programs designed for physicians, lawyers, dentists, pharmacists, nurses, psychologists, and social workers.

These programs are designed to maintain standards of professional conduct and protect the common interests of the professional association and the larger profession. They are also unique in that in addition to self-referral and supervisory referral, these programs rely on clients/patients as a source of identification of problem professionals.

Bibliography

Blum, T. C. and Roman, P. M. (1985). Employee assistance programs and human resources management. In G. R. Ferris and K. M. Rowland (eds.), *Research in Personnel and Human Resources Management*, vol. 7. Greenwich, CT: JAI Press.
Directory of Employee Assistance Program Vendors (1994). *Business Insurance*, 23, 22–4.
Caldwell, B. (1994). EAPs: Survey identifies uses and administration. *Employee Benefit Plan Review*, 9, 36–8.
Smits, S. J. and Pace, L. A. (1992). *The Investment Approach to Employee Assistance Programs*. Westport, CT: Quorum.

Employee Benefit Research Institute

Robert M. McCaffery

The Employee Benefit Research Institute (EBRI) is a private, nonprofit, nonpartisan, public policy research organization in Washington, DC. Established in 1978, EBRI's overall goal is to promote the development of soundly conceived private and public employee benefit programs. To achieve this goal, EBRI staff members interact and cooperate with the academic community, the government, and employee benefit professionals to develop relevant and comprehensive research.

EBRI established a related unit, the Education and Research Fund (ERF), in 1979. EBRI-ERF produces and distributes a wide range of educational publications concerning health, welfare, and retirement policies. These include the periodicals *EBRI Issue Briefs* (monthly) and

Employee Benefit Notes (monthly), as well as the text *Fundamentals of Employee Benefit Programs*, and the *EBRI Databook on Employee Benefits*.

Descriptive information is available on request from: Employee Benefit Research Institute, 2121 K Street, NW, Suite 600, Washington, DC 20037-2121. Telephone 202-659-0670. Fax 202-775-6312. Website: www.ebri.org/.

employee code of conduct

Linda Klebe Treviño

A code of conduct is a formal document that communicates standards of behavior. Its purpose is to encourage conduct that meets organizational or professional standards. Ethics code usage has grown in work organizations in recent years largely in response to the US Sentencing Guidelines passed in 1991 (see www.ussc.gov). These guidelines provide an incentive (reduced fines and sentences for illegal behavior) to organizations that manage ethics and legal compliance via codes of conduct, TRAINING, reporting mechanisms, and other specified means.

In a 2003 Ethics Resource Center study which included employees from organizations of all sizes, 73 percent of respondents reported that the companies they work for had ethics policy standards. When considering only firms with more than 500 employees, that number reached 88 percent, compared to 58 percent for smaller organizations. Written standards of conduct were most prevalent in government organizations (90 percent), followed by nonprofit organizations (82 percent) and for-profit organizations (67 percent). Employees working in organizations with formal ethics standards report that they engage in and observe less unethical conduct. However, unethical conduct is influenced even more by informal systems such as organizational follow through, ethical leadership by executives and supervisors, and perceived fair treatment of employees.

Bibliography

Ethics Resource Center (2003). *National Business Ethics Survey 2003: How Employees View Ethics in Their Organizations*. Washington, DC: Ethics Resource Center.

Treviño, L. K., Butterfield, K., and McCabe, D. (1998). The ethical context in organizations: Influences on employee attitudes and behaviors. *Business Ethics Quarterly*, 8 (3), 447–76.

Treviño, L. K. and Weaver, G. R. (2001). Organizational justice and ethics program follow through: Influences on employees' helpful and harmful behavior. *Business Ethics Quarterly*, 11 (4), 651–71.

Treviño, L. K., Weaver, G., Gibson, D., and Toffler, B. (1999). Managing ethics and legal compliance: What works and what hurts. *California Management Review*, 41 (2), 131–51.

employee empowerment

Charles C. Manz and Christopher P. Neck

The verb empower means to enable, to allow, or to permit. Building upon this simple definition, employee empowerment is synonymous with delegation, or sharing of power with subordinates (Conger, 1989). For example, one specific definition of employee empowerment is to view it as a process whereby an individual's belief in his or her self-efficacy is enhanced. More specifically, Conger and Kanungo (1988: 479) state that empowerment "is a process of enhancing feelings of self-efficacy among organizational members through the identification of conditions that foster powerlessness and through their removal by both formal organizational practices and informal techniques of providing efficacy information." Several empowerment perspectives have been posited that vary in terms of the degree of employee self-influence.

Self-regulation is described in terms of an ongoing cybernetic control model. Self-regulation from this view involves a process of reducing variations from established standards. Much as with a heat-sensitive thermostat, the focus is on sensing and then reducing discrepancies from a relatively steady state (Carver and Scheier, 1981). Within an organization, existing organizational standards or objectives are analogous to the current temperature setting, which is maintained by the organizational control system. In the short run, the process of reducing deviations from standards is largely automatic and self-maintaining. That is, as long as current policies, procedures, and rules are followed, deviations (such as change in temperature) should be reduced. Thus, self-regulation represents a relatively limited level of empowerment because it occurs almost automatically with little conscious thought to serve external demands.

Another empowerment perspective has been labeled *self-management* (Manz and Sims, 1980; Hackman, 1986). Self-management consists of a set of strategies for managing one's own behavior to reduce discrepancies from existing standards (*see* SELF-MANAGEMENT TRAINING). While an individual's immediate behavior can be described as self-controlled, the purpose of the overall process tends to serve the requirements of externally set standards. Self-management strategies address short-run deviations from standards, but not the appropriateness or the desirability of the governing standards themselves. While self-management does allow employees significant self-influence regarding how to complete a task to meet a standard (as defined by the wider system or higher management), it does not provide self-influence regarding what should be done and why. Consequently self-management involves a moderate level of employee empowerment.

Finally, *self-leadership* is described as a broader view of employee empowerment. It includes strategies for self-management as well as for managing the natural motivational value of the task and the patterns in one's thinking (Manz, 1986; Neck and Manz, 1992; Manz and Neck, 2004). Self-leadership jointly focuses on behavior and cognition. It also addresses both the reduction of discrepancies from standards and the appropriateness of those standards. It focuses on *what* should be done and *why*, in addition to *how* it should be done. As a result, the process of self-leadership prescribes a more active and comprehensive role for members in a work system and represents a highly advanced form of employee empowerment.

In order to clarify these various levels of empowerment, consider the following. If the amount of empowerment possessed by organization members is viewed as falling on a continuum from external control to complete self-control, self-leadership falls significantly closer to the "complete" self-influence or empowerment end than does self-regulation and self-management. Under conditions of self-leadership, workers play a greater role in influencing higher-level management decision-making and strategic processes. Thus, employees are more involved in setting the thermostatic standard as well as acting to achieve the standard once it is set. This implies active involvement in both short-term processes of deviation reduction and longer-term processes of deviation amplification.

Lastly, the term empowerment has recently been associated with the concept of SELF-MANAGING TEAMS (SMTs). SMTs are a form of work design that typically involve an increased amount of empowerment at the work-group level (Manz and Sims, 1987). To a large degree, teams (most notably SMTs) have become a central feature and symbol of empowerment efforts in the US and elsewhere. And leading teams of employees to be self-leading represents an advanced form of contemporary employee empowerment (Manz and Sims, 2001).

Bibliography

Carver, C. S. and Scheier, M. F. (1981). *Attention and Self-Regulation: A Control Theory Approach to Human Behavior*. New York: Springer-Verlag.

Conger, J. A. (1989). Leadership. The art of empowering others. *Academy of Management Executive*, 3, 17–24.

Conger, J. A. and Kanungo, R. N. (1988). The empowerment process: Integrating theory and practice. *Academy of Management Review*, 13, 471–82.

Hackman, J. R. (1986). The psychology of self-management in organizations. In M. S. Pollack and R. O. Perlogg (eds.), *Psychology and Work: Productivity Change and Employment*. Washington, DC: American Psychological Association.

Manz, C. C. (1986). Self-leadership: Toward an expanded theory of self-influence processes in organizations. *Academy of Management Review*, 11, 585–600.

Manz, C. C. (1990). Beyond self-managing work teams: Toward self-leading teams in the workplace. In R. Woodman and W. Pasmore (eds.), *Research in Organizational Change and Development*. Greenwich, CT: JAI Press.

Manz, C. C. and Neck, C. P. (2004). *Mastering Self-Leadership: Empowering Yourself for Personal Excellence*. Upper Saddle River, NJ: Prentice-Hall.

Manz, C. C. and Sims, H. P., Jr. (1980). Self-management as a substitute for leadership: A social learning theory perspective. *Academy of Management Review*, 5, 361–7.

Manz, C. C. and Sims, H. P., Jr. (1987). Leading workers to lead themselves: The external leadership of

self-managing work teams. *Administrative Science Quarterly*, **32**, 106–28.
Manz, C. C. and Sims, H. P., Jr. (2001). *The New SuperLeadership: Leading Others to Lead Themselves*. San Francisco: Berrett-Koehler.
Neck, C. P. and Manz, C. C. (1992). Thought self-leadership: The influence of self-talk and mental imagery on performance. *Journal of Organizational Behavior*, **13**, 681–99.

employee handbook

Stuart A. Youngblood

As a business grows in size, management often turns to the use of an employee handbook as a communication tool to inform employees on issues such as company history and products, human resource policies, employee COMPENSATION and BENEFITS, TRAINING assistance, health services, safety, security, employee responsibilities, and work standards.

Handbooks are also useful to supervisors and administrators for insuring consistent implementation and enforcement of company policies. Proponents of employee handbooks argue that they set the parameters of the employment relationship, limit employer liability and responsibility to the employee, and promote employee morale because expectations are communicated and employees know what to expect. Similarly, the disadvantage of a handbook is that it may create unrealistic expectations and liability for the employer, especially when supervisors inconsistently apply company policies.

In the US, employers have confronted the legal issue of whether an employee handbook is a contract, thereby limiting employer rights to manage, especially with respect to employee dismissal. There is no legal requirement for employers to develop handbooks, but those that do usually put a DISCLAIMER in the introductory section to clarify for nonunion employees that EMPLOYMENT-AT-WILL applies to their employment relationship. Employers usually request that employees sign an acknowledgment and receipt form to preserve their option to dismiss at-will.

With the advent of information technology, employee handbooks that previously were published in pocket-sized editions are now being electronically shared on computer networks, accessible to all employees and supervisory personnel. The use of indexing and hypertext to cross-reference material has also made handbooks more user-friendly for employees and supervisors alike. The creation of a handbook is not a static process; thus employers must continuously update and effectively communicate changes in policies to all employees.

employee involvement

Dianna L. Stone

Employee involvement refers to the process of engaging employees in their work and increasing their participation in decision-making. In particular, employee involvement insures that employees who are closest to the work have the power to control work methods, and are able to use their knowledge and skills to improve work processes (Lawler, 1992). This approach also attempts to move information and power downward in the organization, so that employees can work autonomously and regulate their own behavior (Cummings and Worley, 1993). As a consequence, organizations that use this approach typically experience a flattening of the organizational hierarchy.

Although there is no one theoretical basis for employee involvement, it is derived from a number of key human relations assumptions (see, e.g., Argyris, 1957). Specifically, it is assumed that when employees are given challenging work, and allowed to participate in decision-making, they will

1 become more motivated and willing to control their own behavior;
2 become more involved in their work;
3 increase their commitment to organizational goals; and
4 use their skills and abilities to make valuable contributions to organizational goals.

Employee involvement has been used as the foundation for a wide array of management programs, including QUALITY CIRCLES, JOB INVOLVEMENT, QUALITY OF WORK LIFE programs, EMPLOYEE EMPOWERMENT, and TOTAL QUALITY MANAGEMENT.

Bibliography

Argyris, C. (1957). *Personality and Organization.* New York: HarperCollins.
Cummings, T. and Worley, C. (1993). *Organizational Development and Change,* 5th edn. Minneapolis: West Publishing.
Lawler, E. E. (1992). *The Ultimate Advantage: Creating the High-Involvement Organization.* San Francisco: Jossey-Bass.

employee leasing

Stanley Nollen

Leased employees are employees of a staffing company who, as a group, take over the operation of an entire function (such as office management) for a client company on a contractual basis. Usually the leased employees are former employees of the client company who are transferred to the payroll of the leasing company, which in turn handles their pay, BENEFITS, and other personnel administration. Employee leasing is a method for client companies to externalize part of their workforces and outsource some human resource management tasks in a co-employment relationship with the leasing firm, which is a subcontractor of these services.

employee morale

Thomas W. Lee

Employee morale is a term with a long history and multiple meanings (Vroom, 1964), and is infrequently used by contemporary human resource scholars and managers. Employee morale most often refers to a broad collection of mental states that are held by groups of employees; thus, morale is typically regarded as a more macro, summary, and sociological concept. The collection of mental states can include any or all of the following: courage, discipline, confidence, enthusiasm, and willingness to endure hardship. In its earlier usage, employee morale referenced virtually all attitudes toward job features and one's coworkers (Likert and Willitis, 1940). In its later usage, employee morale focused on satisfaction with group goals, desire to maintain group membership, and willingness to strive toward attainment of the group's goals (Vitales, 1953), which resembles contemporary notions about organizational commitment. Still later, employee morale emphasized positive emotional states that referenced future or present circumstances, commonly involving a group of employees (Locke, 1976). These later meanings are quite similar to overall and anticipatory JOB SATISFACTION (Locke, 1976).

Bibliography

Likert, R. and Willitis, J. M. (1940). *Morale and Agency Management,* vol. 1. Hartford, CT: Life Insurance Sales Research Bureau.
Locke, E. A. (1976). The nature and causes of job satisfaction. In M. Dunnette (ed.). *Handbook of Industrial and Organizational Psychology.* Chicago: Rand.
Vitales, M. S. (1953). *Motivation and Morale in Industry.* New York: Norton.
Vroom, V. H. (1964). *Work and Motivation.* New York: John Wiley.

Employee Polygraph Protection Act of 1988

Vida Scarpello

Various lie detector tests, including POLYGRAPH TESTING, have long been used to investigate thefts and other industrial espionage against the employer (see Ones, Viswesvaran, and Schmidt, 1993). They have also been used to screen applicants for sensitive positions. Nevertheless, critics of these tests have pointed to the high rates of people incorrectly identified as having lied (Tiner and O'Grady, 1988a, b). Due to documented claims of invalid results, more than half of the states had passed laws limiting the use of lie detectors and other forms of honesty testing in employment (Ledvinka and Scarpello, 1991).

Given mounting evidence for the invalidity of polygraph testing, as well as the 1977 Privacy Protection Commission's report (*see* PRIVACY ACT OF 1974), which focused attention on the relative lack of privacy protections in the work environment, Congress passed the Employee Polygraph Protection Act.

With three exceptions, the Employee Polygraph Protection Act prohibits private sector employers from using polygraph tests in their employment practices. Government employers are exempted from the Act. Polygraph use is allowed:

1. in ongoing investigations;
2. in the hiring of security employees by security service organizations; and
3. in the hiring of employees by drug companies.

The Act also prohibits employers from retaliating against anyone who exercises any rights under the Act.

The Act gives enforcement authority to the Secretary of Labor, who issues rules and regulations to carry out this Act. The secretary is also instructed to cooperate with regional, state, local, and other agencies and to furnish technical assistance to employers, labor organizations, and employment agencies, as well as investigate violations of the Act. Violators are subject to civil penalty of not more than $10,000, with the amount to be determined by the Secretary of Labor. The secretary also may bring legal action in federal or state court. Employers who violate this Act are liable for "such legal or equitable relief as may be appropriate" (Employee Polygraph Protection Act, 102 STAT. 648). This includes, but is not limited to, employment, promotion, reinstatement, and payment of lost wages and benefits.

Bibliography

Ledvinka, J. and Scarpello, V. (1991). *Federal Regulation of Personnel and Human Resource Management*. Boston: PWS-Kent.

Ones, D. S., Viswesvaran, C., and Schmidt, F. L. (1993). Comprehensive meta-analysis of integrity test validities: Findings and implications for personnel selection and theories of job performance. *Journal of Applied Psychology*, 78, 679–703.

Privacy Protection Study Commission (1977). *Personal Privacy in an Information Society*. Washington, DC: Government Printing Office.

Tiner, M. and O'Grady, D. J. (1988a). Lie detectors in employment. *Harvard Civil Rights-Civil Liberties Law Review*, 23, 85–113.

Tiner, M. and O'Grady, D. J. (1988b). Note: Lie detectors in the workplace, the need for civil actions against employers. *Harvard Law Review*, 101, 806–25.

Employee Retirement Income Security Act of 1974

Ramona L. Paetzold

The Employment Retirement Income Security Act (ERISA) was enacted in 1974 as the first piece of US legislation governing employee pension and welfare benefit plans. Although not mandating pensions for employees, ERISA governs virtually all aspects of employer-sponsored pensions (*see* PENSION PLANS). Because of ERISA's exemption for governmental plans, those pension plans operated by federal, state, or local governments are not covered under ERISA.

ERISA is organized under four titles, with Title I being the most important to the human resource function. In Title I, rules regarding participation and participant vesting, funding, fiduciary responsibility, administration, enforcement, reporting, and disclosure are provided. Some of these rules apply only to pension plans, but rules regarding fiduciary responsibility, administration, enforcement, reporting, and disclosure apply also to welfare benefit plans and many other plans. The remaining Titles (Titles II–IV) provide key language in the Internal Revenue Code for plans seeking or maintaining qualified status (i.e., preferential tax treatment), establish the Pension Benefit Guaranty Corporation and plan termination insurance, and institute other miscellaneous provisions.

ERISA has been amended numerous times, but particularly by the Multiemployer Pension Amendments Act of 1980 (MPPAA), which brought multiemployer plans (in which unions play a significant role) into the plan termination provisions of ERISA. Another important amending Act was the Retirement Equity Act of 1984 (REAct), which attempted to respond to problematic issues for women. In particular, REAct lowered the minimum age for plan participation, weakened the effects of breaks-in-service, particularly due to maternity or paternity leave, mandated spousal rights in pension plans, and provided for enforcement of qualified domestic relations orders against pension distributions. Other amendments have included the CONSOLIDATED OMNIBUS BUDGET RECONCILIATION ACT OF 1985 (COBRA), the TAX REFORM ACT OF 1986 (TRAC), and, most recently, the Retirement Protection Act of 1994.

ERISA's provisions often must be read to overlap with other areas of federal law, particularly antidiscrimination law. In particular, age, sex, and disability antidiscrimination laws often provide claims that overlap with ERISA issues. In recent years, for example, early retirement incentives have produced litigation under the AGE DISCRIMINATION IN EMPLOYMENT ACT OF 1967. Similarly, differential levels of pension contributions (*City of Los Angeles Department of Water and Power* v. *Manhart*, 1978) or levels of pension benefits (*Arizona Governing Committee* v. *Norris*, 1983) for men and women have successfully been challenged under Title VII of the CIVIL RIGHTS ACT OF 1964. Increasingly, an employer's right to amend healthcare plans has been challenged under both ERISA and the AMERICANS WITH DISABILITIES ACT OF 1990, particularly when ceilings for specific illnesses, such as AIDS, are involved.

One major difficulty under ERISA involves federal preemption of state law. Because Congress included welfare benefit plans within the scope of ERISA, a plaintiff's sole claim for benefit-related problems with an employer may lie under ERISA, and not under state law. The scope of preemption is broad: state subrogation laws, prevailing wage laws, contract law, and wrongful discharge laws have all been found to be preempted when they relate to ERISA-covered plans.

Bibliography

Langbein, J. H. and Wolk, B. A. (1995). *Pension and Employees Benefit Law*, 2nd edn. Westbury, NY: Foundation Press.

employee stock ownership plans

Katherine J. Klein

Employee stock ownership plans (ESOPs) are benefit plans through which employees acquire company stock (*see* BENEFITS). An ESOP company annually donates stock, or cash to buy stock, to an ESOP trust. Shares in the trust are allocated to the accounts of individual employees on the basis of salary or a formula designed to proportionately reflect important differences in the workforce. Companies establish ESOPs to offer employees a new benefit, to buy the shares of an existing owner, to borrow money to acquire new capital, and, occasionally, to finance an employee buyout of a company or to offset wage concessions. Research suggests that the more money employees earn through an ESOP and the more participative the company's management practices, the greater employee satisfaction with the ESOP and employee commitment to the organization (Klein, 1987). When combined with participative management practices, ESOPs may lead to improvements in organizational performance (General Accounting Office, 1987; Rosen, 1995).

Bibliography

General Accounting Office (1987). *Employee Stock Ownership Plans: Little Evidence of Effects on Corporate Performance (GAO Report, GAO/PEMD-88-1)*. Washington, DC: General Accounting Office.

Klein, K. J. (1987). Employee stock ownership and employee attitudes: A test of three models. *Journal of Applied Psychology Monograph*, 72, 319–32.

Rosen, C. (1995). *Employee Ownership and Corporate Performance*. Oakland, CA: National Center for Employee Ownership.

employee subcontracting

Stanley Nollen

Employee subcontracting in the human resource management (HRM) context is the outsourcing of business functions from separate suppliers, analogous to the purchase by a manufacturer of components from an outside supplier for final assembly. HRM services can be subcontracted to leased employees (*see* EMPLOYEE LEASING). Other support functions that are not critical to the organization's mission can be subcontracted to other firms to reduce the organization's regular employment levels and provide workforce flexibility. Some of the most common support services that are outsourced include: redeployment, BENEFITS ADMINISTRATION, recruitment, payroll administration, installation and maintenance of human resource information systems, relocation services, EMPLOYEE ASSISTANCE PROGRAMS, WELLNESS programs, and management development programs.

employee turnover

Thomas W. Lee

Employee turnover labels the termination of an individual's formal membership in an organization. Among scholars and managers of human resource management (HRM), the most common meaning for turnover refers to the employee's initiation of leaving the organization; such voluntary turnover implies an employee's volitional quitting. A second meaning for turnover, though slightly less common, refers to the firm's initiation of the employee's leaving the organization. Such involuntary turnover implies the employee's nonvolitional termination. Other terms for involuntary turnover include firing, layoff, DOWNSIZING, and rightsizing (*see* EMPLOYMENT-AT-WILL; STRATEGIC OUTSOURCING; STRATEGIC STAFFING).

VOLUNTARY EMPLOYEE TURNOVER

Knowledge about voluntary turnover is paradigmatically based. That is, research has been theory-driven, empirical results are cumulative, and available information continues to evolve systematically. Currently distinguishable traditional and alternative approaches to understanding voluntary turnover exist.

Traditional research. Traditionally, voluntary turnover has been most often characterized as an intentionally rational psychological process (Simon, 1945). Employees are seen as estimating and comparing the relative desirability and ease of quitting (March and Simon, 1958). If judged desirable and easy, voluntary turnover occurs; if judged less desirable or harder to quit, voluntary turnover does not occur. Mobley (1977) provided substantial clarity to this mental process by specifying the sequential stages that link job dissatisfaction (interpreted as the perceived desirability of quitting), identification and evaluation of work alternatives (interpreted as the perceived ease of quitting), decision to quit (or stay), and the act of quitting. A substantial body of empirical research has accumulated and generally corroborates the Mobley model (Hom and Griffeth, 1995). In an exemplar of normal science (Kuhn, 1970), a growing body of empirical evidence has also sought to improve the specification of the content and ordering of Mobley's stages. In particular, Hom and Griffeth (1995) summarized and integrated the existing scholarly knowledge into a coherent model of voluntary turnover that follows the long tradition of intended rationality.

Unfolding processes. Traditional turnover theory suggests that quitting results from a linear sequence of: (1) job dissatisfaction; (2) search for job alternatives before leaving; and (3) comparisons between job alternatives based on an intendedly rational analysis (e.g., maximization of subjected expected utilities). In a deliberate break from the tradition of intended rationality, Lee and Mitchell (1994) asserted that: (1) factors other than affect can initiate the turnover process; (2) employees may or may not compare the current job with alternatives; and (3) a compatibility judgment (Beach, 1990) is often applied instead of intended rationality. Two particular characteristics are seen as distinguishing their views of the leaving process from more traditional models. First, "a shock to the system" is defined as a jarring event that initiates the psychological processes involved in quitting a job. Second, the amount of mental deliberations that precede quitting varies from a quick "fit" decision that is unencumbered by multiple attributes to a highly rational, expected utilities comparison of alternatives. Integrating their assertions, Lee and Mitchell proposed that turnover can be depicted via four decision paths that are prototypical, dynamic, and nonlinear. Lee et al. (1996) reported empirical results that largely corroborate the Lee and Mitchell model.

Similarity. In another shift from traditional research, scholars have documented an effect of group similarity on voluntary turnover. Derived from research on organizational demography, O'Reilly, Caldwell, and Barnett (1989) reported that heterogeneity in the tenure of group members led to lower social integration within the group, which, in turn, was negatively related to voluntary turnover. Derived from research on environmental psychology and organizational demography, Jackson et al. (1991) found that group heterogeneity (based on age, tenure, educational level, curriculum, alma mater, military service, and career experiences) predicted voluntary turnover.

Consequences. Voluntary turnover is often assumed to be dysfunctional for the firm; yet it is also recognized that some voluntary turnover is likely to be functional for the company. Thus, managers have been advised to manage the leaving process instead of seeking only to minimize it. Researchers have distinguished between functional and dysfunctional quitting for the company (Dalton, Tudor, and Krackhardt, 1982) and between avoidable versus unavoidable leaving for the company (Abelson, 1987). Both aspects of voluntary turnover should be carefully considered by scholars and managers. For example, functional but avoidable quitting implies that the leaver is less valuable to the organization and that such quitting might be encouraged by a manager. Dysfunctional and avoidable quitting implies that the leaver is more valuable to the organization and that such quitting might be discouraged by a manager. Functional or dysfunctional but unavoidable quitting suggests that managers might focus on minimizing disruptions to stayers. Finally, Hom and Griffeth (1995) identified the following actions that might help managers to deal with voluntary turnover: (1) provide REALISTIC JOB PREVIEWS; (2) enrich jobs; (3) alter workspace characteristics; (4) target socialization practices and leader–member exchanges; and (5) include tenure as a criterion for PERSONNEL SELECTION.

INVOLUNTARY EMPLOYEE TURNOVER

In comparison to knowledge about voluntary turnover, knowledge about involuntary turnover is more pre-paradigmatic. That is, research has been more exploratory in nature, empirical results are less cumulative, and available information is more tentative. Currently, no distinguishable or traditional approach to understanding involuntary turnover exists.

Processes and techniques. The available information on the processes and techniques of terminating employees relies heavily on extrapolations from general theories in the organizational sciences. Collarelli and Beehr (1993), for instance, identified five key processes for firings and layoffs, and they suggested specific techniques to enhance the "selection out." The first process involves communication, i.e., warnings and due process that precede firings and advanced notification and frequent information that precede layoffs (see GRIEVANCE PROCEDURE; NONUNION EMPLOYEE GRIEVANCE PROCEDURES). The second process concerns participation, which precedes both firings and layoffs. The third process is control, which suggests that severance pay and some financial options be offered to the terminated persons. The fourth process involves planning, to permit a degree of "orderliness" to precede firings and to permit sufficient time to plan prior to layoffs. The final process addresses organizational support, which might include OUTPLACEMENT assistance for former employees.

Coping with layoffs by former employees. The available information on coping with layoffs derives from preliminary conceptual structures and exploratory empirical research. Leana and Feldman (1992), for example, proposed a four-part conceptual structure to understand layoffs. First, the larger-context factors were identified as characteristics of the JOB LOSS, unemployment rates, and individuals' attachment to the job. Second, reactions to layoffs were seen as including cognitive appraisals, emotions, and physiological changes. Third, two coping strategies were characterized as problem-focused (e.g., JOB SEARCH) or symptom-focused (e.g., seeking social support). Fourth, the primary outcomes were reemployment and psychological adjustment. From two separate samples, Leana and Feldman reported empirical evidence that generally corroborated their model.

Coping with layoffs by the survivors. The available information on layoff survivors began with a preliminary conceptual structure that prompted a subsequent and programmatic body of empirical research. In turn, a stronger, albeit general, conceptual model was developed to guide future empirical efforts. Brockner and his associates (summarized by Brockner, 1988) began with the preliminary ideas that layoffs prompted certain psychological states among employees who are not terminated (e.g., insecurity, inequity, anger, relief). In turn, these mental states should affect organizational meaningful outcomes (e.g., performance, motivation, satisfaction, commitment). Moreover, these effects were likely to be moderated by numerous factors (e.g., nature of the work, individual differences, formal and informal organizational structures, environment). Via seven empirical studies, these basic ideas were tested, and the results were accumulated to suggest a stronger conceptual model for understanding the effects of layoffs on survivors. The subsequent conceptual model consists of three parts. First, the effects of layoffs can occur before (e.g., anticipated notifications), during (e.g., official notifications), or after the actual act of termination. Second, the intervening variables should be expanded beyond psychological states to include group processes and organizational restructuring as well. Third, many of the predicted outcomes and moderating effects were empirically validated.

Bibliography

Abelson, M. (1987). Examination of avoidable and unavoidable turnover. *Journal of Applied Psychology*, 71, 382–6.

Beach, L. R. (1990). *Image Theory: Decision Making in Personal and Organizational Contexts*. New York: John Wiley.

Brockner, J. (1988). The effects of work layoff on survivors: Research, theory, and practice. *Research in Organizational Behavior*, 10, 213–56.

Collarelli, S. M. and Beehr, T. A. (1993). Selection out: Firings, layoffs, and retirement. In N. Schmitt, W. Borman, et al. (eds.), *Personnel Selection in Organizations*. San Francisco: Jossey-Bass.

Dalton, D., Tudor, W., and Krackhardt, D. (1982). Turnover overstated: The functional taxonomy. *Academy of Management Review*, 7, 117–23.

Hom, P. W. and Griffeth, R. W. (1995). *Employee Turnover*. Cincinnati, OH: South-Western Publishing.

Jackson, S. E., Brett, J. F., Sessa, V. I., Cooper, D. M., Julin, J. A., and Peyronnin, K. (1991). Some differences make a difference: Individual dissimilarity and group heterogeneity as correlates of recruitment, promotions, and turnover. *Journal of Applied Psychology*, 76, 675–89.

Kuhn, T. S. (1970). *The Structure of Scientific Revolutions*, 2nd edn. Chicago: University of Chicago Press.

Leana, C. R. and Feldman, D. C. (1992). *Coping with Job Loss*. New York: Lexington Books.

Lee, T. W. and Mitchell, T. R. (1994). An alternative approach: The unfolding model of voluntary employee turnover. *Academy of Management Review*, 19, 51–89.

Lee, T. W., Mitchell, T. R., Wise, L., and Fireman, S. (1996). An examination of the unfolding model of voluntary employee turnover. *Academy of Management Journal*, 39, 5–36.

March, J. G. and Simon, H. A. (1958). *Organizations*. New York: John Wiley.

Mobley, W. H. (1977). Intermediate linkages in the relationship between job satisfaction and employee turnover. *Journal of Applied Psychology*, 62, 237–40.

O'Reilly, C. A., Caldwell, D. F., and Barnett, W. P. (1989). Work group demography, social integration, and turnover. *Administrative Science Quarterly*, 34, 21–37.

Simon, H. A. (1945). *Administration Behavior*. New York: Free Press.

employment-at-will

Leonard Bierman

Employment is deemed to be at-will on the part of both the employer and the employee. An employee can quit his or her job at any time for any reason, while an employer can fire an employee at any time for any reason. Parties seeking a different type of arrangement are free to write contracts stating different terms.

The concept of at-will employment came under heavy attack in academic circles in the 1970s (Summers, 1976). The concept was viewed as being inequitable from the point of view of employees who purportedly lack the bargaining power to obtain written employment contracts from employers, and as being out of step with the broader protections against unjust dismissal provided to workers in other industrialized countries. In the 1980s various state courts began creating judicial exceptions to the at-will doctrine (*Toussaint* v. *Blue Cross and Blue Shield of Michigan*, 408 Mich. 579, 292 N.W. 2d 880, 1980). Various proposals for state legislation dealing with this issue have been advanced, but to date the only legislation enacted in the US has been the state of Montana's Wrongful Discharge from Employment Act (Bierman and Youngblood, 1992).

Bibliography

Bierman, L. and Youngblood, S. A. (1992). Interpreting Montana's pathbreaking Wrongful Discharge from Employment Act: A preliminary analysis. *Montana Law Review*, **53**, 53–74.

Summers, C. W. (1976). Individual protection against unjust dismissal: Time for a statute. *Virginia Law Review*, **62**, 481–532.

employment interview

Robert L. Dipboye

The employment interview is defined as a dialogue initiated by one or more persons to gather and evaluate information on the qualifications of a job applicant (Dipboye, 1992). With the possible exception of REFERENCE CHECKS and application blanks, this is the most frequently used technique of PERSONNEL SELECTION. Even when other selection procedures are used, information often influences the final decision only after it has been filtered through interviewer judgments.

STRUCTURED AND UNSTRUCTURED INTERVIEWS

An important basis for distinguishing among types of interviews is the degree to which they are structured. Most interviews tend to be unstructured in that few constraints are placed on how they go about gathering information and evaluating applicants. At the other end of the continuum are the highly structured interviews in which interviewers are required to ask the same questions in the same way of all applicants, with no follow-up questions or other deviations allowed (Campion, Pursell, and Brown, 1988). An example is the situational interview. The questions are usually focused on specific requirements of the job and the answers of all applicants are quantitatively scored relative to a common set of predetermined standards. The "patterned interview" falls somewhere between these two extremes. One example is the Patterned Behavior Description Interview (Janz, Hellervik, and Gilmore, 1986). Similar to the highly structured interview, the patterned interview is focused on specific requirements of the job and the questioning and evaluation of applicants is standardized. However, interviewers in a patterned interview are allowed more discretion in gathering information and can ask follow-up questions.

THE VALIDITY AND RELIABILITY OF INTERVIEWS

Similar to other selection techniques, employment interviews are evaluated on their reliability and VALIDITY. Typically, reliability has been assessed by examining the extent to which interviewers agree in evaluating the same applicants. Validity is usually assessed by examining the relationship of interviewer judgments at the time of application to the applicants' later performance on the job.

Several meta-analyses have provided insight into the features of interviews that can enhance their reliability and validity (Wiesner and Cronshaw, 1988; Marchese and Muchinsky, 1993; Huffcut and Arthur, 1994; McDaniel et al., 1994). The findings suggest that the questions and rating dimensions used in interviews should be based on formal JOB ANALYSIS and interviewers should not have access to applicants' test scores prior to the interview. On the other hand, the findings do not provide strong support for using "board interviews." The most consistent finding across these meta-analyses is that structured interviews are more valid than those that are unstructured. Indeed, the levels of validity that have been found for structured interviews approach the validities that have been found for mental abilities tests, which are considered to be among the best techniques for employee selection. Exactly how much structure is needed is still open for debate. There is some evidence that interviews with high levels of structure are no more valid than more moderately structured interviews (Huffcut and Arthur, 1994). Another issue that remains unresolved is whether the level of prediction achieved with a highly structured interview can exceed the level of prediction achieved with well-constructed objective procedures such as mental abilities tests, biographical application blanks, or WEIGHTED APPLICATION BLANKS. Some structured interviews may measure attributes that can be more cheaply measured with paper-and-pencil measures at no loss of validity (Dipboye, 1989).

Why Structured Interviews are More Reliable and Valid

The research on interview processes suggests that the subjectivity of the typical interview can lead to a variety of interviewer errors. Structuring the interview may improve the validity and reliability of interviewer judgments because it helps to eliminate these errors. One likely source of advantage is that structured interviewing procedures are based on formal job analyses and are consequently more job-related than unstructured procedures. A second potential advantage of the various structured formats is the manner in which they handle ancillary data. Interviewers usually have other sources of information on applicants, such as test scores, biographical data, reference checks, and school transcripts, and their final impressions also can be influenced, to some extent, by these data (Dipboye, 1989). Structured interviews either do not allow interviewers to preview such ancillary information, or provide for a more structured preview of this information than found in the typical unstructured interview. Finally, structured interviews incorporate a variety of procedures in the judgment phase of the process that have been shown in previous research to enhance the accuracy and reliability of judgment. Interviewers are encouraged to delay their evaluation of the applicant until after the session, thus separating information gathering from the final integration and evaluation of information. Also, well-defined rating scales, such as the BEHAVIORALLY ANCHORED RATING SCALES, are often provided. This is in contrast to the use of graphic rating scales that are so often found in unstructured interviews.

In the formation of a final judgment of the applicant's qualifications, structured procedures statistically combine the information gathered on the applicant, usually through simple averaging or summation of ratings. In contrast, the global evaluations formed with unstructured procedures allow interviewers to combine their impressions of applicants using intuitive and idiosyncratic combinations.

The use of interviews is pervasive in the selection of employees. It should be noted, however, that they serve a variety of other functions in addition to selection. The most notable of these alternative functions is RECRUITING. The research suggests, however, that if the objective is selection, then the interview should be focused solely on the assessment of applicants' job qualifications. To fulfill other functions, such as recruitment, separate interview sessions should be arranged that are kept independent from assessment of the applicant. Moreover, the interview should be structured. Although some individual interviewers may be quite effective in assessing applicants even in the context of an unstructured interview, most interviewers fall far short of what is considered to be acceptable levels of validity and reliability when allowed to follow their intuitions.

Bibliography

Campion, M. A., Pursell, E. D., and Brown, B. K. (1988). Structured interviewing: Raising the psychometric properties of the employment interview. *Personnel Psychology*, **41**, 25–42.

Dipboye, R. L. (1989). Threats to the incremental validity of interviewer judgments. In R. W. Eder and G. R. Ferris (eds.), *The Employment Interview: Theory, Research, and Practice*. Newbury Park, CA: Sage.

Dipboye, R. L. (1992). *Selection Interviews: Process Perspectives*. Cincinnati, OH: South-Western Publishing.

Huffcutt, A. I. and Arthur, W., Jr. (1994). Hunter and Hunter (1984) revisited: Interview validity for entry-level jobs. *Journal of Applied Psychology*, **79**, 184–90.

Janz, T., Hellervik, L., and Gilmore, D. (1986). *Behavior Description Interviewing: New, Accurate, Cost-Effective*. Boston: Allyn and Bacon.

McDaniel, M. A., Whetzel, D. L., Schmidt, F. L., and Maurer, S. (1994). The validity of employment interviews: A comprehensive review and meta-analysis. *Journal of Applied Psychology*, **79**, 599–616.

Marchese, M. C. and Muchinsky, P. M. (1993). The validity of the employment interview: A meta-analysis. *International Journal of Selection and Assessment*, **1**, 18–26.

Wiesner, W. H. and Cronshaw, S. R. (1988). The moderating impact of interview format and degree of structure on interview validity. *Journal of Occupational Psychology*, **61**, 275–90.

environmental scanning

Randall S. Schuler

Change and the constant need for adaptation, renewal, and updating is more prevalent than ever (Schuler, Jackson, and Storey, 2001). While retaining flexibility and a willingness to adapt are critical in successfully dealing with change, it is also important to be able to anticipate change. Anticipating change enables an organization to set in motion the processes to change the procedures and the practices necessary to address the changes. Correct anticipation enables an organization to bring the necessary procedures and practices online just at the time the changes are having their impact (Schrenk, 1989; Schuler, 1989; Storey, 2001).

To insure that correct practices and procedures are online for effective human resource management (HRM), human resource managers and planners are scanning the events occurring and expected to occur in demographics, international affairs, technology, and organization and economics. Changes in these areas have major implications for the practice of HRM.

Because meeting these changes is more important than ever, organizations need to insure that they have the capability to do so. A major way to attain this capability is through environmental scanning. Environmental scanning is a process of systematic surveillance and interpretation designed to identify events, elements, and conditions of the environment that have potential relevance for and impact on an organization (Coates, 1986; Jackson and Schuler, 2003).

THE CONTEXT OF ENVIRONMENTAL SCANNING

The main context of environmental scanning lies in the business environment, which is increasingly global and fast moving. Fundamental changes are occurring and creating new business challenges and opportunities. A business, or a human resource function, that lacks sensitivity to these changes is likely to suddenly discover that it faces serious difficulties (Schrenk, 1989; Storey, 2001).

A second context of environmental scanning is an organization's business planning process and the business strategies that emerge from this process. To succeed, an environmental scanning activity must be consistent with both the method and timing of the relevant business planning activity. In addition, business strategies determine which trends and implications are of concern to an organization. For example, a growing software company might be greatly troubled by an anticipated shortage of programmers, while a similar company that is phasing out of business would not care about such a development. In this way, environmental scanning is closely linked with STRATEGIC HUMAN RESOURCE PLANNING (Storey, 2001; Jackson and Schuler, 2003).

COMPONENTS OF ENVIRONMENTAL SCANNING

Environmental scanning comprises several components, including forecasting future conditions, selecting forecasting techniques, identifying and prioritizing major issues that impact HRM, developing plans that anticipate those issues, and then preparing the organization for successfully dealing with them. Companies regularly monitor the major aspects of the environment for their relevance to and implications for HRM (Jackson and Schuler, 1995). These aspects include workforce demographics, international conditions, economic and organizational trends, and technological trends and developments. While there are many other aspects of the environment, these have major implications for HRM and organizations. Reference to the external environment includes characteristics of the organization itself. While this may not seem to be the external environment to the organization, it is a very important external environment to HRM (Coates, 1987; Jackson and Schuler, 1995, 2003). In description and discussion of these aspects of the external environment, the thrusts are to (1) reveal the current and future (predicted) conditions and characteristics of each component, and (2) suggest some implications of this information for HRM and organizations.

STEPS IN ENVIRONMENTAL SCANNING

1 The first step in an environmental scanning process is to decide which topic areas to

select for analysis. Topic areas are broad categories of trends, such as demographics or economics, that are largely defined by conventional technical disciplines. This step facilitates data gathering, analysis, and reporting (Schrenk, 1989; Jackson and Schuler, 2003).

2 The second step is to gather data. There are an enormous number and variety of possible data sources. The primary problem at this step is deciding what information to use and what to ignore or discard.

3 The third step is to define trends from the data that have been gathered. Trend definition abstracts and simplifies the data. It facilitates further analysis and communication, but the data invariably lose detail. Thus, it can conceal as well as reveal.

4 Once good data have been obtained and trends established, significant implications or likely consequences must be defined. This fourth step is where experience, creativity, and multiple views can all play a role. While some trends may have general implications and consequences, the real key is to specify the important implications for the organization involved. Implications for a particular organization will vary as a function of geographic location, business conditions, strategy, workforce characteristics, and a host of other factors.

5 Once significant implications have been defined, the fifth step is to prioritize them. It often is easy to create long lists of possible consequences, but unless such lists are pruned, they will bury the process in excessive detail. Eliminating relatively unimportant implications basically is a matter of judgment.

6 The sixth step in environmental scanning is to define issues. An issue may arise from a single implication or a combination of them. Here again, judgment is a key ingredient. The question at this point is, "How does one select the most important issues and develop issue statements?" This is a critical step, since it forms the foundation for much of what occurs in strategic HR planning (Jackson and Schuler, 1995).

Human resource environmental scanning has already demonstrated that environmental scans are both feasible and practical. A great deal of valuable information is available, along with effective ways of evaluating it to identify significant trends and human resource implications. Properly used, environmental scans can add significant value to STRATEGIC HUMAN RESOURCE PLANNING PROCESSES. The real challenge at this point is to make environmental scanning accepted and effective within the realities of a specific organization and its planning processes.

Bibliography

Coates, J. F. (1986). *Issues Management*. Mt. Airy, MD: Lomond.

Coates, J. F. (1987). An environmental scan: Projecting future human resource trends. *Human Resource Planning*, 10, 219–89.

Jackson, S. E. and Schuler, R. S. (1995). Understanding human resource management in the context of organizations and their environments. *Annual Review of Psychology*, 46, 237–64.

Jackson, S. E. and Schuler, R. S. (2003). *Managing Human Resources through Strategic Partnerships*. Cincinnati, OH: South-Western Publishing.

Schrenk, L. P. (1989). Environmental scanning. In L. Dyer (ed.), *Human Resource Management Evolves Roles and Responsibilities*. Washington, DC: ASPA/BNA.

Schuler, R. S. (1989). Scanning the environment: Planning for human resource management and organizational change. *Human Resources Planning*, 12, 258–76.

Schuler, R. S., Jackson, S. E., and Storey, J. (2001). HRM and its link with strategic management. In J. Storey (ed.), *Human Resource Management: A Critical Text*, 2nd edn. London: ITL.

Storey, J. (ed.) (2001). *Human Resource Management: A Critical Text*, 2nd edn. London: ITL.

Equal Employment Opportunity Commission

Leonard Bierman

The Equal Employment Opportunity Commission (EEOC) is the federal agency in charge of administering Title VII of the CIVIL RIGHTS ACT, the EQUAL PAY ACT, the PREGNANCY DISCRIMINATION ACT, the AGE DISCRIMIN-

ATION IN EMPLOYMENT ACT, and the AMERICANS WITH DISABILITIES ACT. The major activity of the agency is to process charges of DISCRIMINATION related to these laws, with the resolution of said charges via conciliation and/or legal action. The agency, run by five presidentially appointed commissioners, processes over 90,000 discrimination charges per year.

Equal Pay Act of 1963

Charles H. Fay

An amendment to the FAIR LABOR STANDARDS ACT OF 1938, the Equal Pay Act requires employers to give women equal pay to men performing work of equal (not similar) skill, effort, responsibility, and working conditions. Pay may differ when based on seniority, merit, performance, or any other factor not based on sex. Pay may not be reduced to bring an establishment into compliance. The Equal Pay Act does not provide any assistance to proponents of COMPARABLE WORTH, since it applies only when the jobs are substantially equal.

Bibliography

Dixon, R. B. (2002). *Federal Wage and Hour Laws*, 2nd edn. Washington, DC: SHRM Foundation.
Shilling, D. (2001). *Human Resources and the Law: The Complete Guide with Supplement*. Englewood Cliffs, NJ: Prentice-Hall.
Steingold, F. S. (2003). *The Employer's Legal Handbook*, 5th edn. Berkeley, CA: Nolo Press.

European Union

Susan Cartwright

The European Union (EU) was formally established in November 1993 as an organization of European countries dedicated to increasing economic integration and strengthening cooperation among its members. With its headquarters in Brussels, Belgium, the EU evolved from the formation of the European Community (EC) in 1967. At the time of its formation the EU had 12 member states, Belgium, Denmark, France, Germany, Greece, Ireland, Italy, Luxembourg, The Netherlands, Portugal, Spain, and the UK. In 1995, Austria, Finland, and Sweden joined the EU. More recently, membership has expanded by the admission of Cyprus, the Czech Republic, Estonia, Hungary, Latvia, Lithuania, Malta, Poland, Slovenia, and Slovakia in 2004.

The EU has a number of objectives. Its main goal is to promote and expand cooperation among member states in economics and trade, social issues, foreign policy, security and defense, and judicial matters. Another major goal has been to implement economic and monetary union (EMU), which established a single currency for EU members.

While the EU is primarily concerned with economic harmonization, it has also influenced social and labor relations. The Community Charter of the Fundamental Social Rights of Workers (the Social Charter) was signed by all member states with the exception of the UK in 1989. Although the Charter has no legal force, it sets out a range of basic common employment rights. These include the right of free movement of labor within the EU, the right to join a trade union, the regulation of working time, equal treatment and equal opportunities between men and women, the improvement of health and safety at work, and the provision of adequate social security protection and access for people with disabilities. In 1994, the European Works Council Directive was approved by the Council of Ministers. It seeks to insure that employees are informed of and consulted about the organizations in which they work.

The EU has been very successful in developing a culture of collaboration. However, there is an underlying conflict between supranationalism and intergovernmentalism. Despite broad acceptance of the supranational principle, national governments have been reluctant to cede control over all policy areas to EU institutions, particularly in the case of the UK.

Bibliography

Stirling, J. and Fitzgerald, I. (2001). European works councils: Representing workers on the periphery. *Employee Relations*, 23 (1), 13–25.

executive compensation

Brian K. Boyd

Because senior managers are responsible for creating and implementing the firm's strategy, most companies recognize the need to develop special pay packages for these individuals. Thus, executive compensation addresses the REWARD SYSTEMS used for chief executive officers (CEOs) and members of the top management team (e.g., vice presidents and other officers of the firm). Executive compensation is significant because of its visibility and symbolism, and its ramifications for pay systems at lower levels of the organization.

Executive salaries have shown limited correlation with firm size or performance, have grown at a much faster rate than the salaries for production workers or middle managers, and are substantially higher in the US than overseas. Since 1992, numerous groups have expressed concern with executive pay, including politicians, the Securities and Exchange Commission (SEC), institutional investors, boards of directors, and individual shareholder groups (Boyd, 1994). Still, despite such criticism, a properly designed executive compensation system can help a firm to significantly boost its effectiveness. Key elements to the understanding of executive compensation include its components and implications for design of reward systems.

COMPONENTS

The elements of an executive's pay package include base salary, BONUSES, long-term COMPENSATION, and BENEFITS. Many chief executives also have GOLDEN PARACHUTES, which are severance agreements triggered by a change in firm ownership or control. Base salary is considered a fixed form of compensation, and accounts for one-half to two-thirds of total cash compensation (Gomez-Mejia and Balkin, 1992; Boyd, 1995). Because this is a base, annual salary is generally of little motivational value and difficult to reduce in the face of poor CEO performance or weak economic conditions. Executive pay surveys (Conference Board, 1994; *Wall Street Journal*, 1995) indicate that base salary varies widely both across and within industries.

The sum of annual salary and bonus is called total cash compensation. Bonuses are short-term awards, and are used by a vast majority of firms in compensating key executives (Conference Board, 1994). Experts recommend that both objective (e.g., stock price, return on investment, or market share) and subjective (e.g., the quality of CEO strategic decision-making, as evaluated by the board of directors) criteria be developed for bonus awards. Because bonuses are a form of contingent compensation, they are a source of personal risk. The uncertainty associated with this risk can be a powerful motivational tool, and pay packages which emphasize bonus pay have been linked with higher levels of firm performance. However, excessive emphasis on bonus pay can be ineffective or encourage inappropriate behaviors. Use of either bonus pay or long-term compensation can be considered forms of PAY FOR PERFORMANCE.

The third element of executive pay is long-term compensation. One danger of bonus pay is that it may encourage executives to sacrifice long-term strategic goals in exchange for short-term profit gains. Long-term compensation plans help to balance the emphasis on long- and short-term goals, and can also help to align the interests of senior managers with those of shareholders. Long-term compensation plans are used by a minority of firms, but are gradually gaining in popularity (Conference Board, 1994). Awards for long-term compensation are generally some combination of company stock (in the form of stock options) and cash. The present value of such compensation is complex to calculate, and option losses do not translate to a real loss for executives. So there is still debate about the motivational value of these awards. Additionally, there are many issues associated with the effective administration of long-term compensation programs.

The last element of executive pay is benefits. While some firms offer identical benefits to all employees, most companies provide far more extensive benefits for senior executives. Aside from the ubiquitous company car, common executive perks include financial and tax planning, low-interest loans, and membership in country clubs, health clubs, and other social organizations.

Design Implications

The growing emphasis on STRATEGIC HUMAN RESOURCE MANAGEMENT has prompted many firms to reevaluate their executive pay practices. Increasingly, these firms recognize that the characteristics of an effective executive compensation system will differ substantially across industries, and may even differ for two firms competing in the same industry. Ideally, there will be a strong link between the firm's strategy, key goals, relevant context, and the composition of the executive pay package. To develop a truly strategic system, Hambrick and Snow (1989) recommended that firms begin with a thorough analysis of their situation, including their strategy, pay at competing firms, job mobility of key staff, and so forth. This information should then guide the following steps:

1 selecting the type and amount of incentives (e.g., base versus bonus pay, cash versus stock);
2 setting criteria for receiving incentives (e.g., subjective versus objective criteria, short-term versus long-term goals, difficulty of goals); and
3 administering incentives (e.g., degree of customization for different staff or divisions, levels of visibility and stability of pay packages).

Bibliography

Boyd, B. K. (1994). Board control and CEO compensation. *Strategic Management Journal*, 15, 335–44.
Boyd, B. K. (1995). Board control, compensation mix, and firm performance. Paper presented at the Academy of Management Annual Conference, Vancouver.
Conference Board (1994). *Top Executive Compensation*. New York: Conference Board.
Gomez-Mejia, L. R. (1994). Executive compensation: A reassessment and a future research agenda. *Research in Personnel and Human Resources Management*, 12, 161–222.
Gomez-Mejia, L. M. and Balkin, D. B. (1992). *Compensation, Organizational Strategy, and Firm Performance*. Cincinnati, OH: South-Western Publishing.
Hambrick, D. C. and Snow, C. C. (1989). Strategic reward systems. In C. C. Snow (ed.), *Strategy, Organization Design, and Human Resource Management*. Greenwich, CT: JAI Press.
Wall Street Journal (1995). Special section on executive pay. *Wall Street Journal*, April 12, R1–R16.

executive orders

Ramona L. Paetzold

A variety of executive orders have been issued in the past 60 years to help to eliminate employment DISCRIMINATION by the federal government and by private employers who have contracts with the federal government. In general, executive orders are orders issued by the president having the same force or effect as a statute or other law. A few of the pertinent executive orders are described below.

Order 10925

This executive order, issued by President Kennedy in 1961, required federal contractors to take AFFIRMATIVE ACTION to insure that applicants were employed, and employees treated, without regard to race, creed, color, or national origin. This was the first executive order to contain an affirmative action provision as part of its nondiscrimination prohibitions.

Order 10988

This executive order, issued in 1962, provided COLLECTIVE BARGAINING rights for federal employees.

Order 11141

This order, issued by President Johnson in 1964, prohibited federal contractors and their subcontractors from discriminating on the basis of age. This executive order was the first to extend nondiscrimination to federally assisted construction contracts. The overlap of the AGE DISCRIMINATION IN EMPLOYMENT ACT OF 1967 with this order has attenuated its effect.

Order 11246

This executive order, issued in 1965, provided the basis for the federal government contract compliance program. It required compulsory language to be included in nonexempt federal contracts and in secondary contracts resulting from them (e.g., subcontracts), indicating that contractors did not discriminate on the basis of race, color, religion, or national origin. Additionally, the language provided notification that the contractors would take affirmative action to insure that employees would be hired and treated without regard to their race, color, religion, or national origin. Much of the language of this order was taken from earlier executive orders. The order authorized individual federal agencies to impose sanctions and penalties under the order, which strengthened the enforcement of the order relative to earlier orders.

ORDER 11375

This 1967 amendment to executive order 11246 added prohibitions against discrimination on the basis of sex.

ORDER 11478

This order, issued in 1969 by President Nixon to amend order 11246, stated a federal policy of prohibiting employment discrimination on the basis of race, color, religion, sex, national origin, handicap, or age in each of the executive departments and agencies (and in contractors holding at least $10,000 worth of federal contracts). It established "affirmative program(s) of equal employment opportunity" in all such departments and agencies. It also authorized the EQUAL EMPLOYMENT OPPORTUNITY COMMISSION to issue rules and regulations necessary to implementation of the order. Finally, the order mandated merit as the basis for federal personnel policies.

ORDER 12086

This executive order, issued by President Carter in 1978 as part of the Reorganization Plan, eliminated the enforcement powers of the independent federal agencies and concentrated the enforcement power for executive order 11246 in the Secretary of Labor. The OFFICE OF FEDERAL CONTRACT COMPLIANCE PROGRAMS (OFCCP), under the secretary's direction, has issued an extensive set of regulations to implement the requirements of order 11246. In particular, all contracts and subcontracts exceeding $10,000 must contain an equal opportunity clause (see orders 11246 and 11478). Contractors and subcontractors (nonconstruction) employing 50 or more persons and having a federal contract worth at least $50,000 must also develop a written affirmative action plan. Construction contractors and subcontractors holding federal contracts in excess of $10,000 must engage in affirmative action.

executive search

James A. Breaugh

Executive search refers to the process by which an organization goes about filling senior-level management positions (Lord, 1989). In discussing executive search, writers have generally focused on the use of executive search firms that recruit and screen senior managers employed at other firms. However, this is too narrow a view. Executive positions are frequently filled with candidates from within the organization as well.

THE INTERNAL RECRUITMENT OF EXECUTIVES

Given the advantages of filling job openings internally (*see* RECRUITING SOURCES), organizations often try to fill executive positions from within, before going outside for candidates. Some organizations rely upon SUCCESSION PLANNING for this purpose. Other employers use managerial nominations of candidates when an executive position becomes vacant (Breaugh, 1992). This nomination process involves having executives nominate current employees whom they think have the potential to successfully fill the open position. An organization may then use a formal executive selection process to choose among the final slate of candidates.

THE USE OF EXECUTIVE SEARCH FIRMS

Organizations that decide to go outside to fill an executive position sometimes use such common external recruitment methods as job advertisements and employee referrals. However, they often will utilize an executive search firm, especially if they are recruiting a chief executive officer (Byrne, 1989). Unlike employment agencies, executive search firms do not find jobs for individuals who contact them. Rather, these so-called "headhunters" work for an organization that has a particular executive position to fill.

Typically, an executive search will begin with the search firm getting as much information as it can from its client about the type of individual it wishes to hire, the job opening, and the organization as a whole. The executive search firm can then begin to locate and screen potential executive candidates. In order to locate prospects, a search firm relies on networking (Byrne, 1989). That is, the search firm contacts executives (some of whom it may have previously placed) who may know of viable candidates. These executives may also be asked for the names of other executives who, in turn, may be able to make referrals. Larger executive search firms frequently have computerized databases from previous searches they have conducted which may also provide information on prospective candidates. Conducting an executive search is a time-consuming process that involves confidentiality (both the client and the individuals being contacted may not want their involvement in the search widely known).

Although using an executive search firm minimizes the time an employer needs to spend on recruiting and screening candidates, it is an expensive method for filling a position. Therefore, before hiring a search firm, an organization should do some research on the firms it is considering. Among the questions it might seek answers to are: Does the executive search firm have a good reputation for filling jobs successfully? Does it have a reputation for maintaining confidentiality? Does the firm have sufficient time and resources to carry out the assignment?

Bibliography

Breaugh, J. A. (1992). *Recruitment: Science and Practice*. Boston: PWS-Kent.

Byrne, J. A. (1989). The new headhunters. *Business Week*, February 6, 64–71.

Lord, J. S. (1989). External and internal recruitment. In W. F. Cascio (ed.), *Human Resource Planning, Employment, and Placement*. Washington, DC: Bureau of National Affairs.

executive selection

Lyle F. Schoenfeldt

Executive selection refers to the process whereby individuals are identified for their unique ability to manage (*see* EARLY IDENTIFICATION OF MANAGEMENT TALENT). These managers then progress to an upper-level position to lead, control, and direct the organization or a major component thereof. The key to selecting executives is understanding the challenges facing the organization, and then identifying an individual with the capabilities to be effective in leading the organization to address these challenges.

EXECUTIVE SELECTION AS A STRATEGIC ISSUE

The understanding of challenges facing an organization is a strategic concern, one that has generated a considerable amount of research. Management strategists have been interested in topics such as models of executive tenure (Hambrick and Fukutomi, 1991), executive teams (Keck and Tushman, 1993), and internal versus external executive selection (Cannella and Lubatkin, 1993). The goal of this line of research is to define the job of the executive (or of the top executive team).

HUMAN RESOURCE ASPECTS OF EXECUTIVE SELECTION

As a human resource topic, executive selection is concerned with developing valid selection procedures to screen candidates on the basis of: (1) basic managerial competencies; (2) ideologies, norms, and habits; and (3) special competencies required (Comte and McCanna, 1988). At this senior level, performance measurement is likely to be valuable in providing needed information. The goal would be to scrutinize current and previous performance as indicative of an individual's style and the results of which he or she is capable, and the applicability of this record for the executive position. Mental ability tests and PERSONALITY TESTS are frequently used as part of executive search efforts, although the validity of such procedures varies.

Bibliography

Cannella, A. A. and Lubatkin, M. (1993). Succession as a sociopolitical process: Internal impediments to outsider selection. *Academy of Management Journal*, 36, 763–93.

Comte, T. E. and McCanna, W. F. (1988). Progressive differentiation: Improving the strategic act of CEO selection. *Academy of Management Executive*, 2, 303–10.

Hambrick, D. C. and Fukutomi, G. D. S. (1991). The seasons of a CEO's tenure. *Academy of Management Review*, 16, 719–42.

Keck, S. L. and Tushman, M. L. (1993). Environmental and organizational context and executive team structure. *Academy of Management Journal*, 36, 1314–44.

exit interviews

Robert A. Giacalone

Exit interviewing and surveying (EIS) are used to gather data from separating employees. Organizations use EIS for diagnostic and strategic reasons: identifying reasons for company turnover (*see* EMPLOYEE TURNOVER), training and development needs (*see* TRAINING), and strategic planning goals. Generally, EIS focuses on employee feelings about COMPENSATION and BENEFITS, working conditions, opportunities, workload, and work relationships, although it may focus on a specific problem area such as workplace security. Recent research has shown that the EIS process may be a useful tool in assessing organizational ethics (see Giacalone, Jurkiewicz, and Knouse, 2003). Still, EIS users should be wary of its administrative and methodological shortcomings (Giacalone, 1993; Giacalone et al., 1995).

Bibliography

Giacalone, R. A. (1993). *A Critical Evaluation of the Army Career Transitions Survey: A Suggested Approach for Reformulation*. Research Triangle Park, NC: Battelle.

Giacalone, R. A., Elig, T. W., Ginexi, E. M., and Bright, A. J. (1995). The impact of identification and type of separation on measures of satisfaction and missing data in the exit survey process. *Military Psychology*, 7, 235–52.

Giacalone, R. A., Jurkiewicz, C. L., and Knouse, S. B. (2003). Exit surveys as assessments of organizational ethicality. *Public Personnel Management*, 397–410.

expatriate assignment

Mark E. Mendenhall

An expatriate assignment is a job transfer that takes the employee to a workplace that is outside the country in which he or she is a citizen. There are differences between an expatriate assignment and other job assignments of an international nature. Expatriate assignments are longer in duration than other types of international assignments (e.g., business trips), and require the employee to move his or her entire household to the foreign location. Thus, in an expatriate assignment, the employee's home base of business operations is in the foreign country.

Expatriate assignments offer unique challenges to expatriate employees. Virtually all expatriates run into situations where the home office wants them to do one thing, while local situations dictate that another thing should be done instead. For example, in Japan, local conditions dictate that market-share growth should be the main criterion of a subsidiary's performance, while the home office may force the subsidiary managers into focusing on quarterly profits as the main criterion of organizational performance.

The expatriate assignment requires expatriate managers to face a number of complex issues that their domestic counterparts either do not face, or face with less intensity. Examples of such issues are the integration of large international acquisitions, understanding the meaning of performance and accountability in a globally integrated system of product flows, building and managing a worldwide logistics capability, developing multiple country-specific corporate strategies, managing products and services around the world with differing competitive dynamics in each market, forming and managing collaborative agreements (OEM contracts, licensing, joint ventures), balancing the need for global integration while simultaneously responding to local demands, and managing a MULTICULTURAL WORKFORCE within foreign environments.

Expatriates usually find an expatriate assignment to be one of the biggest challenges of their entire career. Increasingly, firms are investing in cross-cultural training programs to prepare expatriates to operate successfully in their expatriate assignment. Additionally, most companies offer a variety of support systems to employees as part of the expatriate assignment. One of the principal barriers to cross-cultural adjustment is the lack of a way for expatriates – especially nonworking spouses of employees – to become members of a social network. Many firms offer programs of one sort or another that are geared to helping expatriates to develop friendships with other expatriates and host nationals, and to provide support with the day-to-day realities of living in a foreign culture (housing, schooling, transportation, shopping, and so forth).

Expatriate assignments are much more costly than simply hiring local nationals to work in a foreign subsidiary; however, there are advantages to using expatriates over local nationals. Expatriates know how the parent company operates and can pass on this knowledge to local employees. By working overseas they learn how foreign markets operate, and how foreign consumers and clients react to the products or services the company offers. Also, they gain skills in cross-cultural management and develop a global perspective. Expatriate assignments, then, can be a powerful strategic tool in developing global business skills within the senior ranks of a firm's management.

See also *cultural literacy; expatriate human resource issues; expatriate support system; preparation for an international work assignment*

Bibliography

Black, J. S., Gregersen, H. B., and Mendenhall, M. E. (1992). *Global Assignments: Successfully Expatriating and Repatriating International Managers.* San Francisco: Jossey-Bass.

Black, J. S., Mendenhall, M., and Oddou, G. (1991). Toward a comprehensive model of international adjustment: An integration of multiple theoretical perspectives. *Academy of Management Review,* **16,** 291–317.

Mendenhall, M., Punnett, B. J., and Ricks, D. (1995). *Global Management.* Cambridge, MA: Blackwell.

Prahalad, C. K. (1990). Globalization: The intellectual and managerial challenges. *Human Resource Management,* **29,** 27–37.

expatriate human resource issues

Hal B. Gregersen

Strategically designed international assignments can enhance the global competitiveness of firms by increasing coordination and control across units, transferring innovations across geographical boundaries, and developing future executives with global perspectives and local market responsiveness. To obtain these strategic results, firms are increasing the number of managers sent on international assignments as expatriates (Selmer, 1995). Concurrently, human resource scholars have begun to examine various stages of the international assignment cycle, including expatriate selection, TRAINING, PERFORMANCE APPRAISAL, COMPENSATION, and REPATRIATION (Tung, 1988; Adler, 1990; Brewster, 1991; Black, Gregersen, and Mendenhall, 1992; Selmer, 1995).

Selection

Research indicates that firms still select expatriates based on technical criteria, and tend to ignore other important criteria such as cross-cultural competence (Black et al., 1992). While scholars have identified several critical nontechnical criteria for expatriate success (communication, flexibility, and so forth), little empirical evidence exists to corroborate the PREDICTIVE VALIDITY of nontechnical criteria. In addition, firms continue to focus on selecting men instead of women as expatriates in spite of evidence suggesting that female expatriates are at least as competent as male expatriates (Adler, 1990).

Training

Research indicates that well-designed cross-cultural training can facilitate expatriate JOB PERFORMANCE and cultural adjustment after arriving in the host country (Black et al., 1992; Selmer, 1995). Firms can provide cost-effective training at pre-departure or post-arrival intervals for expatriates and their families, yet fewer than one-third of US firms provide any such training (Tung, 1988).

Cross-cultural Adjustment

Adjusting to a new work and nonwork environment is one of the most difficult challenges expatriates and their families encounter. Researchers have identified at least three facets of adjustment: work, interaction with host-country nationals, and general adjustment to the host country. As firms work to facilitate expatriate and family adjustments, evidence indicates that expatriates perform more effectively at work (Black et al., 1992).

Appraisal

Assessing expatriate performance is particularly problematic, since multiple raters in multiple countries must use multiple criteria to evaluate performance accurately. Unfortunately, most firms rely on domestic performance appraisal systems without any modification for international contexts or criteria when evaluating expatriates (Selmer, 1995). Clearly, additional research is needed in this area to assess the generalizability of prior performance appraisal studies to expatriate performance assessment.

Compensation

Since a single international assignment can cost between one and two million dollars, most firms have developed extensive compensation systems to insure that qualified candidates take international assignments, expatriates are not penalized financially during assignments, and overall costs are kept at a minimum. Thus many expatriate compensation consultants provide recommendations on various pay and benefits alternatives. Unfortunately, researchers have paid little attention to expatriate compensation practices and future studies are necessary to evaluate the effectiveness of compensation policies.

Repatriation

Repatriation, or returning home from an international assignment, is generally more difficult than going overseas (Adler, 1990). These challenges arise primarily from expatriates and home office colleagues expecting each other to remain the same during an international assignment. Consequently, most expatriates experience significant culture shock during repatriation. Moreover, upon repatriating, most expatriates fail to receive firm-provided orientation or training or have a formal job assignment. When an assignment is obtained, it is usually a career demotion. While there is a growing literature on expatriation and repatriation adjustment, it is important for future research to assess the adjustment process and the entire international assignment cycle with more systematic longitudinal data from expatriates in a variety of countries.

See also *cultural literacy; expatriate assignment; expatriate support system; international compensation; preparation for an international work assignment*

Bibliography

Adler, N. J. (1990). *International Dimensions of Organizational Behavior*, 2nd edn. Boston: PWS-Kent.
Black, J. S., Gregersen, H. B., and Mendenhall, M. E. (1992). *Global Assignments: Successfully Expatriating and Repatriating International Managers*. San Francisco: Jossey-Bass.
Brewster, C. (1991). *The Management of Expatriates*. London: Kogan Page.
Selmer, J. (ed.) (1995). *Expatriate Management: New Ideas for International Business*. London: Quorum.
Tung, R. (1988). *The New Expatriates: Managing Human Resources Abroad*. New York: Ballinger.

expatriate support system

R. Ivan Blanco

The expatriate support system (ESS) is a set of programs developed by a company to develop and promote multicultural skills among employees who must travel abroad on long-term assignments. The system's effectiveness is measured by its ability to ease an employee's transition from the US (or any other country) to a different country's cultural environment. The system may not eliminate all the pains created by this cultural transition, but it should reduce them to a minimum. The most effective ESS is that which allows employees to become open-minded, to learn how to adapt to a new environment, and even to enjoy the cultural transition as a valuable learning experience. The support system should also address the needs of the employee's spouse and children traveling with him or her.

An ESS includes all or any combination of the following: educational programs to develop employees' multicultural skills; a mentorship or buddy program in the foreign country to help employees during the first weeks abroad; short travel programs to the country of destination prior to the actual assignment to help the employee get acquainted with the country; information supplied to employees about schools, churches, recreational activities, native meals, transportation systems, driver's license, healthcare, and many other aspects of the new country. It must include programs to ease employees' reentry to the US (or home country), to help them cope with the fact that they are now different and that being different is fine. This component should also involve other employees who must interact with a returning colleague. As employees accept the new cultural diversity paradigm and learn how to cope with it, the ESS should be deactivated.

See also *cultural literacy; expatriate assignment; preparation for an international work assignment; repatriation*

expectancy charts

Neal Schmitt

Expectancy charts are a graphical display of the relationship between predictor scores (e.g., ability measures) and JOB PERFORMANCE for a set of employees for whom both performance and predictor measures are available. Both individual and organizational expectancy charts can be constructed. In the construction of an *individual* expectancy chart, the employee group is divided into from five to ten equally sized groups, based on their predictor scores. Within each predictor score range, the proportion of people considered to be high performers is calculated. This percentage is then displayed in a bar graph. When there is a linear and positive relationship between the predictor and performance, the graph should indicate an increasingly larger percentage of high-performing individuals as the predictor score range gets higher.

Organizational expectancy charts display the proportion of successful people hired when one uses a different CUTOFF SCORE on a selection procedure. In this case, the proportion of successful employees is calculated when the selection procedure is not used. Then, the proportion of successful employees is calculated at successively higher cutoff scores. These percentages are then displayed in a bar graph which indicates the performance implications associated with different predictor cutoff scores.

In the construction of expectancy charts, one must be able to define job success in dichotomous terms. It must also be remembered that these charts are based on a particular, finite sample, and that the construction of a similar chart based on data from a different sample may not look the same. Lawshe and Balma (1966) give detailed instructions on the construction of expectancy charts and also provide theoretical expectancy chart values which correct for the sampling problem described above.

Bibliography

Cascio, W. F. (1998). *Applied Psychology in Human Resource Management*. Englewood Cliffs, NJ: Prentice-Hall.

Lawshe, C. H. and Balma, M. J. (1966). *Principles of Personnel Testing*, 2nd edn. New York: McGraw-Hill.

Schneider, B. and Schmitt, N. (1986). *Staffing Organizations*. Prospect Heights, IL: Waveland Press.

external equity/external competitiveness

George F. Dreher

External equity is one of two organizing concepts (along with INTERNAL EQUITY/INTERNAL CONSISTENCY) used to define the structure and form of a traditional job-based pay system. External competitiveness refers to the pay rates of an organization's jobs in relation to its competitors' pay rates. Thus, unlike the concept of internal equity, external equity is concerned with relative pay rates among (not within) organizations (Milkovich and Newman, 1993: 190). The conventional view is that the lower bound of a job-specific pay rate is set by the labor market (this is the point below which it is not possible to attract newcomers to the organization) and the upper bound reflects product market competition. Management sets pay rates within these limits based upon such things as the concern for internal equity, the need to control labor costs, and the organization's ability to pay.

A highly competitive pay rate (a rate that exceeds or leads the market) would be set in an attempt to increase such things as the number and quality of applicants and the likelihood that qualified individuals will accept job offers, and to control voluntary turnover (Williams and Dreher, 1992; see EMPLOYEE TURNOVER). Firms that lag the market rate would, in principle, find it difficult to attract and retain talent but might maintain a labor cost advantage over the competition.

The principle means of establishing external equity is to conduct WAGE AND SALARY SURVEYS to estimate the pay ranges set at competing firms. While the goal is to estimate the market wage for a particular job, the process of collecting relevant data requires considerable judgment, leading some to conclude that the market wage is an illusive concept (Rynes and Milkovich, 1986).

Bibliography

Milkovich, G. T. and Newman, J. M. (1993). *Compensation*. Homewood, IL: Richard D. Irwin.

Rynes, S. L. and Milkovich, G. T. (1986). Wage surveys: Dispelling some myths about the "market wage." *Personnel Psychology*, 39, 71–90.

Williams, M. L. and Dreher, G. F. (1992). Compensation system attributes and applicant pool characteristics. *Academy of Management Journal*, 35, 571–95.

extraterritorial application of employment law

Terry L. Leap

The application of equal employment opportunity (EEO) laws such as Title VII of the CIVIL RIGHTS ACT OF 1964, the AGE DISCRIMINATION IN EMPLOYMENT ACT OF 1967 (ADEA), and the AMERICANS WITH DISABILITIES ACT OF 1990 (ADA) in multinational enterprises (MNEs) has generated a degree of uncertainty. Foreign employers doing business in the US must generally abide by US EEO law (*Sumitomo Shoji America* v. *Avigliano*, 28 FEP Cases 1753, 1982; *MacNamara* v. *Korean Airlines*, 48 FEP Cases 980, 1988). The US Supreme Court ruled in *Boureslan* v. *Aramco*, 55 FEP Cases 449 (1991) that Title VII did not apply to American citizens working abroad for American employers. This ruling was overturned by the CIVIL RIGHTS ACT OF 1991. Section 701 of Title VII now provides language similar to that contained in the ADEA and the ADA. Thus, US citizens working in foreign countries for US companies are protected from various types of employment DISCRIMINATION based on race, sex, religion, national origin, color, age, and disability status. There is an exemption if compliance with Title VII or the ADA would cause the employer to violate the law of a foreign country where the employee is working. Section 702 of Title VII also states that the law "shall not apply to an employer with respect to aliens outside of any State" (Bureau of National Affairs, 1991).

Bibliography

Bureau of National Affairs (1991). *Fair Employment Practices*. Washington, DC: Bureau of National Affairs.

F

face validity

James S. Phillips

Face validity concerns "the extent to which an instrument 'looks like' it measures what it is intended to measure" (Nunnally, 1978: 111). Face validity must be distinguished from CONTENT VALIDITY. Face validity is merely an observation about a test's appearance *after* it has been developed; content-oriented validity is related to the test's construction. Face validity is not considered evidence of the actual validity of a test. It can, however, add a useful dimension to a selection test. Selection tests that "look" valid have a tendency to be viewed more seriously by job applicants and other outside observers (Guion, 1965: 124).

Bibliography

Guion, R. M. (1965). *Personnel Testing.* New York: McGraw-Hill.
Nunnally, J. C. (1978). *Psychometric Theory*, 2nd edn. New York: McGraw-Hill.

factor-comparison job evaluation method

Matthew C. Bloom

Under the factor-comparison method, jobs are evaluated using two standards: a set of compensable factors and the wages for a group of benchmark jobs (Milkovich and Newman, 1996; *see* COMPENSABLE FACTOR). These two standards are combined to form a job comparison scale which is then used to arrange nonbenchmark jobs into the final job hierarchy. The set of benchmark jobs must cover the entire range of each compensable factor. First, each benchmark job is ranked on all the compensable factors, resulting in a matrix which arrays rankings for each benchmark job on each compensable factor. Second, these rankings are translated into dollar amounts by determining how much of the total wage for a benchmark job is associated with each compensable factor. The sum of these dollar values must add up to the total wage for that job. Third, for each compensable factor, two sets of rank orders are created: one arranging the factor's rankings for all benchmark jobs from high to low and another similarly arranging the dollar values. These two rank orders are adjusted until the hierarchy of benchmark jobs is the same for both. (Large discrepancies in rankings usually indicate a benchmark job that should not be used for job evaluation purposes.) This sequential process creates the job comparison scale where the level of each compensable factor has a dollar value assigned to it plus an array of benchmark jobs to serve as anchors. Nonbenchmark jobs can then be slotted into each compensable factor using the benchmark jobs as a standard of comparison. The total wage for each job is simply the sum of its dollar-valued rankings on each compensable factor.

Bibliography

Milkovich, G. T. and Newman, J. M. (1996). *Compensation*, 5th edn. Homewood, IL: Richard D. Irwin.

Fair Labor Standards Act of 1938

Charles H. Fay

The Fair Labor Standards Act (FLSA) contains five major provisions: minimum wage, overtime pay, equal pay (EQUAL PAY ACT OF 1963), record-keeping requirements, and child labor laws. FLSA also is the source of the terms "exempt" and "nonexempt." It is the FLSA from which employees are (or are not) exempt. Typically, but not always, professional, technical, or administrative employees meet the exempt criteria of FSLA. Minimum wage provisions set a floor on wages. Overtime provisions mandate time and one-half pay for all hours worked in excess of 40 hours per week. Record-keeping provisions mandate that employers must collect, store, and report to the Wage and Hour Division of the Department of Labor significant data on all nonexempt employees.

Bibliography

Dixon, R. B. (2002). *Federal Wage and Hour Laws*, 2nd edn. Washington, DC: SHRM Foundation.

Shilling, D. (2001). *Human Resources and the Law: The Complete Guide with Supplement*. Englewood Cliffs, NJ: Prentice-Hall.

Steingold, F. S. (2003). *The Employer's Legal Handbook*, 5th edn. Berkeley, CA: Nolo Press.

Family and Medical Leave Act of 1993

Ramona L. Paetzold

The Family and Medical Leave Act of 1993 is the first federal law mandating that employers provide leaves of absence for childbirth or the care of seriously ill children or other family members. It requires that employers allow eligible workers to take up to 12 weeks of unpaid leave in any 12-month period for qualifying circumstances; only workers who have been employed by the employer for at least 12 months and have at least 1,250 hours of service during that period are eligible for leave under the Act. Employers having fewer than 50 employees are exempt from the Act's coverage.

Qualifying circumstances that trigger the mandated leave include birth or adoption of a child, required care for a child, spouse, or parent having a serious health condition, or the employee's own serious health condition. A "serious health condition" is defined to be a physical or mental condition serious enough to involve inpatient care or continuing treatment by a healthcare provider. Employers are allowed to require medical certification of the need for a leave for the employee's own illness or for the care of the employee's dependant.

Employers may require employees to use accrued paid vacation leave, sick leave, or other leave for any part of the 12-week leave provided by the Act. During the leave the employer must continue to provide healthcare benefits at the same level as if the employee were not on leave. Additionally, the employee must be returned to the same or equivalent position upon returning from leave, without any loss of employment benefits that had accrued prior to the start of the leave.

FASB 106

Ramona L. Paetzold

The Financial Accounting Standards Board (FASB) issued Standard Number 106 in 1990; this standard changed the way that companies account for retiree health benefits. The standard became effective in 1992.

FASB 106 recognizes retiree health benefits as a form of deferred COMPENSATION, which justifies requiring companies to account for them as they are "earned." Instead of being able to use a "pay-as-you-go" approach to expensing retiree BENEFITS, employers are required under FASB 106 to account for these benefits on an accrual basis. They must accrue liabilities for future, potential healthcare expenditures on their financial statements. Additionally, the present value of future retiree health expenditures must be amortized.

As a result of FASB 106, retiree healthcare benefits have been substantially cut through ERISA-governed plan amendments (*see* EMPLOYEE RETIREMENT INCOME SECURITY ACT OF 1974). The standard has had the effect of making retiree healthcare plans appear similar in character to PENSION PLANS, thereby raising (unresolved) issues of vesting and funding for such plans.

Federal Mediation and Conciliation Service

John C. Shearer

The Federal Mediation and Conciliation Service (FMCS) was established by the LABOR MANAGEMENT RELATIONS ACT OF 1947 as an independent agency. It took over all mediation and conciliation functions of the federal government, replacing the former US Conciliation Service, which was in the Department of Labor. The FMCS is headed by a director appointed by the president with Senate approval.

The FMCS is required by statute to offer its services to help to settle labor disputes affecting interstate commerce through the offices of its commissioners located throughout the country. It may act either upon request by one of the parties or on its own initiative.

A party desiring to terminate or modify an existing COLLECTIVE BARGAINING agreement must notify the FMCS of the dispute. When the FMCS has intervened in a dispute, both the union and the employer must participate fully in any meetings called by the service. If MEDIATION or conciliation does not result in a settlement, the service must urge the parties to voluntarily seek other means of settlement, including ARBITRATION. Either party may reject the FMCS suggestion without violating any obligation imposed by the Act. The FMCS also provides arbitration and fact-finding services to parties requesting them. It makes available panels of qualified potential arbitrators or fact-finders for the parties' selection. It publishes annual data on the locations (by states) and nature of the services it has provided. The FMCS also provides and participates in educational programs for the parties and for arbitrators.

Federal Unemployment Tax Act of 1935

Charles H. Fay

This unemployment insurance program, or FUTA, is a mixed federal–state program. Part of the SOCIAL SECURITY ACT OF 1935, FUTA requires employers to pay a 6.2 percent federal tax on the first $7,000 of each covered employee's salary; but they receive a tax credit of up to 5.6 percent, offsetting state unemployment taxes paid. FUTA taxes pay for administration of unemployment insurance and Job Service programs in the states. In times of high unemployment, FUTA taxes also go to pay half the cost of extended unemployment programs. States provide unemployment funds in their state, and determine individual employer state tax rates based on an experience factor, which is a function of the taxes paid in and the benefits claims attributable to an employer.

Bibliography

Beam, B. T. and McFadden, J. J. (2001). *Employee Benefits*, 6th edn. Chicago: Dearborn Financial Publishing, pp. 74–9.

Rejda, G. E. (2001). State unemployment compensation programs. In J. S. Rosenbloom (ed.), *The Handbook of Employee Benefits: Design, Funding and Administration*, 5th edn. New York: McGraw-Hill, pp. 557–71.

final offer arbitration

Peter Feuille

Final offer arbitration (FOA) is a type of INTEREST ARBITRATION used to resolve contract negotiation disputes. In contrast to conventional interest arbitration, where an arbitrator has wide discretion to fashion an award, FOA places severe limits on the arbitrator's decision authority. The arbitrator is required to select the final arbitration offer submitted by the employer or by the union; a compromise outcome is prohibited. In FOA by package, the arbitrator selects one party's entire package of offers on all the disputed issues. In FOA by issue, the arbitrator selects one party's final offer separately on each disputed issue. The underlying rationale for FOA is that its all-or-nothing nature will give each party a strong incentive to submit reasonable offers.

financial assistance plans

Charles H. Fay

Employers offer a number of benefit plans to employees that provide assistance in extraordinary circumstances. Typical programs include dependant care (whether child or elder), family leave programs, legal service plans, relocation assistance, property and liability insurance plans, and educational assistance plans. In most programs, employees pay for at least part of the benefit; the employer acts as a broker and administers the program. Most of these programs are thought to benefit the employer by preventing a covered employee from being preoccupied with family issues. Educational assistance programs serve employee development purposes.

Bibliography

Costello, A. (2001). Dependent care. In J. S. Rosenbloom (ed.), *The Handbook of Employee Benefits: Design, Funding and Administration*, 5th edn. New York: McGraw-Hill, pp. 437–65.
Davidson, C. J. (2001). Educational assistance programs and group legal services plans. In J. S. Rosenbloom (ed.), *The Handbook of Employee Benefits: Design, Funding and Administration*, 5th edn. New York: McGraw-Hill, pp. 467–80.
Mondzelweski, L. (2001). Work/life benefits: An overview. In J. S. Rosenbloom (ed.), *The Handbook of Employee Benefits: Design, Funding and Administration*, 5th edn. New York: McGraw-Hill, pp. 399–421.

Firefighters Local 1784 v. *Stotts*, US Supreme Court (1984)

Leonard Bierman

Sometimes actions taken as part of a BONA FIDE SENIORITY SYSTEM take precedence over voluntary quota systems. In *Firefighters*, the city of Memphis, Tennessee, instituted policies to increase the number of minority firefighters. During a period of layoffs, however, the city implemented a *last hired, first fired* policy that resulted in *adverse impact* for recently hired black firefighters. The Supreme Court held that the seniority-based layoff policy was acceptable. Further, the court ruled that the black firefighters could only claim protection from the policy if they had individually and directly been the object of hiring DISCRIMINATION.

flexible benefit plans

Robert M. McCaffery

Employee benefit programs that offer some degree of choice to employees in selecting types and levels of coverage first appeared in the mid-1970s. Initially employers were motivated to satisfy diverse needs of increasingly heterogeneous workforces. Plan adoptions accelerated in the 1980s as employers realized that the plans were more cost-efficient than traditional BENEFITS. Effectively, employer subsidies can be limited to the costs of basic coverage. Employees can supplement this core by contributing more or, alternatively, choose lower levels and receive cash or credits to apply to other benefits.

Any plan that allows employees to make benefit choices is a "flexible" plan, but only plans that also allow choices between certain benefits and taxable COMPENSATION (e.g., cash) without causing the otherwise nontaxable benefits to become taxable are "cafeteria" plans. Section 125 of the Internal Revenue Code (IRC) specifies benefits that can and cannot be included in cafeteria plans and rules for insuring a tax-favored status.

Currently, most flexible benefit plans are cafeteria plans. At a minimum these plans include: (1) a premium conversion option which allows employees to pay premiums for health benefits on a pre-tax basis; and (2) pre-tax employee contributions to flexible spending accounts (FSAs). Money can be withdrawn throughout the year to pay for healthcare and/or dependant care expenses. Beyond these provisions, many flexible/cafeteria plans include options for employees to choose different levels of coverage for health, disability, and life insurance benefits. Some plans also allow employees to "buy" and "sell" vacation time.

Most large and many medium- and small-sized employers now have some type of flexible program. Continued growth is anticipated.

Bibliography

McCaffery, R. M. (1988). The pioneer plans: A firm foundation for flex. *Topics in Total Compensation*, 2, 225–33.
Nealey, S. N. (1975). Compensation fungibility. *Proceedings of the 28th Annual Meeting of the Industrial Relations Research Association*.

Rosenbloom, J. S. and Hallman, G. V. (1991). *Employee Benefit Planning*, 3rd edn. Englewood Cliffs, NJ: Prentice-Hall.

flexible working hours

Jon L. Pierce and Randall B. Dunham

Flexible working hours represent a work-scheduling arrangement that provides employees with some degree of autonomy (discretion) in the selection of the hours that they will work. While there are a myriad of working-hour arrangements and terms that have been coined to define them, the three basic flexible working-hour variations are:

1 staggered start systems that allow individuals, groups, or organizations to decide when to start their fixed working-hour day;
2 flextime systems that divide the working day into core hours, during which everyone must work, and flex hours, during which time employees can choose either to work or not to work; and
3 variable hour systems that permit employees to contract for a specified amount of time to be worked (e.g., on a daily or weekly basis) without a constraint on when those hours are worked.

Although the theory of flexible working hours has not been well developed, several models predict work-scheduling effects. The QUALITY OF WORK LIFE model suggests that work-scheduling flexibility provides employees with opportunities to meet personal demands, thereby contributing to need fulfillment in both the work and nonwork domains (Ronan, 1981). Interrole conflict is reduced, favorably impacting upon motivation, job attitudes, and behavior (Christensen and Staines, 1990; Kahnweiler and Kahnweiler, 1992). The theory of work adjustment argues that flexible hours have the potential to utilize employees' circadian rhythms more efficiently, permitting a greater alignment between employees' abilities and the requirements of their jobs (Pierce and Newstrom, 1980). Flexible scheduling may encourage employees to increase commitment as an exchange for this benefit (Cohen and Gadon, 1978).

Much of the flextime research is largely anecdotal and impressionistic. While there are some studies that report increases and decreases in performance, the most dominant observation suggests that performance is not detrimentally affected. Flextime can, however, provide for greater flexibility in the use of organizational resources, thereby having a positive effect on PRODUCTIVITY when workers must share those resources.

Most, although not all, employees prefer flexible hours rather than more conventional working-hour arrangements. Flexible hours are commonly associated with increased work and leisure time satisfaction, as well as attitudes toward the schedule and its effect on one's family and social life. The reported impact of flexible work schedules on general satisfaction and organizational commitment has been quite consistent and positive in nature. It has also been observed that flexible schedules lessen interference with one's personal life. There is some evidence that flexible work hours aid in recruiting and retaining employees, as well as reducing short-term leaves and sick-leave usage. Organizations that offer a daily choice on schedule flexibility tend to have reduced tardiness and ABSENTEEISM.

It might be speculated that many of the attitudinal and motivational effects of flexible working hours may stem from "experienced flexibility" potentially afforded by these working-hour arrangements. Reports suggest that there will be increased demands placed upon organizations to provide flexibility and personal work environment control in the individual–organization relationship; some of this flexibility and discretion can be achieved through flexible working hours.

Bibliography

Christensen, K. E. and Staines, G. L. (1990). Flextime: A viable solution to work/family conflict. *Journal of Family Issues*, 11, 455–76.

Cohen, A. R. and Gadon, H. (1978). *Alternative Work Schedules: Integrating Individual and Organizational Needs*. Reading, MA: Addison-Wesley.

Golembiewski, R. T. and Proehl, C. W. (1978). A survey of the empirical literature on flexible workhours:

Character and consequence of a major innovation. *Academy of Management Review*, 3, 837–53.

Hicks, W. and Klimoski, R. J. (1981). The impact of flexitime on employee attitudes. *Academy of Management Journal*, 24, 31–6.

Kahnweiler, W. M. and Kahnweiler, J. R. (1992). The work/family challenge: A key career development issue. *Journal of Career Development*, 18, 251–7.

Kim, J. S. and Campagna, A. F. (1981). Effects of flexitime on employee attendance and performance: A field experiment. *Academy of Management Journal*, 24, 729–41.

Krausz, M. and Hermann, E. (1991). Who is afraid of flexitime: Correlates of personal choice of a flexitime schedule. *Applied Psychology: An International Review*, 40, 315–26.

Martens, M. F. J., Nijhuis, F. J. N., Van Boxtel, M. P. J., and Knottnerus, J. A. (1999). Flexible work schedules and mental and physical health: A study of working population with non-traditional working hours. *Journal of Organizational Behavior*, 20 (1), 35–46.

Pierce, J. L. and Newstrom, J. W. (1980). Toward a conceptual clarification of employee response to flexible working hours: A work adjustment approach. *Journal of Management*, 6, 117–34.

Pierce, J. L. and Newstrom, J. W. (1982). Employee responses to flexible work schedules: An inter-organization, inter-system comparison. *Journal of Management*, 8, 9–25.

Pierce, J. L. and Newstrom, J. W. (1983). The design of flexible work schedules and employees' responses: Relationships and process. *Journal of Occupational Behavior*, 4, 214–62.

Pierce, J. L., Newstrom, J. W., Dunham, R. B., and Barber, A. E. (1989). *Alternative Work Schedules*. Boston: Allyn and Bacon.

Ralston, D. A., Anthony, W. P., and Gustafson, D. J. (1985). Employees may love flextime, but what does it do to the organization's productivity? *Journal of Applied Psychology*, 70, 272–9.

Ronan, S. (1981). *Flexible Working Hours: An Innovation in the Quality of Work Life*. New York: McGraw-Hill.

Schein, V. E., Mauer, E. H., and Novak, J. R. (1977). Impact of flexible working hours on productivity. *Journal of Applied Psychology*, 62, 463–5.

flexible workplace/telecommuting

Randall B. Dunham and Jon L. Pierce

Flexplace involves working at home or other locations away from and without computer links to the traditional office. Telecommuting involves work conducted while away from the traditional office but electronically linked to it. Although many of the advantages and disadvantages discussed in this entry apply to both activities, the trend is to bring the distant worker to the workplace electronically.

As technology advances, working at home becomes more feasible, more affordable, and more commonplace. Today's telecommuters embrace telephones, computers, faxes, email, and online groupware, and are beginning to use desktop video conferencing. With 7.6 million people telecommuting in the US in 1994 and the number growing at 15 percent per year (Hequet, 1994), visible examples are easy to find. Oldsmobile has created five telecommuting virtual zone offices (Laabs, 1995). The US General Services Administration has set up four telework centers near Washington, DC (Maynard, 1994). Bell Atlantic is offering at least partial telecommuting options to 16,000 management employees (Smith, 1994), while 12 percent of AT & T's workforce has telecommuting options (Sears, 1995).

The effective implementation of telecommuting requires technical as well as organizational support. The technical end appears to be developing more quickly. Ameritech and Bell Atlantic, for example, are both providing commercially available telework services. Whether the managers of telecommuting (employers) will do their part of the work remains to be seen. Most employees report that they like the idea of telecommuting but are skeptical about their bosses providing adequate support (Betts, 1995).

Telecommuting is being used to attract and retain skilled employees. It can significantly reduce real estate costs. With fewer cars on the road, air quality can be improved and traffic congestion alleviated. It also has been argued that telecommuting can increase PRODUCTIVITY and heighten EMPLOYEE MORALE.

The cost of the infrastructure to support telecommuting can be quite high. Employees may lose some of the social aspects that make their jobs enjoyable at the workplace. Organizations are less skilled at managing telecommuters than they are workers in their facilities, and may be ineffective at employee selection, TRAINING, and communication. There is concern among some managers that workers will not work all of the hours for which they are paid, although it might be beneficial to shift the focus to work accomplished rather than number of hours worked. In addition, existing supervisory and management models must be modified to deal with distant workers.

It is clear that telecommuting exists today and is rapidly expanding. It presents technical, social, and managerial challenges but promises payoffs for organizations and their members. Effectively utilized, telecommuting will likely give tomorrow's organizations a competitive edge.

Bibliography

Barnes, K. (1994). Tips for managing telecommuters. *HR Focus*, 71, 9–10.

Betts, M. (1995). Workers slow to accept telecommuting. *Computerworld*, 29, 97.

Buckle, T. (1995). Companies keep making the same telecommuting mistakes. *Communications News*, 32, 72.

Connelly, J. (1995). Let's hear it for the office. *Fortune*, 131, 221–2.

Currid, C. (1995). Tips for telecommuting. *Information Week*, January 23, 64.

Greengard, S. (1994a). Making the virtual office a reality. *Personnel Journal*, 73, 66–70.

Greengard, S. (1994b). Workers go virtual. *Personnel Journal*, 73, 71.

Hequet, M. (1994). How telecommuting transforms work. *Training*, 31, 56–61.

Kirrane, D. E. (1994). Wanted: Flexible work arrangements. *Association Management*, 46, 38–45.

Korzeniowski, P. (1995). Telecommuting: A driving concern. *Business Communications Review*, 25, 45–8.

Laabs, J. J. (1995). Oldsmobile replaces zone offices with virtual offices. *Personnel Journal*, 74, 12.

Maynard, R. (1994). The growing appeal of telecommuting. *Nation's Business*, 82, 61–2.

Rockwell, M. (1995a). Ameritech focuses on telecommuting. *Communications Week*, March 27, 49.

Rockwell, M. (1995b). Bell Atlantic to offer package of telecommuting services. *Communications Week*, March 20, 90.

Sears, S. B. (1995). The telecommuting connection. *Credit World*, 83, 6–8.

Smith, R. (1994). Bell Atlantic's virtual work force. *Futurist*, 28, 13.

Stanko, B. B. and Matchette, R. J. (1994). Telecommuting: The future is now. *Business and Economic Review*, 41, 8–11.

forced distribution method of performance evaluation

Rick Jacobs

The forced distribution method of performance evaluation derives its name from the fact that those responsible for providing evaluations, the raters, are "forced" to distribute ratings for the individuals being evaluated into a "prespecified" performance distribution. Typically, the performance distribution is chosen to reflect the normal curve, so that a relatively small percentage of ratees are required to be placed in the extremes (best and worst performers) and larger percentages of ratees are placed in the categories toward the middle of the performance distribution.

For example, an evaluator rating 25 individuals might be instructed to place three individuals in the category labeled "outstanding" and three individuals in the category labeled "poor." The evaluator might further be asked to place five individuals in the category described as "above average" and five more individuals in the category described as "below average." Finally, the evaluator would place nine individuals in the category labeled "average." In this way the evaluator has forced the distribution of ratee performance into a predetermined set of ratings.

In this simple example several issues emerge. First, the criterion on which the performance judgment is made must be defined. It is possible to ask raters to make their judgments based on the "overall performance" or on each of a series of performance dimensions (e.g., long-range planning, employee development, business development, or communications). Next, the designer of the system must decide the number of performance categories to be used and the definitions for each of these categories. In the example above, five categories were specified with simple labels defining distinct levels of effectiveness. In most applications of forced distribution ratings, the number of categories will range from 5 to 11. Definitions of categories can be as brief as a simple word or more elaborate descriptions of performance. Finally, the specification of the number of ratees to be placed in each category must be given as an instruction to the raters. Here the most frequently used strategy is to have the final distribution of ratees reflect an approximation to the normal curve. While this strategy tends to be the "norm," other less statistically oriented distributions can be and are used.

Forced distributions have several advantages for the conducting of performance appraisals. Among these advantages are:

1. the ratings require relatively simple comparative judgments by the rater;
2. the prespecified distribution rules out leniency errors and central tendency errors (see CENTRAL TENDENCY EFFECTS; LENIENCY EFFECTS); and
3. raters know directly the outcome of the ratings.

Forced distribution ratings also have disadvantages. These include:

1. there is no real evaluation of *absolute* performance levels;
2. there is no ability to compare ratings across groups;
3. when multiple criteria are used, raters must separately sort all ratees for each criterion; and
4. this method does not provide specific information for the purpose of APPRAISAL FEEDBACK and PERFORMANCE COACHING.

Bibliography

Cascio, W. F. (1991). *Applied Psychology in Personnel Management*, 4th edn. Englewood Cliffs, NJ: Prentice-Hall.
Muchinsky, P. M. (1995). *Psychology Applied to Work*. Pacific Grove, CA: Brooks/Cole.
Saal, F. E. and Knight, P. A. (1995). *Industrial/Organizational Psychology: Science and Practice*. Pacific Grove, CA: Brooks/Cole.

401(k) plans

Charles H. Fay

Named for the section of the Revenue Act of 1978 authorizing them, these cash or deferred arrangement (CODA) plans allow employees to agree to a reduction in salary in exchange for the employer's equal contribution to a tax-qualified trust. Employees thus can accumulate capital for retirement purposes and defer income tax on both contributed and plan income until retirement. Employers are allowed to match some portion of employee contributions; the most common match is 50 percent. As with all defined contribution PENSION PLANS, there are non-discrimination regulations to assure that plans do not discriminate in favor of highly paid employees.

Bibliography

Beam, B. T. and McFadden, J. J. (2001). *Employee Benefits*, 6th edn. Chicago: Dearborn Financial Publishing, pp. 588–608.
Van Derhei, J. L. and Olsen, K. A. (2001). Section 401(k) plans (Cash or deferred arrangements) and thrift plans. In J. S. Rosenbloom (ed.), *The Handbook of Employee Benefits: Design, Funding and Administration*, 5th edn. New York: McGraw-Hill, pp. 633–60.

Fourteenth Constitutional Amendment

Ramona L. Paetzold

Ratified in 1868, the Fourteenth Amendment, through the Equal Protection Clause, limits the ability of state and local governments to treat persons differentially based on arbitrary classifications. Although any government classification of persons may be challenged, certain classifications (e.g., those based on race, sex, alienage) receive greater scrutiny by courts and require greater governmental justification to survive. In general, three possible levels of judicial scrutiny exist: (1) strict scrutiny (e.g., race-based classifications); (2) intermediate scrutiny (e.g., most sex-based classifications); and (3) rational basis or weak scrutiny (e.g., most other classifications). The Fourteenth Amendment also provides for due process and prohibits states from abridging the privileges and immunities of US citizens.

France

Jacques R. Rojot

The basic characteristic of French labor law and INDUSTRIAL RELATIONS is the predominant part played by statutory law. Beyond this, three legal doctrines are important. First, in opposition to the US, where the collective agreement plays the essential role, the foremost concept is that of the individual contract of employment between employer and employee. It may be in writing and have an actual specific content but need not be so. It is always legally assumed to exist as soon as an employment relationship is materialized in fact, and it has a compulsory implicit legal content: statutory labor law, administrative regulations, customs, applicable collective agreements for their duration, and judicial precedents as they apply to the relationship.

The parties may always add to that implicit content as long as it improves the lot of the employee or it is allowed explicitly by statutes in other cases. Collective agreements play an important, if secondary, role. They are passed between the main union representatives, who have an exclusive right to conclude them, and employers' associations or employers alone at all levels, from national inter-industry to simple undertaking. Therefore, most events occurring within the employment relationship, such as dismissals, resignations, and so forth, have to be analyzed in terms of the interpretation of the individual contract of employment.

Second, the right to manage the business rests mostly on the employer only. On the one hand, there is no system of codetermination, in the German fashion (*see* GERMANY). Works councils have only advisory and consultative power. On the other hand, the courts, which in the past had systematically denied themselves the power to weigh the opportunity or validity of the employer's managerial decisions, have changed their attitudes in several matters, notably collective dismissals. Consequently, managerial decisions, which were unchallenged as long as they remained within the framework of legality, are increasingly submitted to court control as to their opportunity in economic as well as legal terms. Nevertheless, the courts' inroads in that domain, although a new factor, remain moderate in practice.

Third, the right to STRIKE is protected by the constitution. A clear consequence is that there is no peace obligation for the duration of the collective agreement. Generally, a strike can legally be called at any time for any reason by any number of people. The notion of WILDCAT STRIKES is also irrelevant because there is no union monopoly to call a strike whatsoever. However, the right to strike can be abused and in that case deemed unlawful.

Within that general framework, four characteristics should be added, which are of importance in the management of human resources. Individual and collective dismissal, even though requiring the observance of relatively complex statutory regulations, is always possible, except for shop stewards. Legal requirements regarding fair treatment and nondiscrimination do exist, but are minimal as compared to the US. To the contrary, employee representation through works councils, employee delegates, and union representatives, as well as rights on the shop floor, are much stronger. Finally, labor courts and government-appointed labor inspectors monitor the system. In that regard, the nonobservance of labor law requirements is a penal as well as a civil offense.

Bibliography

Despax, M. and Rojot, R. (1977). France. In R. Blanpain (ed.), *The International Encyclopedia for Labor Law and Industrial Relations*. Deventer: Kluwer.

Despax, M. and Rojot, R. (1987). *Labor Law and Industrial Relations in France*. Deventer: Kluwer.

functional job analysis

Ronald A. Ash

Functional job analysis (FJA) is a type of JOB ANALYSIS that focuses on tasks (*see* TASK) and ratings of those tasks on a number of different scales. Tasks describe what a worker does and what gets done on a job. In FJA, a task is defined as "an action or action sequence grouped through time designed to contribute a specified end result to the accomplishment of an objective and for which functional levels and orientation can be reliably assigned" (Fine and Wiley, 1971). In FJA, task statements are written in a standardized format. A task statement consists of an explicit expression of a worker action and an immediate result expected from that action. The action verb is modified by the means (tools, method, equipment) used, by the immediate object of the action, and by some indication of the prescription/discretion in the worker instruction. An example task statement for the job of social worker is: "Suggests/explains to client reasons for making a good appearance and particular areas where he or she can make improvements to conform to local standards in order that client makes applications for jobs appropriately dressed and groomed."

Each task is analyzed according to seven scales. Three are worker function scales (data, people, and things); one is the worker instruction scale; and three are general educational development scales (reasoning, mathematics, and language). See Fine and Wiley (1971) and Fine (1988) for the specific content of the scales and procedures for their use. According to Fine (1988), FJA is concerned with the whole person on the job, both with the person as a functioning instrument to meet specific job requirements, and with the person as an adaptive system relating to a work environment. For this reason, FJA obtains information relevant to functional skills, specific job content, and adaptive skills necessary for satisfactory JOB PERFORMANCE. FJA has been applied widely in both the public and private sectors, and has been used to generate job analysis data for occupational classification, PERSONNEL SELECTION procedures, PERFORMANCE STANDARDS, training curricula, job design, and job evaluation.

Bibliography

Fine, S. A. (1988). Functional job analysis. In S. Gael, E. T. Cornelius, III, E. L. Levine, and G. Salvendy (eds.), *The Job Analysis Handbook for Business, Industry, and Government*. New York: John Wiley.

Fine, S. A. and Wiley, W. W. (1971). *An Introduction to Functional Job Analysis: A Scaling of Selected Tasks from the Social Welfare Field*. Kalamazoo, MI: W. E. Upjohn Institute for Employment Research.

G

gainsharing

Theresa M. Welbourne

Gainsharing is a term used to describe a set of group-based incentive programs that provide employees in a designated work group (usually a business unit, smaller organization, or department) with a share of the financial gains realized due to increases in PRODUCTIVITY, improvements in processes, or reductions in costs. The philosophy supporting these plans is that employees will improve productivity if provided with (1) an incentive that shares the gains with employees, and (2) a mechanism for voicing their suggestions. Most gainsharing plans consist of two components to assure these goals are met. The first is a bonus plan, and the second is a form of employee participation.

Although historically one of three plans was used (i.e., SCANLON PLAN, RUCKER PLAN, or IMPROSHARE), today's programs include customized bonus formulas and participation systems. However, all gainsharing plans share the goal of including *only* criteria that employees can change (cost of production, sales value of production, customer service, quality, and so forth). An additional factor differentiating gainsharing from other forms of organization-based rewards (such as PROFIT SHARING) is that the bonus is paid out more frequently, usually quarterly, although some pay weekly.

The second component of gainsharing is an EMPLOYEE INVOLVEMENT program. Not all gainsharing programs implement the involvement system, but, when used, they are designed to provide employees with a mechanism for communicating ways to improve the production process. More sophisticated involvement plans consist of layers of suggestion committees that are staffed by peers who are empowered with budget authority to approve suggestions.

gender effects in recruiting

Fiona A. E. McQuarrie

RECRUITING is crucial for an organization because it ultimately affects the composition of the workforce. Special consideration must be given to the effects of gender in recruiting because of the potential legal and organizational impacts.

Gender must be considered in all steps of the recruitment process. Planning for recruitment must take into account the current, future, and desired gender characteristics of the organization's workforce, and must be designed to support the desired or mandated gender balance within the organization. The current gender balance within the organization must also be considered in the choice of internal or external recruiting (*see* RECRUITING SOURCES). If a gender imbalance already exists within an organization, internal recruiting may act to perpetuate, rather than solve, such a situation. The organization's internal structure, particularly in the area of career movement, must be considered. For example, in some organizations, formalized structures such as job ladders not only create but also help to maintain gender segregation (Perry, Davis-Blake, and Kulik, 1994).

Whether posted internally or externally, recruiting messages must be framed so that one gender is not favored (inadvertently or otherwise). For example, general terms such as "manager" may evoke gender-based schema in a recruiter's mind. A description of actual job duties may avoid this problem (Kulik, 1989). It is a generally accepted practice (and legally mandated in many cases) for advertisements to indicate whether the company has an equal opportunity policy.

The choice of the target group for recruiting is also important in the identification of potential gender effects. If the target group is mostly populated by one gender (e.g., women in nursing), the recruiter must balance that reality against the demands of the organization, as well as any legal or internal mandates, for gender balance in the workplace. However, the gender identification of the job (a "male" or "female" occupation) and the gender of current job occupants must be noted as a potential source of DISCRIMINATION in the recruiting process. The continuation of existing gender patterns of hiring may result in continued sex segregation in the workplace (Heilman, 1983).

Gender effects can be particularly influential in the selection process. Recruiters generally have limited time and information on which to base their selection decisions and, thus, stereotypes tend to have a strong effect. Gender-based stereotypes (e.g., about one gender's particular talents or aptitudes for a job) may, thus, result in a biased hiring decision (Powell, 1987). Beliefs about appropriate appearance, age, or level of attractiveness for the ideal candidate may also receive more attention in selection than actual job-relevant credentials.

Appropriate TRAINING for those screening or interviewing candidates is one method of alerting those involved in the recruitment process to possible biases.

Bibliography

Heilman, M. E. (1983). Sex bias in work settings: The lack of fit mode. In L. L. Cummings and B. M. Staw (eds.), *Research in Organizational Behaviour*, vol. 5. Greenwich, CT: JAI Press.

Kulik, C. T. (1989). The effects of job categorization on judgments of the motivating potential of jobs. *Administrative Science Quarterly*, **34**, 68–90.

Perry, E. L., Davis-Blake, A., and Kulik, C. T. (1994). Explaining gender-based selection decisions: A synthesis of contextual and cognitive approaches. *Academy of Management Review*, **19**, 786–820.

Powell, G. N. (1987). The effects of sex and gender on recruitment. *Academy of Management Review*, **12**, 731–43.

gender issues in international assignments

Georgia T. Chao

Gender issues in international assignments generally focus on the selection and performance of women who work in foreign environments. Globally, most organizations recognize an international assignment as a critical prerequisite for career advancement to executive ranks. However, the vast majority of managers and expatriates in multinational companies are male (Harris, 2002). Three common reasons are often cited by organizations in their reluctance to assign women to international assignments:

1 women are less interested in international assignments than men;
2 foreigners, especially those in male-dominated cultures, are less likely to accept women professionals; and
3 for safety reasons, organizations prefer to send men to remote locations, developing countries, or isolated work assignments.

Current research has concluded that these reasons are largely without merit (Caligiuri and Tung, 1999; Harris, 2002).

Advantages and disadvantages have been identified for women in international assignments (Mathur-Helm, 2002). Advantages include: higher visibility in the organization due to the rareness of a female expatriate and the general assumption that a female expatriate must be highly qualified since she passed the selection hurdle. Disadvantages include: barriers in selection; limited opportunities for a woman when the home office seeks to protect her by restricting her travel and exposure to outsiders; and dual-career concerns that are more likely to be problematic for married women (*see* DUAL-EARNER AND DUAL-CAREER COUPLES). More research is needed to determine the extent to which international assignments can be managed to maximize the success for women expatriates.

See also *expatriate assignment; expatriate human resource issues*

Bibliography

Caligiuri, P. M. and Tung, R. L. (1999). Comparing the success of male and female expatriates from a US-based multinational company. *International Journal of Human Resource Management*, **10** (5), 763–82.

Harris, H. (2002). Think international manager, think male: Why are women not selected for international management assignments? *Thunderbird International Business Review*, **44** (2), 175–203.

Mathur-Helm, B. (2002). Expatriate women managers: At the crossroads of success, challenges and career goals. *Women in Management Review*, **17** (1), 18–28.

Generation X

Hadyn Bennett

A term used to describe the post-baby-boom generation born between 1964 and 1981. Each generation carries its own perspectives on the world of work and employment, shaped by its experiences of the environment, and responds to differing management practices. Among the characteristics attributed to members of Generation X are self-reliance, independence, and an expectation of immediate gratification (Caudron, 1997), a desire to continue growing and learning (Tulgan, 1995), and high value for factors such as flexible work patterns (*see* FLEXIBLE WORKING HOURS; FLEXIBLE WORKPLACE/TELECOMMUTING), shorter commuting distances, and interesting work cultures (Bova and Kroth, 2001).

Bibliography

Bova, B. and Kroth, M. (2001). Workplace learning and Generation X. *Journal of Workplace Learning*, **13** (2), 57–65.

Caudron, S. (1997). Training for Generation X. *Human Resource Management International Digest*, **5** (5), 32–5.

Tulgan, B. (1995). *Managing Generation X: How to Bring Out the Best in Young Talent*. Santa Monica, CA: Merritt.

genetic screening

Judy D. Olian

Genetic screening for employment purposes is the practice of predicting work-relevant behaviors or dispositions based on genetic marker information. Although this STAFFING practice is still virtually nonexistent among US corporations (see Office of Technology Assessment, 1990), rapidly accelerating advances in genetic research are leading to (1) the identification of "genetic markers" for a vast range of diseases and dispositions, and (2) the development of cost-effective and accurate genetic screening tests for genetic counseling purposes as well as for potential employment applications. The types of work-related behaviors that are potentially predictable from genetic information include interpersonal orientation (based on a marker for extraversion–introversion), cognitive processing (based on a marker for field dependence–independence), and aggression. Susceptibility to disease is also predictable from genetic information. Examples include disposition toward cancer and heart disease, or vulnerability to exposure from chemicals (e.g., oxidizing agents) used in production processes that could increase the probability of pulmonary disease (see Olian, 1984; Rothstein, 1989). This type of predictor information has obvious implications for employer healthcare costs.

Genetic screening has potential utility for staffing purposes to the extent that traditional scientific standards of validity are attained for such tests. For certain diseases or susceptibilities, the low base rate in the population and the complex pattern of interactions among genetic markers in predicting actual disease impose upper limits on the validity of the tests in traditional populations of applicants. More critically, however, the practice of genetic screening introduces profound ethical and public policy challenges (Olian, 1984; Greenfield, Karren, and Zacharias, 1989). These stem primarily from the immutable nature of genetic markers as the basis for employment and allocation decisions, and the fact that many genetic markers are distributed unequally across racial, ethnic, and gender groups. For these and other reasons, various commentators have cautioned against premature adoption of these practices (see Draper, 1991; Strudler, 1994).

Bibliography

Draper, E. (1991). *Risky Business*. Cambridge: Cambridge University Press.

Greenfield, P. A., Karren, R. J., and Zacharias, L. S. (1989). Screening workers: An examination and analysis of practice and public policy. *Employee Relations*, 11 (5), 1–47.

Office of Technology Assessment (1990). *Genetics in the Workplace*. Washington, DC: US Government Printing Office.

Olian, J. D. (1984). Genetic screening for employment purposes. *Personnel Psychology*, 37, 423–38.

Rothstein, M. (1989). *Medical Screening and the Employee Health Cost Crisis*. Washington, DC: Bureau of National Affairs.

Strudler, A. (1994). The social construction of genetic abnormality: Ethical implications for managerial decisions in the work place. *Journal of Business Ethics*, 13, 839–48.

Germany

Eduard Gaugler, Steffen Lichtenberger, and Cornelia Martin

During the past decades, human resource management (HRM) in Germany has undergone a considerable functional change. Up to the 1950s, corporate personnel management chiefly dealt with administrative tasks such as wage and salary payments and the administration of personnel records (administrative phase). Due to an acute lack of manpower, this period was followed by a phase in which the work factor was acknowledged to an increased extent. As a result, the status of HRM in the company was enhanced (acknowledgment phase). This was manifested, for example, by the establishment of the first academic chair for HRM in the German language area at the University of Mannheim in 1961. As a consequence of the incipient change of values and technologies, HRM has experienced a constantly rising acceptance since 1970 (integration phase).

Today HRM has to be classified as a top management task. In large companies, the human resource manager is often a member of the executive board. In addition, by law large corporations must have an executive of labor relations (*Arbeitsdirektor*). This executive is entrusted with human resource and social tasks.

A great number of German companies consider their staff more and more as the decisive factors of success. This attitude is accompanied by greater professionalization of human resource managers. Furthermore, it leads to an increased specialization of HRM into a wide variety of subtasks and to an increased strategic orientation (*see* STRATEGIC HUMAN RESOURCE MANAGEMENT).

ECONOMIC SYSTEM

The existing market organization in unified Germany is a social market economy. Taking into account the given legal and political restrictions, the individual companies have to develop their own strategies in order to engage in free competition with others. In this regard, HRM serves as an instrument to reinforce the company's competitiveness as well as its viability.

Due to its limited domestic market (82.5 million inhabitants), the German economy has to rely to a large extent on the export of goods and services, which also explains the general concentration on goods and capital exports. (Germany's major trading partners are the countries of the European Union with a share of 51.5 percent, the US with 7.7 percent, and the countries of Central and Eastern Europe with 13.5 percent. In 2002, total proceeds from exports amounted to 522.1 billion euros.) Germany only has a few primary raw materials (hard coal, brown coal), a fact which compels its economy to focus on the development and implementation of state-of-the-art technologies. In addition, investments in the vocational training and further education of the existing human resources are high on an international level.

The situation in the labor market of the unified Germany is as follows: in 2001, 36.8 million out of 82.5 million Germans were gainfully employed, 22.0 percent in producing industries, 28.3 percent in service industries; a total of 3.6 million were self-employed; 56.1 percent of all employees were male and 41.2 percent female. The number of part-time employees currently amounts to 6.8 million. In 2002, the average salary per month of an employee was 2,730 euros; the average hourly wage in the industrial sector was 15.17 euros. Due to its high labor costs, which are above average, in particular ancillary wage costs (which in 2002 amounted to approximately 76.8 percent of labor costs, made up of components of statutory, negotiated, and employers' social security contributions), and the smallest number of annual working hours in the world (*see* ANNUAL HOURS), the German economy has to achieve high PRODUCTIVITY. Key factors in this regard are staff know-how and the implemented level of technology. For this reason, Germany's output is mainly composed of products and services that are a combination of these two key factors. Industrial sectors that require a relatively low skill level have increasingly been relocated to countries with lower wages, a strategy designed to secure international competitiveness. This tendency, however, together with the economic structural difficulties that resulted from the reunification of Germany in 1990, caused a rise in unemployment to 10.8 percent in 2002.

German HRM has reacted to this situation with a more individual organization of working time, the introduction of PAY FOR PERFORMANCE systems, and more flexible regulations in the field of employee BENEFITS and services.

LABOR LAW

HRM in Germany is subject to a variety of restrictions tracing back to legal and collective agreement provisions. Labor law consists of a large number of individual provisions that regulate work in dependent employment, i.e., the relation between employer and employee. The historical intention of labor law was to protect the dependent employee. Labor law can be divided into individual labor law, which regulates the form of individual contracts as the basis of the employment relationship, and collective labor law, which includes labor association law (unions, employers' associations), the collective agreements law, as well as the codetermination right at plant level and enterprise level which is particularly relevant for HRM.

The number of unionized employees in Germany is relatively low, at 33.8 percent. However, collective agreements made between employers and unions of a branch industry are often binding for the employees of this branch. Industrial codetermination, which is regulated in the Industrial Constitution Law of 2/2001 (*Betriebsverfassungsgesetz* 2/2001), has a significant effect on HRM. Its main interest is to give employees a right of participation in corporate decisions. In such cases of participation, employees are usually represented by the works council (*Betriebsrat*) elected by them. The works council has different rights of participation. A large number of decisions on human resource matters, such as the start and end of the daily working hours, specific matters of wage structures, and so forth, can only be taken together by the employer and the works council.

AUTHORITIES AND SPHERES OF ACTION FOR INDUSTRIAL HRM

In Germany, all large and medium-sized companies have human resource departments. The human resource department performs its tasks in cooperation with the individual corporate executives who are responsible for direct leading of human resources. The works council, in its function as employees' representation, is another body that participates in the performance of certain tasks. Based on the objectives of corporate human resource policy, which is an integral part of corporate policy, HRM centers on HUMAN RESOURCE PLANNING. This includes complex planning of measures and activities that are aimed at anticipating and satisfying the demand for human resources required to effect future performance. Subsequent areas of planning are staff RECRUITING and human resource marketing, human resource development and further TRAINING, and discharge. These areas of planning serve for optimal satisfaction of planned human resource needs with regard to the forecasted number of employees and to quality, quantity, time, and area requirements. Further tasks are human resource maintenance and the development of corporative incentives. These include the corporate strategic COMPENSATION system, corporate benefits, and the management style. In addition, human resource development and vocational training, including the specific features of the German training system (dual system), are original tasks of HRM.

PRESENT TRENDS OF HRM

Within a short period of time many German companies have adopted management plans for solving urgent problems regarding time, cost, and quality issues. Such management plans include lean management, TOTAL QUALITY MANAGEMENT, and BUSINESS PROCESS REENGINEERING, and they have led to reorganization activities in many companies. Common traits of these concepts are an extensive decentralization of corporate functions and the elimination of unproductive functional areas. These trends lead to changes in the nature of tasks and duties as well as the organization of human resource departments, and have the following consequences:

1. An increased demand for professionalization of human resource managers as a prerequisite for effective human resource work. This implies that human resource managers have comprehensive knowledge of all HRM instruments and the preconditions for their application, as well as knowledge of labor restrictions.
2. The separation of HRM functions; for example, by externalizing parts of the human resource development area. HRM know-how is increasingly procured from human resource consulting organizations (e.g., in the field of staff recruitment or human resource marketing).
3. Rising pressure for the justification of HRM activities due to an increased cost orientation. This often leads to a changing self-image of human resource departments. Human resource work will increasingly be considered as a service to other functional areas of the company. As a result, human resource work will be oriented to a greater extent to the interests and expectations of "internal customers" (executive board, employees' representation, executives, and staff members).
4. A tendency toward increased activities in human resource controlling to enhance corporate human resource work as an equal corporate function, even in an economic sense.
5. A long-term tendency to decentralize human resource work. The demand for closer contact to "internal customers" can only be met by a decentralization of human resource work. It also improves satisfaction of specific demands and the solution of specific problems. However, central "authorities" remain responsible for important HRM issues, such as principles of leadership, PERFORMANCE APPRAISAL, and remuneration.
6. Original leadership tasks will be redelegated from the human resource department to immediate superiors. There is a tendency toward redelegating certain leadership tasks to immediate superiors, such as the selection of new staff, discussions with individual employees, and dismissals.
7. The use of up-to-date automation systems and human resource information systems. The use of such systems reduces the amount of routine work in the field of HRM.

Bibliography

Berthel, J. (1990). Personnel management. In E. Grochla and E. Gaugler (eds.), *Handbook of German Business Management*, vol. 2. New York: Springer-Verlag.

Conrad, P. and Pieper, R. (1990). Human resource management in the Federal Republic of Germany. In R. Pieper (ed.), *Human Resource Management: An International Comparison*. New York: Walter de Gruyter.

Gaugler, E. (1988). Human resource management: An international comparison. *Personnel*, 8, 24–30.

Gaugler, E. (2002). Personalmanagement: Vielfalt seiner Ansatze und Inhalte. In E. Gaugler and R. Kohler (eds.), *Entwicklungen der Betriebswirt: Schaftslehre*. Stuttgart: Schaeffer-Poeschel.

Gaugler, E., Dechsler, W. A., and Weber, W. (2003). *Handwoerterbuch des Personalwesens*, 3rd edn. Stuttgart: Schaeffer-Poeschel.

Gaugler, E. and Mungenast, M. (1995). Human resource management in Germany and European integration. In P. Hermel (ed.), *European and International Management*. Washington, DC: ASPA/BNA.

Gaugler, E. and Wiltz, S. (1992). Federal Republic of Germany. In C. Brewster (ed.), *The European Human Resource Management Guide*. London: Academic.

Gaugler, E. and Wiltz, S. (1993). *Personalwesen im europaeischen Vergleich*. Mannheim: Price Waterhouse Cranfield Project.

glass ceiling

Fiona A. E. McQuarrie

The term "glass ceiling" describes the phenomenon of women rising to certain hierarchical levels in corporations and then being unable to advance any higher, despite their qualifications and abilities to do so (Morrison et al., 1992). While gender is not explicitly stated as a reason for these individuals' inability to advance, gender-related issues and perceptions prevent their ongoing progress; hence, gender acts as an invisible, or "glass," barrier.

Recent research suggests that the glass ceiling phenomenon occurs, in part, due to differential developmental job experiences that male and female managers receive at the same organizational levels. Male managers are more likely to be assigned critical tasks with visibility and broad responsibility than are female managers (Ohlott, Ruderman, and McCauley, 1994). As a result, women managers may not receive the practical experiences considered necessary for promotion. Likewise, the same skills have been found to be better rewarded for men than for women, and training and development has been shown to have a stronger effect on male managers' career advancement than on female managers' advancement (Tharenou, Latimer, and Conroy, 1994).

Among the strategies suggested for "cracking" the glass ceiling are for women managers to be consistently outstanding in their work, to act as advocates for each other within the organization, and to recognize the exceptional pressures caused by work and family demands and demand that the organization adapt to these pressures (*see* WORK–FAMILY CONFLICT). Legislation such as the CIVIL RIGHTS ACT OF 1991 has also been promoted as having a positive effect in removing barriers to advancement.

See also *affirmative action*

Bibliography

Morrison, A. M., White, R. P., Van Velsor, E., and Center for Creative Leadership (1992). *Breaking the Glass Ceiling: Can Women Reach the Top of America's Largest Corporations?* Reading, MA: Addison-Wesley.

Ohlott, P. J., Ruderman, N. M., and McCauley, C. D. (1994). Gender differences in managers' developmental job experiences. *Academy of Management Journal*, 37, 46–67.

Tharenou, P., Latimer, S., and Conroy, D. (1994). How do you make it to the top? An examination of influences on women's and men's managerial advancement. *Academy of Management Journal*, 37, 899–931.

global human resource strategies

Mary Ann Von Glinow

International human resource (HR) managers have a key role to play in effective STRATEGIC MANAGEMENT. However, they can only be effective in this role if they have acute understanding of the development cycles that a firm goes through as it moves from being domestic to more global in its operations, thinking, and management of resources. In this context, a working definition of global human resource strategies seems proper. The HR literature, however, does not define global HR strategies; in general it is a generic term which appears in many strategic texts as well as the literature. To be sure, most firms employ one of four basic strategies to enter and compete in the international environment: an international strategy, a multidomestic strategy, a global strategy, and a transnational strategy. In the multidomestic strategy, companies pursue a path that allows them maximum local responsiveness. In the global strategy, firms will focus on increasing profitability by reaping the cost reductions that come from experience-curve effects and location economies. In other words, they pursue a low-cost strategy in a few favorable global locations.

The human resource management (HRM) literature often utilizes Ghadar and Adler's (1990) or Dowling and Schuler's (1990) four-phase evolution to explain similar concepts from a more focused HR approach: the ethnocentric approach, the polycentric approach, the geocentric approach, and the regiocentric approach. These terms seem more suitable in describing properties of global HR strategies. The ethnocentric approach suggests that if there are foreign subsidiaries, they have little autonomy; strategic decisions are made at headquarters. The polycentric approach is where the multinational enterprise (MNE) treats each subsidiary as a distinct national entity with some decision-making autonomy. Subsidiaries are usually managed by local nationals, who are seldom promoted. The geocentric approach is when the organization ignores nationality in favor of ability. This approach to STAFFING without regard to nationality must be accompanied by a worldwide integrated business strategy to be successful. The regiocentric approach reflects the geographical strategy and structure of the MNE. Like the geocentric approach, it utilizes a wider pool of managers, but in a limited way. Regional managers may not be promoted to headquarters, but enjoy a degree of regional autonomy in decision-making. Dowling and Schuler (1990) use the geocentric approach to describe international HRM practices for firms with a *global strategy*:

> The global firm manages its global workforce in a centralized or at least coordinated way. Corporate policy on human resource management is relatively specific and influential. There are numerous guidelines, policies, principles, and guiding corporate values; desired personnel practices are often prescribed. Specific examples are worldwide policies on open-door grievance procedures, single status, and stance toward unions, a uniform procedure of performance evaluation or global compensation policies; monitoring of human resource management through opinion surveys that compare the performance of business units and divisions, and a code of corporate values that guide the indoctrination of new recruits. (Dowling and Schuler, 1990: 37)

The key assumption underlying this approach is that the MNE has sufficient numbers of good people constantly available for transfer anywhere, anytime. In short, global HR strategies are those strategies that embody a sense of centralized control, but local autonomy, and in particular the HR strategies, are highly sensitive to management development, socialization, and cultural diversity.

Bibliography

Dowling, P. J. and Schuler, R. S. (1990). *International Dimensions of Human Resource Management*. Boston: PWS-Kent.

Ghadar, F. and Adler, N. J. (1990). International strategy from the perspective of people and culture: The North American context. In A. M. Rugman (ed.), *Research in Global Strategic Management: International Business Research for the Twenty-First Century, Canada's New Research Agenda*, vol. 1. Greenwich, CT: JAI Press.

golden parachutes

Nancy A. Bereman

Golden parachutes (more technically "change-in-control" arrangements) are payments made to employees that are contingent on a change of ownership or control of an organization. The US Internal Revenue Code (section 280G) defines a golden parachute provision as any payment contingent on a change of ownership or control. The US Tax Reform Act of 1984 placed constraints on the size of golden parachutes. If such payments are greater than three times the executive's annual salary and BONUSES, the corporation is not permitted to deduct the excess payment (excess of payment over annual salary) as a wage expense. In addition, the executive must pay an excise tax on the excess payment.

Golden parachutes have a number of different purposes. One purpose is to serve as a defense against a hostile takeover. Golden parachutes are made available to top management, which makes the acquisition more expensive. Golden parachutes can also be considered as a type of severance package which may make it easier for companies to attract talent. These severance agreements should include a clause making the contract void if the executive leaves because of incompetence or resignation. One argument made in favor of golden parachutes is that they lessen the likelihood of target firm resistance to takeover bids, as they help to make managers more objective when considering tender offer proposals (Jensen, 1988). At least one study (Buchholtz, 1994) found that this was not the case and that, in fact, takeover resistance increased with the number of parachutes in the target company.

Bibliography

Buchholtz, A. K. (1994). Role of chief executive officers in takeover resistance: Effect of CEO incentives and individual characteristics. *Academy of Management Journal*, **37**, 554–79.

Jensen, M. (1988). The takeover controversy: Analysis and evidence. In J. Coffee, L. Lowenstein, and S. Rose-Ackerman (eds.), *Knights, Raiders, and Targets: The Impact of the Hostile Takeover*. New York: Oxford University Press.

good faith bargaining

Charles R. Greer

The NATIONAL LABOR RELATIONS ACT OF 1935 included the requirement that employers must bargain in good faith with unions. The LABOR MANAGEMENT RELATIONS ACT OF 1947 (Taft-Hartley Act) added the requirement that unions must also bargain in good faith. These Acts, the interpretations of the NATIONAL LABOR RELATIONS BOARD (NLRB), and various court decisions require and prohibit an extensive number of behaviors in defining good faith bargaining (Taylor and Witney, 1992).

More specifically, good faith bargaining requires the parties to begin negotiations in a reasonable time frame, send authoritative agents to the negotiations, and be willing to put any agreement reached in writing. In addition, the parties must be willing to negotiate over issues the law and the NLRB consider mandatory, such as wages, hours, working conditions, and BENEFITS. Furthermore, when rejecting a proposal, a party must respond with a counterproposal, although it is not required to make any concessions. Other prohibited behaviors include continually shifting positions on an issue and bypassing the union to engage in direct bargaining with the union's members. Finally, a catch-all requirement examines the totality of the parties' conduct for consistency with good faith bargaining (Commerce Clearing House, 1987; Taylor and Witney, 1992).

In reality, some employers have not adhered to the spirit of good faith bargaining and have been able to avoid executing a contract with unions that have won REPRESENTATION ELECTIONS. Although employers must bargain with unions that have won elections, they are not legally required to come to an agreement with unions. As a result, some very determined employers have resisted to the point that their unions have gone out on STRIKE and then the employers have replaced striking workers (Freeman and Medoff, 1984).

Bibliography

Commerce Clearing House (1987). *Labor Law Course*, 26th edn. Chicago: Commerce Clearing House.
Freeman, R. B. and Medoff, J. L. (1984). *What Do Unions Do?* New York: Basic Books.
Taylor, B. J. and Witney, F. (1992). *Labor Relations Law*, 6th edn. Englewood Cliffs, NJ: Prentice-Hall.

graphic rating scale method of performance evaluation

Robert L. Cardy

A graphic rating scale, defined as any rating scale consisting of points on a continuum, is a generic label given to a broad category of rating formats (Cascio, 1991). Raters are presented with a description of a dimension on which the ratees are to be evaluated, and a continuum with anchor points that demarcate levels of effectiveness along that continuum. The rater is asked to judge the level of effectiveness for each ratee, using that rating continuum. The number of points on the rating scale can vary from three upward. Research has indicated that five to nine scale points result in the highest quality of ratings (Finn, 1972).

Graphic rating scales are probably the most common rating format. One reason for this popularity is that the graphic rating scale category can be adapted to a wide variety of specific formats. Other reasons for their popularity include: (1) they are fairly easy to construct; (2) they have a fairly high level of user acceptability; and (3) they have FACE VALIDITY (Cardy and Dobbins, 1994).

Graphic rating scales can be differentiated based on the type and amount of information presented in the anchors. The most common format uses ambiguous adjectives (e.g., "marginal," "average," or "outstanding") as anchors. A more sophisticated format would use specific *behavioral descriptions* for each anchor point. Where research is used to help to define the level of effectiveness represented by these specific behavioral statements, the format would be considered as BEHAVIORALLY ANCHORED RATING SCALES or BEHAVIORAL OBSERVATION SCALES.

Graphic rating scales can also be classified based on whether the judgments asked for are of an absolute or relative nature. Graphic scales of an absolute type ask raters to indicate a ratee's specific level on a dimension. In contrast, relative rating scales ask raters to judge a ratee's level on a dimension *relative* to the level exhibited by other ratees. For example, a relative graphic scale might have scale anchors such as "one of the worst," "about on an average with his or her peers," and "one of the best." With an absolute graphic rating scale, everyone could be rated at a high level. With the relative scale format, some ratees must be rated average and low. While absolute judgments theoretically do not include comparisons with other ratees, research has demonstrated that relative comparisons do influence the absolute judgment (Laming, 1985). Research has also identified a number of specific rating errors and methods for minimizing these effects (*see* RATER TRAINING).

Bibliography

Cardy, R. L. and Dobbins, G. H. (1994). *Performance Appraisal: Alternative Perspectives.* Cincinnati, OH: South-Western Publishing.

Cascio, W. F. (1991). *Applied Psychology in Personnel Management*, 4th edn. Englewood Cliffs, NJ: Prentice-Hall.

Finn, R. H. (1972). Effects of some variations in rating scale characteristics on the means and reliabilities of ratings. *Educational and Psychological Measurement*, 32, 255–65.

Laming, D. (1985). The relativity of "absolute" judgments. *British Journal of Mathematical and Statistical Psychology*, 37, 152–83.

graphology

Hannah R. Rothstein

Graphology, or handwriting analysis, is an increasingly used, yet scientifically unsupported, technique for selecting and promoting workers and for retaining managers after mergers or acquisitions. The use of graphology as a personnel STAFFING tool is based on the presumptions that (1) the writer's personality will reveal itself in his or her handwriting, and (2) personality traits are predictive of success on the job (*see* INTEGRITY TESTING; PERSONALITY TESTS; TRAIT).

Scientific research on graphology shows that reliable differences in handwriting are associated with such phenomena as adolescence and psychosis, but not with temporary situational stressors. Furthermore, personality profiles developed by some graphologists on the basis of handwriting samples can be matched to the person whose handwriting was analyzed by friends and relatives of that person. Thus, there is some evidence to link personal characteristics with graphological markers (Nevo, 1987). On the other hand, there is very little to link these analyses with predictions of employee success at work.

Graphological findings are not reliable. In other words, analyses of the same handwriting sample by different graphologists can produce inconsistent or contradictory results (McCarthy, 1988: 19). Furthermore, research suggests that accurate graphological analyses are dependent on the *content* they extract from the handwriting samples, rather than on the writing itself (Ben-Shakhar et al., 1986). Any job-related information that a graphological analysis uncovers can be obtained more directly and less expensively from other devices, such as personality tests, BIOGRAPHICAL HISTORY INVENTORIES, and structured interviews (*see* EMPLOYMENT INTERVIEW). These devices will also gather additional job-related information that is not attainable from handwriting analysis.

Although graphology is very popular in Europe and Israel, and increasingly popular in the US, there is little basis for recommending its use. Finally, US users should be aware that analysis of handwriting without the writer's knowledge (a common practice) may be an illegal invasion of privacy under US employment law.

Bibliography

Ben-Shakhar, G., Bar-Hillel, M., Bilu, Y., Ben-Abba, E., and Flug, A. (1986). Can graphology predict occupational success? Two empirical studies and some methodological ruminations. *Journal of Applied Psychology*, 71, 645–53.

McCarthy, M. (1988). Handwriting analysis as a personnel tool. *Wall Street Journal*, August 25, 19.

Nevo, B. (ed.) (1987). *The Scientific Aspects of Graphology*. Springfield, IL: Charles C. Thomas.

greenfield sites

Annette Cox

Greenfield sites are attempts by employers to create entirely new workplaces, unencumbered by the traditions and history that can prevent long-established organizations from implementing changes and new ideas. They typically involve opening of a new building often in a rural location, purchase of new technology, and recruitment of new employees with no previous sector experience. Managers seek to implement innovative human resource management practices such as multiskilled teamworking, strict recruitment and selection criteria, and variable pay systems. Research has identified problems in applying this ideal since most greenfield sites appear to "brown off" quickly, suffering similar problems to traditional workplaces.

Bibliography

Newell, H. (1991). Fields of dreams: Evidence of "new" employment relations in greenfield sites. Unpublished DPhil thesis, University of Oxford, Oxford.

grievance determinants

Michael E. Gordon

Conjecture abounds about what causes individuals to file GRIEVANCES. The volume of research is modest and many published findings have methodological problems that limit their internal and external validity.

ENVIRONMENTAL DETERMINANTS

Several facets of the work environment are related to the grievance rate in an organization, defined as the number of grievances filed per 100 workers over a given time period, usually one year. Low grievance rates are encountered in relatively stable organizations that are largely free of technological change and that rely on Scanlon-type GAINSHARING (Arthur and Jelf, 1999; *see* SCANLON PLAN). Grievance rates are higher in organizations where there have been reductions in the number of bargaining unit employees (Wagar, 2001) and where strikes are banned (Hebdon and Stern, 1998). Further, the greater the conflict apparent during the union organizing process, the higher is the grievance rate following certification of the union.

GRIEVANT CHARACTERISTICS

Demographic characteristics (e.g., gender or seniority) and attitudes of individual workers are not important determinants of grievance filing behavior (Gordon and Miller, 1984). Further, research results are inconclusive with regard to whether the tendency to file a grievance is related to the level of a worker's JOB PERFORMANCE.

MANAGEMENT BEHAVIOR

Supervisors who are considerate toward subordinates tend to have lower grievance rates. Union members are more likely to file a grievance when they perceive greater threat to contractual rights inherent in a supervisor's actions and when management's actions are judged to be motivated by personal animus toward the worker (Gordon and Bowlby, 1989).

Bibliography

Arthur, J. B. and Jelf, G. S. (1999). The effects of gainsharing on grievance rates and absenteeism over time. *Journal of Labor Research*, **20**, 133–45.

Gordon, M. E. and Bowlby, R. L. (1989). Reactance and intentionality attributions as determinants of the intent to file a grievance. *Personnel Psychology*, **42**, 309–29.

Gordon, M. E. and Miller, S. J. (1984). Grievances: A review of research and practice. *Personnel Psychology*, **37**, 117–46.

Hebdon, R. P. and Stern, R. N. (1998). Tradeoffs among expressions of industrial conflict: Public sector strike bans and grievance arbitrations. *Industrial and Labor Relations Review*, **51**, 204–21.

Wagar, T. H. (2001). Consequences of work force reduction: Some employer and union evidence. *Journal of Labor Research*, **22**, 851–62.

grievance procedure

William H. Holley, Jr.

A grievance procedure is a sequence of steps, negotiated by the union and company, written in their COLLECTIVE BARGAINING agreement for the purpose of resolving GRIEVANCES during the life of the agreement without a STRIKE or LOCKOUT. A grievance procedure is included in 99 percent of the collective bargaining agreements in the US and typically includes three to five steps. As an example, step 1 consists of the aggrieved employee contacting his or her shop steward (or departmental representative) about the alleged violation of a provision of the collective bargaining agreement. A meeting is then held with the first line supervisor within a defined period of time, such as within ten days after the occurrence of the event that caused the grievance, e.g., a denial of PROMOTION. Most grievances are resolved at this step and a resolution at this step helps to build a better relationship between the shop steward and the first line supervisor. If the grievance is not resolved, the first line supervisor then provides a written answer in a defined period, e.g., five working days.

The grievant and/or the union has the option of appealing the grievance to step 2 within a certain number of days. If appealed, the grievance is usually reduced to writing and presented to management. A step 2 meeting is held and this meeting includes higher-level officials of the union and the company. The union will probably add members of the grievance committee, which includes officers of the local union and interested shop stewards; the company will add a representative, such as a labor relations specialist who has plant-wide responsibility for handling employee grievances. A resolution of the grievance at this level will have plant-wide application and may have an effect on the resolution of grievances in other departments. However, the parties may negotiate a settlement and agree that the settlement of the grievance at this step will not set a precedent in future grievances; for example, returning a discharged employee to work on a last-chance agreement but without backpay. In fact, these types of settlements may be reached at any step in the processing of the grievance.

If the grievance is not resolved at step 2, management will provide a written answer in a specified number of days. The union then has a certain number of days in which to appeal the grievance to step 3, which will include a union representative who represents the local union in grievance administration, negotiations, and ARBITRATION. The company will add the corporate labor relations manager to represent the company position on the grievance. Any resolution of the grievance at this step will have company-wide implications and may affect the resolution of grievances at other company facilities and plants. If the grievance is not resolved at step 3, the management will provide a written answer within a specified period of time.

The union then must determine whether to appeal the grievance to the final step in the grievance procedure, which is arbitration. This action usually must be taken within 30 days after the receipt of the company's step 3 answer. This time period allows the local union members to discuss the grievance at a local meeting and determine whether to advance the grievance to arbitration.

The characteristics of a grievance procedure include: (1) three to five steps; (2) time limits for taking each action; (3) additional higher-level officials at each step in the procedure; and (4) arbitration as the last step to bring finality to the grievance.

Grievance procedures are also provided in nonunion settings. These grievance procedures are included in the EMPLOYEE HANDBOOK or policy manual. Although there has been an increase in employer-promulgated arbitration, most grievance procedures in the nonunion sector do not provide for arbitration as the last step for resolving the grievance.

See also *nonunion employee grievance procedures*

Bibliography

Bureau of National Affairs (1992). *Basic Patterns in Union Contracts*. Washington, DC: Bureau of National Affairs.

Gordon, M. E. and Miller, S. J. (1994). Grievances: A review of research and practice. *Personnel Psychology*, 37, 117–46.

Lewin, D. and Peterson, R. B. (1988). *The Modern Grievance Procedure in the United States*. New York: Quorum.

grievances

Michael E. Gordon

Grievances are formal allegations by a party to a COLLECTIVE BARGAINING agreement that relate to the proper interpretation and/or application of the agreement. Some agreements, however, permit the parties to file grievances about issues pertaining to matters not specified in the contract such as company rules and past practice. Contract administration is the process used to resolve grievances. Grievances may be filed by individual employees or by the union on its own behalf when management practices affect a number of workers or union representatives.

Subject Matter of Grievances

Management typically seeks to restrict grievances to alleged violations of specific contract provisions, whereas unions prefer to define grievances more broadly as "any complaint arising out of the workplace, regardless of whether the specific issue in dispute is included in the contract" (Repas, 1984: 41). Most grievances pertain to company disciplinary actions (e.g., demotions, suspensions, or discharges). Grievances often are filed about work rules (e.g., crew sizes and excessive tardiness or ABSENTEEISM), work assignments (e.g., which job classification is entitled to perform certain work), personnel assignments (e.g., shift or overtime assignments, layoffs, or transfers), supervision (e.g., supervisors doing bargaining unit work), administration of wage or seniority BENEFITS, and general working conditions. Increasing reliance on modular organizations (linking companies on the basis of core competencies) has caused subcontracting and outsourcing to become frequent grievance issues.

Bibliography

Repas, B. (1984). *Contract Administration: A Guide for Stewards and Local Officers*. Washington, DC: Bureau of National Affairs.

Griggs v. *Duke Power*, 401 US 424 (1971)

Leonard Bierman

This case involves a charge of *adverse impact* (*see* DISPARATE TREATMENT) against an employer. The Supreme Court held that Title VII of the CIVIL RIGHTS ACT OF 1964 prohibits not only overt DISCRIMINATION, but also employment practices that appear neutral but have a discriminatory effect on a protected class (e.g., blacks), even if unintentional. In *Griggs*, defendant Duke Power required all manual labor applicants to have a high school degree, even though this requirement was unrelated to the duties of the job. Although this policy applied to all applicants, more of blacks were excluded from consideration because the local labor pool contained fewer black high school graduates, therefore creating an adverse impact.

group disability benefits

Robert M. McCaffery

Employers use several approaches to supplement mandatory programs (e.g., social security and workers' COMPENSATION) in replacing employee income during periods of absence due to disability. One common practice is to provide sick pay or salary continuation for a limited period of time. Employee service (seniority) usually determines the maximum duration of payments within a calendar year.

Group benefit plans, frequently requiring employee contributions, are also utilized by employers to help protect disabled employees' income. These include: (1) short-term (e.g., up to 26 weeks) disability plans and (2) long-term (e.g., after 26 weeks) disability plans.

Bibliography

Employee Benefit Research Institute (1990). *Fundamentals of Employment Benefit Programs*, 4th edn. Washington, DC: Employee Benefit Research Institute.

group life insurance/survivor benefits

Robert M. McCaffery

Employers sponsor a variety of insurance plans designed to provide income replacement for survivors and named beneficiaries of deceased employees. Typically, employers pay the full cost for: (1) basic group term life insurance; (2) basic accidental death and dismemberment insurance; and (3) business travel accident insurance.

Usually employees can obtain supplemental coverage at group rates, but they are responsible for all or most of the costs. Some forms of supplemental coverage include: (1) supplemental group term life insurance; (2) supplemental accidental death and dismemberment insurance; (3) group universal life plans (GULP); (4) survivor income benefit insurance (SIBI); or (5) dependant life insurance. Survivor benefits are also payable from most PENSION PLANS.

Bibliography

McCaffery, R. M. (1992). *Employee Benefit Programs: A Total Compensation Perspective*, 2nd edn. Boston: PWS-Kent.

H

halo effects

Angelo S. DeNisi

Halo effects were the first threat to performance appraisals (*see* PERFORMANCE APPRAISAL) identified in the literature (e.g., Thorndike, 1920), and have received a great deal of attention ever since (the most comprehensive review is probably by Cooper, 1981). Although, conceptually, halo effects are believed to result in high intercorrelations among ratings on separate performance dimensions, there has been considerable disagreement over the proper operational definition of halo (e.g., intercorrelations among ratings, standard deviation of ratings across dimensions), as well as the cause for halo effects (e.g., conceptual similarity among performance dimensions, the effects of global evaluations), and even whether halo reflects true relationships among dimensions or some type of rating error (*see* RATING ERRORS).

Much of the interest in halo effects, though, has been based on the assumption that halo effects do reflect a type of rating error, and so can serve as a proxy for rating (in)accuracy (*see* RATING ACCURACY). But, unless we know the "true" underlying covariance among performance dimensions, we cannot be sure that halo reflects the presence of error. Furthermore, the relationship between halo and rating accuracy is debatable, and may be positive rather than negative, although this probably depends upon the definition of accuracy used. Finally, as the relevance of accuracy as a criterion in performance appraisal research is challenged (Ilgen, 1993), the entire issue may become moot. Instead, halo may be important as an index of within-ratee discriminability, which may be related to ratee reactions to ratings. Further research is needed, however, to determine the utility of such a role (*see* DISTRIBUTIONAL EFFECTS IN PERFORMANCE APPRAISAL).

Bibliography

Cooper, W. (1981). Ubiquitous halo. *Psychological Bulletin*, 90, 218–44.
Ilgen, D. R. (1993). Performance appraisal accuracy: An illusive or sometimes misguided goal? In H. Schuler, J. Farr, and M. Smith (eds.), *Personnel Selection and Assessment*. Hillsdale, NJ: Erlbaum.
Thorndike, E. L. (1920). A constant error in psychological ratings. *Journal of Applied Psychology*, 4, 25–9.

handicapped/disabled

Ramona L. Paetzold

Handicapped/disabled is a category of protection under the REHABILITATION ACT OF 1973 and the AMERICANS WITH DISABILITIES ACT OF 1990 (ADA). In general, a handicap or disability is defined as:

1. a physical or mental impairment that substantially limits one or more major life activities of an individual;
2. a record of any such impairment; or
3. being regarded as having such an impairment.

The ADA specifically excludes certain categories from being considered disabilities; these include, for example, homosexuality, current illegal drug use, pedophilia, compulsive gambling, and kleptomania. The disability category does include individuals who have participated in, or are currently participating in, drug rehabilitation programs, as long as they are not currently using illegal drugs.

Hay method and other hybrid job evaluation methods

Matthew C. Bloom

Any job evaluation method (*see* JOB EVALUATION METHODS) which combines features of the CLASSIFICATION JOB EVALUATION METHOD, FACTOR-COMPARISON JOB EVALUATION METHOD, RANKING JOB EVALUATION METHOD, or POINT JOB EVALUATION METHOD is considered a hybrid. A common hybrid system incorporates the classification and benchmark job features of the classification method with the point scores of a point factor plan. Here, jobs are slotted into important compensatory factors by comparing them to anchoring benchmark jobs. Points are then assigned to the job based upon that slotting. These points may then be summed and compared to survey data to determine the job's wage.

One of the most widely used hybrids is the Hay Associates plan. The Hay plan comprises three compensable factors (*see* COMPENSABLE FACTOR): know-how, problem solving, and accountability (Milkovich and Newman, 1993). Each compensable factor is arranged in a two-dimensional grid defining degrees on each factor. For example, the Hay factor of know-how is described by eight levels of *technical know-how* crossed with 12 levels of *managerial know-how*, resulting in 96 possible combinations, each with a different score assigned to it. The evaluator selects the appropriate level on each compensable factor for a particular job and adds up the factor scores. The wage for a job is derived by comparing its factor scores to a grid of wages for a set of benchmark jobs. The proprietary job evaluation plans of most human resource consulting firms are hybrids.

Bibliography

Milkovich, G. T. and Newman, J. M. (1993). *Compensation*, 4th edn. Homewood, IL: Richard D. Irwin.

hazardous materials in the workplace

Donna E. Ledgerwood

An increasing number of production processes and products expose workers to hazardous substances. In addition to designing a safe and healthful workplace, it is management's responsibility to provide adequate personal protective equipment. Proactive and informed managers prevent losses before they occur. As substantiated in a 1991 survey, the appropriate use of personal protective equipment could have prevented as many as 37.6 percent of the occupational injuries and illnesses experienced by respondents to the survey (LaBar, 1991).

See also *reproductive health hazards; safety in the workplace*

Bibliography

LaBar, G. (1991). What do safety pros think of OSHA? *Occupational Hazards*, 53, 107–9.

hazards in the workplace

Donna E. Ledgerwood

When one thinks of health and the loss of health and onset of illness (such as with a breakdown of a person's immune system as in AIDS/AIDS-RELATED COMPLEX cases or other bloodborne pathogens; *see* SAFETY: BLOOD-BORNE PATHOGENS), one thinks of declining physical and mental abilities over a long period of time. But if a person is unaware of a slippery step on a stairway, he or she could fall and break an arm or leg. The slippery step is, thus, the hazardous condition or imminent danger which can cause an immediate loss unless a person manages the situation by: (1) becoming aware of the wet condition; (2) rerouting employee traffic until the condition can be fixed; (3) cleaning up the spill and/or source of the water; and (4) providing follow-up activity to ensure that no repeat activity occurs.

In most professional safety circles today, the word "accident," an unintentional act potentially resulting in loss, has been replaced by the term "incident," an undesired event or "near miss" that, under slightly different circumstances, could have resulted in personal harm, property damage, or other undesired loss of resources.

A hazard, then, is that dangerous condition, potential or inherent, which can bring about an interruption of or interference with the expected orderly progress of an activity. A hazardous condition is the physical condition or circumstance which is causally related to incident occurrence. The hazardous condition is related directly to both the incident type and the agent (the principal object or substance) involved in the incident.

Hazelwood School District v. United States, 433 US 299 (1977)

Leonard Bierman

In *Hazelwood*, the Supreme Court considered whether the given school district engaged in a *pattern* or *practice* of employment DISCRIMINATION. In particular, the court found that where a job requires special training, the comparison should be with those in the labor force who possess the relevant qualifications, rather than with the entire community. The Supreme Court then remanded the case back to the trial court for an evaluation of the school district's hiring practices in relationship to the RELEVANT LABOR MARKET.

health in the workplace

Donna E. Ledgerwood

The differences between safety and health can be explained in terms of temporal and awareness factors. While safety deals with the ability to identify the causes of a recognizable potential loss and to prevent the loss from occurring by taking action *now*, activities related to occupational or work-related health deal with the ability to identify the factors that cause disease or result in a loss of health over time. For example, the problems related to epidemiology assume the ability to: (1) identify the catalysts or causal factors; (2) measure and understand the interactions/associations between all variables; (3) establish an association, correlation, or cause–effect relationship between critical factors; (4) control and neutralize the harmful factors; and (5) conduct follow-up efforts to ensure the validity of the assumptions and methodology.

Most occupational illnesses and epidemics are studied after the fact, when physicians try to assimilate and synthesize all of the factors that led to and hosted the disease or effect (such as a decrease in pulmonary functioning). Use of these data is evident in the control and prevention of future replications of these diseases or effects.

health maintenance organizations

Charles H. Fay

The health maintenance organization (HMO) is the most common form of MANAGED CARE. While there are several types of HMOs, they are all characterized by the provision of comprehensive healthcare to members, limited choice of members for specific medical providers, an emphasis on preventive medicine, and a financial structure that encourages the HMO to keep costs down. The HMO Act of 1973 actively promoted the development of HMOs, requiring employers with more than 25 employees to offer membership to employees as an alternative to regular healthcare coverage. Since costs are typically lower, employers are also active promoters of HMOs.

Bibliography

Pierce, P. D. (2001a). Understanding managed care health plans: The managed care spectrum. In J. S. Rosenbloom (ed.), *The Handbook of Employee Benefits: Design, Funding and Administration*, 5th edn. New York: McGraw-Hill, pp. 135–69.

Pierce, P. D. (2001b). Understanding managed care health plans: Understanding costs and evaluating plans. In J. S. Rosenbloom (ed.), *The Handbook of Employee Benefits: Design, Funding and Administration*, 5th edn. New York: McGraw-Hill, pp. 171–207.

health promotion

James R. Terborg

Health promotion programs at the worksite, sometimes called WELLNESS programs, generally involve:

1 the periodic or continuing delivery of educational and/or behavior change materials and activities that are designed to maintain or improve employee fitness, health, and well-being; and
2 changes in organizational practices and policies conducive to health promotion (Fielding, 1991).

Most worksite health promotion programs focus on educational and skill-building activities. Interventions targeting organizational practices and policies are less common. Worksite health promotion programs vary along several dimensions, including facilities, budget, employee eligibility, and target outcomes. It is difficult to evaluate and compare programs. Legislatively mandated programs in safety and health and programs dealing with existing medical problems generally are independent of health promotion programs in the US. However, these activities often are integrated with health promotion in western Europe and Australia. Typical programs start with assessments of employee lifestyle and health risk, followed with COUNSELING and opportunities to participate in activities designed to reduce risk (e.g., an exercise program for overweight and sedentary employees). Participation is voluntary at little or no cost to the employee.

Health promotion programs have become quite popular in the US. A 1992 survey of over 1,500 private worksites found that 81 percent offered health promotion activities (US Department of Health and Human Services, 1993). The most popular activities included occupational injury prevention, exercise, and SMOKING CESSATION. Notable increases were observed in nutrition, weight control, blood pressure, and cholesterol programs. A similar survey in Australia showed that the most popular activities were back care, accident prevention, and smoking cessation. However, only 27 percent of worksites offered such programs (National Occupational Health and Safety Commission, 1993). The occurrence of worksite health promotion programs should increase worldwide because such programs have been identified as central for meeting national health goals.

The most common reasons for adopting health promotion programs at work include personal interest by senior management, employee requests, moves to new facilities, concern for EMPLOYEE MORALE, reduction in accidents and injuries, and, in the US, reduction in costs of employee healthcare (Terborg and Glasgow, 1996).

Rigorous experimental data evaluating worksite health promotion are almost nonexistent (Terborg and Glasgow, 1996), although numerous anecdotal and nonexperimental reports suggest favorable results (Pelletier, 1993). Programs targeting hypertension and smoking cessation produce the best results. Exercise, nutrition, weight loss, and cholesterol programs produce the poorest results. Activities that look promising include health risk appraisals, EMPLOYEE ASSISTANCE PROGRAMS, healthy back programs, and changes in company policies. Cost effectiveness and cost-benefit analyses show positive results, but these data must be interpreted with caution. To date, no experimental study has adequately demonstrated the causal link between changes in employee health and changes in economic outcomes (Terborg and Glasgow, 1996). Although some companies report highly positive results (Pelletier, 1993), there is considerable variability in success rates across different companies (Terborg and Glasgow, 1996). Much advice has been given, but little is known about how to consistently implement successful worksite health promotion programs.

Bibliography

Fielding, J. E. (1991). Health promotion at the worksite. In G. M. Green and F. Baker (eds.), *Work, Health, and Productivity*. New York: Oxford University Press.
National Occupational Health and Safety Commission (1993). *Health Promotion in the Workplace Programs: Guidelines for Workplaces*. Sydney: National Occupational Health and Safety Commission.
Pelletier, K. R. (1993). A review and analysis of the health and cost effective outcome studies of comprehensive health promotion and disease prevention programs at the worksite: 1991–1993 update. *American Journal of Health Promotion*, 8, 50–62.
Terborg, J. R. and Glasgow, R. E. (1996). Worksite interventions: A brief review of health promotion programs at work. In A. Brown, C. McManus, S. Newman, J. Weinman, and R. West (eds.), *Cambridge Handbook of Psychology, Health, and Medicine*. Cambridge: Cambridge University Press.

US Department of Health and Human Services (1993). 1992 national survey of worksite health promotion activities: Summary. *American Journal of Health Promotion*, 7, 452–64.

healthcare expense

Charles H. Fay

In 1965, private business expenditures on healthcare for employees (including contributions to private health insurance premiums, contributions to Medicare hospital insurance trust funds, worker's compensation and temporary disability insurance, and industrial in-plant health services) amounted to $5.9 billion; in 1995 these costs had increased to $249.4 billion (McDonnell and Fronstin, 1999: 27).

Bibliography

McDonnell, K. and Fronstin, P. (1999). *EBRI Health Benefits Databook*. Washington, DC: Employee Benefit Research Institute.

hiring persons with disabilities

Adrienne Colella

The hiring of persons with disabilities has become an issue of concern to US organizations primarily due to the REHABILITATION ACT OF 1973 and the AMERICANS WITH DISABILITIES ACT OF 1990, both of which prohibit employment DISCRIMINATION against qualified persons with disabilities. Efforts to increase the hiring of persons with disabilities have also been fueled by the public's belief that people with disabilities are an underutilized labor pool (Louis Harris and Associates, 1991), employer surveys reporting that employees with disabilities are a sound investment (e.g., Greenwood and Johnson, 1987), various advocacy groups for people with disabilities, and federal tax credit programs which offer incentives for hiring people with disabilities and reduce the cost of accommodation.

Based on disproportionately low employment rates for persons with disabilities, particularly in higher-level positions, it is often assumed that job applicants with disabilities face discrimination in the hiring process (Braddock and Bachelder, 1994). Thus, there has been a great deal of research examining potential sources of bias in hiring decisions. One line of research has focused on PERSONNEL SELECTION decisions (based on interviews or resumes) regarding applicants with disabilities. This research, mostly conducted in laboratory settings, has led to mixed results, often reporting negative bias against job applicants with disabilities, but occasionally showing bias in favor of applicants with disabilities (see Stone, Stone, and Dipboye, 1992).

Several factors have been shown to influence bias in hiring decisions toward job applicants with disabilities (see Stone and Colella, 1996, for a review of factors influencing the treatment of employees with disabilities). These factors include interviewer characteristics (e.g., empathy), type of disability, perception of personal blame for the disability, perceived unpredictability of behavior, perceived peril associated with the disability, stereotypes of disability job fit, job characteristics (e.g., amount of public contact), and organization size. Reasons for negative bias include negative stereotypes, low performance expectations, concern over co-worker acceptance, and ignorance about the nature of disabilities.

Another issue in the hiring of persons with disabilities is the construction of valid selection procedures and instruments which are not unduly influenced by various disabilities (e.g., Nester, 1984). Testing applicants with disabilities may require that a different testing procedure or medium be used, or that accommodations be made in current procedures. For example, readers may be necessary to give paper-and-pencil exams to visually impaired applicants and time limits may need to be extended in order to accommodate persons with a variety of disabilities. Such changes in standardized testing procedures will also require further validity work to assure that the test remains fair and valid after modifications.

Another area of concern to employers is the recruitment of persons with disabilities. There are many public and private organizations which assist in the vocational rehabilitation and job placement of persons with disabilities, as well as organizations and programs which assist businesses in recruiting persons with disabilities. One such program is Projects with Industry (PWI), a federally established program which promotes collaborative efforts between rehabilitation specialists and business and industry.

Bibliography

Braddock, D. and Bachelder, L. (1994). *The Glass Ceiling and Persons with Disabilities*. Washington, DC: US Department of Labor, Glass Ceiling Commission.

Greenwood, R. and Johnson, V. A. (1987). Employer perspectives on workers with disabilities. *Journal of Rehabilitation*, 53, 37–45.

Louis Harris and Associates (1991). *Public Attitudes towards People with Disabilities*. Washington, DC: National Organization on Disability.

Nester, M. A. (1984). Employment testing for handicapped people. *Public Personnel Management*, 13, 417–34.

Stone, D. L. and Colella, A. (1996). A framework for studying the effects of disability on work experiences. *Academy of Management Review*.

Stone, E. F., Stone, D. L., and Dipboye, R. L. (1992). Stigmas in organizations: Race, handicaps, and physical unattractiveness. In K. Kelley (ed.), *Issues, Theory, and Research in Industrial and Organizational Psychology*. New York: Elsevier Science.

horizontal management

Susan Albers Mohrman

Horizontal management, or lateral management, is using lateral approaches to perform management functions such as planning, resource allocation, coordination and review of activities, decision-making, and issue resolution. It is necessary when the number and complexity of issues to be resolved and activities to be coordinated exceed the capacity of traditional hierarchical mechanisms to be timely and well informed. Lateral mechanisms include use of informal liaison roles, cross-functional work teams, integrating teams, and/or formal management positions that supplement organizational hierarchy. Some forms entail significant EMPLOYEE EMPOWERMENT. Lateral management is an essential element of process management and network forms of organization.

Bibliography

Galbraith, J. R. (1994). *Competing with Flexible Lateral Organizations*. Reading, MA: Addison-Wesley.

Mohrman, S. A., Cohen, S. G., and Mohrman, A. M., Jr. (1995). *Designing Team-Based Organizations: New Forms for Knowledge Work*. San Francisco: Jossey-Bass.

host-country human resource management

Helen L. De Cieri and Peter J. Dowling

Host-country human resource management (HRM) encompasses all HRM functions, policies, and practices related to the host-country operations of a multinational enterprise (MNE). This will include STAFFING, TRAINING and development, PERFORMANCE MANAGEMENT, COMPENSATION, and labor relations. Host-country HRM issues apply to employees of all nationalities who are working in host-country operations: parent-country national (PCN) expatriates and third-country national (TCN) expatriates, as well as host-country nationals (HCNs).

STAFFING POLICIES AND PRACTICES

Host-country staffing policies and practices may vary according to cultural norms and local requirements, organizational characteristics, and task requirements. Difficulties in recruitment and selection of HCNs may include: poor knowledge of the local labor market, local education systems, and qualifications; language and cultural differences; and inappropriate attempts to transfer parent country staffing practices to different countries and cultures. There are advantages and disadvantages in selecting PCNs, HCNs, and TCNs. These relate to varying levels of control and coordination desired or possible, host government requirements, language and cultural barriers, equal opportunity requirements, and impact on career paths of other employee groups (Dowling, Schuler, and Welch, 1994).

CROSS-CULTURAL TRAINING AND DEVELOPMENT

Cross-cultural training and management development programs are intended to facilitate interactions between PCNs, HCNs, and TCNs, and are positively associated with expatriate adjustment and performance (*see* DEVELOPING GLOBALLY COMPETENT EXECUTIVES/MANAGERS) (Black, Gregersen, and Mendenhall, 1992).

PERFORMANCE MANAGEMENT

Host-country PERFORMANCE APPRAISAL requires reconciliation of parent and host-country raters' perceptions of performance. Flexibility in appraisal criteria may be advisable to allow for volatility in the international environment. Host-country compensation management objectives include: fairness and equity; ability to attract, motivate, and retain desired personnel; facilitation of cost-effective transfer of expatriates; and consistency with organizational strategy (Dowling et al., 1994).

DECLINING UTILIZATION OF EXPATRIATES

Increasing involvement of HCNs in MNE managerial levels parallels a global trend toward lesser utilization of expatriate managers. Perceived benefits to MNEs of expatriate reduction may include: lowering costs associated with managing expatriates and operating in uncertain environments; meeting host-country employment requirements; and contributing to host-country managerial and technical development. Where expatriates are employed, the MNE's goal in REPATRIATION is to return and retain an employee who will contribute knowledge, experience, and networks gained overseas.

STRATEGIC AND ENVIRONMENTAL INFLUENCES

Several factors may be expected to influence host-country HRM. Strategic MNE components that influence host-country HRM are the often conflicting needs of global integration, referring to the responsibility for corporate-wide integration of strategies, and local differentiation, referring to flexible responsiveness to host-country market demands (Bartlett and Ghoshal, 1992). General influences related to an MNE's parent and host countries will affect host-country HRM. These include legislation, education levels, societal and workforce demographic characteristics and values, economic conditions, and behavior of organizational stakeholders, such as the host-country government and trade unions. Factors internal to an MNE that influence host-country HRM include organizational strategy, structure, culture, and MNE headquarters' staffing orientation. Overall, goals and concerns for host-country HRM may include: public legitimacy and market viability in the host country; development of a committed, flexible workforce (*see* WORKFORCE FLEXIBILITY); and transfer of knowledge and learning (Schuler, Dowling, and De Cieri, 1993; *see* TRANSFER OF LEARNING).

Bibliography

Bartlett, C. and Ghoshal, S. (1992). *Transnational Management: Text, Cases, and Readings in Cross-Border Management*. Boston: Richard D. Irwin.

Black, J. S., Gregersen, H. B., and Mendenhall, M. E. (1992). *Global Assignments: Successfully Expatriating and Repatriating International Managers*. San Francisco: Jossey-Bass.

Dowling, P. J., Schuler, R. S., and Welch, D. E. (1994). *International Dimensions of Human Resource Management*, 2nd edn. Belmont, CA: Wadsworth.

Schuler, R. S., Dowling, P. J., and De Cieri, H. L. (1993). An integrative framework of strategic international human resource management. *Journal of Management*, 19, 419–59.

human capital theory

Hadyn Bennett

Human capital theory is the application of neo-classical economic capital theory (Fisher, 1906) to human resources, whereby human "capital" is considered analogous to conventional capital with respect to its economic and productive characteristics. Thus, the individual worker's marginal product (assumed equal to wages) can be viewed as a function of time input, individual capacities, and investment in human capital items (such as education, information, and TRAINING) with the potential to increase the individual's PRODUCTIVITY (and therefore earnings). Human capital theory thus argues that individuals will continue to invest in human capital to the point at which additional investments (costs) no longer lead to a net increase in subsequent earnings.

Bibliography

Fisher, I. (1906). *The Nature of Capital and Income.* Reprinted 1965, New York: Augustus M. Kelley.

human factors engineering

William C. Howell

Systematic consideration of the human user or operator in the design of systems, tools, consumer products, and environments is a concept known as human factors engineering (HFE). It is also known as human factors, human engineering, ergonomics, and human-centered design. The underlying philosophy is that a machine and its human operator constitute a human–machine system, the effectiveness of which depends on the integration of human and nonhuman components.

ORIGIN AND RATIONALE

Design professionals, such as engineers and computer scientists, have traditionally sought to develop physical systems that operate reliably and effectively. Nevertheless, there are always some failures, and most (estimates run as high as 60–90 percent) are attributed to "human error" (Wickens, 1992). During World War II, psychologists were recruited to help combat human error in the operation of aircraft, radar, and other advanced systems of that era, error that was occurring despite rigorous selection and training of personnel. In many cases it was discovered that *design* features, such as instruments that were easily misread or controls that were easily confused, were implicated (Christensen, 1958). Consequent design changes based on well-established principles of human performance (e.g., attention, perception, memory, motor ability) produced marked improvements.

Thus was born the idea that systematic consideration of *human* limitations, capabilities, and tendencies in design could pay big dividends. Following the war, the idea persisted and spread. Disciplines other than psychology and engineering became involved, and civilian applications were found in settings as diverse as transportation, manufacturing, and communications (Chapanis, 1959). By 1958, interest had grown sufficiently to prompt the establishment of several organizations committed to the advancement of the HFE concept, notably the Human Factors Society (now the Human Factors and Ergonomics Society), the Society of Engineering Psychologists (a division of the American Psychological Association), and the international Ergonomics Society.

It was recognized early on that HFE would demand more than merely *applying* what is known about human performance to the design and improvement of systems. Often the required knowledge was lacking, making research necessary. Hence the field evolved as a combined science–practice enterprise. Professional journals (e.g., *Human Factors*, *Ergonomics*) were founded that included scientific as well as applied content.

Debate within the HFE community over exactly what mix of science and practice is appropriate, and whether the field is best regarded as an independent discipline or a philosophy that draws a number of disciplines together, has always been lively (Howell, 1994). Some do not consider HFE a psychological specialty despite the disproportionate representation of psychology in its demographics and content (Van Cott and Huey, 1992).

HFE TODAY

Growth in the size, diversity, and visibility of HFE has continued. There are now over 10,000 professionals who identify with the field. They are being produced by some 59 graduate programs in the US alone (Van Cott and Huey, 1992), and served by literally dozens of professional institutions (Salvendy, 1987). The knowledge base has exploded, with the most recent general handbook (which is quite dated) running to nearly 2,000 pages and barely scratching the surface of the 72 topic areas covered (Salvendy, 1987).

The growing impact of the HFE concept on society is now evident in litigation over the safety of consumer products and working conditions, in government and industry regulations, in product advertising, and in ordinary discourse. "User-friendly" has become a household term. Despite such encouraging signs, however, the discipline still functions in relative obscurity, and human factors considerations are all too often subordinated to those of cost, aesthetics, and machine performance in the design process (Howell, 1991).

A related difficulty is the popular misconception that advanced technology (notably automation), rather than human-oriented design, offers the final solution to the "human error problem." The fallacy in this logic is that automation never completely eliminates the human from the system. It merely redefines roles – in general, limiting human participation to broad supervision and decision responsibilities. Unfortunately, demands on the human increase rather than decline in this role, and the consequence of error can be enormous. Widely publicized mishaps such as the USS *Vincennes* incident, in which a civilian airliner was mistakenly shot down by a US cruiser despite the latter's highly sophisticated information system, serve to underscore this point (Wickens, 1992).

Topics of greatest interest to HFE researchers and practitioners have generally been driven by technological developments (Howell, 1993). This accounts for the current emphasis on issues posed by computer-based systems. The human–computer interaction (HCI) area, for example, is concerned with how to design the "interface" – displays, processing software, controls – to maximize human learning and performance. Similarly, the aforementioned supervisory role of the human in increasingly complex and powerful systems has prompted research on the "mental workload" demands of such systems, human capacities for coping with them, and designs for reducing them.

Another driver of HFE activity is social trends. For instance, changing population demography is currently stimulating considerable interest in design for special user groups (such as the elderly and disabled), an increasingly diverse workforce (*see* DIVERSITY), and an altered concept of the workplace (*see* FLEXIBLE WORKPLACE/TELECOMMUTING).

Bibliography

Chapanis, A. (1959). *Research Techniques in Human Engineering*. Baltimore, MD: Johns Hopkins University Press.

Christensen, J. M. (1958). Trends in human factors. *Human Factors*, 1, 2–7.

Howell, W. C. (1991). Human factors in the workplace. In M. D. Dunnette and L. M. Hough (eds.), *Handbook of Industrial and Organizational Psychology*, 2nd edn, vol. 2. Palo Alto, CA: Consulting Psychologists Press.

Howell, W. C. (1993). Engineering psychology in a changing world. *Annual Review of Psychology*, 44, 231–63.

Howell, W. C. (1994). Human factors and the challenges of the future. *Psychological Science*, 5, 1–7.

Salvendy, G. (ed.) (1987). *Handbook of Human Factors*. New York: John Wiley.

Van Cott, H. P. and Huey, B. M. (eds.) (1992). *Human Factors Specialists' Education and Utilization*. Washington, DC: National Academy Press.

Wickens, C. D. (1992). *Engineering Psychology and Human Performance*. New York: HarperCollins.

human relations approach

Fang Lee Cooke

The human relations approach to management was originated in the 1930s as a reaction against the mechanistic view of organizations and the pessimistic view of human nature suggested by the classical approach. The human relations approach argues that people are emotional rather than economic-rational beings; organizations are cooperative social systems rather than mechanical ones; and organizations are composed of informal structures, rules, and norms as well as formal practices and procedures.

The human relations approach represents a distinct break from the classical approach. However, both share two important similarities. First, they see organizations as closed and unchanged entities. Second and relatedly, they believe that there is "one best way" of managing the organization, regardless of the type, nature, or size of the organization, and that their way is "the best way."

Important theoretical advancements in the human relations approach include the famous Hawthorne experiments conducted by Elton Mayo, Chester Barnard's cooperative system, Abraham Maslow's hierarchy of needs, Douglas McGregor's Theory X–Theory Y, and Warren Bennis's "the death of bureaucracy." Despite these intellectual advancements, the human relations school remained operationally weak until the 1950s and 1960s when the advent of the job design movement offered operational guidelines to organizations. Job design proponents argue that jobs can and should be designed to fit human needs. The human relations approach was criticized for a number of reasons and was later taken over by the CONTINGENCY APPROACH in the 1960s.

Bibliography

Burnes, B. (1996). *Managing Change: A Strategic Approach to Organizational Dynamics*, 2nd edn. London: Pitman Publishing.

human resource audits

Mark A. Huselid

A human resource audit is a series of systematic, formal procedures designed to evaluate the efficiency and effectiveness of the firm's human resource management (HRM) system, compare its performance to relevant internal and external benchmarks, evaluate the appropriateness of this system for implementing the firm's strategic and operational objectives, and thereafter provide a framework for improving the way in which the firm manages people. The goal of this process is the development of an HRM system that is internally consistent, mutually reinforcing, and appropriately linked with the firm's competitive strategy and business needs (*see* HUMAN RESOURCE STRATEGY).

Specific areas of analysis include job and organizational design, recruitment and selection, PERFORMANCE MANAGEMENT, COMPENSATION and BENEFITS, employee development and training (*see* TRAINING), HUMAN RESOURCE PLANNING, labor relations, diversity management (*see* DIVERSITY; STRATEGIC ISSUES IN DIVERSITY), and compliance with legal and governmental guidelines (Biles and Schuler, 1986). Where possible, organizations measure both the costs and benefits associated with "people" management, and express these figures in a dollar-denominated metric. Specifically, the impact of the firm's HRM system on outcomes such as sales or profitability per employee, EMPLOYEE TURNOVER, attitudes such as JOB SATISFACTION, JOB INVOLVEMENT, and organizational commitment, number of GRIEVANCES and accidents, and individual employees' performance are generally assessed during this process (see Cascio, 1993).

Conceptually, a human resource audit can be thought of as two distinct but related processes: an assessment of the degree to which the firm is "doing the right things" as well as "doing things right." Ensuring that the firm is "doing the right things" requires an understanding of the firm's operating environment and competitive strategy, and an assessment of the degree to which its HRM system is both operationally appropriate and consistent with its needs. Because this process requires the expert judgment of professionals, it is crucial that the human resource managers involved have an in-depth understanding of how the business operates as well as its competitive environment.

An assessment of the degree to which the firm is "doing things right" requires an evaluation of the efficacy and efficiency of each of the primary HRM functions. To facilitate this process, firms frequently identify internal and external "benchmark" or comparison firms to help identify areas in need of improvement, and to provide inspiration for ways in which they might improve (*see* BENCHMARKING AND COMPETITOR ANALYSIS). Within this context, audit or benchmark data are often used as input into a BUSINESS PROCESS REENGINEERING effort (Florkowski and Schuler, 1994). Sources of benchmarking data for the HUMAN RESOURCE FUNCTION include the SOCIETY FOR HUMAN RESOURCE MANAGEMENT, the Bureau of National Affairs, and management consulting firms. In addition, many firms collect their own benchmarking data from peer organizations. An important element of this process, however, is gaining an understanding of the *context* within which the relevant comparison data are taken, as well as the specific results achieved by the comparison firms. Finally, as a repository of information concerning a wide variety of employment-related data, the firm's HUMAN RESOURCE INFORMATION SYSTEMS frequently play a significant role in the human resource audit process.

Bibliography

Biles, G. E. and Schuler, R. S. (1986). *Audit Handbook of Human Resource Management Practices*. Alexandria, VA: Society for Human Resource Management.

Cascio, W. F. (1993). *Costing Human Resources: The Financial Impact of Behavior in Organizations*, 4th edn. Boston: PWS-Kent.

Florkowski, G. W. and Schuler, R. S. (1994). Auditing human resource management in the global environment. *International Journal of Human Resource Management*, 5, 827–51.

Schuler, R. S. (1995). *Managing Human Resources*. St. Paul, MN: West Publishing.

human resource-based competitive advantage

Scott A. Snell and Shad S. Morris

Combining resource-based theories with human resource management (HRM) perspectives (Wright, Dunford, and Snell, 2001), human resource-based competitive advantage is broadly defined as the utilization of employee capabilities to create value for customers in a way that rival firms cannot. Resource-based theories emerged to show the importance of internal characteristics of the firm as an alternative to looking only at external forces in the industry (Wernerfelt, 1984). Barney (1991) made the case that a firm's resources lead to sustained competitive advantage when they are: (1) valuable, (2) rare, (3) inimitable, and (4) nonsubstitutable. More recently, Hoopes, Madsen, and Walker (2003) showed that considerable research has focused on these four resource characteristics and how they can be maintained and developed over time. Below, we show how these characteristics have been applied to understand human resource-based competitive advantage.

THE VALUE OF HUMAN RESOURCES

Human resources can add value by either improving efficiency or enhancing a firm's ability to satisfy customer needs (i.e., effectiveness). Research shows that programs designed to create a highly skilled workforce can result in higher PRODUCTIVITY, and these improvements provide value to firms over and above the costs incurred (Hunter and Hunter, 1984). For example, EMPLOYEE EMPOWERMENT programs tend to make performance more sensitive to variations in human skills, knowledge, and attitudes and to insure that mental effort rather than physical effort is instrumental for creating value and success (Walton and Susman, 1987).

THE RARENESS OF HUMAN RESOURCES

Human resource-based competitive advantage is also based on the assumption that labor supplies are *heterogeneous* across firms (Wright, McMahan, and McWilliams, 1994; Lepak and Snell, 1999). Many human attributes, such as cognitive ability, are normally distributed in the population, and because of this capability levels even one standard deviation above the mean (i.e., 84th percentile) are, by definition, rare. If companies can attract and retain the best and the brightest employees, and establish programs that maximize their value-added contribution, then they can build a competitive advantage through people.

In addition to the heterogeneity of labor, the question of rareness also depends on the *asset specificity* and *mobility* of the workforce (Becker, 1964). Employee skills that are firm-specific and cannot be transferred to other companies constitute a potential source of sustainable competitive advantage (Lado and Wilson, 1994).

THE INIMITABILITY OF HUMAN RESOURCES

Human capital can be either acquired on the open market or developed internally. If employee capabilities can be duplicated or imitated by another firm, they cannot be a source of sustainable competitive advantage. Resources are difficult to imitate under two conditions: (1) when the link between a firm's resources and its competitive advantage is *causally ambiguous* (Reed and DeFillippi, 1990), and (2) when internal and external relationships are multifaceted and *socially complex* (Barney, 1991). These two conditions imply that while individual skills and capabilities can be important sources of competitive advantage, it may be the complementarity among them that is most distinctive and sustainable (Snell, Youndt, and Wright, 1996).

The Substitutability of Human Resources

In the context of human resource-based competitive advantage, if a competitor can substitute another resource (e.g., technology) and achieve the same benefit vis-à-vis customers, then human resources would not provide a sustainable source of competitive advantage. The key issue here is *functional equivalence* (i.e., alternative resources that serve the same function are substitutes). In the past, organizations have historically substituted capital for labor where possible, and replaced decision-making with rules and procedures. In these ways, human resources have been readily substituted in traditional organizations, particularly in the context of routine aspects of physical work. However, as employees make the shift from touch labor to knowledge work, their value hinges more on cognitive processes such as problem diagnosis, troubleshooting, and decision-making (Snell and Dean, 1992). These aspects of human capital are not easily substitutable.

In summary, human resource-based competitive advantage refers to leveraging employee skills to outperform rival firms. Particularly in knowledge-based industries, competitive advantage increasingly resides in the people-embodied know-how (Prahalad, 1983), and human resources rather than physical or financial resources are what distinguish market leaders.

Bibliography

Barney, J. (1991). Firm resources and sustained competitive advantage. *Journal of Management*, 17, 99–120.

Becker, G. S. (1964). *Human Capital*. New York: Columbia University Press.

Hoopes, D. G., Madsen, T. L., and Walker, G. (2003). Guest editors' introduction to the special issue: Why is there a resource-based view? Toward a theory of competitive heterogeneity. *Strategic Management Journal*, 24, 889–902.

Hunter, J. and Hunter, R. (1984). Validity and utility of alternative predictors of job performance. *Psychological Bulletin*, 96, 72–98.

Lado, A. A. and Wilson, M. C. (1994). Human resource systems and sustained competitive advantage: A competency-based perspective. *Academy of Management Review*, 19, 699–727.

Lepak, D. P. and Snell, S. A. (1999). The human resource architecture: Toward a theory of human capital allocation and development. *Academy of Management Review*, 24, 31–48.

Prahalad, C. K. (1983). Developing strategic capability: An agenda for management. *Human Resources Management*, 22, 237–54.

Reed, R. and DeFillippi, R. J. (1990). Causal ambiguity, barriers to imitation, and sustained competitive advantage. *Academy of Management Review*, 15, 88–102.

Snell, S. A. and Dean, J. W. (1992). Integrated manufacturing and human resource management: A human capital perspective. *Academy of Management Journal*, 35, 467–504.

Snell, S. A., Youndt, M. A., and Wright, P. W. (1996). Establishing a framework for research in strategic human resource management: Merging resource theory and organizational learning. In G. R. Ferris (ed.), *Research in Personnel and Human Resources Management*, vol. 14. Greenwich, CT: JAI Press.

Walton, R. E. and Susman, G. I. (1987). People policies for the new machines. *Harvard Business Review*, 86, 71–83.

Wernerfelt, B. (1984). A resource-based view of the firm. *Strategic Management Journal*, 5, 171–80.

Wright, P. M., Dunford, B. D., and Snell, S. A. (2001). Human resources and the resource-based view of the firm. *Journal of Management*, 27, 701–21.

Wright, P. M., McMahan, G. C., and McWilliams, A. (1994). Human resources and sustained competitive advantage: A resource-based perspective. *International Journal of Human Resource Management*, 5, 301–26.

Human Resource Certification Institute (HRCI)

Rebecca A. Thacker

The Human Resource Certification Institute (HRCI) was founded by the SOCIETY FOR HUMAN RESOURCE MANAGEMENT in 1976 for the purpose of certifying individuals who have mastered the body of knowledge common to the field of human resource management (HRM). HRCI recognizes professionals who have, through HRM experience and the passing of a comprehensive written examination, demonstrated their competence in human resource management. Certification is at one of two levels: Professional in Human Resources Management (PHR) and Senior Professional in Human Resources (SPHR). In addition, HRCI promotes the establishment of standards for the HRM profession. As of 1995, 16,000 individuals were certified by HRCI and, of these, 9,000 are members of the Society for Human Resource Management.

human resource department

Mark A. Huselid

The human resource department is generally a formal unit or group of individuals within a firm who develop and implement policies, programs, and procedures for the acquisition and development of the firm's human capital, consistent with the needs of the firm's primary stakeholders. These stakeholders include shareholders, employees at all levels throughout the firm, governmental agencies, unions, job applicants, and suppliers (Tsui and Milkovich, 1987). Employees within the HUMAN RESOURCE FUNCTION also provide support and consulting services to line managers who are directly responsible for the administration of the firm's human resources (Schuler, 1995).

Bibliography

Schuler, R. S. (1995). *Managing Human Resources*. St. Paul, MN: West Publishing.

Tsui, A. S. and Milkovich, G. T. (1987). Personnel department activities: Constituency perspectives and preferences. *Personnel Psychology*, **40**, 519–37.

human resource department effectiveness

Mark A. Huselid

A human resource department can be considered *effective* to the degree it meets the needs of its primary stakeholders or constituencies. These groups include shareholders, customers, employees at all levels throughout the firm, governmental agencies, unions, job applicants, and suppliers (Tsui and Milkovich, 1987).

As markets have become increasingly competitive, firms have sought out innovative ways to achieve sustainable competitive advantage, and to satisfy these constituencies. An important element of a firm's response to these demands is the development of a "high-performance work system." Such systems require extensive employee TRAINING, COMPENSATION contingent on individual, work group, and overall firm performance, job-related and competency-based selection, and employee participation and involvement (Huselid, 1995). The adoption of such a *system* of interrelated practices helps to produce a workforce with the competencies and flexibility necessary to compete in rapidly changing product markets (*see* WORKFORCE FLEXIBILITY). When successfully implemented, such systems are difficult to imitate and have a potential *strategic* impact through the creation of sustainable competitive advantage. In addition, the outcomes of such a process can generate mutual gains reflected in greater returns for shareholders as well as higher pay, greater job security, and enhanced development opportunities for employees. In essence, the development of a high-performance work organization presents a "win-win" scenario for shareholders, employees, and society (Kochan and Osterman, 1994).

Conceptually, properly deployed human resource management (HRM) systems can influence firm performance by affecting employees in three broad ways (Bailey, 1993). First, HRM practices influence employee *skills* through the acquisition and development of the firm's human capital. Recruiting procedures that provide a large pool of qualified applicants, paired with reliable and valid PERSONNEL SELECTION programs, will have a substantial influence over the skills possessed by new employees. Thereafter, formal and informal training experiences, such as basic skills training, on-the-job experience (*see* ON-THE-JOB TRAINING), coaching, MENTORING PROGRAMS, and management development, can further enhance the development of employees.

Second, the effectiveness of even highly skilled employees will be limited if they are not inspired to perform, and HRM practices can affect employee *motivation* by encouraging employees to work both harder and smarter. Examples include the use of performance appraisals that assess individual and work group performance, the tight linkage of such appraisals with incentive compensation systems, and the use of promotion systems that focus on employee merit (*see* INCENTIVE PAY; PERFORMANCE APPRAISAL; PROMOTION).

Finally, the contribution of even a highly skilled and motivated workforce will be limited if work is so structured or "programmed" that employees do not have the opportunity to use their skills and abilities to design new and improved ways of performing their roles. Thus, HRM practices can also influence firm performance through *work and organizational designs* that encourage employees to participate and allow them to improve *how* their jobs are to be performed. Cross-functional teams, JOB ROTATION, and QUALITY CIRCLES are examples of organizational structures that encourage this type of participation.

The impact of high-performance work systems on firm performance has been the focus of an expanding body of research. Delaney (1996) found the widespread use of "progressive" HRM practices to have a strong and negative effect on organizational turnover (i.e., it reduced EMPLOYEE TURNOVER). Ichniowski, Shaw, and Prennushi (1994) found the impact of "cooperative and innovative" HRM practices to have a positive impact on organizational productivity. Arthur (1994) found that firms emphasizing employee commitment had lower turnover and scrap rates, and higher PRODUCTIVITY, than did firms emphasizing efficiency and lower labor costs. Huselid (1995) found that a one standard deviation improvement in firm deployment of high-performance work practices was associated with 7.05 (relative) percent lower turnover, and on a per employee basis, $27,044 higher sales, $18,641 higher market value, and $3,814 higher profits. Finally, MacDuffie (1995) found that "bundles" of internally consistent HRM practices were associated with higher productivity and quality.

In summary, the developing evidence suggests that human resource departments are effective to the degree that they meet the needs of their constituencies, and that the development of internally consistent *systems* of high-performance work practices has the potential to meet the needs of these constituencies through their statistically significant and economically meaningful impact on the performance of the firm.

Bibliography

Arthur, J. B. (1994). Effects of human resource systems on manufacturing performance and turnover. *Academy of Management Journal*, 37, 670–87.

Bailey, T. (1993). Discretionary effort and the organization of work: Employee participation and work reform since Hawthorne. Working paper, Columbia University, New York.

Delaney, J. T. (1996). Unions, human resource innovations, and organizational outcomes. *Advances in Industrial and Labor Relations*.

Huselid, M. A. (1995). The impact of human resource management practices on turnover, productivity, and corporate financial performance. *Academy of Management Journal*, 38, 635–72.

Ichniowski, C., Shaw, K., and Prennushi, G. (1994). The effects of human resource management practices on productivity. Working paper, Columbia University, New York.

Kochan, T. A. and Osterman, P. (1994). *The Mutual Gains Enterprise: Forging a Winning Partnership among Labor, Management, and Government*. Boston: Harvard Business School Press.

MacDuffie, J. P. (1995). Human resource bundles and manufacturing performance: Organizational logic and flexible production systems in the world auto industry. *Industrial and Labor Relations Review*, 48, 197–221.

Tsui, A. S. and Milkovich, G. T. (1987). Personnel department activities: Constituency perspectives and preferences. *Personnel Psychology*, 40, 519–37.

Human Resource Division, Academy of Management

M. Susan Taylor

The Human Resource Division is the third largest of 21 professional divisions in the US Academy of Management, with approximately 2,600 members in 2004. Its domain is the study of content relating to administering the HUMAN RESOURCE FUNCTION and to external influences upon the administration of work. The division is governed by an executive committee consisting of the past and current chairs, chair-elect, and 12 other members elected by the membership. Human Resource Division services include quarterly newsletters, an electronic bulletin board, Human Resource Net (HRNET) (*see* INTERNET), an international research directory, doctoral and junior faculty consortia, preconference developmental activities, a full conference program, and social hours and receptions (Heneman, 1994).

Bibliography

Heneman, R. (1994). *Professional Division Report, Human Resource Division, 1989–1990 to 1994–1995.* Dallas, TX: Human Resource Division, Academy of Management.

human resource function

Mark A. Huselid

The role of the human resource function is to attract and select qualified job applicants, to develop PERFORMANCE MANAGEMENT and COMPENSATION systems that align employee behaviors with organizational goals, and to assist in the development and retention of a diverse workforce to meet current and future organizational requirements (*see* HUMAN RESOURCE STRATEGY; HUMAN RESOURCE DEPARTMENT EFFECTIVENESS). Employees within the human resource function also provide support and consulting services to line managers, who are directly responsible for the administration of the firm's human resources (Schuler, 1995). Specific areas of responsibility include job and organizational design, recruitment and selection, performance management, compensation and BENEFITS, employee development and training (*see* TRAINING), HUMAN RESOURCE PLANNING, labor relations, diversity management (*see* DIVERSITY; STRATEGIC ISSUES IN DIVERSITY), and compliance with legal and governmental guidelines.

Bibliography

Schuler, R. S. (1995). *Managing Human Resources.* St. Paul, MN: West Publishing.

human resource information systems

John W. Boudreau

Human resource information systems (HRIS) are systematic procedures for collecting, storing, maintaining, retrieving, and validating data needed by an organization about its human resources, personnel activities, and organization unit characteristics (Milkovich and Boudreau, 1993). HRIS need not be complex or even computerized. They can be as informal as the payroll records and time cards of a small boutique or restaurant, or as extensive and formal as the computerized human resource data banks of major manufacturers, banks, and governments.

HRIS can support HUMAN RESOURCE PLANNING with information for labor supply and demand forecasts; STAFFING with information on equal employment opportunity, job postings (*see* JOB POSTING), separations, and applicant qualifications; and training and development with information on training program costs and trainee work performance (*see* TRAINING). HRIS can also support COMPENSATION with information on pay increases, payroll processing, salary forecasts, and pay budgets; and labor–employee relations with information on contract negotiations and employee assistance needs. The purpose is to provide information that is required by human resource stakeholders or supports human resource decisions. HRIS enhance human resource management in several ways, including:

1 reducing the *costs* of gathering, summarizing, and distributing information;
2 BUSINESS PROCESS REENGINEERING, by encouraging decision-makers to carefully consider how to design their human resource information processing to be most efficient and effective; and
3 decision support, by providing data that help the recipient to improve decisions about programs or personal choices (Boudreau, 1992).

HRIS must accomplish three significant processes: (1) *input*, which involves adding data to the system; (2) *maintenance*, which involves updating, integrating, and organizing the data; and (3) *output*, which involves manipulating the data to appear in the appropriate format, and then delivering the data to the appropriate destination or person. A growing number of organizations now use computerized systems to implement their HRIS. Such systems may rely on large centralized databases, but more frequently are evolving to exploit large networks of smaller computers, each containing a portion of the human resources data of the organization (Broderick and Boudreau, 1991). Future systems will very likely provide connections to worldwide networks such as the INTERNET, allowing external information to be imported and combined with the internal information from the organization. Construction of such computerized information requires careful planning, and the cooperation of multiple constituents (Walker, 1993).

As computers become increasingly common in offices, homes, and factories, access to HRIS is rapidly increasing. In the past, only a handful of technicians had the skills to obtain HRIS contents. Today, many managers can acquire such information from their desktops or even by phone, and employees are increasingly able to use computers to change their personal data entries, get information about company policies, and even obtain computerized expert system assistance for decisions such as choosing among FLEXIBLE BENEFIT PLANS or relocation. As access proliferates, the question of PRIVACY IN ORGANIZATIONS will be increasingly important to human resource managers, especially those who support international human resource management (Boudreau, Broderick, and Pucik, 1994).

Bibliography

Boudreau, J. W. (1992). HRIS: Adding value or just cutting costs? *HR Monthly*, May, 8–11.

Boudreau, J. W., Broderick, R. L., and Pucik, V. (1994). Just doing business: Human resource information systems in the global organization. In P. C. Deans and K. R. Karwan (eds.), *Global Information Systems and Technology: Focus on the Organization and Its Functional Areas*. Harrisburg, PA: Idea Group Publishing.

Broderick, R. L. and Boudreau, J. W. (1991). The evolution of computer use in human resource management: Interviews with ten leaders. *Human Resource Management*, **30**, 485–508.

Milkovich, G. T. and Boudreau, J. W. (1993). *Human Resource Management*. Homewood, IL: Richard D. Irwin.

Walker, A. J. (1993). *Handbook of Human Resource Information Systems*. New York: McGraw-Hill.

human resource inventories

Donald W. Jarrell

Inventories, also called stocks, are accumulated stores of employee characteristics within an organization that have value to the organization. Inventories have value to the extent that the characteristics contribute, directly or indirectly, to the achievement of organization objectives.

Characteristics with value to an organization may be either attributes of individual employees or attributes of groups of employees. Individual attributes that may have value are: abilities, age, attitudes, behaviors and traits, beliefs, capitalized value, character or integrity, citizenship, commitment, competencies, condition and health, energy level, knowledge and understanding, longevity or tenure, performance, personality, productivity, protected group classification, satisfaction, skills, service orientation, values, and work ethic. All these attributes may be summed to determine their extent within groups of employees.

In some instances synergistic or critical mass effects tend to occur when many persons in a group have an attribute. The most common synergistic effect is the acting out by employees of a characteristic. Enactment occurs when employees in the group become aware that other persons in the group share the characteristic and when display of the characteristic meets a social need of employees (Weick, 1979).

Individual employee attributes most likely to have synergistic effects within groups are (with their corresponding group attribute in parentheses): behaviors and traits (culture), commitment (loyalty), JOB SATISFACTION (morale), and character or integrity (social character).

ARE CHARACTERISTICS ACTUALLY INVENTORIED?

To inventory usually means that the amount of the item in the stock is counted or measured at a given time. In practice, organizations typically inventory human resources only when the characteristic may easily be counted or measured and/or a count or measure is necessary or highly important. For example, many organizations routinely inventory the age and longevity of their employees because EMPLOYEE TURN-

OVER can have significant financial implications. Organizations doing federal contract work inventory the protected group status of employees since they may be required by a presidential executive order (*see* EXECUTIVE ORDERS) to submit this information to the OFFICE OF FEDERAL CONTRACT COMPLIANCE PROGRAMS. More often, human resource inventories are monitored without actual physical count or measure.

Inventories have long played a central role in the forecasting of workforce availability, as part of the employment planning process. Current changes sweeping the workplace appear to be heightening the need for attention to monitoring human resource inventories. For example, WORKFORCE FLEXIBILITY, widely sought by organizations to allow just-in-time delivery of product and quick response to changing customer needs (*see* JUST-IN-TIME PRODUCTION SYSTEMS), is enhanced by building organizations with flat structures staffed by empowered employees working in teams (*see* SELF-MANAGING TEAMS). These teams require multi-skilled employees, who can perform most of the discrete jobs needed to produce the product or service, and who have problem-solving and interpersonal skills.

STRATEGIC HUMAN RESOURCE MANAGEMENT may identify, often using generic competency models, competencies of special importance to strategic objectives. These competencies, because of their critical importance for organization success, often are measured using ASSESSMENT CENTERS and deficiencies are addressed through corporate universities or academies.

Bibliography

Biles, G. E. and Schuler, R. S. (1986). *Audit Handbook of Human Resource Practices: Auditing the Effectiveness of the Human Resource Functions.* Alexandria, VA: American Society for Personnel Administration.

Grinold, R. C. and Marshall, K. T. (1977). *Manpower Planning Models.* New York: North-Holland.

Jarrell, D. W. (1993). *Human Resource Planning: A Business Planning Approach.* Englewood Cliffs, NJ: Prentice-Hall.

Manzini, A. O. and Gridley, J. D. (1986). *Integrating Human Resources and Strategic Business Planning.* New York: AMACOM, American Management Association.

Weick, K. E. (1979). *The Social Psychology of Organizing.* Reading, MA: Addison-Wesley.

human resource management in the US

John E. Delery

During the first quarter of the twentieth century, the HUMAN RESOURCE FUNCTION in US organizations emerged as the personnel department. Early functions of this department included attempts to keep labor unions from forming and focusing on production efficiency through time and motion studies. In the 1910s and 1920s these departments began to engage in employment testing, focusing on individual differences that predicted JOB PERFORMANCE. Soon after this, with the passage of federal legislation governing labor unions, the focus was again on keeping unions out of the workplace and employees were viewed as adversaries.

From World War II to the late 1960s the human relations movement flourished. This movement was characterized by a belief that more satisfied employees were more productive employees, and it emphasized more supportive supervision and a greater consideration for employees' needs. With the passage of federal civil rights legislation in the 1960s, the personnel department gained importance as the legal watchdog for the organization. The emphasis shifted to organizational compliance with the law, which heightened the importance of many human resource management (HRM) practices, including JOB ANALYSIS.

Over the past three decades, this functional area has changed as the pressures from increasing national and international competition have forced organizations to cut costs and increase PRODUCTIVITY. During this time HRM has emerged as a strategic function for the success of the organization and the practitioners are now viewed as business partners with the chief executives of the firm. Many US organizations today view their human resource departments as value-added service providers and their employees as a source of sustained competitive advantage. This has given rise to the term STRATEGIC HUMAN RESOURCE MANAGEMENT, which emphasizes the need for organizations to manage employees in a manner consistent with strategic business objectives.

LEGAL ENVIRONMENT

The field of HRM is highly regulated in the US. There are federal laws dealing with labor relations, employment DISCRIMINATION/civil rights, health and safety, compensation, and work and family issues, just to name a few. The NATIONAL LABOR RELATIONS ACT OF 1935 gave employees the right to engage in COLLECTIVE BARGAINING through representation by a labor union. This Act also specified the process through which employees gain representation, outlined specific practices of management that were labeled unfair labor practices, and set up the NATIONAL LABOR RELATIONS BOARD (NLRB) to oversee compliance. Later Acts amended this legislation to include unfair union practices and to specify that union leaders be elected by the membership.

Employment discrimination on the basis of race, color, gender, religion, or national origin is prohibited in the US. In addition, there are federal laws that prohibit discrimination against individuals over the age of 40, persons with disabilities, and Vietnam-era veterans (see AGE DISCRIMINATION IN EMPLOYMENT ACT OF 1967; AMERICANS WITH DISABILITIES ACT OF 1990; VIETNAM-ERA VETERANS READJUSTMENT ACT OF 1972). Many communities have enacted even tougher protection at the state and local levels. Some US cities prohibit discrimination based on sexual preference. These laws generally protect individuals from being discriminated at any time in the employment relationship. This includes the hiring process, promotions, terminations, and compensation. The major piece of civil rights legislation was the CIVIL RIGHTS ACT OF 1964. This Act, in addition to prohibiting employment discrimination, established the EQUAL EMPLOYMENT OPPORTUNITY COMMISSION (EEOC) to enforce the provisions of the law. The EEOC is today the primary agency with these duties. The president of the US has also ordered that all federal contractors engage in AFFIRMATIVE ACTION programs to insure that women and minorities are provided equal opportunity. The OFFICE OF FEDERAL CONTRACT COMPLIANCE PROGRAMS oversees this executive order (see EXECUTIVE ORDERS).

In 1970 the OCCUPATIONAL SAFETY AND HEALTH ACT OF 1970, intended to provide US workers a safe and healthy workplace, went into effect. This Act established a national agency, the OCCUPATIONAL SAFETY AND HEALTH ADMINISTRATION (OSHA), charged with the duty of enforcing the provisions of the law. In addition to providing workers with a safe workplace, employers are required to provide workers' compensation benefits. This insurance is a no-fault insurance designed to provide compensation to workers who have been injured on the job.

Other laws have established a minimum wage, child labor regulations, and the requirement that employers document that their employees have the legal right to work in the US. Recent legislation has also required that employers provide employees with up to 12 weeks of unpaid leave if they have a family or medical emergency (see FAMILY AND MEDICAL LEAVE ACT OF 1993).

FUNCTIONAL AREAS IN HRM

Staffing practices vary greatly across organizations and industries in the US. In general, the most common method of external recruitment used by US organizations has traditionally been the newspaper advertisement. Recruiting practices vary, however, depending on the labor market and the level of skill required for the job. Many US organizations have had a long history of hiring from within their organizations. For internal recruitment, job postings and supervisor referrals appear to be the most common (see RECRUITING; STAFFING).

Selection has received a great deal of attention, due in large part to discrimination laws. The most common selection technique is the EMPLOYMENT INTERVIEW. However, many organizations use various forms of cognitive ability testing and PERSONALITY TESTS. Recently, the use of honesty and integrity testing has become commonplace (see INTEGRITY TESTING). One of the largest trends in staffing over the past few years has been for organizations to outsource this function. There is now a growing industry comprised of organizations who do nothing but recruit and screen applicants for other organizations.

Hourly pay for blue-collar jobs and salaries for white-collar jobs still characterize most US organizations. Many organizations, however, have begun to try more innovative PAY FOR PERFORMANCE and skill-based compensation practices (see SKILL-BASED PAY DESIGN). These vary from rather simple MERIT PAY systems, where employees' raises are determined by their annual evaluation, to GAINSHARING systems, where employees receive BONUSES based on cost-cutting, to more complicated stock options plans (see EMPLOYEE STOCK OWNERSHIP PLANS). In all, a trend toward pay for performance or putting a greater proportion of pay at risk rather than pay for hours worked has emerged.

In the US a growing gap between the wages of top management and employees at the bottom of the organization has appeared. In addition, women have traditionally earned less than men, and this continues to be the case today (see WOMEN'S CAREER ISSUES).

Many employers provide a wide range of BENEFITS to employees, the most common of which are healthcare, retirement pay, vacation, and sick leave. Some of the more progressive organizations have begun to provide CHILDCARE BENEFIT, FLEXIBLE WORKING HOURS, and cafeteria or FLEXIBLE BENEFIT PLANS, where employees may choose the benefits they wish to have.

Nonmonetary rewards have also been gaining in popularity. For example, organizations may reward employees with anything from a gold star paperweight or a wrist watch to a better parking space.

Training has become increasingly important to US organizations as they find it more and more difficult to find qualified applicants and as the technological environment continues to change rapidly. Organizations provide this training in a variety of ways, from unstructured ON-THE-JOB-TRAINING to formal classroom and computer-assisted instruction. Recent emphasis has been placed on training individuals to perform a variety of jobs. This practice of CROSS-TRAINING enables organizations to achieve greater flexibility in staffing.

In general, however, organizations have not traditionally measured the success of their training programs. Training effort in organizations has been measured not so much by which training method they use, or how effective it is, as by how much money they spend on it.

US organizations use a wide variety of practices to appraise the performance of their employees (see PERFORMANCE APPRAISAL). These mainly vary across different jobs and different levels in the organization. For instance, many employees are subject to a formal appraisal from their supervisor only once a year, while others are in jobs where performance can be more easily and objectively measured. Besides objective performance measures, such as sales dollars or production output, some organizations have experimented with PERFORMANCE MANAGEMENT programs such as MANAGEMENT BY OBJECTIVES, where the employee and supervisor sit down and outline specific objectives for the coming period and then sit down again at the end of the period to evaluate achievement of those objectives.

Although much of the emphasis in HRM has been on the traditional functional areas of staffing, training, appraising, and compensation, there are countless other practices that are also aimed at managing human resources. For instance, some US organizations provide employees with greater job security through formal policies. Many organizations are also involved in employee participation programs and have attempted to provide greater degrees of EMPLOYEE EMPOWERMENT. Team-based production systems, where teams control much of their work processes, have become widespread.

RECENT TRENDS

The recent trends in HRM in US organizations have included the STRATEGIC OUTSOURCING of much of the traditional human resource function. Staffing and temporary help agencies have grown rapidly. Other functions outsourced include much of compensation and benefits. Organizations that handle the payroll function for other organizations have become quite common, and as benefits packages have become more costly, organizations have turned much of the management of these programs over to organizations specializing in this area.

While some of the traditional human resource functions are being outsourced, the management of human resources has gained greater prominence in the organization. Organizations have placed a greater emphasis on insuring that they are managing their human resources in a manner that will achieve a competitive advantage. This means including human resource professionals in the STRATEGIC HUMAN RESOURCE PLANNING PROCESSES for the organization. The emphasis is shifting from technical competence in functional human resource areas to a more generalist, strategic perspective that focuses on how human resource practices help to support one another and how HRM systems help to support the organization's overall business strategy.

Bibliography

Barney, J. (1995). Looking inside for competitive advantage. *Academy of Management Executive*, **9** (4), 49–61.

Baron, J. N., Jennings, P. D., and Dobbin, F. R. (1988). Mission control? The development of personnel systems in US industry. *American Sociological Review*, **53**, 497–514.

Dulebohn, J. H., Ferris, G. R., and Stodd, J. T. (1995). The history and evolution of human resource management. In G. R. Ferris, S. D. Rosen, and D. T. Barnum (eds.), *Handbook of Human Resource Management*. Cambridge, MA: Blackwell.

Feldblum, P. F. (1993). A short history of labor law. *Labor Law Journal*, February, 67–79.

Pfeffer, J. (1994). *Competitive Advantage through People*. Boston: Harvard Business School Press.

Schuler, R. S. (1990). Repositioning the human resource function: Transformation or demise. *Academy of Management Executive*, **4**, 49–60.

Wright, P. M. and McMahan, G. C. (1992). Theoretical perspectives for strategic human resource management. *Journal of Management*, **18**, 295–320.

human resource planning

James W. Walker

Organizational effectiveness depends on having the right people in the right jobs at the right times to meet rapidly changing organizational requirements (Bechet and Walker, 1993). Human resource planning is a process that uses available information to define skill and capability requirements needed to meet future business needs. Human resource planning originated as manpower planning (Walker, 1969), focusing on the process of balancing talent supply and demand in an organization.

Human resource planning is an approach for dealing with policies, plans, analyses, systems, and methods to establish and implement programs that bring about an effective workforce in the future. It is an approach that seeks to reconcile, to the extent possible, the individual's needs and desires for the future with those of the organization (Burack and Mathys, 1980).

Over the years, the process has been defined and applied more broadly. STRATEGIC HUMAN RESOURCE PLANNING addresses everything an organization does to manage people effectively in support of organizational objectives (Walker, 1992). Almost any finite definition, description, or outlined process may be refuted by examples of how some organizations approach it differently. Planning enables managers to define future scenarios, gaps between the present situation and a selected scenario, and action plans that will bridge these gaps.

Human resource planning lacks the precise definition of other traditional human resource functions such as TRAINING, BENEFITS, or RECRUITING (*see* HUMAN RESOURCE FUNCTION). Human resource planning is variously perceived as:

1 a system of forecasting and information management;
2 a process of influencing management to embrace human resources as a dimension of strategic business planning;
3 an integrating theme for human resource management; and
4 a formalizing and strengthening of long-standing informal practices for managing people (Holbrook, 1994).

A practical definition requires consideration of the applications relevant to a specific organization (Dyer, 1986).

See also *strategic human resource planning*

Bibliography

Bechet, T. P. and Walker, J. P. (1993). Aligning staffing with business strategy. *Human Resource Planning*, **16**, 1–16.

Burack, E. H. and Mathys, N. (1980). *Human Resource Planning: A Pragmatic Approach to Manpower Staffing and Development.* Lake Forest, IL: Brace-Park Press.

Burack, E. H. and Walker, J. W. (1972). *Manpower Planning and Programming.* Boston: Allyn and Bacon.

Dyer, L. (1986). *Human Resource Planning Guide.* New York: Random House.

Holbrook, V. S. (1994). *Human Resource Planning Portfolio.* Phoenix, AZ: Motorola.

Walker, J. W. (1969). Forecasting manpower needs. *Harvard Business Review,* 152–75.

Walker, J. W. (1992). *Human Resource Strategy.* New York: McGraw-Hill.

Human Resource Planning Society

Oliver London

"The Human Resource Planning Society (HRPS) is committed to improving organizational performance by creating a global network of individuals who function as business partners in the application of strategic human resource management practices" (mission statement of HRPS). One focus of the society is identifying state-of-the-art STRATEGIC HUMAN RESOURCE MANAGEMENT issues, utilizing input from human resource experts. Additionally, HRPS conducts a yearly conference for all members, a corporate sponsor's conference, and several professional development workshops, and sponsors human resource-related research. The approximately 2,500 members are typically people who hold more senior and key strategic human resource positions. Most members have responsibilities in organization effectiveness, continuity, and/or organizational development.

For further information contact: Human Resource Planning Society, 41 East 42nd Street, Suite 1509, New York, NY 10017. Telephone 212-490-6387.

human resource programming

Stella M. Nkomo

Human resource programming is a process for developing action plans to close the gap between the supply of human resources and the demand for human resources over a particular planning period. It is part of HUMAN RESOURCE PLANNING and occurs after an organization's human resource needs have been forecasted. Action programs may be needed to increase the supply of employees when demand is greater than supply of employees. Conversely, programs may be required to decrease the number of employees if the forecasts show supply exceeding demand. These gaps may reflect not only quantities of employees but also their quality, skill mix, and diversity. Additionally, some parts of a firm may be in balance while other areas may experience shortages or surpluses. Effective human resource programming involves generating alternative courses of action, evaluating each, and selecting the best course of action to close the gap. Research and practice suggest that organizations have a number of alternative ways to manage surpluses and shortages of human resources.

Human resource surpluses can be addressed through a number of strategies. Because layoffs have such a negative impact on employees, practitioners and researchers alike suggest the use of first-level strategies such as reduction in overtime or work hours and hiring freezes so that attrition may naturally diminish the workforce (Greenhalgh, Lawrence, and Sutton, 1988). Other defenses against layoffs include RETRAINING, REDEPLOYMENT, JOB SHARING, unpaid vacation, and reduction in pay. More companies have been making use of voluntary early retirement programs to manage surpluses. Such programs offer additional years' credit and bonuses to encourage employees not currently eligible for retirement to retire at an earlier age (*see* EARLY RETIREMENT POLICY). A major concern with such programs has been the potential loss of talent. One study of a major employer, however, found no loss in quality of management talent as a result of early retirements (Howard, 1988). Another concern is that employees may feel coerced into retiring through negative changes in their performance evaluations and pressure from supervisors to take the incentive. The Older Workers Benefit Protection Act of 1991, an amendment to the AGE DISCRIMINATION IN EMPLOYMENT ACT OF 1967, lays out guidelines for structuring early retirement programs to minimize risk of adverse impact charges from older employees (Stein, 1991; *see* DISPARATE IMPACT).

Once first-level strategies have been exhausted and surpluses still remain, layoffs and DOWNSIZING may be inevitable. In recent years, because of competitive and economic pressures, organizations have turned to downsizing as a strategy to reconcile gaps between demand and supply of human resources. Downsizing is not without its problems. Cascio (1993) reported that few companies are well prepared for downsizing and that, six months to a year after a downsizing, key firm performance indicators often do not improve. Reasons for this include workload strains on remaining employees, survivors' guilt among those not laid off, and replacement costs for loss of knowledge and skills. Researchers suggest that companies must be careful to plan for downsizing and layoffs. Downsizing should not be undertaken as a short-term, quick-fix solution but should be contemplated in relation to a firm's intended competitive strategies. Attention must be paid not just to headcount reduction but also to fundamental changes in the design of work and the structure of the organization (Cascio, 1993). There are a number of practices that can soften the impact of layoffs on employees. These range from early advance notice to outplacement services. Companies having 100 or more employees are required by the WORKER ADJUSTMENT AND RETRAINING NOTIFICATION ACT OF 1988 (WARN) to provide 60 days' advance notice of plant closings to employees, unions, and state and local officials when 50 or more employees will lose jobs.

Human resource shortages present another kind of challenge. Shortages can be addressed through RECRUITING both internally and externally. Internal recruiting offers the advantage of greater knowledge of job candidates, lower recruitment costs, and less need for orientation. On the downside, reliance on internal recruiting may result in stagnation due to in-breeding. Part of the challenge with external recruiting to fill shortages is identifying those sources that will yield the desired number and quality of employees at the most efficient cost. Instead of recruiting permanent employees, many organizations are increasingly turning to contingent workers to fill employee shortages. Contingent workers include temporaries, part-timers, consultants, subcontractors, and leased employees (Belous, 1989). These approaches offer an organization greater strategic flexibility in matching STAFFING needs with work demands (*see* CONTINGENT EMPLOYMENT; EMPLOYEE LEASING; EMPLOYEE SUBCONTRACTING).

Bibliography

Belous, R. S. (1989). How human resource systems adjust to the shift toward contingent workers. *Monthly Labor Review*, 112, 7–12.

Cascio, W. F. (1993). Downsizing: What do we know? What have we learned? *Academy of Management Executive*, 7, 95–104.

Greenhalgh, L., Lawrence, A. T., and Sutton, R. I. (1988). Determinants of work force reduction in declining industries. *Academy of Management Review*, 13, 241–54.

Howard, A. (1988). Who reaches for the golden handshake? *Academy of Management Executive*, 2, 133–44.

Stein, L. I. (1991). Through the looking glass: An analysis of window plans. *Labor Law Journal*, October, 665–76.

human resource strategy

James A. Craft

The term human resource strategy (HRS) currently lacks definitional precision, but it generally refers to a construct denoting the coherent set of decisions or factors that shape and guide the management of human resources (acquisition, allocation, utilization, development, reward) in an organizational context. It is directly related to the business strategy and focuses on the formulation and alignment of human resource activities to achieve organizational competitive objectives.

HRS is a relatively new concept in the field of human resource management (HRM). It has emerged as the HUMAN RESOURCE FUNCTION has assumed a more strategic perspective and organizations have come to view employees as essential resources to be managed effectively to achieve strategic business goals. At least three basic concepts of HRS have been articulated: the decisional concept, the human resource issue/

action concept, and the human resources priorities concept.

The Decisional Concept

Drawing upon the business strategy literature, Dyer (1984) formulated a longitudinal or retrospective decisional concept of HRS. He defines the organizational HRS as "the pattern that emerges from a stream of important decisions about the management of human resources" (p. 159). This concept requires a review of important HRM-related organizational decisions over a period of time to determine consistencies and observable patterns. In effect, the emergent pattern of coherent and consistent decisions revealed upon retroactive investigation indicates the strategy that guides human resource (HR) activity.

In a later work, Dyer and Holder (1988) offered a more proactive decisional concept of HRS. In this case, the HRS is viewed as the collection of major HR goals and means to be used in pursuit of organizational strategic plans. When an acceptable business strategy is formulated, key HR goals are defined to support this strategy and the necessary means (i.e., programming and policies) are designed and implemented to meet the goals. For example, if an organization chooses a competitive strategy of low-cost producer, major HR goals to support this strategy could be higher performance and lower headcounts. These, in turn, could lead to programs including reduction in force and more increased investment in employee TRAINING. This combined set of HR goals and means would be the organizational HRS.

The HR Issue/Action Concept

This approach is based on an issue-oriented focus to develop an organizational HRS. Schuler and Walker (1990) and Walker (1992) argue that in a dynamic, fast-changing environment, managers must deal effectively with a series of emerging business issues that can have a significant impact on competitive success. Business issues will involve HR issues that are critical to successful strategy implementation.

These HR issues can be considered gaps that represent opportunities for people to contribute more effectively to the achievement of business strategies. Line managers have to respond to these HR issues in their decision processes. As is necessary, they will define directional actions to address the people-related business issues. These managerial actions and plans will focus, mobilize, and direct the HR activities toward the business issues most important to the firm; and they will form the essence of the organizational HR strategies.

The HR Priorities Concept

This concept of HRS posits that each organization has an identifiable set of dominant HR priorities that are used to align its HR activities, policies, and programs with its strategic business goals (Craft, 1988, 1995). This cluster of key HR priorities, which constitutes the HRS, defines the organization's orientation and attitude toward its employees and it guides the development of HR plans that deal with the personnel aspects of basic business issues. For example, in an organization competing on the basis of innovation, core HR priorities might include employee risk taking, initiative, teamwork and high competence.

The priorities will be basic factors guiding and configuring the HR system (acquiring, developing, rewarding) in response to business needs. Each organization's cluster of priorities (HRS) will differ based on the mix of its competitive strategy, internal organizational factors (e.g., culture, technology), and external environmental factors (e.g., labor market, competitor practice).

While the HRS tends to be stable in the short term, over time it is a dynamic concept since the priorities will evolve and be crafted to meet changing business situations.

Bibliography

Craft, J. A. (1988). Human resource planning and strategy. In L. Dyer (ed.), *Human Resource Management: Evolving Roles and Responsibilities*. Washington, DC: Bureau of National Affairs.

Craft, J. A. (1995). Human resources strategy. Unpublished working paper.

Dyer, L. (1984). Studying human resource strategy: An approach and an agenda. *Industrial Relations*, 23, 156–69.

Dyer, L. and Holder, G. W. (1988). A strategic perspective of human resource management. In L. Dyer (ed.), *Human Resource Management: Evolving Roles and Responsibilities*. Washington, DC: Bureau of National Affairs.

Schuler, R. S. and Walker, J. W. (1990). Human resources strategy: Focusing on issues and actions. *Organizational Dynamics*, 19, 4–19.

Walker, J. W. (1992). *Human Resource Strategy*. New York: McGraw-Hill.

Immigration Reform and Control Act of 1986

Vida Scarpello

The US Constitution gives Congress the power to establish a uniform code for naturalization. Accordingly, Congress legislates who can come into the country and who cannot. The Immigration Reform and Control Act (IRCA) replaces the Immigration and Nationality Act of 1952 (INA) (see Legislative History, 1980).

The INA had two goals: (1) to define the terms and conditions of alien admission into the US; and (2) to establish procedures for the subsequent treatment of lawfully admitted aliens. Related to the first goal is INA's prohibition against concealing, harboring, or shielding from detection any alien not lawfully entitled to enter or reside in the US. The law, however, specifically excluded employers from the "harboring" prohibition and, thus, made it legal to hire illegal immigrants.

Various economic problems in the US, along with high unemployment and an increasing illegal immigrant population, motivated Congress to pass the 1986 Immigration Reform and Control Act. The IRCA removed employer exclusion from INA's "harboring" prohibition. This Act, like previous immigration laws, has two major purposes: (1) to control illegal immigration; and (2) to protect US citizens and legal resident immigrants against adverse economic consequences of job competition with illegal immigrants (Ledvinka and Scarpello, 1991). Although the first purpose was motivated by INA's "harboring" provision, the second purpose was motivated by concern for protecting Hispanic and other minority US citizens and legal immigrants from employment DISCRIMINATION. Because illegal immigrants may potentially compete with Hispanic US citizens and other minority groups for employment, IRCA gives citizens preferential status.

The IRCA requires employers to verify the identity, citizenship status, and employment eligibility of all job applicants. It also specifies the employment verification procedures required of both employers and job applicants. All applicants for employment must provide proof of identity and employment eligibility, and all employers must examine that proof to confirm the new hire's identity and right to work in the United States. The one exception to these rules involves hiring applicants referred by a state employment agency. In those cases, the state agency is responsible for verifying the identity, employment eligibility, and citizenship status of the new hires and for keeping certification and attestation records for a period of three years from the initial date of referral (Ledvinka and Scarpello, 1991).

The IRCA includes an antidiscrimination in employment prohibition and also defines a special category of foreign labor for seasonal agricultural employment. The antidiscrimination prohibition (section 1324B(a)(1)) makes it unlawful to discriminate against any individual (other than an unauthorized alien) with respect to recruiting, hiring, and terminating any individual because of national origin or citizenship status. It permits the employer, however, to discriminate in favor of US citizens and those who have filed a declaration of intention to become US citizens (Ledvinka and Scarpello, 1991). Foreign seasonal agricultural workers are considered "eligible individuals" under the IRCA. An eligible individual is neither an illegal alien nor an immigrant. This category of worker is treated as a legal immigrant for the period of employment.

The IRCA allows employers to hire foreigners as seasonal agricultural workers provided the employer (or employer association) petitions the Secretary of Labor for a labor certification to import immigrants as temporary agricultural workers. Once granted, the labor certification can stay in effect for up to three years. To protect employment rights of seasonal foreign workers, the IRCA requires employers to provide wages, benefits, and working conditions (including housing) as specified by the Secretary of Labor. The Act also authorizes the attorney general to adjust the status of the temporary agricultural worker to that of a permanent legal immigrant after the worker has worked 90 days of seasonal work during each of three years of seasonal employment. Given that one hour of work in a given day is counted as one day's work, this provision treats any seasonal agricultural worker as a permanent US resident.

The IRCA applies to all employers with four or more employees. Under the Act, the entity responsible for personnel practices is defined as the employer. This means that in a corporation with decentralized personnel practices, each division with independent personnel activities is considered a separate employer. The IRCA also treats most immigrant workers as employees rather than as INDEPENDENT CONTRACTORS. The significance of this provision is that employers cannot avoid compliance with a myriad of employment laws by arbitrarily calling their immigrant workers "independent contractors" (Ledvinka and Scarpello, 1991).

The IRCA's enforcement and administration is divided among six federal entities as well as state agencies. The Immigration and Naturalization Service is responsible for border patrol, inspection of employment verification records, and other enforcement activities for deterring illegal entry of aliens in the US. The US Department of Labor is responsible for inspection of employment verification records. The Secretary of Labor extends or withholds labor certifications of foreign seasonal agricultural workers. The NATIONAL LABOR RELATIONS BOARD (NLRB) is responsible for union certification elections and resolution of unfair labor practice charges. The US attorney general is responsible for: (1) legalizing the status of immigrant workers; (2) developing procedures for investigating illegal hiring complaints; (3) selecting administrative law judges to rule on IRCA violations; and (4) prosecuting cases in US courts. Other government agencies may also be involved, when the hiring of illegal aliens violates other employment laws.

Bibliography

Ledvinka, J. and Scarpello, V. (1991). *Federal Regulation of Personnel and Human Resource Management.* Boston: PWS-Kent.

Legislative History of the Immigration Reform and Control Act (Public Law 99-603) (1980). Washington, DC: Government Printing Office.

impact of mergers and acquisitions

Martin M. Greller

MERGER AND ACQUISITION: DEFINITION AND PURPOSE

Mergers and acquisitions rapidly reconfigure assets to better implement strategy by combining independent enterprises. This is effected through the purchase of one organization (classic acquisition), exchange of stock, or simple pooling of assets (classic merger). Typically, 80 percent of such combinations are described as failures (Hawkins, 1988), attributable to poorly blended organizations, culture differences, or turnover of key people (Scott, 1981; Schweiger and Weber, 1989).

ROLE OF HUMAN AND ORGANIZATION RESOURCES

Mergers and acquisitions are complex changes, incorporating rapid growth and modification of organizational culture. For the combination to be successful, employees must accept new objectives and functions within a new structure. Employees may be required to engage in new behaviors or continue previous behavior but in a new organization context. Thus, the merger or acquisition plan should include steps to foster employee behaviors necessary to the combination's success.

Mergers and acquisitions also cause disruptions in individual and organizational performance as a byproduct of the changes. Tasks and rules appropriate in the combined organization must be learned or reaffirmed and employees are forced to deal with ambiguity and job stress, which compel attention to a greater extent than the tasks they are expected to perform. In the face of such transition, there may also be an unfreezing of attitudes allowing for rapid change. If this opportunity is squandered as employees cling to old conventions rather than establish new psychological contracts, an important opportunity to guide the success of the combination is lost.

HUMAN RESOURCE MANAGEMENT ACTIONS

The most common role for the HUMAN RESOURCE FUNCTION is fostering communication after the combination is announced. This includes newsletters, telephone hotlines, formal presentations (particularly those explaining BENEFITS and personnel policies), and meetings among counterparts from the different organizations. These programs emphasize one-way communication.

More sophisticated efforts foster employee involvement by soliciting and responding to questions or by establishing project teams. This may involve surveying employees and providing feedback. Teams can decide how things will be done after the combination occurs. Such groups are common at the executive level (e.g., Baxter Healthcare, described in Ulrich et al., 1989), but may also involve supervisory and professional employees (e.g., Ernst and Young, described in Greller, Kesselman, and Ostling, 1994). The participative approach increases acceptance, disseminates information, creates opportunities to influence decisions, and builds relationships across organization boundaries.

Human resource issues can be part of the decision to proceed with a particular combination. This may involve developing an acquisition screening procedure that includes questions dealing with operational aspects of personnel management practices (PERFORMANCE APPRAISAL, COMPENSATION, and so forth), and cultural fit (e.g., Novell, described in Anfuso, 1994). Alternatively, firms may identify a few key indicators, such as sales per employee (Hawkins, 1988), which act as surrogates for more extensive information on culture and BUSINESS PROCESSES.

Currently, human resource managers generally become involved after the decision to combine has been made and even after key policies have been set. Under these circumstances, communication is the major tool available for constructive action. Proactive employee relations can identify concerns and morale problems so that management may address them.

Bibliography

Anfuso, D. (1994). Novell idea: A map for mergers. *Personnel Journal*, 48–54.

Greller, M. M., Kesselman, G. A., and Ostling, P. J. (1994). Merging the service organization: The case of Ernst and Young. In C. H. Fay, K. F. Price, and R. J. Nihaus (eds.), *Achieving Organizational Success through Innovative Human Resource Strategies*, vol. 1. New York: Human Resource Planning Society.

Hawkins, M. D. (1988). Using human resource data to select merger/acquisition candidates. In R. J. Nihaus and K. F. Price (eds.), *Creating the Competitive Edge through Human Resource Applications*. New York: Plenum.

Schweiger, D. M. and Weber, Y. (1989). Strategies for managing human resources during mergers and acquisitions: An empirical investigation. *Human Resource Planning*, 12, 69–86.

Scott, J. H. (1981). *The Effect of Mergers, Acquisitions, and Tender Offers on American Business: A Touche Ross Survey*. New York: Touche Ross.

Ulrich, D., Cody, T., LaFasto, F., and Rucci, A. (1989). Human resources at Baxter Healthcare Corporation merger: A strategic partnership role. *Human Resource Planning*, 12, 87–103.

Improshare

Theresa M. Welbourne

The Improshare plan is a form of GAINSHARING that focuses on sharing physical PRODUCTIVITY gains with employees. Standard hours are calculated for the production of each unit, and Improshare pays a bonus when the time needed in the production process is reduced. Gains realized by working either faster or more efficiently are then split between the employer and employees, and the employee portion is shared among all workers. Improshare does not require any form of employee participation, although participation is compatible with the process.

incentive pay

Nancy A. Bereman

Incentive pay refers to basing payment to employees directly on some objective measure of production or PRODUCTIVITY. Incentive pay differs from PAY FOR PERFORMANCE in that it is based more directly on job output and does not normally become a part of the individual's base pay. There are two basic types of incentive pay systems: individual and group. Probably the oldest form of individual incentive pay is a piece-rate system or PIECEWORK, in which employees are paid a given rate for each unit produced. A variant, a STANDARD HOUR PLAN, provides BONUSES based on performing work in a shorter time than a standard time period. Piece-rate systems rely heavily on setting output standards which establish the base pay an employee earns. Performance above standard results in increased pay to the employee. Piece-rate systems are popular in labor-intensive industries with a high degree of cost competition. Problems include: difficulty in setting the initial standards, providing allowances for problems beyond the control of the employee, and maintaining employee acceptance of the system.

Group incentive plans work on the same basic principles. However, the measure of production or productivity is at the group or the organization level. Group incentive plans are designed to foster performance in situations where teamwork is vital, there is relatively high task interdependence, and it is difficult to measure individual performance. Examples of organization-wide incentive plans include SCANLON PLAN, RUCKER PLAN, and IMPROSHARE plan. These incentive plans are also called cost reduction, PROFIT SHARING, or GAINSHARING plans.

Bibliography

Hills, F. S., Bergmann, T. J., and Scarpello, V. G. (1994). *Compensation Decision Making*, 2nd edn. Fort Worth, TX: Dryden Press.

Milkovich, G. T. and Newman, J. M. (1993). *Compensation*, 3rd edn. Homewood, IL: Richard D. Irwin.

indemnity plans

Charles H. Fay

Indemnity plans are used to provide healthcare benefits to employees. Employers typically provide medical, surgical, and major medical insurance to employees under indemnity plans. The employer may buy coverage from an insurance company or provide self-coverage. Cost controls may be imposed by the use of coinsurance (the employer pays only 80 percent of claims, the employee pays 20 percent) and deductibles (the employee pays the first $100 of any claim). The employee has the most freedom of choice of providers and treatment under indemnity plans. Managed indemnity plans introduce some features of MANAGED CARE to further control costs.

Bibliography

Mahoney, D. F. (2001). Health plan design evolution. In J. S. Rosenbloom (ed.), *The Handbook of Employee Benefits: Design, Funding and Administration*, 5th edn. New York: McGraw-Hill, pp. 109–34.

Pierce, P. D. (2001a). Understanding managed care health plans: The managed care spectrum. In J. S. Rosenbloom (ed.), *The Handbook of Employee Benefits: Design, Funding and Administration*, 5th edn. New York: McGraw-Hill, pp. 135–69.

Pierce, P. D. (2001b). Understanding managed care health plans: Understanding costs and evaluating plans. In J. S. Rosenbloom (ed.), *The Handbook of Employee Benefits: Design, Funding and Administration*, 5th edn. New York: McGraw-Hill, pp. 171–207.

independent contractors

Stanley Nollen

Independent contractors are self-employed people who work at a client company for a specific period of time or to accomplish a specific project. They are used by organizations to achieve WORKFORCE FLEXIBILITY by adding labor input during peak demand periods, or they are used to obtain technical or professional specialty skills whose need is deemed temporary. Contracts are typically for three or six months and renewable. Independent contractors are used more in some European countries, where their maximum length of service is regulated, than in the US, where STAFFING companies sometimes provide alternatives to temporary employment. Independent contractors sometimes are retirees or people who were forced out of their previous employment because of DOWNSIZING and brought back on a contractor basis in CONTINGENT EMPLOYMENT, which sometimes gives rise to legal and tax issues about their employment status and rights.

individual differences

J. Kevin Ford and Deidre Wasson

People differ from one another in the knowledge, skills, abilities, and other characteristics (*see* KSAOS) that they bring to the training situation (*see* TRAINING). These individual characteristics of the trainee affect the capability and motivation of trainees to acquire and transfer trained knowledge and skills to the job. Given that individual learning rates often differ under conditions where people are exposed to the same training program (Fleishman and Mumford, 1989), the characteristics that people bring to the training environments are an essential ingredient of instructional system design. Prior to training, it is critical that individuals have the prerequisite background experiences necessary and a desire to learn. During training, the training program offered may be tailored to individual differences in capabilities and motivation. For example, Cronbach and Snow (1977) have described attempts to provide each trainee with the appropriate model of instruction as the examination of aptitude–treatment interactions. As an example of an aptitude–treatment interaction, high-ability students have been found to benefit more from low-structure, high-complexity training programs, while the opposite tends to be true for lower-ability students (Snow, 1986).

Bibliography

Cronbach, L. J. and Snow, R. E. (1977). *Aptitude and Instructional Methods.* New York: John Wiley.

Fleishman, E. A. and Mumford, M. D. (1989). Individual attributes and training performance. In I. Goldstein et al. (eds.), *Training and Development in Organizations.* San Francisco: Jossey-Bass.

Snow, R. E. (1986). Individual differences and the design of educational programs. *American Psychologist*, 41, 1029–39.

individual retirement accounts

Charles H. Fay

While most employees are covered by private PENSION PLANS, not all are. These employees must build up capital for post-retirement income replacement with after-tax income, which places them at a disadvantage. Under the EMPLOYEE RETIREMENT INCOME SECURITY ACT OF 1974, individuals not participating in an employer-sponsored pension plan may contribute up to $2,000 to an individual retirement account (IRA), deducting contributions from taxable income. Proportional deductions are allowed on contributions to plans by pension plan participants who meet certain maximum income requirements. In addition, nondeductible contributions can be made to a Roth IRA; earnings accrue on a tax-free basis.

Bibliography

Martin, E. L. and Rabel, W. H. (2001). Individual retirement arrangements (IRAs), simplified employee pensions (SEPs) and HR-10 (Keogh) plans. In J. S. Rosenbloom (ed.), *The Handbook of Employee Benefits: Design, Funding and Administration*, 5th edn. New York: McGraw-Hill, pp. 759–76.

industrial relations

Jack Fiorito

Industrial relations refers to workplace and societal interactions between workers and employers, and resulting employment-related outcomes. In the US especially, the term often is used in a narrower sense to refer only to employment relationships where COLLECTIVE BARGAINING is used to establish terms and conditions of employment. In its broadest meaning, industrial relations is "all aspects of people at work" (Kochan, 1980: 1).

Industrial Relations as an Area of Study

The term "industrial" connotes heavy industry to many, but most industrial relations scholars use the term broadly, as in distinguishing industrialized societies from agrarian societies. Thus industrial relations refers to relations between employers and workers in all economic sectors.

Industrial relations remains a common term for describing the field among scholars. The major US professional association is the Industrial Relations Research Association (IRRA), and in Britain, the British Universities Industrial Relations Association. There has been controversy concerning whether the field has become too closely associated with the narrower conception of industrial relations, i.e., union–management relations, and there have been calls for name changes with the intent of better conveying the broad sense of the field. Many firms and academic programs have tended to downplay or even eliminate reference to "industrial relations" (e.g., in department names), and the IRRA Executive Board has recommended a new name to its members, the Labor and Employment Relations Association.

To fully appreciate multifaceted industrial relations issues, one must draw from varied perspectives, including economics, psychology, sociology, political science, and law. Thus industrial relations is often called an interdisciplinary subject. Industrial relations is studied within business schools and in specialized institutes or schools at many colleges and universities.

Theories and Assumptions

Kochan (1980) suggested that an important factor distinguishing industrial relations from its contributing disciplines and related areas (e.g., human resources) is a distinctive set of values and assumptions. These include the following propositions:

1. Labor is more than a commodity.
2. An inherent conflict of interests exists between employers and employees in economic matters (e.g., wages versus profits), but also in terms of friction in supervisor–subordinate relations.
3. Large areas of common interests and important interdependencies between employers and employees remain despite their conflicting interests.
4. An inherent inequality of bargaining power exists in most individual employer–employee relationships.
5. There is pluralism, the notion that there are multiple competing interest groups in society, each with valid interests.

The dominant paradigm or conceptual framework for the study of industrial relations is the industrial relations systems model advanced by Dunlop (1958). The concept of a system is applied in the sense that industrial relations consists of the "processes by which human beings and organizations interact at the workplace and, more broadly, in society as a whole to establish the terms and conditions of employment" (Mills, 1994: 5). Kochan (1980) observed that like any complex social system, industrial relations systems are best understood by analyzing various components and how they interact with one another to produce certain outcomes.

The major components of the industrial relations system are:

1. the actors (workers and their organizations, management, and government);
2. contextual or environmental factors (labor and product markets, technology, and community or "the locus and distribution of power in the larger society"; Dunlop, 1958);
3. processes for determining the terms and conditions of employment (collective bargaining, legislation, judicial processes, and unilateral management decisions, among others);
4. ideology, or a minimal set of compatible or shared beliefs, such as the actors' mutual acceptance of the legitimacy of other actors and their roles, which enhances system stability; and
5. outcomes, including wages and BENEFITS, rules about work relations (e.g., standards for disciplinary action), JOB SATISFACTION, employment security, productive efficiency,

industrial peace and conflict, and industrial democracy.

The basic purposes of the industrial relations systems concept are to provide a conceptual framework for organizing knowledge about industrial relations and for understanding how various components of industrial relations systems combine to produce particular outcomes (and hence why outcomes vary). It is noteworthy that the systems concept does not presume superiority of a particular process for determining employment outcomes.

The precise specification of system components may vary with the level of analysis and from one system to another. Although it has endured, the industrial relations systems concept has been criticized and challenged (e.g., Kochan, Katz, and McKersie, 1986). Although not denying change, several scholars have argued that even though major transformations in industrial relations may be occurring, they are not inconsistent with traditional understandings of industrial relations or the systems concept (e.g., Lewin, 1987).

See also *strategic industrial relations*

Bibliography

Barbash, J. (1984). *Elements of Industrial Relations*. Madison, WI: University of Wisconsin Press.
Chelius, J. and Dworkin, J. (eds.) (1990). *Reflections on the Transformation of Industrial Relations*. New Brunswick, NJ: IMLR Press.
Dunlop, J. T. (1958). *Industrial Relations Systems*. New York: Holt-Dryden.
Fiorito, J. (1996). Industrial relations. In *Gale Encyclopedia of Business*. Detroit: Gale Research.
Kaufman, B. E. (1993). *The Origins and Evolution of the Field of Industrial Relations in the United States*. Ithaca, NY: ILR Press.
Kaufman, B. E. and Kleiner, M. M. (eds.) (1993). *Employee Representation: Alternatives and Future Directions*. Madison, WI: Industrial Relations Research Association.
Kochan, T. A. (1980). *Collective Bargaining and Industrial Relations: From Theory to Policy to Practice*. Homewood, IL: Richard D. Irwin.
Kochan, T. A., Katz, H. C., and McKersie, R. B. (1986). *The Transformation of American Industrial Relations*. New York: Basic Books.

Lewin, D. (1987). Industrial relations as a strategic variable. In M. M. Kleiner et al. (eds.), *Human Resources and the Performance of the Firm*. Madison, WI: Industrial Relations Research Association.
Mills, D. Q. (1994). *Labor Management Relations*, 5th edn. New York: McGraw-Hill.

industrial unions

James B. Dworkin

An industrial union represents all workers in a particular industry regardless of their skill levels. Examples of industrial unions include the United Auto Workers, the United Steel Workers, and the Aluminum Workers of America. These unions bargain collectively over wages, hours, and other terms and conditions of employment. Unlike CRAFT UNIONS, which seek to restrict employment, industrial unions seek to expand membership and employment in the industries within which they operate. Thus, job security becomes a very prominent feature of a typical COLLECTIVE BARGAINING agreement. Industrial unions seek both fair wages and job security for their membership.

Bibliography

Kochan, T. A., Katz, H. C., and McKersie, R. B. (1986). *The Transformation of American Industrial Relations*. New York: Basic Books.
Slichter, S. H., Healy, J. J., and Livenash, E. R. (1960). *The Impact of Collective Bargaining on Management*. Washington, DC: Brookings Institution.

information technology enablers

William H. Glick

Davenport (1993; Davenport and Short, 1990) identified a variety of factors that can provide the means for (enable) process innovation and BUSINESS PROCESS REENGINEERING. Enablers of process change include information technology, organizational forms, and human resources. Information technology is the most visible of these factors, for two reasons. First, the pace of change in information technology is much faster than in organizational or human resource changes. Second, introducing information technology without changing BUSINESS PROCESSES does not appear to lead to the expected financial benefits (Davenport, 1993). Thus, the phrase "information technology enablers" has linked information technology with business process reengineering and has changed the role of many information systems groups within organizations.

Specific examples of information technology enablers include: expert systems that allow individuals to perform much more complex tasks with less outside assistance and less TRAINING; performance monitoring systems that provide information to enable rapid responses to defects in a continuous improvement cycle; electronic data interchange systems that give supplier organizations information that allows the adoption of JUST-IN-TIME PRODUCTION SYSTEMS; and product configurators that allow a salesperson to accurately design and price a complex, customized product in the customer's office.

Bibliography

Davenport, T. H. (1993). *Process Innovation: Reengineering Work through Information Technology*. Boston: Harvard Business School Press.

Davenport, T. H. and Short, J. E. (1990). The new industrial engineering: Information technology and business process redesign. *Sloan Management Review*, 31, 11–27.

integrative bargaining

Paul Jarley

Integrative bargaining refers to situations where the parties' goals are not in direct conflict and each party perceives opportunities for mutual gain. Integrative bargaining is often contrasted with DISTRIBUTIVE BARGAINING, but elements of both may be present in any negotiation.

THE CHARACTER OF INTEGRATIVE BARGAINING

Integrative bargaining focuses on the parties' interests, is cooperative, and stresses the creation of win–win situations. Negotiation is characterized by a joint problem-solving approach whereby problems are identified, solutions proposed, and specific proposals implemented. Negotiators strive to understand the interests and goals each brings to the negotiation and to fashion proposals that meet as many of these objectives as possible. A central notion in integrative bargaining is Pareto optimality. Proposals should be generated and altered until no party can be made better off without the other party being made worse off. Satisfaction of this principle ensures that the parties have realized the full potential for mutual gain inherent in the negotiation.

INTEGRATIVE BARGAINING STRATEGIES

Integrative bargaining strategies support and facilitate a joint problem-solving approach. Negotiators stress their similarities and common interests, downplaying differences. Each party encourages the other to clearly and fully communicate his or her interests and hopes to secure the other's cooperation and trust by fashioning proposals that explicitly recognize and meet the other's needs. Creative suggestions are encouraged and the parties evaluate proposals against both objective standards and notions of equity. Common integrative bargaining strategies include brainstorming, bridging, cost-cutting, and logrolling (*see* NEGOTIATION TACTICS).

Bibliography

Fisher, R. and Ury, W. (1983). *Getting to Yes: Negotiating Agreement without Giving In*. New York: Penguin.

Lewicki, R. J. and Litterer, J. A. (1985). *Negotiation*. Homewood, IL: Richard D. Irwin.

Walton, R. E. and McKersie, R. B. (1965). *A Behavioral Theory of Labor Negotiations: An Analysis of a Social Interaction System*. New York: McGraw-Hill.

integrity testing

Paul R. Sackett

Integrity (or honesty) tests are paper-and-pencil instruments administered primarily to job applicants for the purpose of predicting counterproductive work behavior. Recent estimates suggest that several million such tests are administered in the US annually, primarily to applicants for entry-level jobs with access to money or merchandise (e.g., retailing, financial services). Early integrity tests were billed as paper-and-pencil surrogates for POLYGRAPH TESTING. Current research, however, downplays or eliminates the link to the polygraph. It focuses not only on the prediction of employee theft, but also on a wide variety of counterproductive behaviors, to include violation of work rules, fraudulent workers' compensation claims, and ABSENTEEISM.

Two basic types of tests can be identified. Overt tests measure attitudes toward theft and other forms of counterproductivity. They commonly ask for a self-report of applicant involvement in various illegal and/or counterproductive behaviors. Personality-oriented tests are considerably broader in focus and are not explicitly aimed at theft. They may include items dealing with dependability, conscientiousness, social conformity, thrill-seeking, trouble with authority, and hostility (see BIG FIVE PERSONALITY TESTS; PERSONALITY TESTS).

A large body of validity evidence shows integrity tests to be positively related to both a range of counterproductive behaviors and supervisor ratings of overall performance. However, most of the research has been done by test publishers, leading skeptics to question whether only successes are being publicized.

There is currently no federal regulation on the use of integrity testing. Women, racial minority groups, and older workers do not systematically perform more poorly on these tests. As a result, there have been no successful challenges to integrity tests under federal antidiscrimination laws. However, two states (Massachusetts and Rhode Island) restrict the use of integrity tests.

Critics express concerns about invasion of privacy and the risks of misclassifying honest applicants. Defenders point to the business justification for inquiry into issues of conscientiousness and counterproductivity. They also note that the standard of comparison for any selection system is not perfect accuracy but the degree of predictive accuracy achieved by available alternatives.

Bibliography

American Psychological Association (1991). *Questionnaires Used in the Prediction of Trustworthiness in Pre-Employment Selection Decisions: An APA Task Force Report*. Washington, DC: US Government Printing Office.
Congress of the United States Office of Technology Assessment (1990). *The Use of Integrity Tests for Pre-Employment Screening*. Washington, DC: US Government Printing Office.
Murphy, K. R. (1993). *Honesty in the Workplace*. Pacific Grove, CA: Brooks-Cole.
Sackett, P. R., Burris, L. R., and Callahan, C. (1989). Integrity testing for personnel selection: An update. *Personnel Psychology*, **42**, 491–529.

intelligence tests

Linda S. Gottfredson

An intelligence test is a series of standardized tasks for assessing general cognitive ability. The tasks may be diverse, including, for example, words, numbers, designs, pictures, and blocks. Tests that include more than one item type often arrange them in subtests such as vocabulary, information, block design, comprehension, arithmetic, and picture completion. Factor analyses show that, whatever their differences in manifest content, all IQ tests, mental test batteries, and parts thereof measure primarily a single common factor, called the general mental ability factor (g, for short; Carroll, 1993).

Intelligence tests therefore measure a highly general capability, which is reflected in higher-order thinking skills such as efficient learning, reasoning, problem solving, and abstract thinking. This is in contrast to aptitude and achievement tests. Aptitude tests target narrower abilities, such as verbal, mechanical, or spatial aptitude. Achievement tests assess knowledge of specific school curricula, such as reading, science, or history. Intelligence tests tend to require less specific, more generally available knowledge, sometimes only elementary concepts such as in/out or large/small. The distinctions among the three types of test are not always clear. Some aptitude and achievement tests function like intelligence tests when test takers have been equally exposed to the subject matter being tested.

ORIGINS AND USE

Alfred Binet and his colleague Théophile Simon constructed the first modern intelligence test, in

1905, in response to the French government's desire to develop diagnostic and instructional procedures for mentally retarded children. American psychologists developed the first group intelligence tests (called the Army Alpha and Army Beta tests) during World War I, in response to the Army's need to screen millions of recruits. The Army Alpha required examinees to read; the Army Beta did not.

Interest in mental testing grew rapidly after World War I, and both the federal government and military services in the US developed test batteries for large-scale screening of individuals for jobs. Many schools, colleges, and private employers likewise adopted some of the many new tests on the market for selecting and placing students and employees. Some of the group-administered tests (such as the SAT) are hours long, whereas others (such as the 12-minute, 50-item Wonderlic Personnel Test) are very short. The most widely used individually administered intelligence tests today are, for school-age children, the Wechsler Intelligence Scale for Children-IV (WISC-IV) and, for adults, the Wechsler Adult Intelligence Scale-III (WAIS-III). These IQ batteries are administered orally and most of their subtests are untimed.

The major uses of intelligence tests include clinical diagnosis of individuals' behavior or achievement problems, vocational and educational guidance, PERSONNEL SELECTION, and placement into different education and training programs. Good professional practice requires that test scores be supplemented with other information when high-stakes decisions are being made about individuals (e.g., assigning a child to a special education class).

Individual tests are administered by highly trained professionals who exercise judgment in gaining rapport, administering prompts, and scoring the quality of responses. Group tests can be administered by less-trained individuals because they allow no discretion in administration and scoring. The construction and use of intelligence tests are governed by professional standards, principally the STANDARDS FOR EDUCATIONAL AND PSYCHOLOGICAL TESTING (American Educational Research Association et al., 1999).

TRENDS

The construction of intelligence tests is increasingly guided by explicit theories of intelligence and new evidence on the structure of mental abilities (i.e., the relations between the general factor, g, and the narrower group factors, such as verbal and spatial ability). Multivariate confirmatory factor analysis is often used to evaluate a new test's CONSTRUCT VALIDITY and whether its results are equally construct valid in different race, age, and gender groups (Keith, 1997). Theories on the biological basis of intelligence may someday lead to very different sorts of intelligence tests. For example, the last two decades have produced much research testing the notion that differences in intelligence originate primarily in differences in the speed and efficiency of brain processes (Deary, 2000). A wide variety of structural and physiological features of the brain (such as brain volume, rate of glucose metabolism, latency and shape of brain waves), as well as speed of perceiving exceedingly simple perceptual stimuli (inspection and reaction-time tasks), have been shown to correlate moderately with IQ when considered individually and sometimes strongly when measures are aggregated.

LEGAL AND SOCIAL ISSUES

Test use has risen and fallen during the last century, depending on social and legal currents of the time (Wigdor and Garner, 1982). Public concern has focused on test fairness, because mental tests are often used in ways that affect people's lives. Selection and placement are two such uses. Although often warranted by the tests' predictive value, such uses make tests the focus of longstanding sociopolitical debates over equal opportunity.

Pervasive and sometimes large racial or ethnic disparities in test scores continue to fuel claims that intelligence tests are culturally biased. Extensive research (e.g., Jensen, 1980; Wigdor and Garner, 1982) has shown that they are not biased against native-born, English-speaking Americans, including blacks. Their use, however, often creates DISPARATE IMPACT, which has provoked much litigation. GRIGGS V. DUKE POWER, 401 US 424 (1971), *Larry P.* v. *Riles,*

495 F Supp. 926 (ND Cal., 1979), and similar court decisions have greatly affected the regulation and use of tests in employment and educational settings. Media reports of the foregoing issues have tended to misreport expert opinion on intelligence testing (Snyderman and Rothman, 1988).

Bibliography

American Educational Research Association, American Psychological Association, and National Council on Measurement in Education (1999). *Standards for Educational and Psychological Testing*. Washington, DC: American Educational Research Association.

Carroll, J. B. (1993). *Human Cognitive Abilities: A Survey of Factor-Analytic Studies*. New York: Cambridge University Press.

Cronbach, L. J. (1990). *Essentials of Psychological Testing*, 5th edn. New York: HarperCollins.

Deary, I. J. (2000). *Looking Down on Human Intelligence: From Psychometrics to the Brain*. Oxford: Oxford University Press.

Jensen, A. R. (1980). *Bias in Mental Testing*. New York: Free Press.

Keith, T. Z. (1997). Using confirmatory factor analysis to aid in understanding the constructs measured by intelligence tests. In D. P. Flanagan, J. L. Genshaft, and P. L. Harrison (eds.), *Contemporary Intellectual Assessment: Theories, Tests, and Issues*. New York: Guilford Press, pp. 373–402.

Sattler, J. M. (2001). *Assessment of Children: Cognitive Applications*, 4th edn. San Diego, CA: Jerome M. Sattler.

Snyderman, M. and Rothman, S. (1988). *The IQ Controversy, the Media and Public Policy*. New Brunswick, NJ: Transaction.

Wigdor, A. K. and Garner, W. R. (1982). *Ability Testing: Uses, Consequences, and Controversies. Part I: Report of the Committee*. Washington, DC: National Academy Press.

interest arbitration

Peter Feuille

Interest arbitration is a procedure used to resolve negotiation disputes over new contract terms (or disputes over interests, rather than disputes over rights under an existing contract, as occurs in grievance arbitration; *see* RIGHTS ARBITRATION). Interest arbitration procedures vary according to (1) the basis for the proceedings (voluntary versus compulsory), (2) the number of arbitrators involved (one individual versus a multiple-person panel), (3) the rules governing how the arbitration decision will be made (conventional versus FINAL OFFER ARBITRATION), and (4) the formality of the proceedings, and so on.

Most interest arbitration occurs in negotiating disputes involving public employers and unions of their employees, as a result of state or federal COLLECTIVE BARGAINING legislation that requires that arbitration be used in this manner (it usually is compulsory rather than voluntary). As this implies, arbitration requirements are accompanied by prohibitions on the use of strikes and lockouts (*see* LOCKOUT; STRIKE). These legislative mandates are sought by public employee unions and resisted by public employers, based on their mutual belief that compulsory arbitration enables unions to negotiate new contract terms from a stronger position than would be the case without such laws, and research evidence supports these beliefs. Research also indicates that the existence of a compulsory arbitration requirement sometimes may reduce union and employer incentives to bargain their own contracts.

Because most private sector employers and unions strenuously object to relinquishing their decision authority to arbitrators (which includes their right to strike or lock out), there is little use of voluntary or compulsory interest arbitration in the private sector.

interim management

Hadyn Bennett

The Institute of Interim Management (Taher-Zadeh, 2003) defines an interim manager as "a professionally qualified and independent business executive, who deliberately chooses to work as a supplier of specific skills and knowledge, on a fixed-term and fee basis, for a specific period and scope of work." Interim managers differ from management consultants in that they hold operating (or line) authority for the duration of the fixed-term or project (*see* MANAGEMENT CONSULTANCY). Among the advantages of using interim managers are flexibility and the availability of experienced senior management staff who can bring fresh, external, and unbiased perspectives to organizational issues on a commercial rather than an employment contract basis. Examples of business areas suitable for interim management include mergers and acquisitions, corporate rescue, CHANGE MANAGEMENT, HUMAN RESOURCE STRATEGY, and operational support and project management (Taher-Zadeh, 2003).

Bibliography

Taher-Zadeh, T. (Chairman) (2003). Institute of Interim Management, www.ioim.org.uk.

internal equity/internal consistency

George F. Dreher

Internal equity is one of two organizing concepts (along with EXTERNAL EQUITY/EXTERNAL COMPETITIVENESS) used to define the structure and form of a traditional job-based pay system (*see* JOB-BASED PAY). Internal equity is the degree to which an organization's jobs or positions are ordered hierarchically such that there is congruence with the organization's strategic and business objectives (Milkovich and Newman, 1993: 35). Thus, the relative pay differences between jobs (within a single organization) will reflect each job's unique value to the employing organization when the system is internally equitable (Mahoney, 1979). At a more macro level, the structures of pay hierarchies also are likely to reflect societal norms and values.

A high degree of internal equity should promote a sense of equity and fairness among organization members and thus encourage cooperation and organizational citizenship behaviors. Internally equitable systems also are likely to facilitate a willingness to undertake TRAINING and seek higher-level positions within the hierarchy.

The principal means of establishing internal equity is through the use of JOB EVALUATION METHODS. Here, the job's essential attributes are rated with respect to their perceived value to the organization. Thus, it is possible for there to be a discrepancy between a job's value as defined by the so-called market wage and how it is positioned within the organization's internal structure. This possible tension between internal and external equity represents a central and difficult area for resolution for wage and salary administrators.

Bibliography

Mahoney, T. A. (1979). Organizational hierarchy and position worth. *Academy of Management Journal*, **22**, 726–37.

Milkovich, G. T. and Newman, J. M. (1993). *Compensation*. Homewood, IL: Richard D. Irwin.

internal labor markets

Paul Osterman

Many of the rules which determine economic outcomes and social welfare originate within the firm and are, in a nontrivial sense, chosen by the firm. Because many workers spend long stretches of their careers within the shelter of enterprises, understanding these rules is very important. These rules have come to be characterized as the internal labor market (ILM).

The central idea of ILMs was set forth by Kerr (1954) in his description of "institutional labor markets." Kerr argued that these labor markets created noncompeting groups, and that one of the central boundaries was between the firm and the external labor market. Kerr identified "ports of entry" as the link between the inside and outside and described the implications for labor mobility of the boundaries and rules. Dunlop (1966) coined the term "internal labor market" and provided a description of one of its central rules, that concerning job ladders. In the 1970s, Doeringer and Piore (1971) provided a full description of the rules of blue-collar ILMs as well as the trade-offs among rules (e.g., between hiring criteria and training procedures). Doeringer and Piore also began the process of linking analysis of ILMs back to mainstream labor economics through their discussion of how specific human capital helps to cement employee attachment to firms.

Internal labor markets attract scholars of divergent bents. For mainstream economists the challenge is to explain these rules in a framework that preserves the core ideas of maximization and efficiency. Institutional economists do not deny the impact of standard economic considerations, but they emphasize the interplay of economic, political, and social forces. This orientation has been reinforced by recent interest in international comparisons. There is also a vibrant sociology literature. Since stable work groups lead to the formation of norms, customs, and interpersonal comparisons, ILMs provide sociologists with an opportunity to illustrate and explore the importance of these phenomena. In addition, variation across enterprises in extent and content of rules suggests that sociological models which focus on the diffusion and adaption of institutional practices independent of their efficiency properties (e.g., the search for legitimacy via mimicry) can be fruitfully applied to ILMs.

The nature of research on ILMs has also expanded. The initial investigations were largely field-based, and the ideas rested upon interviews with firms and unions. Our confidence in these observations has, however, been strengthened by studies based upon representative samples of firms as well as more thorough examinations of particular practices, such as firm-based wage setting, long-term tenure, or part-time work. In the course of this research the original concept, while generally affirmed, has been modified in important ways. For example, there is heightened sensitivity to the fact that a firm is not a unitary employment system, but rather consists of a set of ILM subsystems which may operate on quite different principles (Osterman, 1984).

A central ILM idea is that categories of rules fit together in a logical system, and it does not make sense to isolate one rule and ignore the others. For example, narrow job classifications, wages attached to jobs, few restrictions on the ability of the firm to lay off workers, and strict seniority are a mutually reinforcing set of practices. On the other hand, broad classifications, wages attached to individuals rather than jobs, ease of deployment, and high levels of job security constitute another logical cluster. Anyone familiar with the literature will recognize the first cluster as the "traditional" US model, while the second is a model associated (at least until recently) with leading-edge US firms and with the Japanese.

An important development is the transformation of ILMs in America. From the mid-1940s to the mid-1970s, the traditional model – which is essentially what Doeringer and Piore described – dominated both in the union sector and in largely imitative nonunion firms. Toward the end of this era, a competing model emerged, one which placed much greater emphasis upon direct communication with workers and upon innovations such as team production and QUALITY CIRCLES. This structure was motivated in part by its superior performance, and in part by its ability to keep unions at bay. It emerged in a progressive segment of the US nonunion sector (e.g., IBM), but it also gained momentum from the spread of Japanese transplants, such as the Honda factory in Ohio, which organized work along the Japanese model. The more traditional sector, union and nonunion, was torn between adoption of the new (often called "transformed" or "salaried") model and defense of old structures. The playing out and resolving of this tension is the current ILM "story" of greatest interest and importance.

Bibliography

Doeringer, P. and Piore, M. (1971). *Internal Labor Markets*. Lexington, MA: D. C. Heath.

Dunlop, J. (1966). Job vacancy measures and economic analysis. In *The Measurement and Interpretation of Job Vacancies: A Conference Report*. New York: Columbia University Press.

Kerr, C. (1954). The Balkanization of labor markets. In E. W. Bakke (ed.), *Labor Mobility and Economic Opportunity*. Cambridge, MA: MIT Press.

Osterman, P. (1984). *Internal Labor Markets*. Cambridge, MA: MIT Press.

international compensation

Yvonne Stedham

International compensation refers to all forms of financial returns and tangible BENEFITS that employees of an international organization receive from their employer in exchange for providing their labor and commitment.

In an international organization, there are three types of employees. Parent-country nationals (PCNs) or expatriates are employees who are nationals of the country in which the organization is headquartered and are working for the organization in a foreign country. Host-country nationals (HCNs) are employees who are nationals of the foreign country in which the organization is operating and are working and living in that country. Third-country nationals (TCNs) are employees who are not nationals of the country in which the organization is headquartered or nationals of the country in which the organization is operating, but are nationals of a third country.

THEORETICAL CONSIDERATIONS

International compensation must meet requirements for both INTERNAL EQUITY/INTERNAL CONSISTENCY and EXTERNAL EQUITY/EXTERNAL COMPETITIVENESS (Wallace and Fay, 1988). Designing an equitable international compensation system is especially difficult because perceptions of fairness and equity are strongly influenced by an individual's cultural background (Hofstede, 1980). A variety of external forces unique to each country have an impact on the salary structure in a particular country. External equity depends on the labor market of the country in which a unit of an international organization is located. The importance and acceptance of PAY FOR PERFORMANCE varies across countries, depending on the culture and the values prevailing in a country.

PRACTICAL CHALLENGES AND SOLUTIONS

Differences in taxation across countries make it difficult to develop an equitable international compensation system. Two major approaches are used to handle taxation.

1. *Tax equalization*: companies withhold an amount equal to the home-country tax obligation of the PCN, and they pay all taxes in the host country.
2. *Tax protection*: the PCN pays up to the amount of taxes that would have to be paid on compensation in the home country and may keep any windfall gained from lower taxes in the host country.

Legally required employee benefits differ across countries. Most PCNs of US organizations remain under their home country's benefit plan.

Further challenges result from currency fluctuations, differences in inflation rates, and the fact that, in addition to salary and benefits, PCNs receive other payments, such as housing allowances, educational payments, and home leave, as inducement payments or hardship premiums.

There are three approaches to international compensation. The home-based policy links the base salary for PCNs and TCNs to the salary structure of the home country. A host-based policy links the base salary to the salary structure in the host country, but allowances linked to home-country salary structures are provided. The region-based policy compensates PCNs and TCNs who are working in their home regions at somewhat lower levels than those who are working in regions far from home (Dowling, Schuler, and Welch, 1993). The most widely used approach is the home-based approach because it emphasizes keeping the expatriate whole – preventing the expatriate from suffering material loss due to a transfer. Reynolds (1986) recommends a balance-sheet approach designed to equalize the purchasing power of employees at comparable position levels living overseas and in the home country, and to offset qualitative differences between assignment locations.

Bibliography

Briscoe, D. R. (1995). *International Human Resource Management*. Englewood Cliffs, NJ: Prentice-Hall.
Dowling, P. J., Schuler, R. S., and Welch, D. E. (1993). *International Dimensions of Human Resource Management*. Belmont, CA: Wadsworth.
Hofstede, G. (1980). *Culture's Consequences*. Beverly Hills, CA: Sage.
Reynolds, C. (1986). Compensation of overseas personnel. In J. J. Famularo (ed.), *Handbook of Human Resource Administration*. New York: McGraw-Hill.
Wallace, M. J. and Fay, C. H. (1988). *Compensation Theory and Practice*. Boston: PWS-Kent.

International Foundation of Employee Benefit Programs

Robert M. McCaffery

The International Foundation of Employee Benefit Programs (IFEBP) is a private not-for-profit organization dedicated to providing research, education, publications, and information resources for individuals and groups involved in the study and practice of employee BENEFITS. It is located in Brookfield, Wisconsin. Among its extensive information resources for members, IFEBP maintains EBIS, Employee Benefits Infosource, a computerized database service.

In 1976, in conjunction with the Wharton School at the University of Pennsylvania, IFEBP launched the Certified Employee Benefits Specialist (CEBS) program. By completing a specified group of courses, offered throughout the country at colleges and universities, participants earn the equivalent of a college major in benefits management and certification status.

Descriptive information available on request from: International Foundation of Employee Benefit Plans, PO Box 69, Brookfield, WI 53008-0069. Telephone 414-786-6700. Internet: www.ifebp.org.

International Public Management Association for Human Resources

Jannifer David

The International Public Management Association for Human Resources (IPMA-HR) supports the work of over 5,000 human resource professionals in the public sector throughout the world. The organization specializes in providing information and resources relating to the unique aspects of the public employment relationship. IPMA-HR annually hosts international conferences to share information about trends in public employment. Members may also receive IPMA-HR publications (*IPMA-HR News*, *HR Bulletin*, *Public Personnel Management*) that provide information about trends, legislative updates, and research studies about public sector HRM. IPMA-HR also provides professional certifications (IPMA-CP and IPMA-CS) and training opportunities for public sector human resource professionals.

The IPMA-HR can be contacted at 1617 Duke Street, Alexandria, VA 22314. Telephone: 703-549-7100. Fax: 703-684-0948. Website: www.ipma-hr.org.

Internet

John W. Boudreau

The Internet is a general reference to the worldwide network of electronic information sources that can be accessed using personal computers connected by telecommunications technology. Through this network, individuals may send mail, read reference material, share documents electronically, and send computer software directly from one computer to another.

Within a single organization, such connections can include electronic messages (email), centralized repositories of general information (e.g., EMPLOYEE HANDBOOK, announcements, job postings, and so forth), and the capability to "teleconference" using software that allows individuals at various locations to see and hear each other simultaneously. "Virtual" documents can be shared and modified by individuals on a team, despite geographic or temporal dispersion.

However, the term "Internet" is generally associated with inter-organizational connections. Until the 1980s, the "Internet" was used primarily by research scientists in government and universities. It was originally designed as a communication network for scientists and as a precaution against the loss of other communication networks during a national emergency. In the late 1980s, with the widespread proliferation of personal computers and the development of commercial network providers such as America Online (AOL), Compuserve, and Prodigy, virtually anyone with a personal computer connected by modem to a telephone line could obtain mail and join discussion groups on virtually any topic.

As computers, software, and technology links have grown in sophistication, the possibilities for remote communication have grown exponentially. Today, the Internet allows individuals seamless access to repositories of information at virtually every major university or company in the world, as well as the opportunity to send electronic messages to virtually anyone, including the president of the US. A variant of electronic mail is the electronic "discussion list," or "interactive bulletin board," which offers a single location to where many individuals may "post" questions, comments, or ideas, which are then automatically distributed to everyone on the list through email. The responses are also distributed so that everyone can "listen" and participate in discussions. The largest and oldest of such lists, HRNET, was established through Cornell University under the auspices of the Academy of Management's Human Resource Division, and has over 2,600 members worldwide (see HUMAN RESOURCE DIVISION, ACADEMY OF MANAGEMENT). A single message posted to such lists commonly elicits 10 to 100 replies within 24 hours, often from all corners of the world, and can bring together human resource practitioners with researchers and content experts.

In the 1990s, increased speed and technical sophistication spawned the emergence of the worldwide web (WWW). The web uses many of the same communications pathways of the Internet, but it employs technology that makes connecting to remote sites, and sending and receiving text, graphical images, sounds, and video, virtually effortless by simply clicking a mouse. The WWW may become the backbone of a new concept in electronic connectivity, such that individuals will depend less on the particular information in their own computers and rely more on seamless access to remote sources of expertise and information. Virtually any individual or organization may establish a "site" on the WWW, which means that millions of information sources exist. Email, list servers, and access to research libraries are also available through the WWW.

For human resource professionals, the Internet offers extraordinary possibilities, with the promise to fundamentally change many human resource activities. Already, most major companies have websites, where potential customers and employees can learn about products and job openings, and can even submit electronic applications. Similar job-posting systems exist within many organizations. Commercial sites now exist to provide online recruitment, training, and expert advice to virtually any individual who requests it. Major research centers, such as Cornell's Center for Advanced Human Resource Studies and School of Industrial and Labor Relations, have sites that allow human resource professionals to obtain the latest information from governments, academic institutions, and professional associations. Professional organizations, such as the SOCIETY FOR HUMAN RESOURCE MANAGEMENT and the SOCIETY FOR INDUSTRIAL AND ORGANIZATIONAL PSYCHOLOGY, also provide such access. In the future, such access will make it less necessary to physically visit individuals or institutions with expertise, and much easier to obtain such expertise instantly and electronically.

However, the proliferation of such sites makes it ever more difficult to determine the quality and relevance of the information. The Internet has been compared to the "world's largest library," but the information is not as well organized and catalogued as users might prefer. Rather, the Internet more closely resembles an infinitely large magazine and book store, where flashy graphics and compelling marketing are often enticing, but where the quality of the information must be carefully judged.

interviewer errors

Robert L. Dipboye

In conducting employment interviews, interviewers can commit a variety of errors that can threaten the VALIDITY, reliability, and fairness of their judgments. An error is defined as a deviation of the interviewer's judgments from what is true about the applicant. One source of error derives from the effects of the interviewer's behavior on the applicant. For instance, an applicant who is actually highly qualified might appear unqualified as the result of an interviewer's style of questioning. In some cases interviewers' opinions of an applicant may be self-fulfilling (Dougherty, Turban, and Callender, 1994). In other words, interviewers' opinions of an applicant's qualifications may "leak into" the conduct of the session and bias the behavior of the applicant in the direction of confirming the interviewer's opinions.

In addition to errors associated with the conduct of the interview process itself, other errors can occur as a consequence of the ways that interviewers process information about the applicant. Interviewers can show "similar-to-me" effects, in which they give more favorable evaluations to applicants who are perceived as similar to the interviewer on background characteristics, education, attitudes, and other factors (Graves and Powell, 1995). The consistency with which race, disability, gender, and age of the applicant influence interviewer judgments is open to argument, but professional interviewers have been shown to err in the direction of undervaluing the qualifications of minorities, women, and older applicants (Stone, Stone, and Dipboye, 1992). A consistent finding is that physically unattractive candidates receive lower interviewer evaluations than attractive candidates (Stone et al., 1992). For instance, Rynes and Gerhart (1990) found that attractiveness was a more important correlate of recruiter evaluations of firm-specific fit than were objective characteristics of the applicants such as grade point average, sex, business experience, academic major, and extracurricular activities. Another type of error is the attributional error. In explaining why applicants behave the way they do in an interview session, interviewers tend to underestimate how their own conduct influences the applicant, and to overestimate the importance of the applicant's traits. Finally, the same RATING ERRORS that have been observed in PERFORMANCE APPRAISAL also can occur in the interview.

The errors committed by interviewers seem likely to threaten the validity and reliability of their judgments. The use of structured employment interviews, such as the SITUATIONAL INTERVIEW, seems likely to minimize the effects of these errors by making the process more consistent across applicants and by focusing the interviewer on the specific requirements of the job.

See also *employment interview*

Bibliography

Dougherty, T. W., Turban, D. B., and Callender, J. C. (1994). Confirming first impressions in the employment interview: A field study of interviewer behavior. *Journal of Applied Psychology*, **79**, 659–65.
Graves, L. M. and Powell, G. N. (1995). The effect of sex similarity on recruiters' evaluations of actual applicants: A test of the similarity–attraction paradigm. *Personnel Psychology*, **48**, 85–98.
Rynes, S. L. and Gerhart, E. (1990). Interviewer assessments of applicant "fit": An exploratory investigation. *Personnel Psychology*, **43**, 13–35.
Stone, E. F., Stone, D. L., and Dipboye, R. L. (1992). Stigmas in organizations: Race, handicaps, and physical attractiveness. In K. Kelley (ed.), *Issues, Theory, and Research in Industrial and Organizational Psychology*. Amsterdam: Elsevier Science.

intra-organizational bargaining

Paul Jarley

Intra-organizational bargaining refers to the process by which each party to a negotiation determines its own bargaining goals and strategies. Intra-organizational bargaining may involve elements of both DISTRIBUTIVE BARGAINING and INTEGRATIVE BARGAINING.

SOURCES OF INTRA-ORGANIZATIONAL CONFLICT

Each party to a negotiation is comprised of various constituencies, each with different interests to satisfy and opinions about optimal bargaining strategies. Different interests often derive from differences in constituents' jobs, terms and conditions of employment, or nonwork-related (e.g., family) roles. Each constituency wants its negotiator to give its special interests and concerns priority over the parochial interests of others during inter-organizational negotiations. Conflict may also stem from different perceptions about the relative efficacy of bargaining strategies and expectations about what is achievable during inter-organizational negotiations. Such disputes may arise among principals, but often occur because of information asymmetries and perceptual differences between principals not directly involved in the negotiations and their agents at the bargaining table.

IMPORTANCE OF INTRA-ORGANIZATIONAL BARGAINING

Unresolved intra-organizational conflict often produces insufficient formal authority at the bargaining table to execute an agreement. Negotiators will be uncertain about what commitments they can make during negotiations and must guard against opposition attempts to gain concessions directly from the factions most predisposed toward their bargaining proposals. Unresolved intra-organizational conflict greatly increases the likelihood of an impasse since the other party often has little choice but to halt negotiations and put pressure on the various opposition factions to resolve their internal disputes before returning to the bargaining table.

Bibliography

Kochan, T. A., Huber, G. P., and Cummings, L. P. (1975). Determinants of intra-organizational conflict in collective bargaining in the public sector. *Administrative Science Quarterly*, 20, 10–23.

Walton, R. E. and McKersie, R. B. (1965). *A Behavioral Theory of Labor Negotiations: An Analysis of a Social Interaction System*. New York: McGraw-Hill.

ISO 9000

William E. Youngdahl

ISO 9000 is an internationally developed and recognized series of quality standards that focus on a company's *management practices*. Businesses certified by third-party agencies join a registry of ISO-certified companies. This stamp of approval provides comparative advantages to certified companies. Additionally, European Union (EU) companies can minimize certain legal liabilities by applying ISO 9000 standards and choosing ISO-certified suppliers (Chase and Aquilano, 1995).

The ISO 9000 series consists of five separate standards. The ISO 9000 standard provides basic definitions and concepts and summarizes how to select and use the other standards in the series. Essentially, ISO 9000 directs a firm to document what it does and do what it has documented. ISO 9004 lists the essential elements that make up a quality system and contains guidelines for operation. The remaining standards constitute a hierarchical set of quality requirements covering various aspects of the business. ISO 9003, the least stringent, deals only with final testing and inspection. ISO 9002 covers production and installation requirements. ISO 9001, the most comprehensive standard, covers all elements of ISO 9002 and 9003, while also addressing design, development, and service capabilities.

Organizations often ponder the relative merits and timing of ISO 9000 certification and MALCOLM BALDRIGE NATIONAL QUALITY AWARD (MBNQA) application. The MBNQA emphasizes customer satisfaction and business results (Rabbitt and Bergh, 1993). Generally, ISO 9000 is a good starting point to help organizations prepare for MBNQA application. MBNQA assumes that internal processes, the focus of ISO 9000, are in control.

Bibliography

Arter, D. R. (1992). Demystifying the ISO 9000/290 series standards. *Quality Progress*, November, 66.

Chase, R. B. and Aquilano, N. J. (1995). *Production and Operations Management: Manufacturing and Services*. Burr Ridge, IL: Richard D. Irwin.

Huyink, D. S. (1994). *ISO 9000: Motivating the People, Mastering the Process, Achieving Registration!* Burr Ridge, IL: Richard D. Irwin.

Rabbitt, J. T. and Bergh, P. A. (1993). *The ISO 9000 Book*. White Plains, NY: Quality Resources.

Italy

Raoul C. D. Nacamulli

The main characteristics of the human resource policies in Italy are the substantial weight of regional economic differences among North, Central, and South, and the still prominent role played by unions in the overall Italian INDUSTRIAL RELATIONS system.

LABOR MANAGEMENT POLICIES IN THE ITALIAN REGIONS

Fragmentation is a fundamental characteristic of human resource practices in Italy. In fact, labor relations, management style, and personnel policies are different in the so-called First, Second, and Third Italies.

The "First Italy" is the northern part of the country and the center of industrial activities. This area contains most of the main large modern corporations with advanced human resource management (HRM) policies. The situation in the south of Italy (the "Second Italy") is different, with traditional industries, a large agricultural sector, and a significant number of state-owned enterprises. The models of personnel management in the Second Italy tend to be more bureaucratic and hierarchical. The "Third Italy" is situated in the northeast and center of the nation. In this area small and medium-sized entrepreneurial companies and interrelated networks of local firms (local districts) are predominant.

What makes the Third Italy distinctive in respect of human resource policies is the low degree of formalization of labor practices and the distinctive social commitment of the employees. This combination leads to a peculiar organizational model halfway between craft and mass production: the so-called flexible specialization model (Piore and Sabel, 1984).

The Italian Industrial Relations System

The salient features of the Italian industrial relations system are the pattern of a "weak political union" and a marked ritualistic approach in the handling of labor conflicts. The "weak political model" is between the political and the associative modes of trade unions.

The high degree of ritualistic conflict is mainly related to the extreme organizational complexity of the major unions: CGIL (left wing), CISL (Catholic), and UIL (Socialist). Patterns of industrial relations in Italy may be summarized as follows. From 1945 to the beginning of the 1960s, employers and management mostly considered unions, which were very weak, as an external disturbance. In this period, management actually led negotiations with the only purpose of minimizing the cost of labor. From 1962 to 1969, the system became a more pluralistic one as trade unions enjoyed higher recognition and began to play a more important role in COLLECTIVE BARGAINING, particularly at the local level, but the model continued to be that of DISTRIBUTIVE BARGAINING. From 1969 to the early 1970s, the unions began to take the initiative at the bargaining table while the companies retained mainly a reactive posture. State and local authorities played a crucial role in these processes, supporting the interest of the unions. The 1980s were characterized by a new reversal in the distribution of roles and the initiative switched back to management. Currently, industrial relations appear to be more complex and segmented than they used to be, as TOTAL QUALITY MANAGEMENT, participative management, and GAINSHARING policies have been developed within companies. The role of unions seems to be increasing in the public and service sectors while it becomes less significant in industry. Moreover, authorities are now mainly concerned with the DOWNSIZING of the welfare state.

Bibliography

Camuffo, A. and Costa, G. (1993). Strategic human resource management: The Italian style. *Sloan Management Review* (Winter), 59–67.

Clegg, S. E. (1990). *Modern Organizations: Organization Studies in the Postmodern World*. London: Sage.

Nacamulli, R. C. D. (1993). Italy. In M. Rothman, R. M. Briscoe, and R. C. D. Nacamulli (eds.), *Industrial Relations Around the World*. New York: Walter de Gruyter.

Piore, M. J. and Sabel, C. F. (1984). *The Second Industrial Divide: Possibilities for Prosperity*. New York: Basic Books.

J

Japan

Koji Taira

Studies of Japanese business must begin with a basic question: "Who owns the firm?" (Abegglen and Stalk, 1985). The answer to this question in the US would be simple: shareholders. This implies the most important principle of firm governance: management is the agent of the shareholders. The basic problems of the firm arise from the principal–agent relationship with asymmetric information. In this type of firm, workers are resources that management buys, pays, and uses up for the maximization of profits.

The Japanese business law has just caught up with the American concept of the firm. The Commercial Code provides the basic legal framework for all types of private business in Japan. The latest amendments to the Code went into effect in April 2003, introducing, among others, "an American-style board with a chief executive officer (CEO) and more outside directors to help perform the oversight function" (JETRO, 2002). At present, a majority of Japanese firms have no plans to shift to this new system of corporate governance, but several high-profile firms, such as Sony, Hitachi, Toshiba, Mitsubishi Electric, and several others with a significant presence of foreign shareholders have adopted or are likely in the near future to adopt the American-style boards of directors (Japan Institute of Labor, 2003).

In Japan, the answer to the question "who owns the firm?" has never been as straightforward as in the US (Matsumoto, 1991; Aoki and Dore, 1994). Although the stakes of the individual shareholders have recently been gaining increasing attention and respect from management, shareholding has traditionally functioned as a means of strengthening inter-firm alliances. That is, a good proportion of the shares of the firm are held by friendly firms in the enterprise group of which the firm is a member. The firm itself also owns shares of other firms of the group. The member bank of the group is the main bank for the member firms.

Workers employed by the firm are much more than a factor of production. A good proportion of them, "regular employees," are considered "members of the firm" (*shain*) and participate in its management through "bottom-up" management, the employee union and consultative machinery (Koike, 1988). The firm, having slimmed down to its core activities, surrounds itself by a *keiretsu* of subsidiaries, affiliates, subcontractors, and distributors that supply it with parts, components, or services through forward and backward linkages. Managing the firm, then, means a coordination of diverse, sometimes conflicting, interests of various stakeholders while pursuing the firm's goals such as solvency, growth, and market share.

"Human resource," a popular concept in academic discourse, downgrades people to an equal status with other nonhuman resources. It is an especially misleading metaphor when applied to employee-members of the Japanese firm. Closer to the truth is that every employee is a manager in his or her own right, as much committed to the goals of the firm as those conventionally classified as "managers." Although the formal hierarchy of positions and functions within the Japanese firm is not much different from that of any firm in a market economy, practically all the positions and functions above the entry level all the way through top management are filled by internal promotions, owing to the well-developed INTERNAL LABOR MARKET.

The production concept of the Japanese firm is LEAN PRODUCTION, which emphasizes high product quality, *kaizen* (continuous improvements) in process and outcome, and "just-in-time" delivery in work relationships (*see* JUST-IN-TIME PRODUCTION SYSTEMS). This mode of production, unlike "mass production," devolves a maximum of judgment, initiative, and responsibilities to employees on the shop floor, eroding social distance and functional differences between managers and managed (Womack, Jones, and Roos, 1990). In the Japanese firm, those employees who would elsewhere be labeled "blue-collar" are "white-collarized" (Koike, 1988).

The tenure of the regular employees (employee-members of the firm) is indefinite, though subject to mandatory retirement at a stipulated age. The "standard regular" employees are hired at graduation from high school or college and remain in employment "for life," i.e., until mandatory retirement. These employee-members of the firm are immune to layoffs or discharges except under extreme circumstances, although they are free to quit of their own volition any time.

The Japanese firm, like its counterpart anywhere, is subject to output fluctuations due to changes in the conditions of the market, technology, and general business environment. A conventional capitalist firm adjusts workforce up or down as its output fluctuates. Barred from discharging its regular employees at will, the firm uses contingent workers as an adjustment factor (*see* CONTINGENCY EMPLOYMENT). These workers can be flexibly hired or fired according to changes in the firm's volume of business (Taira and Levine, 1985). The regular/contingent duality of employment is a major strategy of the Japanese firm. Contingent workers come in under a variety of contractual arrangements. Most common are temporary, seasonal, casual, or part-time workers hired for specified lengths or hours of service. The firm may also contract with other firms for sending in their employees for specified tasks in it. These firms, "subcontractors," belong to the *keiretsu*. Worker-dispatching firms have grown up in occupations related to data processing, office work, building maintenance, and security under a law passed in 1985.

For ordinary business cycles, the rules of employment adjustment built into the Japanese employment system are adequate for the security of tenure of the regular employees. When a recession is exceptionally long or deep, the terminations of contingency workers alone may not be enough. When this happens, as it did in the mid-1970s after the 1973 oil shock or in the post-bubble 1990s, additional adjustment measures are undertaken, such as a hiring freeze, reduction of working hours, transfers and reassignments, or moderation or suspension of salary increases. In the worst cases, after the exhaustion of all conceivable alternatives, some regular employees may be asked to take voluntary early retirement. Their terminations are costly, involving premiums and other incentives added to the contractual severance pay.

The recruitment and hiring of regular employees is a serious business (Taira and Levine, 1992). The firm begins planning for new hiring 12 months ahead of the actual induction of new employees. The procedure is also regulated by law and the Ministry of Health, Labor, and Welfare. During the spring of a given year, as soon as the new school year begins in April, the firm formulates its hiring plans targeted at college and high school seniors expected to graduate in the following year. In the summer, upon approval of the plans by the Employment Stabilization Office, the firm sends employee search notices to high schools and colleges.

To forestall undue influences on impressionable youth, the law prohibits recruiters from individually meeting high school students. They are only allowed to hold information meetings with groups of students. College students, supposed to be more mature and self-assured, are allowed individual JOB SEARCH activities. In the fall, the firm receives job applications, and holds written and oral examinations. Informal offers of employment (*naitei*) are then made to selected employees-to-be. During the remaining few months before April, the firm makes every effort to hold on to the *naitei* candidates. Depending on economic conditions, inter-firm competition may become so keen that each student receives several *naitei* offers and acquires considerable bargaining strength.

In April, new employees are inducted into the firm's employ at a solemn ceremony. Freshman employees are then put through a year of basic education and training combining classroom instructions and on-the-job practices. After this, each employee is formally assigned to a work unit to begin actual value-adding work. At this stage, a mentor is assigned to each new employee. From here on, the employee engages in lifelong competition for promotions in the firm's internal labor market as skills, knowledge, competence, and performance grow with more ON-THE-JOB TRAINING and experience.

Employee motivation for perpetual learning and effort is strengthened by a steeply rising salary schedule in association with the length of service and age known as the "seniority-based wage system." In principle, every freshman employee has the equal opportunity for rising to the top of the personnel hierarchy. Actual career paths depend upon efforts, merits, and luck that vary among individuals.

The Japanese firm exhibits two contradictory tendencies, one toward a "virtual corporation" and another toward diversification. They are interrelated, however. Like a virtual corporation, the Japanese firm concentrates on core competencies and procures parts, components, and services from other firms in the enterprise group and *keiretsu*. At the same time, the Japanese firm is innovative in generating growth through product differentiation and diversification as well as organizational restructuring and BUSINESS PROCESS REENGINEERING. The firm, overgrown, then spins off activities that have reached a critical mass for viable independence and adds them to the group and *keiretsu*. By this process of cell division, the core firm remains slim, fit, and dynamic.

In summary, in addition to the long-familiar "three treasures" of the Japanese employment system (lifetime employment, seniority-based wages, and enterprise union), recent research calls attention to the nature and strategy of the Japanese firm including characteristics such as enterprise groups, *keiretsu*, lean production, quality, *kaizen*, reengineering, virtual corporation, contingency workers, and many more. The basic point is that firms in a capitalist market economy must survive, make profits, and grow. Toward these goals, the Japanese firm has generated a complex of strategy, structure, organization, and process that appears distinct and fascinating when compared with firm types of other capitalist market economies. Through many stages of abstraction, generalization, and theorizing, the practices of the Japanese firm have been modeled as the "Japanese employment system." Since the last economic bubble burst in 1990, the macro economy of Japan has undergone considerable restructuring under a prolonged stagnation and frequent recessions. Since the Japanese employment system was a product of a growing economy, it has been losing fit with reality at the margins since 1990. An alternative model has not emerged yet, however.

Bibliography

Abegglen, J. and Stalk, G. (1985). *Kaisha: The Japanese Corporation*. New York: Basic Books.

Aoki, M. and Dore, R. (eds.) (1994). *The Japanese Firm: The Sources of Competitive Strength*. New York: Oxford University Press.

Japan Institute of Labor (2003). Revised commercial code introduces US-style corporate governance. *Japan Labor Bulletin*, **42** (5). Tokyo: Japan Institute of Labor.

JETRO (2002). Cover story: Corporate governance. *Focus Japan*, **29** (6). Tokyo: JETRO.

Koike, K. (1988). *Understanding Industrial Relations in Modern Japan*. New York: St. Martin's Press.

Matsumoto, K. (1991). *The Rise of the Japanese Corporate System*. London: Kegan Paul International.

Taira, K. and Levine, S. B. (1985). Japan's industrial relations: A social compact emerges. In H. Juris, M. Thompson, and W. Daniels (eds.), *Industrial Relations in a Decade of Change*. Madison, WI: Industrial Relations Research Association.

Taira, K. and Levine, S. B. (1992). Education and labor skills in postwar Japan. In R. Leestma and H. J. Walberg (eds.), *Japanese Educational Productivity*. Ann Arbor, MI: Center for Japanese Studies.

Womack, J. P., Jones, D. T., and Roos, D. (1990). *The Machine that Changed the World*. New York: Rawson Associates.

job

Robert J. Harvey

A job is a collection of one or more positions that are similar enough in terms of their tasks and duties to allow them to be grouped together and treated interchangeably. Although some cross-position heterogeneity is typically present, as a practical matter the positions that are grouped together to form a job should be sufficiently similar in terms of their tasks and duties to allow them to be described adequately through the use of a single JOB ANALYSIS and job title.

See also *duty; task*

job analysis

Michael T. Brannick and Edward L. Levine

Job analysis is the systematic process of uncovering and describing the components of a job. The process may be all-encompassing or narrower, depending upon the needs of the job analyst. The analyst may explore the goals of the work, the work procedures and processes (duties, tasks, and so forth; Harvey, 1992), the kinds of personal attributes required of people to complete the work (*see* KSAOS), and the work context, broadly defined to include the physical environment as well as the business environment. For example, for the job of police officer, the goals of the work might include enforcing laws, promoting the safety of the public, and maintaining community relations. The work procedures and processes might include such activities as giving traffic citations, resolving domestic disputes, and testifying in court. The personal characteristics might include the ability to remember laws, physical strength, and skill in operating a patrol car. The work context might include such items as working outdoors. The police officer reports to a police sergeant within a particular civic and geographic context (consider, for example, how the job might differ from Miami, Florida, to Ann Arbor, Michigan).

Job analysis can be considered to be a managerial activity because it helps solve so many human resource problems (McCormick, 1979; Gael et al., 1988). However, it may also serve society at large. Among the vast uses of job analysis are producing a written description of the nature of the job (a JOB DESCRIPTION), providing information used to set salaries (JOB EVALUATION METHODS), and planning for the future of people at work in the company (HUMAN RESOURCE PLANNING). Job analysis also forms the basis for training programs (training and development; *see* TRAINING), hiring and promoting workers (STAFFING), defending the JOB-RELATEDNESS of employment practices, and defining the job in such a way that JOB PERFORMANCE can be evaluated (performance measurement). Societal purposes include vocational guidance for students.

Job analysis employs a variety of approaches to uncover and describe components of a job. Such approaches can be captured in four categories: (1) the kinds of job data collected; (2) the methods of gathering data; (3) the sources of job information; and (4) the methods of data analysis (Levine, 1983). The kinds of data collected include such items as responsibilities, products and services, machines, tools, work aids, and equipment, and work and worker activities. The sources of information include the job analyst (the person doing the job analysis), the job holder, the job holder's supervisor, training specialists, and technical experts such as chemists or college professors (*see* JOB ANALYSIS INFORMATION SOURCES). The data analytic approach can include units of work (TASK, DUTY, or job dimensions), worker TRAIT requirements, such as mental and physical capabilities, and quantitative scales applied to the work. For an example of a quantitative approach, job holders could be given a survey that asks them to rate each task in their job in terms of its difficulty to learn. The way we carry out a job analysis will depend on what we are trying to accomplish (Levine, Thomas, and Sistrunk, 1988). We might proceed differently, for example, if we are interested in staffing than if we are interested in job evaluation. In staffing, we would concentrate on what personal characteristics (e.g., skill in word processing) job applicants need in order to be successful on the job. In evaluating jobs to set salaries, we would concentrate on the aspects of jobs that differentiate them in terms of pay, such as degree of fiscal responsibility.

See also *strategic job analysis*

Bibliography

Gael, S., Cornelius, E. T., III, Levine, E. L., and Salvendy, G. (eds.) (1988). *The Job Analysis Handbook for Business, Industry and Government*. New York: John Wiley.

Harvey, R. J. (1992). Job analysis. In M. D. Dunnette and L. M. Hough (eds.), *Handbook of Industrial and Organizational Psychology*, 2nd edn, vol. 2. Palo Alto, CA: Consulting Psychologists Press.

Levine, E. L. (1983). *Everything You Always Wanted to Know about Job Analysis*. Tampa, FL: Mariner.

Levine, E. L., Thomas, J. N., and Sistrunk, F. (1988). Selecting a job analysis approach. In S. Gael, E. T. Cornelius, III, E. L. Levine, and G. Salvendy (eds.), *The Job Analysis Handbook for Business, Industry and Government*, vol. 1. New York: John Wiley.

McCormick, E. J. (1979). *Job Analysis: Methods and Applications*. New York: AMACOM.

job analysis information sources

Michael T. Brannick and Edward L. Levine

The process of discovery of the nature of a job requires that the job analyst pursue one or more sources of job information, such as interviewing a job holder or observing the job holder perform the work.

METHODS EMPHASIZING THE ANALYST

Observation. Probably the most common method is for the job analyst to watch the job holder actually doing the job (practical tips are given by Martinko, 1988). It is important to capture a representative sample of the entire job. It would not do, for example, to observe a surgeon only in his or her office counseling patients away from the operating room.

Doing the work. Although for practical reasons this method is seldom used, a great deal of insight about the difficulties of learning a job and the skills and abilities required to perform it can be learned by actually doing the work.

METHODS EMPHASIZING BOTH INCUMBENT AND ANALYST

Individual interviews. In this method, the analyst asks questions of job holders and their supervisors. The questions need to be carefully structured prior to the interview for best results, but probing and following up on responses to questions allows this method some flexibility.

Group interviews. A knowledgeable group of workers and supervisors may be gathered to discuss a job. An advantage of such a procedure is that consensus can emerge about the nature of a job. Also, group members can say things that trigger responses from other group members resulting in a very complete picture of the job.

METHODS EMPHASIZING THE INCUMBENT

Diary. This method requires job holders to write down periodically the activities they have been doing at a particular time (see Freda and Senkewicz, 1988). Several different methods can be used for sampling times. For example, the job holder may have to write every half hour, each time he or she changes tasks, or whenever a beeper set by a job analyst goes off (*see* PERFORMANCE DIARIES).

Questionnaire. The questionnaire can be considered a structured interview that is self-administered. Often the items on a questionnaire are tasks or activities, and the incumbent is asked to evaluate each task on one or more scales. The US Air Force was instrumental in developing this approach. A good description of the Air Force technique is given in Christal and Weissmuller (1988). The POSITION ANALYSIS QUESTIONNAIRE is another good example of this job analysis method.

OTHER SOURCES

Several other sources of information can be used in conducting a job analysis. These sources tend to be used as supplements to those already listed. They include equipment-based sources, in which the job analyst uses equipment such as a videotape recorder or audiotape recorder to gather information. The analyst may also review records, such as those found in company PERFORMANCE APPRAISAL files or accident reports. Often the job analyst will begin by reviewing literature about the job, such as books, research reports, or other materials produced inside the organization or outside of it. Training materials are especially useful in this regard. Finally, the analyst may resort to studying equipment design; i.e., examining blueprints or schematic drawings when the job is heavily dependent upon equipment or machinery and especially for new jobs when they do not yet have any incumbents.

Bibliography

Christal, R. E. and Weissmuller, J. J. (1988). Job-task inventory analysis. In S. Gael, E. T. Cornelius, III, E. L. Levine, and G. Salvendy (eds.), *The Job Analysis Handbook for Business, Industry and Government*, vol. 2. New York: John Wiley.

Freda, L. J. and Senkewicz, J. J. (1988). Work diaries. In S. Gael, E. T. Cornelius, III, E. L. Levine, and G. Salvendy (eds.), *The Job Analysis Handbook for Business, Industry and Government*, vol. 1. New York: John Wiley.

Martinko, M. J. (1988). Observing the work. In S. Gael, E. T. Cornelius, III, E. L. Levine, and G. Salvendy (eds.), *The Job Analysis Handbook for Business, Industry and Government*, vol. 1. New York: John Wiley.

job-based pay

Thomas H. Stone

Job-based pay refers to pay structures based on any form of JOB EVALUATION METHODS, focusing on job contents and/or job specifications. Job-based pay systems may be contrasted with knowledge-based or skill-based pay systems that use knowledge, skills, abilities, and other characteristics (*see* KSAOS) of each incumbent to determine pay (*see* SKILL-BASED PAY DESIGN). Thus, job evaluation methods of classification, factor comparison, Hay method, and point and ranking would all yield a job-based pay system whereby an incumbent's base pay is determined by the job he or she occupies rather than by KSAOs. Most employers use job-based pay, but knowledge- and skill-based systems are growing.

See also *classification job evaluation method; factor-comparison job evaluation method; Hay method and other hybrid job evaluation methods; point job evaluation method; ranking job evaluation method*

job burnout

Thomas A. Wright and James Campbell Quick

Job burnout is defined as the chronic and negative affective pattern of responses to stressful conditions at work (*see* JOB STRESS). It is related to reduced PRODUCTIVITY and increased ABSENTEEISM and EMPLOYEE TURNOVER. Understanding the causes of job burnout is important to early recognition, prevention of adverse consequences, and early recovery actions.

CAUSES

Freudenberger (1980), who coined the term "burnout," implied that it is caused by the continuous pursuit of success. Cordes and Dougherty (1993: 640) said job burnout results from a high level of chronic work demands, entailing very important obligations and responsibilities. Maslach (1982) suggested that job burnout is caused by constant exposure to emotionally charged interpersonal situations on the job. Hence, high achievement, responsibility, and/or emotionally demanding jobs may cause burnout.

CONCEPTUALIZATION

Maslach's (1982) three-component conceptualization is the most widely accepted. The first component, emotional exhaustion, describes an individual's affect, feelings of depleted emotional resources, and lack of energy. Individuals feel unable to give psychologically. A common symptom is dreading to go to work.

The second component, depersonalization, is characterized by negative, cynical attitudes and feelings about one's clients, who are seen to deserve their lot in life. Prominent symptoms include the use of derogatory, abstract language about one's clients, extensive use of jargon, and withdrawal from direct client contact.

The third component, diminished personal accomplishment, refers to the tendency for negative self-evaluation, resulting in increased dissatisfaction with one's job accomplishments and a heightened perception of minimal work-related progress.

TREATMENT

Job burnout is a potentially reversible condition. EMPLOYEE ASSISTANCE PROGRAMS and STRESS MANAGEMENT PROGRAMS can be helpful in identifying causes of job burnout and in establishing treatment interventions.

Bibliography

Cordes, C. L. and Dougherty, T. W. (1993). A review and integration of research on job burnout. *Academy of Management Review*, 18, 621–56.

Freudenberger, H. J. (1980). *Burnout: The High Cost of High Achievement*. Garden City, NY: Anchor.

Maslach, C. (1982). *Burnout: The Cost of Caring*. Englewood Cliffs, NJ: Prentice-Hall.

job description

Michael T. Brannick and Edward L. Levine

The job description is a written summary of the nature of a job (see Ghorpade, 1988). The most common elements in a job description include:

1. a job identification that includes the job title;
2. a job overview that states the mission of the job and the products and services produced by the worker;
3. the primary tasks involved in the job;
4. a list of equipment, machines, and tools used;
5. raw materials, goods, data, or other materials used in the job;
6. the processes used to transform materials into products and services;
7. guidelines and controls that limit the discretion of the worker, such as supervision;
8. required knowledge, skills, abilities, and other characteristics (*see* KSAOS);
9. a description of the work context, such as working conditions; and
10. a statement of the qualifications required, such as a license or level of education.

Supervisors use job descriptions as a basis for assigning work and clarifying performance expectations. Job holders can use job descriptions to help understand their own jobs and jobs further up the job ladder that they may hold one day. Job descriptions are also a primary tool in PERFORMANCE APPRAISAL, in which supervisors evaluate the JOB PERFORMANCE of incumbents, and in JOB EVALUATION METHODS, with which the salaries of jobs within an organization are determined. Job descriptions may also play a role in RECRUITING and STAFFING functions, where they inform all parties of the nature of the work to be performed, thus helping to insure a good match between people and jobs.

The centrality of the job description to human resource practices is currently being questioned by some organizations because of rapid changes in jobs. Such changes are in response to the dynamic nature of today's business environment. In addition, many organizations have placed increased reliance on teams that require flexible assignment of duties (*see* SELF-MANAGING TEAMS).

Bibliography

Ghorpade, J. (1988). *Job Analysis: A Handbook for the Human Resource Director*. Englewood Cliffs, NJ: Prentice-Hall.

job element method of job analysis

Ronald A. Ash

The job element method of JOB ANALYSIS focuses on the human attributes necessary for superior performance on the job. This approach can be contrasted with other job analysis procedures in that it bypasses the TASK information or descriptions of the work itself, and goes directly to job elements. Elements cover the entire range of job behaviors, intellectual behaviors, motor behaviors, and work habits, and may be called knowledge, skills, abilities, and other personal characteristics (KSAOS; Primoff and Eyde, 1988). The same element may cut across different tasks and different jobs. The significant elements in a job are identified, described, and evaluated by experienced and expert workers in an occupation and their supervisors, typically referred to as subject matter experts (SMEs).

The job element method was originally developed by Ernest Primoff of the US Civil Service Commission (now called the Office of Personnel Management), and since its development has been used in a variety of settings for developing job information used in RECRUITING, PERSONNEL SELECTION, PROMOTION, PERFORMANCE APPRAISAL, and TRAINING.

Specific procedures and rating scales used in the job element method of job analysis are described in Primoff (1975) and Primoff and Eyde (1988).

Bibliography

Primoff, E. S. (1975). *How to Prepare and Conduct Job Element Examinations: Technical Study 75-1, US Civil Service Commission.* Washington, DC: US Government Printing Office.

Primoff, E. S. and Eyde, L. D. (1988). Job element analysis. In S. Gael, E. T. Cornelius, III, E. L. Levine, and G. Salvendy (eds.), *The Job Analysis Handbook for Business, Industry and Government.* New York: John Wiley.

job evaluation administrative issues

Timothy J. Keaveny

Job evaluation administration addresses implementation and utilization of a job evaluation plan. A primary issue is to decide who will participate in job evaluation. The typical choices are COMPENSATION specialists, managers, supervisors, and job incumbents. An effective job evaluation system requires managerial as well as employee acceptance of job evaluation results. In order to help to insure acceptance, participation by managers, supervisors, and employees is essential. Such participation can be through representation on task forces charged with designing a job evaluation system, as well as serving on committees that use the system to evaluate jobs.

Other administrative issues include training in the use of the system (*see* TRAINING), approval of completed job evaluations, communication of results to employees, and appeals procedures. Managers, supervisors, and job incumbents must be trained in the use of the job evaluation system. When the committee completes the evaluation of jobs, the results typically are reviewed by higher levels of management to insure that directions and guidelines were followed. The approved job evaluation results must be communicated to managers, supervisors, and job incumbents. Different methods can be used to explain the results to employees, such as brochures, videotapes, or meetings.

It is possible that some jobs will be incorrectly evaluated and it is quite likely that at least some will question the VALIDITY of some evaluations. As a consequence, it is essential to have procedures for appeal and review of job evaluation results.

After the initial round of evaluating jobs, communicating the results and addressing appeals, the system must provide for updating job descriptions (*see* JOB DESCRIPTION), analysis of newly created jobs, and evaluation of revised as well as new jobs.

Bibliography

Henderson, R. I. (1989). *Compensation Management: Rewarding Performance.* Englewood Cliffs, NJ: Prentice-Hall.

Hills, F. S., Bergmann, T. J., and Scarpello, V. G. (1994). *Compensation Decision Making.* Fort Worth, TX: Dryden Press.

Milkovich, G. T. and Newman, J. M. (1993). *Compensation*, 4th edn. Homewood, IL: Richard D. Irwin.

job evaluation methods

Matthew C. Bloom

Job evaluation is a systematic process designed to aid in establishing pay differentials across jobs within a single employer (Milkovich and Newman, 1996: 127). It is an alternative to person-based (e.g., competency-based pay) and market-pricing approaches (*see* PERSON-BASED PAY). Job evaluation is a judgmental process based on a systematic appraisal of job descriptions (*see* JOB DESCRIPTION). The culmination of this appraisal process is a hierarchy of jobs denoting their relative complexity and value to the organization. When matched with data about market pay rates, job evaluation provides the critical link between the organization's internal job structure and the external market and establishes the organization's pay structure (Schwab, 1980; Milkovich and Newman, 1996). Job evaluation is a crucial process for establishing a pay structure that is internally equitable, externally competitive, and consistent with the goals of the organization (*see* EXTERNAL EQUITY/EXTERNAL COMPETITIVENESS; INTERNAL EQUITY/INTERNAL CONSISTENCY).

Two essential components are usually assessed in job evaluation: job content and job value. Job content refers to the type of work performed, the knowledge, skills, abilities, and other personal characteristics (*see* KSAOS) required to perform that work, working conditions, degree of responsibility assumed, and so on. Job value refers to the relative contribution a job makes to organizational goals, its value in external markets, or its worth relative to some other agreed-upon standard. Job evaluation methods differ in terms of how they appraise job value and content, and how they position jobs based upon these values and content assessments. The most popular job evaluation method is the POINT JOB EVALUATION METHOD.

Bibliography

Milkovich, G. T. and Newman, J. M. (1996). *Compensation*, 5th edn. Homewood, IL: Richard D. Irwin.

Schwab, D. P. (1980). Job evaluation and pay setting: Concepts and practices. In E. R. Livernash (ed.), *Comparable Worth: Issues and Alternatives*. Washington, DC: Equal Employment Opportunity Council.

job family

Robert J. Harvey

A job family is a grouping of different jobs whose tasks and/or duties are deemed sufficiently similar to one another to allow them to be treated as interchangeable (e.g., to share a common employee selection battery). Because subsets of each job's tasks or duties (*see* DUTY; TASK) may be used when assessing similarity, it is quite possible for jobs that are grouped into different job families for one personnel purpose (e.g., employee selection using highly specific skill-based tests) to be grouped into the same job family for a different purpose (e.g., selection using a general cognitive ability test). Typically, job families are formed by clustering jobs within a single organization; in contrast, the term "occupation" is used to describe groupings of jobs that occur across industry and organizational boundaries. However, some authors use the term job family more generally to denote virtually any collection of similar jobs, regardless of the industry or organization in which they are found.

job involvement

Eugene F. Stone-Romero

Job involvement is an attitude toward the work role and its context. Conceptual definitions of job involvement have been of two basic types (see, e.g., Lodahl and Kejner, 1965; Rabinowitz and Hall, 1977). One regards it as reflecting the degree to which a person's sense of esteem is affected by JOB PERFORMANCE. The other views it as the centrality of work and the job context to the individual's self-image. Unfortunately, however, there are many other views on the nature of the job involvement construct and there is currently no consensus on the most appropriate measure of this construct (Rabinowitz and Hall, 1977). Moreover, as is true of the conceptual definitions of many constructs, popular definitions of job involvement tend to confuse it with its antecedents (e.g., work values) and consequences (e.g., performance-based esteem changes; Stone-Romero, 1994).

Researchers and theorists have equated job involvement, directly or indirectly, with such constructs as work centrality, EMPLOYEE MORALE, intrinsic motivation, JOB SATISFACTION, and the Protestant work ethic (Rabinowitz and Hall, 1977). However, Paullay, Alliger, and Stone-Romero (1994) argued that job involvement differs from both the Protestant work ethic and work centrality. The Protestant work ethic is a value orientation that has several components, including the normative belief that individuals should be involved in their work (Weber, 1930; Wollack et al., 1971). Work centrality reflects the degree to which individuals view work (independent of a specific job) as being an important activity in life (Dubin, 1965). Job involvement reflects the degree to which individuals feel attracted or attached to the tasks that make up their jobs (i.e., job involvement role) and the setting in which such tasks are carried out (i.e., job involvement setting). Research by Paullay et al. showed that job involvement role, job involvement setting, work centrality, and Protestant work ethic are distinct, although related, constructs.

Fishbein and Ajzen's (1975) attitude model can aid in the conceptualization of the job involvement construct. The model specifies that:

1. attitudes toward an attitude object are a function of individuals' values and beliefs;
2. attitudes, in conjunction with subjective norms, are precursors of behavioral intentions; and
3. these intentions determine actual behavior.

Applying this framework to the attitude of job involvement suggests that:

1. socialization consistent with such value orientations as the Protestant work ethic leads individuals to value the performance of job-related tasks and to view work as central to their lives;
2. this value orientation predisposes them to become involved with their jobs and their work settings;
3. when such work-related values are combined with beliefs about the nature-specific jobs and their settings, individuals manifest job involvement (i.e., an attitude of attraction to the job and its context); and
4. this attitude leads individuals to develop behavioral intentions that are reflective of it and, thereafter, to behave in attitude-consistent ways (e.g., perform at above-average levels).

This view of job involvement clarifies relationships between job involvement and its antecedents and consequences, helps to explain the results of prior research on relationships between job involvement and other variables (see Rabinowitz and Hall, 1977, for a review), and provides a basis for predicting how such interventions as employee involvement and job redesign programs will affect job involvement and its consequences.

Bibliography

Dubin, R. (1965). Industrial workers' worlds: A study of the "central life interests" of industrial workers. *Social Problems*, 3, 131–42.

Fishbein, M. and Ajzen, I. (1975). *Belief, Attitude, Intention, and Behavior: An Introduction to Theory and Research*. Reading, MA: Addison-Wesley.

Lodahl, T. M. and Kejner, M. (1965). The definition and measurement of job involvement. *Journal of Applied Psychology*, 49, 24–33.

Paullay, I. M., Alliger, G. M., and Stone-Romero, E. F. (1994). Construct validation of two instruments designed to measure job involvement and work centrality. *Journal of Applied Psychology*, 79, 224–8.

Rabinowitz, S. and Hall, D. T. (1977). Organizational research on job involvement. *Psychological Bulletin*, 84, 265–88.

Stone-Romero, E. F. (1994). Construct validity issues in organizational behavior research. In J. Greenberg (ed.), *Organizational Behavior: The State of the Science*. Hillsdale, NJ: Erlbaum.

Weber, M. (1930). *The Protestant Ethic and the Spirit of Capitalism*. Winchester, MA: Allen and Unwin.

Wollack, S., Goodale, J. G., Wijting, J. P., and Smith, P. C. (1971). Development of the survey of work values. *Journal of Applied Psychology*, 55, 331–8.

job loss

Carrie R. Leana

Job loss is used interchangeably with layoffs and generally refers to loss of employment due to plant closings, work slowdowns, corporate DOWNSIZING, or organizational restructuring (Leana and Feldman, 1992).

Evidence exists that job loss has a negative impact on the unemployed, on his or her family, and on friends and coworkers. People who have lost their jobs have been found to be more anxious, depressed, unhappy, and dissatisfied with life in general. Job loss also has strong effects on psychosomatic illnesses such as sleeping disorders, eating disorders, overuse of sedatives, dermatitis, headaches, and listlessness. Spouses of the unemployed often suffer psychological problems similar to those of the job loser. There is also evidence that job loss may contribute to the rate of marital separation and divorce. The results of several laboratory and field studies on coworkers of laid-off employees suggest that these so-called survivors often lower their PRODUCTIVITY, develop poorer job attitudes, and voluntarily leave their employers in the wake of coworkers' layoffs (Brockner, 1988; Leana and Feldman, 1994).

Individuals cope with job loss in a variety of ways. These coping strategies have been categorized as problem-focused coping (i.e., JOB SEARCH, RETRAINING) or symptom-focused coping (i.e., seeking social support). Some level of both is necessary for successful adjustment and reemployment (Leana and Feldman, 1994).

Four corporate interventions have been most frequently used to soften the effects of layoffs. These include: advance notification, severance pay and extended benefits, retraining programs, and outplacement programs (Leana and Feldman, 1992).

Bibliography

Brockner, J. (1988). The effects of work layoffs on survivors: Research, theory, and practice. In B. Staw (ed.), *Research in Organizational Behavior*, vol. 10. Greenwich, CT: JAI Press.

Leana, C. R. and Feldman, D. C. (1992). *Coping with Job Loss: How Individuals, Organizations, and Communities Respond to Layoffs*. New York: Lexington Books.

Leana, C. R. and Feldman, D. C. (1994). The psychology of job loss. In G. R. Ferris and K. M. Rowland (eds.), *Research in Personnel and Human Resources Management*, vol. 12. Greenwich, CT: JAI Press.

job performance

Peter Villanova, James T. Austin, and Walter C. Borman

Job performance is defined as that aspect of the work behavior domain that is of relevance to job and organizational success (Austin et al., 1991). As such, it represents a sample of the universe of behaviors an individual performs in the course of work that is relevant to judging success. Job performance is a key construct in human resource management, because criteria for PROMOTION, as well as for selection validation purposes, are frequently drawn from the job performance domain.

REPRESENTING AND UNDERSTANDING JOB PERFORMANCE

Job performance is a complex construct that is multidimensional, multiply determined, and potentially dynamic. Understanding job performance requires one to recognize that patterns of behavior in organizations can be prescribed through formal, bureaucratic means, such as job descriptions (*see* JOB DESCRIPTION), and through informal and more subjective means, such as role-sending, role-making, and role negotiation. Traditional definitions of job performance have concentrated on the former, more technical, objective and quasi-static job-based domain. More recent conceptualizations of job performance have been expanded to include less formally established activities, such as citizenship behavior and a willingness to assume responsibility and leadership beyond those detailed in a formal job description. No doubt this more inclusive conceptualization of job performance reflects the complexity of today's work organizations.

Job performance is multidimensional. There is abundant evidence that job performance, even for low-complexity jobs, is multidimensional (Campbell, McHenry, and Wise, 1990; Borman, 1991), and reflects both task and contextual aspects of the job (Borman and Motowidlo, 1993). Task proficiency is what has been traditionally studied as job performance and consists of the technical core (i.e., creating goods and services). Contextual performance reflects behaviors that enhance or detract from the environment surrounding the technical core.

Moreover, just as task performance is almost perfectly identified with established task elements of a job, contextual performance consists exclusively of emergent task elements that may be actively constructed or passively accepted by a worker. Because contextual performance more closely resembles "role performance," these activities and contributions may vary from worker to worker, even among those nominally assigned the same job classification. The implications are that performance dimensions may not only vary from one setting to another, as Bailey (1983) has argued, but also within a setting, where multiple roles are enacted by individuals performing the same "job."

Job performance is multiply determined. Just as no single dimension can successfully represent the complexity of performance, no single predictor sufficiently accounts for performance variability, or, more appropriately, for the patterns of behavior that define job success. Moreover, if one accepts that both tasks and contextual aspects of performance are important, the implications for selection include expansion of the predictor domain and acknowledgment that single predictor–single criterion combinations are inevitably deficient, both conceptually and practically. In particular, motivational and personality constructs would appear as logical candidates for providing incremental understanding of contextual performance, just as knowledge, skill, and ability constructs (see KSAOS) would seem to support task performance. Borman, White, and Dorsey (1995) have shown that contextual aspects of performance, such as "dependability," can account for as much, or more, of the variance in supervisor ratings of performance as do knowledge, ability, and proficiency.

Job performance is dynamic. The dynamic nature of performance on most jobs makes its representation by any measure at any one point in time somewhat deficient, contaminated, and less relevant than if measured at another time. Dynamic criteria reflect these shifts in the underlying structure of job success, and are reflected in changes in rank ordering of employees over time (Ghiselli, 1956). For example, the demands of the job, work aids, and worker proficiency may change over time as new technology or work methods are introduced, while performance standards are not calibrated to reflect these changes. The practical implications include timing of appraisals, appraisal accuracy, and the potential for inaccurate estimates of selection validity and utility. Models that reflect the interaction between persons and work systems seem well equipped to explain this dynamic variance.

Bibliography

Austin, J. T. et al. (1991). Construct validation of performance measures: Definitional issues, development, and evaluation of indicators. In G. R. Ferris and K. M. Rowland (eds.), *Research in Personnel and Human Resources Management*. Greenwich, CT: JAI Press.

Bailey, C. T. (1983). *The Measurement of Job Performance*. Aldershot: Gower Press.

Blumberg, M. and Pringle, C. D. (1982). The missing opportunity in organizational research: Some implications for a theory of work performance. *Academy of Management Review*, 7, 560–9.

Borman, W. C. (1991). Job behavior, performance, and effectiveness. In M. D. Dunnette and L. M. Hough (eds.), *Handbook of Industrial and Organizational Psychology*, 2nd edn, vol. 2. Palo Alto, CA: Consulting Psychologists Press.

Borman, W. C. and Motowidlo, S. J. (1993). Expanding the criterion domain to include elements of contextual performance. In N. Schmitt and W. C. Borman (eds.), *Personnel Selection*. San Francisco: Jossey-Bass.

Borman, W. C., White, L. A. and Dorsey, D. W. (1995). Effects of ratee task performance and interpersonal factors on supervisor and peer performance ratings. *Journal of Applied Psychology*, 80, 168–77.

Campbell, J. P., McHenry, J. J., and Wise, L. L. (1990). Modeling job performance in a population of jobs. *Personnel Psychology*, 43, 313–33.

Ghiselli, E. E. (1956). Dimensional problems of criteria. *Journal of Applied Psychology*, 40, 1–4.

job posting

Robert D. Gatewood

Job posting is an internal RECRUITING source that transmits information about open positions to current employees of the organization. Commonly used methods are bulletin boards, organization newsletters, flyers, and computer systems. Job posting has both advantages and disadvantages. Filling a position with a current employee creates other job openings which, in turn, are filled by other employees. This series of moves can result in both career development opportunities and increased motivation to attain them. Job posting often results in an applicant pool for which the organization has detailed information regarding applicants' abilities and work performance, thereby providing relatively complete information for selection decisions. However, since job posting restricts the entrance of new employees into the organization, its use can also restrict the availability of new, innovative ideas about work activities. Also, depending on the demographic composition of the organization's workforce, it could hinder the development of a MULTICULTURAL WORKFORCE that is representative of the RELEVANT LABOR MARKET.

Breaugh (1992) has described guidelines for implementing a job-posting system. Specific suggestions include:

1 publicize openings in ways that employees will see them;

2 list postings for a reasonably long time period;
3 include a detailed JOB DESCRIPTION and JOB SPECIFICATION;
4 include a description of the steps required for applying for the job and how the organization will process applications; and
5 inform applicants about the results of their applications in a timely manner.

Empirical research concerning job posting is very limited. However, related to some of these recommendations, Barber and Roehling (1993) found that the amount of information presented and specifics about location and COMPENSATION were influential in decisions of whether or not to apply.

Bibliography

Barber, A. E. and Roehling, M. V. (1993). Job postings and the decision to interview: A verbal protocol analysis. *Journal of Applied Psychology*, 78, 845–56.
Breaugh, J. A. (1992). *Recruitment: Science and Practice.* Boston: PWS-Kent.

job-relatedness

Barbara A. Lee

One method of proving that an employer practice is a BUSINESS NECESSITY is for the employer-defendant to show that it is job-related. For example, a job-related selection device is one that either measures the knowledge, skills, abilities, and other characteristics (*see* KSAOS) needed for the job or is a valid predictor of an individual's ability to perform the job. The EQUAL EMPLOYMENT OPPORTUNITY COMMISSION 1978 Uniform Guidelines on Employee Selection Procedures require that validation studies be used to establish that the employer practice is job-related (29 CFR, section 1607.2(B)), but most courts have not required that selection devices other than tests be empirically validated (Schlei and Grossman, 1983: 1329).

Bibliography

Schlei, B. L. and Grossman, P. (1983). *Employment Discrimination Law*, 2nd edn. Washington, DC: Bureau of National Affairs.

job rotation

Gary P. Latham and Lucie Morin

This onsite training technique involves giving managerial and nonmanagerial trainees a series of lateral job assignments in various parts of the organization for a specific period of time varying in length from 3 to 12 months (Wexley and Latham, 1991). A primary objective is to improve trainees' decision-making and problem-solving skills by enabling them to gain an overall perspective of the organization, and to increase their understanding of the interrelations among its various units. Job rotation also helps trainees to crystalize their career plans and to increase their JOB SATISFACTION, motivation and organizational commitment (Campion, Cheraskin, and Stevens, 1994). Managers have reported that the most significant learning experiences that have contributed to their development are, in fact, on-the-job experiences (Latham and Seijts, 1995).

Although this training technique is receiving increasing recognition as a form of management development, it can prove to be costly because of the trainee's learning curve, the increase in workload, and a decrease in PRODUCTIVITY for the trainee and for peers. Thus, to maximize the effectiveness of job rotation, trainees should be assigned full functional responsibility with ample opportunity to use new skills and to make decisions (Wexley and Latham, 1991). This responsibility should be complemented by supportive coaching from one's supervisor or peers in each of the job assignments. Job rotation should be tailored to the needs and capabilities of all trainees as well as their career aspirations (Wexley and Latham, 1991).

See also *training; training evaluation*

Bibliography

Campion, M. A., Cheraskin, L., and Stevens, M. J. (1994). Career-related antecedents and outcomes of job rotation. *Academy of Management Journal*, 37, 1518–42.
Latham, G. P. and Seijts, G. H. (1995). Management development. In P. Drenth, C. de Wolff, and H. Thierry (eds.), *European Handbook of Work and Organizational Psychology*. Houten: Bohn Stafleu Van Loghum.

Wexley, K. N. and Latham, G. P. (1991). *Developing and Training Human Resources in Organizations*, 2nd edn. New York: HarperCollins.

job satisfaction

Eugene F. Stone-Romero

Job satisfaction is an affective (i.e., emotional) response to a job or its facets that is based upon individuals' beliefs about differences between (1) the outcomes they perceive to be getting from a job and (2) the outcomes that they expect to get from it (see, e.g., Lofquist and Dawis, 1969; Cranny, Smith, and Stone, 1992). Although perceived outcomes are typically influenced by the *objective* levels of various variables (e.g., workload, pay), relationships between objective and perceived outcome levels are often far from perfect. Moreover, because values, interests, and needs differ considerably across individuals, there are corresponding differences in the outcomes that individuals want or expect from jobs.

OVERALL SATISFACTION VERSUS SATISFACTION WITH JOB FACETS

Job satisfaction may be viewed in terms of individuals' (1) overall affective reactions to a job or (2) reactions to the specific facets of a job. Among the many facets that have been considered in previous job satisfaction research are the work itself, pay/COMPENSATION, achievement, PROMOTION/advancement, supervision–human relations, supervision–technical, coworkers, ability utilization, activity level, authority, company policies and practices, creativity, independence, moral values, recognition, responsibility, job security, social service, social status, task variety, career progress, personal growth, and working conditions (e.g., Lofquist and Dawis, 1969; Smith, Kendall, and Hulin, 1969). Unfortunately, there is little consistency in the satisfaction facets considered by various job satisfaction theorists and researchers (see Cook et al., 1981: 37–74).

RESEARCH ON PUTATIVE CAUSES AND EFFECTS OF SATISFACTION

The construct of job satisfaction has been of considerable interest to individuals in such fields as human resource management, industrial and organizational psychology, industrial sociology, occupational/vocational psychology, and organizational behavior. Not surprisingly, therefore, a tremendous number of empirical studies have had job satisfaction as their focus. As of about 1975, more than 3,300 studies had been conducted on job satisfaction (Locke, 1976). That number has probably more than doubled by now.

Research on job satisfaction has considered measures of both overall job satisfaction and facet satisfactions (Cook et al., 1981). Results of this research show considerable evidence of relationships between measures of job and/or facet satisfactions and (1) a host of hypothesized antecedents or causes (e.g., job design, pay, advancement/promotion, working conditions, career progress, coworkers, and supervision) and (2) a number of assumed consequences (e.g., ABSENTEEISM, EMPLOYEE TURNOVER, GRIEVANCES, physiological strain, psychological strain, general wellbeing, life satisfaction, job involvement, EMPLOYEE MORALE, and organizational commitment) (Locke, 1976; Cook et al., 1981; Cranny et al., 1992). The literature also shows that a number of INDIVIDUAL DIFFERENCES (e.g., work values) moderate relationships between job satisfaction and both its assumed causes and effects. Unfortunately, most of the research on job satisfaction has used nonexperimental designs. As a consequence, it is generally not possible to advance firm conclusions about the causes and effects of job satisfaction or the role that individual differences play in moderating relationships between job satisfaction and other variables.

Bibliography

Cook, J. D., Hepworth, S. J., Wall, T. D., and Warr, P. B. (1981). *The Experience of Work: A Compendium of 249 Measures and Their Use*. London: Academic Press.

Cranny, C. J., Smith, P. C., and Stone, E. F. (1992). *Job Satisfaction: How People Feel About Their Jobs and How It Affects Their Performance*. New York: Lexington Books.

Locke, E. A. (1976). The nature and causes of job satisfaction. In M. D. Dunnette (ed.), *Handbook of Industrial and Organizational Psychology*. Chicago: Rand McNally.

Lofquist, L. H. and Dawis, R. V. (1969). *Adjustment to Work: A Psychological View of Man's Problems in a Work-Oriented Society.* New York: Appleton-Century-Crofts.

Smith, P. C., Kendall, L. M., and Hulin, C. L. (1969). *The Measurement of Satisfaction in Work and Retirement.* Chicago: Rand McNally.

job search

Robert D. Bretz, Jr.

Job search is the process of gathering information about potential job opportunities. It is the individual corollary of RECRUITING and together they form the basis for successful person–job matching (*see* PERSON–JOB FIT). Job search frequently has been embedded within the construct of employee withdrawal under the assumption that it results from the same factors that lead to EMPLOYEE TURNOVER. However, the temporal relationship between intention to search and the intention to quit is ambiguous, suggesting that job search serves many purposes in addition to facilitating turnover. Some employed people search without any intention to leave a current position. For example, job search can be used to establish networks of influential contacts, to leverage improved employment conditions with the current employer, or to convince oneself that the current employment arrangements are attractive relative to alternatives (Bretz, Boudreau, and Judge, 1994).

Job search among the employed is thought to be motivated by a combination of "push" and "pull" factors. The push process reflects the degree to which current life or work situations cause enough dissatisfaction to justify the costs of finding and evaluating alternatives. The pull process reflects the market's reaction to one's human capital, or the degree to which an individual's accomplishments make one a target for external recruitment activity.

Critical aspects of the job search process include: (1) the amount of information sought; (2) the nature of the information sought; and (3) the source of the information (Schwab, Rynes, and Aldag, 1987). The amount of information sought encompasses both extensive and intensive search behaviors. Extensive search involves identifying potential job opportunities. Intensive search involves collecting detailed information about each alternative, and has been shown to relate to many positive outcomes, including shorter unemployment durations and higher probabilities of finding an acceptable job (Rynes, 1991).

The type of information sought changes over the course of the search. At first, people engage in extensive search to generate alternatives, followed at later stages by intensive search to learn more about the alternatives. However, the job choice literature is inconclusive regarding the evaluation process. One model suggests that job offers are evaluated simultaneously against one another, while competing models suggest that job seekers consider alternatives sequentially as they become known (Schwab et al., 1987). Under most circumstances it is reasonable to believe that job search is sequential, and that jobs are evaluated against preestablished standards on a few important criteria, such as (1) the nature of the work required, (2) the rewards the job offers, and (3) the degree of person–organization "fit" based on job requirements, values, personality, or needs (Bretz and Judge, 1994).

Job applicants typically assign greater credibility to informal than to formal sources of job information. Specifically, friends, relatives, and organizational representatives other than the recruiter are presumed more likely to give REALISTIC JOB PREVIEWS and are thus perceived as more credible. These sources generally yield better post-hire results as well. The effects of recruitment on applicant decisions have been debated, but research indicates that recruiting does significantly affect job search and choice behaviors (Rynes, Bretz, and Gerhart, 1991).

Bibliography

Bretz, R. D., Boudreau, J. W., and Judge, T. A. (1994). Job search behavior of employed managers. *Personnel Psychology,* **47,** 275–301.

Bretz, R. D. and Judge, T. A. (1994). The role of human resource systems in job applicant decision processes. *Journal of Management,* **20,** 531–51.

Rynes, S. L. (1991). Recruitment, job choice and post-hire consequences: A call for new research directions. In M. D. Dunnette and L. Hough (eds.), *Handbook of Industrial and Organizational Psychology,* 2nd edn. Palo

Alto, CA: Consulting Psychologists Press, pp. 399–444.

Rynes, S. L., Bretz, R. D., and Gerhart, B. (1991). The importance of recruitment in job choice: A different way of looking. *Personnel Psychology*, 44, 487–521.

Schwab, D. P., Rynes, S. L., and Aldag, R. J. (1987). Theories and research on job search and choice. In G. R. Ferris and K. M. Rowland (eds.), *Research in Personnel and Human Resources Management*, vol. 5. Greenwich, CT: JAI Press, pp. 129–66.

job sharing

Stanley Nollen

Job sharing is a version of PART-TIME EMPLOYMENT whereby two part-time (usually half-time) employees share one regular full-time job (*see* PART-TIME WORK SCHEDULE). The two job sharers agree on the division of responsibilities and coverage of the job, such as by each working half-days or each working two and one-half days per week. Regular full-time pay and BENEFITS are prorated to each job sharer according to time worked. Job sharing usually occurs in organizations on a case-by-case basis and occurs among a wide range of occupations from production workers to professionals.

Bibliography

Olmsted, B. and Smith, S. (1994). *Creating a Flexible Workplace*, 2nd edn. New York: AMACOM.

job-skills training

Timothy T. Baldwin

Job-skills training initiatives are designed to identify and target improvement in the basic skills individuals need to be successful in the workplace. Job-skills training is of increasing interest to employers because new business realities (e.g., global competition, rapid technological change) have created demand for a higher level of skills for all workers. The domain of basic skills includes the traditional "three Rs" (reading, writing, and arithmetic) as well as problem solving, teamwork, and capacity to learn (Carnevale, Gainer, and Meltzer, 1990a). The most effective job-skills training has employed a job-specific methodology which links learning to JOB PERFORMANCE and encourages retention by requiring repeated use of trained skills (Carnevale, Gainer, and Meltzer, 1990b).

Bibliography

Carnevale, A. P., Gainer, L. J., and Meltzer, A. S. (1990a). *Workplace Basics: The Essential Skills Employers Want*. San Francisco: Jossey-Bass.

Carnevale, A. P., Gainer, L. J., and Meltzer, A. S. (1990b). *Workplace Basics: Training Manual*. San Francisco: Jossey-Bass.

job specification

Michael T. Brannick and Edward L. Levine

A job specification is a written description of the human characteristics necessary for the successful performance of a job. The typical sequence of events is to complete a JOB ANALYSIS to understand the nature of the work, to prepare a JOB DESCRIPTION, and then to prepare a more detailed job specification, which is used in RECRUITING and STAFFING. A summary of the job specification may be included in the job description.

The job specification communicates applicant characteristics that employers are looking for to job applicants as well as to recruiters and others in human resources responsible for staffing. In the psychological literature, the job specification usually refers to a list of knowledge, skills, abilities, and other personal characteristics (*see* KSAOS) required by the job, such as verbal comprehension, memorization, or integrity. A job specification is the result of one of several methods of job analysis specifically designed to yield estimates of KSAOs such as the JOB ELEMENT METHOD OF JOB ANALYSIS (Primoff and Eyde, 1988), the POSITION ANALYSIS QUESTIONNAIRE (McCormick and Jeanneret, 1988), the threshold traits analysis system (Lopez, 1988), and the ability requirement scales (Fleishman and Mumford, 1988). In the management literature the job specification tends to be more broadly defined to include such attributes as educational requirements or other minimum qualifications (Wernimont, 1988). In practice, the job specification is sometimes far less than ideal, and often nothing more than a vague paragraph of personality traits written by a manager and given to a college recruiter. Ghorpade (1988) considered "job specification" to be something of a misnomer because it refers to human abilities as opposed to job attributes. He preferred the term "worker specification."

Bibliography

Fleishman, E. A. and Mumford, M. D. (1988). Ability requirements scales. In S. Gael, E. T. Cornelius, III, E. L. Levine, and G. Salvendy (eds.), *The Job Analysis Handbook for Business, Industry and Government*, vol. 2. New York: John Wiley.

Ghorpade J. (1988). *Job Analysis: A Handbook for the Human Resource Director*. Englewood Cliffs, NJ: Prentice-Hall.

Lopez, F. M. (1988). Threshold traits analysis system. In S. Gael, E. T. Cornelius, III, E. L. Levine, and G. Salvendy (eds.), *The Job Analysis Handbook for Business, Industry and Government*, vol. 2. New York: John Wiley.

McCormick, E. J. and Jeanneret, P. R. (1988). Position Analysis Questionnaire (PAQ). In S. Gael, E. T. Cornelius, III, E. L. Levine, and G. Salvendy (eds.), *The Job Analysis Handbook for Business, Industry and Government*, vol. 2. New York: John Wiley.

Primoff, E. S. and Eyde, L. D. (1988). Job element analysis. In S. Gael, E. T. Cornelius, III, E. L. Levine, and G. Salvendy (eds.), *The Job Analysis Handbook for Business, Industry and Government*, vol. 2. New York: John Wiley.

Wernimont, P. F. (1988). Recruitment, selection, and placement. In S. Gael, E. T. Cornelius, III, E. L. Levine, and G. Salvendy (eds.), *The Job Analysis Handbook for Business, Industry and Government*, vol. 1. New York: John Wiley.

job stress

James Campbell Quick, Debra L. Nelson, and Marilyn Macik-Frey

Job stress is defined as the psychophysiological arousal resulting from demands associated with a job. Although more often having negative connotations, job stress is a neutral concept that can also result in positive outcomes. The response to stress is dependent upon individual, interpersonal, and contextual factors associated with the perception and response to the job demands. The goal of individuals and organizations is to increase the functional, healthy consequences, or eustress, and decrease the dysfunctional, unhealthy consequences, or distress (or strain). Eustress may lead to enhanced JOB PERFORMANCE up to an optimal level of stress; conversely, distress may place an employee at risk of physical and psychological illness and occurs when the job stress is too intense, frequent, or chronic (Selye, 1976), or when prevention and coping are suboptimal. Understanding job stress is important to maximize the positive outcomes, minimize the detrimental effects on the person and organization, and provide systematic prevention management programs.

SOURCES OF JOB STRESS

Job stress is triggered by a wide variety of job demands. These include task-specific demands, role demands, interpersonal demands, and physical demands (Quick et al., 1997). These demands are not inherently or necessarily harmful, and the degree of stress they elicit in a person depends in part on the individual's cognitive appraisal of that demand. Lack of control over and uncertainty about aspects of the psychosocial and physical work environments are a major source of job distress. The complex contemporary organization with growing diversity, WORK–FAMILY CONFLICT, globalization, and increasing technology add to the loss of control and predictability (Cooper, 1996). Extreme working environments, such as those of military fighter pilots or oilfield service personnel in arctic climates, create unique physical and/or peak demands. Whether the job-stress level is healthy or unhealthy is determined in part by the prevalence of job strain within a given work population as well as the INDIVIDUAL DIFFERENCES in their response to stress.

COSTS OF JOB STRAIN

Job strain may be costly to organizations and may take one of three individual forms: psychological, medical, or behavioral. Common forms of psychological distress are depression, JOB BURNOUT, anger, and sleep disturbances. Common forms of medical distress are backaches and headaches, ulcer disease, and cardiovascular problems. Common forms of behavioral distress are substance abuse, violence, and accident proneness. High-strain jobs, characterized by high job demands and low employee control, have significantly higher incidence rates of distress, such as myocardial infarction (Karasek et al., 1988).

Organizational costs may accrue from employees' psychological, medical, and behavioral distress. The direct organizational costs of job strain take the form of EMPLOYEE TURNOVER, ABSENTEEISM, performance problems on the job, and workers' compensation. In addition, there are indirect organizational costs of job strain which may be reflected in low EMPLOYEE MORALE, low JOB SATISFACTION, faulty decision-making, and distrust in working relationships.

INDIVIDUAL DIFFERENCE IN THE STRESS–STRAIN RELATIONSHIP

The stress response is universal; the intensity, frequency, and consequences of the stress response are not. Individual differences influence the degree to which job stress may become job strain or eustress. Gender, personality, EMOTIONAL INTELLIGENCE, cognitive complexity, and interpersonal communication competency play a role in the response to stress (Macik-Frey, Quick, and Quick, 2004). Although many of these individual difference variables are inherent traits, there is evidence that focused training in stress management and prevention may improve the stress response outcomes for those people who are predisposed to experience strain in particular situations.

STRESS MANAGEMENT PROGRAMS may help prevent job stress from becoming one or another form of job strain (job distress) and may potentially assist with positive focus of energy (eustress). EMPLOYEE ASSISTANCE PROGRAMS can help employees who experience identifiable job strain, distress, and/or job burnout. HEALTH PROMOTION programs may also help employees to manage job stress.

Bibliography

Cooper, C. L. (ed.) (1996). *Handbook of Stress, Medicine and Health*. Boca Raton, FL: CRC Press.

Karasek, R. A., Theorell, T., Schwartz, J. E., Schnall, P. L., Pieper, C. F., and Michela, J. L. (1988). Job characteristics in relation to the prevalence of myocardial infarction in the US health examination survey (HES) and the health and nutrition examination survey (HANES). *American Journal of Public Health*, 78, 910–18.

Macik-Frey, M., Quick, J. C., and Quick, J. D. (2004). Interpersonal communication: The key to unlocking social support for preventive stress management. In C. L. Cooper (ed.), *Handbook of Stress, Medicine and Health*, rev. edn. Boca Raton, FL: CRC Press.

Quick, J. C., Quick, J. D., Nelson, D. L., and Hurrell, J. J., Jr. (1997). *Preventive Stress Management in Organizations*. Washington, DC: American Psychological Association.

Selye, H. (1976). *Stress in Health and Disease*. Boston: Butterworth.

Johnson v. Transportation Agency, Santa Clara County (1987)

Leonard Bierman

In *Johnson* the court considered whether a voluntary AFFIRMATIVE ACTION plan, developed by the county transportation agency, was justified by the existence of a *manifest imbalance* that reflected underrepresentation of women in *traditionally segregated job categories* rather than purported past *discriminatory* practices. The Supreme Court ruled by six to three that the Santa Clara Transportation Agency was justified in giving a road dispatcher's job to Diane Joyce, who scored two points *less* than a man on a test, but was found to be otherwise qualified by a panel of supervisors. The county's plan passed a three-pronged test set by the justices: it was flexible, temporary, and designed to gradually correct a manifest imbalance in the overwhelmingly white, male workforce. The plan did *not* require the discharge of white workers and their replacement by minority hires, nor did it absolutely bar the advancement of nonminority employees.

just-in-time production systems

James P. Womack

A just-in-time production system (JIT) is a term for the production management system pioneered by Taiichi Ohno and his colleagues at the Toyota Motor Company in the years immediately after World War II. Ohno believed that inventory was the root of most problems in physical production and set out to devise a universally applicable system in which the creation of significant amounts of inventory was impossible. In logic, the best way to do this was the introduction of a "pull" system in which no part or finished unit was made until the ultimate customer or the next stage in the production process specifically requested it. Ohno's mechanism for signaling the previous production stage to make more parts was the *kanban*, an order card returned from the next stage when more parts were needed.

Ohno's system could only work if previous stages were able to quickly switch production to the type of part just requested. Therefore, rapid tool changes were essential. (Methods for rapidly changing tools are often termed "single minute exchange of dies," after the usage of Shigeo Shingo, Ohno's colleague who perfected quick tool changes.)

Ohno's system also required high quality and a high degree of machine availability because, by design, there were no reserve inventories of parts on hand. *Jidoka* (or self-monitoring machines), *poka-yoke* (or mistake-proofing of processes), and total productive maintenance (a set of techniques to assure that all tools are available for work all the time) were accompanying techniques for JIT production, perfected in Japan in the 1950s.

See also *lean production*

Bibliography

Monden, Y. (1983). *The Toyota Production System*. Atlanta, GA: Institute of Industrial Engineers.

Ohno, T. (1988). *Just-in-Time for Today and Tomorrow*. Cambridge, MA: Productivity Press.

key job/benchmark job

Jerry M. Newman

The terms "key job" and "benchmark job" are generally used interchangeably. A benchmark job is a job that matches, in terms of content, a similar job in the external labor market. If the content of a company's job is identical to that of the external market match, the average wage paid for the external job can be taken as the going market rate. Benchmark jobs have several characteristics:

1 they are stable in content across time;
2 they are stable in content across companies;
3 this content is well known across individuals in organizations;
4 their current pay rates are generally acceptable; and
5 the pay differentials among them are reasonably stable.

This stability allows such jobs to be included in salary surveys. COMPENSATION experts, seeking to find what others pay for these jobs, ask for wage data from a number of labor market competitors (or contract with consulting firms). This information across numerous benchmark jobs gives a picture of the external market rate.

knowledge teams

Susan Albers Mohrman

Knowledge teams are groups of employees who perform interdependent knowledge work and who are collectively responsible for a product or service. Knowledge teams are often composed of members with a number of different highly advanced discipline bases. Each carries values, algorithms, information, and skills that may be only partially overlapping (Dougherty, 1992), making communication and collaboration difficult. The team integrates the work of these specialists.

Variants of knowledge teams include:

1 work teams, such as new product development or systems integration teams, that deliver service or produce a product;
2 integrating teams that coordinate across parts of the organization;
3 management teams that integrate parts of the organization by providing strategic and operational direction, allocating resources, and insuring that the organization is appropriately designed, and by insuring that there is an effective PERFORMANCE MANAGEMENT system in place; and
4 process improvement teams that examine and make changes to the work processes of the organization (Mohrman, Cohen, and Mohrman, 1995).

Knowledge teams may be SELF-MANAGING TEAMS, but there are some design challenges that limit team independence. If deep-discipline knowledge bases are required, CROSS-TRAINING is limited and the organization must find ways to keep discipline knowledge current. Knowledge teams are often highly interdependent with other organizational teams and units, requiring integrating mechanisms across teams.

Knowledge teams are examples of HORIZONTAL MANAGEMENT. Team members do the coordination, assignment, and management of tasks among disciplines that have traditionally been done hierarchically. Increased use of knowledge teams reflects pressures for faster time-to-market and better customer responsiveness, as well as for effectively dealing with the complexity of organizational trade-offs and decisions in the global economy (Galbraith, 1994).

See also *knowledge work*

Bibliography

Dougherty, D. (1992). Interpretive barriers to successful product innovation in large firms. *Organizational Science*, 3, 179–202.

Galbraith, J. R. (1994). *Competing with Flexible, Lateral Organizations*. San Francisco: Jossey-Bass.

Mohrman, S. A., Cohen, S. G., and Mohrman, A. M., Jr. (1995). *Designing Team-Based Organizations: New Forms for Knowledge Work*. San Francisco: Jossey-Bass.

knowledge work

Susan Albers Mohrman

Knowledge work refers to work that adds value by applying knowledge bases and processing of information in order to solve problems. Routine knowledge work is the management of structured problems using existing knowledge bases. Accuracy of the information and of the application of knowledge are primary determinants of success. Nonroutine knowledge work requires the application of incomplete knowledge to the management of unstructured problems – problems where there is incomplete cause–effect understanding that introduces uncertainty into the work (Mohrman, Mohrman, and Cohen, 1995). This work demands increased judgment, interpretation, creativity, and discretion. Successful nonroutine knowledge work often requires the generation of information and the creation of new knowledge. Learning is an integral part of such work.

A key challenge in organizing for knowledge work is how to increase the accessibility to knowledge that is needed by its members. Information technology can support knowledge work by providing data, establishing connections between knowledge workers, and building knowledge-based routines into applications that facilitate work. Complex knowledge work, such as new product development or systems integration, requires the integrated application of multiple knowledge bases. It may be accomplished by use of knowledge work teams.

Knowledge work is often performed in an office (Pava, 1983) or in a technical setting, such as a scientific laboratory. As knowledge becomes encoded in software tools that can execute routine tasks, people increasingly perform the judgmental and nonroutine aspects of work. Most work settings, including modern production facilities, house knowledge work, and more work is becoming knowledge work.

See also *knowledge teams*

Bibliography

Mohrman, S. A., Mohrman, A. M., Jr., and Cohen, S. G. (1995). Organizing knowledge work systems. In M. Beyerlein (ed.), *Advances in Interdisciplinary Studies of Work Teams*, vol. 2: *Knowledge Work in Teams*. Greenwich, CT: JAI Press.

Pava, C. (1983). *Managing New Office Technology: An Organizational Strategy*. New York: Free Press.

KSAOs

Paul E. Spector

KSAOs refer to the knowledge, skill, ability, and other personal characteristics required for good JOB PERFORMANCE on a specific job. Knowledge is what a person knows that is relevant to the job (e.g., knowledge of legal procedures for a police officer). Skill is what a person is able to do on the job. This includes both mental tasks (e.g., skill in doing algebra) and physical tasks (e.g., skill in driving an automobile). Ability is the capacity to learn a skill (e.g., cognitive ability is the capacity to learn mental skills). Abilities include mental abilities, physical abilities, and psychomotor abilities. Other personal characteristics, not covered by the first three, include attitudes, beliefs, personality characteristics, temperaments, and values. All four classes of human characteristics can be assessed with psychological tests, as well as with other assessment devices. KSAOs are commonly assessed for purposes of PERSONNEL SELECTION.

Some JOB ANALYSIS methods provide specifications of the KSAOs necessary for a particular job. KSAO requirements can also be tied to individual job tasks (see TASK), which is helpful in designing jobs. The ability to associate KSAOs with individual tasks is important for compliance with the AMERICANS WITH DISABILITIES ACT OF 1990. KSAO requirements that are associated with noncritical tasks can be relaxed to make reasonable accommodation for a disabled employee.

L

labor contract

Charles R. Greer

Labor contracts, also referred to as labor agreements, specify in writing the wages and conditions negotiated between unions representing employees in a BARGAINING UNIT and employers. In addition to specification of wage rates for different job classifications and overtime procedures, labor contracts typically specify BENEFITS, vacations, holidays, disciplinary procedures, grievance procedures (*see* GRIEVANCE PROCEDURE), ARBITRATION procedures, layoff procedures, management prerogatives or rights, dues, check-off arrangements, PROMOTION procedures, the determination of seniority, the duration of the agreement, and other benefits or important rules. Labor contracts are typically negotiated for two- or three-year time periods. In general, labor agreements for CRAFT UNIONS are usually much shorter than those negotiated for INDUSTRIAL UNIONS since elaborate job classifications and wage structures are not applicable to such unions and because craft unions, instead of employers, administer the benefit programs for their members.

Labor Management Relations Act of 1947

Charles E. Krider

The Labor Management Relations Act, or the Taft–Hartley Act, amended the NATIONAL LABOR RELATIONS ACT OF 1935 (the Wagner Act), which encouraged unions and COLLECTIVE BARGAINING. With governmental assistance, unions were able to organize most major industries. The attention of Congress now focused on correcting perceived abuses of unions. The passage of the Taft–Hartley Act in 1947 followed the post-World War II pent-up frustrations of unions, which were prevented from striking during the war. The largest number of work days lost due to strikes in US history was recorded in 1946. Congress's response was to further regulate labor–management relations to: (1) achieve more balance between the interests of labor and management; and (2) limit the power of unions in order to protect employees and the public. The Taft–Hartley Act was strongly opposed by organized labor and was passed by Congress over President Truman's veto.

BALANCE OF INTERESTS

The Wagner Act of 1935 had contained unfair labor practices for employers but not for unions. The Taft–Hartley Act added section 8(b) union unfair labor practices, which mirrored those for employers and added several to regulate picketing and boycotts. Just as employers could not coerce or restrain employees in the exercise of their section 7 rights, it now became an unfair labor practice for a union to "restrain or coerce employees in the exercise of their rights guaranteed in section 7." Similarly, unions could not cause an employer to discriminate against an employee to encourage membership in a union and unions that were recognized as the bargaining agent could not refuse to bargain collectively with an employer.

PROTECT EMPLOYEES

Under the Wagner Act a union is certified to represent employees who may not be supporters or members of the union. This creates an obvious concern for the rights of a minority that may need protection from the union. In Taft-Hartley, Congress separated union membership from the right to be employed. A union may not seek to have an employee discharged as long as the employee is willing to tender periodic dues. A union may still deny an employee membership in the union but the employee cannot be terminated for that reason.

Section 14(b) of the Act also permitted states to pass more restrictive laws regulating union security, namely, RIGHT TO WORK statutes. These statutes, now in 26 states, prohibit unions from negotiating union shop agreements that require employees to join the union as a condition of employment. Section 14(b) has been strongly opposed by unions but all efforts to lobby for congressional repeal have failed.

The Taft-Hartley Act also added an employee right to section 7 to refrain from such activities as organizing a union and striking. Employees are also protected from union picketing that seeks to force employees to accept a union as their bargaining agent.

Protect the Public and Neutrals

A major concern of Taft-Hartley was to protect the public from strikes that endangered the national economy (see STRIKE). If the president determines that an actual or threatened strike which affects an entire industry or substantial part thereof will affect the national health or safety, then he may appoint a board of inquiry to investigate the dispute. He may ultimately seek a temporary injunction from a federal court and, if an injunction is granted, the parties must seek to resolve their dispute through MEDIATION. If that fails the president may seek legislation from Congress to end the strike. In only a few instances has the Congress imposed binding ARBITRATION to end a strike.

Finally, the Act added a prohibition against SECONDARY BOYCOTTS. The intent was to limit the area of economic conflict to the union and employer who had a dispute. Other neutral or secondary employers were not to be subjected to economic pressure by the union. The courts have not interpreted the Act to prohibit all secondary pressures.

Labor Management Reporting and Disclosures Act of 1959

Charles E. Krider

The Labor Management Reporting and Disclosures Act or Landrum-Griffin Act of 1959 was passed in response to congressional investigations in 1957–9 into union corruption and abuse of power. Leaders of some unions were discovered to be abusing their positions so that members did not have effective control over their unions. Congress's strategy was to make unions more democratic and to protect individual rights, so that members would be able to correct the problems that had been identified. This was a further intervention by government into labor–management relations through the regulation of the internal affairs of unions.

The objective of the Landrum-Griffin Act was to promote union democracy. The critics of the Act responded that unions are inherently adversarial organizations that must be able to effectively do battle with employers. The effort to make unions more democratic would inevitably make unions weaker. If that analysis is correct, society has chosen to pursue democratic unions even at the possible cost of weakening unions for COLLECTIVE BARGAINING. The Act was opposed by organized labor.

Bill of Rights

The Act provides that union members have the following rights.

1 Equal rights – to nominate candidates, to vote in elections, to attend and participate in membership meetings, all subject to reasonable rules.
2 Freedom of speech and assembly – to meet and assemble with other members, to express any views or opinions at meetings or upon candidates.
3 Dues – dues of a local can be increased only by a majority of secret ballot votes by members at a meeting or by referendum.
4 Right to sue – unions may not limit the right of members to sue the union or officers.
5 Safeguards against improper discipline – no union may discipline members except for

nonpayment of dues unless the member has been provided with due process.

Elections

Local unions must have a secret ballot election for officers every three years and national unions must have such elections every five years. All candidates have access to mailing lists and equal opportunities to distribute information.

Reports of Officers and Unions

Every union officer must file an annual financial report with the Secretary of Labor in order to allow identification of any improper financial arrangements, particularly with employers the union has dealings with. Employers must also report all financial dealings with unions and their officers. Unions must provide reports on their receipts, expenditures, assets, and liabilities to the Secretary of Labor and to members.

These provisions are intended to provide union members with enough information about their unions and officers to identify misuses of funds and then to protect the individual rights of members so that members can vote out any corrupt officials in democratic elections.

labor mobility

Hadyn Bennett

Theories of competitive labor market equilibrium argue that workers are allocated to firms so as to maximize the value of labor's product. Thus, within a competitive labor market individuals will search constantly for jobs in which they can be more productive and thus earn higher wages, while companies will also engage in search activities to attain more productive employees. Labor mobility is the term used to describe the movement of workers from one position within the labor market to another. Since the labor market is never perfect (e.g., individuals may not be aware of the extent or value of their skills and may have incomplete information about opportunities in other companies; meanwhile, companies may be unaware of the true PRODUCTIVITY of employees) nor static, perfect equilibrium will not be established and an element of labor mobility will always remain a feature of the market.

lean production

James P. Womack

Lean production is a term introduced in the late 1980s by the participants in the International Motor Vehicle Program at MIT. It describes a set of techniques for product development, supply-chain management, customer relations, and production operations pioneered by Japanese companies, led by Toyota, in the years immediately after World War II.

Lean production may be thought of as the general case for producing goods and services in a condition of *continuous flow*. This is a situation in which product designs, orders, and physical products proceed, respectively, from concept to production launch, from sale to delivery, and from raw materials to the hands of the customer, with no interruptions, backflows, or waste. By contrast, Henry Ford and his associates in the years just prior to World War I had pioneered continuous flow in the special condition of a completely standardized product made at very high volume and with no significant change in the product's specification for years. Ford termed this special case "mass production."

In the late 1940s, Taiichi Ohno (1912–91) at Toyota concluded that the special conditions permitting mass production could never be attained in Japan because of the small, fragmented Japanese market. He set out to achieve continuous flow (with its accompanying benefits of low cost and immediate response to customer desires) in the production of low-volume products, made in a wide variety of specifications and with short product lives. As mass markets across the world began to fragment into many niches in the 1970s and product lives began to fall, it became apparent that lean production was the general application of flow production, appropriate for the vast majority of manufacturing activities across the globe.

To achieve lean production, Ohno and his colleagues pioneered many innovations in physical production: (1) quick tool changes (perfected by Shigeo Shingo); (2) automatic machine stopping (*jidoka*) and mistake-proofing (*poka-yoke*) so that one worker could tend many machines without producing a bad part; (3) level scheduling (*heijunka*) to avoid production of large batches of the same item; (4) just-in-time or "pull" systems for scheduling production (*see* JUST-IN-TIME PRODUCTION SYSTEMS); and (5) miniaturizing of machinery, so that fabrication of entire products could be conducted almost instantly in "single-piece flow."

As Ohno worked on physical production, many Japanese firms including Toyota pioneered single-piece flow in product development by deploying dedicated, multidisciplinary teams under strong team leaders (called *shusa* at Toyota). These teams were instructed to work steadily on a design until it was ready for production, with no interruptions or backflows for rework.

Similar innovations in order taking and dealing with the customer made it possible to better understand customer desires and to deliver products built to customer specifications within only a few days. Shotaro Kamiya, who developed Toyota's "aggressive selling" system, was the pioneer.

The final element in lean production is a new way of relating to supplier firms by including them directly in product development and production operations. Toyota began to pioneer this approach in 1949 when it started spinning off its in-house suppliers as separate companies that, nonetheless, still "shared a destiny" with Toyota.

Bibliography

Cusumano, M. A. (1985). *The Japanese Automobile Industry*. Cambridge, MA: Harvard University Press.

Kamiya, S. (1976). *My Life with Toyota*. Tokyo: Toyota Motor Sales Company.

Monden, Y. (1983). *The Toyota Production System*. Atlanta, GA: Institute of Industrial Engineers.

Ohno, T. (1988). *Toyota Production System: Beyond Large-Scale Production*. Portland, OR: Productivity Press.

Shingo, S. (1988). *A Study of the Toyota Production System*. Portland, OR: Productivity Press.

Womack, J. P., Jones, D. T., and Roos, D. (1990). *The Machine that Changed the World*. New York: Rawson/Macmillan.

learning organization

Vinod K. Jain

Learning, most fundamentally, is the process of acquiring knowledge or skill. The underlying process is "thinking," which includes observing facts and integrating them into valid conclusions. Acquisition of skill involves repeated application of knowledge, so that it becomes partly automatized or routinized. The desired organizational outcome of learning is often continuous improvement or better performance (Locke and Jain, 1995).

All learning is individual learning, and organizations learn through their individual members (Argyris and Schon, 1978; Senge, 1990; Simon, 1991). Learning at the organization level occurs through shared insights, knowledge, and mental models, and builds on the past knowledge and experiences of organization members (Stata, 1989). A "learning organization" is an organization "where people continually expand their capacity to create the results they truly desire, where new and expansive patterns of thinking are nurtured, where collective aspiration is set free, and where people are continually learning how to learn together" (Senge, 1991: 1). According to Garvin (1993: 80), "a learning organization is an organization skilled at creating, acquiring, and transferring knowledge, and at modifying its behavior to reflect new knowledge and insights." Nonaka (1991) goes so far as to characterize a learning (or a knowledge-creating) organization as one where inventing new knowledge is not a specialized activity, "it's a way of behaving, indeed, a way of being, in which everyone is a knowledge worker."

The primary tasks of a learning organization are, thus, to create and apply new knowledge. According to Senge (1990), a learning organization represents a significant evolution of organizational culture – a culture that encourages and rewards the application of new learning. In addition to a continuous improvement culture, a learning organization must also have structures that foster cross-disciplinary teamwork, collaboration, and learning (Kiernan, 1993).

There are several views on how one may go about building a learning organization, ranging from somewhat conceptual approaches (e.g., Senge, 1990) to the more practical approaches (e.g., Garvin, 1993). Senge (1990) suggests the use of five "component technologies" for building learning organizations: systems thinking, personal mastery, mental models, shared vision, and team learning. Nonaka (1991) suggests using metaphors and organizational redundancy to focus thinking, encourage dialogue, and make tacit ideas explicit. And, according to Garvin (1993), a learning organization must be skilled at systematic problem solving, experimentation, learning from its own experiences and from past history, learning from the experiences and best practices of others, and transferring knowledge quickly and efficiently throughout the organization.

Bibliography

Argyris, C. and Schon, D. (1978). *Organizational Learning*. Reading, MA: Addison-Wesley.
Garvin, D. A. (1993). Building a learning organization. *Harvard Business Review*, 71, 78–91.
Kiernan, M. J. (1993). The new strategic architecture: Learning to compete in the twenty-first century. *Academy of Management Executive*, 8, 7–21.
Locke E. A. and Jain, V. K. (1995). Organizational learning and continuous improvement. *International Journal of Organizational Analysis*, 3, 45–68.
Nonaka, I. (1991). The knowledge-creating company. *Harvard Business Review*, 69, 96–104.
Senge, P. M. (1990). *The Fifth Discipline: The Art and the Practice of the Learning Organization*. New York: Doubleday.
Simon, H. A. (1991). Bounded rationality and organizational learning. *Organization Science*, 2, 125–34.
Stata, R. (1989). Organizational learning: The key to management innovation. *Sloan Management Review*, 30, 63–74.

learning reinforcement – feedback

J. Kevin Ford and Deidre Wasson

Feedback is a condition of learning where information is supplied or obtained by the learner regarding progress toward skill mastery and/or the errors being committed in the skill performance (Goldstein and Ford, 2002). Without feedback, learning cannot occur. Feedback can increase motivation by increasing a trainee's perception of task competence (Hays and Blaiwes, 1986). To be effective, feedback should be regular and frequent, specific and informative, and measure both successes and failures immediately after or during performance. To facilitate skill retention and transfer, feedback should be gradually withdrawn as the learning process progresses (Lintern, 1991).

See also *learning reinforcement – practice*

Bibliography

Goldstein, I. L. and Ford, J. K. (2002). *Training in Organizations: Needs Assessment, Development, and Evaluation*, 4th edn. Wadsworth, CA: Brooks/Cole.
Hays, R. T. and Blaiwes, A. S. (1986). Knowledge of results in training device design: Individual and team applications. *Journal of Educational Technology Systems*, 15, 171–89.
Lintern, G. (1991). An informational perspective on skill transfer in human–machine systems. Special issue: Training theory, methods, and technology. *Human Factors*, 33, 251–66.

learning reinforcement – practice

J. Kevin Ford and Deidre Wasson

Practice is a condition of learning that focuses on the amount of repetition allowed in the performance of skills (Goldstein and Ford, 2002). Successful practice involves varying examples and increasing difficulty as practice time progresses (Gagne and Dick, 1983). A task may be performed as a single unit or broken down into components that are practiced separately (Goldstein and Ford, 2002). With increasing complexity and lower interrelatedness among task components, a component learning strategy to practice is often more effective. Practice can only be an effective condition of learning if the content and the sequencing of training material are appropriate (Campbell and Campbell, 1988).

See also *learning reinforcement – feedback*

Bibliography

Campbell, J. P. and Campbell, R. J. (1988). Training design for performance improvement. In J. P. Campbell and R. J. Campbell (eds.), *Productivity in Organizations: New Perspectives from Industrial and Organizational Psychology*. San Francisco: Jossey-Bass.
Gagne, R. M. and Dick, W. (1983). Instructional psychology. *Annual Review of Psychology*, 34, 261–95.

Goldstein, I. L. and Ford, J. K. (2002). *Training in Organizations: Needs Assessment, Development, and Evaluation*, 4th edn. Wadsworth, CA: Brooks/Cole.

lecture method

J. Kevin Ford and Deidre Wasson

Lectures are characterized by one-way communication of basic information from trainers to trainee groups of any size in short periods of time (Camp, Blanchard, and Huszczo, 1986). By far the most popular training method, lectures can be effective when they introduce a new topic, provide an introduction to learning a task, are given by highly skilled lecturers, and cover simple topics. The lecture format, though, lends itself to frequent criticism, giving little opportunity to deliver or receive feedback, low transfer of training back to the workplace, and individual ability differences that cannot be accounted for in instruction (Wexley and Latham, 1991).

See also *training*

Bibliography

Camp, R. R., Blanchard, P. N., and Huszczo, G. E. (1986). *Toward a More Organizationally Effective Training Strategy and Practice*. Englewood Cliffs, NJ: Prentice-Hall.

Wexley, K. N. and Latham, G. P. (1991). *Developing and Training Human Resources in Organizations*, 2nd edn. New York: HarperCollins.

leniency effects

Angelo S. DeNisi

Leniency effects have been traditionally considered a type of rating error (*see* RATING ERRORS), where ratings are skewed so that the mean rating given is substantially higher than the midpoint of the rating scale. There would appear, however, to be little basis for assuming that the mean of a set of ratings *should* be at the midpoint of the scale, especially since various HR practices, such as PERSONNEL SELECTION and TRAINING, are designed to insure that the employees are "better than average." Nonetheless, there has been disagreement over the proper operational definition of leniency (e.g., elevated mean for ratings, skewed ratings distribution; see Saal, Downey, and Lahey, 1980, for a review), as well as the cause of leniency (e.g., desire to be liked, avoiding the need to provide negative feedback).

Although leniency effects have been assumed to be a type of rating error (and so could potentially serve as a proxy measure for RATING ACCURACY), some views of leniency have moved beyond simple assumptions that higher ratings can be equated with leniency effects (*see* DISTRIBUTIONAL EFFECTS IN PERFORMANCE APPRAISAL). Instead, more recent views assert that raters tend to elevate ratings when they lack clear standards upon which to base their evaluations (e.g., Hauenstein, 1992). Furthermore, although leniency effects may not represent rating errors, they may indicate other problems for an organization, since elevated ratings are believed to undermine INCENTIVE PAY systems, as well as pose legal problems for organizations when they try to terminate employees for poor performance (e.g.,Ticket al., 1996).

Bibliography

Hauenstein, N. (1992). An information processing approach to leniency in performance judgments. *Journal of Applied Psychology*, 77, 485–93.

Kane, J. S., Bernardin, H. J., Villanova, P., and Peyrefitte, J. (1996). The stability of rater leniency: Three studies. *Academy of Management Journal*, 38.

Saal, F. E., Downey, R. G., and Lahey, M. A. (1980). Rating the ratings: Assessing the quality of ratings data. *Psychological Bulletin*, 88, 413–28.

lockout

David A. Gray

A lockout is the employer's counterpart of the union's STRIKE, where the employer closes the workplace during a labor dispute. However, the employer may attempt to continue operations with managers and other nonunion employees. The lockout, while common in the 1920s and 1930s, is rarely used today. Its purpose is to apply economic pressure on union employees through lost wages in order to convince the union to accept the employer's COLLECTIVE BARGAINING terms (wages, hours, and working conditions). Nearly all labor agreements contain a "no lockout" as well as a "no strike" clause, which specifies that the employer will not lock out employees during the term of the contract.

Lorance v. AT&T, 490 US 900 (1989)

Leonard Bierman

A new 1979 COLLECTIVE BARGAINING agreement eliminated the transferability of plant-wide seniority to employees moving into tester positions. In 1982, female employees who were promoted to tester positions in 1978 and 1980 received demotions that they would not have sustained under the old seniority system. They filed charges with the EQUAL EMPLOYMENT OPPORTUNITY COMMISSION alleging that adoption of the new seniority system resulted in DISCRIMINATION. The court held that the charges had not been filed within the permitted time period after the alleged unlawful employment practice occurred and were therefore invalid. The CIVIL RIGHTS ACT OF 1991 overturned this holding, now permitting suits when individuals are injured by the application of seniority systems and lengthening the time period permitted after an alleged discriminatory practice for the filing of a Title VII claim.

M

McDonnell Douglas v. Green, 411 US 722 (1973)

Leonard Bierman

DISPARATE TREATMENT discrimination occurs when an employer intentionally treats an employee differently based on a prohibited factor under Title VII (race, color, religion, sex, or national origin). In *McDonnell Douglas*, the Supreme Court held that once an employee establishes a prima facie case, there is a presumption that the employer has unlawfully discriminated against the employee. The defendant then has the BURDEN OF PROOF to rebut the plaintiff's case by showing that the adverse employment action was taken for legitimate, nondiscriminatory reasons. The plaintiff can then dispute the defendant's rebuttal.

McNamara-O'Hara Service Contract Act of 1965

Charles H. Fay

Under this prevailing wage law, any employer with a federal government service contract in excess of $2,500 must pay wages and BENEFITS found to be prevailing locally (as determined by the Department of Labor), or the level found in a previous existing contract. The employer must in any case pay at least minimum wages under the FAIR LABOR STANDARDS ACT OF 1938. The impact of the Service Contract Act (as is the case with the DAVIS-BACON ACT OF 1931 and the WALSH-HEALY ACT OF 1936) is that employers pay local union rates and provide benefits similar to those negotiated by local unions.

Bibliography

Dixon, R. B. (2002). *Federal Wage and Hour Laws*, 2nd edn. Washington, DC: SHRM Foundation.

Shilling, D. (2001). *Human Resources and the Law: The Complete Guide with Supplement*. Englewood Cliffs, NJ: Prentice-Hall.

Steingold, F. S. (2003). *The Employer's Legal Handbook*, 5th edn. Berkeley, CA: Nolo Press.

make-whole/compensatory remedies

Barbara A. Lee

Make-whole remedies are intended to restore the plaintiff-employee to the position and the benefits that the employee would have been entitled to absent the discriminatory treatment. They include reinstatement or hiring, backpay, retroactive pension payments, vacation time or pay, retroactive seniority, promotions that would have been received, reimbursement for medical costs incurred that would have been covered by the employer's benefit plan, and recovery of other costs incurred by the plaintiff-employee as a result of the discrimination.

Bibliography

Kirp, D. L., Yudof, M. G., and Franks, M. S. (1986). *Gender Justice*. Chicago: University of Chicago Press.

Schlei, B. L. and Grossman, P. (1983). *Employment Discrimination Law*, 2nd edn. Washington, DC: Bureau of National Affairs.

Malcolm Baldrige National Quality Award

Richard S. Blackburn

To improve the quality of American goods and services, the US Congress established the Malcolm Baldrige National Quality Award (MBNQA) in 1987. Named for a former Secretary of Commerce, the award originally recognized US manufacturing and service organizations for "business excellence and quality achievement." Three other award categories have been added in the past few years so that small businesses, healthcare, and educational organizations can now seek recognition for their approaches to quality management.

The 2003 award criteria framework for large-scale manufacturing and service organizations combines seven categories (each contributing points to a total of 1,000): (1) leadership (120 points); (2) strategic planning (85 points); (3) customer and market focus (85 points); (4) measurement, analysis, and knowledge management (90 points); (5) human resource focus (85 points); (6) process management (85 points); and (7) business results (450 points). This last category requires applicants to provide information on their results with regards to customer focus, products and services, financial and markets, human resources, organizational effectiveness, and governance and social responsibility. Similar templates with different categories and weightings also exist for educational and healthcare applicants.

The MBNQA competition involves a multi-stage process including the determination of eligibility, review and evaluation of applications, site visits to finalists' facilities, and the judge's review and final recommendations. Although the competition is sponsored by the US government, there are fees associated with various steps in the process. Applicants must pay a nonrefundable $150 fee to determine their eligibility. If eligible, applicants pay fees on a sliding scale depending on their classification. Small not-for-profit educational organizations pay $500, while large manufacturing and service organizations pay $5,000. Additional fees may be required, if organizations move further into the process. Annual MBNQA winners are expected to share information on their quality strategies with other US organizations at "quest for excellence conferences."

Some organizations pursue the MBNQA to get an assessment of their standing relative to this benchmark of quality performance. Other organizations do not actually enter the competition, but use the published criteria as the basis for an internal audit of their current quality status. Most of the entrants view the competition not as an attempt to actually "win" something, but as an effort to change their corporate culture. They view the MBNQA not as an end in itself, but as a first step on a journey to ever-improving quality (Blackburn and Rosen, 1993).

The MBNQA is one of a number of quality awards offered around the world, including the Deming prize awarded by the Union of Japanese Scientists and Engineers and the European Quality Award presented by the European Foundation for Quality Management.

Copies of the MBNQA award criteria, application forms, and a variety of other related materials are available from Baldrige National Quality Program, National Institute of Standards and Technology, 100 Bureau Drive, Stop 1020, Gaithersburg, Maryland 20899-1020. Telephone 301-975-2036. Fax 301-948-3716. Email: nqp@nist.gov. Website: www.quality.nist.gov/.

Bibliography

Blackburn, R. and Rosen, B. (1993). Total quality and human resources management: Lessons learned from Baldrige Award-winning companies. *Academy of Management Executive*, 7, 49–66.

Evans, James R. and Jack, Eric P. (2003). Validating key results linkages in the Baldrige Performance Excellence Model. *Quality Management Journal*, 10, 7–25.

Wilson, Darryl D. and Collier, David A. (2000). An empirical investigation of the Malcolm Baldrige National Quality Award causal model. *Decision Sciences*, 31, 361–90.

managed care

Charles H. Fay

Managed care refers to a variety of approaches employers take to control the increase in the cost of healthcare benefits. Initially the emphasis was on such specific management techniques as peer review and requiring second opinions prior to surgery. The emphasis now is on a general approach to designing, financing, and delivering healthcare benefits to employees. The CIVIL RIGHTS ACT OF 1991, HEALTH MAINTENANCE ORGANIZATIONS (HMOs), preferred provider organizations (PPOs), and point of service plans are all managed-care approaches featuring restricted access to healthcare providers and utilization of management programs.

Bibliography

Pierce, P. D. (2001b). Understanding managed care health plans: Understanding costs and evaluating plans. In J. S. Rosenbloom (ed.), *The Handbook of Employee Benefits: Design, Funding and Administration*, 5th edn. New York: McGraw-Hill, pp. 171–207.

management by objectives

Donald J. Campbell

At the individual level, management by objectives (MBO) is an interactive process whereby a manager and an employee (1) jointly identify and agree upon the subordinate's work goals, (2) define each of their responsibilities for achieving the agreed-upon goals, and (3) then use goal accomplishment as a guide for examining and evaluating the subordinate's performance (Odiorne, 1965). At the organizational level, MBO is a process for managing and guiding the firm in a consistent and logical way. At this level, MBO requires senior management to develop clear, long-range organizational objectives. Mid-level management then uses these objectives to form appropriate shorter-range objectives. In turn, these become the basis for the traditional manager–employee MBO discussion and individual goal setting. Conducted properly, this cascading process insures that objectives at different levels of the organization and within different groups mesh together, and result in the attainment of the firm's overall goals. Regardless of individual or organizational level, the defining characteristics of MBO are the creation of specific, measurable goals in important areas, and the use of these goals to monitor and guide progress.

THEORETICAL UNDERPINNINGS OF MBO

Although Drucker (1954) and a number of other practitioners championed MBO in the 1950s, the research of Locke (1968) and his colleagues on goal setting provides the theoretical foundation for understanding the workings of MBO. Goal-setting research explains why objectives should be specific and challenging, why participation in setting objectives may be important, and why periodic feedback on goal attainment is essential.

EFFECTIVENESS OF MBO

In spite of being a widely implemented motivation and PERFORMANCE APPRAISAL technique, the evidence supporting MBO effectiveness is mixed. While MBO has great potential for improving performance, practical difficulties abound, and firms have often found successful implementation difficult. Top management must first create an organizational culture supportive of an objectives-oriented approach. Without this, MBO effects are likely to be short term, with benefits dissipating within a year or two.

Common criticisms of MBO are that such systems generate too much paperwork, and that they over-emphasize quantitative goals at the expense of more qualitative objectives. However, these criticisms do not point up any theoretical weakness in the technique, and may simply underscore the need for thoughtful, careful implementation.

MBO may also create a conflict of interest for the employee. Since financial and other rewards are typically tied to successful goal achievement, it is in the subordinate's interest to set easily achievable goals. Yet goal-setting research consistently demonstrates that performance is highest with challenging goals. Thus, the goal-setting aspect of MBO may take the form of a struggle, with the employee attempting to set easy targets (to insure achievement), while the supervisor strives to set more challenging goals (to increase performance and insure unit success). This possibility highlights the critical roles mutual trust and supportiveness play in any effective MBO implementation. Without these qualities, the firm will not reap the full benefits of MBO's substantial potential.

Bibliography

Carroll, S. and Tosi, H. (1973). *Management by Objectives: Applications and Research*. New York: Macmillan.

Drucker, P. (1954). *The Practice of Management*. New York: Harper.

Locke, E. (1968). Toward a theory of task motivation and incentives. *Organizational Behavior and Human Performance*, 3, 157–89.

Odiorne, G. (1965). *Management by Objectives: A System of Managerial Leadership*. New York: Pitman.

Raia, A. (1974). *Managing by Objectives*. Glenview, IL: Scott Foresman.

management consultancy

Sandra Fielden

The Institute of Management Consultants (2002) defines management consultancy as "the provision to management of objective advice and assistance relating to the strategy, structure, management and operations of an organization in pursuit of its long-term purpose and objectives." It involves a wide range of activities based on different philosophical and theoretical approaches, with varying consulting types, consulting roles, and client goals. At one end of the continuum consultancy is very prescriptive, where the client presents a problem and the consultant provides expert advice and guidance to assist the client in overcoming that problem, e.g., employment law. At the other end of the continuum, the consultant facilitates the client in determining and defining the problem and assists the client in exploring ways in which to achieve a solution. Effective management consultants, through client discussions, need to recognize which approach would be most appropriate in their business and problem-solving roles. They need to have a clear understanding of the business needs of their clients and be able to meet the changing demands of the sector in which they work, demonstrating a high level of competency and engagement.

Bibliography

Institute of Management Consultants (2002). *Competence Framework*. IMC: London.

management development

Richard W. Beatty

In the private sector, especially in the US, concepts of management development continue to change rapidly. At every level of the firm, ideas about what managers do or should do, from supervisors to executives, are evolving. Most of these changes are driven by the significant competitive challenges many firms are facing – often related to reaching maturity in a product or firm life cycle and not changing either reactively or proactively to the marketplace.

Firms are vanishing at a much faster rate than ever before, so much so that the average firm life span is now less than the life span of the people who comprise their workforce. This has led to a rethinking of the relationship between firms and their workforce and the nature of career development. Workers are now often developing not within the firm but across firms. From the perspective of today's worker, in climbing the corporate ladder it may be more useful to move out in order to move up – i.e., to leave the firm to gain additional skills and return. Large firms can create such developmental experiences through rotational assignments (*see* JOB ROTATION), but workers in smaller firms (the fount of greatest growth in the economy and employment) may be on a self-guided journey in managing their development (i.e., across firms before joining their "dream" firm).

A major driver in this trend is a reconception of the traditional notion of a firm's strategic capabilities (e.g., logistics, distribution, marketing, research and development, mergers and acquisitions). Many firms are now adding leadership, or perhaps more accurately, strategic leadership, to their strategic capabilities. The rapidly changing, intensely competitive environment has generated the need to develop strategic leaders. Such strategic leaders typically possess two competencies heretofore omitted in traditional competency models of leadership: strategic thinking and change leadership. Acquiring robust competencies in these areas is becoming critical for firms.

It has become evident that the competency models proffered by many consulting firms and normed on existing firm leaders have seriously underestimated the leadership requirements for a firm to win its future. The past is not prologue. Today's leaders are not necessarily what is needed to enable a firm to win tomorrow. Making the competencies of strategic change leadership and strategic thinking critical elements of leadership development efforts is essential. Efforts to develop these elements require not only intellectual comprehension, but practice in demonstrating them and feedback on the extent to which leaders have acquired these competencies.

For executive team members feedback on the ability to think strategically and build executive teams to create and implement strategic change initiatives can come from several sources. Most important are individual feedback from bosses and from the 180-degree (i.e., subordinate feedback) component of a 360-degree survey on leadership efficacy. "If you want to find out who the leaders are, ask the led" – a truism often paid lip service, but which is nevertheless true. A 360-degree survey that includes friends and bowling buddies is not nearly as useful in identifying leadership talent as feedback that comes directly from the led (*see* 360-DEGREE APPRAISALS).

Another leadership competency of growing importance is knowing and understanding a workforce. Firms don't change unless people change. Leaders must continue to change themselves and change their workforces to ultimately improve their firm's success. This is the only way firms will succeed – by finding ways to continually change and evolve such that they are impacting their environments and creating turbulence for present or potential competitors. This means that firms must change *before they have to*. This is a particularly difficult challenge for leaders. Because they have achieved a leadership role in the first place by demonstrating specific skills and behaviors to meet today's requirements, momentum tends to keep them on the same track. Thus, leaders must buck this momentum and fight the fantasy that they and their firms can remain unchanged (and still successful) in a rapidly changing environment. In the long run, being able to create change before it is absolutely necessary is a competitive advantage.

In the inventory of leadership competencies, it is increasingly important for leaders to be able to determine which work is valuable and which is not. In the assessment of all direct reports, each executive must ask: Who is the work's customer? What is the strategic value of each piece of work? How well is that work being done? How well does it need to be done? Clearly, work that is strategic and done well is to be recognized and rewarded. Work that is strategic but not done well must be fixed. And it goes without saying that work that is not strategic, regardless of how well it is done, needs to be removed. Such an analysis is a significant challenge for mature firms and is often difficult to address, but it is an essential competency for tomorrow's leaders.

Finally, the provision of honest and candid feedback is a *major* challenge for leaders. Many lawsuits have occurred because leaders have not created an atmosphere where candor and honesty can flourish. In providing feedback on performance, many managers prefer to tell employees what they wish to hear, rather than what needs to be done to enhance their performance. By the same token, subordinates are reluctant to be messengers of bad news. Candor and honesty is a two-way street. But many leaders (and employees) would rather be liked than right. Lacking candor and honesty, several major American firms have gone up in flames in a matter of months.

Whatever the rhetoric about management development and competencies, the bottom line is that executives must know to execute strategy by asking six simple questions about their firm:

1 How grow?
2 What strategic capabilities and culture?
3 What obstacles? How overcome?
4 How accelerate?
5 What business metrics?
6 How reward?

The questions may be simple – the answers are not. The challenge for management development is to find ways to grow executives who have the competencies to provide these answers.

See also *early identification of management talent*

Bibliography

Bossidy, L., Charan, R., and Burck, C. (2002). *Execution: The Discipline of Getting Things Done*. New York: Crown.
Burns, J. M. (2003). *Transforming Leadership: The Pursuit of Happiness*. New York: Atlantic Monthly Press.
Finkelstein, S. (2003). *Why Smart Executives Fail: And What You Can Learn from Their Mistakes*. New York: Portfolio.
Gerstner, L. V. (2002). *Who Says Elephants Can't Dance? Inside IBM's Historic Turnaround*. New York: HarperBusiness.

Goldsmith, M. (2003). *Adding Value – But at What Cost?* Fast Company, July 21, pp. 1–2.
Joyce, W. F. and Nohria, N. (2003). *What Really Works: The 4+2 Formula for Sustained Business Success.* New York: HarperBusiness.
Kotter, J. P. (1996). *Leading Change.* Boston: Harvard Business School Press.
Sonnenfeld, J. A. (1988). *Hero's Farewell: What Happens When CEOs Retire.* New York: Oxford University Press.
Tichy, N. M. and Cardwell, N. (2002). *The Cycle of Leadership: How Great Leaders Teach Their Companies to Win.* New York: HarperBusiness.
Welch, J. and Byrne, J. A. (2001). *Jack: Straight from the Gut.* New York: Warner.

management games

Gary P. Latham and Lucie Morin

A management game is a simulated business training environment ranging from the simple to the complex, computerized to noncomputerized, interactive to noninteractive, and single participant to multiple participants. Examples of such games include the leaderless group discussion, in-basket techniques, complex decision-making, and large-scale behavioral SIMULATIONS (Latham and Seijts, 1995).

Management games, which have been developed for low, middle, and upper management, facilitate skill development by allowing for active practice where outcomes of one's actions occur much faster than in the actual business world. They are a safe place where participants can explore alternative policies, learn about extreme situations, develop a shared understanding of business dynamics, and evaluate future consequences of actions and experience without causing risk for themselves or their firm (Senge, 1990). Moreover, since trainees are drawn into the learning process by being required to actively participate, management games can also be used to increase self-beliefs about one's managerial capabilities (*see* SELF-EFFICACY).

A drawback of management games is that they can foster a misleading impression of precision and certainty by presenting an organization in an overly structured and simplified way (Latham and Seijts, 1995). Although there are often no right answers to organizational problems, and no ideal way to manage in the real world, management games can inadvertently suggest otherwise (Linstead, 1990).

To maximize learning, management games should be combined with structured training delivery methods, such as lectures, discussions, and reading assignments that provide an important conceptual framework generally lacking from such participative learning methods (Latham and Seijts, 1995).

Bibliography

Keys, B. J. and Wolfe, J. (1990). The role of management games and simulations in education and research. *Journal of Management*, 16, 307–36.
Latham, G. P. and Seijts, G. H. (1995). Management development. In P. Drenth, C. de Wolff, and H. Thierry (eds.), *European Handbook of Work and Organizational Psychology.* Houten: Bohn Stafleu Van Loghum.
Linstead, S. (1990). Beyond competence: Management development using computer-based systems in experiential learning. *Management Education and Development*, 21, 61–74.
Senge, P. M. (1990). *The Fifth Discipline: The Art and Practice of the Learning Organization.* New York: Doubleday.

management localization

Manuel G. Serapio, Jr.

Management localization is a term which takes on different meanings depending on the specific international human resource management (HRM) context under consideration. In extreme circumstances, the term may indicate complete nationalization of the enterprise or that ownership is transferred to foreign-country nationals. In less extreme contexts, the term means that the enterprise's managerial practices and approaches have been adapted to those appropriate for the foreign country or local conditions (Negandhi and Welge, 1984).

The term is also used to describe greater flows over time of host-country nationals into subsidiaries' key managerial positions and the delegation to them of greater decision-making authority (Serapio, 1995). Scholars have argued that, in the absence of host-country managers having authority to make decisions, real management localization does not occur just because host-country nationals have been placed in key managerial positions.

Research on international HRM literature has typically defined management localization more narrowly to describe the flow of host-country nationals into management positions, the promotion of host-country nationals, and the corresponding replacement of home-country nationals over time (Negandhi and Welge, 1984; Serapio, 1995). Other variations in the use of the term occur in its operationalization for research purposes. One such study, involving the subsidiaries of Japanese companies in the US, has operationalized the term as the percentage of total managers accounted for by host-country (US) nationals, and has traced these percentages over a five-year time series, beginning with the start of operations in the host country (Serapio, 1995). Another example of the term's operationalization is provided by a study of subsidiaries of companies having their corporate headquarters in the US, Germany, and Japan. In this study, comparisons are made of the percentages of managers accounted for by host-country nationals at top-, middle-, and lower-level positions (Negandhi and Welge, 1984).

Bibliography

Negandhi, A. and Welge, M. (1984). *Beyond Theory Z: Globalization Strategies of American, German, and Japanese Multinational Companies.* Greenwich, CT: JAI Press.

Serapio, M. (1995). Management localization in Japanese subsidiaries in the United States. In O. Shenkar (ed.), *Global Perspectives on Human Resource Management.* Englewood Cliffs, NJ: Prentice-Hall.

management prerogatives

John C. Shearer

Management prerogatives are those rights of a management to direct its workforce which have not been restricted by COLLECTIVE BARGAINING. Many labor agreements specify a "management rights" or "residual rights" clause that all those rights which have not been specifically restricted or modified by a specific provision of the labor agreement remain exclusively with management.

managerial performance assessment

James T. Austin

Problems associated with conceptualizing and measuring JOB PERFORMANCE in general extend to the area of managerial performance. In addition, there are some unique characteristics of managerial jobs that distinguish them from other jobs. These include less structured activities, greater autonomy, and considerable resource dependence. These differences often require the adoption of alternative methods to measuring performance.

DESCRIBING THE JOB OF MANAGER

Classic theories of management (e.g., Fayol, 1949) emphasized the functions that management activities were to support. Fayol's five classic management functions included planning, organizing, commanding, coordinating, and controlling. Campbell et al. (1970) reviewed managerial performance using a person–process–product framework. Mintzberg's (1971) observations of chief executive officers concentrated instead on the activities of managers engaged in work. He found that managers' activities consisted of many brief episodes, involved interaction with many different people both inside and outside the organization, and resulted in gathering more information than they transmitted to others. More recently, Carroll and Gillen (1987) integrated diverse perspectives on managerial work using a goal-driven "work agenda" model. Agendas determine activities (e.g., interpersonal interactions), and they are supported by managers' skills, competencies, and knowledge base, to produce performance. The manager's job requires constant monitoring of progress toward goals, frequent revision of agenda items, and commitment to activities that sustain the agenda or may contribute information about previously unrecognized threats and opportunities.

A significant obstacle to describing managerial performance is the relatively unstructured and highly autonomous nature of management jobs. Unlike many jobs that lend themselves to direct observation, interview, or standardized task inventories for the purpose of JOB ANALYSIS, the description of managerial jobs often requires less traditional methods, including diary-keeping and the use of inventories designed specifically for these jobs (e.g., the professional and managerial position questionnaire).

PERFORMANCE APPRAISAL FOR MANAGEMENT JOBS

Two most frequently used approaches to measuring management performance are MANAGEMENT BY OBJECTIVES (MBO) and work planning and review (WP&R). Approximately 40 percent of the Fortune 500 companies use some form of MBO. MBO is a management philosophy that combines elements of Theory Y management with the strict accountability provisions championed by Drucker (1954). MBO attempts to increase compatibility between individual and system goals through increased subordinate participation in the goal-setting process, an emphasis on results and accomplishments, and periodic review to assess progress or modify objectives. In practice, MBO approaches vary widely from one organization to another in terms of level of subordinate participation, frequency of review, and use of objective criteria.

Many MBO programs closely resemble the WP&R method in that they include a goal-setting component in addition to separate subjective judgments of performance relative to those goals. WP&R methods are frequently used in instances where objective measures of unit performance are unavailable or suspected to be contaminated and/or deficient.

Research generally supports the effectiveness of MBO programs. Rodgers and Hunter (1991) found that 68 of 70 studies that evaluated MBO programs reported PRODUCTIVITY gains. In addition, it appears that more effective MBO programs are characterized by high levels of top management commitment and participation. In these instances, the average productivity gain was about 57 percent, whereas when commitment was low the programs exhibited marginal productivity gains (6 percent).

Bibliography

Campbell, J. P., Dunnette, M. D., Lawler, E. E., and Weick, K. E., Jr. (1970). *Managerial Behavior, Performance, and Effectiveness.* New York: McGraw-Hill.
Carroll, S. J. and Gillen, D. A. (1987). Are the classical management functions useful in describing managerial work? *Academy of Management Review*, 12, 38–51.
Drucker, P. F. (1954). *The Practice of Management.* New York: Harper.
Fayol, H. (1949). *General and Industrial Management.* London: Pitman.
Mintzberg, H. (1971). *The Nature of Managerial Work.* New York: Harper and Row.
Rodgers, R. and Hunter, J. E. (1991). Impact of management by objectives on organizational productivity. *Journal of Applied Psychology*, 76, 322–36.

managerial value differences

David A. Ralston

Managerial value differences in the cross-cultural context require that we take into consideration the interaction of the personal values of managers – as influenced by their cultural heritage – and the work environment demands – as influenced by the political and economic ideology of the country. Specifically, cultural influences are those that differentiate one society or one societal cluster from another (e.g., eastern, western). History, religion, and proximity tend to be important factors in differentiating the cultural values of societies (Ronen and Shenkar, 1985). Conversely, ideological influences (e.g., capitalism, socialism) tend to emanate from the economic and political systems within which an individual must function (Ricks, Toyne, and Martinez, 1990). Therefore, cultural influences tend to reflect regional differences, while ideological influences tend to be more cosmopolitan in that these influences tend to be shared across societies with common business ideologies.

Thus, both culture and ideology shape managerial values. The more unique one culture is from another and/or the more unique one ideology is from another, the more likely it is that the managers from these various culture–ideology mixes will differ in their values and the resultant work behaviors that they exhibit to perform their managerial duties (Ralston et al., 1993). The importance of recognizing the causes of these differences and understanding how to deal with them lies in the need to function efficiently and effectively in the global environment, even when this environment is markedly different from the typical domestic situation with which the manager is familiar.

Managerial value differences manifest themselves in organizations in a wide variety of ways and behaviors. These differences frequently can be observed in managers' degree of delegation, respect for authority, individual versus group orientation, means of communications, ethical standards, and style of motivation and leadership.

Bibliography

Ralston, D. A., Gustafson, D. J., Cheung, F., and Terpstra, R. H. (1993). Differences in managerial values: A study of US, Hong Kong, and PRC managers. *Journal of International Business Studies*, **24**, 249–75.

Ricks, D. A., Toyne, B., and Martinez, Z. (1990). Recent developments in international management research. *Journal of Management*, **16**, 219–53.

Ronen, S. and Shenkar, O. (1985). Clustering countries on attitudinal dimensions: A review and synthesis. *Academy of Management Review*, **10**, 435–54.

managing the human resource planning process

Donald W. Jarrell

Human resource planning may be done in response to the organization business planning process or as an integral part of the business planning process. Whichever the approach, certain initial steps need to be followed (Jarrell, 1993: 146–53):

1 Set objectives for the planning process. Although specific objectives will vary depending on the needs of particular organizations, the main objective must be to bring about focused management of the human resources of the organization.

2 Identify key participants. Planning should begin with participants who played key roles in the management of human resources in the past. Participants may change as the planning process evolves, but at a minimum should include the chief executive officer, the chief human resource officer, and selected line managers. Human resource specialists, as well as other members of the organization, may be added as the need for specific planning knowledge and skills becomes apparent.

3 Establish that part of the organization philosophy or mission statement that concerns human resources.

4 Collect information about that part of the organizational environment of importance to human resource management (*see* ENVIRONMENTAL SCANNING). Sectors of the environment of special importance to human resource planning are cultural, demographic, economic, political, social, and technological.

5 Compare the human resource competencies of the organization with those of competitors. This comparison will help to determine strategies appropriate for the organization.

6 Formulate a human resource strategy. A strategy may be as simple as the decision to excel in one of the classic human resource management functions, such as STAFFING or development. Or a strategy may be a bundle of interrelated human resource activities that cut across traditional functional lines (MacDuffie, 1995).

7 Implement the chosen strategies. Implementation requires a long-term collaborative effort by human resource professionals and line managers. Steps must be taken to insure that control systems applied to this strategy implementation are appropriate for the longer term (Hain, 1983).

8 Evaluate the planning process in terms of its expected outcomes, both direct and indirect (Hax, 1985).

9 Manage issues that arise under the strategic plan. Issues should be used as feedback for

improving the planning process and keeping it current. Issues management normally is more efficient if done for the HUMAN RESOURCE FUNCTION as part of an organization-wide effort.

The planning process outlined above can be used where a formal approach is needed as a guide and where little or no preexisting information and planning methodology have been accumulated. As the planning process evolves, planners should tailor the planning process to their unique needs.

See also *human resource planning; strategic human resource planning; strategic human resource planning processes*

Bibliography

Hain, T. (1983). Commentary on Dyer. *Human Resource Management*, 22, 272–3.
Hax, C. (1985). A new competitive weapon: The human resource strategy. *Training and Development Journal*, 89, 76–82.
Jarrell, D. W. (1993). *Human Resource Planning: A Business Planning Approach*. Englewood Cliffs, NJ: Prentice-Hall.
MacDuffie, J. P. (1995). Human resource bundles and manufacturing performance: Organizational logic and flexible production systems in the world auto industry. *Industrial and Labor Relations Review*, 48, 197–221.

mandatory bargaining issues

Terry L. Leap

Labor and management are required to bargain in good faith over mandatory bargaining subjects. If, for example, union negotiators want to discuss the mandatory topic of healthcare insurance, management must negotiate with them on this topic until either an agreement or impasse is reached. Mandatory subjects are those related directly to wages, hours, and other conditions of employment. Subjects falling into the broad mandatory category include wages, salaries, INCENTIVE PAY, shift differentials, subcontracting of BARGAINING UNIT work, random DRUG TESTING, vacations, retirement benefits, rest and lunch periods, job duties, work assignments, and seniority provisions, to name a few. The distinction between mandatory, permissive, and illegal bargaining issues was made by the US Supreme Court in *NLRB* v. *Borg Warner*, 356 US 342 (1958).

maquiladora

Mark C. Butler

In colonial Mexico, a *maquila*, from which the term *maquiladora* is derived, was the fee that a miller collected for processing grain. Today's *maquiladoras* are still processing facilities. They process and assemble myriad products, including consumer and industrial electronic goods, automotive components, wood, leather and clothing, toys, and medical supplies. Some *maquilas* also process paperwork – the labor-intensive sorting of grocery discount coupons, for example. *Maquiladoras* are frequently referred to as *maquilas*, and the terms are used interchangeably. The *maquiladora* program is also known as the "twin plant," "production sharing," or "in-bond" program. The terms "twin plant" and "production sharing" stem from the notion that paired plants would be established in physical proximity, one on either side of the US–Mexico border. The labor-intensive production processes would occur in Mexico, with the remaining processes in the US (production sharing). The term "in-bond" stems from a provision that materials for manufacture are imported into Mexico under a bond that guarantees the finished product will be exported. Although they were originally confined to locations along the border, the passage of the North American Free Trade Agreement (NAFTA) has seen a proliferation of *maquiladora*-type organizations throughout Mexico.

Bibliography

DeForest, M. E. (1994). Thinking of a plant in Mexico? *Academy of Management Executive*, 8, 33–40.
Noll, C. L. (1992). Mexican *maquiladora* workers: An attitude toward working. *Southwest Journal of Business and Economics*, 9, 1–7.
Shaiken, H. (1988). High tech goes third world. *Technology Review*, 91, 39–47.

Teagarden, M. B., Butler, M. C., and Von Glinow, M. A. (1993). Mexico's *maquiladora* industry: Where strategic human resource management makes a difference. *Organizational Dynamics*, **20**, 34–7.

Markov analysis

Marcus Hart Sandver

Markov analysis is named for the Russian mathematician Andrei Andreevich Markov, who died in 1922. A Markov chain or a Markov process is defined as a sequence of events in which the probability of each event depends upon the outcome of previous events.

USE IN ORGANIZATIONS

At the organizational level, Markov analysis may be applied to describe and forecast the process of human resource flows or movements within, into, and out of the organization. Since there are a finite number of human resource movements which may occur in an organization (PROMOTION, demotion, transfer, exit, new hire), Markov analysis may be used for investigating the rates of such movements over time or between two time periods (t and $t + k$).

The Markov analysis process begins by translating the existing organizational structure into a series of mutually exclusive and exhaustive states which individuals may occupy. These states correspond to job titles and are created on the basis of organizational function (marketing, accounting, operations, and so forth) and hierarchical level within function (Walker, 1980). In addition, an exit state is created to reflect movement out of the organization. States are arranged in a matrix, with the rows representing the states at time t and the columns representing the states at time $t + k$.

For the individuals in each state at t, the number and proportion occupying each state at $t + k$ is computed. For each row, the numbers of individuals in the cells represent the distribution of people by job title who stayed in the same position during the year, who moved to another position, or who exited the organization. For each row the number of individuals in each cell at $t + k$ is divided by the row total at time t. The resultant proportions are defined as *transitional probabilities*, the probability of remaining in the initial state, of moving to another state or cell within the matrix, or exiting the organization (Heneman and Sandver, 1977).

The cell proportions form a *transitional probability matrix*. The diagonal elements of the matrix represent the proportion of individuals who did not change states from t to $t + k$. The off-diagonal elements of the matrix represent the proportion of persons who moved from one state to another or who exited the organization from t to $t + k$. For each row of the matrix, the sum of the probabilities must equal 1 because the number of moves in the system is finite and the states are mutually exclusive and exhaustive. The matrix may be multiplied by itself to represent the movement of people in the organization over successive time periods.

MARKOV ANALYSIS AS A FORECASTING TOOL

Markov analysis may prove useful to human resource planners to help forecast shortages of employees in certain critical job titles over time (Mahoney and Milkovich, 1971). Some applications of Markov analysis employ the technique as a tool in STRATEGIC HUMAN RESOURCE MANAGEMENT (Bechet and Maki, 1987).

LIMITATIONS OF MARKOV ANALYSIS

Some authors have pointed out the limitations of Markov analysis and warn human resource managers to view personnel flows as stochastic or probabilistic rather than as deterministic and forecastable events (Vroom and MacCrimmon, 1968). Methodological problems such as sample size, choice of the time interval between t and $t + k$, multiple employee moves during a time period, and accuracy of personnel data may limit the usefulness of Markov analysis for HUMAN RESOURCE PLANNING purposes (Heneman and Sandver, 1977).

Bibliography

Bechet, T. P. and Maki, W. R. (1987). Modeling and forecasting focusing on people as a strategic resource. *Human Resource Planning*, **10**, 209–17.

Heneman, H. G. and Sandver, M. G. (1977). Markov analysis in human resource administration: Applications and limitations. *Academy of Management Review*, **2**, 535–42.

Mahoney, T. A. and Milkovich, G. T. (1971). The internal labor market as stochastic process. In D. J. Bartholomew and A. R. Smits (eds.), *Manpower and Management Science*. Lexington, MA: Lexington Books.

Vroom, V. H. and MacCrimmon, K. R. (1968). Toward a stochastic model of managerial careers. *Administrative Science Quarterly*, 13, 26–46.

Walker, J. W. (1980). *Human Resource Planning*. New York: McGraw-Hill.

Martin v. Wilks, 490 US 755 (1989)

Leonard Bierman

In this case the Supreme Court held that white employees who were disadvantaged by an AFFIRMATIVE ACTION consent decree established in litigation in which they did not intervene, but of which they had notice, could challenge under Title VII decisions made pursuant to that decree. Section 703(n) of the CIVIL RIGHTS ACT OF 1991, however, modified the court's decision and provided that a consent judgment that resolves federal claims of employment discrimination cannot be challenged.

mediation

Deborah M. Kolb

While mediation has traditionally been an adjunct to labor negotiations and international conflict, its use is increasingly being extended to resolve differences in families and communities, at work, and across levels of government. As a mode of dispute processing, mediation involves an outsider, a so-called third party, who assists the principal parties in the resolution of their differences. Mediation is generally a voluntary process where the mediator lacks formal decision-making authority. Because of its voluntary nature, the ability of parties to actively participate in the resolution of their own differences, and the relative speed of the process, mediation is often seen as a better, more satisfying and harmonious, more efficient, less costly way for society to deal with its conflicts.

Although mediation has long been part of labor negotiations, only recently has it spread to other disputing arenas in organizations. Mediation is being used to settle legal claims between firms, and is now a step in many grievance and complaint procedures (*see* GRIEVANCE PROCEDURE), including the role of ombudsman. In addition, informal mediation is coming to be recognized as a necessary part of teamwork and organizational change, and as a function of management generally.

Mediators assist parties by giving them a forum to air their differences, vent their feelings and frustrations, explore options for settlement, and appreciate the consequences of no agreement (Moore, 1986). What mediators actually do in a dispute, whether they push for settlement or try to alter how parties relate to and communicate with one another, is a function of their diagnosis of the conflict, their relationships with the parties, and their background and training, among other factors (Kressel and Pruitt, 1989; Bush and Folger, 1994; Kolb et al., 1994).

Bibliography

Bush, R. B. and Folger, J. (1994). *Mediation at the Crossroads*. San Francisco: Jossey-Bass.

Kolb, D. M. et al. (1994). *When Talk Works: Profiles of Mediators*. San Francisco: Jossey-Bass.

Kressel, K. and Pruitt, D. (1989). *Mediation of Social Conflict*. San Francisco: Jossey-Bass.

Moore, C. (1986). *The Mediation Process*. San Francisco: Jossey-Bass.

mental abilities

Paul E. Spector

Mental ability refers to the capability or capacity to develop and learn mental skills, such as mathematics and verbal comprehension. Overall cognitive ability is termed intelligence, but there are many specific cognitive abilities that are only moderately related to one another. As a result, some mental abilities are separately measured. For example, mathematical ability and verbal ability are often separated in INTELLIGENCE TESTS. Mental abilities are used frequently in PERSONNEL SELECTION because mental ability tests have been found to be valid predictors of JOB PERFORMANCE on a wide range of jobs (e.g., Schmitt et al., 1984; Smith and George, 1992).

Bibliography

Schmitt, F. L., Gooding, R. Z., Noe, R. A., and Kirsch, M. P. (1984). Meta-analyses of validity studies published between 1964 and 1982 and the investigation of study characteristics. *Personnel Psychology*, 37, 407–22.

Smith, M. and George, D. (1992). Selection methods. In C. L. Cooper and I. T. Robertson (eds.), *International Review of Industrial and Organizational Psychology*. Chichester: John Wiley.

mentoring programs

Kathy E. Kram

Mentoring programs are initiatives designed to encourage relationships that support learning and development of targeted employee populations (e.g., new hires, high potentials, individuals from diverse backgrounds). They are generally established to create *accountability for development* and *accessibility to developmental relationships* (*see* STRATEGIC ISSUES IN DIVERSITY). Mentoring programs vary in specific objectives, degree of structure, number of participants, associated training and education, and monitoring and evaluation methods.

Sometimes formally assigned relationships remain superficial or become destructive, participants have unrealistic expectations for the program and fail to seek other opportunities for development, and/or those who do not participate feel unfairly excluded. These unintended negative consequences are minimized when program objectives and design are aligned with an organization's culture and human resource strategy, participation is voluntary, and adequate education and training are provided.

There are a number of alternatives to mentoring programs that can foster developmental relationships for a wide range of employees. These include:

1 job assignments that require individuals who have complementary development needs to collaborate;
2 PERFORMANCE APPRAISAL and COMPENSATION strategy practices that recognize and reward mentoring and coaching behaviors;
3 SUCCESSION PLANNING processes that explicitly monitor the mentoring and coaching needs of candidates for leadership positions;
4 work teams that have mentoring as one of their primary purposes; and
5 various homogeneous and heterogeneous groups whose purposes are to promote personal learning through dialogue.

Given trends of globalization, flatter and team-oriented organizations, increasing workforce diversity, and rapid technological change, multiple strategies to promote mentoring are essential. The maximum value of mentoring programs is achieved when they are implemented (and aligned) with related human resource practices.

Bibliography

Kram, K. E. and Hall, D. T. (1996). Mentoring in a context of diversity and turbulence. In S. Lobel and E. Kossek (eds.), *Human Resource Strategies for Managing Diversity*. Oxford: Blackwell.

Murray, M. (1991). *Beyond the Myths and Magic of Mentoring: How to Facilitate an Effective Mentoring Program*. San Francisco: Jossey-Bass.

Noe, R. A. (1988). An investigation of the determinants of successful assigned mentoring relationships. *Personnel Psychology*, 41, 457–79.

merit pay

Robert L. Heneman

Merit pay refers to pay increases based on PERFORMANCE APPRAISAL (Heneman, 1992). The higher the rating of an employee's performance, the larger the pay increase granted to the employee. The size of the pay increase allocated is dependent upon the employee's position in the rate ranges as assessed by the compa-ratio (*see* COMPA-RATIOS). The larger the compa-ratio for an employee, the smaller the size of the increase granted in order to keep the employee's salary within the rate range. Under a traditional merit pay plan, pay increases are made a permanent addition to the employee's salaries. Under a lump sum merit pay plan, pay increases are one-time BONUSES not made as permanent additions to employees' salaries. Merit pay plans are used in over 80 percent of US organizations, primarily for exempt employees (Peck, 1984). Merit pay is one form of PAY FOR PERFORMANCE.

Merit pay has been shown to be related to positive attitudes toward work, including pay satisfaction (see JOB SATISFACTION). The evidence regarding the relationship of merit pay to subsequent PRODUCTIVITY is mixed, with some studies showing an improvement in productivity and others a decrease (Heneman, 1992). Merit pay is often criticized as being associated with an entitlement culture (see REWARD SYSTEMS).

In order for merit pay plans to be effective, two conditions must be met (National Research Council, 1991). First, performance appraisal ratings must have CRITERION RELEVANCE, be free from RATING ERRORS, and be accurate. Second, pay increases must be large enough to differentiate poor from excellent performers.

Bibliography

Heneman, R. L. (1992). *Merit Pay: Linking Pay Increases to Performance Ratings*. Reading, MA: Addison-Wesley.
National Research Council (1991). *Pay-for-Performance: Evaluating Performance Appraisal and Merit Pay*. Washington, DC: National Academy Press.
Peck, C. (1984). *Pay and Performance: The Interaction of Compensation and Performance Appraisal*. New York: Conference Board.

Meritor Savings Bank v. *Vinson*, 1986

Kelly A. Vaverek

Meritor Savings Bank v. *Vinson* (477 US 57, 1986) is the first Supreme Court decision involving a SEXUAL HARASSMENT case. In its holding, the Supreme Court acknowledged that *hostile environment* is a form of sexual harassment forbidden by Title VII. Although there was no evidence that Ms. Vinson's career had suffered because of the harassment, the court said "the language of Title VII is not limited to 'economic' or 'tangible' discrimination." It also said that the critical issue was not whether the relationship between supervisor and teller was voluntary. Rather, it was whether the supervisor's sexual advances were unwelcome. If they are unwelcome, and they rise to the level of abusive, then they are illegal.

Bibliography

Martell, K. and Sullivan, G. (1994). Sexual harassment: The continuing workplace crisis. *Labor Law Journal*, 45, 195–207.

Mexico

Mary B. Teagarden and Mark C. Butler

Mexican labor laws regulate individual labor relations, collective labor relations, labor litigation, and federal and state conciliation and arbitration boards made up of labor, management, and government representatives. These boards are empowered to make final enforceable judgments.

The Mexican commitment to workers' rights is rooted in its 1917 Constitution. Article 123 established the jurisdiction of the Mexican Congress and the state legislatures to issue labor laws responsive to local regional needs in accordance with the Constitution's guiding principles, which include improving the living and working conditions of Mexican workers and honoring workers' inherent liberty and dignity.

The Mexican Constitution guarantees basic rights, such as workplace health and safety, minimum wage, maximum hours of work, freedom of association, and the right of workers to strike. It also guarantees employment security, PROFIT SHARING, annual leave, worker training, and many other benefits and protections. These rights and benefits are implemented by *Ley Federal de Trabajo*, the Federal Labor Law, which was originally drafted in 1931, canceled and reissued in 1971, and amended numerous times since. The Federal Labor Law recognizes the two types of workers, union and confidential, to which the law applies. Confidential workers are those who handle functions of administration, supervision, control, vigilance, or inspection.

Specific Provisions of the Federal Labor Law

Fringe benefits. Vacation bonus amounts to 25 percent of the worker's salary for the vacation period and a Christmas bonus equal to 15 days paid before December 20 each year.

Health and safety. The formation of health and safety committees consisting of management and employee representatives is required to insure that the employer meets minimum requirements for health and safety. These committees work in conjunction with labor authorities to analyze and investigate causes of work-related accidents and illnesses, develop safety practices and procedures, communicate these procedures to the workforce, and oversee compliance. Both the Social Security (IMSS) and the Labor Ministries are empowered to issue safety regulations and to inspect sites to evaluate compliance with minimum work standards, to develop special standards in accordance with the type of industry or activity, and to impose sanctions for noncompliance.

Housing. Employers contribute the equivalent of 5 percent of their annual payroll to a special fund for worker housing (INFONAVIT).

Maternity benefits. Workers are entitled to six weeks off before and six weeks after the expected delivery of a baby. Employers must retain the mother as an employee at this time, without pay, but they must pay her social security contribution. Her salary is paid by the IMSS during her maternity leave. Nursing mothers are allowed two hours off at midday to feed their baby.

Minimum wage. Minimum wages are established by occupation categories and the minimum wage also varies by region. Border regions and the Federal District (Mexico City) have higher wage rates.

Medical benefits. Under the country's social security laws, all workers are registered to receive medical care and social services, paid for by the employer.

Non-waiver of rights. The minimum rights of workers, as well as those later acquired, cannot be waived by workers.

Overtime. Overtime up to nine extra hours per week is paid at 100 percent of the worker's salary. Overtime in excess of this and work on holidays is paid at 200 percent of the regular wage. Work on Sundays or the weekly rest day is paid at 225 percent over the regular wage.

Pension. In February 1992, the Mexican government established a mandatory occupational pension program, *Sistema de Ahorro para el Retirel*, that requires employers to establish a defined contribution plan for retirees. Under the program, employers must contribute 2 percent of covered pay of each employee into individual, interest-bearing accounts.

Profit sharing. Employers must provide profit-sharing packages equal to 10 percent of the company's adjusted pre-tax profits. These must be distributed each year.

Strikes. A strike is considered "existent" if it is called by a majority and is for legal purposes. Legal purposes include: (1) to obtain equilibrium between factors of production, harmonizing the rights of labor with the rights of capital; (2) to obtain from the employer or employers the signing of a COLLECTIVE BARGAINING agreement and to demand its revision upon expiration; (3) to obtain from the employers the signing of a law contract and to demand its revision upon expiration; (4) to demand compliance with the collective bargaining agreement or the law contract in the enterprises or establishments in which it has been violated; (5) to demand compliance with the legal provisions of profit sharing; (6) to support a strike, which meets the objectives identified above; and (7) to demand a revision of the contractual salaries. A strike is considered "nonexistent" if: (1) it does not meet the objectives listed above; (2) it is not supported by the majority of the workers; and (3) the legal process was not followed.

Termination/severance. Employers have a 30-day period during which a worker can be released without obligation; after this the employee is considered permanent. If a permanent worker is fired or laid off, the company must provide severance pay equaling three months' wages, plus 12 additional days for each year of employment. This is increased to 21 days for each year of employment if the employee terminates the work relationship for causes attributable to the employer, or if the employer refuses to reinstate the employee after being required to do so by the labor board. A 30-day severance notification is required.

Training. Employers are required to provide their employees with minimum training. Training should allow workers to improve skills, prepare for higher positions that may become available, improve worker PRODUCTIVITY and general welfare, and minimize work accidents. Training committees with representatives from both management and labor are required. Details of the training program must be filed with the Labor Ministry Board for approval.

Vacations. Employees have a right to six days of paid vacation after completing a year of service and this increases by two days per year until a total of 12 days is reached. Vacations cannot be forfeited or compensated with pay and must be used within six months of the employment anniversary date.

Work week. The work week is 48 hours, with one day a week for compulsory rest, although a 40-hour week is becoming more common practice. The work day shift is eight hours; a night shift is seven hours. Employees are generally paid for 56 hours of work each week.

MEXICAN LABOR UNIONS

Article 123 of Mexico's Constitution defines labor unions as "associations formed for the study, betterment, and defense of the interests of workers and their employers." Two major categories of unions are distinguished in Article 123. Section A identifies industrial workers, agricultural day laborers, domestic employees, artisans, and, in general, all workers covered by private labor contracts. Section B identifies all public sector workers employed by the national government, the various Mexican states, and all municipalities.

Five official classifications of labor unions exist in Mexico: (1) *gremiales*, or workers in the same profession; (2) *de empresa*, or workers from a single company; (3) *industriales*, or workers from two or more companies in the same industry; (4) *nacionales de industria*, or those in one or more states; and (5) *oficios varios*, those including fewer than 20 workers of the same profession, in the same municipal location. These unions have also been characterized as "official unions," "independent unions," and "white unions."

The alliance between the Mexican government and organized labor is unique in Latin America and is credited with contributing to the stability of the Mexican state by serving as a mediating structure which promotes the general welfare of the working class through intervention at the political level. The first official labor union, CTM, was established in 1918 as a result of the Mexican Revolution. Official labor unions have historically been affiliated with Mexico's former ruling party, the Institutional Revolutionary Party (PRI). This included support in elections, voluntary wage suppression, and a very low incidence of strikes. In return, PRI suppressed independent unions from challenging the power of official unions, guaranteed union officials a fixed quota of candidates for federal and state government positions, persuaded local labor boards to favor unions in decisions, and provided social services to union members through the IMSS and other social agencies. In 2000, however, the PRI was defeated by Vicente Fox's National Action Party (PAN) and the new government has adopted policies more supportive of global integration of Mexico's economy.

NAFTA-ERA DYNAMICS AND GLOBAL INTEGRATION CHALLENGES

The North American Commission on Labor Cooperation (NACLC) was established under the North American Free Trade Agreement (NAFTA) to mediate labor-related disputes. Any North American group or individual may file a complaint. The complaint first goes to one of three national administration offices; each NAFTA country has one in its capital city. Then, if necessary, the complaint goes to the NACLC's ministerial council, which is comprised of the three countries' trade ministers and is usually the first step in the dispute process. The NACLC's international secretariat helps coordinate work with the council. Under NAFTA, labor complaints are filed with the US National Administrative Office (NAO) of the Labor Department's Bureau of International Labor Affairs, an office established to monitor labor policies in the US, Mexico, and Canada. The labor secretaries of the three nations can, by a two-thirds vote, impose fines or trade sanctions on a country that fails to enforce its laws for cases involving minimum wages, child labor, or health and safety.

Human resource management (HRM) in Mexico in the NAFTA era reflects profound political, economic, and social change – a dynamism more dramatic than any the republic has ever experienced. This dynamism includes a shift from an economic orientation of protectionism, a developmental model of import substitution, substantial government ownership of business, and few competitors, to a competitive economic orientation, development based on open markets, private ownership of business, and many global competitors. During this dynamic transition there has been very high inflation and a peso devaluation. Both of these events have adversely affected wages, salaries, the value of benefits packages, and ultimately the purchasing power of workers.

Prior to NAFTA the sources of competitiveness for firms in Mexico were low cost and reasonable productivity. The traditional HRM challenges faced by firms in Mexico were high EMPLOYEE TURNOVER, ABSENTEEISM, and variable quality. The primary objective for most firms in this pre-NAFTA era was maintaining the status quo. However, in the NAFTA era the sources of competitiveness have become globalized and include low cost, high quality, speed, flexibility, and innovation. The primary objective for most firms has become survival. Firms face a host of strategic challenges in the NAFTA era, including: an abundant workforce comprised often of young, inexperienced, and unskilled workers; strong labor laws that have traditionally favored the worker; cross-cultural challenges, given the diversity encountered in the Mexican workforce; and an expectation of meeting global standards. These strategic challenges are compounded by shortages of skilled technical and managerial employees. In this dynamic global competitive arena, the HRM designs firms use are helping them meet competitiveness challenges. Mexican employers and foreign investors have used three HRM designs: (1) a control design, (2) a paternalistic design, and (3) a developmental design. Firms using these designs have encountered varying degrees of success. The first two yield short-term benefits and are the ones most often used by Mexican employers. The developmental design, on the other hand, yields longer-term strategic benefits but is often overlooked in the quest for short-term benefits and survival in the face of global competition.

The control design focuses on control of worker behavior (often through punishment) to achieve economies and accomplish corporate goals. Little attention is paid to motivating or developing the worker. From the employer's perspective, the agreement is a day's pay for a day's work – these workers are not seen as assets. Employers using this design provide extensive, specific training, usually on every aspect of one particular job. This limits the firm's flexibility in the long term.

The paternalistic design uses a different approach to control and motivation. This style "takes care" of workers. Rewards and promotion are based on workers "being in favor" with supervisors or management. This design uses absolute top-down authority and workers are often afraid to ask any questions. These firms use limited training (at best) that focuses on narrow, task-specific requirements. Training often takes the form of a worker being assigned to observe another "for a couple of hours" before beginning a new task. Firms using this design invest moderate to low levels in plant and equipment and in training and development. In return, they encounter variable costs and variable quality.

Neither of these designs is as effective as the developmental design for meeting NAFTA-era competition. The developmental design, currently used most often by foreign investors, integrates control, motivation, and developmental needs of workers. It is based on a sophisticated reward system (see REWARD SYSTEMS) that provides an extensive array of culturally appropriate benefits, such as transportation, subsidized food and beverages, social activities, and education (many Mexican workers highly value education as a reward). These rewards are closely matched to local worker needs.

This design provides training and development programs designed to reduce overall costs and improve quality and is targeted at the developmental and general needs of workers. In addition to training during working hours, these employers offer onsite, work-related, and general education for workers, usually two hours each day after work, often subsidized by the government. Courses include basics such as high school equivalency education and specialized courses such as supervision and leadership, computer skills, and English.

Employers who implement this design commonly have high levels of investment in plant and equipment, including state-of-the-art robotics. This capital investment requires higher skill levels, which the emphasis on training and development provides. This design results in low cost, high quality, manufacturing flexibility and speed, and high levels of cultural capability. Some of these employers, most notably foreign investors, have the highest quality of *any* of their global operations. This reflects their skillful blending of sophisticated manufacturing and service delivery processes and world-class, culturally consistent HRM practices. While foreign investors have championed the developmental HRM design in Mexico, the lessons learned are being incorporated into HRM practices by Mexican employers in meeting the global competition introduced in the NAFTA era.

See also *maquiladora*

Bibliography

Butler, M. C. and Teagarden, M. B. (1993). Strategic management of worker health, safety, and environmental issues in Mexico's *maquiladora* industry. *Human Resources Management*, 32, 479–504.

Carillo, V. J. (1991). The evolution of the *maquiladora* industry: Labor relations in a new context. In K. J. Middlebrook (ed.), *Unions, Workers, and the State in Mexico*. San Diego, CA: University of California San Diego, Center for US–Mexican Studies.

Cerda Gastelum, J. and Nunez, F. J. (1990). *La administracion en desarrollo: Problemas y avances de la administracion en Mexico*. Mexico: Editorial Xaxhe-te.

DeForest, M. E. (1994). Thinking of a plant in Mexico? *Academy of Management Executive*, 8, 33–40.

Kras, E. S. (1991). *La administracion Mexicana en transicion*. Mexico, DF: Grupo Editorial Iberoamerica.

La Botz, D. (1988). *The Crisis of Mexican Labor*. New York: Praeger.

Meyers, F. (1979). *Mexican Industrial Relations from the Perspective of the Labor Court*. Los Angeles: UCLA Institute of Industrial Relations Publications.

Millan, J., Perera, M., and Lowe, J. (1990). The ABCs of Mexican labor relations. *Twin Plant News*, May, 2–8.

Morales, R. A. (1993). Mexico. In M. Rothman, D. R. Briscoe, and R. C. D. Nacamulli (ed.), *Industrial Relations Around the World: Labor Relations in Multinational Companies*. New York: DeGruyter.

Pail, Y. and Teagarden, M. B. (1995). Strategic international human resource management approaches in the *maquiladora* industry: A comparison of Japanese, Korean, and US firms. *International Journal of Human Resource Management*, 6, 566–87.

Roxborough, I. (1984). *Unions and Politics in Mexico: The Case of the Automobile Industry*. Cambridge: Cambridge University Press.

Shaiken, H. (1988). High tech goes third world. *Technology Review*, 91, 39–47.

Teagarden, M. B., Butler, M. C., and Von Glinow, M. A. (1993a). Mexico's *maquiladora* industry: Where strategic human resource management makes a difference. *Organizational Dynamics*, 20, 34–7.

Teagarden, M. B., Butler, M. C., and Von Glinow, M. A. (1993b). Capturing the competitive edge: Strategic human resource management in Mexican *maquiladoras*. In T. Agmon and R. Drobnick (eds.), *Small Firms in Global Competition*. Oxford: Oxford University Press.

Trueba Urbina, A. (1972). *Nuevo derecho del trabajo: Teoria integral*. Mexico, DF: Editorial Porrua.

Trueba Urbina, A. and Barrera, J. T. (1991). *Ley federal del trabajo: Comentarios, prontuario*. Mexico, DF: Editorial Porrua.

Williams, E. J. and Passe-Smith, J. T. (1992). *The Unionization of the Maquiladora Industry: The Tamaulipan Case in National Context*. San Diego, CA: San Diego State University, Institute for Regional Studies of the Californias.

Zapata, F. (1989). Labor and politics: The Mexican paradox. In E. C. Epstein (ed.), *Labor Autonomy and the State in Latin America*. Boston: Unwin-Hyman.

mixed-standard scales

H. John Bernardin

Mixed-standard performance rating scales consist of sets of conceptually compatible statements (usually three) that describe high, medium, and low levels of performance within a job dimension. Statements are randomized on the rating form, and the dimension that each statement represents is not obvious. The rater then indicates whether a ratee's performance is "better than," "as good as," or "worse than" the behavior described in the statement.

Introduced by Blantz (1965), mixed-standard scales were designed to inhibit error in ratings, particularly the tendency to be lenient (*see* LENIENCY EFFECTS; RATING ERRORS). In the first test of the method, Blantz and Ghiselli (1972) found that ratings from mixed-standard scales resulted in less leniency than those from "ordinary rating scales" and that "assessments obtained from different raters are quite comparable" (p. 189). Unfortunately, because Blantz and Ghiselli did not actually obtain ratings from any other format, relative comparisons could not be made on any psychometric characteristics. There have since been several comparisons of ratings from mixed-standard scales with ratings from other formats, such as BEHAVIORALLY ANCHORED RATING SCALES and BEHAVIORAL OBSERVATION SCALES, and no strong evidence was found suggesting that this format is superior to others.

Bibliography

Blantz, F. (1965). A new merit rating method. Unpublished doctoral dissertation, University of Stockholm.
Blantz, F. and Ghiselli, E. E. (1972). The mixed standard scale: A new rating system. *Personnel Psychology*, 25, 185–99.
Saal, F. E. and Landy, F. J. (1977). The mixed standard scale: An evaluation. *Organizational Behavior and Human Performance*, 18, 19–35.

multicultural workforce

R. Roosevelt Thomas, Jr. and Catherine A. Ouellette

A multicultural workforce contains participants with varying backgrounds reflecting the assumptions, or cultures (Schein, 1985), of the organizations through which they were socialized. Socializing entities include family, community, religious, and educational institutions. To the extent that individuals experienced socialization by organizations with different driving assumptions, they can be considered to be of different cultures. While the common practice has been to link culture with race, ethnicity, and gender, these factors are not necessarily the principal determinants of cultural differences.

See also *diversity; strategic issues in diversity*

Bibliography

Cox, T. H., Jr. and Blake, S. (1991). Managing cultural diversity: Implications for organizational competitiveness. *Academy of Management Executive*, 5, 45–56.
Schein, E. H. (1985). *Organizational Culture and Leadership*. San Francisco: Jossey-Bass.
Thomas, R. R., Jr. (1991). *Beyond Race and Gender: Unleashing the Power of Your Total Workforce by Managing Diversity*. New York: AMACOM.

multinational bargaining

Richard L. Rowan

Multinational bargaining is a concept developed in the 1970s, when the growth and spread of firms operating in more than one nation appeared vulnerable to activity orchestrated by unions known as international trade secretariats. Some of these union bodies with worldwide memberships, such as the International Chemical and Energy Workers, the International Union of Food and Allied Workers, and the International Metalworkers' Federation, all based in Geneva, claimed that a new concept encompassing union and management delegates bargaining across national borders would be the wave of the future. The European Trade Union Confederation, based in Brussels, and its industry groups were also seen as active participants in this process. A number of serious obstacles have prevented the development of multinational COLLECTIVE BARGAINING:

1 *Different legislation*: No two countries have the same labor laws or practices. Bargaining rights, union structures, and bargaining structures are different and difficult to reconcile from one country to another.
2 *Employer opposition*: Employers almost universally oppose multinational bargaining

since they see nothing to be gained from the process. Most business leaders see multinational bargaining as a potential complicating factor that would add a third level of risk to work stoppages.

3 *Union opposition*: Some unions fear that multinational bargaining will result in a transfer of power from national union officials to those who lead multinational organizations.

4 *Lack of employee interest*: Employee interest in multinational union action is close to being nonexistent. Workers in one country are not likely to support their fellow employees in another country.

Bibliography

Northrup, H. R. and Rowan, R. L. (1974). Multinational collective bargaining activity: The factual record in chemicals, glass, and rubber tires. *Columbia Journal of World Business* (Spring and Summer), 112–24 and 49–63.

Northrup, H. R. and Rowan, R. L. (1979). *Multinational Collective Bargaining Attempts: The Record, the Cases, and the Prospects*. Philadelphia: Industrial Research Unit, Wharton School, University of Pennsylvania.

Rowan, R. L. and Northrup, H. R. (1975). Multinational bargaining in the telecommunications industry. *British Journal of Industrial Relations*, 13, 257–62.

multiple cutoff selection procedures

Neal Schmitt

When a job applicant is removed from consideration if the score on at least one selection device falls below some prespecified value, the employing organization is using a multiple cutoff selection procedure (*see* CUTOFF SCORE). The assumptions underlying this procedure are: (1) if the applicant scores below the cutoff values on any predictor, his or her performance on the job will be unsatisfactory; and (2) individual differences in performance by those scoring above the cutoffs are unimportant. The procedure is simple to employ and easy to explain, but very difficult to devise or change. A change in the cutoff value for even one score in such a system necessitates changes in the values for all cutoff scores.

Bibliography

Cascio, W. F. (1998). *Applied Psychology in Human Resource Management*. Englewood Cliffs, NJ: Prentice-Hall.

Schneider, B. and Schmitt, N. (1986). *Staffing Organizations*. Prospect Heights, IL: Waveland Press.

multiple-hurdle selection procedures

Neal Schmitt

In a multiple-hurdle selection procedure, decisions to reject a job applicant or to collect more information on applicants' capabilities are made at each of several, sequential hurdles. Hurdles are usually ordered in such a way that the least expensive, and/or least difficult to collect, information is used in the initial hurdles, while a more intensive examination of a smaller number of applicants is conducted at subsequent hurdles. While cost-effective for both the organization and the applicant, the procedures used in the final hurdles may not display a great deal of validity (*see* CRITERION-RELATED VALIDITY), because important job-related individual differences may have been reduced by the decisions made at previous selection hurdles.

Bibliography

Cascio, W. F. (1998). *Applied Psychology in Human Resource Management*. Englewood Cliffs, NJ: Prentice-Hall.

Schneider, B. and Schmitt, N. (1986). *Staffing Organizations*. Prospect Heights, IL: Waveland Press.

narrative method of performance evaluation

Rick Jacobs

The narrative method of performance evaluation is perhaps the simplest and oldest method of assessing employees. Raters are asked to provide a description, usually in writing, of the employee's performance. Often, the evaluator is given the instruction to describe an individual's strengths, weaknesses, and potential for advancement/new assignments, and to provide a plan for further development of job-relevant skills. While such a system of performance evaluation is simple, straightforward, and nothing more than a formalization of daily supervisory observations, it does represent a method of performance evaluation with both serious advantages and disadvantages.

Advantages of this method include: (1) ratings are descriptive and offer more complete information about performance; (2) the very process of gathering the necessary information for the evaluation can result in more interaction between rater and ratee; and (3) details for APPRAISAL FEEDBACK and PERFORMANCE COACHING with the ratee are part of the rating process. Disadvantages include: (1) ratings may be as much a reflection of the rater's willingness to spend time on the evaluation process and/or level of verbal skills as they are related to performance level of the ratee; (2) no numeric outcome is inherent with this qualitative method; (3) there is no standardization across raters; (4) there is no guarantee that important aspects of the job will be evaluated; and (5) there is limited or no ability to compare employees within or across groups.

Bibliography

Cascio, W. F. (1998). *Applied Psychology in Human Resource Management*. Englewood Cliffs, NJ: Prentice-Hall.

National Academy of Arbitrators

I. B. Helburn

The National Academy of Arbitrators consists of experienced labor–management arbitrators with proven general acceptability within the union–management community. Neither a selecting nor an appointing agency, the Academy holds an annual meeting, an annual educational conference, and regional meetings designed to improve the understanding of ARBITRATION and its role in the resolution of union–management and other workplace disputes. The proceedings of the annual meeting are published yearly. The Academy enforces the "Code of Professional Responsibility for Arbitrators of Labor–Management Disputes," to which members are expected to adhere.

National Institute for Occupational Safety and Health

Donna E. Ledgerwood

The OCCUPATIONAL SAFETY AND HEALTH ACT OF 1970 mandated the existence of the National Institute for Occupational Safety and Health (NIOSH), which is part of the Department of Health and Human Services (HHS), to initiate studies related to safety and health, to make recommendations to the OCCUPATIONAL SAFETY AND HEALTH ADMINISTRATION (OSHA), and to help train managers in critical areas related to occupational safety and health. NIOSH and OSHA were to coordinate with other health-related HHS governmental agencies, such as the Public Health Service, the National Institutes for Health, the Environmental Protection Agency (EPA), and the Social Security Administration. Labor and industry representatives have also played an active part in recommendations concerning public health policies.

A sister agency to OSHA, the EPA was given the task of monitoring health and safety-related hazards (chemical spills, air pollutants, and so forth) which are generated by the manufacturing processes of an organization or the transportation of its products. These activities involve functions external to the walls of the organization. Managers and nonmanagerial employees not only have the obligation to have knowledge of OSHA and EPA laws, they are also increasingly responsible for knowing and complying with these laws.

National Labor Relations Act of 1935

Charles E. Krider

The National Labor Relations Act (NLRA), or the Wagner Act, was passed by Congress in 1935. It provides legal protection for employees in the private sector who wish to organize unions and participate in COLLECTIVE BARGAINING. Employees who perceive that their individual bargaining power is inadequate to set acceptable terms of employment may join with other employees to enhance their bargaining power. A major objective of the Act is to promote labor peace by encouraging collective bargaining to resolve disputes between employees and employers.

The heart of the Act is the rights in section 7 that are recognized for employees: (1) to form and join unions; (2) to bargain collectively through a union; and (3) to strike and engage in other concerted activities. These rights are made effective by: (1) the NATIONAL LABOR RELATIONS BOARD; (2) REPRESENTATION ELECTIONS; and (3) unfair labor practices.

NATIONAL LABOR RELATIONS BOARD

The National Labor Relations Board (NLRB) is the agency that is responsible for enforcing the NLRA. Its five members are appointed by the president. The regional offices of the NLRB are responsible for: (1) conducting representation elections to determine if employees wish to have a union; and (2) investigating charges of unfair labor practices. If warranted, the regional office will prosecute the unfair labor practice charge before an administrative law judge, whose decision can be appealed to the NLRB and then to the federal courts. The board is the judicial branch of the NLRB and the general counsel is the prosecutorial branch. The general counsel of the NLRB is appointed separately by the president and is responsible for supervising the regional offices.

REPRESENTATION ELECTIONS

Employees who seek to have union representation may petition the regional office of the NLRB for a representation election. If 50 percent plus 1 of *those voting* support the union, then it is certified by the NLRB as the employees' bargaining agent. Such a union will be the exclusive bargaining representative for all employees in the unit, including those who did not vote or who voted against the union. The employer then must bargain in good faith with the union and seek to reach an agreement.

The NLRB's election process means that unions gain the right to represent employees through a political process rather than on the basis of their economic power to strike and force an employer to grant recognition. Unions win approximately 50 percent of the elections.

UNFAIR LABOR PRACTICES

Section 8 of the NLRA sets forth illegal acts for employers (called unfair labor practices) that protect the section 7 rights of employees. These are practices: (1) to interfere, restrain, or coerce employees in the exercise of section 7 rights; (2) to dominate or interfere with the formation or administration of any labor organization; (3) to encourage or discourage membership in any labor organization by DISCRIMINATION in regard to employment or any term or condition of employment; and (4) to refuse to bargain collectively with a union that represents a majority of the employees. Similar unfair labor practices for unions were added by the LABOR MANAGEMENT RELATIONS ACT OF 1947.

The NLRB is limited in most cases to a make-whole remedy (*see* MAKE-WHOLE/COMPEN-

SATORY REMEDIES). For example, employees who have been discharged because of union activity can be ordered reinstated with backpay; there is an offset for any other earning of the employee during the time he or she was discharged. The NLRB may not impose fines, punitive damages, or jail sentences. Also, if an employer does not bargain in good faith, the NLRB can issue an order for the employer to bargain in good faith.

The outcome of negotiations is not directly regulated by the NLRB but is determined by the relative bargaining power of the employees. Unions can strike in support of their demands and employers can lock out employees and hire permanent replacements if there is a strike (see LOCKOUT; STRIKE).

Bibliography

Cihon, P. and Castagnera, J. (1993). *Labor and Employment Law*. Boston: PWS-Kent.

Cox, A., Bok, D., Gorman, R., and Finkin, M. (1991). *Labor Law*. Westbury, NY: Foundation Press.

Weiler, P. C. (1990). *Governing the Workplace*. Cambridge, MA: Harvard University Press.

National Labor Relations Board

David A. Gray

The National Labor Relations Board (NLRB) is a federal agency created under the NATIONAL LABOR RELATIONS ACT OF 1935. The NLRB is headquartered in Washington, DC, with approximately 40 regional and field offices scattered across the US. Its five-member board is appointed by the president and confirmed by the US Senate. The board has two functions: (1) preventing, investigating, and remedying unfair labor practices committed by employers and unions; and (2) conducting secret ballot elections of designated bargaining units (see BARGAINING UNIT) to determine whether employees desire union representation. Unfair labor practice charges are initially handled by the regional offices, with appeals to the five-member board. REPRESENTATION ELECTIONS are usually held on the premises of the employer.

national origin

Ramona L. Paetzold

National origin is one of the protected categories under Title VII of the CIVIL RIGHTS ACT OF 1964. This category of protection is interpreted synonymously with ancestry; it protects individuals based on the country of origin of the individuals themselves or of their forebears. It also protects individuals from discrimination based on their *perceived* ancestries. The term "national origin" is not synonymous with citizenship; although it is illegal to discriminate on the basis of national origin, it is not illegal to discriminate (under Title VII) on the basis of alienage *per se*. Aliens are protected under Title VII only to the extent that they are discriminated against on the basis of race, color, religion, sex, or national origin.

negligent hiring

Barbara A. Lee

Negligent hiring claims are made when an employee injures another individual (whether or not the victim is a coworker) and the victim can prove not only that the employee was unfit for the position, but also that the employer knew that the employee was unfit, or, had the employer investigated the employee's background prior to hiring that individual, the employer would have known that the employee was unfit. The victim must show that the injury was a direct result of the employment relationship, such as an assault committed by an employee who comes into a customer's home to repair an appliance.

negligent retention

Barbara A. Lee

Negligent retention claims may be filed against an employer when one of its employees injures or otherwise harms another individual, and the victim asserts that the employer knew that the employee was either dangerous or unfit for the job. Employers who know that an employee has been violent, has engaged in sexual, racial, or other unlawful forms of harassment, or has been dishonest may be liable under this legal theory if the employee repeats the behavior and someone, whether another employee, a client or customer, or a member of the general public, is harmed.

negligent supervision

Barbara A. Lee

Similar to claims of NEGLIGENT HIRING and NEGLIGENT RETENTION, claims of negligent supervision may be made when an employee injures another person and the victim asserts that the employer knew or should have known that the individual could engage in this behavior, and thus should have supervised the individual more closely. In order for an employer to be found liable, the victim must show that the injury was foreseeable and that the employer's failure to supervise the employee more effectively was the proximate cause of the injury.

negotiation biases

Peter H. Kim

Negotiation biases are systematic deviations from rationality that occur during negotiations. All biases are based on the heuristics (mental rules) people use to simplify their decision processes. While these heuristics can promote more efficient decision-making when they are used appropriately, they can systematically limit performance when their use is inappropriate. Negotiation researchers have identified four individual-level mental rules that can bias performance in negotiations and three biases that are unique to the complexities of negotiation interaction (see Neale and Bazerman, 1991).

Individual-level Biases Relevant to Negotiation

Framing describes the tendency to be risk averse when confronting potential gains and risk seeking when confronting potential losses (Kahneman and Tversky, 1979). Depending on a negotiator's reference, that individual may perceive an offer as a potential gain and accept it (the risk-averse decision), or perceive the offer as a potential loss and hold out for future, potential concessions (risk seeking).

Anchoring and adjustment describes the tendency to estimate values for unknown objects or events by starting from an initial anchor value and adjusting from there to reach a final answer. This bias affects negotiations because even arbitrarily chosen reference points will significantly influence how individuals estimate value, and those estimates will be insufficiently adjusted away from such arbitrary reference points (Slovic and Lichtenstein, 1971).

Availability describes how vivid information exerts a much greater impact on final decisions than equally informative, but pallid, information. The control of information (both the amount and mode of presentation) in negotiation can, therefore, provide the potential for manipulating negotiated outcomes (Neale, 1984).

Overconfidence describes the tendency of decision-makers to demonstrate unwarranted levels of confidence in their judgment abilities. This bias leads negotiators to consistently overestimate the probability that their side's final offer will be accepted (Neale and Bazerman, 1983). This overconfidence may inhibit settlements even when there is room for a mutually beneficial agreement.

Biases Unique to Negotiation Interaction

The *mythical fixed-pie of negotiations* describes the tendency of negotiators to approach negotiations with the perception that their interests necessarily and directly conflict. This bias often inhibits the discovery of mutually beneficial solutions. For some issues, negotiator interests may be entirely consistent; for others, negotiators may jointly gain if they each trade off less-valued issues for issues they value more.

The *nonrational escalation of conflict* describes the tendency of negotiators to become trapped by their initial course of action. In negotiations, disputants commonly make extreme initial demands, and if negotiators become committed to these initial public statements, they may nonrationally adopt and fortify a nonconcessionary stance and risk nonagreement.

Ignoring the cognitions of others describes the tendency of negotiators to not consider the cognitions of their opponents. To improve performance, negotiators must adopt strategies for routinely examining the thoughts and perceptions of their opponents. Further, since individuals may have such a strong bias against considering the cognitions of others, negotiators need to incorporate the fact that their opponent may not be fully considering the cognitions of the focal negotiator either.

See also *negotiation tactics*

Bibliography

Kahneman, D. and Tversky, A. (1979). Prospect theory: An analysis of decision under risk. *Econometrica*, **47**, 263–91.

Neale, M. A. (1984). The effect of negotiation and arbitration cost salience on bargaining behavior: The role of arbitrator and constituency in negotiator judgement. *Organizational Behavior and Human Performance*, **34**, 97–111.

Neale, M. A. and Bazerman, M. H. (1983). The role of perspective-taking ability in negotiating under different forms of arbitration. *Industrial and Labor Relations Review*, **36**, 378–88.

Neale, M. A. and Bazerman, M. H. (1991). *Cognition and Rationality in Negotiation*. New York: Free Press.

Slovic, P. and Lichtenstein, S. (1971). Comparison of Bayesian and regression approaches to the study of information processing in judgement. *Organizational Behavior and Human Performance*, **6**, 649–744.

negotiation tactics

Jeffrey T. Polzer

Negotiation tactics are the methods used by bargainers to reach their negotiation goals. Most negotiation scholars distinguish between tactics intended to attain a high distributive outcome (i.e., claim value) and those intended to attain a high integrative outcome (i.e., create value) (Walton and McKersie, 1965; Raiffa, 1982; Lewicki et al., 1994; *see* DISTRIBUTIVE BARGAINING; INTEGRATIVE BARGAINING). This distinction is useful for understanding negotiation tactics, provided it does not obscure the idea that, in practice, attempting to claim and create value simultaneously is a fundamental tension faced by negotiators (Lax and Sebenius, 1986). As such, tactics of both types may be used in combination, or one tactic may even be used to accomplish both goals.

Because each negotiation party typically has incomplete information about the opponent's true preferences, tactics are used to convey and gather information. Tactics intended to claim value may convey information to the opponent about one's own bargaining situation (e.g., unwillingness to concede) or one's commitment to undertake a course of action (e.g., threats to reach an impasse). Tactics intended to create value may, for example, convey information to the opponent about one's true preferences on the issues being negotiated. Other tactics, such as those intended to gather information about the opponent's preferences, may be used to either claim or create value. This latter example demonstrates that while certain tactics are often used to send or gather particular types of information, it is often the use of the information and the accuracy with which it is transmitted that link the tactic to a particular outcome.

Many specific tactics are described in the negotiation literature. Some examples include making an extreme first offer, threatening to walk away if concessions are not granted, or using silence to elicit information from the opponent. Most tactics involve risk. Distributive tactics may increase the chance that the opponent will become more competitive. Some integrative tactics, such as revealing one's true preferences, create the opportunity for an opponent to take advantage of this information. Because of these risks, choosing an appropriate tactic or set of tactics can be difficult. Adding further complexity, the timing with which tactics are employed can moderate their effectiveness. Ethical considerations also frequently arise when a negotiator considers using tactics that convey incomplete, misleading, or even false information.

Contextual factors typically have a strong influence on the probability that various tactics will succeed. One of the most important factors in choosing tactics is the opponent. For example, while some opponents are likely to reciprocate contentious tactics, others may give in to them.

Of course, being able to predict the reactions of the other party to a particular tactic can greatly simplify the decision regarding which tactics to use. Frequently, however, tactics are most effective when applied forcefully, and this very force decreases the predictability of the opponent's reaction. Choosing appropriate tactics remains, in Raiffa's (1982) words, an art as well as a science.

See also *negotiation biases; strategic negotiations*

Bibliography

Lax, D. A. and Sebenius, J. K. (1986). *The Manager as Negotiator: Bargaining for Cooperation and Competitive Gain*. New York: Free Press.
Lewicki, R. J., Litterer, J. A., Minton, J. W., and Saunders, D. M. (1994). *Negotiation*. Boston: Richard D. Irwin.
Neale, M. A. and Bazerman, M. H. (1991). *Cognition and Rationality in Negotiation*. New York: Free Press.
Raiffa, H. (1982). *The Art and Science of Negotiation*. Cambridge, MA: Harvard University Press.
Walton, R. E. and McKersie, R. B. (1965). *A Behavioral Theory of Labor Negotiations*. Ithaca, NY: ILR Press.

nepotism policies

Cynthia D. Fisher

Nepotism is showing favoritism toward relatives, spouses, or children of current employees when hiring new employees. The term also includes giving preference to a relative who is already employed when making any subsequent personnel decision, such as PROMOTION, work assignment, or pay adjustments. While some organizations feel that employing relatives results in a loyal and congenial workforce, most worry about the potential for actual or perceived unfairness, favoritism, or conflicts of interest when relatives work closely together.

To prevent potential problems, many organizations have adopted antinepotism policies. The broadest form of antinepotism policy prohibits the employment of a relative of an employee anywhere in the organization, even at another site. Less broad policies prohibit the employment of related people at the same site, or in the same department. The narrowest type of antinepotism policy is a no-supervision rule, which states that an employee may not have decision-making authority (regarding job assignment, PERFORMANCE APPRAISAL, hiring, or COMPENSATION) over a relative.

Antinepotism policies were invented to prevent abuses and served this role reasonably well until the explosion of dual-career couples (*see* DUAL-EARNER AND DUAL-CAREER COUPLES). Suddenly rules that were intended to prevent the hiring of unqualified relatives were prohibiting the hiring of very qualified individuals who just happened to be married to current employees. An even more difficult situation arose when coworkers met at work, fell in love, and married. Presumably both were hired on their own merits, but an antinepotism policy may decree that one must transfer to another department or leave the organization altogether.

Antinepotism policies have been challenged in US courts on the basis that they violate the First Amendment right to marry, have DISPARATE IMPACT on women, or violate state laws prohibiting marital status discrimination. While cases taking the latter approach have been relatively more successful, the courts have generally upheld no-supervision rules. Employers who wish to have an antinepotism policy are advised to adopt a narrow policy (no-supervision versus no relatives employed), have a compelling business rationale for the policy, and enforce the policy even-handedly.

Bibliography

Bierman, L. and Fisher, C. D. (1984). Anti-nepotism rules applied to spouses: Business and legal viewpoints. *Labor Law Journal*, 35, 634–42.
Massengill, D. (1997). Not with your husband (or wife) you don't! The legality of no spouse rules in the workplace. *Public Personnel Management*, 26, 61–76.
Steiner, J. M. and Steinberg, S. P. (1994). Caught between Scylla and Charybdis: Are anti-nepotism policies benign paternalism or covert discrimination? *Employee Relations Law Journal*, 20, 253–67.
Werbel, J. D. and Haines, D. S. (1992). Are two birds in hand worth more than one in the bush? The case of paired employees. *Human Resource Management Review*, 2, 317–28.

new employee orientation

Cynthia D. Fisher

New employee orientation is among the most common type of training offered by organizations (see TRAINING). A carefully planned orientation program creates a favorable first impression of the organization among new hires, builds organizational commitment, provides new employees with the information they need to get started in a new job, helps to reduce the stress of coping with an unfamiliar environment, speeds socialization, and may improve retention.

A new employee orientation program should have two components, administered by different individuals. First, there should be one or more formal presentations by human resource professionals aimed largely at administrative and organization-wide issues. Some of these issues must be dealt with on the first day at work; others can wait for several weeks until there is a small group of newcomers who can be oriented as a class. The formal sessions might include the following: (1) rules and procedures (pay and BENEFITS, work hours, EMPLOYEE HANDBOOK); (2) safety procedures, fire evacuation procedures; (3) administrative formalities (payroll forms, insurance enrolment forms); (4) tour of the facility; and (5) information about the organization's history, mission, goals, and values (perhaps including a talk by a senior manager or a videotaped message from the chief executive officer).

The second component of new employee orientation is conducted on-the-job by the immediate supervisor (see ON-THE-JOB TRAINING). A checklist provided to the immediate supervisor assures that all relevant information is covered over the course of the first few weeks on the job. Topics to be included in the orientation by the superior include: (1) information about the job, duties, procedures, manuals, performance expectations, workstation, equipment, location of needed resources, authority to make decisions, and so forth; (2) introduction to coworkers, including possible assignment of a "buddy" to answer questions; (3) information about the department, goals, rules, schedules, work flow, and relationships to other departments and clients; and (4) discussion of career goals, training needs, PERFORMANCE APPRAISAL and PROMOTION practices, and so on.

See also *organizational socialization*

Bibliography

Barbazette, J. (2001). *Successful New Employee Orientation: Assess, Plan, Conduct, and Evaluate Your Program.* New York: John Wiley.

Garvey, C. (2001). The whirlwind of a new job. *HR Magazine*, 46, 110–15.

Klein, H. J. and Weaver, N. A. (2000). The effectiveness of an organizational-level orientation training program in the socialization of new hires. *Personnel Psychology*, 53, 47–66.

Sims, D. (2001). *Creative New Employee Orientation Programs: Best Practices, Creative Ideas and Activities for Energizing Your Orientation Program.* New York: McGraw-Hill.

non-compete agreements

Barbara A. Lee

If an employer employs an individual or individuals with specialized training or knowledge, or whose skills are highly valuable to that employer and its competitors, the employer may require the employee to sign a non-compete agreement. These agreements restrict the employee from working for competing organizations, typically for a limited period of time and within a limited geographic area. Non-compete agreements that completely bar an employee from any employment in his or her occupation are usually not enforced by the courts because they are viewed as unreasonable.

nonunion employee grievance procedures

Douglas M. McCabe

Nonunion employee grievance procedures, defined as the procedural requirements with respect to the processing of employees' complaints in nonunion companies, are a form of employee voice, ALTERNATIVE DISPUTE RESOLUTION procedures, and industrial justice systems (McCabe and Lewin, 1992). To be valid within a nonunion organizational context, nonunion complaint procedures must provide for both PROCEDURAL JUSTICE and DISTRIBUTIVE JUSTICE (McCabe, 1988a, b). Three types of nonunion complaint procedures in ascending order of complexity and formality are: (1) open-door policies; (2) peer review systems and internal corporate tribunals; and (3) nonunion grievance arbitration systems (McCabe, 1988a, b; McCabe and Peterson, 1994). A description of each of these three types of procedures follows.

Open-door Policies

An open-door policy is one in which management is motivated by a desire for employees to feel comfortable – and without fear of retribution – in going over the heads of their immediate supervisors in search for just and equitable answers to personal and organizational problems. But, inasmuch as management deems it impractical for all its doors to be open at all hours and under all circumstances to employees, a more or less formally structured system is prescribed for an employee's appeals upward through management to the highest level authorized in the firm's EMPLOYEE HANDBOOK. In short, management's doors are open to employees but only under very limited conditions, which differ from company to company (McCabe, 1990).

Peer Review Systems and Internal Corporate Tribunals

An increasingly large number of firms and organizations – sometimes totally disenchanted with seemingly underutilized open-door complaint and grievance procedures – are establishing internal tribunals and peer review panels to resolve conflicts over promotions, disciplinary actions, and discharges. Some consist of three peers of the aggrieved employee and two management representatives, and their decisions are final and binding on both employer and employee (McCabe, 1988a, b). While numerous variations exist among companies in the composition of their internal tribunals, the favored type is a tribunal whose members include both management personnel and nonsupervisory employees. On one issue agreement exists among the companies that provide internal tribunals for the resolution of employees' grievances: the desire of their top management that the members of the tribunals perform their work with the impartiality and objectivity which are the foundation for justice in the jury system (McCabe, 1988a, b).

Nonunion Grievance Arbitration Systems

ARBITRATION of employees' grievances in the nonunion arena or setting is similar in structure and procedure to arbitration in the unionized company. An arbitrator is a neutral third party who renders a final and binding decision between the employer and the employee (the two contending parties), who cannot mutually arrive at a satisfactory resolution of their conflict (in this case, the employee's complaint).

An important feature of nonunion grievance arbitration is that the scope of the arbitrator's authority is limited to that stipulated by the contending parties. Furthermore, the selection of an arbitrator is by mutual agreement of the parties.

Why would a company permit its employees to invoke arbitration? The inducement is that its availability should assure employees that their company is fair-minded because employee grievances are settled on neutral ground. However, this nonunion grievance procedure is rare in practice because most firms do not wish to grant a right of third-party arbitration of complaints and grievances to nonunionized employees (McCabe, 1989; McCabe and Rabil, 2002a, b).

Bibliography

McCabe, D. M. (1988a). *Corporate Non-Union Complaint Procedures and Systems: A Strategic Human Resources Management Analysis*. New York: Praeger.

McCabe, D. M. (1988b). Grievance processing: Nonunion setting. Peer review systems and internal corporate tribunals: A procedural analysis. *Labor Law Journal*, **34**, 496–502.

McCabe, D. M. (1989). Corporate non-union grievance arbitration systems: A procedural analysis. *Labor Law Journal*, **40**, 432–7.

McCabe, D. M. (1990). Corporate non-union grievance procedures: Open door policies – a procedural analysis. *Labor Law Journal*, **41**, 551–7.

McCabe, D. M. and Lewin, D. (1992). Employee voice: A human resource management perspective. *California Management Review*, **34**, 112–23.

McCabe, D. M. and Peterson, R. B. (1994). The nonunion grievance system in high performing firms. *Labor Law Journal*, 45, 529–34.

McCabe, D. M. and Rabil, J. M. (2002a). Administering the employment relationship: The ethics of conflict resolution in relation to justice in the workplace. *Journal of Business Ethics*, 36, 33–48.

McCabe, D. M. and Rabil, J. M. (2002b). Ethics and values in non-union employment arbitration: A historical study of organizational due process in the private sector. *Journal of Business Ethics*, 41, 13–25.

nonunion firms

P. B. Beaumont

Nonunion firms do not recognize trade unions for COLLECTIVE BARGAINING purposes. This may be the case in single-establishment firms or in multi-establishment firms; in the latter case all of the individual employment establishments or plants of the firm may be nonunion or only a (minority) proportion of them. If the firm is a multinational one it may operate on a nonunion basis in its country of origin, but recognize unions for collective bargaining purposes in other countries (or vice versa). This is the case with a number of well-known US firms. For example, IBM recognizes unions in Germany; McDonald's recognizes unions in Germany, Spain, China, and Mexico.

Historically, INDUSTRIAL RELATIONS researchers have paid relatively little attention to nonunion firms, concentrating instead on the processes and outcomes of collective bargaining in unionized organizations. This position has begun to change in recent years as a result of the decline in union membership and collective bargaining in a number of advanced industrialized economies, and the rise of more individual employee-oriented human resource management (HRM) practices. The small, but growing, body of research on nonunion firms had its origins in work carried out in the US and Britain, but has more recently spread to other countries, most notably Australia, Canada, and Ireland.

A Comparative Perspective

As an initial perspective on nonunion firms it is useful to distinguish between (1) centralized European and (2) decentralized North American industrial relations systems, with nonunion firms being much more a feature of North American industrial relations systems. Britain fits, somewhat awkwardly, in the latter because of its decentralized operations.

In the European systems the extensive coverage and influence of multi-employer, centralized (national, industry, or regional levels) collective bargaining arrangements account for the limited presence of nonunion firms. In such systems the decision of individual firms to join an employer's association, as the bargaining agent or representative at, for example, the industry level, is the all-important decision that effectively accords recognition to unions for collective bargaining purposes. Why are so many firms willing to make this decision in the European context? Partially because of frequent system-wide incentives to do so. For instance, in countries like Germany and Finland, national-level legislation extends collectively bargained terms and conditions to all employers; hence the incentive to be a party to the initial bargaining. Furthermore, many firms appear to view the "costs" of collective bargaining to be much lower in centralized systems. For example, the size of the union relative wage effect is much smaller in such systems (Freeman, 1994), and a relatively high degree of MANAGEMENT PREROGATIVES can be maintained at the plant level. If works councils are mandated at the plant level they are more likely to act as cooperative, joint problem-solving bodies (Freeman and Rogers, 1993), because the centralized bargaining arrangements handle the more contentious issues.

The Priority Attached to Union Avoidance

Some nonunion firms apparently do not attach, at least in answers to survey questionnaires, a particularly high priority to union avoidance. Such organizations are likely to be relatively small-sized, single-establishment firms that can rely on their low visibility (and appeal) to unions, particularly given the severe organizing constraints facing unions in many systems in more recent times.

In contrast, research in the US has indicated that in a sizable (and growing) proportion of nonunion firms, managements attach a high priority to union avoidance, particularly where they face severe product market pressures and low levels of workforce unionization (Kochan and Katz, 1986: 195–8; Cooke, 1990: 72–3). In Britain, one establishment-level survey indicated that approximately one-third of nonunion establishments attached a relatively high priority to union avoidance (Beaumont and Harris, 1994). These were establishments that had similar organizational and workforce characteristics to traditionally unionized establishments; hence their concern about being a target for union organizing efforts. That is, they were relatively large-sized, manufacturing sector establishments that employed a high proportion of male skilled workers. In other words, they were very different to the *average* nonunion establishment in Britain, which is a relatively small-sized, service sector establishment that is not part of a large, multi-establishment organization.

One of the most important individual findings to emerge from British establishment-level research is the strong, positive relationship between new or younger establishments and nonunion status. This relationship, which has become much closer from the 1980s compared to previous years, seems to reflect a combination of increased management opposition to unions and the limitations of contemporary union organizing efforts. A similar relationship has been reported for both the US and Japan (Freeman, 1989: 116).

The Means of Avoiding Unions

Given the priority which some nonunion firms attach to union avoidance, it is important to explore the mechanisms or means used to attain this end. Statutory union recognition provisions are much more a feature of decentralized (North American) industrial relations systems than of centralized (European) ones. Accordingly, a great deal of research in the US has concentrated on the forms and outcomes of employer opposition to union organizing efforts in the context of union REPRESENTATION ELECTIONS. The central conclusion of this research is that employer opposition can take a variety of forms (both legal and illegal), and is the major determinant of union losses in representation election, or, given an election victory, a failure to negotiate a first contract (Freeman and Medoff, 1985: 221–45). In Canada the statutory recognition provisions appear to have yielded more favorable outcomes to the unions because of the use of membership card checks, the imposition of time limits on elections, and the use of ARBITRATION for first contract disputes.

In Britain in the 1980s and 1990s, where statutory recognition provisions were not in operation (they were reintroduced from 1999), considerable research focused on organizations where management reverses its previous (voluntary) decision to recognize unions in individual bargaining units (*see* BARGAINING UNIT) or individual plants. Such reversals of recognition cases have attracted considerable media publicity, although they are relatively few in number and occur predominantly in situations where existing union membership levels are already low and falling. In both Britain and the US, increased research attention is being given to large, multi-establishment firms which operate their establishments on both union and nonunion bases. In the US, research has indicated that this practice is particularly associated with firms where existing workforce unionization levels are relatively low and where greenfield site plants are opened with the extensive use of HRM practices (Kochan, McKersie, and Chalykoff, 1986; *see* GREENFIELD SITES). In Britain this particular manifestation of employer opposition has grown through time, and is especially associated with the opening of new plants by firms pursuing a relatively diverse business strategy and growing through the process of mergers and amalgamations.

The Role of HRM

The initial emergence of HRM was largely associated with certain well-known nonunion firms in the US, a relationship which obviously helps to account for some of the early union concerns about such practices. Within the nonunion sector one would expect such practices to be associated with the better-standard "union substitutionists" (Kochan and Katz, 1986: 191–5), which seek to limit their employees' demand for union representation by providing a relatively high level of JOB SATISFACTION via a favorable set of employment terms and conditions; job dissatisfaction and positive perceptions of union instrumentality remain the best predictors of "union interest among nonunion employees." This approach contrasts with the lower-standard "union suppressionists," who provide relatively poor terms and conditions of employment, and instead rely on their small size (and low visibility) and recruitment and dismissal practices to avoid union organization.

Some US research certainly indicates that HRM practices have been influential in helping some nonunion organizations to maintain this status (Foulkes, 1980; Fiorito, Lowman, and Nelson, 1987). But both US and British survey evidence (Sisson, 1993; Kochan and Osterman, 1994) suggests that many HRM practices are currently more a feature of the union than the nonunion sector. One partial explanation of this finding is that the union substitutionists only constitute a minority of the nonunion sector as a whole. This suggests that more research attention be given to trying to account for variation in the use of such practices within the nonunion sector, rather than solely concentrating on inter-sectoral comparisons.

In summary, nonunion firms are of growing importance in decentralized systems of industrial relations, a relationship which has produced a growing body of research. This research is primarily concerned with the characteristics of such organizations, the priority attached by management to union avoidance, and the methods used to achieve this end. The nature and impact of employee voice mechanisms in nonunion organizations has become a particular center of research interest in most recent years.

Bibliography

Beaumont, P. B. and Harris, R. I. D. (1994). Opposition to unions in the non-union sector in Britain. *International Journal of Human Resource Management*, 5, 457–72.

Cooke, W. N. (1990). *Labor–Management Cooperation*. Kalamazoo, MI: W. E. Upjohn Institute for Employment Research.

Fiorito, J., Lowman, C., and Nelson, F. D. (1987). The impact of human resource policies on union organizing. *Industrial Relations*, 26, 113–26.

Foulkes, F. A. (1980). *Personnel Policies in Large Nonunion Companies*. Englewood Cliffs, NJ: Prentice-Hall.

Freeman, R. B. (1989). The changing status of unions around the world. In W. C. Huang (ed.), *Organized Labor at the Crossroads*. Kalamazoo, MI: W. E. Upjohn Institute for Employment Research, pp. 111–38.

Freeman, R. B. (1994). American exceptionalism in the labor market: Union–nonunion differentials in the United States and other countries. In C. Kerr and P. D. Staudohar (eds.), *Labor Economics and Industrial Relations*. Boston: Harvard University Press.

Freeman, R. B. and Medoff, J. (1985). *What Do Unions Do?* New York: Basic Books.

Freeman, R. B. and Rogers, J. (1993). Who speaks for us? Employee representation in a nonunion labor market. In B. E. Kaufman and M. M. Kleiner (eds.), *Employee Representation: Alternatives and Future Directions*. Madison, WI: Industrial Relations Research Association.

Kochan, T. A. and Katz, H. C. (1986). *Collective Bargaining and Industrial Relations*. Homewood, IL: Richard D. Irwin.

Kochan, T. A., McKersie, R. B., and Chalykoff, J. (1986). The effects of corporate strategy and workplace innovations on union representation. *Industrial and Labor Relations Review*, 39, 487–501.

Kochan, T. A. and Osterman, P. (1994). *The Mutual Gains Enterprise*. Boston: Harvard Business School Press.

Sisson, K. (1993). In search of HRM. *British Journal of Industrial Relations*, 31, 201–10.

norms

Linda S. Gottfredson

A score on a standardized test is interpreted by comparing it to some external standard. When scores are compared to those of some reference population, they are called norm-referenced; when compared to some absolute performance standard, they are criterion-referenced. Norms are the distributions of scores (means, standard deviations, etc.) for a test's various reference groups. Normed test scores are most commonly reported as percentile ranks or standard scores, such as z, T, or IQ scores. Age- and grade-equivalents are sometimes reported, especially for achievement tests in elementary school, but they have more technical disadvantages and are prone to misinterpretation. Latent TRAIT or "scaled" scores provide a new form of developmental norms that solve some but not all the interpretive problems of age- and grade-equivalents.

Norm groups (also called reference groups, normative samples, or standardization samples) may be national or local, and represent different age, grade, or social groups. Broad or narrow, however, they must be representative of the populations in question, clearly defined and described, and appropriate for their intended purposes. Intelligence testing compares scores of children of the same age (*see* INTELLIGENCE TESTS). Academic achievement tests typically compare the scores of children in the same grade and often from the same school or geographic area. An employer might compare the aptitude scores of job applicants to those of individuals hired at particular plants in the last five years. PERSONALITY TESTS and VOCATIONAL INTEREST INVENTORIES often provide separate norms for males and females for COUNSELING purposes. The US CIVIL RIGHTS ACT OF 1991 outlawed the use of scores normed separately by race, color, religion, sex, or national origin for purposes of selection or referral in employment.

Bibliography

American Educational Research Association, American Psychological Association, and National Council on Measurement in Education (1999). *Standards for Educational and Psychological Testing*. Washington, DC: American Educational Research Association.

Cronbach, L. J. (1990). *Essentials of Psychological Testing*, 5th edn. New York: HarperCollins.

Kampaus, R. W. (1993). *Clinical Assessment of Children's Intelligence*. Boston: Allyn and Bacon.

Norris-LaGuardia Anti-Injunction Act of 1932

Charles E. Krider

The Norris-LaGuardia Act was passed by Congress to limit the ability of courts to intervene in labor disputes by issuing injunctions. The Act did not create any new rights for unions.

At the time Congress had passed no statutes, except for the RAILWAY LABOR ACT OF 1926, that either encouraged or discouraged unions. The courts, however, were able to intervene in labor disputes without statutory guidance by issuing injunctions to regulate tactics or objectives that were not viewed favorably. For example, a STRIKE for a union shop might have been subject to an injunction even if no statute made such an objective illegal. PICKETING and SECONDARY BOYCOTTS could be stopped by an injunction. Injunctions were almost always used by courts against unions, which gave rise to the charge that unions were subject to government by injunction.

The Norris-LaGuardia Act sought to limit injunctions by defining the term labor dispute more broadly than the Supreme Court had previously done. The key provision of the Norris-LaGuardia Act is that "No court of the United States shall have jurisdiction to issue any restraining order or temporary or permanent injunction in any case involving or growing out of any labor dispute." The term labor dispute was defined to include cases that involve persons (not just employees) "who are engaged in the same industry, trade, craft, or occupation; or have direct or indirect interests therein; or who are employees of the same employer; or who are members of the same or an affiliated organization of employers or employees." This made clear that the courts were *not* to narrowly construe the definition of a labor dispute, and, thereby, avoid the injunction prohibition of this Act. The Act did not affect the legality of union activities but only said federal courts could not issue injunctions.

The Act permits the issuance of an injunction in a few instances, particularly when there are unlawful acts or if there are substantial and irreparable injuries to property. This includes violent acts. Other exceptions are for a National Emergency Strike under the LABOR MANAGEMENT RELATIONS ACT OF 1947 and for strikes in violation of a no-strike promise.

The meaning of the Norris-LaGuardia Act is that the federal government for the first time in US history was neutral in disputes between unions and management. Each was able to use its economic power to achieve its labor relations objectives without the opposition or support of the federal courts. The time from 1932 to 1935 was a brief period of *laissez-faire* for unions and management. Governmental neutrality ended in 1935 with the passage of the NATIONAL LABOR RELATIONS ACT OF 1935, which encouraged unions and COLLECTIVE BARGAINING. The

Norris-LaGuardia Anti-Injunction Act also made "yellow dog" contracts illegal. These were promises made by employees that they were not union members and would not join a union during the duration of their employment.

Bibliography

Taylor, B. J. and Witney, F. (1992). *US Labor Relations Law*. Englewood Cliffs, NJ: Prentice-Hall.

occupational choice

Jeffrey H. Greenhaus

Occupational choice refers to the process by which individuals select an occupation or career field to pursue CAREER CHOICE. Comprehensive reviews of the theoretical approaches to occupational choice may be found in Brown and Brooks (1990) and Osipow (1990). An examination of the research on occupational choice and related phenomena is published annually in the October issue of the *Journal of Vocational Behavior*.

THEORETICAL APPROACHES TO THE STUDY OF OCCUPATIONAL CHOICE

Several different, although not mutually exclusive, theoretical perspectives on the occupational choice process have emerged over the years. One of the most popular has been the *matching approach*, which asserts that individuals tend to choose occupations that match their unique set of needs, motives, values, and talents. Holland's (1985) typology of personality and occupational environment and the work adjustment theory of Dawis and Lofquist (1984) are prominent examples of this approach.

The *developmental* approach views occupational choice as a process that unfolds and evolves over time. The most influential developmental perspective has been provided by Super (1990), who proposed that people progress through different stages of career development that permit them to form a self-concept and express that self-concept in an occupational decision.

Other researchers focus on the psychological *decision-making process* that guides a person in the selection of a specific occupation. This perspective has examined how people combine and weigh information about different occupations to arrive at an occupational choice, and has studied the reasons why people may become undecided about what occupational path to pursue. One decision-making approach, social learning theory, emphasizes the role of SELF-EFFICACY expectations – personal beliefs about competence in a particular area – in occupational choice (Hackett and Betz, 1981). It is believed that people tend to enter occupations for which they hold strong self-efficacy expectations.

ADDITIONAL ISSUES IN THE STUDY OF OCCUPATIONAL CHOICE

In addition to the ongoing development and refinement of theories on how people select occupations, it is expected that research will continue to address a number of significant and timely issues. One burgeoning area of study is the role of gender in occupational choice. It is increasingly questioned whether the theories on men's occupational choice are applicable to women or whether unique theories of women's occupational choices need to be developed (Fouad, 1994). A similar question has been raised about the occupational choices of American minorities (Smith, 1983). It is possible that the unique barriers and obstacles experienced by minority group members render traditional theories of occupational choice less relevant for this group. Finally, research on the occupational choices of adult employees is likely to expand in the years ahead. Corporate DOWNSIZING and restructuring will require adults of all ages to reevaluate their career goals and redirect their careers into different occupational areas. Considerable research will be required to help this growing segment of the population.

Bibliography

Brown, D. L. and Brooks, L. (eds.) (1990). *Career Choice and Development: Applying Contemporary Theories to Practice*. San Francisco: Jossey-Bass.

Dawis, R. V. and Lofquist, L. H. (1984). *A Psychological Theory of Work Adjustment*. Minneapolis: University of Minnesota Press.

Fouad, N. A. (1994). Annual review 1991–1993: Vocational choice, decision-making assessment, and intervention. *Journal of Vocational Behavior*, 45, 125–76.

Hackett, G. and Betz, N. E. (1981). A self-efficacy approach to the career development of women. *Journal of Vocational Behavior*, 18, 326–39.

Holland, J. L. (1985). *Making Vocational Choices: A Theory of Vocational Personalities and Work Environments*, 2nd edn. Englewood Cliffs, NJ: Prentice-Hall.

Osipow, S. H. (1990). Convergence in theories of career choice and development: Review and prospect. *Journal of Vocational Behavior*, 36, 122–31.

Smith, E. J. (1983). Issues in racial minorities' career behavior. In W. B. Walsh and S. H. Osipow (eds.), *Handbook of Vocational Psychology*, vol. 1. Hillsdale, NJ: Erlbaum.

Super, D. E. (1990). A life-span, life space approach to career development. In D. Brown and L. Brooks (eds.), *Career Choice and Development: Applying Contemporary Theories to Practice*. San Francisco: Jossey-Bass.

occupational injury/illness measurement

Donna E. Ledgerwood

In the past, measurement of occupational injuries was calculated strictly in terms of frequency rates and severity rates. The American National Standards Institute (ANSI) provides employers with voluntary guidelines for measuring and reporting these same factors, which today are called incidence rates. Incidence rates are also known as "safety ratios," and are defined as an injury/illness rate based upon 200,000 employee-hours, which is approximately the hours worked by 100 employees during a 50-week period at 40 hours per week (Editorial, 1993a, b). (For more information on incidence rates or safety ratios, contact the National Safety Council.)

New guidelines for hiring competent persons with relevant knowledge, skills, abilities, and other factors (*see* KSAOS) are being explicitly stated by standards of the ANSI. Related to the ANSI standards are the International Standards Organization's 9000 and 14,000 standards (*see* ISO 9000).

The world is becoming increasingly aware that health and safety standards are not theories which should be confined to the bookshelves of a safety officer or in the human resource department of a firm. These standards are the realities of all managers and should be a part of each employee's JOB DESCRIPTION and PERFORMANCE APPRAISAL.

Bibliography

Editorial (1993a). Council updates work-death statistics. *Safety and Health*, 147, 80–1.

Editorial (1993b). Council expands into global arena. *Safety and Health*, 147, 82–4.

Occupational Safety and Health Act of 1970

Vida Scarpello

The purpose of the Occupational Safety and Health Act of 1970 (OSHA) is to provide safe or healthful employment. The passage of OSHA was motivated by: (1) ineffectiveness of state workers' compensation laws as a means of solving safety and health problems; (2) inadequate safety and health regulation at the federal level; and (3) increased industrial injuries (Ledvinka and Scarpello, 1991).

OSHA covers nearly every private sector place of employment. The Act is reasonably brief and straightforward. Voluminous and technically complex, however, are the written regulations issued pursuant to OSHA.

Part 1 of section 5(a) specifies that each employer must provide each employee a place of employment that is free from recognized hazards which either are causing or are likely to cause serious physical harm or death. This mandate is usually referred to as the "general duty" clause because not only does it impose the obligation to comply with specific safety and health standards, promulgated under the Act, but it also imposes the general duty of eliminating safety and health hazards that are not covered by any standard (Ledvinka and Scarpello, 1991).

Part 2 of section 5(a) presents a different kind of burden on employers, that of comprehending and complying with an exceptionally long and detailed set of mandatory safety and health standards. Those standards, promulgated by the Secretary of Labor (section 6) are defined in section 3(8) of the Act as standards which are reasonably necessary or appropriate to providing safe or healthful employment. The employer is also obligated to allow the government to inspect the workplace at reasonable times (section 8(a)(1)); to investigate, and to question privately, employers, owners, operators, agents, or employees (section 8(a)(2)); to make available records regarding activities related to the Act (section 8(c)(1)); and to refrain from retaliating against employees who exercise their right to request inspections when they believe that there is a violation of a safety or health standard that threatens physical harm, or when they believe an imminent danger exists.

During congressional hearings on OSHA, management and unions agreed that health hazards were the major problems warranting government regulation (Ashford, 1976; Bingham, 1978; Mendeloff, 1979). Consequently, section 6(b)(7) mandates that any standard must prescribe use of labels or other warnings to insure that employees know of all hazards to which they are exposed and the consequences of those exposures. The hazard communication standard requires employers to inform and train all employees who may be exposed to hazardous chemicals, either during foreseeable emergencies or during their work routines, and to inform them when a new hazard is introduced into the workplace (Editorial, 1988). Additionally, the hazards communication standard states that employees must be provided with a master list of hazardous chemicals and told where those chemicals are located in the workplace. The employer must also keep material safety data sheets (MSDs) on all hazardous chemicals present in the workplace. Besides employer obligations, section 5(b) imposes a broad set of obligations on employees. Nevertheless, the Act does not contain penalties for violation of employee obligations. For all practical purposes, the OSHA law regulates employer compliance but not employee compliance.

OSHA is enforced and administered by a complicated regulatory apparatus with responsibilities divided among five agencies. These agencies are as follows.

1. The OCCUPATIONAL SAFETY AND HEALTH ADMINISTRATION, a branch of the US Department of Labor, is responsible for (a) establishing safety standards, (b) allowing variances from those standards, (c) conducting inspections of workplaces, (d) issuing citations for OSHA violations, (e) safety consultation, and (f) research of selected injuries.
2. The Occupational Safety and Health Review Commission (OSHRC) issues citations and thus operates as a trial court, similar to the way US district courts operate in violations of Title VII of the CIVIL RIGHTS ACT OF 1964 (Ledvinka and Scarpello, 1991).
3. US Court of Appeals, which serves as the appeal for OSHRC rulings.
4. NATIONAL INSTITUTE FOR OCCUPATIONAL SAFETY AND HEALTH (NIOSH), which has two principal functions: (a) training, with emphasis primarily on training OSHA inspectors and other personnel associated with OSHA enforcement; and (b) research into job safety and health, focused primarily toward creating new safety and health standards.
5. States, which have approved occupational safety and health plans. OSHA allows individual states to take over the responsibilities for occupational safety and health, provided the state's standards are at least as rigorous as those under the federal OSHA law.

Bibliography

Ashford, N. A. (1976). *Crisis in the Workplace: Occupational Disease and Injury*. Cambridge, MA: MIT Press.

Bingham, E. (1978). OSHA: Only beginning. *Labor Law Journal*, 29, 131–6.

Editorial (1988). *Occupational Safety and Health Reporter*, May 18, 1851.

Ledvinka, J. and Scarpello, V. (1991). *Federal Regulation of Personnel and Human Resource Management*. Boston: PWS-Kent.

Mendeloff, J. (1979). *Regulating Safety: An Economic and Political Analysis of Occupational Safety and Health Policy*. Cambridge, MA: MIT Press.

Occupational Safety and Health Administration

Donna E. Ledgerwood

As mandated in the OCCUPATIONAL SAFETY AND HEALTH ACT OF 1970, the Occupational Safety and Health Administration (OSHA) was established as a part of the Department of Labor. OSHA was given the responsibility for seven major activities:

1. to encourage employers and employees to reduce workplace hazards and to implement new or improve existing safety and health programs;
2. to provide for research in occupational safety and health to develop innovative ways of dealing with occupational safety and health problems;
3. to establish separate, but dependent, responsibilities and rights for employers and employees for the achievement of better safety and health conditions;
4. to maintain a reporting and record-keeping system to monitor job-related injuries and illness;
5. to establish training programs to increase the number and competence of occupational safety and health personnel;
6. to develop mandatory job safety and health standards and enforce them effectively; and
7. to provide for the development, analysis, evaluation, and approval of state occupational safety and health programs.

Basically, OSHA was established to set forth and to monitor safety and health programs related to workplace conditions within the physical parameters of the organization itself. The major areas of concern were to be studied and reported by the NATIONAL INSTITUTE FOR OCCUPATIONAL SAFETY AND HEALTH (NIOSH), along with recommendations to assist OSHA in enforcing these industry standards.

Standards which are industry-specific are called vertical standards, while general standards applying to all industries are called horizontal standards. The Code of Federal Regulations (CFR) is the vehicle which prints all vertical and horizontal federal standards. Guidelines for managing workplace safety are described in OSHA's pamphlet, *All About OSHA*, published by the US Department of Labor.

Bibliography

US Department of Labor, Occupational Safety and Health Administration (1991). *All About OSHA*. Washington, DC: US Department of Labor, Occupational Safety and Health Administration.

Office of Federal Contract Compliance Programs

Leonard Bierman

The Office of Federal Contract Compliance Programs (OFCCP) of the US Department of Labor enforces various presidential EXECUTIVE ORDERS relating to employment DISCRIMINATION and AFFIRMATIVE ACTION with respect to federal contractors. The principal executive order administered by the OFCCP is executive order 11246 promulgated by President Lyndon Johnson in 1965. The agency's most severe sanction is "debarment," or prohibiting a company from receiving federal government contracts. The role of the agency has come into question given recent US Supreme Court decisions limiting affirmative action programs in the context of federal government contracting.

on-the-job training

Timothy T. Baldwin

On-the-job training (OJT) involves assigning trainees to jobs and encouraging them to observe and learn from experienced job incumbents or supervisors. OJT is the most widely used training strategy and is favored for its low cost and the opportunity it provides for immediate feedback. It also facilitates positive transfer of training by allowing trainees to learn with the actual materials, personnel, and machinery that comprise the job. Unfortunately, OJT is often used haphazardly and its success is contingent on the capacity and willingness of job incumbents to take time from regular work duties to provide effective instruction and guidance.

See also *training*

organization development and change

Richard W. Woodman

Organization development and change, also known as organization development (OD), is a field of applied behavioral science focused on understanding and managing organizational change. OD is both a field of social and managerial action and a field of scientific inquiry (Cummings and Worley, 2001). The action side of the field is of greatest interest for human resource managers and professionals, although successful change programs rely on valid, scientifically acquired knowledge of individual, group, and organizational behavior. OD is not a single CHANGE MANAGEMENT technique, but rather a collection of techniques that have a certain philosophy and body of knowledge in common.

Definitions and Characteristics

Some formal definitions of organizational change and development help to frame the boundaries and identify the focus of the field. According to Cummings and Worley, OD "is a systemwide application of behavioral science knowledge to the planned development, improvement, and reinforcement of the strategies, structures, and processes that lead to organization effectiveness" (2001: 1). French and Bell focus on organizational participants: "Basically, organization development is a process for teaching people how to solve problems, take advantage of opportunities, and learn how to do that better and better over time" (1999: xiii). Woodman suggests that organization development and change "means creating adaptive organizations capable of repeatedly transforming and reinventing themselves as needed to remain effective" (1993: 73).

Organization development is typically characterized by: (1) developing individual commitment to needed change; (2) changing whole systems and processes, in contrast to piecemeal change approaches; (3) relying on action research and other collaborative change philosophies and techniques; and (4) emphasizing both organizational effectiveness and human fulfillment through the work experience. In addition, another key characteristic of OD is particularly instructive for the training function in organizations (*see* TRAINING). OD typically places equal emphasis on solving immediate organizational or work team problems and on the long-term development of an effective, adaptive organization. Thus, the most effective training, from the OD perspective, is that which not only helps employees solve current problems but also prepares them to solve future problems facing the organization.

Organization Development and Human Resource Management

Church, Waclawski, and Berr (2002) surveyed internal and external human resource management (HRM) and OD professionals with regard to what types of OD-related services are currently most in demand. Their respondents reported that executive coaching and development, team building and team effectiveness (*see* TEAM-BUILDING TRAINING), facilitating strategic organizational change, systemic integration of change initiatives, and diversity and multiculturalism programs were receiving the most attention.

In addition, surveys of the Fortune 500 industrials and the Fortune 500 service firms indicate that the practice of organization development, as well as the location of OD staff in these large corporations, is most commonly found within the HRM function (McMahan and Woodman, 1992). Further, among the change management issues identified by these surveys as crucial to organizational success is the problem of linking human resource activities to organizational strategy. The human resource training function can make major contributions to organizational effectiveness by linking with and supporting the firm's internal OD activities as well as the overall strategy and goals of the organization (Woodman and Pasmore, 2002). In general, the field of organization development and change provides a promising arena for human resource managers to contribute to organizational effectiveness.

Bibliography

Church, A. H., Waclawski, J., and Berr, S. A. (2002). Voices from the field: Future directions for organization development. In J. Waclawski and A. H. Church (eds.), *Organization Development: A Data-Driven Approach to Organizational Change.* San Francisco: Jossey-Bass, pp. 321–36.

Cummings, T. G. and Worley, C. G. (2001). *Organization Development and Change*, 7th edn. Cincinnati, OH: South-Western Publishing.

French, W. L. and Bell, C. H. (1999). *Organization Development: Behavioral Science Interventions for Organization Improvement*, 6th edn. Upper Saddle River, NJ: Prentice-Hall.

McMahan, G. C. and Woodman, R. W. (1992). The current practice of organization development with the firm. *Group and Organization Management*, 17, 117–34.

Woodman, R. W. (1993). Observations on the field of organizational change and development from the lunatic fringe. *Organization Development Journal*, 11, 71–4.

Woodman, R. W. and Pasmore, W. A. (2002). The heart of it all: Group- and team-based interventions in organization development. In J. Waclawski and A. H. Church (eds.), *Organization Development: A Data-Driven Approach to Organizational Change*. San Francisco: Jossey-Bass, pp. 164–76.

organizational culture and selection

Benjamin Schneider and D. Brent Smith

The predominant model for PERSONNEL SELECTION is one based on a fit or match of people's knowledge, skills, abilities, and other characteristics (*see* KSAOS) to the demands of a job. While this approach has proven effective for the prediction of JOB PERFORMANCE, there are other kinds of performance, referred to as "contextual performance" (Motowidlo and Van Scotter, 1994), that are necessary for an organization to survive and prosper. Behaviors consistent with contextual performance include cooperating with others, protecting the organization from harm, offering suggestions for improvement, and so forth. While an organization can promote such a culture by erecting policies, practices, procedures, and REWARD SYSTEMS consistent with the display of contextual behaviors, it can also be facilitated through the selection of people most likely to display these behaviors.

Most consider the maintenance and perpetuation of organizational culture a byproduct of the process of socialization and acculturation (*see* ORGANIZATIONAL SOCIALIZATION) whereby the basic values and beliefs of an organization are transmitted to and subsequently internalized by newcomers. The culture to which newcomers are exposed is, in turn, maintained by the policies, practices, procedures, and reward systems that have emerged over time in the organization. Both the traditional personnel selection model that focuses on task performance and the socialization and acculturation models of newcomer entry have ignored the potential for hiring people who will display contextual performance in their everyday behavior. Thus, as Schein (1992: 243) suggests, "One of the most subtle yet most potent ways through which cultural assumptions get embedded and perpetuated is the process of selecting new members." Schneider (1987) places similar emphasis on the importance of selection for the preservation of organizational culture, as do Bowen, Ledford, and Nathan (1991).

There is mounting evidence to indicate that organizations might be able to select newcomers who are more likely to display the kinds of contextual performance organizations require. O'Reilly, Chatman, and Caldwell (1991), for example, have shown that when people's values fit the values of the organizational culture they are more committed to the organization – and more committed people display higher levels of contextual performance. Motowidlo and Van Scotter (1994) have shown that personality attributes (such as dependability, cooperativeness, and internal control) predict contextual performance more strongly than they predict task performance. While there is as yet sparse literature on the relationship between culture and selection, these few studies suggest that particular personalities are more likely to display contextual performance and, further, that people whose values fit the culture of the organization are also more likely to display these behaviors.

Although there are certainly positive consequences associated with increased contextual performance, one caveat is worth noting. To the extent that contextual performance is promulgated, "healthy dissent" may be suppressed because it runs counter to the prevailing values embedded in the organization's culture. Reminiscent of the predictions of Schneider's ATTRACTION–SELECTION–ATTRITION model, Borman and Motowidlo (1992: 94) caution that when contextual criteria are valued in the extreme, it could lead to "a severely homogeneous, inbred organization and inhibit its ability to be flexible and to change when market or other external factors require a sharp departure from the status quo."

Bibliography

Borman, W. C. and Motowidlo, S. J. (1992). Expanding the criterion domain to include elements of contextual performance. In N. Schmitt and W. Borman (eds.), *Personnel Selection in Organizations*. San Francisco: Jossey-Bass.

Bowen, D. E., Ledford, G. E., and Nathan, B. E. (1991). Hiring for the organization, not the job. *Academy of Management Executive*, **5**, 35–51.

Motowidlo, S. J. and Van Scotter, J. R. (1994). Evidence that task performance should be distinguished from contextual performance. *Journal of Applied Psychology*, **79**, 475–80.

O'Reilly, C. A., Chatman, J., and Caldwell, D. F. (1991). People and organizational culture: A profile comparison approach to assessing person–organization fit. *Academy of Management Journal*, **34**, 487–516.

Schein, E. H. (1992). *Organizational Culture and Leadership*. San Francisco: Jossey-Bass.

Schneider, B. (1987). The people make the place. *Personnel Psychology*, **40**, 437–54.

organizational socialization

Cynthia D. Fisher

Organizational socialization is the process of learning the ropes in an organization, or moving from naive newcomer to fully informed insider. As newcomers become socialized, they learn about the organization and its history, values, jargon, culture, and procedures. They also learn about their work group, the specific people they work with on a daily basis, their own role in the organization, the skills needed to do their job, and both formal procedures and informal norms. Socialization functions as a control system in that newcomers learn to internalize and obey organizational values and practices.

Socialization takes place over weeks or months. It occurs through both formal methods, such as NEW EMPLOYEE ORIENTATION, TRAINING, coaching, and MENTORING PROGRAMS, and by informal methods, such as advice from coworkers, observation, experience, and trial and error.

Some authors have distinguished three stages in the socialization process. The first stage is anticipatory socialization, and includes the learning and adaptations newcomers make prior to actually joining the organization. The selection process can be one source of information about the organization, and correct anticipatory socialization should be facilitated by REALISTIC JOB PREVIEWS. The second stage is sometimes called "encounter." In this stage, the newcomer may suffer from reality shock and unconfirmed expectations if anticipatory socialization was found to be inaccurate. This is often a traumatic period of rapid learning, during which the newcomer is regarded as a rookie by others in the organization. The third stage has been called mutual acceptance, adaptation, or metamorphosis. In this stage, the newcomer makes a place for himself or herself and becomes accepted as a full insider. The newcomer may change his or her values or work styles to fit the organization, but also may negotiate some accommodation by the organization for his or her own preferences.

Effective socialization results in greater JOB SATISFACTION, organizational commitment, and self-confidence at work, and reduces stress and the likelihood of EMPLOYEE TURNOVER.

Bibliography

Chao, G. T., O'Leary-Kelly, A. M., Wolf, S., Klein, H. J., and Gardner, P. D. (1994). Organizational socialization: Its contents and consequences. *Journal of Applied Psychology*, **79**, 730–43.

Fisher, C. D. (1986). Organizational socialization: An integrative review. *Research in Personnel and Human Resource Management*, **4**, 101–45.

Saks, A. M. and Ashforth, B. E. (1997). Organizational socialization: Making sense of the past and present as a prologue for the future. *Journal of Vocational Behavior*, **51**, 234–79.

Wanous, J. P. (1992). *Organizational Entry: Recruitment, Selection, Orientation and Socialization of Newcomers*. Reading, MA: Addison-Wesley.

outplacement

Mark L. Lengnick-Hall

Outplacement is the process by which an individual whose employment has been terminated makes the transition from one employer to another work situation with the assistance of reemployment professionals and appropriate support services, provided by the former employer (Lee, 1991). In its most basic form, the purpose of outplacement is to help a terminated employee find a new job or career. While assistance is offered, the responsibility for finding a new job or changing careers remains with the employee. In addition to job and career counseling, outplacement services typically include some form of emotional support and assistance in coping with the stress of JOB LOSS.

About 90 percent of all major companies now use outplacement, as do a great many smaller organizations (Lee, 1991). Men are the predominant recipients of outplacement services. Women who receive outplacement services tend to be younger than men by about five years, and they are more often single (Lee, 1991). Worldwide, women represent a very small percentage of outplacement recipients, largely due to their underrepresentation in the managerial and professional workforce.

Outplacement is a relatively recent organizational activity. The earliest efforts to provide outplacement occurred after World War II in the US, when the armed forces greatly reduced their numbers. However, outplacement did not become a common practice in business organizations until the 1980s.

Researchers have theorized that terminated employees react to job loss and unemployment through a series of stages (Latack and Dozier, 1986). Stages of job loss include: (1) denial (refusal to believe in the reality of the situation); (2) grief and depression (questioning personal competence, feelings of guilt); (3) anger (blaming others and the organization for creating the situation); and (4) acceptance (willingness to let the past go, taking from it the experience needed to build one's future). Stages of unemployment include: (1) relaxation and relief (a release of the tension built up as the individual anticipated the layoff and a chance to catch up without the daily pressure of a job); (2) concerted effort (an optimistic JOB SEARCH campaign); (3) vacillation and doubt (questioning EMPLOYABILITY and anger at continued unemployment); and (4) resignation (withdrawal and reduced and infrequent job seeking).

Outplacement activities are designed to ease the difficulties associated with job loss and unemployment. Key components of outplacement programs include: (1) departure assistance; (2) personal support; (3) career assessment and counsel; (4) personal assessment and counsel; (5) career planning; (6) job search; (7) marketing counsel; and (8) administrative services (Lee, 1991). Outplacement services can be provided in-house or contracted out to a consulting service. The primary advantage of providing in-house outplacement services is lower costs. Consulting services typically charge organizational clients a fee of 15 percent of the individual employee's total annual COMPENSATION, and there may be additional administrative charges. The duration of services provided can range from two weeks to 18 months or more. Consulting services offer some advantages that cannot be achieved through in-house outplacement. For example, consulting services provide professional advice on proper pre-termination planning, consulting services can provide terminated employees more candid feedback about reasons for their termination, the human resource staff is relieved from much of the time-consuming details, and the consulting service provides space away from the organization for the terminated employee to use during outplacement activities.

Programs for senior executives, middle managers and professionals, and first-level supervisors usually differ in form and content. Senior employees receive longer, more individualized outplacement benefits than more junior employees. According to the Corporate Leadership Council (CLC) brief (2002), which focused on the pharmaceutical industry, companies offer counseling sessions and office space either off-site or on a different floor for senior employees. Counseling sessions can include assessment workshops to understand if exiting employees want to change their field, and/or interpersonal reflection to help employees deal with job loss. Another CLC study (2001) looked at outplacement trends in the energy (utilities), consumer products, and heavy manufacturing industries. They also found that the outplacement benefit depended on the employee's corporate grade and salary level. Senior officers could receive up to $30,000 in customized services, and nonexempt employees receive approximately $3,000 in basic services such as workshops in interviewing skills and resume writing. In some companies, officers may receive different outplacement help contingent on stipulations in their employment contracts or employees can negotiate their outplacement deal.

Both the organization and the individual may benefit from effective outplacement services (Lee, 1991). According to Drake Beam Morin, a leading provider of strategic human resource solutions, the top five benefits of outplacement to the organization are that it:

1   improves the organization's internal and external image (78 percent);
2   helps reduce litigation (72 percent);
3   reduces stress on managers responsible for implementing organizational changes (68 percent);
4   provides a good return on investment (64 percent);
5   improves the morale of retained employees (59 percent).

The individual benefits by: (1) receiving professional support to adjust to the job loss; (2) receiving assistance in career planning, self-assessment, and job search strategies; and (3) having access to resources, such as databases, reference libraries, personal computers, and so forth.

Organizations should have outplacement policies before the need arises. Several issues addressed ahead of time can facilitate effective and efficient delivery when needed. Outplacement policies should clarify: (1) who is eligible to receive it; (2) what services are provided; (3) the duration of services provided; and (4) how services will be provided.

Research suggests that outplacement activities can be effective. One study (Stybel, 1981) compared two groups of 60 persons, in which one group received outplacement while the other did not receive any assistance. At the end of three months, 90 percent of the employees who received outplacement had obtained jobs, while only 55 percent of the other group had obtained jobs. The average salary was 36 percent higher for the employees who receive outplacement. In a US Department of Labor study (Wegman, 1979), 1,000 persons were assigned to one of five job search assistance programs or to a control group receiving no assistance. The job search assistance groups were almost twice as likely to be successful as the control group.

In summary, outplacement is a human resource program designed to ease the transition of a terminated employee to another job or career. It can benefit both the organization and the terminated employee. Specific outplacement programs differ, depending upon the managerial level of the employee (executive, middle, and so forth) and occupational type (e.g., professional versus nonprofessional). While some organizations may choose to provide outplacement services in-house and thereby reduce their costs, others prefer to hire outside consulting services, which offer additional benefits at a greater cost. Even though little research has been done on this human resource practice, evidence suggests that outplacement activities can improve the probabilities of terminated employees' reemployment.

Bibliography

Latack, J. C. and Dozier, J. B. (1986). After the ax falls: Job loss as a career transition. *Academy of Management Review*, **11**, 375.

Lee, R. J. (1991). Outplacement counseling for the terminated manager. In J. W. Jones, B. D. Steffy, and D. W. Bray (eds.), *Applying Psychology in Business: The Handbook for Managers and Human Resource Professionals*. Lexington, MA: Lexington Books, pp. 489–508.

Stybel, L. J. (1981). How managers react to their own dismissal: Implications for intervention theory and practice. Paper presented at the Academy of Management Conference, August.

Wegman, R. (1979). Job search assistance: A review. *Journal of Employment Counseling*, **12**, 197–225.

P

paid time off

Robert M. McCaffery

When the US shifted from an agrarian to an industrial society in the nineteenth century the tradition of long hours of work (from dawn to dusk) continued. Vacations and holidays, with or without pay, were rarely granted to workers. Later, management became aware that work without rest could adversely affect PRODUCTIVITY. This led to a shortening of the work week and a variety of provisions for paid time off.

Today employees at all levels and in all industries receive a set of paid time off allowances. Typically these payments cost employers 10 to 12 percent of payroll and include:

1. Vacations – from one to five weeks per year depending on length of service.
2. Holidays – from eight to 14 days per year (employees in retailing tend to receive the fewest number of days, public sector employees the most).
3. Sick days (*see* GROUP DISABILITY BENEFITS) – a maximum of five to 130 days per year, depending on length of service and level.
4. Jury duty – the difference between regular pay and court payments for up to two or three weeks.
5. Short-term military service – the difference between regular pay and military pay.
6. Funeral leave – three days per incident for the immediate family, one day for other relatives.
7. Severance pay – minimally one or two weeks of extended pay or a lump sum payment (greater allowances for long service and management employees); severance pay may supplement unemployment compensation.

A recent innovation is the concept of "total time off" (TTO), which combines many of the above categories into a single annual allowance. Also some industries (e.g., automobiles and steel) have reduced paid time off in an effort to improve productivity and become more competitive with foreign (especially Japanese) manufacturers.

Bibliography

Employee Benefit Research Institute (1995). *EBRI Databook on Employee Benefits*, 3rd edn. Washington, DC: Employee Benefit Research Institute.

McCaffery, R. M. (1983). *Managing the Employee Benefits Program*, rev. edn. New York: AMACOM.

US Chamber of Commerce (annual). *Employee Benefits*. Washington, DC: US Chamber of Commerce.

part-time employment

Jill Rubery

Part-time employment implies an average working week shorter than the standard – or full-time – week in the same job. Part-time work is associated with the service sector and with female employment, but its incidence varies (O'Reilly and Fagan, 1998; Rubery, Smith, and Fagan, 1999) according to country-specific patterns of industrial organization, labor market regulation, and gender relations (Pfau-Effinger, 1998). Part-time work adds to the flexibility of employment arrangements, allowing for variations in working and operating time at lower costs than full-time work. Its advantages to employers include the opportunity to adjust labor hours to meet variable demand during the day or week, to extend operating hours, to cover unsocial hours, and to increase work intensity through minimizing paid rest periods. Other advantages include opportunities to minimize employment during periods of slack demand, to reduce variable and overhead costs through paying lower basic pay rates, and to exclude part-timers from BONUSES, unsocial hours premia, fringe benefits, or social protection contributions.

Under European law, application of inferior terms and conditions for part-timers may be regarded as indirect DISCRIMINATION against women. Part-time work can be used to meet employee needs, to facilitate women staying in or reentering employment, to provide employment opportunities for students, or a transition into retirement. Even so, the question remains as to whether part-time work is a bridge, facilitating access to employment, or a trap (Buchtemann and Quack, 1989), confining workers, particularly women, to low-paid jobs with limited career prospects.

See also *part-time work schedule*

Bibliography

Buchtemann, C. and Quack, S. (1989). Bridges or traps? Non-standard employment in the Federal Republic of Germany. In G. Rodgers and J. Rodgers (eds.), *Precarious Jobs in Labor Market Regulation: The Growth of Atypical Employment in Western Europe*. Geneva: International Labor Organization.

O'Reilly, J. and Fagan, C. (eds.) (1998). *Part-Time Prospects: Part-Time Work in Europe, North America and the Pacific Rim*. London: Routledge.

Pfau-Effinger, B. (1998). Culture or structure as explanations for differences in part-time work in Germany, Finland and the Netherlands? In J. O'Reilly and C. Fagan (eds.), *Part-Time Prospects: Part-Time Work in Europe, North America and the Pacific Rim*. London: Routledge.

Rubery, J., Smith, M., and Fagan, C. (1999). *Women's Employment in Europe: Trends and Prospects*. London: Routledge.

part-time work schedule

Stanley Nollen

A part-time work schedule consists of two different STAFFING and scheduling options. First, it is regular, voluntary employment with fewer hours of work per day, week, month, or year than normal full-time employment. Regular part-time employees have stable work schedules, prorated pay and BENEFITS, and as much expectation of continuing employment as full-time employees. Second, PART-TIME EMPLOYMENT is CONTINGENT EMPLOYMENT consisting of casual or hourly paid work without job security, regular work hours, or benefits; it may be chosen by employees who have other primary interests, or it may be involuntary because no other employment is available.

pattern bargaining

Daniel G. Gallagher

Pattern bargaining is an approach to COLLECTIVE BARGAINING where the objective is to spread the terms of employment achieved in one union–management relationship to other bargaining relationships within an industry (automotive, rubber, airlines, and so forth). In pattern bargaining a union negotiates a favorable or "model" agreement with a single employer (or one firm). The union subsequently seeks to reach similar wage and contract terms with other firms in the industry with which the union has a bargaining relationship. Pattern bargaining may also reflect NEGOTIATION TACTICS within one company. The union (or the employer) in a decentralized bargaining arrangement seeks to apply an early contractual settlement to other sites within the same company.

Bibliography

Ready, K. J. (1990). Is pattern bargaining dead? *Industrial and Labor Relations Review*, 43, 272–9.

pattern or practice cases

Ramona L. Paetzold

Technically, "pattern or practice" cases are brought by the US government under section 707 of Title VII of the CIVIL RIGHTS ACT OF 1964. In these cases the EQUAL EMPLOYMENT OPPORTUNITY COMMISSION (in its role as plaintiff) must prove that DISCRIMINATION against a protected group results from the employer's usual practices or standard operating procedures (i.e., that there is a "pattern or practice" of discrimination on the part of the employer).

Private plaintiffs may bring a close analogue of "pattern or practice" suits by filing class action discrimination suits. In class action suits, the plaintiff class must establish a pattern of discrimination based on its protected group membership. If successful, the burden of persuasion shifts to the employer to try to show that individual class members were not discriminated against. The employer will not be liable to those individuals whom it can establish were not recipients of discriminatory treatment.

Pattern or practice cases should not be confused with systemic DISPARATE TREATMENT cases. Pattern or practice cases refer to situations in which discrimination is alleged against an entire protected group; systemic disparate treatment refers to a model of proof in which statistical evidence is used to establish disparate treatment discrimination. Thus, if pattern or practice cases rely primarily on anecdotal treatment of individual class members, they are not systemic disparate treatment cases, but can be viewed as multiple individual disparate treatment cases joined together. Pattern or practice cases coincide with systemic disparate treatment cases when the pattern or practice is primarily established through the use of statistical analysis of the employer's conduct.

pay for knowledge, skills, and competencies

Gerald E. Ledford, Jr.

Plans that pay employees for their knowledge, skills, and competencies are called pay for knowledge, pay for learning, skill-based pay, and many other names. Here we use the shorthand "skill-based pay" and "SBP" to refer to these plans.

SBP plans pay employees for their repertoire of knowledge, skills, and competencies, not the job they are performing at one point in time. Pay increases are associated with increases in knowledge, skills, or competencies that the organization values, not job changes or increased seniority. Typically, employees must pass some type of formal certification of increased skill before obtaining pay increases. This contrasts with JOB-BASED PAY systems, where pay typically changes immediately when the job changes. Advancement opportunities for employees tend to be greater under SBP than under job-based pay.

Different types of learning may be rewarded through SBP. Skill depth reflects increasing knowledge about one topic. The skilled trades apprenticeship systems and the technical ladder for professionals are examples of depth-oriented SBP systems. Skill breadth refers to increasing knowledge that is relevant to but different from the employee's job or position. For example, employees may be rewarded for learning all the jobs in a work team or manufacturing plant. This is the form most commonly associated with the term "skill-based pay." SBP plans may also reward the development of self-management skills.

Skill-based pay is the most widely used form of person-based pay. In 1993, 60 percent of Fortune 1,000 firms used SBP with at least some employees, up from 40 percent in 1987 (Lawler, Mohrman, and Ledford, 1995). Firms using SBP typically cover less than 20 percent of the workforce. SBP plans are now found in every type of manufacturing and service delivery technology and in almost every kind of organizational setting (Jenkins et al., 1992).

Research on skill-based pay is limited. Available research includes survey studies, including one survey of 97 SBP plans (Jenkins et al., 1992), and some case studies (e.g., Ledford, 1991). The results suggest that employees tend to respond favorably to skill-based pay. Most organizations using SBP report few problems and a wide variety of organizational benefits, such as increased PRODUCTIVITY and quality. These benefits appear to result from employee flexibility and the facilitation of employee self-management. A consistent finding is that SBP appears more often and is more successful in settings with a high level of EMPLOYEE INVOLVEMENT.

An area of great practitioner interest is the application of the concept to knowledge workers, such as managers and professionals (*see* KNOWLEDGE WORK). The SBP concept often is relabeled "competency-based pay" in these settings. There is virtually no research on this type of pay system. Boyatzis's (1982) study of managerial competencies is the foundation for much consulting practice in this area. The differences in the nature of professional work have led to the evolution of new forms of SBP (Ledford, 1995). For example, employees in some firms negotiate learning contracts as part of the PERFORMANCE APPRAISAL system. Others reward employees with BONUSES rather than base pay increases where the underlying knowledge base quickly becomes obsolete.

See also *skill-based pay design*

Bibliography

Boyatzis, R. E. (1982). *The Competent Manager: A Model of Effective Performance*. New York: John Wiley.

Jenkins, G. D., Jr., Ledford, G. E., Jr., Gupta, N., and Doty, D. H. (1992). *Skill-Based Pay: Practices, Payoffs, Pitfalls, and Prospects*. Scottsdale, AZ: American Compensation Association.

Lawler, E. E., III, Mohrman, S. A., and Ledford, G. E., Jr. (1995). *Creating High Performance Organizations: Practices and Results of Employee Involvement and Total Quality Management in Fortune 1,000 Companies*. San Francisco: Jossey-Bass.

Ledford, G. E., Jr. (1991). Three case studies on skill-based pay: An overview. *Compensation and Benefits Review*, 23, 11–23.

Ledford, G. E., Jr. (1995). Paying for the skills, knowledge, and competencies of knowledge workers. *Compensation and Benefits Review*, 27, 55–62.

pay for performance

Ian Kessler

Pay for performance, defined as the explicit link of financial reward to individual performance, covers a variety of different pay systems. These systems do, however, share a common structure. Any performance-based pay scheme is founded upon three features: (1) setting performance criteria for the individual employee; (2) assessing whether those criteria have been met; and (3) linking the assessment to financial reward. The various types of systems can be distinguished using these three features. Performance criteria may be related to what the individual brings to the job in terms of behavioral traits or competences (*see* MERIT PAY) or more tangible outputs, targets, or goals (*see* BONUSES).

The assessment of those criteria may take different forms in terms of who carried it out (line manager, personnel specialist, peers), when it is carried out (once a year or more frequently), and how it is conducted (formally or informally). The linking of the assessment to reward may be through a consolidated or nonconsolidated payment and a general cost of living increase may or may not be incorporated. There has been much rhetoric surrounding the value and viability of pay for performance. Policy-makers in Britain, for example, have been strongly supportive of the principle. Other commentators, including some of the major management gurus, such as Deming, Peters, and Moss Kanter, have been more critical, highlighting its negative impact upon teamwork and cooperation.

Beyond the rhetoric, the evidence suggests that in the US pay for performance is extensive, while in Britain it is spreading. A survey by the American Association in the late 1980s found that practically all firms relied on annual PERFORMANCE APPRAISAL by supervisors as an input into pay decisions. In Britain, the Workplace Employment Relations survey found that 37 percent of manual workers and 44 percent of nonmanual staff were covered by some form of payment by results (Millward, Bryson and Forth, 2000).

It is nevertheless apparent that paying for individual performance is to some degree culturally bound. The Anglo-American emphasis on rewarding individual performance is not matched in certain eastern countries. Trompenaars (1993) has stressed the limited attraction of such a pay system in Japan, where seniority and group-based pay have predominated (*see* JAPAN).

The managerial reasons for introducing performance-related pay have varied. It has been used as an ad hoc and opportunistic response to immediate pressures (Smith, 1992). Thus, in Britain many organizations have implemented such schemes as a way of RECRUITING and retaining scarce staff groups. Alternatively, some have sought to control their paybill more effectively through targeted pay increases. Other organizations have used pay for performance more strategically to develop a performance culture, to encourage communication between managers and their staff, to facilitate the development of certain management skills, and to foster greater employee commitment (Kessler, 2001).

A number of operational difficulties with such schemes have been highlighted. Major problems have been noted in setting performance criteria for employees involved, for example, in routine or caring work. Subjectivity has been a major concern in relation to assessment. Moreover, the limited amounts of money devoted to paying for performance have often been too small to motivate.

The effectiveness of pay for performance has been challenged by studies which suggest that pay for performance has very little positive impact on motivation (Thompson, 1993). At the same time it is clear that many of the objectives underlying the use of performance pay are less easily measured. The use of performance pay to pursue the longer-term goal of changing organization culture suggests that such schemes may well have considerable life left in them yet.

See also *pay for performance plans*

Bibliography

Kessler, I. (2001). Reward system choice. In J. Storey (ed.), *Human Resource Management: A Critical Text*. London: Thomson.

Millward, N., Bryson, A., and Forth, J. (2000). *All Change at Work?* London: Routledge.

Smith, I. (1992). Reward management and HRM. In P. Turnbull and P. Blyton (eds.), *Reassessing Human Resource Management*. London: Sage.

Thompson, M. (1993). *Performance Related Pay: The Employee Experience*. Brighton: Institute of Manpower Studies.

Trompenaars, F. (1993). *Riding the Waves of Culture*. London: Economist Books.

pay for performance plans

Robert L. Heneman

PAY FOR PERFORMANCE is defined as the rewarding of employee contributions to organizations with pay (Milkovich and Newman, 1993). Pay for performance is the policy which guides performance-based pay, REWARD SYSTEMS, INCENTIVE PAY, MERIT PAY, and some pay innovations. The policy of pay for performance draws upon reinforcement theory. Pay for performance plans are increasingly being used by organizations as a source of competitive advantage.

Pay for performance plans vary by type of measure and level of measurement. Types of measures for contribution include skill blocks, PERFORMANCE APPRAISAL, sales, costs, time, profits, output, and PRODUCTIVITY. Levels at which the contribution can be measured include the individual, group or team, and organizational. Several pay for performance plans are commonly used. Merit pay provides pay for performance appraisal at the individual level. PIECEWORK provides pay for service and goods output at the individual level. SKILL-BASED PAY DESIGN methods reward individuals for the mastery of skill blocks. Standard hour (*see* STANDARD HOUR PLAN) and TIME-BASED PAY provide rewards for the time individuals spend at work. COMMISSION-BASED PAY provides pay for individual sales. Team-based pay (*see* TEAM-BASED INCENTIVES) pays for team-level outputs. GAINSHARING plans, including the RUCKER PLAN and SCANLON PLAN, pay for group-level outcomes such as labor costs and productivity. PROFIT SHARING pays on the basis of the profitability of the entire organization. BONUSES can be awarded at individual, team, group, or organizational levels.

Pay for performance plans have been subject to considerable study over the years (Schuster and Zingheim, 1992). The research indicates that while pay for performance is a preferred method of granting pay increases in the US, managers are more in favor of pay for performance plans than are employees. Pay for performance plans have been shown to be related to improved attitudes, behaviors, and financial outcomes (Lawler, 1971; McAdams and Hawk, 1994). Some research suggests that pay for performance plans may lower employees' satisfaction with the job itself (Deci, 1972; *see* JOB SATISFACTION).

In order for pay for performance plans to be effective, several conditions must be met. First, the pay for performance plan must be consistent with STRATEGIC HUMAN RESOURCE PLANNING and the corporate culture. Second, there must be EMPLOYEE EMPOWERMENT. Third, performance measures must be criterion relevant (see CRITERION RELEVANCE), accurate, and free from RATING ERRORS.

Bibliography

Deci, E. L. (1972). The effects of contingent and noncontingent rewards and controls on intrinsic motivation. *Organizational Behavior and Human Performance*, 8, 217–29.

Lawler, E. E., III (1971). *Pay and Organizational Effectiveness: A Psychological View*. New York: McGraw-Hill.

McAdams, J. L. and Hawk, E. J. (1994). *Organizational Performance and Rewards: 665 Experiences in Making the Link*. Scottsdale, AZ: American Compensation Association.

Milkovich, G. T. and Newman, J. M. (1993). *Compensation*. Homewood, IL: Richard D. Irwin.

Schuster, J. R. and Zingheim, P. K. (1992). *The New Pay*. New York: Lexington Books.

pay grade

Jerry M. Newman

Pay grades are classes into which jobs of similar value to the firm are grouped. Because job evaluation is a somewhat subjective process (see JOB EVALUATION METHODS), small differences in the value of jobs may be attributable to subjective error. To lessen the impact of this error on job holders, jobs of similar value (as determined by job evaluation) are grouped together. Jobs in the same pay grade have the same minimum worth, the same maximum worth, and movement between these two figures depends on individual performance and other measures of individual worth.

pay satisfaction

Robert L. Heneman

Pay satisfaction is defined as the amount of positive or negative feelings that individuals have toward their pay (Miceli and Lane, 1991). It can be measured using the pay satisfaction questionnaire (PSQ), which is broken down into several pay dimensions toward which individuals have feelings (Heneman and Schwab, 1985). These dimensions are pay level, pay raise, BENEFITS, and structure or administration. Satisfaction with pay level is the perceived satisfaction with direct wages or salaries, whereas satisfaction with pay raises refers to perceived satisfaction with changes in pay level. Satisfaction with structure or administration is defined as perceived satisfaction with the internal pay grades (see PAY GRADE) and with the methods used to distribute pay. Satisfaction with benefits concerns perceived satisfaction with indirect payments to the employees.

Pay satisfaction is important as research has shown it to be related to ABSENTEEISM, EMPLOYEE TURNOVER, and union vote (Heneman, 1985). Possible causes of pay satisfaction include perceived and actual job characteristics (e.g., autonomy), person characteristics (e.g., seniority), and pay plan characteristics (e.g., JOB EVALUATION METHODS, PAY SECRECY, MERIT PAY, pay innovations, REWARD SYSTEMS). Each dimension of pay satisfaction may have different causes. Hence, for example, the amount of dental insurance offered by an employer is likely to impact benefits satisfaction, but not impact satisfaction with structure or administration.

Bibliography

Heneman, H. G., III (1985). Pay satisfaction. In G. R. Ferris and K. M. Rowland (eds.), *Research in Personnel and Human Resources Management*, vol. 3. Greenwich, CT: JAI Press.

Heneman, H. G., III and Schwab, D. P. (1985). Pay satisfaction: Its multidimensional nature and measurement. *International Journal of Psychology*, 20, 129–41.

Miceli, M. P. and Lane, M. C. (1991). Antecedents of pay satisfaction: A review and extension. In G. R. Ferris and K. M. Rowland (eds.), *Research in Personnel and Human Resources Management*, vol. 9. Greenwich, CT: JAI Press.

pay secrecy

Steve H. Barr

An important element of a COMPENSATION plan is the decision of whether to allow organizational members to know the wage or salary levels of others in their group or organization. *Private* pay plans, also known as closed plans, generally ask employees to not discuss their compensation levels with their peers. Proponents of this approach note that the contract (formal or implied) between employee and employer is a private matter. *Public* pay plans, referred to as open plans, allow members information about the compensation levels of others. Proponents of this approach note that individuals compare their wage/salary levels to others regularly to insure that they are being treated equitably. Thus, allowing some information may decrease common misperceptions about how others are compensated.

peer ratings

Walter C. Borman

To obtain peer evaluations of JOB PERFORMANCE in organizations, typically coworkers of the organization member to be evaluated are asked to rate him or her on overall performance or on multiple dimensions of performance (job knowledge, planning and organizing, etc.). Reasons for generating peer ratings include providing feedback on performance, obtaining criterion scores for selection or other kinds of research, making predictions of future performance, providing information to aid in PROMOTION decisions and salary allocation, or some other administrative action.

An advantage of peer assessment (relative to SUPERVISORY RATINGS) is that often peers work more closely with the organization member being evaluated than does his or her supervisor. Thus, peers should have better knowledge of his or her performance. A disadvantage is that peers will often have less experience than supervisors of making performance evaluations; therefore, they may tend to provide ratings with more error or bias (*see* RATING BIAS; RATING ERRORS).

The quality of peer ratings has usually been evaluated according to inter-rater reliability (i.e., how closely two or more peers agree in their independent evaluations of the same organization members), agreement with other rating sources (e.g., supervisor or SELF-RATINGS), leniency (i.e., whether the ratings are overly high; *see* LENIENCY EFFECTS), or, when appropriate, accuracy regarding the prediction of subsequent performance (*see* RATING ACCURACY). We now summarize the results in each of these areas.

Kane and Lawler (1978) reviewed 14 studies using peer ratings and found a mean inter-rater reliability of 0.45. This is not very high, but it suggests at least a moderate level of agreement between peer raters evaluating the same persons. Regarding agreement across different rating sources, Harris and Schaubroeck (1988) conducted a meta-analysis of inter-rater agreement across supervisor, peer, and self-ratings. Results for peer ratings were: mean peer–supervisor reliability = 0.62; mean peer–self reliability = 0.35. The peer–supervisor agreement results are encouraging for the reliability of both rating sources.

Regarding leniency, research has shown that self-ratings are most lenient and supervisor ratings are least lenient (Borman, 1991). Peer ratings fall between these two sources. Finally, research, primarily in the military, has demonstrated that peer assessments of leadership can successfully predict subsequent performance as a leader (e.g., Hollander, 1965).

A prevailing opinion about peer ratings is that they are a valuable source of performance information. Peers are likely to provide performance data somewhat different to what the more commonly gathered supervisor ratings provide. Accordingly, experts recommend obtaining performance ratings from multiple sources (e.g., supervisors and peers); *see* 360-DEGREE APPRAISALS.

Bibliography

Borman, W. C. (1991). Job behavior, performance, and effectiveness. In M. D. Dunnette and L. M. Hough (eds.), *Handbook of Industrial and Organizational Psychology*, 2nd edn, vol. 2. Palo Alto, CA: Consulting Psychologists Press.

Harris, M. M. and Schaubroeck, J. (1988). A meta-analysis of self–supervisor, self–peer, and peer–supervisor ratings. *Personnel Psychology*, 41, 43–62.

Hollander, E. P. (1965). Validity of peer nominations in predicting a distant performance criterion. *Journal of Applied Psychology*, 49, 434–8.

Kane, J. S. and Lawler, E. E. (1978) Methods of peer assessment. *Psychological Bulletin*, 85, 555–86.

pension plans

Charles H. Fay

The goal of a pension plan is to provide replacement of a percentage (usually between 50 and 80 percent) of an employee's income after retirement (SOCIAL SECURITY BENEFITS and personal savings should supplement this so the standard of living does not change appreciably, given the lower costs retirees have). There are two categories of pension plans in use today. The first form is the defined benefit pension, in which the employer promises a level of benefit to the employee, typically in the form of replacement income. The second form is a defined contribution plan, in which the employer provides a specific annual contribution to an employee's retirement account; no promise is made as to the retirement income such an account will provide.

Defined benefit programs offer advantages to the employee, because the retirement benefit is known (typically as a percentage of average career earnings or of final average earnings) and all risk is assumed by the employer. Plans may be integrated with social security, so that higher-income employees and lower-income employees receive a similar percentage of income replacement. The pension fund is managed by the employer or employer's designated administrator, and is a unitary fund for all plan participants. The employer pays insurance premiums to the Pension Benefit Guaranty Corporation, which insures payments to plan participants.

Defined contribution programs focus on the amount contributed on an annual basis by the employer. Each employee has an individual account (or accounts), and assumes the risk for managing the account. Defined contribution programs are more likely to allow or mandate employee contributions. Typical defined contribution programs include 401(K) PLANS, PROFIT SHARING, and SAVINGS OR THRIFT PLANS.

A recent innovation is a cash balance plan, i.e., a defined benefit plan that looks like a defined contribution plan, and changes the schedule of contributions by the employer so that they are spread more evenly throughout the employee's worklife, rather than backloaded, as in a typical defined benefits plan. They are designed to be more portable for younger employees, but are considered by many to discriminate against older employees.

Bibliography

Allen, E. T. (2001). Retirement plan design. In J. S. Rosenbloom (ed.), *The Handbook of Employee Benefits: Design, Funding and Administration*, 5th edn. New York: McGraw-Hill, pp. 575–99.

Beam, B. T. and McFadden, J. J. (2001). *Employee Benefits*, 6th edn. Chicago: Dearborn Financial Publishing, pp. 465–623.

Coleman, D. R. and Sher, L. J. (2001). Cash balance pension plans and other evolving hybrid pension plans. In J. S. Rosenbloom (ed.), *The Handbook of Employee Benefits: Design, Funding and Administration*, 5th edn. New York: McGraw-Hill, pp. 661–80.

performance appraisal

Robert L. Cardy and Gregory H. Dobbins

Performance appraisal is the process of identifying, observing, measuring, and developing human performance in organizations (Carroll and Schneir, 1982). This description is a widely accepted definition of appraisal (Cardy and Dobbins, 1994). Each of the components of this definition refers to an important portion of the appraisal process. The *identification* component refers to the process of determining what areas are to be focused on. Identification typically involves JOB ANALYSIS as a means of identifying performance dimensions and developing rating scales. In terms of the rater, identification means that the evaluator must somehow determine what to examine concerning the ratees. What is identified, of course, should be performance-related criteria and not performance-irrelevant characteristics.

The *observation* component indicates that all appraisal criteria must be sufficiently observed so that fair and accurate judgments can be made. Infrequent observation or observation of non-performance characteristics will lead to poor ratings.

The *measurement* component refers to the central feature of appraisal. The rater must somehow translate the observations into a value judgment representing the level of the ratee's performance. As pointed out by Banks and Roberson (1985), raters are, in essence, human testing devices. As such, they need to be similarly calibrated (i.e., use similar standards to evaluate ratees' performance). The comparability of measurement standards across raters is an important but under-researched area.

The *development* component suggests that performance appraisal should be more than simply the assessment of past performance. To be complete, appraisal should also focus on improving future performance. This requires that raters be effective performance coaches (*see* PERFORMANCE COACHING) and that ratees accept APPRAISAL FEEDBACK. Problems with any of the other components may make the development phase an impossibility.

This definition is a description of what appraisal should be. Unfortunately, characteristics of the typical appraisal system often fall far short of this ideal (*see* DYSFUNCTIONAL PERFORMANCE APPRAISALS).

Performance appraisal is a central human resource management (HRM) function, since it is an input or component of so many other HRM activities (e.g., Landy, Farr, and Jacobs, 1982). Subjective performance ratings are the common criteria against which performance is evaluated. The ratings may also be used to assess the effectiveness of a training program (*see* TRAINING) or the validity of a selection mechanism.

Performance ratings also drive a variety of personnel actions. For example, promotions are often largely determined by performance ratings (*see* PROMOTION). Training, salary increases, layoffs, and terminations may also be directly tied to performance appraisal.

While appraisal is important in its own right, its involvement in so many other HRM activities makes it a critical HUMAN RESOURCE FUNCTION.

Bibliography

Banks, C. G. and Roberson, L. (1985). Performance appraisers as test developers. *Academy of Management Review*, **10**, 128–42.

Cardy, R. L. and Dobbins, G. H. (1994). *Performance Appraisal: Alternative Perspectives*. Cincinnati, OH: South-Western Publishing.

Carroll, S. J. and Schneir, C. E. (1982). *Performance Appraisal and Review Systems: The Identification, Measurement, and Development of Performance in Organizations*. Glenview, IL: Scott Foresman.

Landy, F., Farr, J. L., and Jacobs, R. R. (1982). Utility concepts in performance measurement. *Organizational Behavior and Human Performance*, **30**, 15–40.

performance coaching

Lisa M. Collings and Oliver London

Performance coaching is the process of giving verbal performance feedback and development suggestions at regular intervals to direct reports, colleagues, or external clients. It is often done as part of a PERFORMANCE MANAGEMENT program. However, rather than expecting employees to "just know" how they are performing or to wait for an annual review, coaching involves giving feedback when needed, along with providing development tips and ideas. This process can be as formal as creating a development plan or menu, and then following up on a regular basis to see if the involved employees are having success or if they need more guidance. It is a shift from the traditional paradigm of control/order/prescription to a partnership that rests on acknowledging and empowering people (Evered and Selman, 1989).

Performance coaching requires specific skills from both the coach and the employee receiving the coaching. The four main skills required of the performance coach are observational, analytical, interviewing, and feedback skills (Orth, Wilkinson, and Benfari, 1987). The coach needs to know when to give feedback and when not to give feedback; how to approach the employee and phrase the feedback so that resistance to the feedback is low; how to validate and recognize strengths while highlighting areas for improvement; and how to make developmental suggestions without directing the employee to accomplish yet another list of tasks. The employee needs to know how to ask for feedback, rather than assuming that her or his performance must be acceptable in the absence of feedback; how to hear the feedback, tips, and suggestions nondefensively; how to hear the feedback as advice, not as directives; and how to take responsibility for updating the coach on developmental progress.

Successful coaching is a complex interaction between management behaviors, time, and manager–employee relationships (Graham, Wedman, and Garvin-Kester, 1993). Knowing when and how to provide feedback is part of establishing a trusting relationship. Trust is a crucial component of performance coaching; without it, feedback, regardless of its value, will not be accepted. In the same vein, if an employee is not trustworthy, a coach may choose not to provide feedback to that employee. Trusting the coach means the employee knows the coach is providing honest feedback to the employee. Trusting the employee means the coach knows the employee is willing to accept the honest feedback of the coach (see MENTORING PROGRAMS).

In order to help employees improve their performance, coaches need to use their observational skills in providing employees with examples of their behavior that can be understood and acted upon. Subjective personality statements (e.g., you are lazy) do not provide information which can be acted upon and improved. Behavioral observations (e.g., you were 15 minutes late for work on Monday and 20 minutes late on Friday) do provide the data necessary for an employee to understand the feedback. It should be descriptive, nonevaluative, factual, specific, and observable. Once employees receive specific behavioral performance information, they can know what behaviors are impacting their JOB PERFORMANCE.

The coach also needs to frame the performance feedback within the larger context of career development. According to Popper and Lipshitz (1992), coaching consists of two components: (1) improving performance at the skill level; and (2) establishing relations that allow coaches to enhance trainees' psychological development. This can be achieved by soliciting input from the employee on her or his future career aspirations (e.g., where would you like to be in five years?). Again, this is predicated on a trusting relationship, because the employee may reveal goals that would require her or him to leave the organization in order to achieve them. After the aspiration has been established, each time feedback is given, the coach needs to relate it to the career goal. It is more likely that the employee will accept and act on the suggestions if there is both an organizational and a personal gain.

Underlying all of the above is a foundation of active listening skills. After delivering the feedback, the coach must allow for a response from the employee. This requires an open, nonjudgmental attitude and a respect for the employee's thoughts and feelings. Throughout the response, the coach can demonstrate active listening by paraphrasing, commenting, asking questions, clarifying, restating, and using reflective statements.

Once the coach has established an environment of trust, provided behavioral observations, and linked them to the employee's career goals, a development plan can be established. This includes concrete, actionable steps to address the feedback. It is comprised of various activities, such as training courses, readings, and on-the-job assignments. The coach would then periodically check in with the employee to discuss how the accomplishment of the plan is progressing and to offer support if the employee is finding any of the developmental activities to be a challenge.

In order to reinforce the feedback given throughout the coaching process, it is important to provide regular recognition and rewards for the employee's professional development (see REINFORCEMENT). This can occur in a multitude of ways. Some examples include praising the employee when improvement is observed, sharing positive feedback from a third party that relates to the development areas the employee has identified, or offering a quarterly incentive solely based on behavioral improvements. Without the development plan and reinforcement through reward and recognition, performance coaching simply becomes performance feedback.

Bibliography

Evered, R. D. and Selman, J. C. (1989). Coaching and the art of management. *Organizational Dynamics*, **18**, 16–32.

Graham, S., Wedman, J. F., and Garvin-Kester, B. (1993). Manager coaching skills: Development and application. *Performance Improvement Quarterly*, **6**, 2–13.

Orth, C. D., Wilkinson, H. E., and Benfari, R. C. (1987). The manager's role as coach and mentor. *Organizational Dynamics*, 15, 66–74.

Popper, M. and Lipshitz, R. (1992). Coaching on leadership. *Leadership and Organization Development Journal*, 13, 15–18.

performance diaries

Kevin J. Williams

Performance diaries are typically used for PERFORMANCE APPRAISAL purposes. Raters use diaries to record critical work behaviors of ratees whom they observe during the appraisal period (Bernardin and Walter, 1977). Diaries also may be used in other ways, such as when role incumbents are asked to record their own behaviors as part of a JOB ANALYSIS, criterion validation, or self-management study. In performance appraisal, the purpose of a performance diary is to document the occurrence of target behaviors and the conditions under which they occur, thereby facilitating evaluations of performance and related personnel decisions.

Event-Contingent Sampling

Performance diaries can be thought of as a behavior sampling technique. Raters are encouraged to keep diaries in order to increase the sample of observations upon which evaluations are made. Several behavior sampling techniques exist (see Wheeler and Reis, 1991), but the most common technique for performance diaries is event-contingent sampling. In event-contingent sampling, individuals record specific events (e.g., task behaviors) each time they are observed and note important characteristics of the event. This type of sampling represents a CRITICAL INCIDENTS TECHNIQUE approach to performance measurement.

The Promise of Performance Diaries

RATING ACCURACY has been a longstanding concern among human resource management (HRM) practitioners and researchers. Research on raters' cognitive processes suggests that memory decay and biased observation result in a low correspondence between actual behaviors and ratings. For example, raters use different cues, such as knowledge about the ratee or job, as well as the purpose of the appraisal, to form impressions of ratees, which then influence the amount and types of information to which raters attend (Ilgen, Barnes-Farrell, and McKellin, 1993). Performance diaries have been offered as a way to reduce memory and observation biases (Lee, 1985).

There are several ways in which performance diaries may increase rating accuracy. First, diaries reduce memory demands placed on raters. They provide raters with a "hard copy" of their observations at the time ratings are made, thereby reducing subjectivity and bias in recall (DeNisi, Robbins, and Cafferty, 1989).

Second, diary-keeping reinforces the importance and relevance of certain behaviors at the time of observation. By making behaviors more salient, diaries may reduce the influence of global impressions on observation. Combining diaries with BEHAVIORALLY ANCHORED RATING SCALES may be an especially effective technique for focusing rater attention on critical behaviors (Bernardin and Walter, 1977; Bernardin and Beatty, 1984).

A third benefit, proposed by cognitive researchers, is that diaries structure the way information is organized in memory. The organization of performance information in memory has been related to recall and rating accuracy (Williams, Cafferty, and DeNisi, 1990), and organizing performance diaries by person categories, as opposed to task categories or no specific categories, may hold the most promise for improving accuracy (DeNisi et al., 1989; DeNisi and Peters, 1992).

A fourth benefit of diaries is that they improve estimates of the frequency, distribution, and intensity of ratee behavior. Such information is often under-utilized in traditional performance appraisals.

Concerns Surrounding the Use of Diaries

A common problem with performance diaries is response decay: rates of responding by raters tend to decrease over time due to fatigue or motivation loss. A second concern is participant cooperation. The benefits of performance diaries will only be realized to the extent that raters are willing to use them properly. Also, diary-keeping is not immune to the observational biases mentioned earlier. Impressions of ratees and contextual cues will influence how behavior is interpreted and recorded, in addition to how it is observed.

SUMMARY

If managed properly, performance diaries may be a useful tool in the performance appraisal process. Current research suggests that diary-keeping should emphasize specific behaviors related to task success, and should be organized by persons. Rater training and incentives should be used to insure that a sufficient number of incidents are sampled, that a distribution of performance is attained, and that environmental conditions affecting performance are identified (Bernardin and Beatty, 1984).

Bibliography

Bernardin, H. J. and Beatty, R. W. (eds.) (1984). *Performance Appraisal: Assessing Human Behavior at Work.* Boston: Kent.

Bernardin, H. J. and Walter, C. S. (1977). Effects of rater training and diary-keeping on psychometric error in ratings. *Journal of Applied Psychology*, 62, 64–9.

DeNisi, A. S. and Peters, L. H. (1992). Diary keeping and the organization of information in memory: A field extension. Paper presented at the Annual Meeting of the Society for Industrial and Organizational Psychology, Montreal, Canada, May.

DeNisi, A. S., Robbins, T., and Cafferty, T. P. (1989). Organization of information used for performance appraisals: Role of diary-keeping. *Journal of Applied Psychology*, 74, 124–9.

Ilgen, D. R., Barnes-Farrell, J. L., and McKellin, D. B. (1993). Performance appraisal research in the 1980s: What has it contributed to appraisals in use? *Organizational Behavior and Human Decision Processes*, 54, 321–68.

Lee, C. (1985). Increasing performance appraisal effectiveness: Matching task types, appraisal process, and rater training. *Academy of Management Review*, 10, 322–31.

Wheeler, L. and Reis, H. T. (1991). Self-recording of everyday life events: Origins, types, and uses. *Journal of Personality*, 59, 339–54.

Williams, K. J., Cafferty, T. P., and DeNisi, A. S. (1990). The effect of appraisal salience on recall and ratings. *Organizational Behavior and Human Decision Processes*, 46, 217–39.

performance management

Robert L. Cardy and Gregory H. Dobbins

Performance management should be the primary goal of any PERFORMANCE APPRAISAL system. While measurement is important, what is critical is what is done with the evaluations. A complete appraisal process includes informal day-to-day interactions between managers and workers as well as formal face-to-face interviews, all aimed at improving ratees' levels of effectiveness.

Appraisal interviews, part of the formal performance management system, are typically done annually to provide feedback to ratees. The appraisal interview often involves discussion of both performance and salary. However, some companies have shifted to a system, referred to as split reviews, in which performance and salary discussions occur in separate interviews. However, research has found that discussion of salary in an appraisal review session has a positive impact on how employees perceive the usefulness of the review (Prince and Lawler, 1986). Discussion of salary may have a positive impact by increasing the meaningfulness of the interview session for both the rater and the ratee.

Formal appraisal interviews are typically conducted once a year and, thus, may not have a lasting impact on performance (Bernardin and Beatty, 1984). Informal day-to-day performance feedback is probably more useful for that purpose.

Effective performance management requires: (1) identifying and controlling system influences on performance; (2) developing an action plan and empowering workers to reach solutions; and (3) directing communication at performance, rather than at the performer (Gomez-Mejia, Balkin, and Cardy, 1995).

Identification of system factors involves careful study of the work situation by the rater and ratee. System factors are any influences on performance that are external to the worker. A joint and systematic consideration of possible external influences on performance can help to create a partnership between the rater and ratee and be an important basis for the improvement of performance. Once the system factors are identified, the rater and ratee can work together to try to eliminate or reduce their influences on performance.

Developing an action plan and taking an empowered approach means that the rater should help the ratee to identify ways to effectively deal with the work situation. Empowering the worker to deal with the work situation requires that the rater be a coach rather than a director or controller (see PERFORMANCE COACHING). Making suggestions, providing immediate feedback, helping to eliminate unnecessary constraints, and other coaching activities can create a supportive work environment and lead to meaningful and long-lasting performance improvement.

Communication between a rater and ratee is critical to effective performance management. How a rater communicates with a ratee about performance can determine whether performance improves or declines. Communication should address the characteristics of the performance and not characteristics of the performer. In addition, communication that might cause the ratee to be defensive should be avoided.

Bibliography

Bernardin, H. J. and Beatty, R. W. (eds.) (1984). *Performance Appraisal: Assessing Human Behavior at Work*. Boston: Kent.

Gomez-Mejia, L. R., Balkin, D. B., and Cardy, R. L. (1995). *Managing Human Resources*. Englewood Cliffs, NJ: Prentice-Hall.

Prince, J. B. and Lawler, E. E. (1986). Does salary discussion hurt the developmental appraisal? *Organizational Behavior and Human Decision Processes*, 37, 357–75.

performance outcome

Jeanette N. Cleveland

The term "performance outcome" is used to refer to a variety of measures used to assess effectiveness at the individual, work group, and organization level. Example outcomes would include profit, customer satisfaction, market share, sales, sales revenues, costs, quality, and defects. PRODUCTIVITY is a ratio of performance outcomes to the inputs (e.g., capital, labor) needed to produce these outcomes, and thus assesses the efficiency with which performance outcomes are produced.

Bibliography

Campbell, J. P., Campbell, R. J., et al. (1988). *Productivity in Organizations*. San Francisco: Jossey-Bass.

performance standards

Adrienne Colella

Performance standards are criteria against which individuals' behaviors and outcomes are judged in order to evaluate their performance. There are three features which define performance standards (Bobko and Colella, 1994). First, standards have an *evaluative* component. That is, they serve as criteria for judging effectiveness. Second, standards are *externally established*. Finally, performance standards are usually considered to be *established entities*, which usually remain stable over time and across individuals. Locke and Latham (1990: 7) define performance standards as "a rule to measure or evaluate things." They distinguish between standards and goals, by defining the latter as the "aim or end of an action." Bobko and Colella (1994) further distinguish between goals and standards by pointing out that standards are usually consistent across individuals, whereas goals are usually assigned on an individual basis.

Performance standards are essentially ubiquitous in organizations. Common examples include sales quotas, standards for making partners in a law firm, and manufacturing piece-rate systems. Standards are used in a variety of personnel decisions, including, but not limited to, PERFORMANCE APPRAISAL, TRAINING, PROMOTION, and PAY FOR PERFORMANCE. Despite the frequent presence of performance standards in organizational life, little research has directly focused on issues such as how organizations currently set standards, how they should set standards, and the consequences of various standard-setting procedures (Murphy and Cleveland, 1991). Much more research has been conducted on selection standards than on performance standards. The education literature, in particular, has focused a great deal on standard setting in education (see Pulakos et al., 1989, for a review).

Despite this lack of research, several practical guides to setting performance standards exist. For example, Carlyle and Ellison (1984) suggest that standards should be concrete and specific, practical to measure, meaningful, realistic and based on a sound rationale, and consistent across similar jobs.

Bobko and Colella (1994) suggested that standards that exist for evaluative purposes can also influence the motivation and JOB SATIS-FACTION of those to whom the standards are applied. These authors reviewed a variety of literatures related to standard setting (e.g., goal setting and feedback literatures) and proposed characteristics of standards that are likely to influence employee job motivation and satisfaction. These characteristics include who sets the standards, whether outcomes and rewards are tied to meeting these standards, the difficulty of the standards, whether some standards conflict with other standards, the specificity of the standards, whether the standards are focused on behaviors versus outcomes, the valence of the standards, how standards are framed, whether employees participated in standard setting, single versus multiple standards, and whether the standard is static or can be expected to change.

Bibliography

Bobko, P. and Colella, A. (1994). Employee reactions to performance standards: A review and research propositions. *Personnel Psychology*, **47**, 1–29.

Carlyle, J. and Ellison, T. (1984). Developing performance standards. In H. J. Bernardin and R. W. Beatty (eds.), *Performance Appraisal: Assessing Human Behavior at Work*. Boston: Kent.

Locke, E. and Latham, G. (1990). *A Theory of Goal Setting and Task Feedback*. Englewood Cliffs, NJ: Prentice-Hall.

Murphy, K. and Cleveland, J. (1991). *Performance Appraisal: An Organizational Perspective*. Boston: Allyn and Bacon.

Pulakos, E., Wise, L., Arabian, J., Heon, S., and Delaplane, S. E. (1989). *A Review of Procedures for Setting Job Performance Standards*. Alexandria, VA: US Army Research Institute.

person-based pay

Timothy J. Keaveny

Typically, COMPENSATION systems base pay on the value of work associated with a job (*see* JOB-BASED PAY). An alternative approach is to base an employee's pay on characteristics associated with capacity to do work; that is, skills, abilities, and competence. The focus can be on the breadth or range of work or jobs one can perform or the focus can be on the depth of knowledge in a particular type of work (*see* SKILL-BASED PAY DESIGN).

Bibliography

Jenkins, G. D., Jr., Ledford, G. E., Jr., Gupta, N., and Doty, D. H. (1992). *Skill-Based Pay: Practices, Payoffs, Pitfalls, and Prospects*. Scottsdale, AZ: American Compensation Association.

person–job fit

Peter Villanova and Paul M. Muchinsky

Person–job fit is a state of congruence between job demands and resources on the one hand, and individual abilities and proclivities on the other. Although the preponderance of work on person–job fit has focused on PERSONNEL SELECTION, training and development activities (*see* TRAINING) may also enhance correspondence between employee and job features.

DEVELOPMENT OF THE PERSON–JOB FIT CONCEPT

Historically, most attempts at person–job fit have focused on applicant knowledge, skills, and abilities, with some collateral attention to other applicant characteristics, such as attitudes and motivation (*see* KSAOS). The primary vehicle used to assess these personal orientations continues to be the EMPLOYMENT INTERVIEW. However, recent conceptual and technological developments have expanded interest in the "fit" concept.

According to Edwards (1991), one conceptual perspective on person–job fit maintains that fit represents the extent of congruence between a person's desires and the job's ability to satisfy those desires (see also Dawis and Lofquist's

(1993) discussion of the theory of work adjustment). This aspect of fit is more relevant to issues of employee JOB SATISFACTION and traces its heritage to work adjustment theory, goal setting, need theories, and vocational interest. A second perspective is more consistent with the traditional view of fit that concentrates on the congruence between job demands and employee capabilities. A major integrative review of person–job fit has been presented by Kristof (1996).

Methodologically, advances have largely taken the form of adopting different profile-matching measurement technologies from related fields and applying them to the selection context, as exemplified in the work of Caldwell and O'Reilly (1990; the profile comparison process) and Villanova et al. (1994; job compatibility) (see PROFILE-MATCHING SELECTION PROCEDURES). Not all approaches to person–job fit are equally preferable in all situations, and the issue of how best to represent person–job fit remains a major obstacle to understanding.

Bibliography

Caldwell, D. F. and O'Reilly, C. A. (1990). Measuring person–job fit with a profile comparison process. *Journal of Applied Psychology*, 75, 648–57.

Dawis, R. V. and Lofquist, L. H. (1993). From TWA to PEC. Special issue: The theory of work adjustment. *Journal of Vocational Behavior*, 43, 113–21.

Edwards, J. (1991). Person–job fit: A conceptual integration, literature review, and methodological critique. In C. L. Cooper and I. T. Robertson (eds.), *International Review of Industrial and Organizational Psychology*. New York: John Wiley.

Kristof, A. L. (1996). Person–organization fit: An integrative review of its conceptualizations, measurement and implications. *Personnel Psychology*, 49, 1–49.

Villanova, P., Bernardin, H. J., Johnson, D. L., and Dahmus, S. A. (1994). The validity of a measure of job compatibility in the prediction of job performance and turnover of motion theater personnel. *Personnel Psychology*, 47, 73–90.

personal development plans

Hadyn Bennett

Personal development plans (PDPs), which became popular in the 1990s (Tamkin, 1996), seek to move career ownership from the organization to the individual, resulting in a process of self-managed learning in which the individual adopts responsibility for personal development. PDPs are reflective of a changing business environment (Tamkin, 1996) in which the concept of a job for life has become a historic one and in which it has therefore become increasingly important for individuals to have PDPs. Within this context, organizations no longer stand to benefit to the same extent from heavy investment in training and development (see TRAINING), and, coupled with increased pressure for greater cost efficiency, are no longer so willing to incur high expenditure on staff development. Furthermore, increasing environmental uncertainty has developed a need for flexible, autonomous, and responsible employees; taking personal responsibility for career management is seen as one way of developing such staff.

The development of PDPs requires genuine collaboration between the organization and the individual, whereby the manager's (and the organization's) expectations are considered alongside the individual's "whole life" aspirations and how these might best be achieved. The process thus facilitates self-actualization on the part of the individual through responsibility and autonomy, while the organization benefits from utilizing the creative energy released within employees.

Bibliography

Tamkin, P. (1996). Practical applications for personal development plans. *Management Development Review*, 9 (7), 32–6.

personality tests

Michael K. Mount

Personality tests can be classified into two types: personality inventories and projective tests. Each is designed to assess the unique organization of characteristics that define an individual's pattern of interactions with the environment. An individual's personality is believed to be of critical importance in JOB PERFORMANCE, and, therefore, personality tests are frequently used as part of the selection process. For example, sales or customer service jobs require individuals to interact with others, whereas jobs such as air traffic controller and police officer require individuals to cope with highly stressful situations. Personality tests are used to identify individuals' relative standing on the traits believed to be relevant for effective job performance on these jobs (see TRAIT).

Personality Inventories

Personality inventories are paper-and-pencil instruments that attempt to measure any of the literally hundreds of specific aspects, or traits, that can be used to distinguish among persons. Example traits would include ambition, sociability, achievement, adjustment striving, and dependability. Typically, personality inventories are comprised of a set of questions that a person responds to using a self-report format. Respondents answer questions by indicating whether an item is true or false or whether they agree or disagree. This structured format allows tests to be objectively or computer scored. Commonly used personality inventories of this type include the California Psychological Inventory (CPI), the Edwards Personal Preference Schedule (EPPS), and the Guilford–Zimmerman Temperate Survey (G–ZTS).

There has been some debate in the research literature about the usefulness of personality measures in forecasting future job performance. In the mid-1960s the dominant belief was that personality inventories were of limited value in employment settings. Studies conducted more recently have demonstrated that there are meaningful relationships between personality constructs and a variety of criterion types for different occupations (Barrick and Mount, 1991; Tett, Jackson, and Rothstein, 1991; Mount and Barrick, 1996). Under certain circumstances the CRITERION-RELATED VALIDITY of personality measures can approach the magnitude of validities typically found for other selection devices, such as BIOGRAPHICAL HISTORY INVENTORIES, structured interviews (see EMPLOYMENT INTERVIEW), and ASSESSMENT CENTERS.

Because personality inventories are self-report measures, they have been criticized as being susceptible to response distortion. That is, individuals may consciously or unconsciously alter their responses in order to make themselves "look good." The available research indicates that individuals frequently do distort their scores on these inventories when applying for jobs, but such distortion does not seem to affect the validity of personality measures. It has also been found that when personality measures are completed by observers who are familiar with the person, they yield higher validities than if those measures were based on self-ratings (Mount and Barrick, 1996).

Projective Tests

Projective tests differ in several important ways from personality inventories. They consist of one or more relatively ambiguous stimuli, such as vague pictures or inkblots. Typically, the person is asked to make up a story about each stimulus. Another form of projective test may ask a person to complete a sentence such as "My father..." or "My favorite...." The pictures, inkblots, and sentence stems are purposefully chosen to elicit a wide variety of responses. These techniques are referred to as "projective tests" because they require the individual to *project* his or her organization and interpretation on to ambiguous stimuli that have no inherent organization or meaning. Responses are believed to be an extension of the individual's personality. Commonly used projective tests include the Rorschach Inkblot Technique, the Thematic Apperception Test (TAT), and the Miner Sentence Completion Scale (MSCS).

One difficulty with the use of projective tests is that there is no a priori scoring system, or, if there is, considerable disagreement exists about which system is best. (The TAT and MSCS are notable exceptions.) This underscores the need for rigorous training in the use of projective tests, particularly with respect to the application of standardized guidelines for the constructs purportedly being measured. Although projective tests are not generally held in high regard by most selection researchers, there is some evidence that they yield significant validity coefficients when reliable scoring procedures are used (Cornelius, 1983).

See also *Big Five personality tests*

Bibliography

Barrick, M. R. and Mount, M. K. (1991). The Big Five personality dimensions and job performance: A meta-analysis. *Personnel Psychology*, **44**, 1–26.

Cornelius, E. T. (1983). The use of projective techniques in personnel selection. In G. R. Ferris and K. M. Rowland (eds.), *Research in Personnel and Human Resources Management*. Greenwich, CT: JAI Press.

Mount, M. K. and Barrick, M. R. (1996). The Big Five personality dimensions: Implications for research and practice in human resources management. In G. R. Ferris (ed.), *Research in Personnel and Human Resources Management*. Greenwich, CT: JAI Press.

Tett, R. P., Jackson, D. N., and Rothstein, M. (1991). Personality measures as predictors of job performance: A meta-analytic review. *Personnel Psychology*, **44**, 703–42.

personnel selection

David J. Snyder and Michael A. McDaniel

Personnel selection is concerned with accepting or rejecting individuals on the basis of INDIVIDUAL DIFFERENCES in knowledge, skills, or abilities (*see* KSAOS). The primary goal is to capitalize on individual differences that are deemed most important for success on the job. Personnel selection involves the prediction of JOB PERFORMANCE based on one or more individual difference variables. Those who possess greater amounts of a characteristic which is considered important for job success are selected before those who possess lesser amounts of the characteristic.

pest analysis

Fang Lee Cooke

Pest (political/legal, economic, social, technological) analysis is a broad framework that is used to analyze the business environment of an organization with the aim of formulating or revising its strategy. Political/legal factors include government stability, monopolies legislation, foreign trade regulations, and employment law. Key economic influences refer to stages in the business cycle, unemployment, inflation, and interest rate. Social factors include demographic and population change, income distribution, education and training, attitudes to work and leisure. Technological factors include innovation and development, government spending on and promotion of research and development, speed of technology transfer, and rates of obsolescence.

Bibliography

Johnson, G. and Scholes, K. (1993). *Exploring Corporate Strategy*, 3rd edn. Hemel Hempstead: Prentice-Hall.

physical abilities

Paul E. Spector

Physical ability refers to the capability or capacity to develop or learn a physical skill, such as climbing a ladder or hammering nails. Many individual physical abilities exist that involve both motor (e.g., running speed) and perceptual (e.g., visual acuity) functions. Abilities that combine both physical and psychological factors (e.g., information processing or perception) are termed PSYCHOMOTOR ABILITIES. An example would be eye–hand coordination. Many job tasks require a combination of specific physical abilities involving both motor and psychological components. In PERSONNEL SELECTION, however, a physical equivalent to INTELLIGENCE TESTS does not exist. Where PHYSICAL ABILITY TESTING is used, it tends to focus on specific abilities rather than overall physical capability.

physical ability testing

Richard D. Arvey

Physical ability testing has to do with methods and procedures used by organizations to assess the capacity of applicants and employees to perform physically demanding work. Such assessment may be useful in the selection, TRAINING, and job placement of employees, and for the reduction of potential workload injuries. The first step in physical ability testing is to assess the physical demands of work through careful job analyses (see JOB ANALYSIS). Here, work is examined to identify important skeletal and movement requirements (e.g., distances involved, spatial requirements), workload requirements (e.g., weight, repetition), physiological requirements (e.g., oxygen uptake, heart rate), and task- or duty-level demands (e.g., running short distances, climbing walls). Researchers often characterize the underlying abilities associated with these various job demands as constructs. Hogan (1992), for example, showed that the structure of several physically demanding jobs (e.g., coalmining maintenance, chemical operating jobs) could be characterized and described as involving the following seven physical ability constructs: muscular tension, muscular power, muscular endurance, cardiovascular endurance, flexibility, balance, and coordination.

Once the physical features of a job or jobs are known, a variety of assessment methods and measures are available, or can be developed, to determine INDIVIDUAL DIFFERENCES on the corresponding performance of the tasks involved, or on the physical ability constructs underlying the performance of those tasks. Simple basic measurement systems (e.g., height, weight, arm length) may be used to infer the degree to which individuals can perform major job functions (e.g., lifting packages overhead). A number of medically based physiological measures exist to assess such variables as oxygen uptake capacity, blood pressure, and susceptibility to environmental toxins, and to help in inferring the degree to which individuals can perform job features which call into play such physiological requirements. In addition, a number of tests exist that directly tap different physical ability constructs (Hogan, 1991). For example, test events such as push-ups, leg lifts, ergometer measurements, and sit-ups may be used to assess muscular endurance. Another method used to assess physical abilities is WORK SAMPLES or SIMULATIONS of the job's tasks and duties themselves, such as having applicants run up stairs, carry fire hoses, or run through obstacle courses in order to assess their physical abilities.

Organizations using these methods to assess physical abilities sometimes find themselves in legal difficulties because of the adverse impact of such tests on females and the physically handicapped (see DISPARATE IMPACT). If such protected groups are greatly disadvantaged on such tests, the organization must show evidence of JOB-RELATEDNESS or VALIDITY (Arvey and Paley, 1988). This evidence may be produced using several methodologies: (1) CONTENT VALIDITY, where the organization demonstrates that the tasks, duties, and/or underlying physical requirements of the job are reproduced with good fidelity in the tests or test events; (2) CRITERION-RELATED VALIDITY, where scores on the tests or test events are significantly related to some external measure of job performance; or (3) CONSTRUCT VALIDITY, where evidence is marshaled to confirm that data fit a specified model of relationships between the posited physical ability constructs, test events, job performance measures, and other variables embedded in the model (Arvey et al., 1992). Meta-analysis methods might also represent another means of providing validity evidence for the use of physical ability tests in selection processes.

Bibliography

Arvey, R. D., Landon, T. E., Nutting, S. M., and Maxwell, S. E. (1992). Development of physical ability tests for police officers: A construct validation approach. *Journal of Applied Psychology*, 77, 996–1009.

Arvey, R. D. and Paley, R. H. (1988). *Fairness in Selecting Employees*. Reading, MA: Addison-Wesley.

Hogan, J. C. (1991). Physical abilities. In M. D. Dunnette and L. Hough (eds.), *Handbook of Industrial and Organizational Psychology*, 2nd edn. Palo Alto, CA: Consulting Psychologists Press.

Hogan, J. C. (1992). Structure of physical performance in occupational tests. *Journal of Applied Psychology*, 76, 495–597.

picketing

Hoyt N. Wheeler

Picketing, in its usual (primary) form, is the stationing of persons outside the premises of an employer with which a union has a labor dispute

(Cihon and Castagnera, 1993). This is done for the purpose of giving notice of the existence of the dispute, and is usually intended to persuade persons not to deal with the employer. It has at times been described as inherently coercive (*Cory Corporation*, 84 NLRB 972, 1949) and at times as free speech (*Thornhill* v. *Alabama*, 310 US 88, 1940). Currently US law permits peaceful picketing unless it is mass picketing, is pursued for purposes of gaining union recognition, or is part of SECONDARY BOYCOTTS.

Bibliography

Cihon, P. J. and Castagnera, J. O. (1993). *Labor and Employment Law*, 2nd edn. Belmont, CA: Wadsworth.
Taylor, B. J. and Witney, F. (1992). *Labor Relations Law*, 6th edn. Englewood Cliffs, NJ: Prentice-Hall.

piecework

Robert L. Heneman

Piecework refers to pay granted to employees for products or services produced at or beyond a specified standard. There are several variations of piecework. With the basic version of straight piecework, the employee is paid a wage rate to produce at a standard level of production per hour. For production above the standard, there are incentives for each unit produced. With piecework, pay is allocated on the basis of products or services provided by the individual, rather than the team or entire organization; hence, piecework is used when identifiable products or services are developed by individual employees. Piecework is one example of PAY FOR PERFORMANCE. The available research indicates that piecework has a large impact on the quantity of output. A potential problem with piecework is that quality may suffer because pay BONUSES are based on quantity rather than quality.

Bibliography

Jenkins, D. G., Jr. (1986). Financial incentives. In E. A. Locke (ed.), *Generalizing from Laboratory to Field Settings*. Lexington, MA: D. C. Heath.
Locke, E. A., Feren, P. B., McCaleb, V. M., Shaw, K. N., and Denny, A. J. (1980). The relative effectiveness of motivating employee performance. In K. D. Duncan, M. M. Gruneberg, and D. Wallis (eds.), *Changes in Working Life*. New York: John Wiley.
Milkovich, G. T. and Newman, J. M. (1993). *Compensation*, 4th edn. Homewood, IL: Richard D. Irwin.

placement

David J. Snyder and Michael A. McDaniel

Placement is concerned with maximizing institutional outcomes by placing individuals who are already hired into one of two or more treatments (i.e., jobs) on the basis of a single criterion score. In placement, one tries to capitalize on INDIVIDUAL DIFFERENCES on a certain job-relevant characteristic by dividing a single criterion scale into two or more sections. Individuals falling in different sections on the scale are then assigned to different treatments. Placement can be contrasted with CLASSIFICATION, in which one tries to optimally match persons to treatments on the basis of multiple criteria.

point job evaluation method

David B. Balkin

The point job evaluation method has the following characteristics:

1 it uses compensable factors (*see* COMPENSABLE FACTOR);
2 each factor is subdivided into degrees which are numerically scaled; and
3 each factor is given a weight that reflects its relative importance (Milkovich and Newman, 1993: 131).

A job receives a point total in this method that represents the sum of points for each degree of compensable factor associated with the job. This provides a quantitative measure of the relative worth of each job, which facilitates the development of a pay structure and pay grades (*see* PAY GRADE).

The advantage of the point job evaluation method is that the quantitative rating scales provide for relatively stable and consistent results (Belcher and Atchison, 1989: 196). The disadvantages of the point job evaluation method are that it is costly and takes time to develop and implement unless a ready-made plan is purchased.

See also *job evaluation methods*

Bibliography

Belcher, D. W. and Atchison, T. J. (1989). *Compensation Administration*, 2nd edn. Englewood Cliffs, NJ: Prentice-Hall.
Milkovich, G. T. and Newman, J. M. (1993). *Compensation*, 4th edn. Homewood, IL: Richard D. Irwin.

political action committees and labor unions

Marick F. Masters

Labor unions have used political action committees (PACs) to influence elections and lawmakers. PACs raise money that may be contributed to political candidates. Research has indicated that PAC contributions may have considerable impact on the electoral and legislative processes (Kau and Rubin, 1981; Masters and Zardkoohi, 1987).

THE ROLE OF LABOR PACs

Labor unions formed PACs in the New Deal era to raise money to channel to candidates for elective office (Delaney and Masters, 1991). Since the LABOR MANAGEMENT RELATIONS ACT OF 1947 (Taft-Hartley Act) and, more recently, the Federal Election Campaign Act of 1971, unions have been prohibited from using regular sources of income (e.g., dues) for contributions to congressional and presidential candidates (Epstein, 1976). Federal election law, however, allows unions to raise money from their members on a strictly voluntary basis for PACs, which, in turn, may contribute up to $5,000 to each federal candidate per election.

PACs are one of the most important means unions have to influence politics, although in-kind assistance (e.g., get-out-the-vote drives) is also quite significant (Masters and Delaney, 1987). Since the 1970s, union PAC receipts and contributions have grown considerably, offsetting the decline in union membership (Masters, Atkin, and Delaney, 1989–90). Union PAC receipts (adjusted for inflation) rose from nearly $35 million in 1980 to nearly $50 million in 1992, despite unions losing several million members during this period. Research has shown that union PAC activity is correlated with a union's membership composition and industry location (Delaney, Fiorito, and Masters, 1988).

PAC INFLUENCE

The impact of PACs has been widely debated and researched (Masters and Delaney, 1987). While no singular conclusion has been reached, several studies indicate that union PAC contributions may have offset the decline in union membership in maintaining union political influence (Moore et al., 1995).

Bibliography

Delaney, J. T., Fiorito, J., and Masters, M. F. (1988). The effects of union organizational and environmental characteristics on union political action. *American Journal of Political Science*, 32, 616–41.
Delaney, J. T. and Masters, M. F. (1991). Unions and political action. In G. Straus, D. Gallagher, and J. Fiorito (eds.), *The State of Unions*. Madison, WI: Industrial Relations Research Association.
Epstein, E. M. (1976). Labor and federal elections: The new legal framework. *Industrial Relations*, 15, 257–74.
Kau, J. B. and Rubin, P. H. (1981). The impact of labor unions on the passage of economic legislation. *Journal of Labor Research*, 2, 133–46.
Masters, M. F., Atkin, R., and Delaney, J. (1989–90). Unions, political action, and public policy. *Policies Studies Journal*, 18, 471–80.
Masters, M. F. and Delaney, J. T. (1987). Empirical research on union political activities: A review of the literature. *Industrial and Labor Relations Review*, 40, 336–53.
Masters, M. F. and Zardkoohi, A. (1987). Labor and Congress: PAC allocations and legislative voting. In D. Lewin, D. B. Lipsky, and D. Sockell (eds.), *Advances in Industrial and Labor Relations*, vol. 4. Greenwich, CT: JAI Press, pp. 79–118.
Moore, W. J., Chachere, D. R., Curtis, T. D., and Gordon, D. (1995). The political influence of unions and corporations on COPE votes in the US Senate, 1979–1988. *Journal of Labor Research*, 16, 203–22.

political influences in career planning

Kevin W. Mossholder and Jixia Yang

Traditional career planning is based on rational self-assessments of fit between individual characteristics and organizational needs, framed within human capital theories of career attainment (*see* HUMAN CAPITAL THEORY). A political perspective on careers recognizes that organizations involve an interplay of competing interests and finite resources. In such environments, career planning may be defined more in terms of self-interest and power than the efficiency with which individual characteristics meet organizational needs.

Both organizational and individual variables can act as political influences on careers. The primary organizational influence is power. Cohort and interest groups with power shape career-relevant processes such as hiring, internal mobility, and succession so as to maintain their power (Pfeffer, 1989). Factors such as congruence with power groups' demographic composition and cultural values are important to CAREER SUCCESS, as is position in both formal and informal organizational networks. Networking, such as developing a close personal relationship with a mentor, is related to upward mobility (Brass, 1995). Because social capital engendered by the fabric of social relations offers several benefits (Adler and Kwon, 2002), people with political skills may profit from the personal investments and social connections they make. To the degree that such actions inspire trust and confidence in others, this can allow them to effectively leverage social capital to maximize career success (Ferris et al., 2000).

Individual-focused variables involve political tactics that are used to enhance career opportunities. Of several classifications of political behavior, Kipnis's taxonomy has generated the most organizational research (Ferris and Judge, 1991). Self-promotion and impression management may be accomplished by several tactics, including assertiveness, ingratiation, rationality, sanctions, exchange, upward appeal, blocking, and coalitions. Judge and Bretz (1994) noted that tactics encouraging the appearance of job competence (e.g., taking credit for others' accomplishments) seem to be ineffective in promoting career success, whereas tactics that elicit positive affect from superiors and important decision-makers (e.g., ingratiation) appear to be effective. Tharenou (2001) found that masculinity and managerial inspiration were predictive of advancement. Seibert, Kraimer, and Crant (2001) discovered that having a proactive personality could strongly influence career success, and identified key characteristics of a proactive personality: speaking up, being innovative, exhibiting career initiative, and displaying political knowledge of the organization.

Bibliography

Adler, S. A. and Kwon, S. (2002). Social capital: Prospects for a new concept. *Academy of Management Review*, 27, 17–40.

Brass, D. J. (1995). A social network perspective on human resources management. *Research in Personnel and Human Resources Management*, 13, 39–79.

Ferris, G. R. and Judge, T. A. (1991). Personnel/human resources management: A political influence perspective. *Journal of Management*, 17, 447–88.

Ferris, G. R., Perrewé, P. L., Anthony, W. P., and Gilmore, D. C. (2000). Political skill at work. *Organizational Dynamics*, 28 (4), 25–37

Judge, T. A. and Bretz, R. D. (1994). Political influence behavior and career success. *Journal of Management*, 20, 43–65.

Pfeffer, J. (1989). A political perspective on careers: Interests, networks, and environments. In M. G. Authur, D. T. Hall, and B. S. Lawrence (eds.), *Handbook of Career Theory*. New York: Cambridge University Press.

Seibert, S. E., Kraimer, M. L., and Crant, J. M. (2001). What do proactive people do? A longitudinal model linking proactive personality and career success. *Personnel Psychology*, 54, 845–74.

Tharenou, P. (2001). Going up? Do traits and informal social process predict advancing in management? *Academy of Management Journal*, 44, 1005–17.

polygraph testing

Paul R. Sackett

Polygraph testing is a specialized procedure used for the purpose of identifying persons who fail to answer questions honestly. The polygraph, commonly referred to as a "lie detector," is used for this purpose. It monitors physiological responses, including cardiovascular, respiratory, and electrodermal patterns, as an examinee answers a set of questions.

Research makes it clear that there is, in fact, no direct physiological response that indicates deception on the part of the examinee. A sharp jump in one or more physiological indicators in response to a direct question about the theft of money, for example, still leaves unanswered the "reason" for that physiological response. Many plausible reasons might exist (e.g., the individual has stolen and fears being detected, the individual has not stolen but fears being wrongly accused, the individual suddenly remembers that he or she forgot to feed the parking meter), making a conclusive inference of dishonesty unwarranted. As a result, examination techniques have been developed in an attempt to differentiate between various possible causes for a physiological response to a particular question.

The accuracy of polygraph examinations remains a matter of considerable dispute. Levels of accuracy above 90 percent have been reported in some technically sound studies investigating a single specific event (e.g., "who took the money from the safe?"). However, the vast majority of polygraph investigations in the employment context have not been investigations into a specific criminal act, but, rather, are broad, multifaceted pre-employment inquiries. Even if accuracy were as high as 90 percent in the inquiry into a single event, error rates would compound in a pre-employment inquiry where the range of issues might include theft, drug use, and work habits, among others. The American Polygraph Association concludes that there is a high accuracy rate with trained examiners and proper examination procedures. In contrast, the American Psychological Association concluded that the scientific evidence in support of polygraph use is unsatisfactory.

Use of the polygraph by private employers was heavily restricted by the EMPLOYEE POLYGRAPH PROTECTION ACT OF 1988, which prohibited requiring or requesting that applicants or employees submit to a polygraph examination. Exemptions are provided for highly regulated examinations of employees who are suspects in an ongoing investigation, and for examination of applicants by a very limited set of employers (e.g., manufacturers of controlled substances). Most states also regulate or restrict polygraph exams, with some state regulations also covering government employees.

Federal regulation covers mechanical devices used to diagnose an individual's honesty. Thus, devices such as voice stress analyzers are covered. However, federal regulation does not cover oral or written inquiries into honesty, such as written honesty tests or INTEGRITY TESTING.

Bibliography

Ben-Shakar, G. and Furedy, J. J. (1990). *Theories and Applications in the Detection of Deception*. New York: Springer-Verlag.

Congress of the United States Office of Technology Assessment (1983). *Scientific Validity of Polygraph Testing*. Washington, DC: US Government Printing Office.

Raskin, D. C. (1986). The polygraph in 1986: Scientific, professional, and legal issues surrounding application and acceptance of polygraph evidence. *Utah Law Review*, 29, 29–74.

Saxe, L., Dougherty, D., and Cross, T. (1985). The validity of polygraph testing: Scientific analysis and public controversy. *American Psychologist*, 40, 355–66.

Portal to Portal Act of 1947

Charles H. Fay

The Portal to Portal Act amends portions of the DAVIS-BACON ACT OF 1931, FAIR LABOR STANDARDS ACT OF 1938, and WALSH-HEALY ACT OF 1936 to specify that employers need not pay employees for time spent in activities preliminary to their starting work or for time spent in activities after work ends, including travel to and from the actual place of performance. Contract provisions or custom may require such payments. The Act also allows courts to reduce or deny damages against employers who act in "good faith," and have a reasonable belief that their actions do not violate provisions of the laws noted above.

Bibliography

Dixon, R. B. (2002). *Federal Wage and Hour Laws*, 2nd edn. Washington, DC: SHRM Foundation.

Shilling, D. (2001). *Human Resources and the Law: The Complete Guide with Supplement*. Englewood Cliffs, NJ: Prentice-Hall.

Position Analysis Questionnaire

James B. Shaw

The Position Analysis Questionnaire (PAQ), developed by Ernest J. McCormick and his associates (McCormick, Jeanneret, and Mecham, 1972; McCormick, 1979), is a worker-oriented JOB ANALYSIS instrument that assesses the human behaviors, mental processes, and personal job demands required of an employee while doing the job. As opposed to job-oriented methods such as the TASK INVENTORY APPROACH TO JOB ANALYSIS, the PAQ focuses on *how* the job gets done, not *what* gets done.

STRUCTURE OF THE PAQ

The 194 items (referred to as job elements) of the PAQ are grouped into six divisions.

1. "Information input" includes items concerning the methods for obtaining and the sources of information that an employee uses in doing the job.
2. "Mental processes" assesses the reasoning, decision-making, planning, and information-processing activities required to do the job.
3. "Work output" examines what physical activities, machines, tools, and other equipment are involved in performing job activities.
4. "Relationships with other persons" focuses on the interpersonal interactions required by the job.
5. "Job context" assesses the physical environment in which the work is done.
6. "Other job characteristics" is a category that includes a variety of other work-related issues, such as job structure, work pace, and schedule.

THE ANALYSIS PROCEDURE

The PAQ requires a fairly high level of literacy to fully understand, and, as a result, may be inappropriate for job incumbents to "self-administer" on some jobs. Typically, the PAQ is completed by a job analyst, or trained supervisor, who interviews a job incumbent and helps the incumbent rate each of the PAQ items using one of several rating scales: (1) extent of use; (2) importance to the job; (3) amount of time; (4) possibility of occurrence; (5) applicability; and (6) a variety of special code scales that have been constructed for specific items and vary in their exact format. Several employees with the same job title are usually interviewed, with their individual PAQ ratings averaged to get a more reliable picture of the job.

OUTPUT FROM A PAQ ANALYSIS

The items of the PAQ have been factor analyzed and grouped into 32 divisional and 13 overall job dimensions. Divisional job dimensions were formed by factor analyzing the items within each of the six PAQ divisions separately. Overall job dimensions were formed by factor analyzing 187 PAQ items together (with seven of the items excluded since they dealt only with wage rates). Each job dimension represents a group of worker-oriented activities that tend to co-occur on the job.

Data from a PAQ analysis are typically scored using a centralized PAQ computer scoring service. Output from an analysis includes scores on each of the 32 divisional and 13 overall job dimensions. The job dimension scores represent the actual levels of these activities that occur on the job being analyzed. In addition to job dimension scores, Marquardt and McCormick (1972) developed procedures linking the PAQ job dimension scores to 76 human attributes. These human attribute scores indicate the levels at which various physical, cognitive, and situational abilities are involved in JOB PERFORMANCE.

A final type of data resulting from a PAQ analysis focuses on job evaluation (*see* JOB EVALUATION METHODS). Job dimension scores are used to predict appropriate monthly wage rates based on the relative similarities or differences in their behavioral content (see McCormick, Jeanneret, and Mecham, 1977).

USES AND EVALUATION OF THE PAQ

The PAQ has been used extensively for PERSONNEL SELECTION, job classification, and job evaluation. However, its use in PERFORMANCE APPRAISAL and TRAINING systems is limited. The worker-oriented PAQ items make analyzing a wide variety of jobs easier, but they also make it difficult to translate PAQ scores directly into specific performance standards or training content. A comparison of the PAQ with several other job analysis methods can be found in Levine et al. (1983).

Bibliography

Levine, E. L., Ash, R. A., Hall, H., and Sistrunk, F. (1983). Evaluation of job evaluation methods by experienced job analysts. *Academy of Management Journal*, 26, 339–48.

McCormick, E. J. (1979). *Job Analysis: Methods and Applications*. New York: AMACOM, pp. 347–68.

McCormick, E. J., DeNisi, A. S., and Shaw, J. B. (1979). Use of the Position Analysis Questionnaire for establishing the job component validity of tests. *Journal of Applied Psychology*, 64, 51–6.

McCormick, E. J., Jeanneret, P. R., and Mecham, R. C. (1972). A study of job characteristics and job dimensions as based on the Position Analysis Questionnaire (PAQ). *Journal of Applied Psychology*, 56.

McCormick, E. J., Jeanneret, P. R., and Mecham, R. C. (1977). *Position Analysis Questionnaire (PAQ) Technical Manual (System II)*. Logan, UT: PAQ Services.

McCormick, E. J. and Mecham, R. C. (1970). Job analysis data as a basis for synthetic test validity. *Psychology Annual*, 4, 30–5.

Marquardt, L. D. and McCormick, E. J. (1972). *Attribute Ratings and Profiles of the Job Elements of the Position Analysis Questionnaire (PAQ)*. West Lafayette, IN: Department of Psychological Sciences, Purdue University.

Marquardt, L. D. and McCormick, E. J. (1974). *The Utility of Job Dimensions Based on Form B of the Position Analysis Questionnaire (PAQ) I: A Job Component Validation Model*. West Lafayette, IN: Occupational Research Center, Purdue University.

positive discipline

Mark R. Sherman

The definitional core of positive discipline is the rejection of traditional PROGRESSIVE DISCIPLINE as dysfunctionally punitive. Nonpunitive or positive discipline, by contrast, is an approach to disciplining employees that focuses on instilling self-discipline by reasoning with them, rather than externally imposing discipline by punishing them. Positive discipline's rejection of punitive, progressive discipline leads many of its proponents to claim that it represents discipline without punishment (Redeker, 1989).

Outwardly, positive discipline resembles the operational characteristic of progressive discipline in that successive managerial responses to misconduct are increasingly severe. However, more emphasis is placed on COUNSELING employees instead of simply warning them. Furthermore, no suspensions are involved in positive discipline systems. The step prior to termination is a *paid* day off work, variously referred to by names such as "decision-making leave" or "decision day." The purpose of paid time off is to provide the disciplined employee with a last opportunity to reflect on his or her ability to conform to the organization's behavioral expectations. Therefore, at least until the point of termination, management imposes no penalties on employees in an effort to encourage them to conform to organizational standards.

Positive discipline systems have come under fire from some managers who question the provision of paid time off for marginal employees. Moreover, some arbitrators have expressed skepticism over whether employees are genuinely "put on notice" when they are not penalized for prior instances of misconduct (Sherman and Lucia, 1992). Nevertheless, the high-profile success that numerous employers have experienced with nonpunitive discipline systems (Bryant, 1984) has led to continuing interest in such programs.

Bibliography

Bryant, A. (1984). Replacing punitive discipline with a positive approach. *Personnel Administrator*, 10, 79–87.

Redeker, J. R. (1989). *Employee Discipline*. Washington, DC: Bureau of National Affairs.

Sherman, M. R. and Lucia, A. J. (1992). Positive discipline and labor arbitration. *Arbitration Journal*, 47, 35–41.

predictive validity

Chester A. Schriesheim

Predictive validity is one of two subdomains of CRITERION-RELATED VALIDITY, the other being CONCURRENT VALIDITY. Predictive validation procedures assess the degree to which scores on an instrument (the predictor) are statistically associated with values obtained by a theoretically appropriate outcome measure (the criterion), when both are measured at *different* points in time.

As in concurrent validity, the statistical procedures commonly used in predictive validation most typically involve simple and multiple correlation and regression (although other data-analytics are sometimes employed).

Evidence of predictive validity is particularly appropriate when the purpose of applying an instrument is for prognosis or to predict a future status or situation. For example, correlating a selection test which is administered to applicants for employment with their JOB PERFORMANCE one year after being hired provides predictive validity evidence on that test. Another appropriate use of predictive validation is when a network of longitudinal relationships is required as evidence for the construct validation process (see the description of this process under CONSTRUCT VALIDITY).

Bibliography

American Educational Research Association, American Psychological Association, and National Council on Measurement in Education (1999). *Standards for Educational and Psychological Testing*. Washington, DC: American Educational Research Association.

Pregnancy Discrimination Act of 1978

Ramona L. Paetzold

The Pregnancy Discrimination Act of 1978 (PDA) amended Title VII of the CIVIL RIGHTS ACT OF 1964 to make clear that DISCRIMINATION due to sex includes discrimination on the basis of pregnancy, childbirth, and other related medical conditions (such as abortion). In an earlier case, *General Electric v. Gilbert* (1976), the US Supreme Court had ruled that employers could deny disability benefits to all employees, even though such a policy would have a DISPARATE IMPACT on women. Congress effectively reversed the *Gilbert* decision in passing the PDA.

The PDA therefore requires that pregnant workers be compared to others who are similar in their ability or inability to perform on the job; persons cannot be differentially singled out for adverse treatment due to their pregnancy or related conditions. The US Supreme Court has adopted this view of the PDA in cases such as *Newport News Shipbuilding and Dry Dock Co. v. EEOC* (1983), in which the employer was found to have violated the PDA because, although it offered pregnancy benefits to female employees, it did not extend pregnancy benefits to the spouses of male employees. Thus, employee families were treated differently solely on the basis of pregnancy.

In *California Federal Savings and Loan v. Guerra* (1987), the US Supreme Court held that a state may offer reinstatement to pregnant workers even though reinstatement was not given to other workers returning from disability leave, because the effect was to provide equal opportunity to all workers to have families without losing their jobs. This interpretation of the PDA suggests that pregnancy be realized as distinct from disability, so that women, like men, do not have to experience a conflict between having a job or career and having children.

preparation for an international work assignment

Stewart Black

The preparation of expatriates and their families prior to embarking on a foreign work assignment is at least as important as selecting the right candidate in the first place (see EXPATRIATE ASSIGNMENT). Research indicates that high expatriate failure rates are due to failure to adjust by the expatriate and/or family (Shaffer, Harrison, and Gilley, 1999). Despite results that indicate that preparation and training (see TRAINING) facilitate cross-cultural adjustment (Eschbach, Parker, and Stoeberl, 2001), American firms tend to provide less preparation in the form of training than European and Pacific Rim companies (Tung, 1982; Ronen, 1986; Black et al., 1999).

The fundamental difference between domestic and international work assignments lies in the contrasting cultural features that are likely to prevail in the foreign assignment. Training beyond that generally required for domestic transfers should be concentrated on the cultural dissimilarities that characterize foreign work assignments, and such training has been shown to add value to the preparation of expatriates for foreign work assignments (Black and Gregersen, 1991; Deshpande and Viswesvaran, 1992; Giacalone and Beard, 1994). In particular, a review of the research literature on cross-cultural training effectiveness by Black and Mendenhall (1990) found substantial supporting evidence that cross-cultural training positively influences cross-cultural skill development, adjustment, and performance.

To achieve these positive outcomes, cross-cultural training resources would be well spent on language acquisition, cultural awareness, or cross-cultural skills (e.g., conflict resolution, evaluation), always with an eye to the level of rigor appropriate for the cultural context in which the expatriate will be working (Black and Gregersen, 2000). Given that expatriates identify family adjustment problems as a primary reason for failure to complete foreign work assignments (Tung, 1987; Harris, 1989), it is crucial that the family be considered and included when training and preparation needs for an international work assignment are addressed (Black and Stephens, 1989).

A number of useful approaches to cross-cultural training have been developed, with varying degrees of rigor and depth. Mendenhall and Oddou (1986) have proposed a classification framework that clusters cross-cultural training methods with respect to the amount of interaction the expatriate will have with host-country nationals, and the degree of cultural novelty of the foreign assignment location. They have argued that longer and more culturally novel foreign assignments should be preceded by more extensive, rigorous, and intensive training and preparation. "Immersion approaches" (e.g., ASSESSMENT CENTERS, field experiences, SIMULATIONS, extensive language training) are appropriate for assignments that are protracted or very different from the expatriate's cultural background. "Affective approaches" are useful where moderately rigorous training is necessary (e.g., ROLE PLAYING, cases, moderate language training, critical incidents; see CRITICAL INCIDENTS TECHNIQUE). Where less rigor is required, training approaches that rely primarily on information dissemination (e.g., cultural briefings, films, reading material, basic language skills) are appropriate. Black and Mendenhall (1989) have extended previous research on cross-cultural training, and have offered a cross-cultural training model grounded in the principles of social learning. Their model integrates culture novelty, job novelty, and training rigor, and generates specific recommendations regarding training rigor, duration, and methods. It should be noted that no single training method is best for all situations; different combinations of methods will yield superior results, depending on the cultural context of the assignment (Gudykunst, Hammer, and Wiseman, 1977; Harrison, 1992).

Cross-cultural mastery, although a crucial goal of training, should not be considered the only important facet of preparation for an international work assignment. Other issues that should often be considered include implications for DUAL-EARNER AND DUAL-CAREER COUPLES, potential dependant care problems, compensation/tax equalization (see INTERNATIONAL COMPENSATION), benefits/healthcare, and networking/professional development. Additionally, REPATRIATION issues are coming to the fore as an important and necessary aspect of international preparation. Repatriation issues that often require attention include home-country reintegration and readjustment, career management, and organizational utilization of the skills and understandings gained by the expatriate (Black, Gregersen, and Mendenhall, 1992). Finally, preparation for foreign work assignments should not be limited to home-country nationals; preparation and training of host-country and third-country nationals may also be a necessary part of expatriate success.

See also *cultural literacy; expatriate human resource issues; expatriate support system; gender issues in international assignments*

Bibliography

Black, J. S. and Gregersen, H. B. (1991). Antecedents to cross-cultural adjustment for expatriates in Pacific Rim assignments. *Human Relations*, **44**, 497–515.

Black, J. S. and Gregersen, H. B. (2000). High impact training: Forging leaders for the global frontier. *Journal of Human Resource Management*, **39** (2 and 3), 173–84.

Black, J. S., Gregersen, H. B., and Mendenhall, M. E. (1992). Toward a theoretical framework of repatriation adjustment. *Journal of International Business Studies*, 23, 737–60.

Black, J. S., Gregersen, H. B., Mendenhall, M. E., and Stroh, L. K. (1999). *Globalizing People through International Assignments*. Reading, MA: Addison-Wesley.

Black, J. S. and Mendenhall, M. E. (1989). A practical but theory-based framework for selecting cross-cultural training programs. *Human Resource Management*, 28, 511–39.

Black, J. S. and Mendenhall, M. E. (1990). Cross-cultural training effectiveness: A review and a theoretical framework for future research. *Academy of Management Review*, 15, 113–36.

Black, J. S. and Stephens, G. K. (1989). The influence of the spouse on American expatriate adjustment and intent to stay in Pacific Rim overseas assignments. *Journal of Management*, 15, 529–44.

Deshpande, S. P. and Viswesvaran, C. (1992). Is cross-cultural training of expatriate managers effective? A meta-analysis. *International Journal of Intercultural Relations*, 16, 295–310.

Eschbach, D., Parker, G., and Stoeberl, P. (2001). American repatriate employees' retrospective assessments of the effectiveness of cross-cultural training on their adaptation to international assignments. *International Journal of Human Resource Management*, 12, 270–87.

Giacalone, R. A. and Beard, J. W. (1994). Impression management, diversity, and international management. *American Behavioral Scientist*, 37, 621–36.

Gudykunst, W. B., Hammer, M. R., and Wiseman, R. L. (1977). An analysis of an integrated approach to cross-cultural training. *International Journal of Intercultural Relations*, 1, 99–110.

Harris, J. E. (1989). Moving managers internationally: The care and feeding of expatriates. *Human Resource Planning*, 12, 49–54.

Harrison, J. K. (1992). Individual and combined effects of behavior modeling and the cultural assimilator in cross-cultural management training. *Journal of Applied Psychology*, 77, 952–62.

Mendenhall, M. E. and Oddou, G. R. (1986). Acculturation profiles of expatriate managers: Implications for cross-cultural training programs. *Columbia Journal of World Business*, 21, 73–9.

Ronen, S. (1986). *Comparative and Multinational Management*. New York: John Wiley.

Shaffer, M., Harrison, D., and Gilley, M. (1999). Dimensions, determinants and differences in expatriate adjustment processes. *Journal of International Business Studies*, 30, 557–81.

Tung, R. L. (1982). Selection and training procedures of US, European, and Japanese multinationals. *California Management Review*, 25, 57–71.

Tung, R. L. (1987). Expatriate assignments: Enhancing success and minimizing failure. *Academy of Management Executive*, 1, 117–26.

Price Waterhouse v. Hopkins

Kelly A. Vaverek

In *Price Waterhouse* v. *Hopkins* (490 US 228, 1989), the Supreme Court decided the substantive and evidentiary burdens that Title VII imposes upon the litigants in a *mixed motives* discrimination case. Price Waterhouse decided to table Ms. Hopkins's application for partnership based on permissible factors (personality) and impermissible factors (gender). The Supreme Court held that the law requires the plaintiff to show that the impermissible reason was a substantial, significant, or motivating factor in the employment-related decision. The plaintiff need not show that the impermissible factor was the only, principal, or true reason. The burden then shifts to the defendant employer to show, by a preponderance of the evidence, that its permissible reason, standing alone, would have induced it to make the same decision. The CIVIL RIGHTS ACT OF 1991 removes this defense.

Bibliography

Ledvinka, J. and Scarpello, V. G. (1991). *Federal Regulation of Personnel and Human Resource Management*, 2nd edn. Boston: PWS-Kent.

Zimmer, M. J. (1994). Pretext and mixed motive after the 1991 Act (Civil Rights Act of 1991). *New Jersey Law Journal*, 138, 11–13.

Principles for the Use of Personnel Selection Procedures

Robert M. Guion

This booklet, produced by the SOCIETY FOR INDUSTRIAL AND ORGANIZATIONAL PSYCHOLOGY (SIOP, 1987), presents professionally accepted principles for conducting selection research and using valid selection procedures. It also includes information intended to help those who authorize or implement validation efforts. It is an official policy statement of SIOP, although not necessarily of the American Psychological Association (of which SIOP is Division 14).

The phrase "personnel selection procedures" encompasses a wide variety of assessment procedures and their uses. The procedures include a variety of psychological tests and inventories, and non-test assessments such as interviews, biodata, ASSESSMENT CENTERS, educational or experience or physical requirements, ratings of future potential, or any other information (usually quantifiable) that can be used in making personnel decisions. In addition to hiring decisions, personnel decisions include any decisions that affect a person's employment status. The booklet is intended to help researchers and managers develop a solid foundation of logic, theory, and data for such decisions.

Topics covered include VALIDITY, validation and validation strategies, JOB ANALYSIS, VALIDITY GENERALIZATION, and the operational use of validation research. Included are a glossary and a list of references. Throughout, the *Principles* are intended to be consistent with the STANDARDS FOR EDUCATIONAL AND PSYCHOLOGICAL TESTING (American Educational Research Association et al., 1999), although the standards focus on psychometrics and the *Principles* focus on personnel decisions and the foundations for them.

Bibliography

American Educational Research Association, American Psychological Association, and National Council on Measurement in Education (1999). *Standards for Educational and Psychological Testing.* Washington, DC: American Educational Research Association.

Society for Industrial and Organizational Psychology (1987). *Principles for the Validation and Use of Personnel Selection Procedures,* 3rd edn. College Park, MD: Society for Industrial and Organizational Psychology.

Privacy Act of 1974

Vida Scarpello

Privacy has been a concern in the US since the colonial days. Privacy protections were written into the Bill of Rights of the US Constitution and later into the FOURTEENTH CONSTITUTIONAL AMENDMENT. Concern over privacy, in the 1970s, due in part to incidents such as the Watergate break-in which led to the downfall of the Nixon presidency, culminated in the passage of the Privacy Act of 1974 (Duff and Johnson, 1983; Ledvinka and Scarpello, 1991). The underlying philosophy of the Privacy Act of 1974 is that any disclosure of private information without the consent of the individual is an invasion of privacy (Duff and Johnson, 1983).

The Privacy Act's purpose is to protect the privacy of citizens employed by the US government by requiring all agencies, departments, and employees of the executive branch to observe defined constitutional rules in the collection, computerization, management, use, and disclosure of personal information about individuals. Because the Constitution governs government, privacy protections apply also to public sector employees (Ledvinka and Scarpello, 1991). The Act also gives federal government employees the right to: (1) determine what information is being kept on them by their government employers; (2) review information kept on them by their government employers; (3) correct erroneous information in their personnel records; and (4) prevent the use of their personnel information for any purpose other than that for which it was collected (Rice, 1978). Subject to certain exceptions, the Act prohibits the government from releasing any record maintained on an individual or employee, without the consent of that individual or employee.

Section 3(b) of the Act specifies the exceptions to the Act's disclosure requirements. These are when the information is given: to agency officers or employees in the ordinary course of performing their duties (3(b)(1)); to the Bureau of Census, which is bound by other confidentiality laws, for the purpose of carrying out a census or survey (3(b)(4)); for sole use as a statistical research or group-based reporting record, where individuals cannot be identified (3(b)(5)); to the National Archives of the US (3(b)(6)); to law enforcement agencies (3(b)(8)); to save the life or protect the safety of that individual in a unique emergency situation (3(b)(8)); to either House of Congress or congressional committees (3(b)(9)); to the comptroller general or his or her authorized representatives in the course of performing duties of the General Accounting Office (3(b)(10)); or pursuant to the order of a court of competent jurisdiction (3(b)(11)).

The Act does not assign administrative authority to any agency to insure compliance. Rather, it authorizes any aggrieved person to enforce the Act by seeking a Federal District Court adjudication. Furthermore, section 3(g) specifies that the aggrieved person can collect compensation for actual damages, punitive damages, and, in the case of successful action, attorney's fees as determined by the court.

Section 5 of the Act also established a Privacy Protection Study Commission for the purpose of establishing standards and procedures for the protection of personal information and to recommend to the president and Congress how the privacy protection principle should be protected in the future, while meeting the legitimate needs for information by government and society. In 1977, the commission issued a report focusing attention on the relative lack of privacy protections in the work environment. The commission also made recommendations for further privacy legislation. Those recommendations led to the passage of the EMPLOYEE POLYGRAPH PROTECTION ACT OF 1988 and the COMPUTER MATCHING AND PRIVACY PROTECTION ACT OF 1988.

See also *privacy in organizations*

Bibliography

Duff, K. J. and Johnson, E. T. (1983). A renewed employee right to privacy. *Labor Law Journal*, 34, 747–62.
Ledvinka, J. and Scarpello, V. (1991). *Federal Regulation of Personnel and Human Resource Management*. Boston: PWS-Kent.
Privacy Protection Study Commission (1977). *Personal Privacy in an Information Society*. Washington, DC: US Government Printing Office.
Rice, J. D. (1978). Privacy legislation: Its effect on pre-employment reference checking. *Personnel Administrator*, 23, 46–51.

privacy in organizations

Eugene F. Stone-Romero and Dianna L. Stone

Organizational privacy is a state or condition in which an individual (i.e., job applicant, current employee, or former employee) can (1) control the release and possible subsequent dissemination of personal information, (2) regulate both the amount and nature of social interaction in the workplace, (3) exclude or isolate himself or herself from unwanted (auditory, visual, etc.) stimuli in the workplace, and, thus, (4) behave free from the control of others (Stone and Stone, 1990). Organizational privacy is of considerable importance because organizations collect, store, and use large amounts of information about individuals for such purposes as PERSONNEL SELECTION, PERFORMANCE APPRAISAL, TRAINING, needs assessment, HUMAN RESOURCE PLANNING, and attitude assessment (*see* ATTITUDE SURVEYS) (Privacy Protection Study Commission, 1977; Stone and Stone, 1990). Organizations also structure the physical and social environments of work (e.g., through office and plant layout, structuring of work roles) in ways that facilitate the attainment of organizational goals. Unfortunately, the same actions may be viewed as intrusive by individuals because they have the potential to violate expectations of organizational privacy or legal rights to privacy (e.g., PRIVACY ACT OF 1974). In response to such violations, individuals may form negative attitudes toward the organization, engage in counterproductive behaviors at work, file GRIEVANCES against the organization, institute litigation against the organization, and engage in other acts aimed at insuring organizational privacy (Privacy Protection Study Commission, 1977; Harris and Westin, 1979; Stone and Stone, 1990). In view of this, organizations must be sensitive to organizational privacy issues.

Bibliography

Harris, L. and Westin, A. F. (1979). *The Dimensions of Privacy: A National Opinion Research Survey of Attitudes toward Privacy*. Stevens Point, WI: Sentry Insurance Company.
Privacy Protection Study Commission (1977). *Personal Privacy in an Information Society*. Washington, DC: US Government Printing Office.
Stone, E. F. and Stone, D. L. (1990). Privacy in organizations: Theoretical issues, research findings, and protection mechanisms. *Research in Personnel and Human Resources Management*, 8, 349–411.

procedural justice

Robert Folger

Procedural justice involves the fairness of means (methods for determining results), much as DISTRIBUTIVE JUSTICE involves the fairness of ends (outcomes, the results themselves). Thibaut and Walker (1975) suggested that people want "process control" over dispute resolution or allocation methods, akin to participation or a "voice" in decision-making. People want a say in decisions affecting them. Expressing opinions and arguments about one's interests can substitute (somewhat) for not choosing outcomes directly. People value this fairness substitute both as a means of trying to influence a decision-maker (instrumental value) and for the inherent satisfaction of speaking out (expressive value).

Other procedural fairness criteria exist (Leventhal, Karuza, and Fry, 1980). One, representativeness, overlaps with voice, process control, and participation: a fair procedure reflects the concerns of each affected group (e.g., GRIEVANCE PROCEDURE with union steward representing labor's interests). Additional criteria include consistency (same procedure each time, for everyone), accuracy (e.g., objective data collection), correctability (e.g., appeal systems), bias suppression (no favoritism), and ethicality (norms of socially appropriate conduct). With respect to ethicality as fair interpersonal treatment, some writers distinguish between the procedural justice of making decisions and the "interactional justice" of implementing them (e.g., prior notice, timeliness). The latter refers especially to fairness perceived because of adequate, sincere explanations and interpersonally sensitive conduct (e.g., politeness, consideration). The perceived fairness of both a procedure itself and its implementation increases decision acceptance along with the degree to which outcomes are also considered fair.

Bibliography

Cropanzano, R. and Folger, R. (1991). Procedural justice and worker motivation. In R. Steers and L. Porter (eds.), *Motivation and Work Behavior*. New York: McGraw-Hill.

Folger, R. and Greenberg, J. (1985). Procedural justice: An interpretive analysis of personnel systems. In G. R. Ferris and K. M. Rowland (eds.), *Research in Personnel and Human Resources Management*, vol. 3, Greenwich, CT: JAI Press.

Greenberg, J. (1990). Organizational justice: Yesterday, today, and tomorrow. *Journal of Management*, 16, 399–432.

Leventhal, G. S., Karuza, J., and Fry, W. R. (1980). Beyond fairness: A theory of allocation preferences. In G. Mikula (ed.), *Justice in Social Interaction*. New York: Springer-Verlag.

Lind, E. A. and Tyler, T. R. (1988). *The Social Psychology of Procedural Justice*. New York: Plenum.

Thibaut, J. and Walker, L. (1975). *Procedural Justice: A Psychological Analysis*. Hillsdale, NJ: Erlbaum.

Tyler, T. R. and Smith, H. J. (1996). Social justice and social movements. In D. Gilbert, S. T. Fiske, and G. Lindzey (eds.), *Handbook of Social Psychology*, 4th edn. New York: McGraw-Hill.

productivity

Jeanette N. Cleveland

Productivity is an efficiency concept. It is generally defined in terms of a *ratio* of output variables, including performance outcomes (*see* PERFORMANCE OUTCOME), to input variables (Cascio, 1987). Output variables include the value of goods and services produced by the organization. Input variables include the costs of capital, labor, equipment, and materials (Murphy, 1990). Conceptual distinctions can be made between total factor productivity and partial factor productivity. Total factor refers to the efficiency of transforming all input into outputs (total process); partial factor relates to the output attributable to a single input (Mahoney, 1988).

Productivity definitions and measures are somewhat arbitrary. Definitions and measures depend on the purpose for which they are developed (e.g., to compare individuals, work groups, or organizations; see Mahoney, 1988). However, different productivity improvement programs may address different input and output variables, depending upon the definition of productivity used. Such interventions might be designed to encourage employees to increase the amount of products made (outputs) or to minimize costs or errors (input) (Murphy, 1990). Behavioral science can contribute to productivity improvement on the input side (i.e., labor) through valid selection procedures, effective training programs, relevant performance feedback with goal-setting programs, and meaningful worker involvement programs (Campbell, Campbell, et al., 1988).

Bibliography

Campbell, J. P., Campbell, R. J., et al. (1988). *Productivity in Organizations*. San Francisco: Jossey-Bass.

Cascio, W. F. (1987). *Applied Psychology in Personnel Management*, 3rd edn. Englewood Cliffs, NJ: Prentice-Hall.

Mahoney, T. A. (1988). Productivity defined: The relativity of efficiency, effectiveness, and change. In J. P. Campbell, R. J. Campbell, et al. (eds.), *Productivity in Organizations*. San Francisco: Jossey-Bass.

Murphy, K. R. (1990). Job performance and productivity. In K. R. Murphy and F. E. Saal (eds.), *Psychology in Organizations*. Hillsdale, NJ: Erlbaum.

professional ethics

Linda Klebe Treviño

Society grants professionals certain powers based in part upon their willingness to conduct themselves in a manner consistent with society's values. The term "professional ethics" refers to the standards of conduct expected of a member of a profession. Human resource professionals face a variety of legal and ethical issues in their work (e.g., conflicts of interest, employee fairness issues such as privacy, confidentiality, and so forth). They are also guided by a number of professional organizations, some of which have written codes of conduct that human resource professionals are expected to observe (*see* SOCIETY FOR HUMAN RESOURCE MANAGEMENT).

Bibliography

Frankel, M. S. (1989). Professional codes: How, and with what impact? *Journal of Business Ethics*, 8, 109–15.

Wallace, F. A. (1985). Walking a tightrope: Ethical issues. *Personnel*, 62, 32–6.

profile-matching selection procedures

Neal Schmitt

When decisions about the selection or rejection of job applicants are made on the basis of their pattern of relative strengths and weaknesses on several different ability dimensions, a profile-matching selection procedure is being employed. In developing this strategy, attention must be paid to the development of a *target profile* against which applicants' profiles are judged. This target profile may be based on a JOB ANALYSIS specifying what levels of various abilities are required for satisfactory performance of a job. Target profiles can also be based on the average measured abilities of currently successful job incumbents. In both cases, a hiring decision would then be made on the basis of whether or not an applicant's profile of scores *matched* the target profile.

The development of indices of profile fit is complicated by the fact that profiles of scores can differ in terms of both *level* and *shape*. For example, a person may have the same relative strengths and weaknesses as the target profile, but be uniformly lower in measured ability on all dimensions in the profile. Or an applicant may be higher than the target profile averages on some dimensions and lower on others, but on average across all dimensions, the applicant and target scores may be very similar. The measurement of profile similarity is discussed in detail by Nunnally and Bernstein (1994: 601–10).

When one is using a profile-matching selection strategy, it is very important that each ability measure display a high degree of reliability and low intercorrelations with other ability measures. If this is not the case, then it will be impossible to discriminate among the ability dimensions and the profiles of different applicants.

Bibliography

Cascio, W. F. (1998). *Applied Psychology in Human Resource Management*. Englewood Cliffs, NJ: Prentice-Hall.

Nunnally, J. C. and Bernstein, I. H. (1994). *Psychometric Theory*. New York: McGraw-Hill.

Schneider, B. and Schmitt, N. (1986). *Staffing Organizations*. Prospect Heights, IL: Waveland Press.

profit sharing

David B. Balkin

Profit sharing is a type of variable COMPENSATION policy that provides employees with income that is based on the profitability of the entire organization or selected subunits (Florkowski, 1987: 622). Profit sharing can instill in employees a sense of partnership with other employees and managers across organizational units, because each employee is entitled to receive a share in the success of the organization, as measured by profits. Profit sharing gives the firm's managers some flexibility to reduce its labor costs when resources are scarce and profits are low by reducing employee earnings, as an alternative to using layoffs (Gomez-Mejia and Balkin, 1992). Employees may gain additional job security from this practice.

The three basic types of profit-sharing plans are (1) cash, (2) deferred, and (3) combination cash–deferred plans (Kruse, 1993). Cash profit-sharing plans provide a cash bonus payment to employees on a quarterly or annual basis. Deferred profit-sharing plans put the employee's share of the profits into a tax-deferred profit-sharing trust, which is a retirement benefit. The income is not taxed until the employee retires. The combination cash–deferred plan combines cash and deferred contributions in one plan.

Bibliography

Florkowski, G. W. (1987). The organizational impact of profit sharing. *Academy of Management Review*, 12, 622–36.

Gomez-Mejia, L. R. and Balkin, D. B. (1992). *Compensation, Organizational Strategy, and Firm Performance*. Cincinnati, OH: South-Western Publishing.

Kruse, D. L. (1993). *Profit Sharing: Does It Make a Difference?* Kalamazoo, MI: W. E. Upjohn Institute for Employment Research.

profit-sharing variations

Charles H. Fay

Two forms of PROFIT SHARING occur. In one form, annual payouts are made to employees as short-term incentive compensation. In the other form, profit sharing is a device employers use to fund a defined contribution retirement plan. Kruse (1993) notes that profit sharing, when used as incentive compensation, is associated with a significant increase in yearly growth in sales per employee and yearly growth in value added per employee; such results do not occur with deferred profit sharing. Tax deferral by employees occurs only with deferred profit sharing. Profit sharing as short-term incentive is not covered by the EMPLOYEE RETIREMENT INCOME SECURITY ACT OF 1974 (ERISA). Deferred profit sharing is subject to ERISA compliance.

Bibliography

Beam, B. T. and McFadden, J. J. (2001). *Employee Benefits*, 6th edn. Chicago: Dearborn Financial Publishing, pp. 569–87.

Kruse, D. L. (1993). *Profit Sharing: Does It Make a Difference?* Kalamazoo, MI: W. E. Upjohn Institute for Employment Research.

Palmer, B. A. (2001). Profit-sharing plans. In J. S. Rosenbloom (ed.), *The Handbook of Employee Benefits: Design, Funding and Administration*, 5th edn. New York: McGraw-Hill, pp. 601–31.

programmed instruction

Raymond A. Noe

Programmed instruction (PI) is a self-directed training method that includes: (1) clearly defined objectives; (2) trainee-selected pacing; (3) logical sequencing of training material into discrete steps or frames; (4) active responses by the trainees before moving to the next frame; and (5) immediate provision of knowledge of results to trainees. PI has been used in COMPUTER-ASSISTED INSTRUCTION and programmed textbooks.

See also *training*

progressive discipline

Mark R. Sherman

Until the growth in popularity of POSITIVE DISCIPLINE, the relationship between progressive discipline and CORRECTIVE DISCIPLINE has been viewed as inextricable. In the early 1950s, Arbitrator Shister illustrated this close definitional relationship in the *Bell Aircraft* case. He reinstated a worker because management failed to use "proper corrective disciplinary procedures." He went on to identify those procedures as progressive discipline and defined the term as follows: "What progressive discipline does mean is that progressively more severe penalties may be imposed on each given employee each time any offense is repeated. Progressive discipline also means that after a specified number of offenses, regardless of whether the offenses are identical or not, the company may have the right to discharge the given employee" (Redeker, 1989).

The normal stages of progressive discipline include oral warning, written warning, suspension, and ultimately termination. The presumption is that each successive phase will "place the employee on notice" that the type of misconduct exhibited will be met with increasingly severe consequences. Labor contracts and employee handbooks that incorporate progressive discipline provisions generally specify a series of disciplinary steps, a limitation period preventing the consideration of old discipline, and a DISCLAIMER for types of gross misconduct that may be met with summary discharge (*see* EMPLOYEE HANDBOOK; LABOR CONTRACT). Where management inappropriately ignores the principles of progressive discipline in a COLLECTIVE BARGAINING context, arbitrators have shown no reluctance to overturn discipline. Even outside the context of grievance ARBITRATION, courts in some states have been willing to give legal force to progressive discipline policies embodied in employee handbooks.

Bibliography

Elkouri, F. and Elkouri, E. (1985). *How Arbitration Works*, 4th edn. Washington, DC: Bureau of National Affairs.

Fairweather, O. (1984). *Practice and Procedure in Labor Arbitration*, 2nd edn. Washington, DC: Bureau of National Affairs.

Redeker, J. R. (1989). *Employee Discipline*. Washington, DC: Bureau of National Affairs.

promotion

David J. Snyder and Michael A. McDaniel

Promotion involves the advancement of an individual from a particular position to one higher in rank within the organizational hierarchy. An individual who receives a promotion usually has an increase in responsibility. In addition, a promotion is almost always associated with an increase in salary and organizational BENEFITS.

psychological contract

Denise M. Rousseau

A psychological contract is an individual's system of belief, shaped by the organization, regarding the terms of an exchange agreement between himself or herself and the organization. It encompasses the actions employees believe are expected of them (e.g., performance demands) and what response they expect in return from the employer (e.g., rewards, BENEFITS, employment duration). The ideal contract in employment would detail the expectations of both the employee and the organization. Typical contracts, however, are incomplete due to bounded rationality, which limits individual information seeking, and to a changing organizational environment that makes it impossible to specify all conditions upfront. The popularity of the concept grew in the 1980s as a consequence of worker displacement from mergers, acquisitions, and restructurings.

Bibliography

Rousseau, D. M. (1995). *Psychological Contracts in Organizations: Written and Unwritten Agreements*. Newbury Park, CA: Sage.

psychological test

Kevin R. Murphy

A psychological test is a sample of behavior, obtained under standardized conditions, that employs specific scoring rules to obtain quantitative information from those behaviors about the attribute(s) the test is designed to measure (Murphy and Davidshofer, 1994). Written, standardized tests of knowledge, skills, or abilities (see KSAOS) are the most familiar test type, but the domain of psychological tests includes a number of other methods of measurement. In general, psychological tests include: (1) tests of performance, in which a person performs some specific task and is evaluated in terms of the accuracy, speed, correctness, and so forth, of responses; (2) behavioral observations, i.e., observations of an individual's behavior in a specific context, such as an interview or a school setting; and (3) self-reports, measures that ask a person to report or describe feelings, attitudes, beliefs, perceptions, and so forth.

All three types of tests are used in work settings. Tests designed to measure mental abilities and psychomotor abilities (i.e., performance tests) are widely used in PERSONNEL SELECTION. Examples of such tests include the Armed Services Vocational Aptitude Battery and the Wonderlic Personnel Test (see Murphy and Davidshofer, 1994). PERSONALITY TESTS (self-reports; e.g., the NEO Personality Inventory) might also be used for this purpose, although their use in making employment decisions is not as widespread as is the use of ability tests. VOCATIONAL INTEREST INVENTORIES provide the foundation for most types of career counseling, and can have a substantial impact on individuals' decisions about which jobs or careers to pursue. WORK SAMPLES and SITUATIONAL TESTS (i.e., behavioral observation tests) are used in both selection and management development (Thornton and Cleveland, 1990).

There is an important distinction between tests that are designed for individual or for group administration. A number of tests (e.g., the Wechsler Adult Intelligence Scale) are designed to be administered on an individual basis, by a trained examiner. Group tests, on the other hand, can be administered individually or in groups, are often machine scored, and do not require the use of highly trained test administrators. Group tests are much more common than individually administered tests in work settings. Many group tests are now administered via computer, and the use of computerized adaptive testing (in which the choice of test items to administer is determined on the basis of iterative estimates of the subject's standing on the attribute being measured) in work settings is growing rapidly.

Standards for the development, validation, and interpretation of psychological tests are described in the STANDARDS FOR EDUCATIONAL AND PSYCHOLOGICAL TESTING (American Educational Research Association et al., 1999); this document is periodically updated and revised. Detailed reviews of specific tests are published regularly, notably in the *Mental Measurements Yearbook* and *Test Critiques* series. Other reference works (e.g., Sweetland and Keyser, 1991) provide a comprehensive listing of tests that are commercially available; these works contain several hundred entries describing tests that are used, or that might reasonably be used, in work settings.

Bibliography

American Educational Research Association, American Psychological Association, and National Council on Measurement in Education (1999). *Standards for Educational and Psychological Testing*. Washington, DC: American Educational Research Association.

Kramer, J. J. and Conoley, J. C. (1993). *The Eleventh Mental Measurements Yearbook*. Lincoln, NE: Buros Institute of Mental Measurements.

Murphy, K. R. and Davidshofer, C. O. (1994). *Psychological Testing: Principles and Applications*, 3rd edn. Englewood Cliffs, NJ: Prentice-Hall.

Sweetland, R. and Keyser, D. (1991). *Tests: A Comprehensive Reference for Assessments in Psychology, Education, and Business*, 3rd edn. Austin, TX: Pro-Ed.

Thornton, G. C., III and Cleveland, J. N. (1990). Developing managerial talent through simulation. *American Psychologist*, **45**, 190–9.

psychomotor abilities

Paul E. Spector

Psychomotor ability is the capability or capacity to develop or learn a skill that involves both physical and psychological functions. PHYSICAL ABILITIES involve motor activities of the body or limbs, such as running or throwing. Psychological functions include information processing and perception. Examples of psychomotor abilities include eye–hand coordination and balancing. Combinations of physical and psychological functions are important in the performance of many job tasks, including the operation of machinery and the use of hand tools.

public sector bargaining

Peter Feuille

This term refers to the structure and practice of COLLECTIVE BARGAINING between government employers and unions of their employees. As in the private sector, collective bargaining in government consists of (1) the contract negotiation process between union and management representatives over wages, hours, and other employment terms; and (2) the contract administration process whereby union and management representatives handle disagreements over how the contract's terms should be applied to workplace situations on a day-to-day basis (*see* GRIEVANCE PROCEDURE; GRIEVANCES).

Collective bargaining emerged on a large scale in the public sector during the 1965–75 period, accompanied by great controversy. Supporters argued that public employees need unions and bargaining to advance their workplace interests as much as private employees do. In contrast, opponents argued that it is inappropriate for public employees to deal with their employers through a power-based interaction process, and that public employee strikes are especially inappropriate. While these arguments raged, most states and the US government enacted legislation which protects unionization and bargaining rights for their employees, and government employees by the millions joined unions and engaged in bargaining. Most public sector laws limit the scope of negotiations and prohibit work stoppages, and some mandate INTEREST ARBITRATION. Government is now the most highly unionized sector in the American economy, with 45 percent (in 1994) of public employees represented by unions. Research evidence indicates that unionized public employees usually are paid more than their nonunion counterparts.

punitive damages

Barbara A. Lee

Punitive damages may be awarded to the plaintiff against a private sector employer (but not against a public employer) when a finding of intentional DISCRIMINATION is made and the plaintiff has demonstrated that the employer "engaged in a discriminatory practice or discriminatory practices with malice or with reckless indifference to the federally protected rights of an aggrieved individual" (42 USC, section 1981A(b)(1)). Punitive damages are intended to punish the defendant for the unlawful conduct, and need bear no relationship to the plaintiff's actual loss. Title VII caps the total of compensatory and punitive damages; the amount of the cap depends upon the size of the employer. For companies with 500 or more employees, damages are capped at $300,000; the size of the cap declines as the size of the company declines.

quality circles

Susan Albers Mohrman

Quality circles are small groups of employees who get together regularly to identify and solve problems and to generate improvements in the way their work area functions. They deal with issues of quality, PRODUCTIVITY, and cost, and generate solutions that are within their area of control. Some quality circles are within a function, and some are cross-functional. Members are generally chosen from volunteers and are trained in problem-solving, group process, and decision-making skills. They utilize systematic data-based processes and statistical tools to address organizational issues. A facilitator is often present to train the team and guide it through its initial problem-solving efforts. Generally quality circles have the power only to make recommendations; higher-level management teams must approve their recommendations before they can be implemented.

Quality circle advocates tout the desirability of having people close to the work provide meaningful input to decisions. Suggested benefits include better decision-making and greater intrinsic motivation, because people have a chance to participate and influence their work setting. Attitudinal benefits of quality circles, however, have been found to accrue primarily to quality circle participants (e.g., Rafaeli, 1985), not to the entire workforce. This argues that it is the experience of participating, rather than the changes that are made in the workplace, that results in positive attitudes. Participants generally do not get paid for their suggestions, despite many accounts of companies experiencing large financial savings as a result of implementing them. Individual suggestion award programs may be expanded to include quality circle awards. Companies using GAINSHARING programs sometimes introduce quality circles so that employees can generate performance improvements that may result in their receiving a bonus.

Quality circles are parallel structures that focus on change and improvement. They complement the primary organizational structure that focuses on stable execution. Often quality circles are an initial approach to the involvement of employees. They are easy to set up because they do not require a rethinking of the traditional hierarchy. However, they have difficulty attaining organizational legitimacy, since they vie with the regular organization for time, resources, and attention from management (Lawler and Mohrman, 1985). Many suggestions do not get implemented and/or institutionalized. For these reasons, quality circle programs often have a short life cycle. It begins with a period of initial problem solving, often with some highly visible successes, and proceeds through an active period. When the negative dynamics emerge, payoff declines, leading frequently to the demise of the program.

Quality circles were first successfully employed in Japan, where they remain an important mode for improving work processes. US adoption during the 1980s was accompanied by significant quality circle activity in many companies, much of which has now declined or ceased. National differences have been attributed to higher levels of education and commitment among Japanese workers as well as to a greater group orientation (Ishikawa, 1968; Cole, 1979). In the US, some quality circle programs have evolved into TOTAL QUALITY MANAGEMENT programs, also patterned after Japanese quality improvement methodologies. This multifaceted and strategically driven approach to improving work processes generally includes employee participation groups as a key element.

Bibliography

Cole, R. E. (1979). Made in Japan: Quality-control circles. *Across the Board*, 16, 72–7.

Ishikawa, K. (1968). *QC Activities*. Tokyo: Union of Japanese Scientists and Engineers.

Lawler, E. E., III and Mohrman, S. A. (1985). Quality circles after the fad. *Harvard Business Review*, January/February, 65–71.

Ledford, G. E., Jr., Lawler, E. E., III, and Mohrman, S. A. (1988). The quality circle and its variations. In J. P. Campbell, R. J. Campbell, et al. (eds.), *Productivity in Organizations*. San Francisco: Jossey-Bass.

Rafaeli, A. (1985). Quality circles and employee attitudes. *Personnel Psychology*, 38, 603–15.

quality of work life

Lawrence H. Peters

Quality of work life (QWL) is a term that is used to describe system-wide efforts to improve the work environment and satisfy the human needs of its employees. It has been referred to in terms of actual changes in the work setting (e.g., changes in work design aimed at involving employees more in decision-making) as well as in terms of employees' perceptions of those changes and their impact. QWL is an umbrella term that encompasses many different, specific changes. Walton (1974) divided QWL changes into eight specific categories: (1) adequate and fair compensation; (2) a safe and healthy work environment; (3) jobs that develop human capabilities; (4) a chance for personal growth and security; (5) a social environment that provides personal identity, freedom from prejudice, a sense of community, and upward mobility; (6) employee rights to privacy, dissent, and due process; (7) a work role that minimizes infringement on personal leisure and family needs; and (8) socially responsible organizational actions. Changes in one, or several, of these categories would be expected to impact employees' perceptions of the extent to which their needs are being met. As Cascio (1995) notes, not all persons will respond positively to QWL changes designed to increase participation or enrich work. To the extent that QWL changes have their intended effect, however, EMPLOYEE MORALE and commitment should increase, as would the extent to which employees actually feel more empowered to contribute, and actually do contribute, to their organization's success. This involves more than just "cosmetic or piecemeal changes." It requires creating an organization that consistently makes its workforce a key stakeholder, that invests in their competencies and wellbeing, and that encourages and taps their potential for contribution.

Bibliography

Cascio, W. F. (1995). *Managing Human Resources: Productivity, Quality of Work Life, Profits*. New York: McGraw-Hill.

Walton, R. E. (1974). Improving the quality of work life. *Harvard Business Review*, May/June, 12–16.

R

race

Ramona L. Paetzold

Race is one of the protected categories under federal antidiscrimination law (for example, Title VII of the CIVIL RIGHTS ACT OF 1964, section 1981 of the CIVIL RIGHTS ACT OF 1871). Although the definition of race is not specifically provided in the statutes, it is typically broadly interpreted to include persons of all racial or ethnic groups. For example, discrimination against whites as well as against other racial or ethnic groups is proscribed. Examples of nonwhite groups that have received protection under the race category include Hispanics, Jews, and Asian Americans, as well as African Americans.

Railway Labor Act of 1926

Charles E. Krider

The Railway Labor Act of 1926 (amended in 1937) governs labor–management relations in the railroad and airline industries. A separate law for railroads was passed first because they were clearly involved in interstate commerce and Congress could regulate labor relations in the industry under the commerce clause. In addition, it was thought necessary to reduce railroad strikes because of the impact the industry had on the economy at that time.

The Act has two major objectives: to protect the right of employees to organize unions and to provide alternatives to strikes for resolving disputes. The Act is enforced by the National Mediation Board, whose three members are appointed by the president.

RIGHT TO ORGANIZE

Congress recognized for the first time that a group of employees "shall have the right to organize and bargain collectively through representatives of their own choosing." Employers are prohibited from denying in any way the right of employees to join, organize, or assist a union. If there is a dispute over union representation then the National Mediation Board is authorized to determine the issue, and may conduct a secret ballot election to determine the employees' representative.

DISPUTE RESOLUTION

The Act seeks to reduce the occurrence of strikes by providing for alternative mechanisms to resolve disputes. First, either party may refer a dispute over GRIEVANCES or the application of an agreement to the National Railroad Adjustment Board. Its awards are final and binding on the parties and are enforceable in federal court.

Second, disputes over changes in wages or terms of employment may be submitted to the National Mediation Board. The Mediation Board seeks to resolve the dispute through MEDIATION and may seek to have the parties agree to ARBITRATION. If either party does not agree to arbitration then the Mediation Board must notify the president, who can appoint an emergency board to investigate the dispute and make a report with a recommendation on how the dispute should be settled. Neither side can make a unilateral change during these procedures, except by agreement, and the union may not strike.

These procedures obviously delay strikes and make COLLECTIVE BARGAINING more difficult. Each side has an incentive to hold something back during negotiations in order to have something to give during mediation or later. The availability of mediation, arbitration, and presidential boards almost guarantees that they will be used.

ranking job evaluation method

David B. Balkin

The ranking method of job evaluation rank orders the relative worth of jobs based on comparison of each job as documented in the JOB DESCRIPTION. One way to achieve this ranking is with paired comparisons for all the jobs until they can be ranked from most to least valuable (Milkovich and Newman, 1993). The ranking method of job evaluation is the quickest, easiest, and least costly method to use. It is mainly used in smaller firms with a modest number of different jobs, since evaluators need to be familiar with all the jobs in order to make reliable comparisons between jobs for purposes of evaluation (Belcher and Atchison, 1989).

See also *job evaluation methods*

Bibliography

Belcher, D. W. and Atchison, T. J. (1989). *Compensation Administration*, 2nd edn. Englewood Cliffs, NJ: Prentice-Hall.

Milkovich, G. T. and Newman, J. M. (1993). *Compensation*, 4th edn. Homewood, IL: Richard D. Irwin.

ranking method of performance evaluation

Robert L. Cardy

The ranking method of performance evaluation requires a rater to order all ratees from highest to lowest. While it is possible to rank order ratees on each of several performance dimensions, simply ordering ratees on an overall performance dimension seems most common.

An important advantage of the ranking method is that it forces raters to differentiate among ratees (Cardy and Dobbins, 1994). The ranking method, therefore, controls RATING ERRORS such as leniency (*see* LENIENCY EFFECTS) and severity, and forces distinctions among workers.

Disadvantages of the ranking method include:

1 The task can become time consuming and difficult when there are a large number of ratees.
2 The ordinal nature of ranking data does not allow for a determination of the relative distances among ratees. That is, while rankings can tell you that one person is judged to be better than another, they cannot indicate "how much" better that person might be.
3 Rankings cannot be compared across different groups of raters. For example, one group may be better performers than another group, but the separate rankings cannot reflect this performance difference. A top-ranked performer in one group may have a performance level of only an average-ranked worker in another group.
4 Finally, it should also be recognized that ranking does not provide information as to *why* the worker received his or her ranking. Thus, the ranking method is not effective for feedback and development purposes, particularly when ranking is done only for overall JOB PERFORMANCE.

Bibliography

Cardy, R. L. and Dobbins, G. H. (1994). *Performance Appraisal: Alternative Perspectives*. Cincinnati, OH: South-Western Publishing.

rate ranges

Thomas H. Stone

A rate or pay range is the minimum to maximum level of pay assigned to a PAY GRADE/JOB FAMILY or class in a pay structure. The midpoint of a range usually corresponds to the employer's wage or pay policy line. Employees paid at this level are judged to be performing at a satisfactory level. Range minimum reflects the lowest value placed on jobs in the range while the maximum indicates the most the job(s) are worth to that employer. Setting rate ranges involves issues of both INTERNAL EQUITY/INTERNAL CONSISTENCY and EXTERNAL EQUITY/EXTERNAL COMPETITIVENESS. Conceptually, rate ranges are related to SD_y in staffing (*see* SD_y; SELECTION UTILITY MODELS).

rater training

Elaine D. Pulakos

Rater training is used in a variety of different situations in which raters are required to provide subjective judgments of another person's performance effectiveness. For example, rater training is used to teach supervisors how to provide appropriate performance appraisals of their subordinates (*see* PERFORMANCE APPRAISAL). It is also used to train interviewers and assessors in how to properly evaluate candidates in employment interviews (*see* EMPLOYMENT INTERVIEW) and ASSESSMENT CENTERS, respectively. Rater training is important because subjective judgments of performance tend to introduce distortion into the measurement process. Well-developed rater training programs have been shown to increase the quality and effectiveness of subjective ratings.

CHARACTERISTICS OF EFFECTIVE RATER TRAINING PROGRAMS

In general, effective rater training applies the basic principles of learning. Successful rater training programs have been characterized by four key learning components:

1. *Lecture*. Trainees receive oral instruction on the training objectives (*see* LECTURE METHOD).
2. *Practice*. Trainees are given an opportunity to practice making ratings. This is often accomplished by having trainees practice observing and rating videotaped performances.
3. *Group discussion*. Trainees are provided with an opportunity to discuss and provide rationales for their practice ratings.
4. *Feedback*. Trainees are given immediate feedback on their practice ratings. The content of the feedback is specific and reflects the training objectives.

RATER TRAINING APPROACHES

Although different rater training techniques have been advocated, these programs can generally be classified into two major categories: rater error training and rater accuracy training (*see* RATING ACCURACY; RATING ERRORS).

Rater error training. Performance evaluations are often affected by various rating errors, or faults in human judgment that occur when one individual evaluates another. These rating errors (e.g., HALO EFFECTS, LENIENCY EFFECTS, and CENTRAL TENDENCY EFFECTS) can lessen the reliability, validity, accuracy, and usefulness of ratings. Accordingly, early rater training programs focused on teaching raters how to avoid making common rating errors by providing definitions and examples of the errors and how they can be avoided in a rating situation (see Latham, Wexley, and Pursell, 1975, for an example of an error training program). Although rater error training approaches have been shown to successfully reduce common rating errors, they have not been particularly effective in increasing rating accuracy, which is the crucial criterion in judging the quality of ratings.

Rating accuracy is the extent to which a set of ratings reflects a ratee's true or actual performance level. Although error training is still an aspect of some rater training programs, recent approaches to rater training have focused more directly on improving rater accuracy.

Rater accuracy training. Several approaches for increasing the accuracy of ratings have been offered. For example, Banks and Robertson (1985) describe an approach to accuracy training called assessment skills training. This training focuses on training raters in how behavior relevant to different performance dimensions of interest might be manifested in different job situations. Hedge and Kavanaugh (1988) describe observational training in which raters are taught how to make appropriate and accurate behavioral observations. These authors also describe a decision training program, which focuses on the processes by which accurate judgments about performance effectiveness are made.

One approach to accuracy training, in particular, has received considerable research attention.

The strategy, labeled frame-of-reference (FOR) training (Bernardin and Buckley, 1981), typically involves training raters about the multidimensional nature of performance, defining the different performance dimensions relevant to the situation or job, providing sample behaviors that represent different levels of effectiveness on the different dimensions, and providing practice and feedback to trainees in how to make accurate ratings. The primary objective of FOR training is to train raters to use common conceptualizations about performance and what constitutes different levels of effectiveness when they are making evaluations of others. This FOR approach to training has been shown to be more effective in increasing rating accuracy than other types of (or no) training (McIntyre, Smith, and Hassett, 1984; Pulakos, 1984, 1986; Athey and McIntyre, 1987).

In summary, rater training programs that focus directly on increasing rater accuracy yield higher-quality ratings than other approaches to rating training. The design of any rater training program should, however, incorporate the key learning components (i.e., lecture, practice, discussion, and feedback) to achieve optimal results.

Bibliography

Athey, T. R. and McIntyre, R. M. (1987). Effect of rater training on rater accuracy: Levels of processing theory and social facilitation theory perspectives. *Journal of Applied Psychology*, 72, 567–72.

Banks, C. G. and Robertson, L. (1985). Performance appraisers as test developers. *Academy of Management Review*, 10, 128–42.

Bernardin, H. J. and Buckley, M. R. (1981). Strategies in rater training. *Academy of Management Review*, 6, 205–12.

Hedge, J. W. and Kavanaugh, M. J. (1988). Improving the accuracy of performance evaluations: Comparison of three methods of performance appraiser training. *Journal of Applied Psychology*, 73, 68–73.

Latham, G. P., Wexley, K. N., and Pursell, E. D. (1975). Training managers to minimize rating errors in the observation of behavior. *Journal of Applied Psychology*, 60, 550–5.

McIntyre, R. M., Smith, D., and Hassett, C. E. (1984). Accuracy of performance ratings as affected by perceived purpose of rating. *Journal of Applied Psychology*, 69, 147–56.

Pulakos, E. D. (1984). A comparison of error training programs: Error training and accuracy training. *Journal of Applied Psychology*, 69, 581–8.

Pulakos, E. D. (1986). The development of training programs to increase accuracy with different rating tasks. *Organizational Behavior and Human Decision Processes*, 38, 76–91.

rating accuracy

Kevin R. Murphy

Rating accuracy refers to the correspondence between PERFORMANCE APPRAISAL ratings and actual performance levels. Because acceptable measures of actual performance (often referred to as "true scores") are often difficult to obtain in field settings, rating accuracy is often inferred on the basis of the psychometric characteristics of the ratings. For example, a number of rating errors measures (e.g., measures of HALO EFFECTS, LENIENCY EFFECTS, CENTRAL TENDENCY EFFECTS) might be used to evaluate ratings. In the absence of such errors, accuracy is sometimes assumed. However, research on rater error measures and other indirect measures of accuracy suggests that these measures cannot be used to determine the accuracy of performance ratings (Sulsky and Balzer, 1988; Murphy and Balzer, 1989). The measurement of rating accuracy requires the development of some normative standard or true score.

STANDARDS FOR EVALUATING ACCURACY

Rating accuracy measures are most often encountered in laboratory research studies (e.g., Borman 1977; Murphy et al., 1982), where it is possible to videotape the performance being evaluated and develop normative true scores. These scores are obtained from multiple expert raters, who have opportunities to observe and evaluate ratings under optimal conditions (e.g., multiple observations of each tape, freedom from distractions). If adequate evidence of convergent and discriminant validity can be demonstrated in these expert ratings, the mean over several experts is accepted as a good approximation of the true performance level, and rating accuracy can be evaluated by comparing an individual rater's evaluations with these expert true scores.

Alternatively, accuracy can be assessed using behavior-recognition measures. In this method, raters are asked whether or not they have observed certain behaviors, and their ratings are checked against videotapes of the performance observed. A number of indices based on signal detection theory can be used to assess raters' sensitivity and biases in remembering or recognizing specific behaviors (Sulsky and Balzer, 1988; Murphy, 1991). Behavior-based methods are thought to assess the accuracy of observation and memory, whereas true score-based measures are thought to assess the accuracy of evaluative judgments about performance.

ACCURACY MEASURES

Measures of accuracy based on comparisons between performance ratings and some normative true score must often be broken down into multiple components; simple differences between ratings and true scores are generally uninterpretable. Cronbach (1955) showed that differences between any rating and some set of standards reflected at least four distinct facets of accuracy: (1) accuracy of the overall mean rating (elevation); (2) accuracy in distinguishing among ratees (differential elevation); (3) accuracy in distinguishing overall strengths from overall weaknesses (stereotype accuracy); and (4) accuracy in distinguishing individual patterns of JOB PERFORMANCE (differential accuracy). There is considerable evidence that these aspects of accuracy are largely independent of one another, unrelated to a number of alternative accuracy measures, and unrelated to a number of indirect measures of accuracy (Sulsky and Balzer, 1988; Murphy and Balzer, 1989).

IS ACCURACY ALWAYS DESIRABLE?

As Murphy and Cleveland (1995) note, performance ratings have a number of purposes in organizations, and the accurate measurement of job performance might be only one of the many goals pursued by raters, ratees, and organizations. Rating accuracy is most desirable when ratings lead directly to administrative decisions (and when there is clear consensus that these decisions should be made on the basis of current job performance), or when they are used for strictly development purposes. Accuracy may be less desirable (and may even interfere with more important uses of performance appraisal) when ratings are used to motivate employees, or to communicate implicit standards and norms (Murphy and Cleveland, 1995).

Bibliography

Borman, W. C. (1977). Consistency of rating accuracy and rater errors in the judgment of human performance. *Organizational Behavior and Human Performance*, 20, 238–52.

Cronbach, L. J. (1955). Processes affecting scores on "understanding of others" and "assumed similarity." *Psychological Bulletin*, 52, 177–93.

Murphy, K. R. (1991). Criterion issues in performance appraisal research: Behavioral accuracy vs. classification accuracy. *Organizational Behavior and Human Decision Processes*, 50, 45–50.

Murphy, K. R. and Balzer, W. K. (1989). Rater errors and rating accuracy. *Journal of Applied Psychology*, 74, 619–24.

Murphy, K. R. and Cleveland, J. N. (1995). *Understanding Performance Appraisal: Social, Organizational and Goal-Oriented Perspectives*. Thousand Oaks, CA: Sage.

Murphy, K. R., Garcia, M., Kerkar, S., Martin, C., and Balzer, W. K. (1982). The relationship between observational accuracy and accuracy in evaluating performance. *Journal of Applied Psychology*, 67, 320–5.

Sulsky, L. M. and Balzer, W. K. (1988). The meaning and measurement of performance rating accuracy: Some methodological concerns. *Journal of Applied Psychology*, 73, 497–506.

rating bias

Kevin R. Murphy

Rating bias refers to a wide variety of distortions in PERFORMANCE APPRAISAL ratings. Rating biases can be distinguished from RATING ERRORS in the sense that bias usually refers to the systematic effect of some presumably irrelevant variable on the mean rating (and sometimes the variability of ratings). LENIENCY EFFECTS are an example of a widely studied rating bias. As this example suggests, however, some rating biases might lead to rating errors.

The source of performance ratings is often considered a potential source of bias. For example, SELF-RATINGS are usually higher than ratings obtained from other sources, which may indicate a self-serving bias (Gioia and Sims, 1985), PEER RATINGS might be upwardly biased by friendship, or might be unduly severe when peers are in direct competition. Ratings could be biased by demographic characteristics, such as race (Kraiger and Ford, 1985), gender, or age, but most reviews of performance appraisal research suggest that demographic effects of rating bias are small.

Rating bias might also reflect differences in performance appraisals due to organizational climates and cultures, work group norms, or simple differences in supervisors' tendencies to use specific parts of the rating scale (Wherry and Bartlett, 1982). While rating biases are thought to reduce RATING ACCURACY, the evidence linking rating biases to inaccuracy is weak.

Bibliography

Gioia, D. A. and Sims, H. P. (1985). Self-serving bias and actor–observer differences in organizations: An empirical analysis. *Journal of Applied Social Psychology*, 15, 547–63.

Kraiger, K. and Ford, J. K. (1985). A meta-analysis of race effects in performance appraisal. *Journal of Applied Psychology*, 70, 56–65.

Wherry, R. J. and Bartlett, C. J. (1982). The control of bias in ratings: A theory of rating. *Personnel Psychology*, 35, 521–55.

rating errors

Kevin R. Murphy

Rating errors refer to distortions in PERFORMANCE APPRAISAL ratings that are assumed to reduce RATING ACCURACY. A wide variety of rating errors have been described in the research literature (Saal, Downey, and Lahey, 1980), but most discussions of these errors focus on HALO EFFECTS, LENIENCY EFFECTS, and CENTRAL TENDENCY EFFECTS.

Rating errors represent differences between characteristics of the ratings and assumed characteristics of the performance to be evaluated. Halo errors are thought be the result of raters generalizing from their overall impressions of each subordinate when evaluating specific aspects of performance (Murphy, Jako, and Anhalt, 1993). Errors of this sort will inflate the intercorrelations among ratings of separate aspects of performance, and can make it difficult to validly distinguish individual strengths and weaknesses. Leniency errors occur when ratings are unrealistically high; rating inflation is often assumed to result from raters' unwillingness to face the consequences of giving low ratings, even when they are clearly deserved (Murphy and Cleveland, 1995). Central tendency errors occur when raters do not distinguish between individuals and/or between specific aspects of performance.

CAUSES AND CONSEQUENCES OF RATING ERRORS

Although some rating errors may be the result of conscious distortions on the part of the rater (e.g., raters might knowingly inflate ratings to avoid confrontations with ratees; Murphy and Cleveland, 1995), they are usually thought to reflect faulty cognitive processes used by raters in evaluating their subordinates. The cognitive processes that contribute to halo errors have been widely studied and there is extensive evidence that attention, encoding, and memory biases can all contribute to halo (Murphy et al., 1993). While leniency and central tendency errors may have both cognitive and motivational causes, they are likely to be strongly affected by rating norms in an organization.

Rating error indices have long been used as indirect measures of rating accuracy, based on the assumption that the sorts of cognitive and motivational distortions that lead to these errors will also decrease the accuracy of ratings. However, there is little evidence that rating errors in fact lead to inaccuracy (Murphy and Balzer, 1989), and the use of rating error measures as criteria for evaluating ratings has been widely criticized (Murphy et al., 1993). Indeed, there is evidence that some "rating errors" (e.g., halo) can *increase* the accuracy of performance ratings (Nathan and Tippins, 1990).

Two strategies have been pursued in attempting to reduce halo, leniency, and/or central tendency. First, a number of RATER TRAINING programs have been developed. Although it is possible to train raters to avoid halo, leniency, and the like, this type of training does not appear to increase the accuracy or usefulness of rating. Second, a number of behaviorally oriented rating scale formats have been developed, with the goal of increasing the accuracy of ratings (e.g., BEHAVIORAL OBSERVATION SCALES, BEHAVIORALLY ANCHORED RATING SCALES). However, there is little evidence that the use of these rating scales reduces rating errors or inaccuracy. To date, no method of reducing rating errors *and* increasing the accuracy and usefulness of ratings has been developed.

ARE RATING ERRORS A SERIOUS PROBLEM?

Measures of halo, leniency, and central tendency have long been used as criteria for evaluating performance ratings, training programs, rating scales, and so forth. Use of rating error measures as criteria, however, is no longer justified. They do not provide information about the accuracy of ratings, the success of training, or the usefulness of scale formats. Obtaining information about the means, variances, and intercorrelations among ratings has some value, but none of these measures permits direct inferences about the *quality* of rating data.

Bibliography

Murphy, K. and Balzer, W. (1989). Rater errors and rating accuracy. *Journal of Applied Psychology*, 74, 619–24.

Murphy, K. R. and Cleveland, J. N. (1995). *Understanding Performance Appraisal: Social, Organizational, and Goal-Oriented Perspectives*. Thousand Oaks, CA: Sage.

Murphy, K., Jako, R. A., and Anhalt, R. L. (1993). The nature and consequences of halo error: A critical analysis. *Journal of Applied Psychology*, 78, 218–25.

Nathan, B. R. and Tippins, N. (1990). The consequences of halo "error" in performance ratings: A field study of the moderating effects of halo on validity study results. *Journal of Applied Psychology*, 75, 290–6.

Saal, F. E., Downey, R. G., and Lahey, M. A. (1980). Rating the ratings: Assessing the quality of rating data. *Psychological Bulletin*, 88, 413–28.

realistic job previews

John P. Wanous

The realistic job preview (RJP) is an external RECRUITING strategy. An RJP contains accurate information about job duties, which can be obtained from a JOB ANALYSIS. It also contains information about an organization's culture, which can be obtained from EXIT INTERVIEWS and/or surveys. There are three criteria for something being included in an RJP: (1) it is important to most recruits, (2) it is not widely known outside the organization, and (3) it is a reason that leads newcomers to quit.

This information is communicated to job applicants *prior* to organizational entry. For example, the RJP can be posted on a website, discussed during the EMPLOYMENT INTERVIEW, be handed out as a brochure, be shown as a video, or be discussed during a job visit (with, for example, potential coworkers). Combining two or more of these methods may increase the impact of the RJP. Realistic information disseminated *after* organizational entry is newcomer orientation (*see* NEW EMPLOYEE ORIENTATION) or ORGANIZATIONAL SOCIALIZATION (Wanous and Reichers, 2000).

The purpose of an RJP is to increase the degree of "fit" between newcomers and the organizations they join, with the ultimate goal of increasing both the retention and performance of new hires (Wanous, 1992). Although the RJP may initially increase stress for job candidates, it will eventually increase newcomer JOB SATISFACTION, commitment to the organization, and, as a result, increase the retention of new hires. RJPs have also been found to increase JOB PERFORMANCE, but only if the videotape format is used (Premack and Wanous, 1985; Phillips, 1998). The most probable reason for this is that role models of effective job performance can be shown to recruits.

There are several explanations for the effects of RJPs on retention. First, the information provided in an RJP helps job candidates to choose more effectively among job offers. Second, the RJP can "vaccinate" expectations against disappointment after organizational entry, because the most dissatisfying job/organizational factors have already been anticipated. Third, the information in an RJP can help newcomers to cope more effectively with their job duties as well as the stress associated with being in a new environment. Finally, an RJP can enhance the perceived trustworthiness of the organization to job candidates, thus increasing their initial commitment to the organization.

Several guidelines for designing an RJP have been suggested (Wanous, 1992: 61–4; Phillips, 1998: 684–7). First, self-selection should be explicitly encouraged; that is, job candidates should be advised to carefully consider whether to accept or reject a job offer. Second, the RJP "message" must be credible. This can be facilitated by using actual employees as communicators. Third, interviews are an excellent method when job candidate questions are expected, because a two-way conversation can take place. Interviews have been shown to be the single most effective medium for increasing retention (Phillips, 1998). Fourth, how typical employees feel about the organization, not just sterile facts, must be part of an RJP. Fifth, the balance between positive and negative information should closely match the realities of the job itself. Finally, the RJP should normally be done early in the recruiting process, before job candidates expend too much energy trying to obtain a job offer. (An exception would be to position the RJP at the end of executive recruitment.)

Research continues to uncover the boundaries for RJPs. First, if the retention rate for new hires is very low (e.g., most newcomers quit before one year), the job may be so undesirable that RJPs will have little effect. Similarly in organizations with very high retention, RJPs may not be able to improve on an already high level. Thus, the RJP is most effective when the one-year job retention rate for newcomers is in the 50–80 percent range, increasing the retention rate by about 10 percent, e.g., from 50 percent to 55 percent (Wanous, 1992). Second, if the RELEVANT LABOR MARKET has relatively few job openings, the RJP will have little effect on a job candidate's job choice. Third, RJPs appear to be more effective when job candidates have some previous job knowledge or work experience, because they can fully understand the information provided to them (Meglino, DeNisi, and Ravlin, 1993). Fourth, RJPs increase newcomer retention more so in business organizations than in the military (Wanous, 1992; Phillips, 1998).

RJPs may also be relevant for other aspects of human resource management. They could easily be used for preparing managers for international assignments (Black et al., 1999; see EXPATRIATE ASSIGNMENT). Some STAFFING techniques also communicate realistic information and may complement the RJP. These include: the SITUATIONAL INTERVIEW. "inside" recruiting sources (i.e., employee referrals and rehires; see Zottoli and Wanous, 2000), and ASSESSMENT CENTERS (e.g., Thornton and Byham, 1982).

Bibliography

Black, J. S., Gregersen, H. B., Mendenhall, M. E., and Stroh, L. K. (1999). *Globalizing People through International Assignments*. Reading, MA: Addison-Wesley.

Meglino, B. M., DeNisi, A. S., and Ravlin, E. C. (1993). Effects of previous job exposure and subsequent job status on the functioning of a realistic job preview. *Personnel Psychology*, **46**, 803–22.

Phillips, J. M. (1998). Effects of realistic job previews on multiple organizational outcomes: A meta-analysis. *Academy of Management Journal*, **41**, 673–90.

Premack, S. L. and Wanous, J. P. (1985). A meta-analysis of realistic job preview experiments. *Journal of Applied Psychology*, **70**, 706–19.

Thornton, G. C. and Byham, W. C. (1982). *Assessment Centers and Managerial Performance*. San Diego, CA: Academic Press.

Wanous, J. P. (1992). *Organizational Entry: Recruitment, Selection, Orientation, and Socialization of Newcomers*. Reading, MA: Addison-Wesley.

Wanous, J. P. and Reichers, A. E. (2000). New employee orientation programs. *Human Resource Management Review*, **10**, 435–51.

Zottoli, M. A. and Wanous, J. F. (2000). Recruitment source research: Current status and future directions. *Human Resource Management Review*, **10**, 353–82.

recruiting

James A. Breaugh

Recruiting consists of organizational activities that provide a pool of applicants for the purpose of filling job openings. Successful recruitment requires careful planning and strategy development, well-designed recruitment actions, and the evaluation of past recruitment efforts (Rynes, 1991).

RECRUITMENT PLANNING

Recruitment planning should be carefully integrated with an employer's HUMAN RESOURCE STRATEGY. Among the issues that an employer should address in recruitment planning are: (1) does it wish to fill positions internally or externally (see RECRUITING SOURCES); (2) what are the job specifications for the open positions (see JOB SPECIFICATION); (3) is AFFIRMATIVE ACTION a consideration; and (4) what are its budgetary constraints?

RECRUITMENT STRATEGY DEVELOPMENT

In developing a recruitment strategy, an employer should address numerous issues. Among the most important of these are (1) what is the RELEVANT LABOR MARKET from which it will recruit; (2) what is the recruitment message it wants to convey; and (3) what recruitment method(s) will it use to communicate this message?

In deciding upon the relevant labor market from which to recruit (e.g., PhD chemists), an employer should consider a variety of factors (e.g., are members of the targeted group likely to be qualified for and interested in the jobs the employer has to fill?). For legal compliance reasons, employers have made special efforts to recruit members of protected groups. To effectively recruit members of protected groups, an employer needs to carefully plan its actions. For example, some recruitment methods (e.g., employee referrals) may be less effective in reaching members of protected groups than other methods (e.g., publicizing positions at a minority job fair). In a similar vein, recruiters who are comparable in relevant background characteristics (e.g., race) to the type of persons being recruited may be seen as having more credibility (Breaugh, 1992).

A key issue in recruitment strategy development is deciding what information about the job and the organization to convey to applicants (Rynes, 1991). If an employer's goal is to attract a large number of applicants, then its recruitment message is likely to present only the positive features of a job. However, such a recruitment message is one-sided, can be perceived as deceptive, and can result in undesirable outcomes (e.g., EMPLOYEE TURNOVER) for the organization (Wanous, 1992). In contrast to a deceptive recruitment message, REALISTIC JOB PREVIEWS provide applicants with an accurate view of the job. The provision of accurate information has been shown to have benefits for both individuals (JOB SATISFACTION) and employers (less turnover). In making decisions about the design of recruitment communications, an employer should consider whether it is conveying the type of information that will help applicants make good job choice decisions.

Once it has determined the information that it wants to convey, an employer needs to decide upon the recruitment method(s) that will most effectively fill positions. Early recruitment communications should attract attention and generate interest (Breaugh, 1992). During the course of the recruitment process, other recruitment methods (e.g., conversations with job incumbents) can provide detailed information about the job opening. Given the number of recruitment methods that can be utilized (e.g., JOB POSTING, EXECUTIVE SEARCH), it is impossible to discuss all of them. Nevertheless, each recruitment method has its pros and cons. For example, the use of employee referrals allows current employees to screen prospective employees and provide realistic job previews. However, the use of employee referrals tends to have adverse impact on protected groups.

RECRUITMENT ACTIVITIES AND RECRUITMENT EVALUATION

Given that an employer has carefully considered its recruitment strategy, carrying out recruitment activities (e.g., writing job advertisements, training recruiters) should be a fairly straightforward process. Once an organization has completed its recruitment actions for filling a job opening, it should evaluate those efforts (Heneman and Heneman, 1994). Among the criteria an employer could assess are: (1) the number of applications generated by each recruitment method; (2) the YIELD RATIO for each step of the recruitment process; (3) the cost per recruit; (4) the number of minority job applicants recruited; and (5) first year performance of new hires. The results of an employer's evaluation of recruitment activities can be used in future recruitment planning and strategy development.

See also *strategic recruiting*

Bibliography

Breaugh, J. A. (1992). *Recruitment: Science and Practice*. Boston: PWS-Kent.

Heneman, H. H. and Heneman, R. L. (1994). *Staffing Organizations*. Middleton, WI: Mendota House.

Rynes, S. L. (1991). Recruitment, job choice, and post-hire consequences. In M. D. Dunnette and L. M. Hough (eds.), *Handbook of Industrial and Organizational Psychology*, 2nd edn. Palo Alto, CA: Consulting Psychologists Press.

Wanous, J. P. (1992). *Organizational Entry: Recruitment, Selection, Orientation, and Socialization of Newcomers*. Reading, MA: Addison-Wesley.

recruiting sources

Robert D. Gatewood

Recruiting sources are methods used by organizations to transmit information about open positions to potential applicants. These sources can differ in the type of applicants reached, amount of information transmitted, and cost. Recruiting sources can be categorized into two types: *internal* and *external* recruiting sources. Internal recruiting sources refer to methods that transmit information to *current* employees. The most common internal source is JOB POSTING, in which position information is directly provided to employees. Interested employees may choose to apply. Breaugh (1992) describes "closed" internal sources whereby applicants may *not* know that they are being considered for a position. Examples include nominations by supervisor(s), replacement charts developed by top management, and computerized job–person matching systems.

External recruiting sources refer to methods directed to individuals who are not current employees. The most common external sources are: brochures, videotapes, advertisements in newspapers, magazines, and professional periodicals, announcements on radio, television, and electronic networks, job fairs, employee referrals, internships, and educational site visits.

Research has attempted to compare the results of various recruiting sources in terms of such variables as JOB SATISFACTION, tenure, and JOB PERFORMANCE. Rynes (1991) concludes that no consistent differences among sources have been determined. These inconsistencies may partially reflect the fact that satisfaction, tenure, and performance are influenced by several factors, besides recruitment. In addition, Williams, Labig, and Stone (1993) found that applicants frequently use multiple recruiting sources. Therefore, the effects of an individual recruitment source may be difficult to assess.

Bibliography

Breaugh, J. A. (1992). *Recruitment: Science and Practice*. Boston: PWS-Kent.

Rynes, S. L. (1991). Recruitment, job choice, and post-hire consequences. In M. D. Dunnette and L. M. Hough (eds.), *Handbook of Industrial and Organizational Psychology*, 2nd edn, vol. 2. Palo Alto, CA: Consulting Psychologists Press.

Williams, C. R., Labig, C. E., Jr., and Stone, T. H. (1993). Recruitment sources and posthire outcomes for job applicants and new hires: A test of two hypotheses. *Journal of Applied Psychology*, 78, 163–72.

red circle jobs

Thomas H. Stone

A red circle job indicates that the incumbent is paid more than the maximum for the job or range rate. Many red circle-rate jobs suggest pay structure control problems, such as managers who have raised employees' pay above rate-range maximums. However, red circle rates may also occur if a new job evaluation results in a lower evaluation of some jobs. The common practice for handling red circle jobs is to freeze the pay at that level for the current incumbent until either the job moves within the rate range as a result of wage structure adjustments over time or the incumbent leaves the job.

redeployment

Stanley Nollen

Redeployment refers to the lateral movement of a group of employees from one type of job or

reference checks

Craig J. Russell

Reference checks are a form of BACKGROUND CHECKING (GENERIC). Applicants provide names of individuals who can verify information provided by the applicant and/or provide additional information. Many organizations perform routine reference checks to avoid embarrassment or legal liability for future events (e.g., disclosure by an investigative news reporter that a high school principal had been hired based on false college transcripts) (Sloane, 1991). However, reference checks generally do not target issues of personal integrity beyond confirmation of information provided by the applicant (*see* INTEGRITY TESTING). Reference checks can also target knowledge, skills, and abilities (*see* KSAOS), tasks, and behavioral requirements obtained from a JOB ANALYSIS.

Like background checks, reference checks are usually conducted by telephone and can be used to verify information obtained from WEIGHTED APPLICATION BLANKS and BIOGRAPHICAL HISTORY INVENTORIES (Muchinsky, 1979). Lack of standardized procedures greatly decreases reliability, causing CRITERION-RELATED VALIDITY to generally be poor.

Bibliography

Muchinsky, P. M. (1979). The use of reference reports in personnel selection: A review and evaluation of value. *Journal of Occupational Psychology*, **52**, 287–97.

Sloane, A. A. (1991). Countering resume fraud within and beyond banking: No excuse for not doing more. *Labor Law Journal*, 303–10.

Rehabilitation Act of 1973

Stuart A. Youngblood

DISCRIMINATION against handicapped workers is not covered by Title VII of the CIVIL RIGHTS ACT OF 1964. Instead, the Rehabilitation Act and the AMERICANS WITH DISABILITIES ACT OF 1990 (ADA) provide coverage for these workers. The Rehabilitation Act applies only to government contractors or other government-financed organizations and requires AFFIRMATIVE ACTION. A handicap is defined very broadly as: (1) a physical or mental impairment; (2) a record of such impairment; or (3) a person who is regarded as having such an impairment. The Act does, however, exclude individuals defined as alcoholics or drug abusers (*see* EMPLOYEE ASSISTANCE PROGRAMS) or any individual who has a currently contagious disease or infection that constitutes a threat to other employees or customers or who is unable to perform the duties of the job. Conditions that have been held to constitute a protected handicap include diabetes, high blood pressure, heart conditions, epilepsy, dyslexia, and post-traumatic stress disorder.

Similar to the ADA, the Rehabilitation Act requires employers to make a "reasonable accommodation" to the handicapped, which typically means providing job access and in some cases job redesign. Reasonable accommodation is a gray area of the law and has been clarified by case law and reliance on the concepts of BUSINESS NECESSITY and financial costs and expenses. Employers have mistakenly interpreted the Rehabilitation Act by tolerating lower JOB PERFORMANCE from handicapped workers and hesitating to discipline and terminate alcoholic and drug-dependent employees for poor job performance. Moreover, in some jobs, refusal to hire an applicant with a handicap may be a BONA FIDE OCCUPATIONAL QUALIFICATION.

Bibliography

Ledvinka, J. and Scarpello, V. G. (1991). *Federal Regulation of Personnel and Human Resource Management*, 2nd edn. Boston: PWS-Kent.

reinforcement

David J. Cherrington

Reinforcement refers to the consequences following a target behavior that increase the likelihood of its occurrence. Positive reinforcers are positive stimuli that have the effect of increasing the probability of a response, while negative reinforcers are aversive stimuli that decrease the probability of a response. In a work setting, some of the most popular positive reinforcers include money, pay increases, promotions, praise, and recognition. Negative reinforcers include criticism, fatigue, boring work assignments, injuries, and unpleasant working conditions.

A distinction is often made between primary and secondary reinforcers. Primary reinforcers are satisfying events associated with physiological needs, such as food, water, sex, rest, and the removal of pain. Secondary reinforcers are learned reinforcers acquired through a process of value internalization, such as social approval, recognition, pride in craftsmanship, and money.

The relationship between behavior and subsequent reinforcement is called a reinforcement contingency. Contingencies include: (1) positive reinforcement contingency, where the occurrence of a target behavior is followed by a positive reinforcer; (2) negative reinforcement contingency, where the occurrence of the target behavior is followed by a decrease in the negative reinforcer; (3) punishment, where a decrease in the target behavior is required to eliminate the presence of an aversive stimulus; (4) extinction, where all reinforcement is withheld to eliminate a response; and (5) combination strategies, where, for example, extinction and positive reinforcement are used to weaken an undesirable response and strengthen a different, desirable response.

Reinforcement schedules refer to the timing of reinforcement. A continuous reward schedule rewards every correct response. An intermittent schedule rewards every Nth response, where N can be either a fixed or a variable number. An interval schedule rewards the first correct response after an interval of time, where the length of the interval can be either fixed or variable. Variable ratio and variable interval schedules create a high response rate and are very resistant to extinction.

relevant labor market

Stuart A. Youngblood and Lawrence H. Peters

The relevant labor market is a term used by the US Department of Labor OFFICE OF FEDERAL CONTRACT COMPLIANCE PROGRAMS (OFCCP) and US federal courts (*see Wards Cove Packing Co. v. Antonio*, 490 US 642, 1989) in matters associated with employment DISCRIMINATION and AFFIRMATIVE ACTION. Determination of the relevant labor market is necessary when employers conduct a UTILIZATION ANALYSIS and an availability analysis as required by Revised Order No. 4 issued by the OFCCP for federal contractors. A utilization analysis consists of describing the percentages of a protected group (e.g., race or sex) of employees by occupation within the current employer's workforce. An availability analysis reports a similar percentage breakdown by protected class, but for applicants and prospective employees who reside within a geographic area that defines the employer's relevant labor market. A discrepancy between these percentages, where the employer's workforce percentage of protected class members is less than the percentage observed for the relevant labor market, is described as "underutilization." Underutilization may call for voluntary or court-ordered affirmative action to close identified gaps. Clearly, a showing of underutilization may very well depend on how the employer defines the relevant labor market. Relevant labor market is determined by commuting patterns as well as search, recruitment, and hiring practices of employers within a geographic area. In general, lower-level positions in organizations, those with relatively low wages and relatively lower skill requirements (*see* KSAOS) are associated with labor markets defined in terms of a "reasonable" daily commuting distance. Sometimes, employers will use decennial census data to establish commute patterns for a given geographic area to assist in the definition of the relevant labor market. The relevant labor market for some professional, managerial, and executive positions, on the other hand, might extend far beyond the local area to reflect a regional, national, or global applicant pool.

Bibliography

Cascio, W. F. (1995). *Managing Human Resources: Productivity, Quality of Work Life, Profits*. New York: McGraw-Hill.

reliability

Larry J. Williams

Classic measurement theory proposes that the variability in the measures used in behavioral science research contain two distinct components: true score variance and random error variance. True score variance reflects variability observed within sample data that is due to the construct that is being measured. Random error variance (i.e., "noise") may reflect a number of causes, to include temporary fatigue, fluctuations of memory or mood, and other factors that are temporary and changing. For a given measure used with a given sample, the total observed variance is equal to the *sum* of the true score variance and random error variance. Reliability is a property of a measure that reflects how much of the total observed variance is due to true score variance. Specifically, reliability is defined as the ratio of true score variance to observed variance (Bohrnstedt, 1983). The higher the reliability, the more observed variability reflects true score differences rather than random error. This is a desirable property of any measure. As such, reliability refers to the accuracy or precision in a measuring instrument, and synonyms include dependability, stability, consistency, predictability, and accuracy (Kerlinger, 1973).

Reliability is important because statistical estimates of relationships between variables are influenced by the reliabilities of the measures. Correlation coefficients are always attenuated by low reliabilities of measures, although it is possible to adjust for this problem by using the correction for attenuation formula (e.g., the correlation is divided by the product of the square roots of the reliabilities of the two measures). The consequences of low reliability with regression coefficients are more complicated (e.g., signs of coefficients can be reversed, significant coefficients can be made to appear nonsignificant, and nonsignificant coefficients can appear as significant; Kenny, 1979). To account for measurement error with regression models, more advanced structural equation techniques must be used (e.g., Joreskog and Sorbom, 1993).

There are several ways to assess the reliability of a measure, including those based on stability and those based on equivalence. One estimate of reliability is obtained by correlating a variable with itself, at two different points in time. This results in a measure of stability referred to as *test–retest reliability*. A similar estimate is obtained by randomly splitting the measure into two forms, which are administered at two points in time, and this process yields a parallel forms test–retest coefficient. A major problem with both of these approaches is that true change in the variables cannot be distinguished from unreliability (Bohrnstedt, 1983). Alternatively, one of the earliest varieties of equivalence is the split-half method, in which the total number of items in a composite is divided into two halves and the summated scores on each half are then correlated. Generally, the split-half approach has been replaced by internal consistency methods. The most popular version of a measure of equivalence is called *coefficient alpha*, which reflects the correlations among all items of the composite.

A different set of reliability estimates is obtained from exploratory and confirmatory factor analysis. *Omega* is one reliability estimate linked to exploratory factor analysis, and it is based on the covariance matrix among the items and the uniqueness estimates from the factor solution. The reliability of a latent variable from a confirmatory factor analysis can also be calculated. In this case, the factor loadings and error variances are used in the calculations. Finally, it should be noted that in judging any estimate of reliability for a measure, criteria have been provided. It has been suggested that in the early stages of research on a measure, a value of 0.70 or higher will be adequate. For basic research, a threshold of 0.80 should be considered. For applied settings, a reliability of 0.90 should be considered the minimum (Nunnally, 1978).

Bibliography

Bohrnstedt, G. (1983). Measurement. In P. Rossi, J. Wright, and A. Anderson (eds.), *Handbook of Survey Research*. San Diego, CA: Academic Press.

Joreskog, K. G. and Sorbom, D. (1993). *LISREL 8: Structural Equation Modeling with SIMPLIS Command Language*. Hillsdale, NJ: Erlbaum.

Kenny, D. (1979). *Correlation and Causality*. Toronto: John Wiley.

Kerlinger, F. (1973). *Foundations of Behavioral Research*. New York: Holt, Rinehart, and Winston.

Nunnally, J. (1978). *Psychometric Theory*. New York: McGraw-Hill.

religion

Ramona L. Paetzold

Religion is one of the protected categories under Title VII of the CIVIL RIGHTS ACT OF 1964. It is defined in the Act to include "all aspects of religious observance and practice, as well as belief" (section 701(j)). Courts have interpreted religion to include moral or ethical beliefs that play the role of religion in a person's life (as long as they are sincerely held), but courts have also held that religion does not include beliefs that are viewed to be political in nature, or that form the basis of a social ideology. Atheists receive protection under this protected category, because atheism fits within the statutory definition of religion.

repatriation

Hal B. Gregersen

International assignments can enhance the global competitiveness of firms by increasing coordination and control across units, transferring innovations across geographic boundaries, and developing future executives (*see* EXPATRIATE ASSIGNMENT). To obtain these results, firms are increasing the number of managers sent on international assignments as expatriates (Selmer, 1995). Concurrently, human resource scholars have begun to examine various stages of the international assignment cycle and have more recently focused their efforts on the repatriation process or returning home from international assignments (Adler, 1981; Black and Gregersen, 1991; Black, Gregersen, and Mendenhall, 1992; Selmer, 1995).

Research indicates that: (1) repatriation is as difficult, if not more difficult, than the original expatriation adjustment; (2) a significant majority of repatriated employees are dissatisfied with the repatriation process; and (3) approximately 25 percent of repatriated employees leave their firm within one year after returning home (Black et al., 1992; Selmer, 1995). In addition, most expatriates do not have a formal job assignment upon repatriation and, when a formal assignment is obtained, it is usually a career demotion compared to the international assignment position (Black and Gregersen, 1991).

While some research has assessed the repatriation process, it is all cross-sectional and future research must assess repatriation with more systematic longitudinal data from a variety of countries.

See also *expatriate human resource issues*

Bibliography

Adler, N. J. (1981). Re-entry: Managing cross-cultural transitions. *Group and Organization Studies*, 6, 341–56.

Black, J. S. and Gregersen, H. B. (1991). When Yankee comes home: Factors related to expatriate and spouse repatriation adjustment. *Journal of International Business Studies*, 22, 671–95.

Black, J. S., Gregersen, H. B., and Mendenhall, M. E. (1992). *Global Assignments: Successfully Expatriating and Repatriating International Managers*. San Francisco: Jossey-Bass.

Selmer, J. (ed.) (1995). *Expatriate Management: New Ideas for International Business*. London: Quorum Books.

repetitive motion strain injury

Donna E. Ledgerwood

Repetitive motion strain is a term synonymous with carpal tunnel syndrome (CTS), hand–arm vibrations, and muscular/skeletal disorders. Three of the physical ailments that workers complain about most often are CTS, back pain, and headaches. According to the NATIONAL INSTITUTE FOR OCCUPATIONAL SAFETY AND HEALTH (NIOSH) (US Department of Health and Human Services, 1993), CTS was first studied as it relates to "primary" Raynaud's phenomenon. Raynaud's phenomenon was first described as a condition of local loss of blood circulation, in which one or more fingers become white and cold all at once. Primary Raynaud's phenomenon, originally described by Dr. Maurice Raynaud, occurs spontaneously in less than 15 percent of the general population. The ratio of female to male patients is five to one. Secondary Raynaud's phenomenon has the same signs and symptoms and progresses through the same stages of severity, but may be correlated with a specific cause, such as another medical condition, vinyl chloride, or vibrating hand tools.

Early stages of vibration syndrome are characterized by tingling or numbness in the fingers. Temporary tingling or numbness during or soon after use of a vibrating hand tool is *not* considered CTS. To be diagnosed as vibration syndrome, these neurologic symptoms must be more persistent and occur without provocation by immediate exposure to vibration. Other symptoms of vibration syndrome include blanching, pain, and flushing. The symptoms usually appear suddenly, and are precipitated by exposure to cold. With continuing exposure to vibration, the signs and symptoms become more severe and the pathology may become irreversible. The exact point at which vibration syndrome becomes irreversible has not yet been firmly established.

CTS and other repetitive motion strains are all issues of ergonomics. As such, these physical disorders will be unlikely to receive standards from NIOSH or the OCCUPATIONAL SAFETY AND HEALTH ADMINISTRATION (OSHA). A greater probability exists that standards will emerge for ergonomic safety and health which will be applicable to the traditional workplace and the virtual office.

Bibliography

US Department of Health and Human Services (1993). Vibration syndrome (NIOSH/PHS/CDC). *Current Intelligence Bulletin*, **38**, US Department of Health and Human Services.

replacement charts

Nicholas J. Mathys

Replacement charts are a human resource forecasting technique that describe a firm's organization structure in terms of individuals who occupy various managerial and professional positions. For each position the incumbent and potential replacements are identified along with information such as potential for advancement, experience or skills needed to qualify for next position, gender (for aid in diversity planning), and age (only for retirement planning).

Replacement charts should be computerized and provide a description of how vacancies can be filled by a firm's INTERNAL LABOR MARKETS. They should be updated annually or when changes in strategic directions occur. Updates should be guided by ongoing assessments of potential replacements – matching their current knowledge, skills, abilities, and other characteristics (*see* KSAOS) against not only present position requirements but also those needed to meet anticipated future needs of the position. Assessments should include KSAOs needed for horizontal as well as vertical moves. The former require more broad-based experience and responsibilities, often of a cross-functional nature, to meet the needs of today's flatter structures.

Before the number of qualified replacements for a current or future position can be determined, a method of comparing potential replacement candidates with the position's requirements is needed. This requires sound JOB ANALYSIS techniques and an up-to-date HUMAN RESOURCE INVENTORIES bank (Gatewood and Rockmore, 1986). When it is done properly, job families (*see* JOB FAMILY; PAY GRADE) can be developed that serve to identify potential CAREER PATHING and aid in individual career planning.

Bibliography

Gatewood, R. D. and Rockmore, B. W. (1986). Combining organizational manpower and career development needs: An operational human resource planning model. *Human Resource Planning*, **9**, 81–96.

representation elections

Charles R. Greer

Representation elections, which are conducted by the NATIONAL LABOR RELATIONS BOARD (NLRB), are the most common method by which employees obtain union representation. While representation elections typically involve only one union, in some circumstances more than one union may seek to represent the same group of employees and, as a result, multiple unions may be on the election ballot in addition to the no union alternative. Although the criterion for winning an election is the majority of votes cast (50 percent plus one vote), if an insufficient number of employees vote in the election, the NLRB will not consider the election as being representative and will not certify the union on the basis of the election.

During the period beginning after the NLRB is petitioned and before the actual election is conducted, the employer and union may choose to present arguments at a hearing with the NLRB as to an appropriate definition of the election unit, which means the groups of employees that should be allowed to vote (Feldacker, 1990). Because of differences in employees' desires for unionization, both sides may perceive an advantage if certain groups are excluded or included. In addition, after the NLRB orders an election, the employer must provide the union with the names and addresses of employees eligible to participate in the election (Feldacker, 1990; Jacobs, 1993).

During the pre-election period the employer must not violate the NLRB's laboratory conditions for a fair election. This means that the employer cannot intimidate employees against voting for the union, such as by threatening to terminate operations if the union wins the election, terminate employees active in organizing efforts, implement an unscheduled increase in wages for the purpose of discouraging unionization, and so forth. If an employer's conduct is especially egregious, and the NLRB determines that a fair election cannot be held, it will issue a bargaining order which requires the employer to bargain with the union. On the other hand, if the employer is successful in winning the election and does not violate the laboratory conditions, the NLRB cannot order another election for 12 months.

See also *union representation procedures*

Bibliography

Feldacker, B. (1990). *Labor Guide to Labor Law*. Englewood Cliffs, NJ: Prentice-Hall.

Jacobs, R. B. (1993). *Legal Compliance Guide to Personnel Management*. Englewood Cliffs, NJ: Prentice-Hall.

reproductive health hazards

Donna E. Ledgerwood

The OCCUPATIONAL SAFETY AND HEALTH ADMINISTRATION (OSHA) has identified reproductive hazards as one of the arenas most likely to experience an increase in litigation. Exposure to substances such as lead, ethylene oxide, cadmium, formaldehyde, mercury, and ionizing radiation is generally believed to introduce potential reproductive hazards. Since these substances may affect the reproductive capacity of men as well as women, fetal protection policies of employers have been the focus not only of health and safety litigants, but of cases involving equal employment opportunity as well.

Zielinski (1990) observed a profound lack of risk assessment and scant evidence of primary research directed at reproductive health hazards in the workplace. Such deficiencies in research efforts are problematic, particularly with the increasing use of potentially harmful substances and an exponential growth in the development and application of new chemicals. The combination of more employee threats of litigation and limited organizational awareness of such issues as reproductive hazards promises to remain as an issue of concern (Stewart, Ledgerwood, and May, 1996).

Bibliography

Stewart, W., Ledgerwood, D., and May, R. (1996). Educating business schools about safety and health is no accident. *Journal of Business Ethics*, **51**, August.

Zielinski, C. (1990). The toxic trap. *Personnel Journal*, **69**, 40–9.

retraining

Daniel C. Feldman

Retraining refers to teaching individuals the knowledge, skills, and abilities (*see* KSAOS) that will be necessary for them to obtain jobs in new occupations or organizations. In contrast to TRAINING, retraining refers to teaching individuals knowledge, skills, and abilities related to jobs outside their current occupations or outside their current organizations. Retraining is frequently used to retool individuals whose career paths (see CAREER PATHING) have become obsolete due to changes in technology, to prepare individuals to assume jobs in different industries or organizations after they have been laid off, or to prepare individuals to take new positions after a structural reorganization of the firm has led to the elimination of their present jobs (Leana and Feldman, 1992).

Bibliography

Leana, C. R. and Feldman, D. C. (1992). *Coping with Job Loss: How Individuals, Organizations, and Communities Respond to Layoffs*. New York: McGraw-Hill.

reverse discrimination

Barbara A. Lee

This term refers to DISCRIMINATION against an individual who is not a member of a group that historically has endured discrimination. Discrimination against Caucasians is race discrimination, but is popularly called reverse discrimination. Discrimination against men is sex discrimination, but is also popularly known as reverse discrimination.

Reverse discrimination claims are brought when an employer engages in voluntary or court-ordered AFFIRMATIVE ACTION that uses racial or gender preferences in hiring or promotions (see AFFIRMATIVE ACTION FOR NON-VICTIMS). The response of the US Supreme Court to these claims has varied, depending upon whether the plaintiffs were charging a refusal to hire or promote, or were challenging a layoff. In JOHNSON V. TRANSPORTATION AGENCY (480 US 616, 1987), the Supreme Court approved a gender-conscious promotion made under the aegis of an affirmative action plan. Using the criteria established in *United Steelworkers of America* v. *Weber* (443 US 193, 1979), the court determined that women were manifestly underrepresented in the job category, that the affirmative action plan did not require the discharge of any male employees and was not an absolute bar to the promotion of men, and that the plan was a temporary measure designed to eliminate gender imbalance rather than to achieve a certain quota of women. However, in *Wygant* v. *Jackson Board of Education* (476 US 267, 1986), the same court ruled unconstitutional a layoff plan that attempted to preserve the racial balance of the teaching staff by laying off more senior white teachers rather than less senior black teachers.

reward systems

Steve H. Barr

Also known as COMPENSATION systems and pay systems, reward systems refer to outcomes that an individual receives in an organization. Such outcomes occur in a variety of types. For example, *extrinsic* rewards include wages, salaries, BONUSES, and fringe benefits (insurance, healthcare, retirement plan, and so forth; see BENEFITS). *Intrinsic* rewards include praise, recognition, esteem, self-competence, and so forth. To enhance organizational effectiveness, reward systems should be designed to reinforce organizational objectives. Thus, they are tied to and should be integrated with the processes of setting goals and evaluating performance.

Reward systems can contribute to the organization's effectiveness in three ways:

1 the reward system can help attract the best human assets to the firm;
2 the reward system can help retain good performers;
3 the reward system can motivate to affect performance.

Reward systems reflect one of two underlying organizational cultures or orientations about rewards. The first is a *performance culture*, also referred to as PAY FOR PERFORMANCE and merit-based systems (see MERIT PAY). These can occur at the individual level (piece rate or bonus/commission plans; see COMMISSION-BASED PAY; PIECEWORK), group level (profit centers, cost reduction sharing), and plant or company level (PROFIT SHARING, SCANLON

PLAN). Performance culture reward systems link intrinsic and extrinsic rewards to measured outcomes of individuals, groups, or the organization. These outcomes should reflect individual, group, or organization-level goals. In this culture, a larger percentage of an employee's pay is at risk (*see* AT-RISK PAY).

A second culture or orientation about rewards is the *entitlement culture*. In this system, rewards are distributed based on factors such as seniority, job level or grade, education, or training. Persons meeting certain levels of each factor receive predetermined levels of reward for that factor. In this culture, a smaller proportion of the employee's pay is at risk.

Bibliography

Henderson, R. I. and Risher, H. W. (1987). Influencing organizational strategy through compensation leadership. In D. B. Balkin and L. R. Gomez-Mejia (eds.), *New Perspectives on Compensation*. Englewood Cliffs, NJ: Prentice-Hall.

Kerr, J. L. (1988). Strategic control through performance appraisal and rewards. *Human Resource Planning*, 11, 215–24.

Lawler, E. E., III (1984). The strategic design of reward systems. In R. S. Schuler and S. A. Youngblood (eds.), *Readings in Personnel and Human Resource Management*. St. Paul, MN: West Publishing.

Markham, S. E. (1988). Pay-for-performance dilemma revisited: Empirical example of the importance of group effects. *Journal of Applied Psychology*, 172–80.

Newman, J. M. (1987). Selecting incentive plans to complement organizational strategy. In D. B. Balkin and L. R. Gomez-Mejia (eds.), *New Perspectives on Compensation*. Englewood Cliffs, NJ: Prentice-Hall.

right to work

John T. Delaney

Section 14(b) of the US NATIONAL LABOR RELATIONS ACT OF 1935 allows states to prohibit unions from negotiating COLLECTIVE BARGAINING agreements that require workers to become union members to obtain or retain employment. Proponents of state right to work laws argue that workers should be allowed to choose freely whether to join a union or not. Because unions are legally obligated to represent members and nonmembers equally, unionists argue that right to work laws unfairly allow nonmembers to receive the benefits of unionization (e.g., negotiated wage increases) without incurring any costs (e.g., union dues). As of 2003, 22 states had such laws.

Bibliography

Haggard, T. R. (1977). *Compulsory Unionism, the NLRB, and the Courts: A Legal Analysis of Union Security Agreements*. Philadelphia: Wharton School, Industrial Research Unit.

Kuhn, J. W. (1961). Right to work: Symbol or substance? *Industrial and Labor Relations Review*, 14, 587–94.

rights arbitration

William H. Holley, Jr.

Rights (grievance) arbitration is the type of ARBITRATION that stems from employee rights negotiated and written in COLLECTIVE BARGAINING agreements. These rights accrue to employees by the fact that they are employees in positions covered under the collective bargaining agreement; in other words, they are BARGAINING UNIT employees.

Typically, the final step in the GRIEVANCE PROCEDURE involves rights arbitration, which takes place in a hearing before a neutral arbitrator selected by the parties. At the hearing the union advocate and management advocate present their respective positions through evidence provided by witnesses and documents related to the relevant contract language and the issue being decided by the arbitrator. At the conclusion of the hearing, the parties decide whether to present oral closing arguments or submit a post-hearing brief (a written version of the facts, relevant contract language, arguments supported by arbitral authority, rebuttals to the opposite party's position, and the requested decision of the arbitrator). The arbitrator then studies the evidence presented by the parties and makes a decision based on the relevant contract language in the collective bargaining agreement and the evidence presented by the parties.

The rights arbitration procedure is considered a peaceful and effective mechanism for resolving disputes that arise during the life of a collective bargaining agreement and is a substitute for the

STRIKE by the union and the LOCKOUT by the employer. Rights arbitration is an example of workplace self-governance in that the parties themselves design the system which best fits their needs. The parties determine whether there will be a single arbitrator or a board of arbitrators and whether to have a permanent or ad hoc (for only one case) arbitrator(s). They also define the authority of the arbitrator by negotiating an arbitration clause in the collective bargaining agreement and by defining the issue to be presented to the arbitrator prior to presenting the evidence at the hearing. The arbitrator interprets the contract language that the parties have negotiated to apply to their workplace. The parties themselves select the arbitrator who will rule on the evidence which the parties present through witnesses and documents. The Code of Professional Responsibility for Arbitrators in Labor–Management Disputes has been established by the NATIONAL ACADEMY OF ARBITRATORS and the major appointing agencies to govern behavior of arbitrators and their relationships with the union and management. The appointing agencies are the American Arbitration Association, the FEDERAL MEDIATION AND CONCILIATION SERVICE, and the National Mediation Service.

The arbitrator's decision is usually written and includes the facts in the case, the issue(s) presented, the relevant contract provisions, positions of the parties, analysis of the parties' evidence and positions, and the final decision. Arbitrator decisions are rarely overturned by appeal to the courts as long as the arbitrator bases his or her decision on the contract language and evidence presented.

After decades of experience with rights arbitration in the US, arbitral standards and guidelines have been developed for arbitral decision-making (see bibliography). These include BURDEN OF PROOF, levels of proof, past practice, intent of the parties, and so forth, which guide the arbitrator's decision-making. About 10 percent of the decisions submitted by the arbitrators to the major reporting services (*Labor Arbitration Reports* by Bureau of National Affairs and *Labor Arbitration Awards* by Commerce Clearing House) are published.

Because of its success in the union–management arena, rights arbitration has been introduced in the nonunion sector through employee-promulgated arbitration (see NONUNION EMPLOYEE GRIEVANCE PROCEDURES). This type of arbitration typically occurs in situations where the EMPLOYEE HANDBOOK specifies that termination will be only for just cause and/or where arbitration is used for resolving conflicts over statutory claims, such as employment DISCRIMINATION on the basis of age, disability, race, or gender. In these types of cases, rights arbitration is considered more of a substitute for a court trial than a substitute for a strike or lockout. In some cases, the introduction of employer-promulgated arbitration is viewed as a union avoidance instrument or union substitution device.

Bibliography

Bornstein, T. and Gosline, A. (eds.) (1990). *Labor and Employment Arbitration*. New York: Matthew Bender.
Cooper, L. and Nolan, D. R. (1994). *Labor Arbitration: A Coursebook*. St. Paul, MN: West Publishing.
Elkouri, F. and Elkouri, E. A. (1985). *How Arbitration Works*, 4th edn. Washington, DC: Bureau of National Affairs.
Schoonhoven, R. J. (ed.) (1991). *Fairweather's Practice and Procedure in Labor Arbitration*, 3rd edn. Washington, DC: Bureau of National Affairs.
Zack, A. M. (ed.) (1984). *Arbitration in Practice*. Ithaca, NY: Cornell University.

role playing

Timothy T. Baldwin

Role playing is one form of simulation (see SIMULATIONS) used primarily for the training of interpersonal skills (e.g., interviewing, giving effective feedback, handling customer complaints). Role playing gives trainees opportunity to experience a situation first-hand and to "learn by doing." Role playing is also frequently used to promote attitude change via a variant known as role reversal. Role reversal involves the exchange of roles among trainees from different backgrounds or perspectives with the goal of heightening awareness and understanding of others. Role playing is often used in conjunction with lectures and other training techniques, and is a key element of BEHAVIOR MODELING training.

Rucker plan

Theresa M. Welbourne

The Rucker plan is a form of GAINSHARING that utilizes a bonus formula based on value added (which is defined as sales minus raw materials and services) rather than net sales, revenue, or sales value of production (which are used in the SCANLON PLAN). Although value added is in the denominator, the ratio still uses cost of labor in the numerator. The rationale behind using this formula is that effects not controllable by employees, such as inflation and market factors, are not included in the formula. The Rucker plan is similar to the Scanlon plan in that it also suggests using employee participation programs (*see* EMPLOYEE INVOLVEMENT).

rule of thumb

Nicholas J. Mathys

The rule of thumb is a qualitative forecasting technique used to predict the demand for human resources. Sometimes called STAFFING tables, this decision aid or heuristic links the required number of direct and indirect staff required to external changes in demand, such as number (or value) of sales, number of customers, and so forth. For example, a retail chain specifies that for every ten new stores an additional regional manager will be hired or for every $10,000 in weekly sales an additional checkout clerk and stock person are needed. See Burack and Mathys (1996) for more details.

Bibliography

Burack, E. H. and Mathys, N. J. (1996). *Human Resource Planning: A Pragmatic Approach to Manpower Staffing and Development.* Lake Forest, IL: Brace-Park.

Russia

Sheila M. Puffer

Like virtually every aspect of Russian society, the labor force is undergoing dramatic change as Russia makes the difficult transition from a communist-controlled, centrally planned system to a market-oriented economy. Since 1991, which marked the fall of communism and the breakup of the Soviet Union, the government's policies to privatize large sectors of the economy have resulted in dramatic changes in job security and social benefits that had been guaranteed to all citizens.

In the mid-1990s, gross national product suffered annual declines in the range of 15 percent. Production dropped dramatically in thousands of privatized enterprises that once received government subsidies and whose suppliers and customers had been designated by central ministries. Unprecedented layoffs and unemployment as well as delayed wage payments ensued. Despite these onerous problems, other government legislation opened up opportunities for entrepreneurship and job creation in the rapidly growing private sector.

In 1998 the country suffered a financial crash, resulting in a highly devalued ruble and massive losses of citizens' savings. The Russian economy gradually recovered, with changes from 2001 to 2002 including an 8.8 percent increase in real disposable income, a 16.6 percent increase in real wages, and a 27 percent increase in the average monthly wage to US$141, reaching US$185 in December 2002. Wages constituted approximately 46 percent of gross domestic product (GDP) in 2002, and the official unemployment rate declined slightly from 9 percent to 8.6 percent. In 2002, one-quarter of the population was reported living below the subsistence level of 1,800 rubles a month or US$57 (World Bank, 2003).

HUMAN RESOURCE PRACTICES

Understandably, the transitional environment resulted in the human resource field consisting of a mix of policies and practices from the former communist regime, as well as new approaches used primarily by the emerging private sector. Two large surveys in 1998 and 2000 found a major drive toward implementing modern human resource management (HRM) practices. However, most HRM innovations were implemented through trial and error rather than drawing from international practices (Gurkov, 2002). The unique time perspective and other cultural vestiges of the communist era tended to make much of the workforce resistant to coordination and integration, thus requiring managers to be flexible in their approaches (Fey and Denison, 2003). Implementing ways of making employees more accountable for their decisions was another important cultural characteristic of the workplace (May, Bermann-Young, and Ledgerwood, 1998).

New Labor Code Enacted in 2002

The Russian Federation's Labor Code was substantially amended in 2002, the first major overhaul since the end of the communist regime, and aimed at being more suited to a market economy. The 100-page law is the primary legislation regulating labor practices such as disciplinary action, overtime, holidays, retirement age, and extra compensation for jobs in remote regions or hazardous occupations. The new code applies to all persons working in the country, including all foreign nationals. The standard work week is 40 hours, and time off includes a minimum of 24 working days for vacation, including 14 taken as consecutive calendar days, and an additional ten public holidays.

Unions

Under the new code, unions have decreased in influence. Unions are to be consulted but their input is not binding, with labor and management negotiating directly with each other. The largest union by far, the Federation of Independent Trade Unions, is the successor to the Soviet government-run organization and is viewed by some as being closer to the political establishment than to the workers (Hooson, 2002). The proliferation of smaller unions throughout the 1990s has subsided, with the new code stipulating that the largest union in a company can petition to be the sole representative of employees in making collective agreements with management. Union approval is no longer required in dismissals, and employers have more latitude in dismissing workers for economic reasons. The right to strike has been curtailed, requiring support of at least half of a meeting attended by at least two-thirds of a company's employees.

Recruitment and Selection

Recruitment and selection are typically conducted on an informal and personal basis, primarily through networks of contacts. As during the communist era, personal characteristics, especially trustworthiness, and friendship and family ties are still the major selection criteria, although skills are becoming considerably more important, especially in entrepreneurial start-ups. Recruitment is also possible through the long-established but largely ineffective state employment agency, as well as new private search firms.

Compensation and Benefits

In 2001 the government implemented a flat personal income tax of 13 percent. As during the communist period, BONUSES were an expected component of COMPENSATION (Puffer, 1993). Employees were accustomed to receiving bonuses based on group or enterprise performance rather than individual results (Welsh, Luthans, and Sommer, 1993). Private start-ups typically paid vastly higher salaries and bonuses than state sector enterprises, but were much less inclined to provide housing, day care, vacation resorts, and medical services (Puffer and Shekshnia, 1994).

All employers are required to make contributions to state funds for medical care, education, employment, and social security, with pension fund contributions being the largest at 28 percent. In 2003 the government was considering a new multi-pillar pension system that would include private sector management of pension assets.

Bibliography

Fey, C. F. and Denison, D. R. (2003). Organizational culture and effectiveness: Can American theory be applied in Russia? *Organization Science*, December.

Gurkov, I. (2002). Innovations and legacies in Russian human resource management practices: The survey of 700 CEOs. *Post-Communist Economies*, 14 (1), 137–44.

Hooson, B. (2002). The new labor code in Russia changes the rules of the game: A new era of Russian labor. *Business Review Journal*, 1.

May, R., Bermann-Young, C., and Ledgerwood, D. (1998). Russian human resource management. *European Management Journal*, 16 (4), 447–59.

Puffer, S. M. (1993). Three factors affecting reward allocations in the former USSR: An empirical study. In J. B. Shaw, P. S. Kirkbride, and K. M. Rowland (eds.), *Research in Personnel and Human Resources*

Management: International Human Resources Management (Supplement 3). Greenwich, CT: JAI Press.

Puffer, S. M. and Shekshnia, S. V. (1994). Compensating local employees in post-communist Russia: In search of talent or just looking for a bargain? *Compensation and Benefits Review*, September/October, 35–43.

Shekshnia, S. V. (2002). *Upravlenie Personalom Sovremennoy Organizatsii (Personnel Management in Contemporary Organizations)*, 7th edn. Moscow: Biznes-Shkola "Intel-Sintez."

Welsh, D. H. B., Luthans, F., and Sommer, S. (1993). Managing Russian factory workers: The impact of US-based behavioral and participative techniques. *Academy of Management Journal*, 36, 58–79.

World Bank (2003). *Russian Economic Report*. Washington, DC: World Bank, Russian Country Department.

S

safety: blood-borne pathogens

Donna E. Ledgerwood

Healthcare employees are subjected to numerous biological risks in the daily course of performing their jobs. But while AIDS/AIDS-RELATED COMPLEX has been the focus of mass media, the actual number of healthcare workers infected with the human immunodeficiency virus (HIV) has been limited, compared to an estimated 12,000 healthcare workers who are infected with the hepatitis B virus annually (Minter and Moretz, 1989). Additionally, the incidence of tuberculosis is growing at an alarming rate. These are but three of a host of communicable diseases existing in the workplace today. Managers must become more aware of the rights of: (1) the infected worker; (2) the coworkers of the infected worker; and (3) the employer. Managers will face many challenges in dealing with the regulations mandated by the AMERICANS WITH DISABILITIES ACT OF 1990, the structure of fines imposed by the OCCUPATIONAL SAFETY AND HEALTH ADMINISTRATION (OSHA), and emerging regulations for personal protective equipment and other aspects related to employee health and safety.

Bibliography

Minter, S. G. and Moretz, S. (1989). Summit interests. *Occupational Hazards*, 51, 80–3.

safety: rights and responsibilities

Donna E. Ledgerwood

The concept of individual rights is unique to the American labor force. In most countries, the right to command resides unilaterally and exclusively with managers and executives, limited only by labor contracts (*see* LABOR CONTRACT), conciliation agreements, or consent decrees.

American labor unions occasionally have had a major influence in the passage of legislation such as the OCCUPATIONAL SAFETY AND HEALTH ACT OF 1970 and have successfully challenged management decisions where labor has shown management to be unwilling to remove work-related hazards. The OCCUPATIONAL SAFETY AND HEALTH ADMINISTRATION (OSHA) was established by congressional intent and requires that every employer assure, as far as possible, the safety and healthful working conditions of every employee. The Department of Labor assumes that every manager is also part of the labor force.

Where OSHA has not promulgated specific standards, employers are responsible for following the Act's General Duty clause. This clause states that employers "shall furnish . . . a place of employment which is free from recognized hazards that are causing or are likely to cause death or serious physical harm to his or her employees."

Employers who are found to be negligent in their health and safety practices (those found to have willful, repeated practices in violation of the law, or those who fail to correct prior conditions found to be OSHA violations) can be cited and receive penalties up to $70,000 per violation, per day, per incident. Citations are written documents which serve as OSHA's vehicle to inform employers of alleged violations. Administrative penalties reflect violations of public policy, whereas fines connote punitive damages imposed by the court for criminal activities. When the potential for state penalties is added to those imposed by the federal government, an employer can see that failure to provide safe and healthful practices can be costly in more than one way. Moreover, safe and healthful work practices allow the employer to remain competitive in the long run, with a proper paper trail to use as a defense in the event the employer is sued or an employee dies in a job-related incident. For example, employers who participate in OSHA-recommended programs (e.g., voluntary protection programs) can have fines reduced as much as 85 percent due to their good faith efforts.

In another important arena, the courts are demonstrating an increasing acceptance of the concept of culpability. For culpable actions which "managers knew or should have known" and prevented, managers and executives are being personally fined and even going to jail for murder or manslaughter. For example, on September 3, 1991, a fire killed 25 people in a North Carolina poultry plant because of inadequate and unmarked exits, with locked doors and poor lighting. There were no functioning fire alarms or sprinklers in the plant. Having been cited previously for safety violations, management was held liable for the loss of life on the grounds of culpability.

The North Carolina incident is not an isolated case of managerial unawareness or negligence. Rather, this tragedy serves as an ominous reminder that employee safety and health remains inadequately addressed as the costs and liabilities of losses mount. In 1988 alone there were 6.2 million job-related injuries in the US, and 240,000 cases of occupational illnesses (Feare, 1990). Nine million injuries and illnesses were reported in 1990 (Westlund, 1991), and OSHA issued 99,225 citations for serious violations of safety standards, while imposing $63 million in fines (Garland, 1991). These statistics demonstrate the relevance of the employee safety and health issue and the concomitant challenge for managers to provide a safe working environment.

Whether due to civil or criminal litigation, managers must become aware of how unaware they are. In addition to fines from federal and state agencies, USC 3571 sets forth an alternative fine structure under federal law for noncompliance with laws related to safety and health. Managerial and nonmanagerial employees can be fined individually up to $250,000 for a misdemeanor and up to $250,000 for a felony which is their first offense (Waska and Monce, 1991). Thus, with additional authority comes additional responsibility. Now there is individual liability for corporate acts as well as corporate liability for individual acts. For more information on specific rights and responsibilities of employers and employees, see *All About OSHA* (US Department of Labor, 1991).

EMPLOYER RESPONSIBILITIES

According to OSHA, employer responsibilities include: (1) meeting a general duty responsibility to provide a workplace free from recognized hazards that are causing or are likely to cause death or serious physical harm to employees, and comply with standards, rules, and regulations issued under the Act; (2) being familiar with mandatory OSHA standards and making copies available to employees for review upon request; (3) informing all employees about OSHA; (4) examining workplace conditions to make sure they conform to applicable standards; (5) removing the hazard or, if the hazard cannot be eliminated, minimizing and reducing it; (6) making sure employees have and use safe tools and equipment, including appropriate personal protective equipment, and that such equipment is properly maintained; (7) using color codes, posters, labels, or signs when needed to warn employees of potential hazards; (8) establishing or updating operating procedures and communicating them so that employees follow safety and health requirements; (9) providing medical examinations when required by OSHA standards; (10) providing training required by OSHA standards; (11) reporting to the nearest OSHA office within *eight* hours any fatal accident or one that results in the hospitalization of five or more employees; (12) keeping OSHA-required records of work-related injuries and illnesses, and posting a copy of the totals from the last page of OSHA Publication No. 200 during the entire month of February each year (this requirement applies to employers with 11 or more employees); (13) posting, at a prominent location within the workplace, the OSHA poster (OSHA No. 2203) informing employees of their rights and responsibilities (in states operating OSHA-approved job safety and health programs, the state's equivalent poster and/or OSHA 2203 may be required); (14) providing employees, former employees, and their representatives access to the Log and Summary of Occupational Injuries and Illnesses (OSHA No. 200) at a reasonable time and in a reasonable manner; (15) cooperating with the OSHA compliance officer by furnishing names of authorized employee representatives who may be asked to accompany the compliance officer during an inspection and, if there are no representatives, allowing the compliance officer to consult with a reasonable number of employees concerning safety and health in the workplace; (16) not discriminating against employees who properly exercise their rights under the Act; (17) posting OSHA citations at or near the worksite involved and leaving each citation, or copy thereof, posted until the violation has been abated, or for three working days, whichever is longer; and (18) abating cited violations within the prescribed period.

Employer Rights

Employer rights include: (1) seeking advice and offsite consultation as needed by writing, calling, or visiting the nearest OSHA office; (2) being active in industry association involvement in job safety and health; (3) requesting and receiving proper identification of the OSHA compliance officer prior to inspection; (4) being advised by the compliance officer of the reason for an inspection; (5) having an opening and closing conference with the compliance officer; (6) accompanying the compliance officer on the inspection; (7) filing a Notice of Contest with the OSHA area director within 15 working days of receipt of a notice of citation and proposed penalty; (8) applying to OSHA for a temporary variance from a standard if unable to comply because of the unavailability of materials, equipment, or personnel needed to make necessary changes within the required time; (9) applying to OSHA for a permanent variance from a standard if proof can be furnished that facilities or methods of operation provide employee protection at least as effective as that required by the standard; (10) taking an active role in developing safety and health standards through participation in OSHA Standards Advisory Committees, through nationally recognized standards-setting organizations, and through evidence and views presented in writing or at hearings; (11) being assured of the confidentiality of any trade secrets observed by an OSHA compliance officer during an inspection; and (12) submitting a written request to the NATIONAL INSTITUTE FOR OCCUPATIONAL SAFETY AND HEALTH (NIOSH) for information on whether any substance in the workplace has potentially toxic effects in the concentrations being used.

Employee Responsibilities

Although OSHA does not cite employees for violations of their responsibilities as it can with employers, the law requires each employee to comply with all occupational safety and health standards and all rules, regulations, and orders issued under the Act that are applicable. Employee responsibilities include: (1) reading the OSHA poster at the job-site; (2) complying with all applicable OSHA standards; (3) following all employer safety and health rules and regulations, and wearing or using prescribed protective equipment while engaged in work; (4) reporting hazardous conditions to the superior; (5) reporting any job-related injury or illness to the employer, and seeking treatment promptly; (6) cooperating with the OSHA compliance officer conducting an inspection if he or she inquires about safety and health conditions in the workplace; and (7) exercising one's rights under the Occupational Safety and Health Act in a responsible manner.

Employee Rights

Employees have a right to seek safety and health on the job without fear of punishment. This right is spelled out in Section 11(c) of the Occupational Safety and Health Act. The law says that employers shall not punish or discriminate against workers for exercising rights such as: (1) complaining to an employer, union, OSHA, or any other government agency about job safety and health hazards; (2) filing safety or health GRIEVANCES; (3) participating on a workplace safety and health committee or in union activities concerning job safety and health; (4) participating in OSHA inspections, conferences, hearings, or other OSHA-related activities;

(5) reviewing copies of appropriate OSHA standards, rules, regulations, and requirements that the employer should have available at the workplace; (6) requesting information from one's employer on safety and health hazards in the area, on precautions that may be taken, and on procedures to be followed if an employee is involved in an accident or is exposed to toxic substances; (7) receiving adequate training and information on workplace safety and health hazards; (8) requesting the OSHA area director to investigate if one believes hazardous conditions or violations of standards exist in the workplace; (9) having one's name withheld from one's employer, upon request to OSHA, if one files a written and signed complaint; (10) being advised of OSHA actions regarding one's complaint and having an informal review, if requested, of any decision not to inspect or to issue a citation; (11) having one's authorized employee representative accompany the OSHA compliance officer during the inspection tour; (12) observing any monitoring or measuring of hazardous materials and having the right to see these records, and one's medical records, as specified under the Occupational Safety and Health Act; (13) having one's authorized representative, or oneself, review the Log and Summary of Occupational Injuries (OSHA No. 200) at a reasonable time and in a reasonable manner; (14) requesting a closing discussion with the compliance officer following an inspection; (15) submitting a written request to NIOSH for information on whether any substance in the workplace has potentially toxic effects in the concentration being used and have one's name withheld from one's employer if requested; (16) objecting to the abatement period set in the citation issued to the employer by writing to the OSHA area director within 15 working days of the issuance of the citation; (17) participating in hearings conducted by the Occupational Safety and Health Review Commission to which an employer goes to appeal a citation or penalty which the employer received by an OSHA inspector; (18) being notified by one's employer if he or she applies for a variance from an OSHA standard, and testifying at a variance hearing and appealing the final decision; and (19) submitting information or comment to OSHA on the issuance, modification, or revocation of OSHA standards and requesting a public hearing.

Bibliography

Feare, T. (1990). Workplace safety: Where we stand, what we need to do. *Modern Materials Handling*, 45, 48–50.

Garland, S. B. (1991). What a way to watch out for workers. *Business Week*, 3232, 42.

US Department of Labor, Occupational Safety and Health Administration (1991). *All About OSHA*. Washington, DC: US Department of Labor, Occupational Safety and Health Administration.

Waska, D. J. and Monce, H. N. (1991). Letter of the law. *Oklahoma Bar Journal*, September, 15, 23.

Westlund, M. C. (1991). First-aid training benefits employer and employees alike. *Safety and Health*, 54, 58–61.

safety in the workplace

Donna E. Ledgerwood

Safety is defined in the Glossary of the American Society of Safety Engineers (ASSE) as a general term denoting an acceptable level of risk of, relative freedom from, and low probability of harm (ASSE, 1993). Called occupational safety during the 1970s and 1980s, the area today typically described as workplace safety refers to the ability to manage (prevent, avoid, and control) job-related losses due to sudden changes in process, material, resources, or energy. Safety could also be defined as those things we presently *should* see that can cause us immediate harm.

See also *safety: rights and responsibilities*

Bibliography

American Society of Safety Engineers (1993). ASSE Professional Development Conference and Exposition. *Professional Safety*, 38, 20–2.

salesforce compensation

David W. Cravens

Salesforce compensation consists of the financial and nonfinancial rewards given to salespeople whose primary responsibilities include contacting customers and prospects with the objective of obtaining commitments to buy the goods or services offered by the salesperson (Ingram and LaForge, 1992). The salespeople may also be responsible for providing supporting services to customers. COMPENSATION is provided by the organization (or individual) employing the salesperson in return for the salesperson's satisfactory JOB PERFORMANCE.

Financial compensation for salespeople may include a salary and/or some form of incentive compensation (see INCENTIVE PAY). Incentives may be a commission paid on sales results or a bonus determined by the amount sold, activities sold, activities performed, or the sales manager's assessment of the salesperson's performance (see BONUSES; COMMISSION-BASED PAY). Team incentives may be used to reward team selling performance. Financial compensation systems range from 100 percent salary to 100 percent commission. Nonfinancial compensation may include various forms of recognition of the salesperson's contribution to the organization (e.g., President's Club).

The method of financial compensation is usually determined by the job requirements and the extent of control and direction that sales management wishes to have over the salesperson's efforts (Anderson and Oliver, 1987). Salary-only compensation provides the most control over the salesperson, whereas commission-only compensation essentially allows the salesperson to determine the amount and allocation of his or her selling effort. Most compensation plans include some opportunity for incentive compensation. For example, salary might represent 70 or 80 percent of compensation, with the remainder comprised of bonus or commission pay (Cravens, 1995).

Bibliography

Anderson, I. and Oliver, R. L. (1987). Perspectives on behavior-based and outcome-based salesforce control systems. *Journal of Marketing*, October, 85–6.

Cravens, D. W. (1995). The changing role of the sales force. *Marketing Management*, 4 (Fall), 49–57.

Ingram, T. N. and Laforge, R. W. (1992). *Sales Management*, 2nd edn. Fort Worth, TX: Dryden Press, pp. 414–15.

salting

Stuart A. Youngblood

Salting refers to a union organizing tactic of covertly placing paid union organizers on an employer's payroll. Employers have argued that a paid union organizer who applies for and is selected to work for an employer cannot be considered an employee under the NATIONAL LABOR RELATIONS ACT OF 1935. The US Supreme Court rejected this argument and unanimously upheld a NATIONAL LABOR RELATIONS BOARD (NLRB) ruling that paid union organizers on an employer's payroll are employees under the National Labor Relations Act. The Supreme Court case, *NLRB v. Town and Country Electric*, involved contractors in the building trades, but the ruling affects all employers in any industry. "Salts" are costly to employers because they can file unfair labor practices, GRIEVANCES, or DISCRIMINATION complaints that require staff and legal resources to resolve. Salting appeals to union organizers in the building trades, which is composed of many smaller employers who hire highly mobile workers for short durations.

Bibliography

Grossman, R. J. (1996). Employers brace for salting after high court ruling. *HR News*, 15 (1), 4–5.

savings or thrift plans

Charles H. Fay

Savings or thrift plans are common defined contribution PENSION PLANS which promote savings on the part of employees. Employers typically match some portion (usually 50 percent) of employee savings. Most such plans have been converted to, or replaced by, 401(K) PLANS, which allow both contributions to such plans and the earnings of the plan to enjoy deferred tax treatment. All EMPLOYEE RETIREMENT INCOME SECURITY ACT OF 1974 requirements apply to tax-qualified thrift plans.

Bibliography

Van Derhei, J. L. and Olsen, K. A. (2001). Section 401(k) plans (Cash or deferred arrangements) and thrift plans. In J. S. Rosenbloom (ed.), *The Handbook of Employee Benefits: Design, Funding and Administration*, 5th edn. New York: McGraw-Hill, pp. 633–60.

Scanlon plan

Theresa M. Welbourne

The Scanlon plan is a GAINSHARING plan that uses a bonus formula based on improvements in historical production. The ratio used is the cost of labor to some measure of PRODUCTIVITY (revenue, sales value of production, or net sales). Assuming a stable historical ratio, a bonus is realized when the ratio improves. The amount of savings creates a bonus pool that is shared between the employer and employees (often a 50:50 split). The employee share is then distributed among all employees in the work group (usually as a percentage of basic pay). The Scanlon plan recommends suggestion committees.

scientific management

Fang Lee Cooke

Scientific management (also known as Taylorism) is a movement founded by Frederick Winslow Taylor (1856–1917), who was an engineer by training. Taylor believed that the principal object of management should be to secure the maximum prosperity for the employer, coupled with the maximum prosperity of each employee. For the employer, maximum prosperity means not just large profits in the short term but the development of all aspects of the enterprise to a state of permanent prosperity. For the employees, maximum prosperity means not just immediate higher wages, but their development so that they may perform efficiently in the highest grade of work for which their natural abilities fit them. Taylor held that there were three causes for antagonism and inefficiency at workplaces: first, the fallacious belief of the workers that any increase in output would inevitably result in unemployment; second, the defective systems of management which make it necessary for workers to restrict output in order to protect their interests; and third, inefficient rule-of-thumb effort-wasting methods of work. Taylor argued that the aim of "scientific management" was to overcome these obstacles by means of systematic observation and measurement. Taylor also believed that it was necessary to increase management control to improve efficiency and that there was a need to reform managerial authority: to base it on competence rather than the power to hire and fire. Taylorism has been widely criticized by scholars from other schools such as the human relations school.

Bibliography

Pugh, D. S. and Hickson, D. J. (1989). *Writers on Organizations*. Harmondsworth: Penguin.

SD_y

Michael J. Burke

The standard deviation of JOB PERFORMANCE in dollar terms, SD_y is a key component of Brogden's selection utility model (*see* SELECTION UTILITY MODELS) and of some TRAINING UTILITY models. Several methods for estimating SD_y include the CREPID (which relies on JOB ANALYSIS information, PERFORMANCE APPRAISAL information, and labor costs) and global SD_y (which relies on subject matter expert judgments of the dollar value of employee performance) procedures. Research related to SD_y estimation procedures (see Boudreau, 1991, for a review) has assisted the field in gaining a better understanding of the economic impact of human resource programs, such as PERSONNEL SELECTION and TRAINING programs.

Bibliography

Boudreau, J. W. (1991). Utility analysis for decisions in human resource management. In M. D. Dunnette and L. M. Hough (eds.), *Handbook of Industrial and Organizational Psychology*, 2nd edn, vol. 2. Palo Alto, CA: Consulting Psychologists Press.

secondary boycotts

Hoyt N. Wheeler

Secondary boycotts are union efforts, usually involving PICKETING, to force a second employer to "refrain from doing business with" an employer with whom the union has a labor dispute (Gould, 1986: 53). The term "boycott," which has the same meaning in several languages, derives from the name of an infamous 1879 Irish estate manager whose tenants isolated him (Funk, 1972). Such actions are illegal for most workers under American labor law (section 8(b)(4)(B), NATIONAL LABOR RELATIONS ACT OF 1935), and give rise to swift legal penalties. However, the variation aimed at consumers is a technique used to good effect in the US by farm workers, who are not covered by the National Labor Relations Act.

Bibliography

Cihon, P. J. and Castagnera, J. O. (1993). *Labor and Employment Law*, 2nd edn. Belmont, CA: Wadsworth.
Funk, C. E. (1972). *Thereby Hangs a Tale*. New York: Warner.
Gould, W. B., IV (1986). *A Primer on American Labor Law*, 2nd edn. Cambridge, MA: MIT Press.

selection models

Neal Schmitt

Selection models are descriptions of the ways in which organizations collect and use information to make decisions about the assignment of people to various treatments (e.g., hire, reject, promote, train). Decision-makers must first collect data using psychological tests (see PSYCHOLOGICAL TEST) or other assessment procedures that yield information relevant to the examinees' abilities to perform relevant job tasks. Decision-makers then need to combine that information in a way that provides correct predictions about the examinees' subsequent JOB PERFORMANCE.

MECHANICAL VERSUS JUDGMENTAL DATA COLLECTION

Through JOB ANALYSIS, an organization identifies the type of knowledge, skills, abilities, and other characteristics (see KSAOS) required to perform the tasks that comprise a job. Human resource specialists have developed a wide variety of techniques to assess the degree to which individuals possess these critical KSAOs. These data collection procedures include mechanical procedures such as psychological tests (or documentation of experience and education requirements), which are relatively easily and objectively scored. In contrast, other data collection procedures involve subjective judgments on the part of an evaluator as to whether an examinee possesses or lacks the required KSAOs. The most common judgmental approach to data collection is the EMPLOYMENT INTERVIEW, though there are certainly subjective elements in other data collection procedures, such as various work SIMULATIONS (see ASSESSMENT CENTERS), or even the evaluation of the degree to which particular credentials indicate the possession of a desired job-relevant attribute.

ACTUARIAL VERSUS CLINICAL DECISION-MAKING

Once relevant KSAO data are collected, the organizational decision-maker must determine *how* to combine that information to predict each applicant's expected job success. If the organization adopts an *actuarial* approach to the use of information, it combines the information using a statistical formula that is based on the statistical relationship between KSAOs and subsequent job success as established in previous research studies. This procedure assumes that the KSAO–job performance relationship is the same in the current group of examinees as it was in those samples in which the research was conducted. Decision quality is dependent solely on the adequate identification of KSAO–job performance relationships.

In *clinical* decision-making, a person considers the entire array of information regarding an applicant's KSAOs. This information is compared to his or her own experience with the job and organization, and prior experience evaluating previous candidates (and those candidates' subsequent job performance). This approach to decision-making is much more individualistic and subjective; the skill of the decision-maker in integrating this array of information is a critical determinant of decision quality.

Noncompensatory and Compensatory Models

One other concern that is important when information is combined to make selection decisions is whether to use that information in a compensatory or noncompensatory fashion. A *compensatory* combination rule is one in which low levels on one ability can be compensated for by high levels on other abilities. For example, an applicant whose computer keyboarding skills are not great would be able to perform a job requiring such skills if he or she was motivated to attain the required level of skill. In effect, superior motivation would compensate for a current lack of keyboarding skills. Occasionally, a *noncompensatory* rule is appropriate. For example, one's technical competence in operating some piece of machinery would not compensate for a lack of color vision if the machine controls were color coded. In this case, no amount of technical competence could compensate for a lack of color vision.

Both compensatory and noncompensatory approaches to combining information are possible with either clinical or actuarial decision-making.

Bibliography

Cascio, W. F. (1998). *Applied Psychology in Human Resource Management.* Englewood Cliffs, NJ: Prentice-Hall.

Schneider, B. and Schmitt, N. (1986). *Staffing Organizations.* Prospect Heights, IL: Waveland Press.

selection ratio

Michael J. Burke

The selection ratio is the proportion of individuals in the applicant population who are hired. For a definition of the hiring rate and its relation to the selection ratio, see Alexander, Barrett, and Doverspike (1983).

Bibliography

Alexander, R. A., Barrett, G. V., and Doverspike, D. (1983). An explication of the selection ratio and its relationship to hiring rate. *Journal of Applied Psychology*, 68, 3424.

selection utility models

Michael J. Burke

A selection utility model is a theoretical equation for translating the results of a CRITERION-RELATED VALIDITY study into terms that are meaningful to organizational decision-makers, such as dollar-valued increases in JOB PERFORMANCE, percent increases in output, and reduction in the number of employees needed. The most frequently applied selection utility models provide decision-makers with a framework for systematically considering the benefits and costs of alternative PERSONNEL SELECTION procedures or decisions.

Brogden's Selection Utility Model

Brogden's (1949) contributions are still the basis for much of the utility analysis work done by human resource researchers and practitioners today. Brogden demonstrated that an estimate of the dollar value, or utility, of a selection program is a function of the number of individuals hired, the correlation between the selection procedure scores and job performance scores, the standard deviation of job performance in dollar terms (SD_y), the mean selection procedure score (expressed in a standard score form, with mean and standard deviation equal to 0 and 1, respectively) of the newly hired employees, and the total cost of the selection program. As noted by several authors, a slightly modified version of Brogden's model can be used for examining the gain in utility of a new selection program over an existing one.

One of the most difficult quantities to estimate when applying Brogden's model is SD_y. Strictly speaking, one would need information about the dollar value of the performance of each employee to compute SD_y. Given the difficulties in obtaining such individual-level data, several simpler methods for estimating SD_y have been proposed.

Global SD_y estimation procedures. Schmidt et al.'s (1979) procedure has subject matter experts (e.g., supervisors) estimate the dollar value, to the organization, of the goods and services produced by the average employee as well as by employees at the 15th and 85th percentiles. Under the assumption that the dollar value of employee performance is normally distributed, the differences between the values associated with the 50th and 15th percentiles and the 85th and 15th percentiles each represent estimation of SD_y. These separate estimates are then averaged to obtain a final estimate of SD_y. Alternative global SD_y estimation procedures, which employ consensus-seeking processes or anchoring (feedback) and adjustment processes, have been evaluated (Burke and Frederick, 1984).

Cascio–Ramos estimate of performance in dollars (CREPID). Cascio and Ramos (1986) proposed an SD_y estimation procedure which relies on JOB ANALYSIS information, performance ratings, and labor costs. Essentially, the CREPID procedure produces a dollar value for each employee based on multiplying mean salary for the employee's job times the employee's weighted overall performance rating. The standard deviation of these employee dollar values is assumed to be equal to SD_y. Modifications to CREPID which rely on existing job analysis and employee PERFORMANCE APPRAISAL information have been proposed. Other types of SD_y estimates, which rely on rules of thumb (such as 40 percent of mean salary; *see* RULE OF THUMB) or which have relevance to particular settings (e.g., military), have also been suggested. A number of studies (see Boudreau, 1991, for a review) have assisted us in gaining a better understanding of the relationships between alternative SD_y estimation procedures. A typical finding is that SD_y estimates based on the CREPID procedure and 40 percent of mean salary are somewhat consistent, whereas global estimates tend to be greater. These results are understandable given how utility is defined for each procedure as well as our knowledge of the mathematical relationships between the various SD_y estimation procedures.

Extensions and Modifications to Brogden's Selection Utility Model

The significant work of Cronbach and Gleser (1965) addressed the utility of classification, placement, and sequential selection. The work of Boudreau (1991) and his colleagues more directly focused on extending Brogden's utility model to incorporate economic concepts (variable costs, taxes, and discounting), the effects of recruitment activities, and the flow of employees into and out of the organization. In addition, Cronshaw and Alexander (1985) incorporated capital budgeting techniques into Brogden's model and subsequently argued that dollar utility can be defined in terms of costs, revenues, and investments. Finally, regression-based utility equations which do not require correcting validity coefficients for range restriction (typically considered in VALIDITY GENERALIZATION analyses) have been presented (Raju, Burke, and Maurer, 1995).

The above adjustments to Brogden's utility model have given researchers and practitioners a better understanding of the complexities involved in estimating selection program utility. In addition, discussions in the literature concerning changes in performance levels over time, possible decays in the predictive effectiveness of selection procedures over time, and the assumed effects of labor market conditions on selection utility have advanced our understanding of the factors impacting selection utility estimates. Overall, this line of research has assisted organizations in gaining a better sense for the economic value of validated personnel selection programs.

Notwithstanding the complexities of estimating selection utility, researchers have discussed how one can deal with the uncertainty of these utility estimates in decision contexts. Among several approaches, focusing on break-even values (minimum values necessary for utility gain to meet the costs associated with a personnel selection program) offers a practical means for decision-making.

Raju, Burke, and Normand's Selection Utility Model

Based on a different set of assumptions than Brogden about the relationship between behavioral performance and the dollar value of job performance, Raju, Burke, and Normand (1990) presented another regression-based utility model and set of equations for estimating selection utility. Whereas Brogden's model requires an estimate of SD_y to compute selection utility in dollar terms, the Raju et al. model requires an estimate of the economic value of the job (the constant "A" in their equations) to express selection in dollars. Recently, researchers have debated the promise of this model for overcoming problems in the estimation of selection program utility.

It should also be noted that the criterion variable in both Brogden's and Raju et al.'s models (typically job performance expressed in dollars) is assumed to be continuous. Several researchers have proposed utility models for evaluating selection procedures based on a dichotomized criterion (i.e., when all individuals in the "unsuccessful group" are assigned the same low value on the criterion and all of those in the "successful group" are assigned the same high value on the criterion).

Jarrett's Selection Utility Model for Estimating Percentage Increase in Output

Jarrett (1948) presented a general formula for estimating the percentage increase in *output* for a validated personnel selection program. He showed that an estimate of the percentage increase in output was a direct function of the validity coefficient, the coefficient of variation (the ratio of the standard deviation of output to mean output), and the mean standard score on the selection procedure of the selected group. In recent years, researchers have examined the extent to which the coefficient of variation (sometimes referred to as SD_p) varies as a function of job complexity. Jarrett's utility model and subsequent research related to estimating the coefficient of variation have increased our understanding of the percentage increase in output resulting from the use of validated selection programs, especially for jobs where performance is quantifiable.

Bibliography

Boudreau, J. W. (1991). Utility analysis for decisions in human resource management. In M. D. Dunnette and L. M. Hough (eds.), *Handbook of Industrial and Organizational Psychology*, 2nd edn, vol. 2. Palo Alto, CA: Consulting Psychologists Press.

Brogden, H. E. (1949). When testing pays off. *Personnel Psychology*, 2, 171–83.

Burke, M. J. and Frederick, J. T. (1984). Two modified procedures for estimating standard deviations in utility analyses. *Journal of Applied Psychology*, 69, 482–9.

Cascio, W. F. and Ramos, R. A. (1986). Development and application of a new method for assessing job performance in behavioral/economic terms. *Journal of Applied Psychology*, 71, 20–8.

Cronbach, L. J. and Gleser, G. C. (1965). *Psychological Tests and Personnel Decisions*. Urbana, IL: University of Illinois Press.

Cronshaw, S. F. and Alexander, R. A. (1985). One answer to the demand for accountability: Selection utility as an investment decision. *Organizational Behavior and Human Decision Processes*, 40, 270–86.

Jarrett, R. F. (1948). Percent increase in output of selected personnel as an index of test efficiency. *Journal of Applied Psychology*, 32, 135–45.

Raju, N. S., Burke, M. J., and Maurer, T. (1995). A note on direct range restriction corrections in utility analyses. *Personnel Psychology*, 48, 143–9.

Raju, N. S., Burke, M. J., and Normand, J. (1990). A new approach for utility analysis. *Journal of Applied Psychology*, 75, 3–12.

Schmidt, F. L., Hunter, J. E., McKenzie, R. C., and Muldrow, T. (1979). The impact of valid selection procedures on work force productivity. *Journal of Applied Psychology*, 64, 609–24.

self-awareness training

Timothy T. Baldwin

Students of human behavior have long suggested that knowledge of oneself (self-awareness) is essential to productive personal and interpersonal functioning. Dimensions of self-awareness include personal values, cognitive style, interpersonal orientation, personality, and interests. Self-awareness training typically consists of the trainee completing and interpreting one or more self-assessment instruments (e.g., Myers–Briggs type indicator) and then receiving feedback from others, sometimes in an unstructured format known as sensitivity training. An increasingly popular form of self-awareness training involves "360-degree feedback" (Van Velsor and Leslie, 1991), which refers to feedback collected from all those within a trainee's sphere of influence (e.g., superiors, subordinates, peers, and customers; *see* 360-DEGREE APPRAISALS).

Bibliography

Van Velsor, E. and Leslie, J. B. (1991). *Feedback to Managers: A Review and Comparison of Sixteen Multi-Rater*

Feedback Instruments (Technical Report No. 150), vol. 2. Greensboro, NC: Center for Creative Leadership.

self-efficacy training

Collette A. Frayne

Self-efficacy is defined as an individual's judgment of his or her capabilities to organize and execute courses of action required to attain certain types of performances (Bandura, 1986). These expectations regarding personal mastery determine whether people will try to cope with difficult situations. In addition, efficacy expectations serve to determine how much effort people will expend and how long they will persist in their efforts to overcome obstacles or aversive events. The stronger the efficacy expectations, the more active one's efforts (Bandura, 1986).

Self-efficacy training programs are designed to directly improve the individual's competencies, primarily through the use of mastery, modeling, and persuasion experiences, in performing the task. Studies have indicated that some training methods can enhance self-efficacy in the areas of, among others, SELF-MANAGEMENT TRAINING (Frayne and Latham, 1987), cognitive modeling, and BEHAVIOR MODELING (Gist, Schwoerer, and Rosen, 1989).

Bibliography

Bandura, A. (1986). *Social Foundations of Thought and Action*. Englewood Cliffs, NJ: Prentice-Hall.

Frayne, C. A. and Latham, G. P. (1987). The application of social learning theory to employee self-management of attendance. *Journal of Applied Psychology*, 72, 387–92.

Gist, M. E., Schwoerer, C., and Rosen, B. (1989). Effects of alternative training methods on self-efficacy and performance in computer software training. *Journal of Applied Psychology*, 74, 884–91.

self-management training

Collette A. Frayne

Self-management (Mills, 1983) is an effort by an individual to control his or her own behavior. Thus, an essential characteristic of self-management is that the individual is the primary agent for increasing or decreasing one or more response patterns.

Training in self-management teaches people how to assess problems, to set specific hard goals in relation to those problems, to monitor ways in which the environment facilitates or hinders goal attainment, and to identify and administer REINFORCEMENT for working toward, and punishment for failing to work toward, goal attainment (Karoly and Kanfer, 1982).

The potential usefulness of self-management in modifying behavior has been supported in laboratory and clinical settings (e.g., Karoly and Kanfer, 1982). In organizational settings, self-management training has improved both employee attendance (Frayne and Latham, 1987) and JOB PERFORMANCE and has enabled employees at various hierarchical levels to manage themselves more effectively (Manz, 1983).

Bibliography

Frayne, C. A. and Latham, G. P. (1987). The application of social learning theory to employee self-management of attendance. *Journal of Applied Psychology*, 72, 387–92.

Karoly, P. and Kanfer, F. H. (1982). *Self-Management and Behavior Change: From Theory to Practice*. Elmsford, NY: Pergamon Press.

Manz, C. (1983). *The Art of Self-Leadership*. Englewood Cliffs, NJ: Prentice-Hall.

Mills, P. (1983). Self-management: Its control and relationship to other organizational properties. *Academy of Management Review*, 8, 445–53.

self-managing teams

Susan Albers Mohrman

Self-managing teams are groups of people who (1) perform interdependent work, (2) are collectively responsible for the accomplishment of a product or service, and (3) self-regulate their work. They are also referred to as semi-autonomous or autonomous work teams and self-regulating teams. Although they vary in their authority limits and amount of autonomy, they are all characterized by increased internal control that results when management tasks such as planning, scheduling and staffing, organizing, and monitoring work are made a team responsibility. By one typology (Hackman, 1982), a self-designing team also controls its team's design, including its goals and composition. Self-managing teams are a form of HORIZONTAL MANAGEMENT.

Self-managing teams extend the principles of motivating job design, or job enrichment, to the team level (Hackman and Oldham, 1984). Teams are appropriate when an individual cannot perform a whole task, so whole-product identification is only possible at the group level. Work technology also determines the appropriateness of teams. Self-managing teams are appropriate when work is interdependent and uncertain, requiring a great deal of online interaction and mutual adjustment. The determination of the appropriateness of the use of self-managing teams is often accomplished through a sociotechnical analysis aimed at jointly optimizing the technical and social design of the work system (Pasmore, 1988).

Three conditions are especially important for successful application of self-managing teams (Cummings, 1978). First, the task of the team must be differentiated and self-contained. Second, the team must have boundary control over its inputs and outputs. These first two conditions exist when the team contains the necessary resources and skills to perform its production tasks and to do its own support tasks and quality control. It also interfaces directly with its suppliers and customers. The third condition is task control, the ability to self-regulate team behavior in converting inputs into products or services. These factors enable the team to be held accountable for its performance.

Implementation of self-managing teams requires the redesign of many aspects of the organizational system. Team members are generally cross-trained (see CROSS-TRAINING) to facilitate mutual coordination, provide flexibility in task assignment, and enable the team to perform expanded functions. Salary is often based, in part, on the skills that have been mastered by each individual. In addition, team BONUSES are sometimes used to reward team performance. Personnel and PERFORMANCE MANAGEMENT functions such as goal setting, feedback, appraisal, interviewing and hiring, disciplining, and firing may all be team responsibilities. In some cases these are joint responsibilities with management.

Management structures and roles change significantly to provide a context suitable for self-managing teams. Supervisors may be responsible for several teams. Their role changes from day-to-day direction to helping to develop the team to manage itself (Manz and Sims, 1989). In some instances, the supervisory level may be eliminated altogether, as team leaders perform management tasks or leadership roles are dispersed among team members. Support functions such as maintenance or quality may be radically reduced in size, and remaining functional experts may be used in a consulting role to the teams.

The historical roots of self-managing teams lie in the sociotechnical tradition and originated in Europe (e.g., Trist and Bamforth, 1951). Early applications focused on the shop floor, largely in production settings characterized by continuous process technology. Recently, use has spread to KNOWLEDGE WORK settings (see KNOWLEDGE TEAMS). Self-managing teams are frequently part of high-involvement (Lawler, 1986) organizational approaches that create conditions that motivate employees to contribute to high performance. Supporting design changes include flattening the organization, distributing performance-related information to employees, extensive training and development, eliminating status differences, rewarding for performance and skills, and creating conditions for EMPLOYEE EMPOWERMENT.

Research on self-managing teams finds modest evidence of positive impact on attitudinal and organizational performance results (Cohen, 1994). Results are believed to be best when they are used in a supportive context and when adequate attention is given to examining and co-optimizing the technical system. Although dissemination of this approach has been slow, data show that the application of self-managing teams is steadily increasing. For example, over 60 percent of the largest US firms now employ self-managing teams in some operations (Lawler, Mohrman, and Ledford, 1995).

Bibliography

Cohen, S. G. (1994). Designing effective self-managing work teams. In M. Beyerlein (ed.), *Advances in Interdisciplinary Studies of Work Teams*, vol. 1. Greenwich, CT: JAI Press.

Cummings, T. G. (1978). Self-regulating work groups: A socio-technical synthesis. *Academy of Management Review*, 3, 625–34.

Hackman, J. R. (1982). The design of work teams. In J. W. Lorsch (ed.), *The Handbook of Organizational Behavior*. Englewood Cliffs, NJ: Prentice-Hall.

Hackman, J. R. and Oldham, G. R. (1984). *Work Redesign*. Reading, MA: Addison-Wesley.

Lawler, E. E., III (1986). *High Involvement Management*. San Francisco: Jossey-Bass.

Lawler, E. E., III, Mohrman, S. A., and Ledford, G. E., Jr. (1995). *Creating High Performance Organizations*. San Francisco: Jossey-Bass.

Manz, C. M. and Sims, H. P. (1989). *Super-Leadership: Leading Others to Lead Themselves*. Englewood Cliffs, NJ: Prentice-Hall.

Pasmore, W. A. (1988). *Designing Effective Organizations: The Sociotechnical Systems Perspective*. New York: John Wiley.

Trist, E. L. and Bamforth, K. W. (1951). Some social psychological consequences of the longwall method of coal-getting. *Human Relations*, 338.

self-ratings

Walter C. Borman

Self-ratings in an organizational setting involve asking organization members to evaluate themselves on overall performance, or, more often, on several individual dimensions of performance (e.g., job knowledge, planning, and organizing). Self-evaluations are used most often for developmental purposes, and often are used in conjunction with SUPERVISORY RATINGS or subordinates' ratings (see 360-DEGREE APPRAISALS). Employees are then given these other ratings so that they can judge how they may have under- or overestimated their performance in each area. In addition, self-ratings are occasionally used as criterion scores for selection or other kinds of research when ratings from other sources are not available.

An obvious advantage of self-ratings is that the "rater" has a lot of knowledge about "ratee" performance. A disadvantage is that self-ratings may often overestimate actual performance levels. In fact, research shows that self-ratings are typically more lenient than PEER RATINGS or supervisory ratings (Borman, 1991; see LENIENCY EFFECTS). Further, a meta-analysis (Harris and Schaubroeck, 1988) found that inter-rater agreement between self-ratings and either peer ratings or supervisor ratings was low ($r = 0.35$ and 0.36, respectively) compared to the agreement between peers and supervisors ($r = 0.62$).

Finally, the issue of self-rating validity was explored by Mabe and West (1982). They conducted a meta-analysis of correlations between self-ratings of abilities and criterion scores (mostly test scores or supervisory ratings). The mean validity coefficient was 0.29, but these validities varied considerably. Relatively high validity coefficients were obtained when raters (1) made relative rather than absolute judgments, (2) had comparatively more experience providing ratings, (3) were told that their ratings were anonymous, (4) rated past rather than future performance, and (5) were told that their ratings would be compared to criterion scores.

Bibliography

Borman, W. C. (1991). Job behavior, performance, and effectiveness. In M. D. Dunnette and L. M. Hough (eds.), *Handbook of Industrial and Organizational Psychology*, 2nd edn, vol. 2. Palo Alto, CA: Consulting Psychologists Press.

Harris, M. M. and Schaubroeck, J. (1988). A meta-analysis of self–supervisor, self–peer, and peer–supervisor ratings. *Personnel Psychology*, 41, 43–62.

Mabe, P. A. and West, S. G. (1982). Validity of self-evaluation of ability: A review and meta-analysis. *Journal of Applied Psychology*, 67, 280–96.

service quality

David E. Bowen

The most widely accepted definition of service quality in the management and marketing literature is the extent to which customers' perceptions of service meet and/or exceed their expectations (e.g., Zeithaml, Parasaraman, and Berry, 1990). This subjective, customer-based definition of quality is a departure from earlier definitions of quality based on the extent to which measurable attributes of the products or services themselves conformed to objective, predetermined specifications (Reeves and Bednar, 1994).

Zeithaml et al. (1990) determined that customers evaluate service on five dimensions: reliability, responsiveness, assurance, tangibles, and empathy (these five factors have a mixed track record of replication by other researchers). Overall, service quality is a function of both outcome (e.g., a properly prepared meal) and process (e.g., how the meal was delivered by the waiter).

Managing the delivery of service quality must take into account the unique nature of services that are primarily intangible, are often produced and consumed simultaneously, and frequently involve customers as coproducers of the service they receive (Bowen and Schneider, 1988). These characteristics pose distinct challenges to human resource managers. For example, service quality must be managed in real time in the service encounter between contact employee and customer. This makes quality control an integral part of the HUMAN RESOURCE FUNCTION because the selection and training of contact employees helps to determine quality. Also, customers who help to coproduce their service (e.g., bringing the right documents to their tax consultant) can be viewed as "partial employees" who also must be managed as human resources (e.g., thoughtfully selected and trained).

Bibliography

Bowen, D. E. and Schneider, B. (1988). Services marketing and management: Implications for organizational behavior. In B. Staw and L. L. Cummings (eds.), *Research in Organizational Behavior*, vol. 10. Greenwich, CT: JAI Press.

Reeves, C. A. and Bednar, D. A. (1994). Defining quality: Alternatives and implications. *Academy of Management Review*, 19, 419–45.

Zeithaml, V. A., Parasaraman, A., and Berry, L. L. (1990). *Delivering Quality Service*. New York: Free Press.

sex

Ramona L. Paetzold

Sex is one of the protected categories under federal antidiscrimination law (e.g., Title VII of the CIVIL RIGHTS ACT OF 1964, EQUAL PAY ACT OF 1963). The interpretation of "sex" has broadened over the years to include not only the biological categorization, but also the cultural and social categorization scheme known as gender (particularly under Title VII). Thus, protection flows to males and females as biological entities, and to men and women as they are culturally understood. For example, the use of sex- and/or gender-based stereotypes can lead to discrimination on the basis of sex. In general, "sex" has not been interpreted to include SEXUAL ORIENTATION.

sex-role stereotypes

Ellen A. Fagenson-Eland

Sex-role stereotypes are biased assumptions made about individuals based upon their membership in a particular sexual group. Sex-role stereotypes assume that all members of one sex have similar characteristics and these characteristics are different from those possessed by members of the other sex. For example, women are often stereotyped as being emotional, nurturing, and passive; men are stereotyped as being independent, decisive, and strong (Powell, 1993). Research has shown, however, that women and men managers are more alike than they are different, suggesting that sex-role stereotypes are inaccurate (Freedman and Phillips, 1988). They can also be harmful.

Women managers cite sex-role stereotypes as the primary barrier they face in securing higher-level management positions (Heidrick and Struggles, 1986; see WOMEN'S CAREER ISSUES). Research has consistently shown that, according to male managers, women managers are less likely to possess the characteristics of successful managers than male managers (Schein, 1973; Brenner, Tomkiewicz, and Schein, 1989; Heilman et al., 1989). In the 1970s, women managers made similar attributions. According to more recent research, however, women managers now perceive that successful managers possess the sex-role stereotypical traits characteristic of both men and women (Brenner et al., 1989; Heilman et al., 1989).

Sex-role stereotyping is most likely to occur when little information other than an individual's sex is known about him or her (Powell, 1993). Consequently, stereotyping of men and women in the workplace could be reduced if (1) information beyond their sex is known to those making judgments and decisions about them, and (2) opportunities to interact with those decision-makers are provided (Fagenson, 1993).

Researchers often measure sex-role stereotypes in the workplace by asking individuals to rate others or themselves on a set of attributes that people generally believe are more desirable or typical of each gender group. The Bem Sex Role Inventory (Bem, 1974), the Woman As Managers Scale (Peters, Terborg, and Taynor, 1974), the Spence and Helmreich Personal Attributes Questionnaire (Spence and Helmreich, 1978), and the Schein Descriptive Index (Schein, 1973) are four instruments commonly employed for this purpose. Hypothetical work situations which may vary the sex of the individual described in the situation are also used by researchers to measure individuals' propensity to stereotype individuals on the basis of their sex.

Bibliography

Bem, S. L. (1974). The measurement of psychological androgyny. *Journal of Consulting and Clinical Psychology*, **42**, 155–62.

Brenner, O. C., Tomkiewicz, J., and Schein, V. E. (1989). The relationship between sex role stereotypes and requisite management characteristics revisited. *Academy of Management Journal*, **32**, 662–9.

Fagenson, E. A. (1993). *Women in Management: Trends, Issues and Challenges in Managerial Diversity*. Newbury Park, CA: Sage.

Freedman, S. and Phillips, J. (1988). The changing nature of research on women at work. *Journal of Management*, **14**, 231–63.

Heidrick and Struggles (1986). *The Corporate Woman Officer*. Chicago: Heidrick and Struggles, Inc.

Heilman, M. E., Block, C. J., Martell, R. F., and Simon, M. C. (1989). Has anything changed? Current characterizations of men, women and managers. *Journal of Applied Psychology*, **74**, 935–42.

Peters, L. H., Terborg, J. R., and Taynor, J. (1974). Women As Managers Scale (WAMS): A measure of attitudes toward women in managerial positions. *American Psychological Association: Journal Supplement Abstract Service*, 585.

Powell, G. (1993). *Women and Men in Management*, 2nd edn. Newbury Park, CA: Sage.

Schein, V. (1973). The relationship between sex role stereotypes and requisite management characteristics among female managers. *Journal of Applied Psychology*, **60**, 340–4.

Spence, J. T. and Helmreich, R. L. (1978). *Masculinity and Femininity: Their Psychological Correlates and Antecedents*. Austin, TX: University of Texas Press.

sexual harassment

Barbara A. Lee

Sexual harassment is a form of SEX DISCRIMINATION and is defined by the EQUAL EMPLOYMENT OPPORTUNITY COMMISSION (EEOC) as follows. Unwanted sexual advances, requests for sexual favors, and other verbal or physical conduct of a sexual nature constitute sexual harassment when: (1) submission to such conduct is made either explicitly or implicitly a term or condition of employment; (2) submission to or rejection of such conduct by an individual is used as the basis for employment decisions affecting said individual; or (3) such conduct has the purpose or effect of substantially interfering with an individual's work performance or creating an intimidating, hostile, or offensive working environment (EEOC Guidelines on Sex Discrimination, 29 CFR section 1604.11).

Employers can be held legally liable for "quid pro quo" sexual harassment (harassment by a supervisor that involves threats or promises of changes in employment terms) (*see* BARNES V. COSTLE, 1977; MERITOR SAVINGS BANK V. VINSON, 1986), as well as for the creation of a hostile or offensive environment by a supervisor (*Harris* v. *Forklift Systems*, 114 S Ct 367, 1993), a coworker, or a nonemployee. In *Harris*, the court ruled that the plaintiff need not prove any physical, psychological, or financial harm as a consequence of the harassment. It is the conduct itself that is unlawful if a reasonable person would find that the conduct had created a hostile or offensive work environment.

The courts have differed as to whether the "reasonable person" test should be used, or the "reasonable woman" test (if the target of the harassment is female) should apply. In *Ellison v. Brady* (924 F 2nd 872, 9th Circuit, 1991), the court ruled that, because research shows that men and women react differently to sexual behavior and because women are more likely to be offended by such behavior, the reasonable woman test should be used. In the *Harris* case, the court appeared to use the "reasonable person" test, but did not address this issue explicitly.

Employers may prevent sexual harassment from occurring and may present a successful defense against sexual harassment claims for hostile or offensive environment harassment if they have: (1) a clear policy that spells out what sexual harassment is and what its consequences will be; (2) a reporting policy that provides multiple avenues for a target of harassment to use so that the target need not report the harassment to the alleged harasser; (3) training programs for, at a minimum, managers and supervisors on how to recognize and respond to harassment; and (4) a monitoring mechanism that enables the employer to identify and stop harassment before it escalates into a legal claim.

The federal courts do not agree on whether Title VII permits a claim of same-sex sexual harassment. While some courts have ruled that such claims relate to SEXUAL ORIENTATION, others have stated that harassment of a man by a gay man, or a woman by a lesbian, can be viewed as a form of sex discrimination because it is gender-targeted conduct.

Bibliography

Kirp, D. L., Yudof, M. G., and Franks, M. S. (1986). *Gender Justice*. Chicago: University of Chicago Press.

Schlei, B. L. and Grossman, P. (1983). *Employment Discrimination Law*, 2nd edn. Washington, DC: Bureau of National Affairs.

sexual orientation

Ramona L. Paetzold

Sexual orientation is generally viewed as including homosexuality and bisexuality, and is not specifically protected under federal antidiscrimination laws. Some states and/or cities and counties do protect individuals from discrimination by private employers on the basis of sexual orientation, however. Public employers may be restricted in their ability to discriminate on the basis of sexual orientation because of Constitutional protections that have been found to flow to gays and lesbians (under the equal protection guarantees of the Fifth Constitutional Amendment and FOURTEENTH CONSTITUTIONAL AMENDMENT).

simulations

Timothy T. Baldwin

Simulations are instructional activities designed to maximize learning by replicating essential characteristics of a real-world task. Although physical similarity between a simulation and the work context is important, the key element in the effectiveness of any simulation is psychological fidelity. Attaining high psychological fidelity requires representation of those conditions which make trainees "feel" as if they are performing the real task. Traditional examples of simulations include flight simulators and business games, but advanced computing technology now enables creation of "virtual reality" in many different contexts (e.g., simulated surgery) and is creating extraordinary opportunities for the use of simulations.

single-group validity

Larry James

Boehm (1972) provided a definition of single-group validity that distinguished it from DIFFERENTIAL VALIDITY. She explained that single-group validity exists when (1) a predictor demonstrates validity that is statistically different from zero for one group but not another group, and (2) there is no statistically significant difference between the validities of two groups. Boehm (1972) argued that the occurrences of single-group validity far outnumbered the instances of differential validity. However,

Schmidt, Berner, and Hunter (1973) presented evidence that when differences in sample sizes are taken into account, there is little support for the single-group validity argument. Furthermore, when the issue is taken to the population level, it becomes untenable. Two population validities cannot be equal and, at the same time, have one be equal to zero and another one not equal to zero. Thus, the usefulness of single-group validity has been questioned.

Bibliography

Boehm, V. R. (1972). Negro–white differences in validity of employment and training selection procedures: Summary of research evidence. *Journal of Applied Psychology*, 56, 33–9.

Schmidt, F. L., Berner, J. G., and Hunter, J. R. (1973). Racial differences in validity of employment tests: Reality or illusion. *Journal of Applied Psychology*, 58, 5–9.

situational interview

Robert L. Dipboye

The situational interview is a type of highly structured procedure used in employment interviews (*see* EMPLOYMENT INTERVIEW) and first introduced by Latham et al. (1980). The basic assumption underlying this approach is that the future performance of applicants can be best predicted by finding out their goals and intentions for dealing with the dilemmas that they might encounter in specific job situations. The first step in developing a situational interview is to analyze the job using the CRITICAL INCIDENTS TECHNIQUE. From the incidents generated in this step, performance dimensions are identified that are then evaluated in the interview. Those incidents that best represent each of the dimensions are turned into interview questions by asking the applicant to consider "what they would do if" they were confronted with the situations described in the incidents. Interviewers ask the same questions of all applicants in exactly the same way, with no opportunity provided for follow-up questions or other conversation with the applicant. Also, interviewers are not given access to applications, test scores, or other ancillary data on the applicant until after they have finished evaluating the applicant. Interviewers evaluate the applicants on BEHAVIORALLY ANCHORED RATING SCALES, in which possible examples of good, average, or poor answers are used to anchor the points on the rating scale. After the applicant is asked each of the questions and rated on the performance dimensions, the ratings on the dimensions are then averaged to form a composite evaluation of the applicant.

The research has provided impressive support for the validity and reliability of the situational interview (McDaniel et al., 1994). Moreover, the JOB-RELATEDNESS of the situational interview makes it more defensible against charges of DISCRIMINATION than the typical unstructured interview.

Bibliography

Latham, G. P., Saari, L. M., Pursell, E. D., and Campion, M. A. (1980). The situational interview. *Journal of Applied Psychology*, 65, 422–7.

McDaniel, M. A., Whetzel, D. L., Schmidt, F. L., and Maurer, S. (1994). The validity of employment interviews: A comprehensive review and meta-analysis. *Journal of Applied Psychology*, 79, 599–616.

situational tests

Richard Klimoski

Situational tests are assessment devices that require applicants, or candidates, to respond to a set of standardized instructions and stimuli *as if* they were doing so under natural conditions. Behavior is directly observed or recorded (sometimes on videotape), and trained staff then score these observations in standardized ways (*see* ASSESSMENT CENTERS; WORK SAMPLES). Examples of situational tests include the in-basket test, the SITUATIONAL INTERVIEW, the leaderless group discussion, and assigned role-playing exercises (*see* MANAGEMENT GAMES; ROLE PLAYING; SIMULATIONS). Situational tests are usually administered in selection contexts, but can also be used in personnel development work.

Most situational tests are based on some aspects of a target job. These tests can vary in terms of "mundane realism" versus fidelity (Weick, 1965). The highest-fidelity situational tests use very realistic materials and equipment to represent the task situation and provide applicants with an opportunity to respond almost as if they were in the job situation. Low-fidelity simulations might merely present a verbal or a written description of a hypothetical work circumstance and ask for verbal reactions (Motowidlo, Dunnette, and Carter, 1990).

Another important distinction is whether or not the situational test provides an opportunity to assess actual performance or inference about underlying job-relevant knowledge, skills, abilities, or other dispositions (see KSAOS) (Russell and Domm, 1995). The development of situational tests to assess actual performance calls for evidence of job relevance (see CONTENT VALIDITY; CRITERION-RELATED VALIDITY), while the development of inferences about underlying KSAOs requires that the inferences made really do get at the underlying traits or qualities of interest (see CONSTRUCT VALIDITY).

Finally, situational tests can be designed for one-on-one assessment or may involve the applicant/candidate in a group context. The latter can require a given candidate to interact with other individuals who are also being assessed, or with staff who are trained to act in standardized ways.

Bibliography

Motowidlo, S. J., Dunnette, M. D., and Carter, G. W. (1990). An alternative selection procedure: The low-fidelity simulation. *Journal of Applied Psychology*, 75, 640–7.

Russell, C. J. and Domm, D. R. (1995). Two field tests of an explanation of assessment center validity. *Journal of Occupational and Organizational Psychology*, 68, 25–47.

Weick, K. (1965). Laboratory experimentation with organizations. In J. G. March (ed.), *Handbook of Organizations*. Chicago: Rand-McNally.

skill

Paul E. Spector

Skill refers to a person's current level of proficiency on a particular task or family of tasks. Examples include driving an automobile or operating a computer. Skills can be classified as either mental (e.g., report writing) or physical (running a machinist's lathe), although most job tasks involve elements of both. Skill reflects a person's current level of proficiency. In contrast, ability (see KSAOS) reflects the capability or capacity to develop a skill. Skills can be assessed by a variety of devices, including ASSESSMENT CENTERS, psychological tests (see PSYCHOLOGICAL TEST), SITUATIONAL TESTS, and WORK SAMPLING.

skill-based pay design

Gerald E. Ledford, Jr.

Three sets of issues are important in a skill-based pay design (Ledford, 1991). First, the plan must be tailored to its context – the business strategy, organizational structure, and organizational culture. Second, pay plan mechanics must be developed, including definition of compensable units of skill and creation of relevant training and assessment materials. Third, a plan for transition from the existing pay system is needed. Of these factors, the fit of the design with its context is probably the most important in determining effectiveness (Jenkins et al., 1992). Plans for knowledge workers (see KNOWLEDGE WORK) are relatively new and present many special design challenges (Ledford, 1995).

Bibliography

Jenkins, G. D., Jr., Ledford, G. E., Jr., Gupta, N., and Doty, D. H. (1992). *Skill-Based Pay: Practices, Payoffs, Pitfalls, and Prospects*. Scottsdale, AZ: American Compensation Association.

Ledford, G. E., Jr. (1991). The design of skill-based pay plans. In M. L. Rock and L. Berger (eds.), *The Compensation Handbook*, 3rd edn. New York: McGraw-Hill.

Ledford, G. E., Jr. (1995). Paying for the skills, knowledge, and competencies of knowledge workers. *Compensation and Benefits Review*, 27, 55–62.

smoke-free work environment

Michael R. Manning

A smoke-free work environment results from organizational policy prohibiting smoking within all company premises. Smoking bans have risen due to opposition from nonsmokers, evidence about the harmful effects of secondhand smoke, and a plethora of new local, state, and federal laws. A 1994 survey suggested that 96 percent of American businesses wanted a smoke-free work environment by 2002 (Laabs, 1994). Since SMOKING CESSATION has been shown to have short-term work-related consequences (Manning, Osland, and Osland, 1989), implementing smoking policies that involve the workforce in policy development and compassionately encourage behavioral changes in smokers seems prudent (Yandrick, 1994).

Bibliography

Laabs, J. J. (1994). Companies kick the smoking habit. *Personnel Journal*, 73, 38–48.

Manning, M. R., Osland, J. S., and Osland, A. (1989). Work-related consequences of smoking cessation. *Academy of Management Journal*, 32, 606–21.

Yandrick, R. M. (1994). More employers prohibit smoking. *HR Magazine*, 39, 68–71.

smoking cessation

James R. Terborg

Smoking cessation is defined as a complete discontinuation of smoking for a period of six months. A 1992 national survey in the US found that 40 percent of worksites provided information or sponsored activities on smoking cessation and 59 percent had formal policies restricting smoking at work. Cigarette smoking is the chief preventable cause of premature death and disability in the US. Compared to nonsmokers, smokers have 40 percent higher estimated lifetime healthcare expenses, consistently sustain more occupational injuries, have higher use of drugs and alcohol, and have higher rates of ABSENTEEISM (Kaman, 1995). The overall effect of smoking on JOB PERFORMANCE is less clear, but appears to be negative because of lost work time due to smoking (Kaman, 1995). Exposure to environmental tobacco smoke, a documented carcinogen, by nonsmokers is also associated with negative health effects. Cascio (1991) estimated the annual cost of employing smokers and allowing them to smoke at work to be $2,853 per smoker, in 1991 US dollars. Meta-analysis suggests that smoking cessation programs at work conservatively produce a 13 percent quit rate, compared to 6 percent of smokers who quit on their own (Fisher, Glasgow, and Terborg, 1990). Smoking cessation programs appear to be cost beneficial. Policies toward a SMOKE-FREE WORK ENVIRONMENT decrease employee exposure to environmental tobacco smoke, modify worksite norms toward smoking, reduce smokers' cigarette consumption while at work, and, in some instances, increase smoking cessation. Considerable variability exists across worksites with respect to the content, implementation, and effectiveness of smoking cessation programs.

Bibliography

Cascio, W. F. (1991). *Costing Human Resources: The Financial Impact of Behavior in Organizations*, 3rd edn. Boston: PWS-Kent.

Fisher, K. J., Glasgow, R. E., and Terborg, J. R. (1990). Worksite smoking cessation: A meta-analysis of long-term quit rates from controlled studies. *Journal of Occupational Medicine*, 32, 429–39.

Kaman, R. L. (ed.) (1995). *Worksite Health Promotion Economics: Consensus and Analysis*. Champaign, IL: Human Kinetics.

social influence in the performance evaluation process

Dwight D. Frink, Darren C. Treadway, and Gerald R. Ferris

Drawing from sociologists such as Erving Goffman (Brissett and Edgley, 1990), social influence in performance evaluations envisions actors engaging in "performances," or acts, delivered to help shape definitions of reality. This broad domain includes impression management, self-presentation, influence tactics, and organizational politics, among others (Ferris et al., 2002). Some acts may be specifically targeted toward managing impressions in hopes of more favorable evaluations. Others may be a part of a social fabric that unintentionally affects perceptions and performance evaluations. Typically, the focus is on the former class of acts.

The general model includes an actor (the ratee) that engages in various activities designed to dispose the audience (the rater) toward giving a favorable rating. The objective typically is a positive disposition toward the actor, but may at times focus on the outcome, as when blackmailing someone in authority over you to get better ratings. Thus, a social influence perspective focuses on the *process*. Employees can employ a number of forms of influence, and the usefulness of different tactics appears to be contingent on the context, source, and target of the influence efforts (Ferris et al., 2002). Typically, the dependent variable is performance ratings, although other outcomes such as perceptions of fairness (Dulebohn and Ferris, 1999) and promotability (Wayne et al., 1997) are relevant.

Research consistently has supported that general model, initially focusing on specific influence tactics. Some effort in that direction remains, although increasingly the emphasis is on moderating variables, such as actor and target INDIVIDUAL DIFFERENCES, including positive affectivity (Castro et al., 2003), self-monitoring (Snyder, 1987), and political skill (Ferris et al., 2004). Other moderators may include social capital and accountability conditions (Frink and Klimoski, 1998), among others.

NATURE AND FORMS OF SOCIAL INFLUENCE

Tactics of influence. Kipnis and his colleagues developed one program of research focusing on subordinate/ratee influence efforts (Kipnis, Schmidt, and Wilkinson, 1980). This produced a typology, and findings indicate that subordinate ingratiation correlates with higher performance ratings. Furthermore, a tactician strategy (emphasizing reason) was more successful for male subordinates, and an ingratiator strategy (emphasizing friendliness) was more effective for female subordinates in receiving higher performance ratings (Kipnis and Schmidt, 1988).

Ferris, Wayne, and colleagues emphasized the performance evaluation process and outcomes in a second program of research. Findings demonstrate that influence tactics operate through supervisor affect, perceived competence, and perceived similarity to the supervisor. Furthermore, Ferris et al. (1994) supported a positive link between supervisor-focused (i.e., ingratiation) tactics and performance evaluation through liking, but a negative link between job-focused (i.e., self-promotion) tactics and performance evaluation through liking. Wayne et al. (1997) used three intermediate linkages (i.e., supervisor affect, perceived competence, and perceived similarity to supervisor), and tangible outcomes (i.e., promotions and salary increases), finding that reasoning, favor-doing, and assertiveness positively influenced, and bargaining negatively influenced, human resource decisions through managers' perceptions of subordinate skills, competence, and similarity to the subordinate. Thus, not all influence tactics are similarly perceived or equally effective (Kipnis and Schmidt, 1988).

These streams are based on the influence typology of Kipnis et al. (1980). However, recent scholarly activity suggests that other forms of influence tactics warrant investigation. Dulebohn and his colleagues (Dulebohn, 1997; Dulebohn and Ferris, 1999) suggest that influence tactics serve as a voice mechanism, and Ferris et al. (2002) suggest that the strategic expression of emotion can be a form of influence.

Also, research is needed that employs longitudinal research designs because of the temporal nature of the phenomenon. To date, only two studies (Wayne and Liden, 1995; Dulebohn, Ferris, and Ree, 1999) have done so. Research investigating longitudinal performance evaluation processes with cross-sectional research designs must be interpreted with caution because one hypothesis may be that findings are merely an artifact of cross-sectional designs.

Accountability as social influence. Interest in accountability as a framework of performance evaluations is increasing because it is a key social context feature, actors and audiences can be held to answer for decisions and actions, and performance evaluations themselves are accountings (Frink and Klimoski, 1998; Klimoski and Inks, 1990; Tetlock, 1992). Research indicates that individuals generally seek out and consider accountability context features, including timing and likelihood of being held accountable, the standards being employed, and the number and characteristics of the various audiences holding that person accountable. Decisions and acts are then tailored to achieve the desired outcome, which may range from avoidance, deflection, and denial to opportunistically reaping rewards (i.e., minimizing losses to neutralizing the accounting to gaining rewards) (Frink and Klimoski, 1998). This embraces the dramaturgical notion that the rate considers how particular influence tactics may be received by the rater, making choices based on the anticipated response.

When accountable, both ratees and raters alter intensity of cognitive processing in order to successfully cope with the accounting. Thus, the rater may rate more conscientiously and the ratee may work more conscientiously when accountable (Klimoski and Inks, 1990). Alternatively, simple decision heuristics and free-riding can occur if they provide easy justifications (Adelberg and Batson, 1978). Hall et al. (2003) presented a conceptualization and empirical results concerning accountability in performance evaluation contexts, and others have investigated the effects of accountability (e.g., Fandt and Ferris, 1990; Ferris et al., 1997). For example, Frink and Ferris (1998) found that personal accountability for goals was related to higher self-set goals, although actual performance did not differ across conditions, implying goal setting can influence impressions. Also, Greenberg (1985) implied that high self-set goals could be used as a self-handicapping strategy to deflect a negative accounting.

Conclusion

Although the greater portion of performance evaluation theory and research has been directed toward measurement issues, forms of influence in performance evaluation are recognized as critical components of the larger focus of social contexts of human resource decisions. This focus is a vital part of human resource management practice and research (Ferris et al., 2002; Ferris and Mitchell, 1987).

Bibliography

Adelberg, S. and Batson, C. D. (1978). Accountability and helping: When needs exceed resources. *Journal of Personality and Social Psychology*, 36, 343–50.

Brissett, D. and Edgley, C. (1990). The dramaturgical perspective. In D. Brissett and C. Edgley (eds.), *Life as a Theater: A Dramaturgical Sourcebook*, 2nd edn. New York: Walter de Gruyter, pp. 1–46.

Castro, S. L., Douglas, C., Hochwarter, W. A., Ferris, G. R., and Frink, D. D. (2003). The effects of positive affect and gender on the influence tactics–job performance relationship. *Journal of Leadership and Organizational Studies*, 10, 1–18.

Dulebohn, J. H. (1997). Social influence in justice evaluations of human resources systems. In G. R. Ferris (ed.), *Research in Personnel and Human Resources Management*, vol. 15. Greenwich, CT: JAI Press pp. 241–91.

Dulebohn, J. H. and Ferris, G. R. (1999). The role of influence tactics in perceptions of performance evaluations' fairness. *Academy of Management Journal*, 42, 288–303.

Dulebohn, J. H., Ferris, G. R., and Ree, M. J. (1999). A longitudinal investigation of influence tactics effects on performance ratings. Paper presented at the 14th Annual Conference of the Society for Industrial and Organizational Psychology, Atlanta.

Fandt, P. M. and Ferris, G. R. (1990). The management of information and impressions: When employees behave opportunistically. *Organizational Behavior and Human Decision Processes*, 45, 140–58.

Ferris, G. R., Dulebohn, J. H., Frink, D. D., George-Falvy, J., Mitchell, T. R., and Matthews, L. M. (1997). Job and organizational characteristics, accountability, and employee influence. *Journal of Managerial Issues*, 9, 162–75.

Ferris, G. R., Hochwarter, W. A., Douglas, C., Blass, R., Kolodinsky, R. W., and Treadway, D. C. (2002). Social influence processes in organizations and human resources systems. In G. R. Ferris and J. J. Martocchio (eds.), *Research in Personnel and Human Resources Management*, vol. 21. Oxford: JAI Press/Elsevier Science, pp. 65–127.

Ferris, G. R., Judge, T. A., Rowland, K. M., and Fitzgibbons, D. E. (1994). Subordinate influence and the performance evaluation process: Test of a model. *Organizational Behavior and Human Decision Processes*, 58, 101–35.

Ferris, G. R. and Mitchell, T. R. (1987). The components of social influence and their importance for human resources research. In K. M. Rowland and G. R. Ferris (eds.), *Research in Personnel and Human Resources Management*, vol. 5. Greenwich, CT: JAI Press.

Ferris, G. R., Treadway, D. C., Kolodinsky, R. W., Hochwarter, W. A., Kacmar, C. J., Douglas, C., and Frink, D. D. (2004). Development and validation of the political skill inventory. *Journal of Management*.

Frink, D. D. and Ferris, G. R. (1998). Accountability, impression management, and goal setting in the performance evaluation process. *Human Relations*, 51, 1259–83.

Frink, D. D. and Klimoski, R. J. (1998). Toward a theory of accountability in organizations and human resource management. In G. R. Ferris (ed.), *Research in*

Personnel and Human Resources Management. vol. 16. Stamford, CT: JAI Press, pp. 1–51.

Greenberg, J. (1985). Unattainable goal choice as a self-handicapping strategy. *Journal of Applied Social Psychology*, 15, 87–101.

Hall, A. T., Frink, D. D., Ferris, G. R., Hochwarter, W. A., Kacmar, C. J., and Bowen, M. G. (2003). Accountability in human resources management. In C. A. Schriesheim and L. Neider (eds.), *New Directions in Human Resource Management*. Greenwich, CT: Information Age Publishing, pp. 29–63.

Kipnis, D. and Schmidt, S. M. (1988). Upward influence styles: Relationship with performance evaluations, salary, and stress. *Administrative Science Quarterly*, 33, 528–42.

Kipnis, D., Schmidt, S. M., and Wilkinson, I. (1980). Intraorganizational influence tactics: Explorations in getting one's way. *Journal of Applied Psychology*, 65, 440–52.

Klimoski, R. and Inks, L. (1990). Accountability forces in performance appraisal. *Organizational Behavior and Human Decision Processes*, 45, 194–208.

Snyder, M. (1987). *Public Appearances and Private Realities: The Psychology of Self-Monitoring*. New York: W. H. Freeman.

Tetlock, P. E. (1992). The impact of accountability on judgment and choice: Toward a social contingency model. In M. P. Zanna (ed.), *Advances in Experimental Social Psychology*, vol. 25. New York: Academic Press, pp. 331–77.

Wayne, S. J. and Liden, R. C. (1995). Effect of impression management on performance ratings: A longitudinal study. *Academy of Management Journal*, 31, 232–60.

Wayne, S. J., Liden, R. C., Graf, I. K., and Ferris, G. R. (1997). The role of upward influence tactics in human resource decisions. *Personnel Psychology*, 50, 979–1006.

Social Security Act of 1935

Charles H. Fay

This Act established the Old Age, Survivor, Disability, and Health Insurance Program (OASDHI). Included under OASDHI are: provisions for retirement, survivors and disability insurance, known collectively as SOCIAL SECURITY BENEFITS; hospital and medical insurance for the aged and disabled, known as Medicare/Medicaid; black lung benefits for coal miners; Supplemental Security Income; unemployment insurance (FEDERAL UNEMPLOYMENT TAX ACT OF 1935); and public assistance and welfare services, including aid to families with dependent children (AFDC). Social Security and Medicare are paid for by taxes on employers and employees, authorized under the Federal Insurance Contributions Act (hence, FICA taxes). Medicaid is funded by the states; matching grants are made by the federal government from general revenues.

FICA taxes are not levied on total salaries: in 2003 the salary subject to FICA taxes for Old Age and Survivor Insurance was $87,000; the tax rate was 6.2 percent for both employers and employees. Medicare taxes are levied on total salaries; in 2003 the tax rate was 1.45 percent for both employers and employees. Social Security was designed to be part of the "three-legged stool" of retiree income replacement: company pensions and personal savings were to account for most retirement income. Social security benefits generally become available on retirement or disability; covered survivors receive benefits in case of the employee's death.

Medicare consists of two parts. HI (Hospital Insurance) provides hospital insurance, with varying deductibles and coverage; eligibility begins at age 65 or with disability. SMI (Supplemental Medical Insurance) provides medical insurance; enrollee premiums cover about 25 percent and the rest is covered by government funds.

Bibliography

Beam, B. T. and McFadden, J. J (2001). *Employee Benefits*, 6th edn. Chicago, IL: Dearborn Financial Publishing, pp. 45–73.

Myers, R. J. (2001). Social Security and Medicare. In J. S. Rosenbloom (ed.), *The Handbook of Employee Benefits: Design, Funding and Administration*, 5th edn. New York: McGraw-Hill, pp. 499–534.

social security benefits

Robert M. McCaffery

Social Security is a term commonly used in the US to describe two separate, but related, federal benefit programs that are funded by employee payroll taxes and matching (100 percent) employer contributions. Old Age, Survivor, and Disability Insurance (OASDI) protects employees and family members against income losses due to the lifetime events cited in the title. Benefits vary according to earnings of the employee, the number of years covered by the program, and, in some cases, age. Medicare or Health Insurance (HI) covers a portion of hospital (Part A) and medical (Part B) costs for people aged 65 or older and certain disabled individuals. Participants must contribute to the costs of Part B coverage.

Bibliography

Bernstein, M. C. (1989). The viability of Social Security and Medicare in an aging society. *Houston Law Review*, 26, 799–812.

Bernstein, M. C. and Bernstein, J. B. (1989). *Social Security: The System that Works*. New York: Basic Books.

McCaffery, R. M. (1990). Raising employee awareness of social security benefits. *Compensation and Benefits Management*, 6, 275–82.

Society for Human Resource Management

Rebecca A. Thacker

The Society for Human Resource Management (SHRM) is the leading voice of the human resource profession, representing the interests of more than 64,000 professional and student members from around the world. SHRM provides its membership with education and information services, conferences and seminars, government and media representation, and publications that equip human resource professionals for their roles as leaders and decision-makers within their organizations. The society is a founding member and Secretariat of the World Federation of Personnel Management Associations (WFPMA), which links human resource associations in 55 nations. SHRM relies upon the efforts of committed volunteers and an empowered staff in establishing its reputation as the voice of the profession on workplace issues and in guiding the advancement of the human resource profession.

For further information, contact: Society of Human Resource Management (SHRM), 606 North Washington Street, Alexandria, Virginia 22314-1997. Telephone 703-548-3440. Fax 703-836-0367. Website: www.shrm.org.

Society for Industrial and Organizational Psychology

Stuart A. Youngblood

The Society for Industrial and Organizational Psychology (SIOP) is a professional organization of approximately 3,600 members, who are scientists, teachers, practitioners, consultants, staff psychologists, and students in private and public sector organizations. Industrial organizational psychologists typically work in a variety of areas: selection and placement, training and development (*see* TRAINING), ORGANIZATION DEVELOPMENT AND CHANGE, performance measurement and evaluation, QUALITY OF WORK LIFE, consumer psychology, and engineering psychology. SIOP is a division (Division 14) within the American Psychological Association (APA), is affiliated with the American Psychological Society (APS), and is also separately incorporated as a nonprofit organization.

SIOP hosts an annual three-day, midyear conference preceded by concurrent professional workshop sessions, and also runs a five-day program of symposia, papers, and special addresses at the annual APA convention. SIOP produces several useful publications, including a casebook on ethics and standards for the practice of psychology, a graduate training program catalog of industrial/organizational and organization behavior PhD programs, guidelines for education and training at the doctoral level, PRINCIPLES FOR THE USE OF PERSONNEL SELECTION PROCEDURES, Frontiers in I-O Psychology (a series of edited books on cutting-edge topics), the Professional Practice Series, and The Industrial Organizational Psychologist (TIP), which can also be accessed on the Internet (cmit.unomaha.edu/TIP). Membership in SIOP requires good standing in APA or APS, completion of a doctoral degree, based in part on a psychological dissertation, conferred by a graduate school of recognized standing, and engagement in professional work and activities that are primarily psychological in nature.

SIOP can be reached at: The Society for Industrial and Organizational Psychology, Administrative Office, 657 East Golf Road, Suite 309, Arlington Heights, IL 60005. Telephone 708-640-0068. Website: www.siop.org.

South Korea

Marianne J. Koch and Richard M. Steers

The HUMAN RESOURCE FUNCTION in South Korean firms can be characterized by two major influences. First, the Confucian tradition has formed the basis for Koreans' attitudes toward work, self-discipline, desire for education, and loyalty to country and employer. Paternalistic leadership, owner-managers, and top-down decision-making have long prevailed as characteristics of the dominant management style in Korean businesses. Recently, there has been a push to "modernize" the human resource function in larger Korean businesses by hiring professional managers (including professional human resource managers) and approaching human resource management (HRM) in a more "scientific" manner.

The second development accrues, in part, from both limited, domestic, skilled human capital and the growth in recent years of unionism in South Korea. Increasing demands for more equitable wealth distribution have also led to severe labor disputes since the late 1980s (which is an interesting deviation from the Confucian ethics tradition). Proficiency in HRM is now seen as a necessary means of avoiding further union organizing and growth and PRODUCTIVITY loss.

Korean businesses are currently grappling with an increasingly diversified workforce. Labor force participation among Korean women is increasing, as is the number of workers from other countries who have been migrating into Korea in order to work. This influx of new types of workers in the historically all-male, all-Korean workforce in South Korea presents new challenges to the relatively new professional HRM staffs in Korean organizations.

Bibliography

Amsden, A. H. (1989). *Asia's Next Giant: South Korea and Late Industrialization*. New York: Oxford University Press.

Clifford, M. L. (1994). *Troubled Tiger: Businessmen, Bureaucrats, and Generals in South Korea*. New York: M. E. Sharpe.

Kirk, D. (1994). *Korean Dynasty: Hyundai and Chung Ju Yung*. New York: M. E. Sharpe.

Koch, M. J., Nam, S. H., and Steers, R. M. (1995). Human resource management in South Korea. In L. F. Moore and P. D. Jennings (eds.), *Human Resource Management on the Pacific Rim: Institutions, Practices, and Attitudes*. Berlin: Walter de Gruyter.

Steers, R. M., Shin, Y. K., and Ungson, G. R. (1989). *The Chaebol: Korea's New Industrial Might*. New York: Harper and Row.

staffing

David J. Snyder and Michael A. McDaniel

Staffing is concerned with the recruitment, selection, placement, classification, evaluation, and promotion of individuals in an organization. Staffing has its roots in the fact that individuals differ from one another. Thus, staffing programs in an organization are concerned with recruiting, selecting and promoting persons based on those INDIVIDUAL DIFFERENCES which are deemed valuable for successful JOB PERFORMANCE.

Staffing begins with recruitment of individuals for a position. This involves attracting a number of qualified individuals to apply for the job. Recruitment can be within or outside the organization. Some methods often used to recruit individuals for a position include postings within the organization (*see* JOB POSTING), advertisement (e.g., newspapers, television, radio), employment agency referrals, and employee referrals.

Another aspect of staffing is PERSONNEL SELECTION. Selection is concerned with hiring those individuals who are best qualified for the position. This involves selecting individuals on the basis of knowledge, skills, and abilities (*see* KSAOS) which are judged necessary for successful job performance. Once persons are hired, organizations often must decide in which of two or more jobs they should be placed. This is accomplished either by the use of a single criterion scale (*see* PLACEMENT) or by the use of many criteria (*see* CLASSIFICATION).

Staffing is also concerned with appraisal and PROMOTION of employees. Once an individual is on the job, the focus turns to making judgments about performance. Promotion

standard hour plan

Timothy J. Keaveny

A standard hour plan is an INCENTIVE PAY plan which establishes a fixed unit of time for completion of a task or job. An employee receives the wage for the standard unit of time for completion of the task without regard to the actual time needed. For example, assume that in an automobile repair shop the standard time for replacing a muffler is one hour. Under a standard hour plan an employee would receive one hour's wage for replacing a muffler, regardless of the actual time required. Such a plan requires accurate measurement of time necessary for each job or task. Standard hour plans are more appropriate than a PIECEWORK incentive plan when the tasks or jobs are longer in cycle, nonrepetitive, and require many skills for completion (Patten, 1977). One must monitor the quality of work when a standard hour plan is used.

Bibliography

Milkovich, G. T. and Newman, J. M. (1993). *Compensation*, 4th edn. Homewood, IL: Richard D. Irwin.

Patten, T. (1977). *Pay: Employer Compensation and Incentive Plans*. New York: Macmillan.

Standards for Educational and Psychological Testing

Robert M. Guion

The *Standards for Educational and Psychological Testing* is the fifth in a series of publications dating from 1954 (American Educational Research Association et al., 1954) setting forth requirements for excellence in developing, documenting research on, reporting, and using psychological and educational tests. Each was developed by representatives of three organizations concerned with testing: the American Educational Research Association, the American Psychological Association, and the National Council on Measurement in Education. The 1999 revision (American Educational Research Association et al., 1999), like the previous versions, provides technical standards for developing and evaluating tests. These include rules of good practice, information to appear in manuals for test users, and requirements for scaling or equating scores. They have also offered more than rules. They have defined and codified key concepts and principles, such as (1) the nature of VALIDITY and the various aspects and types of evidence required for inferring it; (2) concepts of reliability and measurement error; and (3) problems of equivalence across different forms of a test. The 1999 version also addresses standards of effective test use in various settings – using tests with linguistic minorities and people with handicapping conditions, administering and scoring tests and reporting results, and protecting the rights of test takers.

Bibliography

American Educational Research Association, American Psychological Association, and National Council on Measurement in Education (1999). *Standards for Educational and Psychological Testing*. Washington, DC: American Educational Research Association.

American Educational Research Association, American Psychological Association, and National Council on Measurements Used in Education (1954). Technical recommendations for psychological tests and diagnostic techniques. *Psychological Bulletin*, 51, 2.

statistical process control

Richard S. Blackburn

Statistical process control (SPC) is a tool to examine the variability associated with process output. Processes of interest might include grinding components to some desired width or filling cereal boxes to some desired weight. Measurement and analysis of process output provides better understanding of why unacceptable variability (rejects) occurs and how to reduce this variability to acceptable levels. SPC is closely associated with the quality perspective of W. Edwards Deming, one of the early proponents of TOTAL QUALITY MANAGEMENT (Deming, 1986).

SPC assumes that process observations are normally distributed. Process observations will yield a large number of data points clustered around a mean, with 99.8 percent of the observations within three standard deviations (plus or minus) of that mean. Process data can be presented visually in a control chart (see figure 1).

Given the vagaries of human and mechanical interactions, the likelihood of particular observations being exactly at the mean is low. Rather, most of the observations will be within three standard deviations of the mean, in an area defined by the lower and upper "control limits."

The mean value for a process may or may not be at a level that will satisfy customers, and output within the lower and upper control limits may or may not be acceptable to those same customers. Management must decide the acceptable mean level for any particular process and how broad the variability can be and still meet customer expectations. When measures of process results fall *within* the control limits, the process is said to be "in control," and efforts are directed at maintaining this process. When many observations fall outside the control limits, the process is said to be "out of control," and efforts are directed at bringing the process back "in control" (Deming, 1986).

According to Deming, two categories of causes can contribute to a process being out of control. "Common causes" include such organizational problems as poor raw materials, malfunctioning equipment, poor manufacturing process design, or poor supervision. "Special causes" include errors of commission or omission attributable to employees. Deming believed that managers too often attribute out-of-control processes to employee shortcomings, when most of the real causes of such variability are common causes. That is, Deming asserted that most problems were beyond the control of the employee; they were the responsibility of management. Deming argued that organizational shortcomings explain more variance in process quality than managing the performance levels of individual employees. Thus, admonishing employees to work harder, rewarding them for better results, or punishing them for poorer results was believed to have little impact on overall process quality if the underlying quality problems are organizational (or "common") in nature.

Organizations use SPC to determine if process changes are reducing error rates, creating improvements in the mean value of the output, and/or successfully "tightening" the control limits around the desired mean.

SPC requires adequate data collection systems to gather the needed information and appropriate training so that employees can understand the information and determine the most effective way to reduce out-of-control process variability.

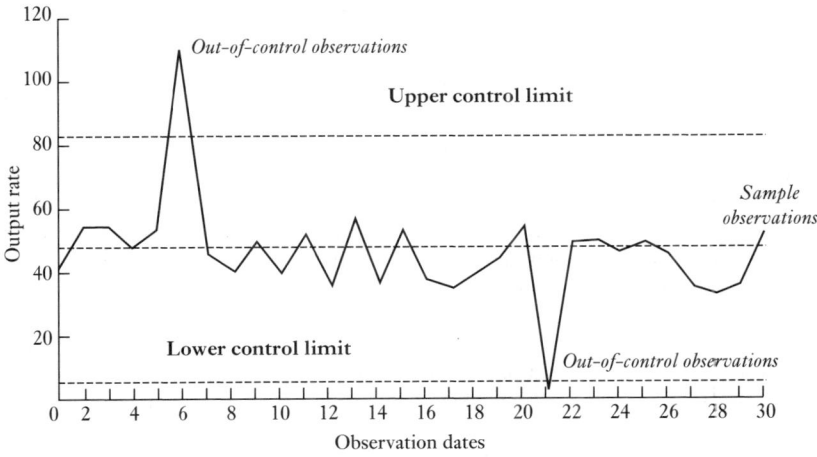

Figure 1 Statistical process control chart

Bibliography

Deming, W. E. (1986). *Out of Crisis*. Cambridge, MA: MIT Center for Advanced Engineering Study.

Evans, J. R. (1991). *Statistical Process Control for Quality Improvement: A Training Guide for Learning SPC*. Englewood Cliffs, NJ: Prentice-Hall.

Shewart, W. (1931). *The Economic Control of Quality of Manufactured Products*. New York: D. Van Nostrand.

Steelworkers v. Weber, 443 US 193 (1979)

Leonard Bierman

In *Steelworkers* the Supreme Court ruled that a quota system used by employer Kaiser Aluminum and Chemical Corporation to admit production workers into a craft training program did not constitute illegal REVERSE DISCRIMINATION. The court held that the specific features of the Kaiser AFFIRMATIVE ACTION program were within the spirit of Title VII because the quota system was designed to correct the effects of the company's past discriminatory practices against blacks. The court highlighted the plan's characteristics of being *temporary*, of not having a *permanent* adverse impact on individuals, and of intending to *correct* a manifest racial imbalance.

strategic alliances

David Lei

Strategic alliances are transitional mechanisms that enable firms to manage highly complex or fast-changing environments, to gain access to desired complementary resources or capabilities, and to learn new competencies that enhance and sustain its competitive strategy. Alliances represent linkages between firms to achieve economic benefits and resources not available through arms-length market transactions, internal development, or acquisition (Lei and Slocum, 1992; Eisenhardt and Schoonhoven, 1996; Inkpen, 1996; Das and Teng, 2000; Lei, 2003). Firms can design strategic alliances as platforms to accelerate organizational learning of new skills and capabilities, especially those that are highly tacit or organization-embedded (Badaracco, 1991; Hamel, 1991; Lei and Slocum, 1992).

FACTORS PROMOTING THE RISE OF ALLIANCES

All alliances are motivated by the need to reduce economic risk and to gain access to firm-based knowledge or capabilities. Several environmental forces have accelerated alliance formation, including (1) sharing costs of commercializing cutting-edge technologies in research and development-intensive industries, (2) shaping or transforming standards in fast-changing industries, (3) pooling resources for global economies of scale in value-adding activities, (4) accelerating entry into new markets, and (5) learning skills and technologies from partners.

FORMS OF ALLIANCES

A variety of governance structures exist to support alliance implementation. Generally, alliances can span the spectrum from licensing agreements and cross-marketing arrangements to more interwoven cooperative mechanisms such as technology development pacts, equity ownership stakes, and formalized joint ventures (Osborn and Baughn, 1990). Regardless of the specific organization design, each alliance entails sharing knowledge among partners (Hamel, 1991; Inkpen, 1996; Inkpen and Beamish, 1997; Khanna, Gulati, and Nohria, 1998). The type of knowledge shared among partners is more important in determining the alliance's role in building competitive advantage than the specific alliance design used.

Shared knowledge may be broadly categorized as migratory and embedded; hence, its form fosters alliances classified as product links and knowledge links, respectively (Badaracco, 1991). Product links share knowledge that is easily understood, highly transparent, mobile, and embodied in specific product technologies or designs (thus the term migratory). Partners cooperate to lower product development, production, and distribution costs or obstacles. Product links govern a division of labor among partners across value-adding activities. Yet one distinguishing factor in these relationships is that each firm utilizes its partner's skills and capabilities, but does not seek to internalize them. Many alliances involve STRATEGIC OUTSOURCING of different functions.

Knowledge links share highly tacit, organization-embedded skills deeply rooted in the firm's core competencies. Embedded knowledge is tightly interwoven within the organization's dynamic routines, communication paths, and operating practices. Alliances predicated on learning seek to develop new capabilities that are future sources of competitive advantage, often spanning multiple products and technologies. Organizational learning and knowledge flows are more complex and difficult to manage in knowledge links than in product links. Partners in these relationships seek to internalize the other firm's skills and capabilities, often leading to a race in which competence-based competition results in opportunism, risks for asymmetric resource dependencies, and control difficulties related to alliance-based knowledge application. Firms in these relationships seek not only to access other firms' new resources, but also to guard their own from high transparency and potential expropriation.

ORGANIZATIONAL CHARACTERISTICS

Alliances reduce the boundaries between firms, thereby facilitating speedier product and technology development. However, the more complex forms of alliances also generate significant coordination issues, particularly concerning knowledge sharing, joint investment costs, and the integration of managers and personnel from different firms (Gulati and Singh, 1998). As such, alliances are organization designs between markets and hierarchies; they evolve with firm strategy (Osborn and Baughn, 1990; Ring and Van de Ven, 1992; Das and Teng, 2000). Rate of organizational learning determines competitive advantage and bargaining power within the alliance (Hamel, 1991). Firms can structure alliances to create transitional, modular networks of relationships to specialized activities; knowledge transmission becomes highly permeable across boundaries, thus amplifying high levels of external interdependence. In some industries, a variety of firms can simultaneously cooperate and compete with one another in a larger "network" configuration that serves as the locus for resource, knowledge, and information flows; consequently, actions among partnering firms lead to strongly embedded relationships (Gnyawali and Madhavan, 2001).

COOPERATION, COMPETITION, AND FUTURE GROWTH

Alliances compel firms to balance cooperation with competition. Knowledge flows (particularly tacit skills) can unintentionally strengthen future competitors, particularly if underlying technologies are applicable across numerous products (Hamel, 1991; Lei and Slocum, 1992), and can result in alliance-based "co-opetition" (Brandenburger and Nalebuff, 1996). Carefully managed alliances enable firms to learn new skills from multiple sources, thereby strengthening their core competencies and strategic flexibility. From a corporate strategy perspective, alliances represent strategic options for future expansion; they leverage firm-specific capabilities with managed growth. Excessive dependence on alliances can "hollow out" the firm's core competencies and skills.

Bibliography

Badaracco, J. L. (1991). *The Knowledge Link: How Firms Compete through Strategic Alliances*. Boston: Harvard Business School Press.

Bleeke, J. and Ernst, D. (1993). *Collaborating to Compete*. New York: John Wiley.

Brandenburger, A. M. and Nalebuff, B. J. (1996). *Co-opetition*. New York: Doubleday

Das, T. K. and Teng, B. S. (2000). A resource-based theory of strategic alliances. *Journal of Management*, **26**, 31–61.

Doz, Y. L. (1996). The evolution of cooperation in strategic alliances: Initial conditions or learning processes? *Strategic Management Journal*, **17SI**, 565–83.

Eisenhardt, K. and Schoonhoven, C. B. (1996). Resource-based view of strategic alliance formation: Strategic and social effects in entrepreneurial firms. *Organization Science*, **7**, 136–50.

Gnyawali, D. R. and Madhavan, R. (2001). Cooperative networks and competitive dynamics: A structural embeddedness perspective. *Academy of Management Review*, **26**, 431–45.

Gulati, R. and Singh, H. (1998). The architecture of cooperation: Managing coordination costs and appropriation concerns in strategic alliances. *Administrative Science Quarterly*, **43**, 781–814.

Hagedoorn, J. (1993). Understanding the rationale of strategic technology partnering: Interorganizational modes of cooperation and sectoral differences. *Strategic Management Journal*, **14**, 371–85.

Hamel, G. (1991). Competition for competence and interpartner learning within international alliances. *Strategic Management Journal*, **12**, 83–103.

Harrigan, K. R. (1988). Joint ventures and competitive strategy. *Strategic Management Journal*, 9, 141–58.

Inkpen, A. C. (1996). Creating knowledge through collaboration. *California Management Review*, 39, 123–40.

Inkpen, A. C. and Beamish, P. W. (1997). Knowledge, bargaining power, and the instability of international joint ventures. *Academy of Management Review*, 22, 177–203.

Kanter, R. M. (1994). Collaborative advantage: The art of alliances. *Harvard Business Review*, 72, 96–108.

Khanna, T., Gulati, R., and Nohria, N. (1998). The dynamics of learning alliances: Competition, cooperation, and relative scope. *Strategic Management Journal*, 19, 193–210.

Lei, D. (2003). Competition, cooperation and learning: The new dynamics of strategy and organization design for the innovation net. *International Journal of Technology Management*, 26, 694–716.

Lei, D. and Slocum, J. W., Jr. (1992). Global strategy, competence building and strategic alliances. *California Management Review*, 35, 81–97.

Osborn, R. N. and Baughn, C. C. (1990). Forms of interorganizational governance for multinational strategic alliances. *Academy of Management Journal*, 33, 78–86.

Ring, P. S. and Van de Ven, A. (1992). Structuring cooperative relationships between organizations. *Strategic Management Journal*, 12, 483–98.

communications downward, upward, and across the organization to shape and reshape strategy; and (3) cohesiveness among managers to coalesce around an emerging strategic vision. Strategic development is critical when implementation consists of the processes through which the organization comes to understand, accept, and commit to an evolving strategy. It is also critical to organizations that seek growth either by extension of their current businesses or by internally based diversification into very similar product lines or services (steady-state organizations). This is in contrast to organizations that seek growth by acquisition or mergers (evolutionary organizations), in which external selection plays a more important role in managerial alignments (Kerr and Jackofsky, 1989).

Bibliography

Kerr, J. L. and Jackofsky, E. F. (1989). Aligning managers with strategies: Management development versus selection. *Strategic Management Journal*, 10, 157–70.

Schuler, R. S. (1992). Strategic human resource management: Linking the people with the strategic needs of the business. *Organizational Dynamics*, 21, 18–31.

strategic development

Ellen F. Jackofsky

Strategic development is one approach to STRATEGIC STAFFING where management development programs are designed and implemented to be aligned with the strategic direction of the organization. Strategic development implies that management development activities should be responsive to strategic business needs, consistent with strategy formulation, and serve a role in strategy implementation (Schuler, 1992).

Strategic development is congruent with a fluid, organic view of organizations where both the manager's value to the organization (in terms of behaviors, skills, knowledge, attitudes, and motives) and strategic demands are viewed as evolving over time. In such situations, management development should influence at least three essential components of the strategic implementation process: (1) flexibility to take advantage of unanticipated events; (2) ongoing

strategic human resource management

Patrick W. Wright

Strategic human resource management (SHRM) is "the pattern of planned human resource deployments and activities intended to enable an organization to achieve its goals" (Wright and McMahan, 1992: 298). SHRM is primarily concerned with understanding how the HUMAN RESOURCE FUNCTION attempts to integrate its activities with the strategic planning process in firms (Greer, 1995). In other words, SHRM is the macro-organizational approach to understanding the role of human resource management in the organization (Butler, Ferris, and Napier, 1991). Researchers and practitioners believe that integrating the human resource function and its activities into the strategic management process results in higher organizational performance.

SHRM plays a role in both the strategy formulation and strategy implementation components of the strategic planning process. Strategy formulation entails the top managers' identification of the external opportunities to be exploited and threats that may potentially negatively impact the firm. This analysis is conducted in conjunction with the identification of internal strengths that the firm can capitalize on and the internal weaknesses that might limit alternatives (known as SWOT analysis) to determine the most effective strategy for the firm to pursue. The human resource function contributes to this process by identifying human resource issues or developments that might be considered opportunities (e.g., new business opportunities for which the firm's human resources might be uniquely qualified to exploit), threats (e.g., possible labor market shortages), strengths (e.g., the unique culture or skills of the firm's human capital pool), or weaknesses (e.g., lack of skills or morale problems).

In response to the choice of a strategic plan, the human resource function attempts to align its activities, such as selection, training, appraisal, compensation, labor relations, and so forth, in a way that insures that the plan will be successfully implemented. This requires two types of integration: vertical and horizontal. Vertical integration consists of linking human resource practices and policies to the firm's strategy. For example, a vertical linkage might entail focusing leadership development efforts on the enhancement of skills in international management when the firm is pursuing a global expansion strategy. Horizontal integration requires coordination among the various human resource practices to ensure that each is supporting, rather than detracting from, the others. An example of horizontal integration might involve a firm engaging in global expansion. Such a firm might systematically identify the skills needed for selection of potential global managers (foreign language skills, flexibility, and so forth) versus what might be taught in training (specific cultural norms). The firm might also identify the type of compensation system necessary to attract individuals who would be willing and able to succeed in a global assignment (*see* INTERNATIONAL COMPENSATION).

SHRM is aimed at increasing organizational performance, and the relationship between SHRM and firm performance has been viewed in three ways: best practices, contingency, and configuration. The best practices approach posits that certain human resource practices will result in increased organizational performance across all situations (Ichniowski, 1990). The contingency approach argues that the effectiveness of human resource practices depends upon the organization's strategy (Schuler and Jackson, 1987). The configuration approach assumes that maximal organizational performance stems from developing the proper set of matching human resource practices that support one another (Arthur, 1994).

See also *strategic management*

Bibliography

Arthur, J. (1994). Effects of human resource systems on manufacturing performance and turnover. *Academy of Management Journal*, 37, 670–87.

Butler, J., Ferris, G., and Napier, N. (1991). *Strategy and Human Resource Management*. Cincinnati, OH: South-Western Publishing.

Greer, R. (1995). *Strategy and Human Resources: An Applied Managerial Perspective*. Englewood Cliffs, NJ: Prentice-Hall.

Ichniowski, C. (1990). *Human Resource Management Systems and the Performance of US Manufacturing Businesses (NBER Working Paper Series No. 3449)*. Cambridge, MA: National Bureau of Economic Research.

Schuler, R. and Jackson, S. (1987). Linking competitive strategies with human resource management practices. *Academy of Management Executive*, 1, 207–19.

Wright, P. and McMahan, G. (1992). Theoretical perspectives for strategic human resource management. *Journal of Management*, 18, 295–320.

strategic human resource planning

James W. Walker

Organizations conduct broad human resource planning to align the management of human resources with business strategy. Plans are strategic when they address significant change of direction, not merely continuity. However, human resource planning has had many definitions as the process has evolved in practice. For some organizations, it is narrowly defined, focusing on the forecasting and addressing of STAFFING needs, management SUCCESSION PLANNING, or other aspects of planning for human resources. For others, it is an integral element of business strategic planning, addressing a wide range of organizational and human resource issues (Director, 1985; Butler, Ferris, and Napier, 1991).

Human resource strategies define how a company will manage its people toward the achievement of business objectives – setting priorities for action (Walker, 1992). Like any strategy, a human resource strategy provides a directional plan of action for managing change. It provides a business perspective of actions necessary to gain and sustain competitive advantage through the management of human resources – a focus on priorities in managing people in a changing environment. Human resource strategies are guides to help organizations to recognize and address issues that call for actions and to give them the opportunity to manage these changes effectively. These strategies focus on the concerns of greatest importance and create a window of opportunity for bringing management to action. Strategic planning creates air time for discussion of key issues among managers.

When applied in best practices, the process of developing and implementing human resource strategies is an integral element of overall business strategic planning. Explicitly or implicitly, human resource strategies are regarded as management strategies, developed and implemented by managing executives in the same manner as other functional business strategies.

Strategies can involve multiple programs and activities, typically involving multiple functions and extending several years. Issues of strategic importance are not easily or speedily resolved. Plans are typically rolled out (top-down) and rolled up (bottom-up) in the context of both business plans and functional human resource plans (staff departmental plans) at each level of an organization.

Human resource strategic planning defines the relationship between people and competitive advantage – and then defines how to systematically manage people to attain this advantage. The process enables organizations to gain competitive advantage through people as well as through management of costs, effective use of people, and people management systems (Ulrich, 1987a). A primary agenda of strategic human resource planning is the design and delivery of people management programs (e.g., selection, development, appraisal, rewards). These encompass a large variety of human resource actions (organization planning, selection, staffing, performance, development, rewards).

Effective human resource plans are simple and focus on action plans. They present a business rationale for human resource actions, stated in business language. Strategies often raise more questions, requiring further analysis and planning, rather than merely a series of near-term action (Ulrich, 1987b). Some human resource strategies build unity between customers and employees by focusing on opportunities to align internal organizational capabilities with services and resulting benefits valued by customers (Ulrich, 1992).

See also *strategic human resource planning processes*

Bibliography

Butler, J. E., Ferris, G. R., and Napier, N. K. (1991). *Strategy and Human Resources Management*. Cincinnati, OH: South-Western Publishing.
Director, S. M. (1985). *Strategic Planning for Human Resources*. New York: Pergamon Press.
Ulrich, D. (1987a). Organizational capability as a competitive advantage: Human resource professionals as strategic partners. *Human Resource Planning*, **10**, 169–84.
Ulrich, D. (1987b). Strategic human resource planning: Why and how. *Human Resource Planning*, **10**, 37–56.
Ulrich, D. (1992). Strategic and HR planning: Linking customers and employees. *Human Resource Planning*, **15**, 47–62.
Walker, J. W. (1990). Human resources planning, 90s style. *Human Resource Planning*, **13**, 229–40.
Walker, J. W. (1992). *Human Resource Strategy*. New York: McGraw-Hill.

strategic human resource planning processes

Randall S. Schuler

The term strategic human resource planning processes refers to the efforts of firms to identify the human resource implications of organizational changes and of key business issues, in order to align their human resources with needs resulting from those changes and issues (Schuler, Jackson, and Storey, 2001; Jackson and Schuler, 2003). Earlier, in times of environmental stability, strategic human resource planning focused on matching human resource demand with human resource supply (Milkovich, Dyer, and Mahoney, 1983). At that time, forecasting human resource needs and planning the steps necessary to meet these needs was largely a numbers game. This process typically consisted of developing and implementing plans and programs to insure that the right number and type of people were available at the right time and place to serve relatively predictable business needs. For example, if a business were growing at 10 percent per year, top management would continue to add to the workforce by 10 percent; it worked before, it "should" work again.

From Numbers to Issues and Objectives

Today, because the environment is changing organizations so dramatically, human resource planning has become more of a dynamic, volatile issues game (Schuler and Walker, 1990; Schuler et al., 2001), and the processes have changed. The question is, "What are the issues and objectives of most importance to the business?" Increasingly, the key business issues and objectives flow from dynamic organizational changes, but they can also result from situations associated with great changes in the external environment, such as increasing global competition. Once knowing these issues and objectives, the question then is, "What are the human resource implications?" Yes, strategic human resource planning still involves numbers, but its processes often involve much more: (1) crafting mission and value statements consistent with the strategies and goals; (2) insuring that employees understand the needs of the business and what changes are necessary for the organization to be successful and then accept the changes necessary as well as the process of change itself; (3) systematically aligning the appropriate human resource activities based upon an explicit understanding of the business; and (4) creating a dynamic human resource planning process that mirrors the business planning process and that identifies key changes and implications for managing human resources for line managers as well as human resource managers (Jackson and Schuler, 2003).

Strategic human resource planning processes must consider both the long-term and short-term human resource implications of organizational changes. In fact, firms might typically go out five years in their planning and then work back to the present. Using strategic human resource planning helps to ensure that the human resource implications of organizational changes and key business issues are dealt with systematically and thoroughly. Regardless of the time horizon or the issues, strategic human resource planning processes can be described in five broad phases (Smith, Boroski, and Davis, 1992; Schuler et al., 2001).

Phase 1: Identify the Key Business Issues and Objectives

The first phase of strategic human resource planning involves gathering data to learn about and understand all aspects of the organization's environments, both its internal and external environments. This helps the organization to anticipate and plan for issues arising from both stable and dynamic conditions based on the organization's strategy, vision, mission, goals, and values. For example, planning for increased global competition based on a strategy of cost reduction could involve assessing current labor PRODUCTIVITY, probable future productivity, and wage levels worldwide. If a company is going to expand its revenue by 10 percent over each of the next five years, it *may* need more employees. Or perhaps improved technologies will mean a need for fewer employees. Human resource planners and line managers together figure out just what the STAFFING implications are. To do this, they might use their HUMAN RESOURCE INFORMATION SYSTEMS (HRIS) to measure performance levels in specific divisions, offices, occupational groups, or positions.

Phase 2: Analysis to Determine Human Resource Implications

The objectives of the analysis phase are (1) to develop a clear understanding of how the information generated during phase 1 impacts the future *demands* of the organization, and

(2) to develop an accurate picture of the current *supply* available internally.

Forecasting human resource demands. A variety of forecasting methods – some simple, some complex – can be used to determine an organization's demand for human resources. The type of forecast used depends on the time frame and the type of organization, the organization's size and dispersion, and the accuracy and certainty of available information. The time frame used in forecasting the organization's demand for human resources frequently parallels that used in forecasting the potential supply of human resources and the needs of the business. Comparing the demand and supply forecasts then determines the firm's short-, intermediate-, and long-term needs.

Forecasting human resource supplies. Forecasting supply can be derived from both internal and external sources of information. Internal sources of supply are generally the focus at this stage of planning. External sources are considered in later phases, as part of the process of designing the practices needed to prepare for the future.

PHASE 3: ESTABLISHING HUMAN RESOURCE OBJECTIVES

After phase 2 is completed, a great deal of descriptive information about current and future conditions is available. The next phase involves interpreting this information and using it to establish priorities and set objectives and goals.

With a short time horizon, which is often the time frame adopted for DOWNSIZING efforts, objectives are often easy to state in quantifiable terms. Examples of short-term human resource objectives include: increasing the number of people who are attracted to the organization and apply for jobs (the applicant pool); attracting a different mix of applicants (with different skills, in different locations, and so forth); improving the qualifications of new hires; increasing the length of time that desirable employees stay with the organization; and helping current and newly hired employees to quickly develop the skills needed by the organization. Such objectives can generally be achieved in a straightforward way by applying state-of-the-art human resource management techniques and working with line managers to insure agreement with and understanding of the program objectives.

PHASE 4: DESIGN AND IMPLEMENT HUMAN RESOURCE POLICIES, PROGRAMS, AND PRACTICES

Whereas the focus of phase 3 was establishing *what* to accomplish, phase 4 addresses *how* to accomplish it. What specific human resource policies, programs, and practices will help the organization achieve its stated objectives? A great variety of activities can be designed during this phase. These include: diversity programs to make organizations more attractive to a broader array of applicants; programs to improve the socialization efforts so that good employees want to remain with the organization; programs to downsize the organization, such as early retirement incentives and generous severance packages to complement the normal attrition process; and programs to empower employees and increase participation in order to insure success in a change to TOTAL QUALITY MANAGEMENT (*see* EMPLOYEE EMPOWERMENT). Increasingly, organizations and their human resource professionals are realizing that many if not all of their human resource policies and practices have to change as new strategies and new directions require different behaviors, competencies, and motivations from their employees (Schuler et al., 2001).

PHASE 5: EVALUATE, REVISE, AND REFOCUS

In this phase, the objectives set during phase 3 again come into play, for these define the criteria to be used in evaluating whether a program or initiative is successful or is in need of revision. For example, if personal self-development is the only objective one hopes to achieve from holding diversity awareness workshops, then asking employees whether the workshop experience was valuable may collect the only data needed. However, when large investments are made for the purposes of reducing EMPLOYEE TURNOVER, attracting new or different employees to the firm, improving team functioning, or all three, then data relevant to these objectives should be examined. Likewise, remuneration schemes may need to be revised if the current schemes are rewarding inappropriate or unnecessary behaviors amongst the employees and consequently the organization is not attaining its strategic business goals and objectives.

Bibliography

Burack, E. H. (1988). A strategic planning operational agenda for human resources. *Human Resource Planning*, 11, 63–8.

Caudron, S. (1994). Contingent work force spurs HR planning. *Personnel Journal*, July, 52–5.

Dyer, L. (1984). Studying human resource strategy: An approach and an agenda. *Industrial and Labor Relations Review*, 23, 156–69.

Jackson, S. E. and Schuler, R. S. (2003). *Managing Human Resources through Strategic Partnerships*. Cincinnati, OH: South-Western Publishing.

McKinlay, K. S. and McKinlay, A. (1993). *Strategy and the Human Resource Management Processes*. Oxford: Blackwell.

Milkovich, G., Dyer, L., and Mahoney, T. (1983). The state of practice and research in human resource planning. In S. J. Carroll and R. S. Schuler (eds.), *Human Resource Management in the 1980s*. Washington, DC: Bureau of National Affairs.

Schuler, R. S. and Jackson, S. E. (1990). Human resource planning: Challenges for industrial/organizational psychologists. *American Psychologist*, February, 26–57.

Schuler, R. S., Jackson, S. E., and Storey, J. (2001). HRM and its link with strategic management. In J. Storey (ed.), *Human Resource Management: A Critical Text*, 2nd edn. London: ITL.

Schuler, R. S. and Walker, J. W. (1990). Human resources strategy: Focusing on issues and actions. *Organizational Dynamics* (Summer), 4–19.

Smith, B. J., Boroski, J. W., and Davis, G. E. (1992). Human resource planning. *Human Resource Management* (Spring/Summer), 81–93.

Storey, J. (ed.) (2001). *Human Resource Management: A Critical Text*, 2nd edn. London: ITL.

Walker, J. W. (1995). The ultimate human resource planning: Integrating the human resource function with the business. In G. R. Ferris (ed.), *Handbook of Human Resources Management*. Oxford: Blackwell.

strategic industrial relations

Cynthia L. Gramm

Strategic industrial relations is an approach for analyzing the strategic choices made by the actors – employers, workers and their organizations, and policy-makers – in INDUSTRIAL RELATIONS systems and the implications of those choices for industrial relations outcomes. Strategic industrial relations is based on the premise that these actors deliberately choose the strategies and institutional structures that they believe will best facilitate attainment of their objectives. Like its sister approach, STRATEGIC HUMAN RESOURCE MANAGEMENT, strategic industrial relations builds on concepts drawn from two bodies of research: STRATEGIC MANAGEMENT and industrial organization economics. Strategic industrial relations, however, differs from strategic management and strategic human resource management in a key respect. Whereas strategic management and strategic human resource management focus on the identification and implementation of choices that advance the employing organization's objectives, strategic industrial relations has a broader focus. Specifically, strategic industrial relations focuses on identifying and implementing choices that advance the individual or joint objectives of workers, worker organizations, and industrial relations policy-makers as well as the objectives of employing organizations.

STRATEGIC INDUSTRIAL RELATIONS MODELS

The most general model of strategic industrial relations is articulated by Kochan, Katz, and McKersie (1994). Their model integrates concepts from the literature on business strategy with the more traditional industrial relations systems models (e.g., Dunlop, 1958). Whereas traditional industrial relations systems models emphasize the role of environmental factors in determining industrial relations processes and outcomes, their model portrays industrial relations processes and outcomes as determined by the "*interaction* of environmental pressures and organizational responses" (Kochan et al., 1994: 13). This model is useful for specifying broad categories of factors (e.g., external environment, values, business strategy, history) likely to influence the strategic choices made by industrial relations actors. Kochan et al. also posit a three-level institutional structure in which strategic industrial relations choices are made: (1) a long-term strategy and policy-making level; (2) a COLLECTIVE BARGAINING and personnel policy level; and (3) a workplace and individual/organization relationships level. They provide detailed descriptive evidence of strategic choices made at each of these levels. As Lewin

(1987) observed, however, the Kochan et al. model has several limitations. In particular, the concept of industrial relations strategy is never defined precisely and the model does not generate unambiguous, testable hypotheses. Perhaps as a result, the model has not yet stimulated much empirical research.

Other recent models based on the strategic industrial relations approach focus more narrowly on the determinants or consequences of specific strategic choices faced by an industrial relations actor(s). Fiorito, Gramm, and Hendricks (1991), for example, develop a model of the determinants of a union's choice of organizational structure. Their model identifies four general union strategies and generates testable hypotheses linking the union's choice of organizational structure to its dominant strategy and the environment in which it operates. Similarly, Walton, Cutcher-Gershenfeld, and McKersie (1994) develop a model of strategic collective bargaining negotiations that generates some testable propositions.

Empirical Research on Strategic Industrial Relations

Empirical research on strategic industrial relations has the potential to provide answers to the following questions.

1. Faced with a particular choice situation, what alternative strategies are available to the industrial relations actor(s)?
2. What factors influence the actor's choice of strategy?
3. Does the choice of strategy contribute to the attainment of the actor's goals or have an impact on other industrial relations outcomes?

Empirical research addressing these questions, however, remains in its infancy. As was true at the time of Lewin's (1987) earlier review of this literature, most of the empirical work continues to rely on qualitative case studies and/or descriptive statistics instead of formal hypothesis testing in the context of multivariate models. A few studies, however, model and test empirically the effectiveness of an industrial relations actor's decision to engage in particular strategic behaviors. Examples of studies of this type include Fiorito, Jarley, and Delaney's (1995) analysis of the effects of a set of innovative union organizing tactics on several indicators of organizing effectiveness, and Gramm and Schnell's (1994) investigation of the effects of alternative employer strategies for operating during strikes on measures of the value of the settlement and the employer's success at continuing operations during the strike.

Bibliography

Dunlop, J. T. (1958). *Industrial Relations Systems.* New York: Holt, Rinehart, and Winston.

Fiorito, J., Gramm, C. L., and Hendricks, W. E. (1991). Union structural choices. In G. Strauss, D. G. Gallagher, and J. Fiorito (eds.), *The State of Unions.* Madison, WI: Industrial Relations Research Association.

Fiorito, J., Jarley, P., and Delaney, J. T. (1995). National union effectiveness in organizing: Measures and influences. *Industrial and Labor Relations Review,* 48, 613–35.

Gramm, C. L. and Schnell, J. F. (1994). Effects of using permanent striker replacements. *Contemporary Economic Policy,* 12, 122–33.

Kochan, T. A., Katz, H. C., and McKersie, R. B. (1994). *The Transformation of American Industrial Relations.* Ithaca, NY: ILR Press.

Lewin, D. (1987). Industrial relations as a strategy variable. In M. M. Kleiner, R. N. Block, M. Roomkin, and S. W. Salzburg (eds.), *Human Resources and the Performance of the Firm.* Madison, WI: Industrial Relations Research Association.

Walton, R. E., Cutcher-Gershenfeld, J. E., and McKersie, R. B. (1994). *Strategic Negotiations.* Boston: Harvard Business School Press.

strategic issues in diversity

R. Roosevelt Thomas, Jr. and Catherine A. Ouellette

Before one can determine the strategic importance of managing workforce diversity (*see* DIVERSITY), one needs to understand (1) what strategy is (i.e., a plan for achieving competitive advantage) and (2) the factors (e.g., environment, mission, vision, culture, and key success variables) that influence effective strategic management. In this context, the strategic importance of workforce diversity is a function of its relevance to the enterprise's strategy, and the management of diversity becomes strategic itself when it is critical to successful strategy implementation.

Below, we list factors that some organizations consider strategic and then examine their relationship with workforce diversity. In doing so we will demonstrate how the management of workforce diversity can be strategic.

Employer of Choice

Many organizations aspire to attract the "cream of the crop" and consider this capability to be a potential source of competitive advantage. When recruiting for the best talent available, managers in some organizations have come to recognize that the pool from which they are drawing is diverse. Further, they believe that effective *management* of this diverse "cream" will give them a competitive edge in becoming the employer of choice (Thomas, 1993).

Empowerment

To gain a competitive advantage, some managers have identified empowerment of employees as strategic (*see* EMPLOYEE EMPOWERMENT). If the workforce is diverse, empowerment cannot be done to an optimal degree without an ability to effectively manage diversity.

Teaming

An increasing number of managers are contending that cross-functional teams and self-directed teams will be sources of competitive advantage. To the extent that team membership reflects diversity in significant aspects, the management of that diversity will be a critical determinant of the manager's ability to tap teaming as a strategic source. The challenge will be to meld team members into an effective unit without unnecessarily compromising the diversity they bring.

Right-sizing

Operating with the optimal number of human resources has been seen for many years as a basic strategic requirement. However, right-sizing places a premium on tapping the full potential of the remaining human resources. If the remaining participants are diverse, diversity management becomes a requirement for realizing the full benefit of right-sizing.

Customer-focused

With a rise in competitive pressures, many managers are stressing being customer-focused as a potential source of competitive advantage. The customer base, however, like workforce participants, is becoming increasingly more diverse. The ability to deal with this external diversity is enhanced by an ability to deal with internal workforce diversity (Cox and Blake, 1991).

Enhance Creativity

Influenced by research (Cox and Blake, 1991) and/or anecdotal experiences, more managers are becoming convinced that a diverse workforce is more creative than one comprised of homogeneous participants. These managers see this enhanced creativity and innovation as a potential source of competitive advantage. An international corporation, for example, with a worldwide research operation will need to manage its global diversity as a means of enhancing creativity. Thus, in general, moving beyond simply creating diversity to harnessing it for enhanced innovation requires diversity management.

Total Quality

This approach to management has gained in popularity as a potential source of competitive advantage (*see* TOTAL QUALITY MANAGEMENT). One of its basic premises is the engagement of the workforce. If the workforce is diverse, diversity management becomes a prerequisite for engaging organizational participants and realizing the strategic importance of total quality (Thomas, 1991).

The management of workforce diversity is clearly strategic for many organizations. Managers need to determine the strategic significance of diversity management by relating it to the organization's strategic factors. In this context, the management of workforce diversity is no longer solely a legal, moral, or social responsibility issue, but a strategic force as well.

See also *strategic management, strategy*

Bibliography

Cox, T. H., Jr. and Blake, S. (1991). Managing cultural diversity: Implications for organizational competitiveness. *Academy of Management Executive*, 5, 345–56.

Morrison, A. M. (1992). *The New Leaders: Guidelines on Leadership Diversity in America*. San Francisco: Jossey-Bass.

Ohmae, K. (1982). *The Mind of the Strategist: Business Planning for Competitive Advantage*. New York: McGraw-Hill.

Schein, E. H. (1985). *Organizational Culture and Leadership*. San Francisco: Jossey-Bass.

Thomas, R. R., Jr. (1991). *Beyond Race and Gender: Unleashing the Power of Your Total Workforce by Managing Diversity*. New York: AMACOM.

Thomas, R. R., Jr. (1993). Managing diversity: Utilizing the talents of the new work force. In A. R. Cohen (ed.), *The Portable MBA in Management*. New York: John Wiley.

strategic job analysis

Benjamin Schneider and D. Brent Smith

Strategic job analysis refers to a process of specifying the tasks to be performed (*see* TASK) and the knowledge, skills, abilities, and other characteristics (*see* KSAOS) required to effectively perform those tasks for a job as it is predicted to exist in the future (Schneider and Konz, 1989). Strategic job analysis acknowledges the potential volatility faced by organizations resulting from such factors as technological innovation and increasingly competitive markets. These factors force fundamental changes in the nature of the work performed and, concomitantly, changes in the requisite KSAOs of the workforce.

In volatile environments, traditional JOB ANALYSIS, focusing on jobs as they currently exist, can fail to anticipate future needs. Schneider and Konz (1989) suggest explicitly incorporating in the job analysis process information from relevant subject matter experts (planners, strategists) about issues, both within the organization (new technology initiatives) and outside the organization (new markets to be entered), that might affect the tasks to be accomplished in jobs and the KSAOs required to do those jobs. This can be accomplished by adding to the traditional job analysis process a workshop composed of subject matter experts who can comment on these issues. The original tasks and KSAOs generated during earlier phases of job analysis can now be revised and supplemented with the information from this workshop. The workshop participants then produce a new set of ratings of the tasks and KSAOs in light of the future issues they identified. Comparing present and future ratings allows an assessment of the extent to which changes facing the organization will affect the job in question.

Bibliography

Schneider, B. and Konz, A. M. (1989). Strategic job analysis. *Human Resource Management*, 28, 51–63.

strategic management

Benjamin M. Oviatt

Strategic management is both a process and a field of study involving the design, selection, or evolution and management of organizational strategy. It is a decision-making and action-taking process that some scholars depict as the deliberate design of organizational plans and actions to achieve organizational aims (Pearce and Robinson, 1994). In contrast, other scholars emphasize the unplanned and emergent nature of organizational strategy (e.g., Mintzberg, 1987). Yet whether deliberate or emergent, its aim is the "survival and growth of those organizations that through their outputs have distinctive competencies, compared to other competing organizations, to produce outputs that serve society" (Summer et al., 1990). As a field of study, it attempts to understand the conditions under which that aim can be achieved.

Strategic management is distinctive in its comprehensiveness. It assumes that survival and growth require a long-run alignment between the network of external environmental elements that an organization faces and its network of internal elements (Miller and Friesen, 1984). The primary actors of interest are usually high-level managers, owners, and entrepreneurs, but it is increasingly clear that due to its comprehensiveness a variety of actors at all levels may be important to successful strategic management.

LEVELS OF STRATEGIC MANAGEMENT

Three levels of strategic management are usually recognized: corporate, business, and functional. Corporate-level strategic management involves the choices of businesses in which to compete and the allocation of resources to those businesses. Research suggests that a corporation with a collection of businesses that share some resources, activities, and/or knowledge performs slightly better on average than corporations with a portfolio of unrelated businesses.

Business-level strategic management involves decisions about how to compete against other businesses in the same or proximate industries. Much of the research at the business level has attempted to identify a small number of generic business strategies used to compete across most industries (*see* STRATEGY for a discussion of some of them).

Functional-level strategic management focuses on how various business functions (human resources, finance, marketing, and so forth) may be aligned to form a coherent business strategy. In recent years, the interest in resources, BUSINESS PROCESSES, BUSINESS PROCESS REENGINEERING, and specific organizational activities has highlighted the need for the separate functions to avoid forming their own distinct strategies, and, instead, to integrate their disparate activities in a way that provides unique customer value and, therefore, a competitive advantage.

A FRAMEWORK OF STRATEGIC MANAGEMENT

Andrews (1980) provided what may be the most comprehensive and enduring framework for explaining the process of strategic management. He noted that organizations must decide what they *might do* in terms of the environmental opportunities and threats they face, what they *can do* in terms of their internal resources and competence, what they *should do* in terms of their social responsibility, and what they *want to do* in terms of the owner's/managers' personal desires and values.

The understanding of external environmental opportunities and threats begins with the study of broad technological, sociological, economic, natural resource, and political changes (*see* PEST ANALYSIS). This is followed by analysis of forces more proximate to relevant industries, perhaps using Porter's (1980, 1985) well-known five forces of incumbent rivals, potential entrants, substitutes, suppliers, and buyers.

Internal competence may depend on access to a scarce asset, such as ownership of a diamond mine or a patent on a pharmaceutical. However, resource-based theory (Barney, 1991) depicts internal organizational competencies and incompetencies as more frequently derived from socially complex routines that are difficult to describe, imitate, and substitute. The inertia naturally inherent in those routines means they are slow to change. That goes for both beneficial and destructive routines, but when they produce outputs of unique value to customers, such as can be achieved by organizational culture that promotes innovation, a sustainable competitive advantage may emerge.

Social responsibility is usually depicted as attempting to solve the complex calculus of competing organizational stakeholders (Freeman, 1984). Inevitably, strong owners and managers project their own personal desires and values on to the strategic management of an organization. Finally, Andrews (1980) emphasizes that understanding these four aspects of strategic management, difficult though that may be, is nothing compared to the creative act of reconciling their always conflicting forces into a proactive statement of organizational strategy.

Bibliography

Andrews, K. R. (1980). *The Concept of Corporate Strategy*, 2nd edn. Homewood, IL: Richard D. Irwin.

Barney, J. (1991). Firm resources and sustained competitive advantage. *Journal of Management*, 17, 99–120.

Freeman, R. E. (1984). *Strategic Management: A Stakeholder Approach*. Boston: Pitman.

Miller, D. and Friesen, P. H. (1984). *Organizations: A Quantum View*. Englewood Cliffs, NJ: Prentice-Hall.

Mintzberg, H. (1987). Five Ps for strategy. *California Management Review*, 30, 11–24.

Pearce, J. A., II and Robinson, R. B., Jr. (1994). *Strategic Management: Formulation, Implementation, and Control*, 5th edn. Burr Ridge, IL: Richard D. Irwin.

Porter, M. E. (1980). *Competitive Strategy: Techniques for Analyzing Industries and Competitors*. New York: Free Press.

Porter, M. E. (1985). *Competitive Advantage: Creating and Sustaining Superior Performance*. New York: Free Press.

Summer, C. E., Bettis, R. A., Duhaime, I. H., Grant, J. H., Hambrick, D. C., Snow, C. C., and Zeithaml, C. P. (1990). Doctoral education in the field of business policy and strategy. *Journal of Management*, 16, 361–98.

strategic negotiations

Joel E. Cutcher-Gershenfeld and J. William Breslin

The term strategic negotiations joins two concepts, each with ancient roots. Negotiation implies two or more interacting parties with a mixture of common and competing interests; strategy extends that interdependence by introducing a time horizon – where present actions by one party anticipate future actions by other parties. Combined, these concepts define the modern paradigm of bargaining in such varied contexts as international diplomacy, labor relations, and managerial decision-making.

In the modern literature, Schelling (1960) was the first to trace systematically the strategic implications of tactical actions in negotiations, exploring the various uses and limitations of threats, commitments, delegation, MEDIATION, and information. Strategy subsequently became an integral part of the emerging negotiation literature, whether the focus was on the bargaining process (Walton and McKersie, 1965; Lax and Sebenius, 1986), the structure of negotiations (Strauss, 1978; Bacharach and Lawler, 1984), the psychology of negotiations (Pruitt, 1981; Bazerman and Neale, 1991), or general negotiations theory (Walton and McKersie, 1965; Breslin and Rubin, 1991; Walton, Cutcher-Gershenfeld, and McKersie, 1994). The book *Getting to YES* by Roger Fisher and William Ury (1981) is notable in the negotiations literature for elevating a set of integrative tactics into a normative strategy that has achieved broad acceptance.

Among frameworks for analyzing strategic choices, Pruitt (1983) identifies four strategies available to negotiators: problem solving, contending, yielding, and inaction. He points out that choices among the strategies can be explained through the use of both Blake and Mouton's dual concerns model (1964) and a feasibility analysis. More recently, Walton et al. (1994) identified two concurrent outcomes of negotiations: substantive agreements and social contracts. Changes in social contracts are particularly likely to take on strategic significance. They then identify three strategies for negotiated change: forcing, fostering, and escape from the relationship. These strategies can be pursued separately, sequentially, or in combination. In addition, they interact with structural constraints and the dynamics of the negotiations process. Across all efforts to link the concepts of strategy and negotiations lie two core principles: (1) the identification and utilization of strategy serves both to enable and to constrain bargaining tactics; and (2) the dynamics of negotiation provide similar constraints and opportunities for change strategies. Thus, bringing together the ancient concepts of strategy and negotiations reveals the many ways in which they are intertwined.

See also *negotiation tactics; strategy*

Bibliography

Bacharach, S. B. and Lawler, E. (1984). *Bargaining: Power, Tactics, and Outcomes*. San Francisco: Jossey-Bass.

Bazerman, M. and Neale M. (1991). *Negotiating Rationally*. New York: Free Press.

Blake, R. R. and Mouton, J. A. (1964). *The Managerial Grid*. Houston, TX: Gulf.

Breslin, J. W. and Rubin, J. Z. (eds.) (1991). *Negotiation Theory and Practice*. Cambridge, MA: Harvard Law School, Program on Negotiation.

Fisher, R. and Ury, W. (1981). *Getting to YES: Negotiating Agreement without Giving In*. Boston: Houghton-Mifflin.

Lax, D. A. and Sebenius, J. K. (1986). *The Manager as Negotiator: Bargaining for Cooperation and Competitive Gain*. New York: Free Press.

Pruitt, D. B. (1981). *Negotiation Behavior*. New York: Academic Press.

Pruitt, D. B. (1983). Strategic choice in negotiation. *American Behavioral Scientist*, 27, 167–83.

Rubin, J. Z., Pruitt, D. G., and Kim, S. H. (1994). *Social Conflict: Escalation, Stalemate, and Settlement*, 2nd edn. New York: McGraw-Hill.

Schelling, T. C. (1960). *The Strategy of Conflict*. Cambridge, MA: Harvard University Press.

Strauss, A. (1978). *Negotiations: Varieties, Contexts, Processes, and Social Order*. San Francisco: Jossey-Bass.

Walton, R. E., Cutcher-Gershenfeld, J. E., and McKersie, R. B. (1994). *Strategic Negotiations: A Theory of Change in Labor–Management Relations*. Boston: Harvard Business School Press.

Walton, R. E. and McKersie, R. B. (1965). *A Behavioral Theory of Labor Negotiations*. New York: McGraw-Hill.

strategic outsourcing

John Storey

Strategic outsourcing is a particular form of subcontracting for services or components. Outsourcing and insourcing can be seen as reflections of the classic make or buy decision. The outsourcing (or contracting) of certain services, such as security, catering, office cleaning, and information technology, has been a traditional, longstanding practice. However, outsourcing is now recognized as far more widespread and part of an ever-increasing trend. The increase is seen in terms of both the number of companies that now practice outsourcing and the wider span of activities which are now outsourced.

Outsourcing becomes strategic when the decisions do not rest on short-term cost-cutting but are part of a long-term plan which reappraises the core competencies of the organization and perceives enduring and emerging competitive advantage through a partnership alliance with vendors who bring special expertise to the organization.

Rationales and Drivers

One major driver is to reduce headcount and direct labor costs. (This sometimes, though not always, has involved subcontractors using non-union labor in order to pay lower hourly rates; trade unions have therefore often viewed outsourcing as a union-busting device.)

It has also been facilitated by developments in information technology: companies can, for example, now outsource routine customer billing to remote stations in low labor-cost parts of the world. The other main reasons for its growth include the following: (1) flexibility, i.e., the level of service provision can be increased or decreased to meet market circumstances without laying off core staff; (2) scrap levels can, in theory, be eliminated as defective parts can be rejected; and (3) outsourcing is a device to access specialist expertise which would be too expensive or even too difficult to accumulate in-house.

The more strategic reasons relate to the association with reengineering and root-and-branch decisions about core functions and sources of competitive advantage (*see* BUSINESS PROCESS REENGINEERING). Strategic outsourcing thus ideally results from a rational and far-reaching competitive analysis process, one which seeks world-class standards on an activity-by-activity basis. The device may also be used to gain close-up access to the latest technology and expertise.

The Case Against

There are several dangers associated with outsourcing.

1. One danger is losing control of the service. This may antagonize customers or employees who cannot get timely access to information and who may blame the main company, not the contractor. Legal and tax complications are associated factors, especially in the US.
2. Contract workers may have lower commitment.
3. The costs may in fact turn out to be higher rather than lower. This concern was given credence as a result of a survey of 100 firms by the Boston Consulting Group (*The Economist*, 1991).
4. Companies may lose expertise in the outsourced functions, which may be impossible to regain.
5. Hollowing of the organization may result in long-term decline if the choice of core competencies has been unwise.
6. There are transactions costs in researching, negotiating, administering, and controlling numerous contractors.

Techniques for Successful Outsourcing

Guidelines from consultants emphasize several cautions regarding outsourcing, including: the importance of clarifying very carefully the objectives desired from each outsourcing decision; the need to expect and specify in the service contract high levels of quality, reliability, and other standards; and the need to avoid arbitrary contracting of all support services (the rationale will vary from company to company depending on its own strategy and sustainable competitive advantages) (Jacobs, 1994).

Bibliography

The Economist (1991). The ins and outs of outsourcing. *The Economist*, August 31, 65–6.

Jacobs, R. A. (1994). The invisible workforce: How to align contract and temporary workers with core organizational goals. *National Productivity Review*, 169–83.

Kochan, T. A., Wells, J. C., and Smith, M. (1992). Consequences of a failed IR system: Contract workers in the petrochemical industry. *Sloan Management Review*, 79–89.

Minoli, D. (1995). *Analyzing Outsourcing: Reengineering Information and Communication Systems*. New York: McGraw-Hill.

Quinn, J. B. and Hilmer, F. (1994). Strategic outsourcing. *Sloan Management Review*, **4**, 43–55.

Tully, S. (1993). The modular corporation. *Fortune*, February 8, 106.

strategic recruiting

Robert D. Bretz, Jr.

Strategic recruiting is the process of identifying, and attempting to attract, applicants in the external labor market who possess the characteristics or aptitudes that will enable the organization to achieve its strategic objectives. RECRUITING typically results from needs identified in the employment planning process, and is presumed to be driven by the need to fulfill immediate operational objectives. Strategic recruiting, on the other hand, derives from systematic assessment of the organization's mission and strategic objectives, and is undertaken to facilitate long-term organizational success.

Rynes and Barber (1990) have suggested that organizations facing a current or anticipated labor shortage could employ strategic recruiting as a means of attracting applicants, or could address the shortage through other strategies that do not involve applicant attraction. Olian and Rynes (1984) have indicated how organizational strategy might affect recruitment practices. Bretz and Judge (1994) have suggested that an organization's strategic objectives drive the choice of human resource systems that are implemented, and in doing so reveal to job applicants important contextual information that would otherwise be unknown. Organizational information has a significant effect on applicant attraction because specific types of individuals are attracted to specific types of organizations. Thus, the use of REALISTIC JOB PREVIEWS to deliver accurate contextual information is critical if an organization wishes to use recruiting strategically, because the applicants' perceptions of good organizational fit affect their JOB SEARCH behaviors and their willingness to join the organization.

Bibliography

Bretz, R. D. and Judge, T. A. (1994). The role of human resource systems in job applicant decision processes. *Journal of Management*, **20**, 531–51.

Olian, J. D. and Rynes, S. L. (1984). Organizational staffing: Integrating practice with strategy. *Industrial Relations*, **23**, 170–83.

Rynes, S. L. and Barber, A. E. (1990). Applicant attraction strategies: An organizational perspective. *Academy of Management Review*, **15**, 286–310.

strategic role of human resources

Patrick W. Wright

The strategic role of human resources is to develop and exploit the firm's people as a source of competitive advantage. This must be accomplished through aligning the firm's human resource management (HRM) practices as well as the skills of the firm's employees with the competitive strategy (Wright, 1991).

The strategic role of human resources consists of three components. First, the firm's human resources must be developed as one aspect of the core competence (Hamel and Prahalad, 1994) of the firm. The core competence describes the unique skills or capabilities that a firm possesses that allow it to perform some activity in a manner superior to its competitors. These skills or capabilities cannot be conceived of apart from the people who make up the organization, and thus can be considered a human resource-based competitive advantage. Thus, the underlying strategic role of human resources is to develop and deploy the firm's human resources such that their unique skills and capabilities will allow it to outperform its competitors (Wright, McMahan, and McWilliams, 1994).

A second component of the strategic role of human resources is to provide input regarding human resource issues into the strategic planning process (*see* STRATEGIC HUMAN RESOURCE PLANNING). Consistent with the concept of STRATEGIC HUMAN RESOURCE MANAGEMENT, this entails identifying the environmental opportunities and threats existing in the external environment which might impact human resources. It also involves identifying the internal strengths and weaknesses of the firm's human resources (e.g., the unique capabilities or limitations that exist within the firm's human capital pool). This information provides strategic planners with some of the limits of strategic alternatives (e.g., the firm neither possesses nor can easily obtain the human resource skills necessary for a particular strategy), as well as some potential areas to be exploited (e.g., the high levels of motivation and positive attitudes of employees might be used to differentiate the firm's services from competitors) (Lengnick-Hall and Lengnick-Hall, 1988).

The third component of the strategic role of human resources is to develop and align human resource practices that will enable the firm's human resources to successfully implement the strategic plan. This requires that the HUMAN RESOURCE FUNCTION, based on the strategic plan, identify the variety of human resource skills that are required and in what amounts. The human resource function then develops and applies human resource planning techniques, selection methods, training and development programs, and appraisal and compensation systems to insure that the firm has employees and managers who possess the skills and motivation to implement the strategic plan (*see* HUMAN RESOURCE PLANNING). This demands that the human resource practices be integrated in two ways: (1) vertical integration, which consists of ensuring that the human resource practices are consistent with and supportive of the strategic plan; and (2) horizontal integration, which entails insuring that the various human resource practices are consistent with and supportive of one another (Baird and Meshoulam, 1988; Wright and McMahan, 1992).

Bibliography

Baird, L. and Meshoulam, I. (1988). Managing the two fits of strategic human resource management. *Academy of Management Review*, 14, 116–28.

Hamel, G. and Prahalad, C. (1994). *Competing for the Future: Breakthrough Strategies for Seizing Control of Your Industry and Creating the Markets of Tomorrow*. Boston: Harvard Business School Press.

Lengnick-Hall, C. and Lengnick-Hall, M. (1988). Strategic human resource management: A review of the literature and a proposed typology. *Academy of Management Review*, 13, 454–70.

Wright, P. (1991). Human resources as a competitive weapon. *Advances in Applied Business Strategy*, 2, 91–122.

Wright, P. and McMahan, G. (1992). Theoretical perspectives for strategic human resource management. *Journal of Management*, 18, 295–320.

Wright, P., McMahan, G., and McWilliams, A. (1994). Human resources and sustained competitive advantage: A resource-based perspective. *International Journal of Human Resource Management*, 5, 301–26.

strategic staffing

Stella M. Nkomo

Strategic staffing is a process for identifying and filling future staffing needs to meet long-term business requirements. It has its roots in STRATEGIC HUMAN RESOURCE MANAGEMENT and is viewed as a part of HUMAN RESOURCE STRATEGY implementation. STAFFING is a crucial tool because it affects an organization's ability to successfully execute a particular competitive strategy (Miller, 1984). Strategic staffing begins with identifying the staffing implications of proposed business strategies. By developing and implementing strategic staffing plans, organizations can insure the right mix of talent to meet changing business objectives and strategies.

The strategic staffing process involves the design of strategies for four broad clusters of activities: (1) the identification of talent through JOB ANALYSIS, skills inventories, and recruiting needed to enhance strategy; (2) the acquisition of the talent through recruitment and selection (*see* RECRUITING); (3) the orientation and socialization of employees (*see* NEW

EMPLOYEE ORIENTATION; ORGANIZATIONAL SOCIALIZATION); and (4) the movement of employees to appropriate positions within the organization through PROMOTION, transfer, and demotion (Butler, Ferris, and Napier, 1991: 83). Much of the emphasis in strategic staffing focuses on managerial staffing (*see* SUCCESSION PLANNING). Researchers have developed models for aligning managerial staffing with business strategy (Kerr and Jackofsky, 1989; Bechet and Walker, 1993). Alignment involves matching managers with the appropriate skill mix and characteristics to an organization's strategic direction.

Bibliography

Bechet, T. P. and Walker, J. (1993). Aligning staffing with business strategy. *Human Resource Planning*, **16**, 1–16.

Butler, J. E., Ferris, G. R., and Napier, N. K. (1991). *Strategy and Human Resource Management*. Cincinnati, OH: South-Western Publishing.

Kerr, J. and Jackofsky, E. (1989). Aligning managers with strategic management development versus selection. *Strategic Management Journal*, **10**, 157–70.

Miller, E. L. (1984). Strategic staffing. In C. J. Fombrun, N. M. Tichy, and M. A. Devanna (eds.), *Strategic Human Resource Management*. New York: John Wiley.

strategy

Benjamin M. Oviatt

A strategy is a *pattern* of decisions and actions evident in an organization over time. An effective strategy may be deliberately planned by its managers, or it may emerge as a post hoc observation of a related group of decisions and actions. A distinctive characteristic of an organizational strategy is its comprehensiveness. That is, it includes and affects most parts of an organization. Mintzberg (1987) has noted that the word strategy is actually used in several different senses: a formal plan, a competitive ploy, a position in the mind of customers, a perspective in the mind of employees, and several others. In all cases, however, a pattern of organizational decisions and actions is observable.

There are three levels of strategy (*see* STRATEGIC MANAGEMENT). Corporate-level strategy concerns the identification of the businesses in which the corporation will compete and the allocation of resources to those businesses. Business-level strategy involves how businesses compete in their industries. Functional-level strategy focuses on the integration of disparate parts of a business so that they are consistent with and supportive of the business strategy.

GENERIC STRATEGIES

Much research has gone into discerning a limited number of generic strategies that are used across many different industries. Porter (1980, 1985) defined three generic business-level strategies of differentiation (unique market-wide customer value), cost leadership (lowest costs among all competitors in a market), and focus (marketing to a limited, well-defined group of buyers, sometimes divided into cost focus and differentiation focus). His concepts have been empirically explored by several scholars in various industry contexts.

Miles and Snow (1978) inductively developed four generic strategies of: defender (narrow product line, concentrates on efficient operations), prospector (innovator always looking for new opportunities), analyzer (operating in both stable and turbulent domains with corresponding foci on efficiency and innovation), and reactor (no consistent strategy, changes when forced to by the environment). These strategies cover both the corporate and the business level.

Miller and Friesen (1984) inductively developed several configurations or archetypes of organizational characteristics by studying a collection of business cases. These may also be seen as generic strategies. Six successful and four unsuccessful organizational configurations were found. In addition, they found nine configurations associated with organizational change. The configurations cover both corporate- and business-level strategy.

These are probably the best known, but other typologies and taxonomies of generic strategy exist. Unfortunately, the cumulative empirical evidence indicates that none of them holds across all or even most industries. Thus, the development of effective organizational strategies still requires a large dose of situational art. Of course, it cannot be otherwise in competitive economies because successful strategies are often imitated, thereby eliminating the competitive advantage they once provided.

Bibliography

Miles, R. E. and Snow, C. C. (1978). *Organizational Strategy, Structure, and Process.* New York: McGraw-Hill.

Miller, D. and Friesen, P. H. (1984). *Organizations: A Quantum View.* Englewood Cliffs, NJ: Prentice-Hall.

Mintzberg, H. (1987). Five Ps for strategy. *California Management Review,* 30, 11–24.

Porter, M. E. (1980). *Competitive Strategy: Techniques for Analyzing Industries and Competitors.* New York: Free Press.

Porter, M. E. (1985). *Competitive Advantage: Creating and Sustaining Superior Performance.* New York: Free Press.

stress management programs

Jonathan D. Quick and James Campbell Quick

Stress management programs are defined as strategies for preventing job strain and for channeling job stress into healthy and productive outcomes. They take a variety of forms aimed at individual adaptation and/or organizational change (Quick and Quick, 1984). Ultimately, stress management is good management. Understanding stress management programs is important to enhance health, wellbeing, and PRODUCTIVITY at work. Stress management programs may aim at modifying the demands or stressors to which employees are subject (primary prevention), at changing individual responses to stressors (secondary prevention), or at treating psychological, behavioral, or medical distress (tertiary prevention).

ORGANIZATIONAL AND JOB STRATEGIES

Stress management programs based on organizational and/or structural change strategies are forms of primary prevention. Organizational cultures that are flexible and resilient provide employees greater degrees of freedom to accommodate job stress. Flexible work schedules are among a number of structural mechanisms for enabling employees to accommodate the full spectrum of demands in their work and personal lives (Levi, 1982). Job redesign programs aimed at enhancing employee decision latitude and increasing control over various aspects of the work environment help to reduce job strain and are another form of primary prevention (Karasek, 1979). Supportive supervisory and peer relationships at work are a form of secondary prevention for employees.

INDIVIDUAL STRATEGIES

Stress management programs based on individual strategies may reflect either primary prevention or secondary prevention. Individual strategies that target specific health-risk behaviors, such as drug abuse or smoking, or strategies such as (1) cognitive restructuring to reduce the stressfulness of a demand, (2) planning and organizing activities to manage job demands, and (3) time management skills are all considered to be primary prevention strategies because they target the *source* of the stress.

HEALTH PROMOTION programs and wellness programs (*see* WELLNESS) are secondary prevention strategies because they are designed to enhance employees' overall health, hardiness, and resistance to job strain. The core of many of these programs is physical fitness training. Relaxation training, momentary relaxation, and a variety of relaxation techniques are a second major category of behavioral change strategies for secondary prevention (Benson, 1974). While the mechanisms through which social relationships significantly influence health are not fully understood, social support systems appear to have direct, positive effects on how employees see and interpret job demands, as well as buffering effects that reduce experienced job strain (House, Landis, and Umberson, 1988). Social relationships may be helpful as emotional outlets for employees experiencing stress or strain. Expressive writing in diaries may also be an alternative emotional outlet.

THERAPEUTIC AND CURATIVE STRATEGIES

Stress management programs based on therapeutic or curative strategies are forms of tertiary prevention. EMPLOYEE ASSISTANCE PROGRAMS may help employees to reestablish a healthier balance between work and home life, to make full use of leisure time, to take other actions to reverse unhealthy effects of job stress, and to assist employees with specific forms of distress through referral to appropriate medical and/or psychological services. The need for therapeutic and curative strategies may also suggest a failure of the organization or the individual to recognize a problem and take early action to prevent distress.

Bibliography

Benson, H. (1974). Your innate asset for combating stress. *Harvard Business Review*, **52**, 49–60.
House, J. S., Landis, K. R., and Umberson, D. (1988). Social relationships and health. *Science*, **241**, 540–5.
Karasek, R. A. (1979). Job demands, job decision latitude, and mental strain: Implications for job redesign. *Administrative Science Quarterly*, **24**, 285–308.
Levi, L. (ed.) (1982). *Society, Stress and Disease: Working Life*. Oxford: Oxford University Press.
Quick, J. C. and Quick, J. D. (1984). *Organizational Stress and Preventive Management*. New York: McGraw-Hill.

strike

Hoyt N. Wheeler

Broadly defined, the strike is a collective abstention from work for the purposes of self-protection (Liso and Pisani, 1992). In American labor law, a strike is defined as a concerted stoppage of work, slowdown, or interruption of operations (section 501(2), LABOR MANAGEMENT RELATIONS ACT OF 1947). In order to be protected under American law, it must be part of a controversy over terms and conditions of employment or about who represents the employees.

The strike comes in many types and varieties. In the US there is the important distinction between the unfair labor practice strike (prompted by an employer's violation of labor laws), where the employer may only temporarily replace strikers, and the economic strike (any other lawful strike), where strikers can be permanently replaced. There are also: (1) WILDCAT STRIKES, which are not authorized by a union; (2) the National Emergency Strike, which affects an entire industry or a substantial part of it; (3) the recognition strike, where a union is seeking recognition as the representative of a group of employees; and (4) the jurisdictional strike, where a union is striking to claim work as against another union. There are also political strikes in which workers withdraw their labor as an act of political or social protest.

The possibility of a strike is what moves management to agree to union COLLECTIVE BARGAINING demands, so "the strike, however its shapes and forms change, is ... integral to collective bargaining" (Barbash, 1984: 65). Nevertheless, its use has declined to historic lows in the US in the past decade, leading to doubts of its continued viability.

Bibliography

Barbash, J. (1984). *The Elements of Industrial Relations*. Madison, WI: University of Wisconsin Press.
Bureau of National Affairs (1988). Strikes, picketing, and boycotts. In *Labor Relations Expediter*. Washington, DC: Bureau of National Affairs.
Liso, F. and Pisani, E. (1992). Italy. In H. N. Wheeler and J. Rojot (eds.), *Workplace Justice: Employment Obligations in International Perspective*. Columbia, SC: University of South Carolina Press.
Wheeler, H. N. (1985). *Industrial Conflict: An Integrative Theory*. Columbia, SC: University of South Carolina Press.

succession planning

Arthur K. Yeung

Succession planning refers to the process and actions that aim at identifying and developing a pool of potential successors for senior or key jobs in the future. Unlike replacement planning, succession planning is more strategic, proactive, long-term oriented, and development-focused. It insures the continual supply of qualified executive talent to lead and support business growth.

Such planning is of strategic importance to many corporations like General Electric (Friedman and LeVino, 1984). By adopting a fair and systematic succession planning process, companies are able to reap the following benefits: EARLY IDENTIFICATION OF MANAGEMENT TALENT, retention of high-potential employees, enhancement of managers' readiness for future roles and challenges, and, as a result, the building up of human capital for business continuity and stability. However, where companies require major shifts in strategic direction that call for external recruitment, succession planning through internal resourcing becomes less important.

Succession planning is vulnerable to corporate politics and personal bias that may be counterproductive to business success and realization of individuals' potential. For instance, businesses may be reluctant to release good people to other businesses and different businesses or functional units may wish to advance their candidates for senior management positions. Hence, to maximize the usefulness of succession planning, corporations need to pay attention to the following processes (Nowack, 1994).

Identify Leadership Competencies

Leadership competencies should be based on business strategies, customer requirements, and business cultures. These required competencies should reflect and profile the successful leaders of the corporation in the coming decade. To facilitate assessment, development, and evaluation, the competencies need to be defined and operationalized in observable behaviors and outcomes.

Develop a Comprehensive Database

A comprehensive and current database should be developed for the target population. Once the leadership competencies are identified, appropriate assessment methods can be used to measure the candidates along those competencies. To insure objectivity, multiple sources of information need to be collected on a periodic basis, including in-depth interviews with high-potential candidates, 360-DEGREE APPRAISALS, performance appraisals (*see* PERFORMANCE APPRAISAL), and ASSESSMENT CENTERS ratings. Ideally, the assessments should be conducted by special human resource staff members who have high personal integrity and are able to assess people accurately through multiple methods. To facilitate the organization and retrieval of information, many companies use computer databases to store candidate information.

Conduct Executive Management Review Sessions

The purposes of executive management review sessions are to review the strengths and weaknesses of the candidates, to determine their promotability, and to recommend developmental plans for the candidates. The sessions are usually attended by incumbent executives and related human resource staff. Evaluation of candidates by potential, not by personal relationship, is the key success factor of these sessions. Therefore, it is important to create an open atmosphere to address the concerns of the candidates and to resolve conflicting interests among business units. Built-in check-and-balance mechanisms are also required to insure the integrity and fairness of the process. For instance, a consensus among attending executives, rather than the recommendation of incumbent executives, may be required to determine the promotability and possible career plans of the candidates. Based on the information collected, human resource staff can also contribute to the fairness of the process by advocating or questioning the view of incumbent executives regarding specific candidates.

Provide Feedback and Implement Plans

While succession planning used to be secretive in order to minimize inflated expectations of the candidates and the effects of the self-fulfilling prophecy of the candidates' superiors (Schein, 1987), companies are realizing the importance of providing feedback to the potential candidates because it is important to match the company's succession plans with the candidates' career aspirations. Once the candidates are committed to the plans, development plans with both systematic on-the-job assignments and external training opportunities should be prepared and implemented.

Measure Developmental Progress

The candidates should be carefully reviewed by senior management regarding their career progress and accomplishment. Data should be periodically updated and the promotability and developmental plans of the candidates should be revised as time evolves.

In a nutshell, succession planning has to be managed carefully and systematically. It should be conceived as a strategic planning process from which companies cultivate their most critical resources: high-quality executive talent.

See also *management development; strategic human resource planning*

Bibliography

Friedman, S. D. and LeVino, T. P. (1984). Strategic appraisal and development at General Electric Company. In C. Fombrun, N. M. Tichy, and M. A. Devanna (eds.), *Strategic Human Resource Management*. New York: John Wiley.

Nowack, K. M. (1994). The secrets of succession. *Training and Development*, November, 49–54.

Schein, E. H. (1987). Individuals and careers. In J. Lorsch (ed.), *Handbook of Organizational Behavior*. Englewood Cliffs, NJ: Prentice-Hall.

supervisory ratings

Walter C. Borman

Supervisors are often asked to evaluate the performance of their subordinates. This is done either for administrative purposes, such as to aid in making pay or promotion decisions, or for research purposes, to help, for example, to validate new PERSONNEL SELECTION procedures. The main advantage of supervisor ratings (as compared to PEER RATINGS or subordinate ratings) is that supervisors will typically have worked with many different subordinates and are thus well calibrated to make reasonably accurate ratings.

Recent research on supervisor ratings focuses on the cognitive processes associated with how supervisors arrive at judgments about their subordinates' performance (e.g., Borman, 1991; Murphy and Cleveland, 1991).

See also *performance appraisal; rating accuracy; self-ratings*

Bibliography

Borman, W. C. (1991). Job behavior, performance, and effectiveness. In M. D. Dunnette and L. M. Hough (eds.), *The Handbook of Industrial and Organizational Psychology*, vol. 2. Palo Alto, CA: Consulting Psychologists Press.

Murphy, K. R. and Cleveland, J. (1991). *Performance Appraisal: An Organizational Perspective*. Boston: Allyn and Bacon.

surveillance

Stuart A. Youngblood

The growth of service industries and the increasing use of computer, telephone, and video technology have contributed to an increased level of monitoring in the workplace. Workers in data-processing, word-processing, and customer service operations (e.g., airline reservation clerks, telephone directory assistance operators) are most likely to be monitored by a computer or telephone on the job. In addition, assembly-line workers and retail clerks are likely to be video monitored as an antitheft precaution.

The growing use of digital telecommunications, electronic data communications between computers, and digital video and graphical image transmission as means of surveillance increases privacy concerns in the workplace. Estimates of employees subject to some form of workplace surveillance range from 6 to 15 million workers in the US alone. As employers experiment with telecommuting and other uses of technology that blur the distinction between work and nonwork, privacy concerns among workers are predicted to increase. Employers are faced with the competing interests of the right to know versus each employee's right to privacy when electing to monitor employee behavior on the job. Although electronic surveillance can be misused, many employees believe that objective measures of their JOB PERFORMANCE used in a PAY FOR PERFORMANCE reward system can be more fair than traditional PERFORMANCE APPRAISAL systems (*see* REWARD SYSTEMS).

The Computer and Business Equipment Manufacturers Association advises employers to do the following to minimize problems: (1) explain to employees how, why, and when work is to be monitored; (2) give employees access to their records and regular feedback; (3) measure only behaviors essential to meeting organizational goals; (4) use statistics to spot problems early and take action on them; (5) anticipate INDIVIDUAL DIFFERENCES and permit workers to regulate their workplace as much as possible; (6) reward individuals for performance; and (7) do not continuously drive up production standards. Other experts have advised employers to humanize workplace monitoring by involving employees during the planning stages of a computer installation that will entail monitoring. Observing PROCEDURAL JUSTICE rights by permitting employees the right of rebuttal before a performance appraisal goes on the record and announcing monitoring systems in advance can prevent worker complaints.

See also *privacy in organizations*

Bibliography

Shepard, I. R. and Duston, R. L. (1987). *Workplace Privacy: Employee Testing, Surveillance, Wrongful Discharge, and Other Areas of Vulnerability*. Washington, DC: Bureau of National Affairs.

US Congress, Office of Technology Assessment (1985). *Electronic Surveillance and Civil Liberties*. Washington, DC: US Government Printing Office.

US Congress, Office of Technology Assessment (1987). *The Electronic Supervisor: New Technology, New Tensions*. Washington, DC: US Government Printing Office.

synthetic validity

James S. Phillips

Synthetic validity is "the inferring of validity in a specific situation from a logical analysis of jobs into their elements, and a combination of those elemental validities into a whole" (Balma, 1959: 395).

The process of synthetic validation is related to VALIDITY GENERALIZATION, since the validity of a test battery is *inferred* rather than demonstrated for a specific job and setting. This inference is based on the development of a matrix of (1) job elements common to a family of jobs (*see* JOB FAMILY) and (2) selection tests that are predictive of JOB PERFORMANCE on those individual job elements. A basic assumption of synthetic validation is that different jobs involving the same kinds of behavior should also require the same knowledge, skills, abilities, and other characteristics (*see* KSAOS). Synthetic validity subsequently assumes that if a test is valid for a particular job element, then it will be valid for use with any job involving that same element (McCormick, DeNisi, and Shaw, 1979: 51).

Using the concept of synthetic validity, a test battery can be assembled for a particular job by identifying the elements involved, and then selecting tests that have previously been shown to predict performance on those elements. This approach presumably eliminates the need to validate the new test battery, since each of the elemental validities is already known and should not have changed significantly across jobs. Synthetic validity is especially useful when there are not sufficient numbers of persons performing the same job to conduct a CRITERION-RELATED VALIDITY study (Hollenbeck and Whitener, 1988).

Bibliography

Balma, J. J. (1959). The concept of synthetic validity. *Personnel Psychology*, 12, 395–6.

Hollenbeck, J. R. and Whitener, E. M. (1988). Criterion-related validation for small sample contexts: An integrated approach to synthetic validity. *Journal of Applied Psychology*, 73, 536–44.

McCormick, E. J., DeNisi, A. S., and Shaw, J. B. (1979). Use of the Position Analysis Questionnaire for establishing the job component validity of tests. *Journal of Applied Psychology*, 64, 51–6.

T

task

Robert J. Harvey

A task is the most behaviorally detailed unit of work that is typically contained in a JOB ANALYSIS. It describes a work activity that produces a single, meaningful work product or outcome. Tasks are implicitly or explicitly composed of even more behaviorally specific "elements" that do not produce a meaningful work product or output when considered in isolation (e.g., "turn power switch to 'on' position," "insert pencil into electric sharpener," "remove sharpened pencils from sharpener"). When these elements are combined, however, a meaningful *task statement* is produced, e.g., "Prior to each scheduled course evaluation, sharpen a sufficient number of no. 2 pencils using an electric sharpener to provide each student with two pencils (at least 3 inches in length) for use in completing course evaluation questionnaires, exercising discretion regarding the colors of pencils used."

Various criteria have been advanced for defining the kinds of content that should be present in a task statement. At a minimum, task statements should include: (1) an *action verb* (e.g., "sharpen") that describes what the worker does, using as behaviorally specific language as possible; and (2) the *object* of the action (e.g., "no. 2 pencils"). Often, task statements include supplemental information, such as: (3) the context in which the task is performed (e.g., "prior to scheduled evaluations"); (4) the tools, equipment, or work aids to be used (e.g., "electric sharpener"); (5) criteria for evaluating successful performance (e.g., "pencils at least 3 inches in length," "enough pencils for each student to have two"); and (6) the degree of worker discretion that is allowed when performing the task (e.g., "free to choose pencil color"). Tasks are more behaviorally specific than duties (*see* DUTY).

task inventory approach to job analysis

Ronald A. Ash

Task inventories are structured JOB ANALYSIS questionnaires used to gather information about job components. The typical task inventory consists of task statements (*see* TASK) which are rated by job incumbents and/or their supervisors using one or more rating scales, and a background information section requesting such information as worker/supervisor identification, work experience, education, sex, race, wage/salary, job satisfaction, physical demands, equipment usage, management information, and any other dimension which may add depth to the analytical process.

Typically, a task is defined as a collection of more elemental activities directed toward the achievement of a specific objective (Levine, 1983). An example of a task statement for an accountant job might be: communicates with clients by letter or telephone in order to gather information for tax returns. A thorough job analysis will typically identify from 30 to 100 tasks of this type for a job. The rating scales used in task inventories often include a 7-, 9-, or 11-point relative time spent scale, with extreme anchor points of "very much below average" and "very much above average." US Air Force occupational analysts convert the relative time spent ratings into percentage time spent estimates which serve as their primary units of analysis. Other rating scales occasionally included in task inventories include *importance*, *difficulty*, and *consequence of error*.

The task inventory approach can be used to analyze a single job, but is more typically used to analyze a more inclusive occupational group, or JOB FAMILY. Thus, all tasks performed by employees in the occupational group to be covered must be included in the analysis. Depending upon the intended breadth of coverage of the inventory, from several hundred to two thousand task statements may be included. When such large numbers of tasks are to be rated, task statements are typically shortened (e.g., "communicates with clients by letter or telephone").

Task inventory data can be analyzed using standard statistical packages (e.g., SPSS; SAS), but the US Air Force has developed a set of some 50 general purpose programs designed specifically for analyzing and displaying task inventory information. This statistical package is called Comprehensive Occupational Data Analysis Programs (CODAP) (Christal and Weissmuller, 1988). Task inventory data are often used to group or classify individual positions into jobs or job families for common treatment in terms of PERSONNEL SELECTION, TRAINING, PERFORMANCE APPRAISAL, and COMPENSATION. It is often useful to link task inventory information to human attribute information (see KSAOS) through creation of a task by KSAO matrix or other procedure (Levine, 1983; Drauden, 1988).

Bibliography

Christal, R. E. and Weissmuller, J. J. (1988). Job-task inventory analysis. In S. Gael (ed.), *The Job Analysis Handbook for Business, Industry, and Government*. New York: John Wiley.

Drauden, G. M. (1988). Task inventory analysis in industry and the public sector. In S. Gael (ed.), *The Job Analysis Handbook for Business, Industry, and Government*. New York: John Wiley.

Levine, E. L. (1983). *Everything You Always Wanted to Know about Job Analysis*. Tampa, FL: Mariner.

tax-deferred annuities

Charles H. Fay

Employees of some nonprofit groups and public school systems have been able to purchase tax-deferred annuities (generally called 403(b) plans), deducting the costs of the annuity from income, since the 1940s. The TAX REFORM ACT OF 1986 imposed restrictions on these plans similar to those on 401(K) PLANS. The goal of legislation affecting tax-deferred annuities is the encouragement of employees of covered organizations to save for retirement.

Bibliography

Beam, B. T. and McFadden, J. J. (2001). *Employee Benefits*, 6th edn. Chicago: Dearborn Financial Publishing, pp. 588–608.

Davis, M. F. (2001). Section 403(b) plans for nonprofit organizations. In J. S. Rosenbloom (ed.), *The Handbook of Employee Benefits: Design, Funding and Administration*, 5th edn. New York: McGraw-Hill, pp. 807–20.

Tax Reform Act of 1986

Ramona L. Paetzold

The Tax Reform Act of 1986 (TRAC) amended both the EMPLOYEE RETIREMENT INCOME SECURITY ACT OF 1974 (ERISA) and the Internal Revenue Code (IRC). First, regarding ERISA, the TRAC lowered the maximum cliff vesting period for an ERISA-covered plan from ten years to five years. Thus, after TRAC, ERISA permits either a five-year cliff vesting or a seven-year graded vesting schedule. However, ten-year cliff vesting is permitted for multi-employer PENSION PLANS. The vesting schedules are duplicated in the IRC as part of the requirement for plan qualification (special tax treatment).

Second, TRAC added a separate limitation in the IRC on the total amount of elective deferrals that an individual can exclude from gross income in any year ($7,000, but indexed for inflation). These elective deferrals include, for example, employer contributions to a qualified cash-or-deferred arrangement.

Third, TRAC substantially amended the IRC to provide new tests for satisfying the antidiscrimination norm (required for qualified status). The new minimum coverage tests state that a plan is not qualified unless it satisfies either the ratio percentage test or the average benefits test. The essence of both tests is that plans seeking preferred tax treatment must not benefit too high a percentage of "highly compensated" employees without providing significant benefits to non-highly compensated employees as well.

Bibliography

Langbein, J. H. and Wolk, B. A. (1995). *Pension and Employees Benefit Law*, 2nd edn. Westbury, NY: Foundation Press.

Welbourne, T. M. and Gomez-Mejia, L. R. (1991). Team incentives in the work place. In L. Berger (ed.), *Handbook of Wage and Salary Administration*. New York: McGraw-Hill.

team-based incentives

Luis R. Gomez-Mejia

Team-based incentives consist of financial rewards provided to employees based on the performance of their group. Individuals are expected to have common goals and objectives, work in close collaboration with one another, and be dependent on one another for the performance of the team. The team incentives can be provided based on outcomes that are objectively measured (e.g., cost savings, number of units produced, revenues from a patent) or subjectively assessed (e.g., judgments made by a panel of executives). The goals, measurement criteria, and payment amount may be specified in advance or management may distribute the team rewards on an ad hoc basis (e.g., upon completion of a product design). Payments can be provided in cash, as company stock, or in the form of special nonmonetary awards, such as time off, a trip, a dinner, and the like. Many team-based plans differentially allocate rewards within the team based on individual contributions to the team effort and the extent to which the employee cooperates with other team members and is able to work effectively with others in problem-solving assignments. In general, team-based incentives work better when teams are relatively permanent in their composition and have relatively impermeable boundaries between them, and intragroup interdependencies exceed intergroup interdependencies.

Bibliography

Welbourne, T. M., Balkin, D. G., and Gomez-Mejia, L. R. (1996). Mutual monitoring and gainsharing plans. *Academy of Management Journal*.

team-building training

Richard W. Woodman

Team building, often called team development, is a training process by which members of a work group or team learn to diagnose how they work together and plan changes to improve their effectiveness. Empirical evaluation of team building has indicated that the process can result in positive changes in team functioning, including higher levels of participation, improved communication, and stronger decision-making and problem-solving skills. Team-building training will be most effective when (1) performed in conjunction with actual work on tasks with intact groups, and (2) preceded by a diagnosis that identifies the emotional and task needs of the team being trained (Woodman and Pasmore, 2002).

Bibliography

Woodman, R. W. and Pasmore, W. A. (2002). The heart of it all: Group- and team-based interventions in organization development. In J. Waclawski and A. H. Church (eds.), *Organization Development: A Data-Driven Approach to Organizational Change*. San Francisco, CA: Jossey-Bass, pp. 164–76.

Teamsters v. *United States*, 431 US 324 (1977)

Leonard Bierman

Actions taken because of bona fide seniority systems (*see* BONA FIDE SENIORITY SYSTEM) may be a justification for a company's practice that results in DISPARATE TREATMENT or DISPARATE IMPACT. In *Teamsters* the Supreme Court held pursuant to section 703(h) of Title VII that otherwise neutral legitimate seniority systems do not become unlawful under Title VII simply because they may perpetuate pre-Act DISCRIMINATION.

teleconferencing method

J. Kevin Ford and Deidre Wasson

Teleconferencing is a type of training method used to simultaneously train individuals at a variety of sites. Teleconferencing involves a central broadcasting facility where the trainer is videotaped for instantaneous transmission, a satellite system to transmit the lesson, and multiple receiving locations (hotels, conference rooms, universities, corporate headquarters) where trainees are located (Wexley and Latham, 1991). Trainees may ask questions of the trainer via telephone calls or a console box at any time during the training (Zemke, 1986). Teleconferencing has advantages in a variety of situations, such as: limited time or money availability, large groups of trainees in multiple locations, and limited availability of trainers.

See also *training; training evaluation*

Bibliography

Wexley, K. N. and Latham, G. P. (1991). *Developing and Training Human Resources in Organizations*, 2nd edn. New York: HarperCollins.

Zemke, R. (1986). The rediscovery of video teleconferencing. *Training*, 23, 28–34, 38–9, 42–3.

temporary workers

Stanley Nollen

Temporary workers are employees of staffing companies or agencies who are supplied to client companies as needed, according to the client's order. Temporary employment serves the traditional purpose of providing fill-in workers for regular employees who are absent from work (usually because of sickness or vacation). Temporary employment also enables client companies to quickly adjust the size of their labor input to fluctuating demands for labor (*see* CONTINGENT EMPLOYMENT), and it allows them to obtain specialized workers for specific short-term needs. Some temporary workers are direct hires onto the payroll of the company where they work (rather than being supplied from an agency), where they form a labor pool that is available to take up different jobs as needed by the company.

Temporary workers move from one client company to another frequently and do not have employment security. Few of them get BENEFITS that are not mandated because their length of service with their agency is too short. For some people, temporary employment is a preferred work option while they pursue other interests, while for others it is chosen only instrumentally as a bridge to regular employment.

The use of temporary employment and its regulation by governments varies widely across countries. In the US, the use of staffing companies to supply the labor needs of companies in a wide range of occupations is becoming increasingly common.

test fairness

Larry James

The key to successful PERSONNEL SELECTION lies in the accurate identification of INDIVIDUAL DIFFERENCES that can be applied to meet the varying requirements of different jobs. To this end, measures of individual differences are used to appraise a person's unique patterns of abilities. These measures, if valid, differentiate between individuals. For example, on a valid predictor of JOB PERFORMANCE, a person who scores higher on the measure than someone else should also perform comparatively better on the job. Test fairness is concerned with whether that differentiation is based on valid factors or is grounded in unfair discrimination, or invalid biases.

Guion (1966: 26) states: "Unfair discrimination exists when persons with equal probabilities of success on the job have unequal probabilities of being hired for the job." Underlying this definition is the need to consider criterion performance and predictor performance simultaneously. It is important to note that a selection measure on which one group scores differently than another group is not unnecessarily unfair if those same differences are *also* found in the criterion. In a selection situation, criterion performance is typically represented by actual job performance. If valid differences exist between groups on actual job performance, then parallel differences on the test are indicative of VALIDITY and not bias. Group differences in means on a selection measure are, thus, not in and of themselves indicative of test unfairness (Drasgow, 1987).

As with many social issues, the definition and operationalization of test fairness depends on one's point of view. What seems like a fair test to the owners of a company may not seem fair to job applicants or social commentators. Consequently, there are several definitions and models of test fairness, each with its own measurement system and advocates. The four most prominent models will be presented here. The sometimes subtle and sometimes not so subtle differences in these models point to the underlying issue that fairness ultimately has subjective components.

In the *regression model*, test fairness is defined in terms of test bias for some subgroup of the selection population (e.g., subgroups defined by race, sex, or ethnicity). Cleary (1968: 115) stated: "The test is biased if the criterion score predicted from the common regression line is consistently too high or too low for members of some subgroup." This is the definition set forth in the 1978 UNIFORM GUIDELINES ON EMPLOYEE SELECTION PROCEDURES (Ledvinka, 1979). The regression model is based on least squares regression procedures that minimize errors in prediction. When regression lines for subgroups of applicants are compared and determined to be unequal, there is a potential for bias in selection, if a common regression line is actually used for the total population. Decisions based on a common regression line in this case would overpredict future performance for one group and underpredict performance for another group.

The *equal risk model* of test fairness was proposed by Einhorn and Bass in 1971 and considers the distribution of criterion scores around a regression line. A minimally accepted probability of success on the job is first determined. For example, a company may wish to accept an 80 percent chance that the person selected will be successful on the job. Separate cutoff points on the selection test are then set for the different subgroups to insure that anyone selected would have at least an 80 percent probability of being successful on the job. Thus, fairness is defined in terms of the hiring entity's needs. If a test predicts well for one subgroup but not another (e.g., there is evidence of DIFFERENTIAL VALIDITY), very different cutoff points would need to be set to yield equal probabilities of success.

The *constant ratio model* was presented by Thorndike in 1971. It focuses on the proportion of a subgroup that could be successful on the job in relation to the proportion of people from that subgroup who are selected. If those proportions are equal, the selection system is deemed fair. For example, if 30 percent of minority group members are successful and 50 percent of majority group members are successful *on the job*, then the selection ratio for each group should reflect those proportions. In this case a fair selection process would select 50 percent of the majority applicants and 30 percent of the minority applicants. This model has been criticized as an elaborate way to set quotas for minority hiring, and may lead to more errors in PLACEMENT than other test fairness models.

Finally, the *conditional probability model* looks at differences in both probability of being selected and probability of success on the job. A test is considered fair under this model if people who belong to different subgroups who should be successful on the job have the same probability of being selected based on a common CUTOFF SCORE. If the test predicts equally well for different subgroups, the probability for success should also be equal. If a selection procedure produces a greater number of selection errors for one subgroup than another, it will be considered unfair.

Each model of test fairness presented above has strengths and weaknesses. Both the regression model and the equal risk model provide assurances for the company that their selection process will yield successful employees. The constant ratio model favors the applicant's point of view because it is primarily concerned with selection ratios rather than prediction accuracy. The conditional probability model benefits companies because it focuses on the reduction of prediction errors. When selecting the appropriate model of test fairness, one must consider precisely what one is attempting to achieve, in terms of both technical merit and public policy and social interests.

Bibliography

Cleary, T. A. (1968). Test bias: Predictions of grades of negro and white students in integrated colleges. *American Psychologist*, 30, 15–41.

Drasgow, F. (1987). Study of the measurement bias of two standardized psychological tests. *Journal of Applied Psychology*, 72, 19–29.

Einhorn, H. J. and Bass, A. R. (1971). Methodological considerations relevant to discrimination in employment testing. *Psychological Bulletin*, 75, 261–9.

Guion, R. M. (1966). Employment tests and discriminatory hiring. *Industrial Relations*, 5, 20–37.

Ledvinka, J. (1979). The statistical definition of fairness in the federal selection guidelines and its implications for minority employment. *Personnel Psychology*, 32, 551–62.

Thorndike, R. L. (1971). Concepts of cultural fairness. *Journal of Educational Measurement*, 8, 63–70.

Thirteenth Constitutional Amendment

Ramona L. Paetzold

Ratified in 1865, the Thirteenth Amendment to the US Constitution outlawed slavery and involuntary servitude. The Amendment also authorized Congress to pass legislation to enforce the prohibition of slavery, which Congress did by passing the CIVIL RIGHTS ACT OF 1866. The first two sections of that Act (now more popularly known as sections 1981 and 1982 of the CIVIL RIGHTS ACT OF 1871) are the primary means of enforcing the Thirteenth Amendment.

360-degree appraisals

Walter C. Borman and David W. Bracken

The central idea of a 360-degree appraisal system is to obtain performance evaluations on individual employees from multiple perspectives or sources. Typically, ratings are gathered from supervisors, peers, and subordinates, or some combination of these sources (e.g., Bracken, 1994). SELF-RATINGS and customer ratings may also be elicited. Other terms used to describe 360-degree appraisals include multi-rater systems, upward feedback, and full-circle feedback.

The purpose of 360-degree appraisals is usually to provide feedback to individuals on how their performance is viewed by a number of organizational constituencies (e.g., Edwards, Borman, and Sproul, 1985). The appraisal done for this purpose will be part of a feedback process that encourages an honest self-diagnosis of strong and weak performance areas, and sets in motion developmental efforts to improve effectiveness in the relatively weak areas. These evaluations have also been used as administrative performance appraisals that feed into personnel decisions, such as promotions (*see* PROMOTION) and SUCCESSION PLANNING.

There are a number of issues associated with administering a 360-degree appraisal program. Best practice thinking (e.g., Bracken, 1994) suggests, first, that behavioral rather than trait rating scales should be employed (*see* BEHAVIORALLY ANCHORED RATING SCALES; TRAIT). Second, selection of raters should be managed carefully to avoid, for example, ratees nominating only "friendly raters" to provide them with feedback. Third, ratings should be made anonymously to encourage honest appraisals. Finally, raters should be trained to use the rating form properly to help them make accurate appraisals (*see* RATING ACCURACY).

See also *appraisal feedback; performance appraisal*

Bibliography

Bracken, D. W. (1994). Straight talk about multi-rater feedback. *Training and Development*, 48, 44–51.

Edwards, M. R., Borman, W. C., and Sproul, J. R. (1985). Solving the double-bind in performance appraisal: A saga of solves, sloths, and eagles. *Business Horizons*, 85, 59–68.

time and motion study

James B. Shaw

A time and motion study is a very detailed analysis of the specific body movements and/or procedural steps that are used to perform a particular TASK. Typically, data for a time and motion study are collected by observing employees on the job and/or videotaping employees as they work. The job analyst records the actions taken to complete the task and also the exact amount of time that each action takes. Descriptions of employee behaviors are recorded by using a standard list of basic body motions. These basic motions include actions such as grasping, searching, selecting, transporting, and assembling (McCormick, 1979). Typically, the analyst develops a chart to show the actions associated with performing a task and the time required for each action. This chart typically uses symbols to represent workers' specific actions and the sequence in which they occur.

Time and motion studies provide detailed information about jobs. These studies concentrate on tasks that require relatively standard, repetitive actions to be completed. The methods are objective. They result in data that are particularly useful for the design of equipment to be used on the job and for setting performance standards for those operating the equipment. By observation of several individuals doing the tasks, a normal or standard time-to-complete can be established and used to evaluate the performance of employees. However, time and motion studies provide little information about the broader context in which the job is performed.

Bibliography

McCormick, E. J. (1979). *Job Analysis: Methods and Applications*. New York: AMACOM.

time-based pay

Timothy J. Keaveny

Employee COMPENSATION can be linked either to the amount of time worked or to a measure of the work completed (*see* INCENTIVE PAY; PAY FOR PERFORMANCE). With a time-based pay system, employee compensation equals the rate of pay per unit of time multiplied by the number of time units worked; for example, $8.00 per hour multiplied by 8 hours equals $64.00. Another label for such a system is membership-based compensation. In a simple time-based pay system, all employees in a given job receive the same rate of pay per unit of time. Such a system is easy to administer because management has only to measure the amount of time an employee is on the job rather than measure the amount of work performed. Time-based pay assumes that the amount of work performed per unit of time is quite uniform. Quality of performance is expected to be better with time-based pay compared to performance-based pay. The principal criticism of such systems is that compensation is linked to attendance and not to performance.

Bibliography

Gomez-Mejia, L. R. and Balkin, D. B. (1992). *Compensation, Organizational Strategy, and Firm Performance*. Cincinnati, OH: South-Western Publishing.

Milkovich, G. T. and Newman, J. M. (1993). *Compensation*, 4th edn. Homewood, IL: Richard D. Irwin.

time span of discretion

Timothy J. Keaveny

Elliot Jaques proposed time span of discretion as a measure of the amount of responsibility for work that a person has in a job. Jaques (1961: 10) defines time span of discretion as "the maximum period of time during which the use of discretion is authorized and expected without review of that discretion by a superior." This concept provides a basis for placing a value on the work performed by a person in a job. Time span of discretion can be viewed as a single-factor method of job evaluation, although it is unique in that it provides an objective measure of worth as opposed to a subjective judgment.

Bibliography

Jaques, E. (1961). *Equitable Payment*. New York: John Wiley.

total quality management

Richard S. Blackburn

Total quality management (TQM) is like "art," an acceptable definition lies in the eye of the beholder. Consider the following definitions of TQM:

1 The "constant attainment of customer satisfaction through an integrated system of tools, techniques, and training. This involves the continuous improvement of organizational processes, resulting in high quality products and services" (Sashkin and Kiser, 1991: 25).
2 An "evolving system... for continuously improving products and services to increase customer satisfaction in a rapidly changing world" (Shiba, Graham, and Walden, 1993: 27).
3 A "total, company-wide effort that includes all employees, suppliers, and customers, and that seeks continuously to improve the quality of products and processes to meet the needs and expectations of customers" (Dean and Evans, 1994: 12).

These definitions share several themes: customer focus, systemic thinking, continuous improvement, EMPLOYEE INVOLVEMENT, and a TQM culture. Organizations with a strong commitment to TQM seek to exceed customer expectations, even to delight customers. But TQM is not a cure-all for specific organizational maladies. To be successful, TQM requires systemic thinking and long-term commitment by senior management. The status quo will never suffice under a TQM strategy; continuous improvement is mandatory. Ongoing performance improvements require structures for employee input, such as EMPLOYEE EMPOWERMENT, employee involvement programs, or SELF-MANAGING TEAMS. Finally, a TQM culture provides a set of unstated (and often unstatable) assumptions that guide employee actions to enhance product or service quality. Confronted with conflicting choices, employees in a TQM culture know that choosing the quality response is the right choice.

A Brief History of Quality

Space constraints preclude a detailed consideration of the history of TQM (for a more complete discussion, see Garvin, 1988). Pride in personal craftsmanship initiated quality's earliest era (inspecting-it-in), with personal inspection of outputs to insure quality. This era closed when the industrial revolution, SCIENTIFIC MANAGEMENT, and mass production left employees responsible for smaller pieces of more complex products. Quality control departments and inspectors insured the quality of these products. Defective products were scrapped, with little information fed back to the employees producing the products. Quality feedback that was received typically contributed to adversarial relations between manufacturing and quality control departments.

Publication of *The Economic Control of Quality of Manufactured Products* (Shewart, 1931) heralded the "analyze-it-in" era of quality management. Shewart, a statistician, improved quality at Western Electric by analyzing variations in manufacturing processes. Shewart reasoned that better understanding of processes should improve the output of those processes. These statistical analyses underscored approaches to quality for many years.

In the decades following World War II, US companies sold almost everything they could make – regardless of its quality. A top automotive executive told a class of MBAs in the mid-1970s: "The American consumer will not pay for better quality" (Hayes, 1990: 8). Coincidentally, the phrase "Made in Japan" meant low-quality merchandise. But, while US businesses were complacent in their markets, the Japanese were designing manufacturing and control processes based on the precepts of W. Edwards Deming (see Deming, 1986). Unknown to all but a handful of US companies, a third quality era ("design/build-it-in") had begun. This era was marked by a new appreciation of the costs of (poor) quality, an attempt to spread total quality throughout organizations, and the introduction of zero defects programs and QUALITY CIRCLES (Garvin, 1988). By the late 1970s, the quality philosophy that Deming, Joseph Juran, and others had been preaching (but which had fallen on deaf ears in the US) began to pay off for Japanese firms. Japanese automobile and electronic manufacturers sold products of superior quality at lower prices than their US competitors. Foreign competitors designed and built quality into their products. US firms did not.

The realization that US firms were losing market share to foreign competition forced many US companies to reassess their commitments to quality, prompting the advent of the fourth quality era, strategic quality management ("manage-it-in"). These firms (re)discovered quality and began efforts to transform their organizations via TQM. The US Congress assisted these efforts in 1987 by passing legislation authorizing the MALCOLM BALDRIGE NATIONAL QUALITY AWARD.

BUILDING A TQM ORGANIZATION

Successful implementation of TQM requires recognizing "the revolutionary character" of multiple changes to an organization's architecture. Traditional structures and systems give way to new approaches that are internally consistent and congruent. Relationships with important constituents, particularly customers and suppliers, change. In traditional organizations, customer interactions are the responsibility of sales and marketing. A TQM perspective views every interaction (both internal and external) as involving a potential customer. This customer focus drives decision-making. Suppliers do not compete to provide raw materials on the basis of price alone. TQM organizations view suppliers as partners and work with a limited number of suppliers (perhaps only one) to insure the timely supply of high-quality inputs at reasonable prices.

Structures and jobs change in a TQM organization: from hierarchical, highly specialized functions supporting individualized jobs and predominantly vertical communications to networked functions supporting flexible, team-based learning with communications flowing in directions needed to get the job done. These changes require transformation of the way staff units provide their services. In particular, successful TQM efforts require substantive changes in major human resource systems, including RECRUITING, PERSONNEL SELECTION, TRAINING, MANAGEMENT DEVELOPMENT, performance evaluation (see PERFORMANCE APPRAISAL), COMPENSATION, REWARD SYSTEMS, and employee voice and communications to reflect a customer-oriented human resource management system (Blackburn and Rosen, 1993).

ISSUES OF CONCERN WHEN IMPLEMENTING TQM

When implementing TQM, management at all levels must "walk the TQM talk," changing processes and systems to reinforce TQM, or employees will view such change efforts as just another "flavor of the month" approach to resolving organizational problems. Some firms have been unable to find links between TQM and improved corporate financial performance. Other firms easily "pick the low hanging fruit" in terms of obvious improvements, but lose momentum when more difficult changes must be made. Some firms get caught in what has been labeled "the activity-centered fallacy" (Schaffer and Thompson, 1992), focusing less on specific organizational results and more on undertaking large numbers of activities that management and consultants hope (but are not certain) will influence those results. Firms organize quality circles and self-managed teams, provide quality training and the like, but important results show little change. Eventually such change efforts collapse under their own weight.

At one time TQM was viewed with an almost religious fervor by its advocates. Early disappointments with TQM-change efforts tempered some of this enthusiasm. Still, what once was viewed by some as a fad has moved from being an order-winning characteristic of organizations to being only an order-qualifier. Everyone is doing it now – other characteristics like speed and design have become the current order-winning requirements.

Bibliography

Blackburn, R. and Rosen, B. (1993). Total quality and human resources management: Lessons learned from Baldrige Award-winning companies. *Academy of Management Executive*, 7, 49–66.

Dean, J. and Evans, J. (1994). *Total Quality: Management, Organization, and Strategy*. Minneapolis: West Publishing.

Deming, W. E. (1986). *Out of Crisis*. Cambridge, MA: MIT Center for Advanced Engineering Study.

Garvin, D. (1988). *Managing Quality: The Strategic and Competitive Edge*. New York: Free Press.

Hackman, J. R. and Wageman, R. (1995). Total quality management: Empirical, conceptual, and practical issues. *Administrative Science Quarterly*, 40, 309–42.

Hayes, R. (1990). Design: Putting class into "world class." *Design Management Journal*, 1, 8–14.

Sashkin, M. and Kiser, K. (1991). *Total Quality Management*. Seabrook, MD: Ducochon Press.

Schaffer, R. and Thompson, H. (1992). Successful change programs begin with results. *Harvard Business Review*, 70, 80–9.

Shewart, W. (1931). *The Economic Control of Quality of Manufactured Products.* New York: D. Van Nostrand.

Shiba, S., Graham, A., and Walden, D. (1993). *A New American TQM: Four Practical Revolutions in Management.* Portland, OR: Productivity Press.

training

Irwin L. Goldstein

When learning events are planned in a systematic fashion and are related to events in the work environment, they are called training programs. From this point of view, the training process is defined as the systematic acquisition of skills, rules, concepts, or attitudes that result in improved performance in the work environment (Goldstein and Ford, 2002). This is a time when organizations are facing a very competitive environment, both domestically and internationally. Also, the use of technology is changing both organizations and the types of training they employ. As organizations move toward a knowledge society, they are struggling with how to use training as a way of developing a continuous learning philosophy. Thus, trainers are faced with a series of issues including: how to work with teams; how to develop leaders; and how to respect diversity as well as traditional concerns about resolving gaps in individual skills and competencies. In all of these situations, effective training stems from a systematically designed learning atmosphere based upon a careful assessment of job requirements and the capabilities of the trainees.

Training represents a positive hope for persons first entering the world of work or those individuals changing their work environment. When training is designed well, it gives individuals opportunities to enter the job market with needed skills, to perform in new functions, and to be promoted into new situations. Therefore, not surprisingly, labor unions often include training opportunities as parts of a contract during bargaining negotiations and large companies have designed multi-million-dollar facilities to annually train thousands of craftspersons in new technological innovations.

The American Society for Training and Development's Human Performances Practices Survey (HPPS) of 540 organizations provides considerable information about training programs. Bassi and Van Buren (1998) analyzed these data and found that technical skills training accounted for 30 percent of the training budgets. Professional skills training (such as accounting, computer sciences, information systems management) accounted for another 19 percent of the budget. Interestingly, basic skills training and new employee training accounted for the smallest percentage of the budget, a mere 2 percent. Other data (Olson, 1994) were consistent with these findings and indicated that employees with a college education are three to four times more likely to receive training than employees with a high school degree. A fascinating part of the HPPS found that despite the development of new learning technologies, 84 percent of all training was still classroom based and instructor led. It is also the case that new training technologies such as computer-based training, web-based training, and virtual reality training are being developed and will have an impact on future training development (*see* COMPUTER-ASSISTED INSTRUCTION; INTERNET). The future challenge will be to develop these systems so that it is possible to take advantage of their capabilities and insure that they are used in a way that supports, not interferes with, learner efforts (Goldstein and Ford, 2002).

A complete instructional system model involves three key components: needs assessment, training and development, and evaluation. Effective training endeavors will emphasize careful needs assessment, precisely controlled learning experiences designed to achieve instructional objectives, and use of performance criteria and evaluation information. The purpose of needs assessment is to design instructional objectives which are based on three levels of needs assessment: organization, task, and person analysis. Once instructional objectives are established, instructional programs can be designed and the training delivered. The development of performance criteria and an experimental or quasi-experimental design for evaluating the training program effectiveness permit inferences about the effectiveness of the instructional system. The next three sections elaborate on each of these three key components of the model and then a discussion of workforce issues that are relevant to training concerns follows.

Needs Assessment

Needs assessment consists of a series of analyses that assess the organization, the job, and the persons performing the job to provide input for the design and evaluation of training systems. Several different steps in the needs assessment process exist. Organizational analysis involves a macro-level analysis of the role of training which includes an examination of the system-wide components of the organization that affect a training program's design and development. This phase includes an examination of the organizational goals and organizational climate for training. For example, in this state, the organization addresses whether training is the appropriate strategy to resolve a specific human resource issue facing the organization. In addition, organizational system constraints are examined that may make successful transfer of training to the job difficult (*see* TRANSFER OF LEARNING). An example of such a constraint could be supervisors who do not support the objectives of the training systems being employed. Research by Rouillier and Goldstein (1993) has identified many of the organizational facilitators and inhibitors which help to determine whether what is learned in training will actually be eventually used by trainees when they arrive on the job. Based upon the assessment obtained as a result of the organizational analysis, decisions are then made as to whether the organization should be or is ready to provide training.

As discussed above, another phase of the needs assessment is the determination of which tasks are required on the job and which knowledge, skills, abilities, and other characteristics (*see* KSAOS) are necessary to learn to perform those tasks. In this phase, the researcher determines which KSAOs are critical in the sense that they make a difference in the performance of the important task components of the job. This is a complex process which involves the collection of data identifying tasks and KSAOs as well as determining the answers to questions such as which KSAOs should be learned in training as compared to which should be learned on the job.

Another component of the needs assessment is person analysis, which involves specifying the trainees' capabilities. This involves determining the target population for the training program, which can include persons already in the organization or individuals who are not yet part of the organization. By determining the capabilities of these target populations on the required KSAOs for the job, the training program can focus on critical KSAOs that are not in the repertoire of the target population. From the information obtained in the needs assessment, a blueprint emerges that describes the objectives to be achieved upon completion of the training program. This provides input for the design of the training program as well as for the measures of success (criteria) that will be used to judge the program's adequacy. Thus, objectives communicate the goals of the program to both the learner and the training designer.

Training Environment

Once the tasks, KSAOs, and objectives have been specified, the next step is designing the environment to achieve the objectives. Training is a delicate process that requires a supportive learning environment. Brinkerhoff and Montesino (1995) designed a study where supervisors had discussions with trainees prior to training regarding course content, the importance of training to the job, and expectations of how training would be applied to the job. Then they followed up after training to insure that what was learned was being used. Contrast that with the findings of the Independent Commission on the Los Angeles Police Department following the 1991 riots. The common statement made to new officers on the beat was "Forget everything you learned at the Academy" (Druckman and Bjork, 1994: 36). The training process must be designed to facilitate the learning of the KSAOs required to perform the tasks that the trainee needs for successful JOB PERFORMANCE. The analysis of job tasks and required KSAOs and the design of a matching training environment require very careful analyses (*see* JOB ANALYSIS). For example, most golfers would agree that instructing them to correct a flaw in their golf swing by reading a text description is not nearly as useful as videotapes which allow the instructor to point to the exact flaws in their swing. Similarly, simulators have been found to be very effective in teaching pilots to fly airplanes (*see* SIMULATIONS). Some of the advances in modern technology have resulted in a vast array of very complex training simulation systems. For example, the Federal Aviation Agency in the US decided that flight simulators had become so sophisticated that business jet pilots could use the simulator to meet many of their training requirements, thereby not always requiring actual flying time in the plane.

Another interesting technological innovation is the development of interactive videodiscs. As described by Purcell and Russell (1990), the hardware components of videodisc systems consist of computers, videodisc players, monitors, and connecting equipment. These instruments present information in many different forms, including motion pictures, stills, text, and graphics, along with sound tracks. The most sophisticated of these systems is called interactive videodisc and permits the student and system to interact, providing a large number of individualized learning experiences. Several companies are now employing this technology to provide employees with workstations that have the capability to make changes in manufacturing processes. The system is often used to provide what is called "just-in-time" training as manufacturing systems driven by computer technology shift from one operation to another (*see* JUST-IN-TIME PRODUCTION SYSTEMS). Indeed, simulations built around work situations have been found to be very effective in teaching many skills, including helping managers to develop communication skills.

These latter simulations include techniques known as behavioral role modeling (*see* BEHAVIOR MODELING). A good example of their effective use is presented by Frayne and Latham (1987), who demonstrated the value of the approach in training managers in self-management skills (*see* SELF-MANAGEMENT TRAINING) in an extremely well-controlled study. But again that does not mean that the use of behavioral role modeling or an interactive videodisc will always be the most effective training system to teach learners for all situations. A critical point is that the fanciest gadget does not make for a training system unless it is based on a proper needs assessment and evaluated to insure that it performs its functions. There are dozens (perhaps hundreds) of different types of training methods. Goldstein and Ford (2002) present detailed information about a variety of training approaches, ranging from classroom instruction to complex simulators.

It is now recognized that learning is a very complex and multidimensional construct (Kraiger, Ford, and Salas, 1993). It involves cognitive changes in the learner's knowledge base, and the way the trainee organizes and integrates the new material in his or her existing framework. Following learning, there is also the question of how the trainee will apply the knowledge and skills in the job situations. Cognitive and instructional theorists have progressed to a stage of development where information is emerging concerning the choice of training environments. Tannenbaum and Yukl (1992) have summarized recent advances concerning our understanding of important learning variables that contribute to the enhancement of the training process. For example, they note that learners do best when given the opportunity to actively produce the capability; that feedback should be accurate, credible, timely, and constructive; and that the instructional process should enhance trainee self-efficacy and expectations that training will be successful and lead to valued outcomes (*see* SELF-EFFICACY TRAINING). Obviously, training systems designed to use these variables are more likely to produce better learning. Excellent discussion of this work on learning and instructional theory can be found in Baldwin and Ford (1988), Ford and Kraiger (1995), and Goldstein and Ford (2002).

TRAINING EVALUATION

The number of different types of objectives that organizations hope training programs can achieve vary widely but could, for example, include: producing quality goods in a shorter time period; reducing accidents, with a corresponding decrease in insurance premiums; implementing a management system that is more customer service oriented; or increasing a health-oriented approach to lifestyles as a way of reducing time away from work due to illness and stress. The potential number of goals is unlimited. While training is not a panacea for all the ills of society, well-conceived training programs have achieved beneficial results. Despite an increasing number of thoughtfully developed programs, realistically not all programs are based upon either appropriate needs assessment or systematic evaluation to insure they achieve their objectives. Unfortunately, many organizations do not collect the information to determine the utility of their own instructional programs. Thus, their techniques remain unevaluated, except for the high esteem with which they may be regarded by training personnel. For example, a survey by Saari et al. (1988) of 600 firms provides information about evaluation methods that indicates that the vast majority of evaluations consist of trainee reactions which are written up at the end of the course. While positive reactions are important, these positive feelings do not necessarily mean that the appropriate level of learning has occurred. Relatively few efforts are made to collect information concerning performance changes. On the job, post-training follow-up enables both the trainee and the organization to learn whether the programs are achieving the desired results and whether modifications are necessary to enable the program to work. In the long run, systematic evaluations can provide information that can lead to meaningful revisions, which in turn insure that organizational goals are met.

The evaluation process centers on two procedures: establishing measures of success (criteria) and using research designs to determine what changes have occurred during the training and transfer process. Criteria must be established for both the evaluation of trainees at the conclusion of the training program and the evaluation of on-the-job performance. Recent classifications for this purpose suggest that several different measures are necessary, including: various type of reaction measures from participants; learning measures including immediate knowledge and knowledge retention of participants in the training program; transfer and behavior changes on the job; and the actual utility of the total program (Alliger et al., 1997).

In addition to criterion development, the evaluation phase must also focus on the necessary design to assess the training program. Several different designs can be used to evaluate training programs and to some extent the choice of a design depends on the questions you want to answer. Some examples of questions (from Goldstein and Ford, 2002) are as follows:

1 Do you wish to determine whether the trainees learn during training?
2 Do you wish to determine whether what has been learned in training transfers as enhanced performance in the work organization?
3 Do you wish to determine whether the performance for a new group of trainees in your organization is consistent with the performance of the original training group?
4 Do you wish to determine whether a training program evaluated as being effective in another organization can be used successfully in your organization?

An answer to these different questions helps to determine the components of your evaluation model. For example, the answers to these questions help to determine when you should collect information and how you can use control groups as a way of accounting for extraneous effects. A number of authors have written material to help in the effective design of evaluation programs (e.g., Goldstein and Ford, 2002).

TRAINING AND SELECTION SYSTEMS

Training interventions are just one component within a larger set of interacting organizational and societal systems (see HUMAN RESOURCE PLANNING). Thus, the need for training systems is often determined by other factors, such as when new technology will be introduced, or when groups of persons will retire, thus requiring others to be trained to take their place (see EARLY RETIREMENT POLICY). Clearly, training and selection systems continuously interact both at the entry level and at PROMOTION level. Both training and selection systems stem from a job analysis or needs assessment, which helps an organization to determine both the basis for selection and also what needs to be trained at what point in time. Often, the organization needs to decide whether it wishes to select (or even find) persons with particular capabilities or whether training should be provided. Usually, both selection and training are required to insure the most capable workforce. But the level of training, and at what capability-level training needs to begin, is determined by the types of individuals who have been selected.

The interactions between training and selection systems often go even further, and sometimes the differences between the uses of selection and training systems are hard to distinguish. For example, ASSESSMENT CENTERS are a standardized set of simulated activities, often used as a way of testing and selecting managers. These simulated activities can also be designed to provide information to the candidates about which skills need to be developed further for them to qualify as future managers. Further, these exercises can be designed so the candidate has the opportunity to practice (or be trained) in performing assessment center simulations requiring these various skills and abilities. Sometimes the assessment has to be designed in a slightly different way so that helpful feedback can be given to the candidate. However, many of the simulations and procedures used are very similar. In this latter case, the same instrument can essentially serve both selection and training purposes.

Another example of the overlap between training and selection devices is known as trainability testing. Investigators interested in predicting performance suggest that a person who can demonstrate proficiency in learning to perform on a small job sample will also learn better on the job. Thus, the measure has been named a trainability test. This is not an entire training program but rather a sample of tasks that call forth some of the KSAOs needed on the job. Note that to have a good trainability test, careful needs assessment is necessary to determine the tasks and KSAOs required for the job. Predictably, this emphasis on good needs assessment as the basis of the measure often leads to successful efforts. Research by Robertson and Downs (1989) over a twenty-year period reports on a considerable number of trainability tests that successfully predict later performance for jobs such as carpentry, bricklaying, dentistry, and sewing.

THE TRAINING SCENE TOMORROW

As noted above, training is a big business, with both organizations and employees having high expectations about what can be accomplished. Many conditions suggest even greater expectations concerning what training needs to accomplish in the future (Goldstein and Ford, 2002).

Advances in technology. Already, a significant portion of our lives is spent in educational and training programs. Prognosticators suggest that instructional technology is likely to have an even greater impact. Several reasons exist for such a prediction, including the startling effects resulting from developments in technology. The clear trend is toward distance learning, CD-ROM and interactive media, web-based instruction, intelligent tutoring systems, and virtual reality training. Many countries are investing in technology in the hope that automation will result in increased PRODUCTIVITY and product quality and as a result will permit them to gain a competitive edge in global market competition. Paradoxically, the increases in technology and machine responsibility increase the demands on the human being. As noted by Howell and Cooke (1989), instead of simple procedural and predictive tasks, the demands of operating extremely sophisticated computer systems require the human operator to become responsible for inferences, diagnoses, judgments, and decision-making, often under severe time pressure.

All of these types of developments in automation and computer technology place even greater demands on training systems to produce a highly sophisticated workforce. The training needs that are likely to affect the future of organizations are clearly stated by a description of the expectations of executives at a Mazda car manufacturing plant: "They want employees to be able to work in teams, to rotate through various jobs, to understand how their tasks fit into the entire process, to spot problems in production, to trouble shoot, articulate the problems to others, suggest improvements and write detail charts and memos that serve as a road map in the assembly of the car" (Vobejda, 1987: A14). The effects of failing to provide adequate training were sadly demonstrated in the nuclear power plant accident at Three Mile Island. A major finding of that investigation was that key maintenance personnel did not have adequate training for their jobs.

Interestingly, as discussed in the section above on the training environment, advances in technology have led to increasingly sophisticated training systems. These advanced systems will only work to the degree that the individual is capable of mastering the technology needed to operate the learning system. Thus, an additional feature to designing the learning program on the basis of a thorough needs assessment is also insuring that the workers are capable of operating the system. In a sense, an environment is being created where some of the advanced training systems will take training for a person to learn to operate it. This all becomes another reason to evaluate all training to insure that it functions as well as possible.

Organizations and global markets. A future look at jobs and organizations makes increasingly fluid world market arrangements appear more likely than is already obvious. Most consumers now realize that it is not unusual for a manufacturer to produce a product (e.g., an automobile) which is manufactured in a number of different countries. Sometimes, these involve arrangements between liaison teams directing the overall efforts between different employees in different organizations in different countries, all contributing to the production of a single final product. In these situations, managers will be expected to understand and manage the processes for achieving quality as well as managing team efforts across individuals who have different values and come from different cultures (*see* EXPATRIATE ASSIGNMENT; PREPARATION FOR AN INTERNATIONAL WORK ASSIGNMENT). In discussing the enormous training implications, Ronen (1989: 418) notes that the manager given an assignment in a foreign country must possess the "patience of a diplomat, the zeal of a missionary, and the linguistic skill of a UN interpreter." Ronen is correct, but the issue is likely to become just as complicated for managers working in their own countries because the workplace will need to incorporate individuals who come from environments with very diverse cultures and values. That issue becomes more obvious in discussions of workplace demographics (*see* STRATEGIC ISSUES IN DIVERSITY).

Changing demographics. Projections clearly indicate that the workforce is changing and thus will impact human resource management in a way never experienced before. In some countries in Europe, such as Sweden, the small number of workers available has made it difficult to even employ selection systems because everyone is needed in the marketplace. In other countries, such as the US, data (Braddock, 1999) clearly indicate that the rate of increase in the population available for the workforce will decline significantly in the coming decades and new entrants or those primarily between the ages of 16 and 24 will decrease substantially.

In addition, demographics indicate that a large number of individuals who will be available for entry into the workforce will be under-educated youth lacking basic literacy skills. The impact of this problem is made more dramatic by the corresponding developments in advanced technology, which increase the need for technical skills to enter the job market. In addition, significant numbers of the under-educated youth are members of racial minority groups that society has not completely integrated into the workforce. While many members of these groups have successfully entered professional and technical careers, many of the hard-core unemployed are racial minorities.

As well as the problem of under-educated youth, other serious demographic issues exist. A number of different groups, including women, racial minorities, and older persons, have faced problems of substantial unemployment as well as job DISCRIMINATION related to promotional opportunities. With this focus, the question of training programs and their fairness to these groups has become a serious legal issue in some countries, such as the US. Training techniques that have not been validated and that are discriminatory in promotional and job opportunities are being struck down by the courts in the US. Settlements often result in millions of dollars in backpay to current employees and require training to enable the employees to qualify for better jobs.

The design and implementation of these programs require a special sensitivity to the needs of the applicant population and the job requirements. For example, training programs for older trainees can be more successful if they follow certain principles. Older workers are often highly motivated to learn but sometimes fear failure in competition with younger workers, especially where high technology needs to be utilized in performing the job. Training should be arranged so that materials are organized to insure complete mastery of previous components before moving ahead, and where possible training should build on elements that are familiar to trainees from past learning. In addition, systems should be organized to minimize memory requirements and to avoid paced or time-pressured situations. Finally, the materials should be as job-relevant as possible, provide positive feedback, and encourage the self-confidence of the trainee. Of course, it is possible to point out that many of these principles are important for any type of training program, but they appear particularly pertinent to insuring the success of the older worker. In these situations, an additional training issue is the degree to which the organization is itself willing to make a commitment rather than assuming that all of the changes necessary must come from the trainee. Organizations which are likely to be successful in integrating persons from diverse groups will need to provide mentoring and training for individuals already in their organization as well as the entry-level trainee (see MENTORING PROGRAMS).

It almost seems unnecessary to suggest that the training implications of all the issues discussed above are enormous, especially for training managers who will be working with a very culturally and racially diverse workforce. Managers will need to provide ON-THE-JOB TRAINING to integrate unskilled youth into the workforce, while at the same time working with job incumbents and other managers who may not have previously been a traditional part of the workforce. Supervisors will need to perform these activities at a time when jobs have become increasingly complex, and national and international competition more intense. All of this will make training in areas such as interpersonal skills even more important in the future workplace.

A related impact for training is that there is an increasing emphasis on quality for both service-oriented jobs (see SERVICE QUALITY) and manufacturing-oriented jobs (see TOTAL QUALITY MANAGEMENT). This has important training implications in that more employees will need to be trained in quality techniques and processes. However, for the manager, the training implications for being able to manage such emphases are dramatic. Managers will be expected to understand and manage the processes for achieving quality as well as learning to manage team efforts, which are likely to be emphasized as a way of achieving success. Clearly, training can be a positive force for both the individual and the organization. To meet these expectations, the training agenda for the next decade will provide quite a challenge.

See also *training capabilities; training evaluation; training utility*

Bibliography

Alliger, G. M., Tannenbaum, S. I., Bennett, W., Traver, H., and Shotland, A. (1997). A meta-analysis of the relations among training criteria. *Personnel Psychology*, **50**, 341–58.

Baldwin, T. T. and Ford, J. K. (1988). Transfer of training: A review and directions for future research. *Personnel Psychology*, **41**, 63–105.

Bassi, L. J. and Van Buren, M. E. (1998). The 1998 ASTD State of the Industry Report. *Training and Development*, **52**, 21–43.

Braddock, D. (1999). Occupational employment projections to 2008. *Monthly Labor Review*, **132** (11), 51–77.

Brinkerhoff, R. O. and Montesino, M. U. (1995). Partnership for training transfer: Lessons from a corporate study. *Human Resources Development Quarterly*, **6**, 263–74.

Campbell, D. T. and Peracchio, L. (1990). Quasi-experimentation. In M. D. Dunnette and L. M. Hough (eds.), *Handbook of Industrial and Organizational Psychology*. Palo Alto, CA: Consulting Psychologists Press.

Druckman, D. and Bjork, R. A. (1994). *Learning, Remembering, and Believing*. Washington, DC: National Academy Press.

Ford, J. K. and Kraiger, K. (1995). The application of cognitive constructs and principles to the instructional systems model of training: Implications for needs assessment, design and transfer. In C. L. Cooper and I. T. Robertson (eds.), *International Review of Industrial and Organizational Psychology*. Chichester: John Wiley.

Frayne, C. A. and Latham, G. P. (1987). The application of social learning theory to employee self-management of attendance. *Journal of Applied Psychology*, **72**, 387–92.

Goldstein, I. L. and Ford, J. K. (2002). *Training in Organizations: Needs Assessment, Development and Evaluation*, 4th edn. Wadsworth, CA: Brooks/Cole.

Howell, W. C. and Cooke, N. J. (1989). Training the human information processor: A review of cognitive models. In I. L. Goldstein (ed.), *Training in Development and Organization*. San Francisco: Jossey-Bass.

Kraiger, K., Ford, J. K., and Salas, E. (1993). Application of cognitive, skill-based, and affective theories of learning outcomes to new methods of training evaluation. *Journal of Applied Psychology*, 78, 311–28.

Olson, C. A. (1994, December). *Who Receives Formal Firm-Sponsored Training in the U.S.?* Madison, WI: National Center for the Workplace, University of Wisconsin.

Purcell, E. D. and Russell, J. S. (1990). Employee development. In K. N. Wexley (ed.), *Developing Human Resources*. Washington, DC: Bureau of National Affairs.

Robertson, I. T. and Downs, S. (1989). Work sample test of trainability: A meta-analysis. *Journal of Applied Psychology*, 74, 402–10.

Ronen, S. (1989). Training the international assignee. In I. L. Goldstein (ed.), *Training and Development in Organizations*. San Francisco: Jossey-Bass.

Rouillier, J. Z. and Goldstein, I. L. (1993). The relationship between organizational transfer climate and positive transfer of training. *Human Resource Development Quarterly*, 4, 377–90.

Saari, L. M., Johnson, T. R., McLaughlin, S. D., and Zimmerle, D. M. (1988). A survey of management education practices and training in U.S. companies. *Personnel Psychology*, 41, 731–43.

Tannenbaum, S. I. and Yukl, G. (1992). Training and development in work organizations. In *Annual Review of Psychology*. Palo Alto, CA: Consulting Psychologists Press.

Vobejda, B. (1987). The new cutting edge in factories. *Washington Post*, April 14, A14.

training capabilities

J. Kevin Ford and Deidre Wasson

Before trainees can benefit from any form of training, they must be ready to learn (Goldstein and Ford, 2002). Trainee readiness refers to both the maturational and experiential factors that a learner brings to a training program. Readiness, though, is typically seen as primarily due to the number and kind of previously learned intellectual skills (Gagne, 1985). To examine readiness, the capabilities of the trainees must be investigated in the context of the ability requirements of the training program content (Fleishman and Mumford, 1989). When there is a mismatch between the ability requirements of the training program and the training capabilities of the trainee, the training program will fail. One implication of a mismatch is the need to carefully screen potential trainees for certain ability characteristics to maximize training success. For example, short work-sample tests (*see* WORK SAMPLES) have been shown to be effective in predicting the trainability of individuals to succeed in a subsequent skill-based training program (Robertson and Downs, 1979).

Bibliography

Fleishman, E. A. and Mumford, M. D. (1989). Individual attributes and training performance. In I. L. Goldstein (ed.), *Training and Development in Organizations*. San Francisco: Jossey-Bass.

Gagne, R. M. (1985). *The Conditions of Learning and Theory of Instruction*. New York: Holt, Rinehart, and Winston.

Goldstein, I. L. and Ford, J. K. (2002). *Training in Organizations: Needs Assessment, Development and Evaluation*, 4th edn. Wadsworth, CA: Brooks/Cole.

Robertson, I. T. and Downs, S. (1979). Work-sample tests of trainability: A meta-analysis. *Journal of Applied Psychology*, 74, 402–10.

training evaluation

Neal Schmitt

Training evaluation is a formal attempt to determine the individual and organizational impact of attempts to make people or organizations more effective (*see* TRAINING). In measuring the outcomes of training and development efforts, two important concerns must be addressed. First, the intended outcomes of the training must be specified in ways that allow for their measurement. Traditionally, trainee reactions, learning, behavior, and performance outcomes have all been considered in rigorous evaluation attempts (Kirkpatrick, 1967). In addition, system functioning, or the interrelationship between these outcomes and other organizational variables, should be considered (Schmitt and Klimoski, 1991: ch. 11). Kraiger, Ford, and Salas (1993) have asserted that the potential affective, behavioral, and cognitive outcomes of training should also be specified and measured.

The second major concern is the degree to which a research design with good internal and external validity (Cook and Campbell, 1979) can be implemented. Internal validity refers to the extent to which we can draw the inference that training has caused the desired outcome within the context of our evaluation study. Various types of research designs provide differing degrees of confidence in this regard (see Cook and Campbell, 1979, for a discussion of the strengths and liabilities of various research designs) and vary in the degree to which they may be practically feasible. External validity refers to the extent to which the effects of training, as measured in a training evaluation study, generalize to ongoing practice within an organization.

Training evaluation research should also include consideration of the theoretical and practical significance of the results, and an analysis of the process and content of training.

Bibliography

Cook, T. D. and Campbell, D. T. (1979). *Quasi-Experimentation: Design and Analysis Issues for Field Settings*. Boston: Houghton-Mifflin.

Kirkpatrick, D. L. (1967). Evaluation of training. In R. L. Craig and L. R. Bittel (ed.), *Training and Development Handbook*. New York: McGraw-Hill.

Kraiger, K. J., Ford, J. K., and Salas, E. (1993). Application of cognitive, skill-based, and affective theories of learning outcomes to new methods of training evaluation. *Journal of Applied Psychology*, 78, 311–28.

Schmitt, N. and Klimoski, R. J. (1991). *Research Methods in Human Resources Management*. Cincinnati, OH: South-Western Publishing.

training utility

Wayne F. Cascio

The utility of a training intervention is the extent to which its use improves the performance of those trained beyond what would have occurred had the training not taken place. Depending on the objective of the training intervention, individuals or teams may be the focus of attention. Performance, in turn, may be defined in at least three ways: (1) the proportion of individuals or teams who are considered successful; (2) the average standard score on one or more relevant measures of JOB PERFORMANCE; or (3) the dollar payoff to the organization resulting from the use of a particular training intervention.

Utility models have been proposed that explicitly address each of the alternative ways of defining performance noted above (for fuller descriptions of these methods see Boudreau, 1991; Cascio, 2000; Boudreau and Ramstad, 2003). In this section, however, we will focus only on performance definition (3) above, namely, assessing the dollar payoff to an organization resulting from the use of a particular training intervention. Assessing the utility of training outcomes in financial terms is not easy, but the technology to do it is available and well developed. At a conceptual level, the expression of utility is straightforward: utility = benefits − costs. To compute utility, however, the following formula is used:

$$\Delta U = (N)(T)(d_t)(SD_y) - C$$

where ΔU is the gain to the firm in dollars resulting from the program; N is the number of employees (or teams) trained; T is the expected duration of benefits in the trained group; d_t is the true difference in JOB PERFORMANCE between the trained and untrained groups in standard deviation units; SD_y is the standard deviation of dollar-valued job performance among employees who have not received the training (see SD_y); and C is the total cost of training N employees. The parameter d is the *effect size*. It describes the degree of departure from the null hypothesis that training had no effect – that is, after training, the job performance of the trained group is no different from that of the untrained group:

$$d = \frac{\overline{X}_1 - \overline{X}_u}{SD_y}$$

The parameter d_t represents the *true* difference between the mean job performance of the trained and untrained groups, expressed in standard (Z)-score units:

$$d_t = \frac{d}{\sqrt{r_{yy}}}$$

As shown above, the *true* difference in job performance between trained and untrained groups (d_t) is obtained by taking the difference (d) and correcting it for the unreliability of the job performance measure. The term is $\sqrt{r_{yy}}$ the square root of the reliability of the job performance measure. To illustrate, if the mean number of products produced per hour of a trained group is 7, while the mean for an untrained group is 6.5, with a standard deviation of one unit, then $d = (7 - 6.5)/1$, or 0.5 standard deviation units. When an objective measure of performance is used, d need not be corrected for unreliability (reliability). However, if SUPERVISORY RATINGS or some other less-than-perfectly reliable measures are used, then d must be corrected statistically for unreliability. Failure to do so will produce a biased (conservative) estimate of d.

ILLUSTRATION

In the simplest possible case, let us assume the following parameters: $N = 50$, $T = 1$ year, $d_t = 0.5$, $SD_y = \$10,000$, and $C = \$50,000$. Substituting these values into the general utility equation yields:

$$\Delta U = (N)(T)(d_t)(SD_y) - C \text{ or}$$
$$\Delta U = (50)(1)(0.5)(\$10,000) - (\$50,000)$$

Therefore $\Delta U = \$200,000$. However, as Boudreau (1983a) has pointed out, such an analysis fails to consider the effects of economic factors, such as discounting, variable costs, and corporate taxes that serve to lower expected payoffs from training. Further, to the extent that training is effective, multiple cohorts will likely receive the training, and this will raise estimates of overall payoffs (Boudreau, 1983b). The example above assumes that only one cohort received the training. In practice, therefore, credible estimates of the economic utility of valid training programs must account for: (1) all of the parameters in the general utility equation; (2) the economic factors of discounting, variable costs, and corporate taxes; (3) multiple cohorts of trainees; and (4) employee attrition and decay in the effects of the training (see Cascio, 1989, 2000). Failure to do so may overstate the expected payoffs (utility) by as much as 50 percent or more.

Bibliography

Boudreau, J. W. (1983a). Economic considerations in estimating the economic utility of human resource productivity improvement programs. *Personnel Psychology*, 36, 551–76.

Boudreau, J. W. (1983b). Effects of employee flows on utility analysis of human resource productivity improvement programs. *Journal of Applied Psychology*, 68, 396–406.

Boudreau, J. W. (1991). Utility analysis for decisions in human resource management. In M. D. Dunnette and L. M. Hough (eds.), *Handbook of Industrial and Organizational Psychology*, vol. 2. Palo Alto, CA: Consulting Psychologists Press, pp. 621–745.

Boudreau, J. W. and Ramstad, P. M. (2003). Strategic industrial and organizational psychology and the role of utility analysis models. In I. B. Winer (gen. ed.), W. C. Borman, D. R. Ilgen, and R. Klimoski (vol. eds.), *Handbook of Psychology*, vol. 12: *Industrial and Organizational Psychology*. New York: John Wiley, pp. 193–221.

Cascio, W. F. (1989). Using utility analysis to assess training outcomes. In I. L. Goldstein (ed.), *Training and Development in Organizations*. San Francisco: Jossey-Bass.

Cascio, W. F. (2000). *Costing Human Resources*, 4th edn. Cincinnati, OH: South-Western Publishing.

trait

Jeanette N. Cleveland

A trait is a disposition to behave in a particular way across a range of situations. People with a strong tendency to consistently behave in a particular way are described as being high on these traits. Human behavior can be organized into a hierarchy. At its simplest level, behavior can be examined in terms of specific responses. Some of these responses or behaviors (*see* BEHAVIOR) are linked to one another and form habits. When groups of habits tend to occur together, they form traits (Pervin, 1993). Finally, at a higher level of organization, traits may tend to be linked together (e.g., sociability, liveliness, impulsiveness) to form types (e.g., extraversion). Trait theories suggest that people have broad predispositions to respond in certain ways and that there is a hierarchical organization to personality.

Bibliography

Mischel, W. and Peake, P. K. (1982). Beyond déjà vu in the search for cross-situational consistency. *Psychological Review*, **89**, 730–55.

Pervin, L. A. (1993). *Personality: Theory and Research*. New York: John Wiley.

transfer of learning

Charles R. Williams

Transfer of learning, also called transfer of training, is a process which involves the following steps: (1) trainees learn and retain the skills taught during training; (2) learned skills are transferred, which means using learned skills to perform one's job; and (3) transferred skills are maintained as a part of JOB PERFORMANCE over time. Achieving transfer of learning is difficult. It is estimated that 90 percent of training efforts do not successfully transfer to the job.

Transfer can be improved *before* training by increasing trainees' motivation to learn. Employees who can choose the training sessions they want, or can choose whether to attend training at all, are more motivated than those not given a choice. Supervisors can also encourage trainees to attend training by discussing its benefits, and can set goals with trainees before training for using learned skills on the job. Transfer can be improved *during* training by selecting and teaching job-relevant knowledge and skills, by maximizing the physical and psychological similarity between the work environment and the training environment, by teaching general learning principles, and by exposing trainees to a variety of problem situations, scenarios, and solutions. Transfer can be improved *after* training by having supervisors model the skills learned in training, by giving trainees the opportunity to use what they learned in training, and by rewarding employees when they use those skills while performing their jobs (see Baldwin and Ford, 1988; Tannenbaum and Yukl, 1992; Goldstein and Ford, 2002).

See also *training*

Bibliography

Baldwin, T. T. and Ford, J. K. (1988). Transfer of training: A review and directions for future research. *Personnel Psychology*, **41**, 63–105.

Goldstein, I. L. and Ford, J. K. (2002). *Training in Organizations: Needs Assessment, Development and Evaluation*, 4th edn. Wadsworth, CA: Brooks/Cole.

Tannenbaum, S. I. and Yukl, G. (1992). Training and development in work organizations. *Annual Review of Psychology*, **43**, 399–441.

trend extrapolation

Nicholas J. Mathys

Trend extrapolation is a forecasting technique that can be used to estimate both demand for and supply of human resources. This technique is based on what is called a time series – a set of observations measured at successive points in time (e.g., weekly, monthly, yearly). Usually the most significant underlying characteristic of any data is their trend, mathematically referred to as the slope or average rate of change over a time period. In projecting STAFFING requirements for some time in the future, it may be useful to assume that the relationships that have occurred in the past will continue to hold. Based on this, one can take past data, such as number of employees used at different levels of activity (or time periods) and project (or extrapolate) what would likely occur in the future. This technique lends itself to graphical analyses and simplifies the mathematics involved. An example of this approach is in Burack and Mathys (1996).

Bibliography

Burack, E. H. and Mathys, N. J. (1996). *Human Resource Planning: A Pragmatic Approach to Manpower Staffing and Development*. Lake Forest, IL: Brace-Park.

trends in unionism

Leo Troy

The term trends in unionism means the direction over time of the membership of unions, and/or of union penetration of the labor market. The latter is often referred to as union density, or extent of organization. Union density is analogous to the concept of real wages: just as nominal wages are adjusted to determine real wages, or the buying power of wages, so union membership is adjusted by employment to get a measure of real membership. Density is expressed as a percentage.

Trends in membership may be up, down, or unchanged, but in themselves are insufficient for understanding how well unions are succeeding in organizing; they do not account for changes compared to the labor market. Union density itself is a subtle index. It can rise even if membership is stable, as long as employment falls. Likewise, density can fall even if membership increases but employment rises more quickly. Historically, density usually falls as a result of a decline in union membership relative to a rise in employment.

Economy-wide measures of unions' density are membership figures compared to nonfarm employment, or the civilian labor force. Similarly, density can be calculated relative to employment by industry, occupation, geography, gender, race and age, and cross-classifications of these variables. One of the most significant measures of trends in density compares the public with the private sectors of the labor market. Density can also be compared across countries, but problems of comparability in the statistics of union membership and employment figures may affect levels. Nevertheless, international trends in density are clearly discernible.

two-tiered pay structures

James E. Martin

Under such two-tiered pay structures, employees hired after a specified date, usually the effective date of the COLLECTIVE BARGAINING contract when tiers were first negotiated, are placed on lower pay scales than those hired previously. Tiers can be either *temporary*, where the pay of the low-tier employees gradually increases until it equals that of the higher tier, or *permanent*, where low-tier employees never reach the high-tier pay scales unless the contract is changed. Equity theory predictions that low-tier employees will exhibit poorer job attitudes than high-tier employees have been supported for permanent tiers (McFarlin and Frone, 1990; Martin, 1990), but not for temporary tiers (Cappelli and Sherer, 1990).

Bibliography

Cappelli, P. and Sherer, P. D. (1990). Assessing worker attitudes under a two-tier wage plan. *Industrial and Labor Relations Review*, 43, 225–44.

McFarlin, D. B. and Frone, M. R. (1990). A two-tier wage structure in a nonunion firm. *Industrial Relations*, 29, 145–54.

Martin, J. E. (1990). *Two-Tier Compensation Structures*. Kalamazoo, MI: W. E. Upjohn Institute for Employment Research.

unemployment compensation

Robert M. McCaffery

Unemployment compensation is a US federal–state partnership created by the SOCIAL SECURITY ACT OF 1935 to protect workers who become temporarily unemployed due to no fault of their own. The federal government sets broad guidelines and gives tax incentives to encourages states to enact their own laws. Each state administers its own programs, which typically specify partial income replacement for up to 26 weeks. During periods of high unemployment benefits may be extended with federal subsidies. Payments are usually 50 to 60 percent of recent earnings up to a statutory maximum.

Benefits are funded by an employer tax (employees contribute in a few states) that is essentially tied to involuntary terminations and layoffs.

Bibliography

McCaffery, R. M. (1992). *Employee Benefit Programs: A Total Compensation Perspective*, 2nd edn. Boston: PWS-Kent.

Rosenbloom, J. S. and Hallman, G. V. (1991). *Employee Benefit Planning*, 3rd edn. Englewood Cliffs, NJ: Prentice-Hall.

Uniform Guidelines on Employee Selection Procedures

Stuart A. Youngblood

The Uniform Guidelines on Employee Selection Procedures (UGESP) are employment validation guidelines issued in 1978 by four US governmental agencies (the EQUAL EMPLOYMENT OPPORTUNITY COMMISSION, the Department of Labor, the Department of Justice, and the US Civil Service Commission [now called the Office of Personnel Management]) for enforcement of Titles VII and IX of the CIVIL RIGHTS ACT OF 1964 as amended by the Equal Employment Opportunity Act of 1972 and 1991, and executive order 11246 (*see* EXECUTIVE ORDERS). Due to the highly technical nature of the UGESP, interpretive guidelines were issued in both 1979 and 1980 that provided over 90 questions and answers. The UGESP were designed to consolidate these four agency guidelines into one consistent guide to assist employers in the development, use, and documentation of technical standards needed to justify employment procedures, especially those that may have adverse impact or DISPARATE IMPACT. The UGESP propose that evidence of validity in terms of CONSTRUCT VALIDITY, CONTENT VALIDITY, or CRITERION-RELATED VALIDITY is acceptable and necessary only if an employment practice has adverse impact. The UGESP have been heavily criticized by researchers, employers, and even two previous chairs of the Equal Employment Opportunity Commission because many of the guideline requirements are inconsistent with current professional opinion (*see* PRINCIPLES FOR THE USE OF PERSONNEL SELECTION PROCEDURES issued by the SOCIETY FOR INDUSTRIAL AND ORGANIZATIONAL PSYCHOLOGY) and more recent Supreme Court decisions.

union avoidance

Anil Verma

It is a well-observed and recorded fact that managers generally prefer to work without the presence of unions in the workplace. Explanations offered for such managerial preference range from ideological opposition to managerial need for control to reasons of efficiency (Kochan, Katz, and McKersie, 1986). Bendix (1956: 444), in his seminal work on ideology in the workplace, argued that "ideologies of management can be explained only in part as rationalizations of self-interest; they also result from the legacy of institutions and ideas."

Thus, managers generally avoid unions to the best of their ability within the constraints of legal and political institutions. Three forms of union avoidance can be articulated based on historical experience.

Direct Opposition

For many organizations, the best way to avoid unions is to insure that one is never formed. In the first half of the twentieth century, such avoidance frequently meant intimidation, coercion, dismissal, and on occasion, the use and/or threat of violence to deter employees from joining unions (Rayback, 1959).

Although many of those tactics are illegal in most countries, including Canada and the US, the incidence of dismissal of union activists remains high (Freeman and Medoff, 1984; Cooke, 1985; ICFTU, 1994). In many parts of the US and Canada, employers can also oppose union drives during a campaign that precedes the vote by employees. Some forms of employer intervention (such as free speech) during a campaign are legal in the US. Although there is always a chance that employer opposition could backfire, i.e., workers alienated by employer behavior could punish the employer by voting for the union, there is considerable evidence that employer opposition is effective in preventing employees from voting for a union (Lawler and West, 1985; Lawler, 1990). A substantial consulting industry specializing in union avoidance know-how has taken root in the US (Kilgur, 1978; Sullivan, 1978; Hughes, 1990; Bureau of National Affairs, 1995).

Union Substitution

Another union avoidance response is for managers to offer employees all those services that a union would normally provide: protection from arbitrary treatment, access to a grievance process (see GRIEVANCE PROCEDURE), more say in workplace decisions, better communication, good wages and BENEFITS, and so forth. Though nonunion companies did not provide these benefits to their employees traditionally, by the 1960s a growing number of firms began to adopt such policies and thus were able to sustain their nonunion status despite attempts to organize them (Foulkes, 1980). Notable among these firms were IBM, Polaroid, Eastman Kodak, and Hewlett-Packard. Empirical evidence supports the notion that such policies reduce the chances of unionization (Fiorito, Lowman, and Nelson, 1987).

Disinvestment in Unionized Operations

Yet another route to union avoidance for unionized firms is to disinvest in unionized operations and to channel new investments into new plants that are nonunion. The disinvestment may be gradual over several years, or it may be sudden in the form of relocation, closure, or sale of a unionized facility. It is generally very difficult to find direct empirical evidence for such actions because investment decisions are made for many reasons. Compounded within each investment decision are reasons (proximity to markets, technology, labor costs, raw materials, and so forth) which are difficult to separate from the desire to avoid unions. A few studies have provided limited evidence of such disinvestment behavior (Verma, 1985; Kochan et al., 1986).

Union avoidance strategies of employers have been successful in the US, where managers enjoy greater freedom to oppose unions than in most other industrialized nations. While union densities (see TRENDS IN UNIONISM) have fallen in most industrialized nations since 1980 (Galenson, 1994), the drop in the US from 30 percent in 1965 to 15.5 percent in 1994 is one of the most precipitous (Troy and Sheflin, 1985; Hirsch and Macpherson, 1995). It has been argued that union avoidance has played a major role in this decline (Freeman and Medoff, 1984; Presidential Commission on the Future of Labor–Management Relations, 1995).

A key related issue is the role of public policy, given what we know about union avoidance. Workers in most countries of the world today enjoy the legal right of association. If the employer's instincts are to oppose collective activity by employees, what role can public policy play to insure that workers are able to exercise their legal right to join a union of their choice?

Bibliography

Bendix, R. (1956). *Work and Authority in Industry*. Berkeley, CA: University of California Press.
Bureau of National Affairs (1995). *Labor Relations Consultants: Issues, Trends and Controversies*. Washington, DC: Bureau of National Affairs Special Reports.
Cooke, W. N. (1985). The rising tool of discrimination against union activities. *Industrial Relations*, **24**, 421–42.
Fiorito, J., Lowman, C., and Nelson, F. D. (1987). The impact of human resource policies on union organizing. *Industrial Relations*, **26**, 113–26.
Foulkes, F. K. (1980). *Personnel Policies in Large Nonunion Companies*. Englewood Cliffs, NJ: Prentice-Hall.
Freeman, R. B. and Medoff, J. L. (1984). *What Do Unions Do?* New York: Basic Books.
Galenson, W. (1994). *Trade Union Growth and Decline: An International Study*. Westport, CN: Praeger.
Hirsch, B. T. and Macpherson, D. A. (1995). *Union Membership and Earnings Databook*. Washington, DC: Bureau of National Affairs.
Hughes, C. L. (1990). *Making Unions Unnecessary*. New York: Executive Enterprises.
International Confederation of Free Trade Unions (ICFTU) (1994). *Annual Survey of Violations of Trade Union Rights*. Brussels: ICFTU.
Kilgur, J. G. (1978). Before the union knocks. *Personnel Journal*, **57**, 186–92.
Kochan, T. A., Katz, H. C., and McKersie, R. B. (1986). *The Transformation of American Industrial Relations*. New York: Basic Books.
Lawler, J. J. (1990). *Unionization and Deunionization: Strategy, Tactics and Outcomes*. Columbia, SC: University of South Carolina Press.
Lawler, J. J. and West, R. (1985). Impact of union avoidance: Strategies on representation elections. *Industrial Relations*, **24**, 406–20.
Presidential Commission on the Future of Labor–Management Relations (1995). *Report and Recommendations*. Washington, DC: US Department of Labor.
Rayback, J. G. (1959). *A History of American Labor*. New York: Free Press.
Sullivan, F. L. (1978). Limiting union organizing activity through supervisors. *Personnel*, **55**, 55–64.
Troy, L. and Sheflin, L. (1985). *US Union Sourcebook: Membership, Finances, Structure Directory*. West Orange, NJ: Industrial Relations Data and Information Sources.
Verma, A. (1985). Relative flow of capital to union and nonunion plants within a firm. *Industrial Relations*, **24**, 395–405.

union commitment

Daniel G. Gallagher

Union commitment can be generally defined as an attitudinal concept reflecting the extent to which workers identify with, or are attached to, the goals and values of the union in which they are a member.

Union commitment represents the application of more general organizational commitment concepts to specific situations involving labor unions. The dimensionality and measurement of union commitment has been subject to considerable debate. However, Gordon et al. (1980) have suggested that union commitment is composed of four underlying factors: (1) loyalty to the union, representing a sense of pride in union membership and a desire to remain a member; (2) responsibility to the union, focusing upon the member's willingness to fulfill obligations pertaining to the protection of union interests; (3) willingness to work for the union, reflecting a readiness to do special work on behalf of the union; and (4) belief in unionism, showing the member's ideological belief in the concept of unionism. Alternative definitions or measures suggest that union commitment represents both pro-union attitudes and the intent to engage in activities to support the union.

Union commitment has been identified by many researchers as an important predictor of actual membership participation in union activities (meeting attendance, political action, PICKETING, and so forth). In addition, considerable evidence suggests that union commitment is influenced by a worker's background experiences (e.g., parents' attitudes toward unions) and the degree to which a worker views the union as providing favorable treatment and outcomes for the union membership.

Bibliography

Barling, J., Fullagar, C., and Kelloway, E. K. (1992). *The Union and Its Members: A Psychological Approach*. Oxford: Oxford University Press.
Gallagher, D. G. and Clark, P. F. (1989). Research on union commitment: Implications for labor. *Labor Studies Journal*, **14**, 52–71.
Gordon, M. E., Philpot, J. W., Burt, R. E., Thompson, C. A., and Spiller, W. E. (1980) Commitment to the

union: Development of a measure and examination of its correlates. *Journal of Applied Psychology*, 65, 479–99.

union effects on pay

Nancy Brown Johnson

The primary question addressed in union pay research is the degree to which a union worker earns more than he or she would earn in a non-union environment. Researchers examine this question through studies of union and nonunion workers with similar demographic characteristics, similar union and nonunion establishments, and workers who move in and out of union membership across time. Lewis (1963, 1986) carefully analyzed over 100 union wage studies and estimated that the union wage gap approximately ranged from 10 to 15 percent. Others have drawn similar conclusions (Hirsch and Addison, 1986). These estimates vary across time and labor market conditions. For example, Lewis (1986) found that union gap estimates had reached as high as 19 to 20 percent in the late 1970s and as low as 12 percent in the late 1960s.

The wage gap estimate also varies by demographic group because unions negotiate standard rate policies that do not allow management to pay workers on an individual basis (Freeman and Medoff, 1984). Standard rate pay results in raising the pay of workers who would otherwise receive lower pay. Thus, unions tend to increase younger workers' pay relative to older workers and blue-collar relative to white-collar workers' pay. However, analysis of numerous studies indicates ambiguous wage gap findings by race and sex (Lewis, 1986).

In summary, union pay research clearly shows that unions raise wages, but the amount they raise wages varies across time. This research also indicates that unions raise wages more for groups of workers who would otherwise receive lower pay.

Bibliography

Freeman, R. B. and Medoff, J. L. (1984). *What Do Unions Do?* New York: Basic Books.

Hirsch, B. T. and Addison, J. T. (1986). *The Economic Analysis of Unions: New Approaches and Evidence*. London: Allen and Unwin.

Lewis, H. G. (1963). *Unionism and Relative Wages in the United States*. Chicago: University of Chicago Press.

Lewis, H. G. (1986). *Union Relative Wage Effects*. Chicago: University of Chicago Press.

union–management cooperation

William N. Cooke

Union–management cooperation is a term that has been widely used to characterize cooperative activities undertaken by unions and employers, primarily aimed at improving organizational performance but with a secondary objective of improving the QUALITY OF WORK LIFE (QWL). The underlying purpose or expectation of cooperation is that both labor and management gain more from the employment relationship through cooperation than either can achieve without cooperation (Kochan, Katz, and McKersie, 1986; Cooke, 1990).

STRUCTURE AND OBJECTIVES

Although the act of cooperation may be viewed as a process of joint decision-making informally conducted on a day-to-day basis, union–management cooperation is more generally viewed as relationships having voluntary but formalized decision-making mechanisms (outside of contract negotiations) for input and discussion from union representatives and/or union members. These formalized mechanisms typically include union–management steering or policy committees at various levels in organizations and team-based efforts (e.g., EMPLOYEE INVOLVEMENT programs, QUALITY CIRCLES, quality of work life programs, and SELF-MANAGING TEAMS) dispersed throughout organizations.

Whereas union–management committees are comprised of union leaders and managers who focus on resolving more systemic organizational problems or inefficiencies, work teams are comprised of BARGAINING UNIT employees who focus on identifying barriers and opportunities to improve performance in given work areas. Toward enhancing performance, the parties engage in *direct* efforts at improving quality, PRODUCTIVITY, throughput, speed-to-market, customer satisfaction, timely delivery, and otherwise reducing costs. Toward enhancing the QWL and *indirectly* improving performance, the parties also engage in cooperative efforts that focus on improving JOB SATISFACTION, the work environment, and the labor–management relations climate.

SUPPORTING PRACTICES

A variety of supporting mechanisms and practices generally accompany these cooperative efforts, such as the following.

1. As incentives and rewards for achieving and sharing in improved performance from cooperation, many organizations provide group-based performance compensation (*see* PAY FOR PERFORMANCE), such as PROFIT SHARING, GAINSHARING, and ad hoc recognition BONUSES.
2. To enhance performance-related skills, organizations invest in additional education and TRAINING in joint problem solving, statistical process control, team building (*see* TEAM-BUILDING TRAINING), leadership, facilitation, and communications.
3. To facilitate greater WORKFORCE FLEXIBILITY and to broaden employee understanding of operations, employees frequently learn and take on more job tasks than usual.
4. Cooperation is often marked by less confrontational approaches to contract negotiations than otherwise. The parties, that is, are more inclined to embrace notions of INTEGRATIVE BARGAINING and interest-based negotiation processes.
5. In order to maintain employee commitment to cooperation and teamwork, the parties often agree to stronger employment security provisions, ranging from protection against displacement that might otherwise occur from increased productivity, to opportunities to counter-bid subcontracting bids from external vendors, to guaranteed employment security during the life of negotiated contracts.

POTENTIAL BENEFITS AND COSTS

A wealth of case studies and self-reports identify a wide range of potential benefits and costs to management, employees, and union leaders. For management, the potential benefits include improved performance, cost reductions, stronger employee identity and commitment to organizational goals, better employee–supervisor relations, reduced GRIEVANCES, reduced disciplinary action, lower ABSENTEEISM, increased workforce flexibility, and greater workforce adaptability. Potential costs to management include additional expenditures for reorientation and training, perceived loss of authority and status, displacement of supervisors and middle managers, and lost time in meetings.

Potential benefits to employees include increased intrinsic rewards from participation, involvement, greater input into how work is accomplished, improved working conditions, fewer grievances, quicker resolution of problems, heightened dignity, greater self-esteem, increased pride in work, and added financial rewards from any group-based performance pay arrangements. Potential costs to employees include demands for working harder (not necessarily smarter), displacement or loss of employment from improved productivity, and unwanted peer pressure to participate and be accountable.

Potential benefits to union leaders include recognition from members for QWL improvements, improved communication with managers, greater input in management decisions, reduced day-to-day contract administration problems, more widespread contact with members, and greater membership input into union activities. Potential costs to union leaders include perceptions of being coopted by management, erosion of traditional roles of unions and collective bargaining, heightened political conflict over union leadership roles, increased uncertainty of reelection, and loss of member commitment and union influence. (For citations and further review of these potential benefits and costs see Cooke, 1990.)

STATISTICAL ANALYSES

Empirical analyses of the effect of union–management cooperation on company performance are limited but generally show that cooperation and related team-based activities lead to significant improvements in both productivity and quality (Voos, 1987; Cooke, 1992, 1994; Fernie and Metcalf, 1995). The degree of effects on performance, however, appears to be conditioned by other factors that influence the intensity of and commitment to cooperative activities. Included among these factors are group-based performance pay, concession bargaining, subcontracting out bargaining unit work, technological investments, and layoffs (Cooke, 1990, 1994; Eaton, 1994).

Little empirical evidence is available about the effects of cooperation and related team-based activities on employees and unions. One survey of employees across locations within a large unionized company shows that employees report greater job satisfaction, stronger organizational commitment, and better work group relations in those locations characterized by union–management cooperation and team-based activities than in locations characterized by traditional union–management relations (Batt and Appelbaum, 1995). Juravich, Harris, and Brooks (1993) report from their survey of union leaders across a diverse industry sample that a majority of union leaders believe that cooperation and team-based participation have improved EMPLOYEE MORALE, health and safety, the ability to resolve grievances, and union member satisfaction and identification with their unions. In addition, a majority of union leaders report that cooperation has improved relationships between union officers and union members, between union officers and plant managers, and between union members and supervisors.

CONCLUSION

In summary, the empirical evidence to date, albeit very limited, appears to indicate that the potential benefits of union–management cooperation and related team-based efforts generally (but not always) outweigh the potential costs for employers, union leaders, and union members.

Bibliography

Batt, R. and Appelbaum, E. (1995). Worker participation in diverse settings: Does the form affect the outcome, and if so, who benefits? *British Journal of Industrial Relations*, 33, 353–78.

Cooke, W. N. (1990). *Labor–Management Cooperation: New Partnerships or Going in Circles?* Kalamazoo, MI: W. E. Upjohn Institute for Employment Research.

Cooke, W. N. (1992). Product quality improvement through employee participation: The effects of unionization and joint union–management administration. *Industrial and Labor Relations Review*, 46, 119–34.

Cooke, W. N. (1994). Employee participation programs, group-based incentives, and company performance: A union–nonunion comparison. *Industrial and Labor Relations Review*, 47, 594–609.

Eaton, A. E. (1994). Factors contributing to the survival of employee participation programs in unionized settings. *Industrial and Labor Relations Review*, 47, 371–89.

Fernie, S. and Metcalf, D. (1995). Participation, contingent pay, representation and workplace performance: Evidence from Great Britain. *British Journal of Industrial Relations*, 33, 380–415.

Juravich, T., Harris, H., and Brooks, A. (1993). Mutual gains? Labor and management evaluate their employee involvement programs. *Journal of Labor Research*, 14, 165–85.

Kochan, T. A., Katz, H. C., and McKersie, R. B. (1986). *The Transformation of American Industrial Relations*. New York: Basic Books.

Voos, P. B. (1987). Managerial perceptions of the economic impact of labor relations programs. *Industrial and Labor Relations Review*, 40, 196–208.

union organizing

Richard B. Peterson

Union organizing is the process by which unions (and employee associations) and public and private sector employers try to influence a given grouping of employees to vote to support or not support union representation in their particular workplace.

In reality, the union is the moving party in the process of seeking representation for a particular grouping of employees. The union may have been approached by disgruntled employees in a particular plant, office, or firm. Or the union may take the initial step of contacting nonrepresented employees to ascertain their possible interest in union representation.

Campaign steps usually include initial contacts with such employees. This is followed by the union organizers determining the level of employee interest in union representation (calling meetings, visiting homes, and counting responses to handbills). If there is sufficient interest, an organizing committee will be formed. That committee will then spearhead the process of soliciting signatures on authorization cards (Gagala, 1983; Feldacker, 1990; Holley and Jennings, 1994).

During the period from 1935 to 1955 most American employers were willing to accept union representation based on signed authorization cards. However, in more recent years, employers have usually required an election to be held to show proof that the majority of employees wish union representation (*see* REPRESENTATION ELECTIONS). Research has shown that one-on-one contact, peer contact and persuasion, and effective written communications are the most successful union approaches (Holley and Jennings, 1994: 166).

Most union organizing campaigns are hotly contested by private sector American employers, where the management engages in similar activities to attempt to dissuade their employees from voting in favor of the union in the consent or directed election. Over the years the NATIONAL LABOR RELATIONS BOARD and the courts have clarified what tactics used in the union organizing process are legal and illegal (see Feldacker, 1990). The success of the organizing campaign for the union is negatively related to such factors as size of the BARGAINING UNIT and delays in holding and affirming the election. On the other hand, unions are more likely to win the campaign if the union has a larger membership, or if two or more unions vie for representation rights (Holley and Jennings, 1994: 172).

Bibliography

Feldacker, B. (1990). *Labor Guide to Labor Law*, 3rd edn. Englewood Cliffs, NJ: Prentice-Hall.
Gagala, K. (1983). *Union Organizing and Staying Organized*. Reston, VA: Reston Publishing.
Holley, W. H., Jr. and Jennings, K. M. (1994). *The Labor Relations Process*, 5th edn. Fort Worth, TX: Dryden Press.

union representation procedures

Richard B. Peterson

Representation procedures are defined as those procedures used by the NATIONAL LABOR RELATIONS BOARD (NLRB) in the US to determine the interest of employees in being represented by a union or employee association for the purpose of COLLECTIVE BARGAINING with their employer over wages, hours, and working conditions. These procedures are used as part of the representation election process (*see* REPRESENTATION ELECTIONS). Many state labor relations agencies use a similar process for determining the interest of public and private sector employees in having union representation.

There are three ways in which employee representation may be determined. First, the NLRB may issue a directive where there is a deadlock between the union and employer. Second, the employer may voluntarily recognize the union or employee association based on evidence that the majority of employees in a defined BARGAINING UNIT wish union representation. This determination may be based on valid signed authorization cards (*see* UNION ORGANIZING). Finally, the NLRB may run a secret ballot election where the parties agree to: the proposed bargaining unit jurisdiction; eligibility to vote; and time, place, and rules for voting. This is called a consent election (Feldacker, 1990; Holley and Jennings, 1994).

In order for an election to take place, the union must show the local NLRB staff that at least 30 percent of the employees who would fall under the bargaining unit jurisdiction have signed a petition for such an election. In reality, few unions will request an election unless they have signatures from 50 to 70 percent of those employees who would fall into the proposed bargaining unit.

Bibliography

Feldacker, B. (1990). *Labor Guide to Labor Law*, 3rd edn. Englewood Cliffs, NJ: Prentice-Hall.
Holley, W. H., Jr. and Jennings, K. M. (1994). *The Labor Relations Process*, 5th edn. Fort Worth, TX: Dryden Press.

union shop

John C. Shearer

A union shop is a negotiated union security clause of a labor agreement, which is legal in states not covered by RIGHT TO WORK state laws. A negotiated union shop provision requires that all new employees become union members (or, at least, pay union dues) after at least 30 days after being employed (as provided by the LABOR MANAGEMENT RELATIONS ACT OF 1947). Under most union shop agreements employees may not later rescind their dues obligation.

union unfair labor practices

Terry L. Leap

Sections 8(b)(1) through 8(b)(7) of the LABOR MANAGEMENT RELATIONS ACT OF 1947 (Taft-Hartley Act) contain a number of complex union unfair labor practices. Section 8(b)(1) makes it illegal for a labor organization (union) to restrain or coerce employees and employers with regard to their selection or recognition of a bargaining representative. Section 8(b)(2) prevents a union from forcing an employer to discriminate against an employee in order to influence the employee's union membership. Section 8(b)(3) requires a union to bargain in good faith with an employer (*see* GOOD FAITH BARGAINING). The most complex set of union unfair labor practices is contained in section 8(b)(4). This section places restrictions on hot-cargo agreements (a firm agrees not to handle products produced by another firm), SECONDARY BOYCOTTS (forcing a neutral or secondary employer to become involved in a STRIKE or other labor dispute), UNION ORGANIZING efforts in situations where another union has already been recognized as the employees' exclusive bargaining representative, and strikes over jurisdictional disputes (e.g., disputes in the construction industry over which union is entitled to perform specific work). Section 8(b)(5) forbids unions from charging excessive or discriminatory fees and dues to its members. Section 8(b)(6) prohibits the practice of featherbedding (a union forces an employer to pay workers for work that they did not perform). Section 8(b)(7) regulates organizational and recognition PICKETING by unions. Unions cannot, for example, engage in organizational picketing to encourage a group of employees to sign authorization cards within 12 months after these employees have been subjected to a valid NATIONAL LABOR RELATIONS BOARD representation election (Norris and Shershin, 1992; *see* REPRESENTATION ELECTIONS).

Bibliography

Leap, T. L. (1995). *Collective Bargaining and Labor Relations*, 2nd edn. Englewood Cliffs, NJ: Prentice-Hall.

Norris, J. A. and Shershin, M. J., Jr. (1992). *How to Take a Case Before the NLRB*, 6th edn. Washington, DC: Bureau of National Affairs.

union voice

Paul Jarley

Union voice refers to the mechanisms through which unions provide members with opportunities to communicate their collective concerns to management. Union voice mechanisms include COLLECTIVE BARGAINING and contract administration, particularly grievance procedures (*see* GRIEVANCE PROCEDURE).

How Voice Differs from Exit

Workers have two basic options for expressing dissatisfaction. First, employees may leave the firm. Exit provides employers with information about the preferences of marginal employees – those most willing and able to leave the organization. If enough workers quit, employers will alter their policies in an effort to reduce EMPLOYEE TURNOVER. Second, employees may communicate their concerns directly to management. Voice may be expressed on an individual or collective basis. Individual voice tends to be idiosyncratic, but through collective voice employers can learn about the preferences of their average employee. Research suggests that there are differences in the terms and conditions of employment offered by firms that rely on union (i.e., collective) voice and those that rely on exit as the principal means for learning about worker preferences.

Views on Union Voice

The literature offers two views on union voice. One view holds that union voice can reduce turnover, facilitate worker acquisition of firm-specific skills, and provide a source of productivity-enhancing suggestions (*see* PRODUCTIVITY). The other view argues that employers have other mechanisms to systematically learn about worker preferences and that any advantages are more than offset by the greater labor–management conflict and stifling of individual initiative that accompany union voice. Evidence exists to support both views (*see* UNIONISM EFFECTS).

Bibliography

Freeman, R. B. and Medoff, J. L. (1984). *What Do Unions Do?* New York: Basic Books.

Hirsch, B. T. and Addison, J. T. (1986). *The Economic Analysis of Unions: New Approaches and Evidence.* Boston: Allen and Unwin.

unionism effects

Nancy Brown Johnson

Unionism effects describe the changes that workers, employers, and society experience resulting from labor unions negotiating COLLECTIVE BARGAINING agreements as opposed to employers unilaterally determining the terms and conditions of employment.

UNION EFFECTS ON WORKERS

Historically, business unions have primarily focused on improving the wages, hours, and working conditions of their members through collective bargaining. Thus, traditional union effect research has focused on whether unions have achieved these goals. Studies of UNION EFFECTS ON PAY have found that unions raise the wages of their members around 10 to 15 percent. Additionally, research indicates that unions increase their members' fringe benefit levels over nonunion members by even more than their wage effect (Freeman and Medoff, 1984). Thus, most evidence strongly suggests that unions successfully achieve their objective of increasing their members' COMPENSATION.

Despite the evidence that unions increase members' pay, a number of studies find that union coverage correlates with *decreased* JOB SATISFACTION and EMPLOYEE TURNOVER. Because a large body of research typically finds that job satisfaction and turnover relate inversely, this research has attracted attention. Exit–voice theory (Hirschman, 1970; *see* UNION VOICE) provides one explanation of this apparent contradiction by arguing that union grievance systems (*see* GRIEVANCE PROCEDURE; GRIEVANCES) protect employees who voice discontent, and therefore serve to mobilize co-workers' discontent (Freeman and Medoff, 1984). A second theory argues that because unions affect job outcomes they also affect the importance of outcomes to the union members. Research drawing on this theoretical perspective has found that unions increase satisfaction with pay and this increased satisfaction offsets the decreased satisfaction with supervision and work itself (Berger, Olson, and Boudreau, 1983). However, a later study used a different sample than prior research and did not find evidence of decreased job satisfaction among union members. These researchers argue that the positive relationship between job satisfaction and turnover in union settings does not exist and the results of prior research resulted from statistical artifact (Gordon and DeNisi, 1995).

UNION EFFECTS ON FIRMS

Although unions affect firms in various ways, their PRODUCTIVITY and profitability effects have received a great deal of attention. Controversy surrounds the union effect on productivity, in part because a number of offsetting influences exist. First, unions negotiate higher wages, potentially reducing employment. To enhance employment opportunities and to protect their members, unions negotiate work-rule provisions such as rigid job descriptions (*see* JOB DESCRIPTION) and job requirements that hinder productivity. However, unions also enhance productivity by changing managerial practices and reducing turnover through enhanced employee voice and seniority provisions. In more recent years, some unions have begun working jointly with management to enhance productivity. Because of the offsetting influences, however, researchers can make no definitive productivity predictions. As a result, there is considerable debate on interpretation of the empirical literature. For example, in separate literature reviews, Freeman and Medoff (1984) concluded that unions raise productivity and Addison and Hirsch (1989) found no compelling evidence of positive or negative productivity effects.

The union effect on firm profitability raises much less disagreement than the effect on productivity. Consistently, studies have found that unionized firms have significantly lower profitability than nonunion firms, regardless of the profit measure, unit of analysis, time period, or methods used (Hirsch, 1991).

UNION EFFECTS ON SOCIETY

Economists examine the union effect on society by viewing unions as monopolies that raise wages above competitive levels, crowd the unorganized sector, and depress wages (Freeman and Medoff, 1984; Rees, 1989). Others have raised additional concerns regarding union effects on society as transmitted through their excessive political power and corruption. While acknowledging that unionization can contribute to these problems, others believe that unionization benefits outweigh these costs. They argue that unions through collective voice provide workplace and compensation practices more amenable to employees, improvements in productivity, and a reduction in wage inequality (Freeman and Medoff, 1984). Others also contend that worker protection from managerial authority and the representation of the general interests of workers serve to aid society (Rees, 1989).

SUMMARY

The above discussion has only highlighted key union effects. Clearly, many other important union effects exist, such as strikes and their effects on nonunion organizations, public sector outcomes, politics, inflation, and job security.

There is also a question of whether the union effects described here will continue into the future. Kochan, Katz, and McKersie (1986) have argued that INDUSTRIAL RELATIONS systems have undergone a fundamental transformation, which suggests that future union effects may differ from those of the past. However, Dunlop (1993) states that although the environment has undergone modifications, the underlying elements of the US industrial relations system have remained essentially stable. This scenario suggests that union effects will remain largely unchanged.

Bibliography

Addison, J. T. and Hirsch, B. T. (1989). Union effects on productivity, profits and growth: Has the long run arrived? *Journal of Labor Economics*, 7, 72–101.

Berger, C. J., Olson, C. A., and Boudreau, J. W. (1983). Effects of unions on job satisfaction: The role of work-related values and perceived rewards. *Organizational Behavior and Human Performance*, 32, 289–324.

Dunlop, J. T. (1993). *Industrial Relations Systems*. Boston: Harvard Business School Press.

Freeman, R. B. and Medoff, J. L. (1984). *What Do Unions Do?* New York: Basic Books.

Gordon, M. E. and DeNisi, A. S. (1995). A re-examination of the relationship between union membership and job satisfaction. *Industrial and Labor Relations Review*, 48, 222–36.

Hirsch, B. T. (1991). Union coverage and profitability among US firms. *Review of Economics and Statistics*, 73, 69–77.

Hirschman, A. O. (1970). *Exit, Voice, and Loyalty: Responses to Decline in Firms, Organizations, and States*. Cambridge, MA: Harvard University Press.

Kochan, T. A., Katz, H. C., and McKersie, R. (1986). *The Transformation of American Industrial Relations*. New York: Basic Books.

Rees, A. (1989). *The Economics of Trade Unions*, 3rd edn. Chicago: University of Chicago Press.

unionization determinants

Jack Fiorito

Unionization determinants are the factors that cause workers to form, support, or join unions or employee associations (*see* CRAFT UNIONS; INDUSTRIAL UNIONS). In the US, workers unionize primarily for the purpose of COLLECTIVE BARGAINING. Workers may unionize for collective political activities and to provide mutual assistance as well.

THEORIES OF UNIONIZATION

Theories of unionization generally can be classified as to whether they view unions as revolutionary change agents in an inevitable class struggle between workers and capitalists (a Marxist perspective) or as a means for workers to improve their wellbeing within the existing socioeconomic order (pure and simple unionism or business unionism, a perspective favored by US scholars). The latter perspective encompasses various narrower theories, but common among them is the notion that workers form, support, or join unions out of the belief that unions are an effective means to address workplace (primarily) and/or societal problems.

Forms of Unionization and Levels of Analysis

Hundreds of studies have examined the determinants of unionization. Unionization determinants can be conceptualized for various forms of unionization and at varying levels of analysis. In a narrow sense, unionization refers to whether a particular individual is a union member or the proportion of workers who are members in some aggregate unit (e.g., the US), which is also referred to as union density (*see* TRENDS IN UNIONISM). In a broad sense, unionization ranges from values, beliefs, attitudes, and behaviors concerning unions to actual membership and labor contract coverage. To illustrate the breadth of meaning intended, attitudes toward unions may include those of the general public or nonunion workers, but also attitudes of unionized workers, such as UNION COMMITMENT.

Aggregate-level studies examine unionization and its causes across very broad units, such as industries, states, or nations, change within such units over time, or both. Individual-level studies examine membership, attitudes, and behaviors across individual workers or changes in individual attitudes, and so forth. Unionization also may be analyzed at various intermediate levels, such as a company or election unit.

Unionization determinants vary with the form of unionization in question and the level of analysis. Aggregate-level studies tend to focus on economic influences (such as inflation and unemployment) and public policies (such as RIGHT TO WORK laws and the NATIONAL LABOR RELATIONS ACT OF 1935). Individual-level analyses stress psychological variables such as attitudes toward work, employers, and unions. Intermediate-level studies such as those of REPRESENTATION ELECTIONS often include economic and psychological variables as well as measures of employer and union characteristics and tactics used to persuade workers to support or oppose unionization.

To some extent, the form of unionization examined and the level of analysis dictate the unionization determinants considered, in terms of either measure availability or relevance. An attitudinal measure may not be available for an aggregate unit or may be relatively constant across aggregate units. Conversely, a macroeconomic variable may not make sense at an individual level or may be essentially constant for all individuals in a given employing unit at one point in time. Similar or overlapping constructs may be represented by different measures at different levels of analysis. For example, in an aggregate study, one might specify past wage changes as an indication of union effectiveness; in an individual-level cross-section one might specify a scale of perceived union effectiveness. In both instances the underlying hypothesis is that workers support unions because they believe unions will improve their economic wellbeing.

To some extent the determinants considered also reflect the disciplinary orientation of researchers. Economists naturally tend to stress economic influences and objective measures, such as wage rates and unemployment rates. Psychologists note that persons act on their perceptions, and stress perceptual variables such as JOB SATISFACTION and perceptions of union effectiveness. INDUSTRIAL RELATIONS scholars stress an interdisciplinary approach, recognizing that these and other disciplines can contribute collectively to a fuller understanding than is possible through any single discipline.

Aggregate-level Findings

In recent years, many studies have attempted to account for the fact that US unionization has dropped from roughly one-third of the workforce in the 1950s to about one-eighth in the 2000s (and less dramatic but similar trends elsewhere). Studies suggest that unionization tends to be pro-cyclical, with unions expanding in prosperous times and declining in hard times, although these results find less support in recent decades. Research also indicates that unionization may be affected by "structural" factors, including occupational, industrial, and regional employment shifts, and changes in workforce demographics, as well as public policies and the behavior of unions and employers within a given policy context. On the latter, several studies have cited a large or even dominant role for employer opposition to unions, in both legal and illegal forms (*see* UNION AVOIDANCE). In addition, some suggest that governments' labor market policies have reduced the need for unions, that worker values have become more individualistic, that job satisfaction has risen, or that unions have failed to respond effectively to these and other changes in their environments. Recent studies have given more emphasis to unions' organizing strategies and tactics.

INDIVIDUAL-LEVEL FINDINGS

Studies of individual decisions to form, support, or join unions stress psychological variables, as noted above. These studies consistently show that perceptions of union effectiveness, job dissatisfaction, and favorable general attitudes toward unions increase workers' unionization tendencies. Additional measures for worker, employer, and union characteristics or organizing campaign tactics have been found influential in some studies. To an extent, however, the latter are simply acting as proxies for worker psychological states they may influence. For example, employer counter-organizing tactics and progressive human resource policies are often aimed at reducing perceptions of union effectiveness or increasing job satisfaction. Similarly, worker-demographic effects may simply reflect shared dissatisfactions among particular demographic groups. This does not necessarily imply that such proxies are unimportant. One often cannot observe worker psychological states, and the role of influences such as employer and union tactics are often intrinsically interesting.

Bibliography

Fiorito, J. (2003). Union organizing in the United States. In G. Gall (ed.), *Union Organizing: Campaigning for Trade Union Recognition*. London: Routledge, pp. 191–210.

Fiorito, J., Gallagher, D. G., and Greer, C. R. (1986). Determinants of unionism: A review of the literature. In K. M. Rowland and G. R. Ferris (eds.), *Research in Personnel and Human Resources Management*, vol. 4. Greenwich, CT: JAI Press, pp. 269–306.

Fiorito, J., Jarley, P., and Delaney, J. T. (2002). Information technology, union organizing, and union effectiveness. *British Journal of Industrial Relations*, **40**, 627–58.

Freeman, R. B. and Rogers, J. (1999). *What Workers Want*. Ithaca, NY: ILR Press.

Hirsch, B. T. and Macpherson, D. A. (2003). Union membership and coverage database from the Current Population Survey. *Industrial and Labor Relations Review*, **56**, 349–54.

Jarley, P. and Fiorito, J. (1990). Associate membership: Unionism or consumerism? *Industrial and Labor Relations Review*, **43**, 209–24.

Lawler, J. J. (1990). *Unionization and Deunionization: Strategy, Tactics, and Outcomes*. Columbia, SC: University of South Carolina Press.

Perlman, S. (1928). *A Theory of the Labor Movement*. New York: Macmillan.

Strauss, G., Gallagher, D. G., and Fiorito, J. (eds.) (1991). *The State of the Unions*. Madison, WI: Industrial Relations Research Association.

United Kingdom

Susan Cartwright

ECONOMIC OVERVIEW

The UK is composed of England, Wales, Scotland, and Northern Ireland. The UK occupies a land area of 244,820 km^2 (93,000 sq. miles), which makes it roughly twice the size of New York State. Despite its relatively small size, the UK is one of the most densely populated countries in the world with a population density of 246 persons per km^2. The estimated population as of June 2003 was 60,094,648. Almost 90 percent of the population live in urban areas, with 7 million people living in the capital, London. According to the 1994 population census, more than 94 percent were described as white; of the remaining nonwhite population, 3 percent were Asian, West Indian, and other. Generally, the UK is highly tolerant of ethnic differences and there has been little hostility.

The total labor force is estimated to be 29.418 million. The largest employment sector is services (75 percent). This sector has grown significantly as manufacturing and other primary industries have declined. The UK has been at the forefront of call center technology and call center workers make up over 2 percent of the working population. Currently, more people work in call centers than in the coal, steel, and vehicle manufacturing industries (Cartwright, 2000).

According to 1997 estimates, the manufacturing sector employs 20 percent of the workforce. As well as growth in the service sector, the UK has witnessed a rise in self-employment, which now accounts for 12 percent of the workforce. Another notable trend has been the increased participation of women in the workforce. In 1997, women formed 47 percent of the full-time and 80 percent of the part-time workforce. It is estimated that two-thirds of women between the ages of 15 and 65 are employed. In common with the US, the UK is experiencing an increase in its older population and a continuing decline in new labor force entrants. Currently, 19.5 percent of the UK population is under 15 and 20.5 percent is over 60 years of age. Life expectancy for men is 76 years and for women 80.7 years.

Scase (1999) estimates that over the next ten years the UK population, like that of many European countries, will remain static and may even decline. According to Kandola (2001), it is predicted that soon 40 percent of the population will be over 50 and only 5 percent will be in the 15–19 age range.

However, compared to the US, fewer people go on to higher education. Currently, the figure is approximately one in three of all school leavers. There are clear implications for future skill shortages and employers are seeking to attract more female and retired workers to take jobs. At the same time, the UK government has announced its intention to increase the number of young people in higher education institutions to 50 percent. As UK employees have struggled to recruit highly skilled, qualified job applicants, they have sought to resolve the problem by recruiting staff from overseas. This trend has mainly been in respect of jobs in the catering and health sector, and according to some estimates approximately 48 percent of UK firms employ foreign staff.

The current rate of gross domestic product (GDP) is 3.5 percent and the inflation rate is 3.6 percent. Compared to the rest of Europe, unemployment is low and for the period 1991–5 averaged 9.1 percent.

POLITICAL AND REGULATORY OVERVIEW

For the period 1979–97 the UK had a Conservative government which was strongly influenced by Margaret Thatcher. During this period competition between individuals and organizations was encouraged in the development of an "enterprise" culture. As a result, unemployment rates increased, inflation reduced, and the gap in financial wealth between the richest and poorest sectors of society increased enormously. In May 1997, the Labour Party, under the leadership of Tony Blair, came to power in a landslide victory. New Labour, as the party became known, was elected on a platform of increased employment and improved public services. New Labour was reelected in June 2001 with a somewhat similar majority of seats in the House of Commons. Under New Labour, unemployment has fallen and an ambitious program of modernization has been introduced into the public sector. Modernization has included the setting of aggressive targets to increase diversity in the workforce and has brought more competition into public services, particularly health. PERFORMANCE MANAGEMENT systems have also increased in prominence in the public sector.

Prior to 1979, previous Labour governments passed a great deal of legislation regulating unfair dismissal, compensation for redundancy, equal opportunities and pay, maternity leave, time for union duties, and health and safety at work. In 1963 the Contracts of Employment Act obligated employers to provide a written statement of the principal terms and conditions of employment, so removing the informality of oral contracts and giving employees a minimum notice period based on years of service. The Redundancy Payments Act of 1965 compelled employers to make a payment based on earnings and length of service to employees declared redundant. In the period between 1990 and 1995, there were estimated to be over 4 million redundancies in the UK (Blyton and Turnbull, 1998).

Employment tribunals were established in 1965, primarily to resolve disputes regarding claims of unfair dismissal. Over the years their remit has extended to include almost 80 different kinds of claims such as disability discrimination, equal pay, working time, and breach of contract. Employment tribunals are normally chaired by a barrister or solicitor of at least seven years' standing and two representatives, one from the employee's side and one from the employer's. Since 1993 certain types of cases may be heard by the chairperson sitting alone. The Employers Protection (Consolidation) Act of 1978 permits dismissed employees to grieve a complaint of unfair dismissal to an employment tribunal. A conciliation officer from the Advisory Conciliation and Arbitration Service (ACAS, established in 1974) attempts to find a mutually agreeable solution to the grievance. ACAS has a staff of almost 750 people and is based in London and the regions.

Additional government bodies have been formed to enforce specific laws, such as the Equal Opportunities Commission (EOC) to insure compliance with the Sex Discrimination Act (SDA) 1975. The Commission for Racial Equality (CRE) was established under the Race Relations Act (RRA) 1976 to tackle direct and indirect racial discrimination and to promote racial equality. The RRA was strengthened by an Amendment Act in 2000, following the Macpherson Inquiry into the death of black teenager Stephen Lawrence, to extend protection against racial discrimination by public authorities. Health and safety in the workplace has been addressed by the Health and Safety at Work Act 1974. As well as attending to the physical hazards that may result in accidents or prove dangerous to health, employers are also obliged to safeguard individuals as far as possible from the ill-health effects of psychosocial hazards such as workplace stress. Since 1974, the Health and Safety at Work Regulations (1999) state that employers have a duty to operate a written health and safety policy; to assess the nature and scale of risks to health; and to apply principles of prevention.

As a member state of the European Union (EU), employment law and practices are influenced by EU directives and steps have been taken to harmonize UK practice in the social policy area with the rest of Europe. The Conservative government was highly resistant to commit to the basic employment rights and objectives embodied in the EU Social Charter (*see* EUROPEAN UNION), but following the 1997 change in government, there has been greater acceptance and adherence to the objectives of the Social Charter under New Labour. Notably, in January 2000 the UK government accepted legislation that required companies with more than 1,000 employees and at least 150 employees in each of two or more member states to set up a European works council (EWC) or some other European-level information and consultative procedure.

Prior to 1998, working hours were not subject to any regulation in the UK. The implementation of the Working Time Regulations 1998, a consequence of the EU Working Time Directive (93/104), regulates the number of hours worked including overtime averaged out over a period of four months or as long as 12 months if employees agree. The Regulations also address the issues of rest breaks and holiday entitlement. The EU has also been influential in protecting the rights of employees transferred from one employer to another as a result of corporate acquisition.

TRADE UNIONS

The UK has a strong tradition of trade unionism dating back to the onset of industrialization in the eighteenth century. Webb and Webb (1902) define trade unions as "a continuous association of wage-earners for the purpose of maintaining and improving the conditions of their employment." COLLECTIVE BARGAINING was a common feature of trade unionism during the twentieth century. However, the power of trade unions has been severely weakened over the years mainly as the result of a decline in manufacturing, prolonged high unemployment, and the extensive anti-union legislation introduced by the Thatcher government. Labour is less sympathetic to the trade union movement than it was in the past and, despite the party's return to power, the influence of trade unionism has not significantly increased. In 1975 trade union membership in the UK was 12.2 million; by 1996 membership had declined to 7.2 million, which amounts to about one-third of the workforce. In 1996 there were fewer than 250 strikes or stoppages due to industrial action. The

Trades Union Congress (TUC), established in 1868, is a voluntary body which in 1997 represented 74 trade unions. The TUC holds an annual conference and elects a General Council to make decisions and establish policy on a wide range of issues.

Human Resource Management Practices and Trends

The evolution of human resource management (HRM) in the UK has followed a similar course to the US (Sisson, 1994), with an increased alignment between HUMAN RESOURCE STRATEGY and business strategy. The changing nature of work and work organization will continue to present a number of challenges for HRM in the future and will require the development of new competencies to cope with the changes in work design (Sparrow, 2000).

Predictions from the Institute for Employment (2000) suggest that by 2009, 40 percent of jobs will fall into the managerial, professional, and associate professional class, with only 21 percent in elementary and operative jobs. In an interview for the *Guardian* newspaper in 2000, Graeme Leach, chief economist at the Institute of Directors, claimed that within 20 years one-quarter of the workforce would be temporary workers and that as many as 50 percent would work from home in some form. Furthermore, the mobility of the workforce is predicted to increase, along with greater polarization in cultural, educational, and material living standards (Scase, 1999). If UK employers are to remain competitive in a global economy, they will need to win what Kandola (2001) terms the "war for talent" and recruit more women and ethnic minorities. This will place an increasing emphasis on flexible working and a move in some sectors to VIRTUAL ORGANIZATION. The UK will also likely employ more immigrant labor, particularly from the EU member states.

The changing nature of work has already impacted on worker health. In the UK the average number of hours worked is 44.7 hours, which is significantly higher than in other EU states despite the Working Time Directive. This has been a contributing factor in the incidence of stress-related illness, which has become a growing problem in the UK in recent years. According to the UK Health and Safety Executive, stress-related absence accounts for 60 percent of all work absences and affects one in five employees (Cartwright, 2000). Apart from facing recruitment difficulties and skills shortages, employers will also need to meet the challenge of maintaining workplace health.

Bibliography

Blyton, P. and Turnbull, P. (1998). *The Dynamics of Employee Relations*. London: Macmillan.
Cartwright, S. (2000). Taking the pulse of executive health in the UK. *Academy of Management Executive*, 16–23.
Kandola, B. (2001). The future of diversity. Paper presented at the British Psychology Society Annual Conference, Glasgow, March.
Scase, R. (1999, August). *Britain Towards 2010: The Changing Business Environment*. London: Department of Trade and Industry.
Sisson, K. (1994). *Personnel Management: A Comprehensive Guide to Theory and Practice in Britain*. Oxford: Blackwell.
Sparrow, P. R. (2000). New employee behaviours, work and designs and forms of work organization: What is in store for the future of work? *Journal of Managerial Psychology*, 15 (3), 202–18.
Webb, S. and Webb, B. (1902). *The History of Trade Unionism*. London: Longman.

utilization analysis

Stuart A. Youngblood and Lawrence H. Peters

Utilization analysis is a description of the percentages of protected group members (e.g., non-white or female employees) employed within specific job classifications or job families (*see* JOB FAMILY) for a specific employer. A comparison of these percentages with those obtained from an availability analysis of the RELEVANT LABOR MARKET determines whether an employer has underutilized protected group members for specific jobs. Such analyses are often conducted proactively by employers to determine if voluntary AFFIRMATIVE ACTION programs are needed, or by employers who choose to do business with the federal government and are therefore required to do such analyses. Employers involved in employment DISCRIMINATION litigation may also conduct such analyses to determine if contested employment practices have resulted in DISPARATE IMPACT for protected class members.

Bibliography

Cascio, W. F. (1995). *Managing Human Resources: Productivity, Quality of Work Life, Profits*. New York: McGraw-Hill.

validity

Robert M. Guion and Chester A. Schriesheim

Validity, in psychometrics, is an inference drawn about the soundness of proposed interpretations of scores on instruments such as tests, ratings, and survey questionnaires. Historically, a shorthand use of language referred to the "validity of the instrument," implying that validity was a property of the measurement device itself. However, validity is now recognized as a property of inferences from, or interpretations of, the meanings of scores (Cronbach, 1971).

Validity is currently viewed as a singular or "unitarian" concept judged from a variety of accumulated information. Information needed in making judgments of validity includes that associated with the three interrelated lines of validity evidence, or aspects of validity, known as CONTENT VALIDITY, CRITERION-RELATED VALIDITY, and CONSTRUCT VALIDITY (see American Educational Research Association et al., 1999). Of these, the evidence most closely related to the "unified" concept of validity is construct validity. However, any information relevant to a particular interpretation of an instrument's score is appropriate evidence of validity, whether it fits one of the three categories or not. Guion (1997) classifies the lines of validity evidence as based on instrument development procedures, on reliability, on patterns of correlates, and on outcomes; inferences of validity depend on all such sources of evidence.

Evidence accumulated during instrument development includes the clarity of the intended interpretations of scores (i.e., the behaviors, attributes, or constructs to be measured) and the appropriateness of the content (including the degree of freedom or constraint imposed on possible responses, expected prior knowledge needed to understand and complete the instrument, and what is included and what is excluded in the instrument's content). Reliability evidence identifies sources of error (whether random or systematic) that may cast doubt on proposed interpretations of scores. Patterns of correlates consist of empirical evidence of the association between an instrument's scores and various criteria to which they theoretically should be related (given the proposed interpretations). Patterns of correlates include the traditional aspect of validity known as criterion-related validity. Sometimes the criterion is chosen for its theoretical relevance to the intended interpretation (i.e., as a test of construct validity), but sometimes it is chosen for practical outcomes that are expected given the intended meanings of scores for prediction or classification. Some evidence may favor a proposed interpretation, but some may not. The evaluation of validity depends on the *preponderance* of accumulated evidence supporting that interpretation and refuting alternative interpretations.

In general, many sources of evidence of validity are better than few, but as pointed out in STANDARDS FOR EDUCATIONAL AND PSYCHOLOGICAL TESTING, "a single line of solid evidence is preferable to numerous lines of evidence of questionable quality" (American Educational Research Association et al., 1999: 9). Note, however, that the *Standards* says a single *line* of evidence, not a single *piece* of evidence (such as an isolated correlation coefficient). Validity should not be confused with a validity coefficient.

See also *validity generalization*

Bibliography

American Educational Research Association, American Psychological Association, and National Council on Measurement in Education (1999). *Standards for Educational and Psychological Testing.* Washington, DC: American Educational Research Association.

Cronbach, L. J. (1971). Test validation. In R. L. Thorndike (ed.), *Educational Measurement*, 2nd edn. Washington, DC: American Council on Education.

Guion, R. M. (1997). *Assessment, Measurement, and Prediction for Personnel Decisions.* Hillsdale, NJ: Erlbaum.

validity generalization

Frank Schmidt

Validity generalization refers to the demonstration that the validities of abilities, aptitude tests, and other selection devices generalize across new settings, organizations, and geographic areas. The most important implication of this finding is that it is not necessary to conduct new validity studies in each setting.

Starting early in the twentieth century, selection psychologists observed considerable variability in validity findings from study to study even when the jobs and tests studied appeared to be similar or essentially identical. This variability showed itself both in statistical significance levels and in actual values of the observed validity coefficients. These findings led personnel psychologists to adopt the theory of situationally specific validity. This theory held that the nature of JOB PERFORMANCE differs from setting to setting and that the human observer or job analyst is too poor an information receiver and processor to detect these subtle but important differences. The conclusion was that validity is specific to each situation and must be estimated by a local validity study conducted in each situation or setting. This meant that validities were not generalizable. This led to the belief that a test that was shown to be valid for a job in Company A might well be completely invalid for an apparently identical job in Company B.

The methods used to test for validity generalization are the meta-analysis methods developed by John Hunter and Frank Schmidt (see Schmidt and Hunter, 1977). These methods have since been applied to many other research literatures in different social sciences, in medical research, in finance, in marketing, and in other areas (Hunter and Schmidt, 1990). John Callender, Hobart Osburn, Nambury Raju, and others have also made contributions to the development of validity generalization methods.

A validity generalization study is conducted in the following manner. First, all available validity studies (published and unpublished) are gathered and coded. The dependent variable is typically a measure of either overall job performance or performance in training. The *variance* of these observed validity estimates is then corrected for variability due to various statistical and measurement artifacts, the most important of which is usually sampling error. The mean of the observed validity coefficients is also corrected for downward biases created by measurement error in the performance measure and by range restriction. If 90 percent or more of the values in this corrected validity distribution are in the positive range, it is concluded that validity generalizes. Because not all artifacts that create variability across studies in validity estimates can be corrected for, these methods yield conservative estimates of the generalizability of validity.

Validity generalization studies have been conducted for over 500 research literatures in personnel selection. Predictors studied include cognitive ability tests, evaluations of education and experience, the EMPLOYMENT INTERVIEW, BIOGRAPHICAL HISTORY INVENTORIES, PERSONALITY TESTS, and INTEGRITY TESTING. In many cases, artifacts accounted for all variance across studies. For cognitive tests, the average amount of variance accounted for has been about 80 percent. In most cases, it has been found that validities generalize across settings, and that mean validity is higher than has typically been believed. However, in some cases (such as the point method of evaluating education and experience; *see* POINT JOB EVALUATION METHOD) it has been found that mean validity is quite low and does not generalize.

These methods have been used to determine whether validities generalize across different jobs, as well as across settings for the same job. Validities of cognitive ability tests, employment interviews, and integrity tests, for example, have been found to generalize across widely varying jobs.

The purpose of the research program in validity generalization was to empirically test the theory of situational validity. This research program showed that theory to be false. In retrospect, it is clear that acceptance of the theory of situational validity was based on an inadequate understanding of the extent to which statistical and measurement artifacts cause apparent but false variability in findings across small sample validity studies. The ability of validity generalization and meta-analysis methods to quantify and remove such artifactual variation has made these methods useful in many research areas beyond personnel selection.

Bibliography

Hunter, J. E. and Schmidt, F. L. (1990). *Methods of Meta-Analysis: Correcting Error and Bias in Research Findings.* Newbury Park, CA: Sage.

Schmidt, F. L. and Hunter, J. E. (1977). Development of a general solution to the problem of validity generalization. *Journal of Applied Psychology*, **62**, 529–40.

variable compensation

Gerald E. Ledford, Jr.

Variable compensation refers to forms of pay that vary according to specified criteria and are not fixed in base pay. This contrasts with MERIT PAY, which usually becomes part of the employee's salary. Variable compensation may take many diverse forms, each with its own purposes.

Different forms of variable pay are associated with different organizational levels. Variable compensation for individual performance can include COMMISSION-BASED PAY and manufacturing PIECEWORK. Variable pay for small group performance is team-based pay (*see* TEAM-BASED INCENTIVES). Variable pay at the organizational-unit level (e.g., a manufacturing plant) usually takes the form of GAINSHARING. Finally, pay for corporate performance usually takes the form of PROFIT SHARING, or, in the case of EXECUTIVE COMPENSATION, stock grants or options (*see* EMPLOYEE STOCK OWNERSHIP PLANS). This variety makes it difficult to generalize about characteristics of variable pay plans and organizational conditions affecting their consequences for employees and organizations. Clearly, however, many forms of variable pay are widely used by corporations in the US (Lawler, Mohrman, and Ledford, 1995) and elsewhere.

Variable pay usually is delivered in cash BONUSES. However, there are other options. The organization may vary BENEFITS, such as contributions to employee retirement accounts or profit-sharing plans. Stock options can be a lucrative reward for performance if the stock performs well during the option period.

Most variable pay plans are intended to achieve at least one of two key goals: increasing employee motivation and linking wages to the organization's ability to pay. Variable pay can motivate employees by varying employee wages with the performance of the employee or the organizational unit. To the extent that employees can affect the level of performance measured through the plan, and to the extent that increased performance is tied to rewards that employees value, employees will be motivated to increase their performance (Lawler, 1990). If the plan's metrics are built on financial returns or metrics that covary with financial returns, payments will reflect the organization's ability to pay (Schuster and Zingheim, 1992). This latter goal is often related to employment security, because it permits the organization to vary wages without layoffs. Japanese firms, for example, typically tie 30 to 40 percent of employee compensation to corporate profits.

Motivation and cost control goals often conflict. Unit performance, as measured by PRODUCTIVITY or quality, often changes independently of financial performance, which is largely dependent on market conditions. However, a profitability metric may not have any motivational value, because employees in large firms cannot influence profits significantly.

In general, the more closely variable pay is tied to individual performance, the greater is its motivational effect. This is because of the "line of sight" between employee behavior and monetary return. However, plans at the team and unit levels can also be motivational and can increase cooperation in interdependent work systems. Organizations often attempt to combine the advantages of local line of sight and ability to pay by complex formulas that, for example, pay out based on unit productivity if the company or business unit earns a profit (McAdams and Hawk, 1994).

Bibliography

Lawler, E. E., III (1990). *Strategic Pay: Aligning Organizational Strategies and Pay Systems*. San Francisco: Jossey-Bass.

Lawler, E. E., III, Mohrman, S. A., and Ledford, G. E., Jr. (1995). *Creating High Performance Organizations: Practices and Results of Employee Involvement and Total Quality Management in Fortune 1,000 Companies*. San Francisco: Jossey-Bass.

McAdams, J. L. and Hawk, E. J. (1994). *Organizational Performance and Rewards: 665 Experiences in Making the Link*. Scottsdale, AZ: American Compensation Association.

Schuster, J. R. and Zingheim, P. K. (1992). *The New Pay: Linking Employee and Organizational Performance*. New York: Lexington Books/Macmillan.

vestibule training method

J. Kevin Ford and Deidre Wasson

Vestibule training is a type of instruction using a vestibule, a small area away from the actual worksite, consisting of training equipment exactly duplicating the materials and equipment used on the job (Cascio, 1991). The purpose of vestibule training is to reproduce an actual work setting and place it under the trainer's control to allow for immediate and constructive feedback. Training vestibules are useful because they allow trainees to practice while avoiding personal injury and damage to expensive equipment without affecting production. Training effectiveness is dependent on the fidelity level of the simulated equipment (Saal and Knight, 1988) and the trainee's ability to behave as in his or her work setting (Goldstein, 1993).

See also *training*

Bibliography

Cascio, W. F. (1991). *Applied Psychology in Personnel Management*, 4th edn. Englewood Cliffs, NJ: Prentice-Hall.

Goldstein, I. L. (1993). *Training in Organizations: Needs Assessment, Development, and Evaluation*, 3rd edn. Pacific Grove, CA: Brooks/Cole.

Saal, F. E. and Knight, P. A. (1988). *Industrial/Organizational Psychology*. Pacific Grove, CA: Brooks/Cole.

veteran status

Ramona L. Paetzold

Veteran status is a protected category for some federal antidiscrimination purposes. One of the relevant pieces of legislation is the Veterans' Reemployment Rights Act, which provides that an employee who is called to active duty or inactive duty training must be released from employment-related obligations with a guarantee that he or she may return to the same position with seniority, pay, and other privileges that he or she would have had if the absence from work had not occurred. The US Supreme Court has ruled that the reemployment right lasts as long as the employee is in the armed services.

See also *Vietnam-Era Veterans' Readjustment Assistance Act of 1972*

Vietnam-Era Veterans' Readjustment Assistance Act of 1972

Vida Scarpello

The purpose of this Act, amended in 1974, is to encourage Vietnam veterans to use their general infantry (GI) educational benefits. The 1972 Vietnam Veterans' Act amends Title 38 of the US Code by improving on the GI Education Program so that more veterans take part in the program. At the time of its passage, the GI program's participation rate was more than 20 percent lower than it had been after World War II. Moreover, of the 5.6 million Vietnam-era veterans, 915,000 were discharged with less than a high school diploma or its equivalency. Despite those statistics, only 17.4 percent of the educationally disadvantaged Vietnam veterans had used the Veterans Administration educational benefits. Equally disturbing was evidence that 30 percent of high school graduates in the armed forces scored as poorly or worse on tests conducted by the armed forces as the average score of those who had not completed high school.

To encourage veteran participation in educational programs, this Act attempts to achieve parity with the World War II GI Bill entitlement level. It also provides for advance payment of the GI Bill educational assistance allowance at the start of the school term and prepayment of the allowance on the first of each month thereafter. Additionally, the Act expands on training options for receipt of GI benefits and also includes special employment assistance provisions. These provisions are contained in the Act's six titles.

Besides raising the rates for vocational rehabilitation, educational assistance, and special training allowances, Title I section (1) of the Vietnam Veterans' Act makes vocational rehabilitation training eligible for GI benefits. Title II specifies the rules and exceptions for advance payment of educational assistance or subsistence allowances. Title III provides for: (1) educational benefits for apprenticeship, ON-THE-JOB TRAINING, and correspondence courses; (2) special assistance to the educationally disadvantaged, including the granting of certain educational benefits to wives and widows of eligible veterans; and (3) methods of dealing with overcharges by educational institutions, discontinuance of allowances for programs or courses violating the US Code provisions, examination of records of educational institutions, and resolving false or misleading claims made by the educational institution, singularly or in combination with the veteran. Title IV includes various miscellaneous and technical amendments to the veterans' and war orphans' and widows' educational assistance programs.

Title V focuses on job and training counseling and placement services for veterans. This title mandates the promulgation of policies through a Veterans' Employment Service within the Department of Labor, so that veterans receive the maximum of existing and new employment opportunities and training programs. Title V further assigns all administrative and funding appropriation authority to the Secretary of Labor. The secretary is instructed to assign a representative of the Veterans' Employment Service to serve as the veterans' employment representative in each state. Assistant employment representatives may also be assigned (one per each 250,000 veterans in the state). These veterans' employment representatives are to be attached to the staffs of the state employment services, but are administratively responsible to the Secretary of Labor. Finally, Title V mandates employers to give special preference to the employment and training of disabled and Vietnam-era veterans.

Bibliography

Vietnam-Era Veterans' Readjustment Assistance Act of 1972 (1992). *Legislative History Public Law*, **92-539**, 4331–89.

Vietnam-Era Veterans' Readjustment Assistance Act of 1972, Public Law 92-540; 86 STAT. 1074 (1992). *Laws of the 92nd Congress, 2nd Session*, 1259–91.

virtual organization

Hadyn Bennett

Virtual organization represents a new form of organization which has emerged to enable firms to take advantage of technological developments, particularly in the area of information technology. Typically, virtual organization involves organizing along the value chain, with a number of independent organizations establishing a network in the form of a temporary alliance (Miles and Snow, 1992). Early examples of this form of virtual organization include the use by Nike (Miles and Snow, 1992) and Puma (Voss, 1996) of advanced information technology to establish global networks of organizations to produce sports shoes.

Simultaneously, such patterns of organization will enable companies to operate successfully in the increasingly complex product markets also being brought about by technology developments. For instance, Davidow and Malone (1992) have suggested that more complex patterns of demand will result in ever greater pressure for companies to deliver quickly and globally a high variety of customized products, differentiated not only on the basis of form and function, but also on the basis of services provided with the product and the ability to involve the customer in its design. Such developments, it is argued, have implications for companies' distribution systems and their internal organization as they strive to become more customer-oriented. This also has implications for relationships with suppliers, whereby supplier networks will have to become increasingly integrated with those of the customer to the point where a system of mutual dependency evolves (Davidow and Malone, 1992). Thus, in the terminology of Byrne and Brandt (1992), the virtual organization is "a temporary network of companies that come together quickly to exploit fast-changing opportunities," with such networks able "to share costs, skills and access to global markets, with each partner contributing what it is best at." Such networks, they argue, will be characterized by excellence (with each party bringing its core competence to the effort), use of information technology, opportunism (being established to take advantage of a specific market opportunity), trust (between partners), and the removal of the traditional boundaries of the company (with increased cooperation between competitors, suppliers, and customers making it ever more difficult to establish where one company ends and another begins).

Walters (2000) argues that the virtual organization therefore relies on an "integrated and coordinated approach towards knowledge, technology and relationship management" to enable companies to fully exploit the opportunities on offer. Meanwhile, a significant issue for the individual company lies in identifying its core competencies, where to deploy these along the value chain, and identifying complementary partnership opportunities (Byrne and Brandt, in Davidow and Malone, 1992).

Virtual Teamworking

Advances in information technology and the development of virtual organizations have also facilitated the development of virtual teamworking within organizations and within virtual organizations. Virtual teamworking occurs where team members communicate and work on projects, sharing resources, objectives, and interdependencies, but do not come into direct face-to-face contact, and may not even be employed by the same organization. It has become a subject of increasing interest (Geber, 1995; Greiner and Metes, 1995; Townsend, DeMarie, and Hendrickson, 1996), although there has been considerable disagreement on the ability of virtual teams to function effectively without face-to-face interaction (Geber, 1995; Levinson and Asahi, 1995). Virtual teamworking requires specific training in managing information technology, cross-cultural communication, and the management of remote interdependencies.

Bibliography

Davidow, W. H. and Malone, M. S. (1992). *The Virtual Corporation: Structuring and Revitalizing the Corporation for the 21st Century*. New York: HarperCollins.

Geber, B. (1995). Virtual teams. *Training*, 32 (4), 36–41.

Greiner, R. and Metes, G. (1995). *Going Virtual: Moving Your Organization into the 21st Century*. Upper Saddle River, NJ: Prentice-Hall.

Levinson, N. S. and Asahi, M. (1995). Cross-national alliances and interorganizational learning. *Organizational Dynamics*, 24 (2), 50–62.

Miles, R. E. and Snow, C. C. (1992). Causes of failure in network organizations. *California Management Review*, 34, 53–72.

Townsend, A. M., DeMarie, S. M., and Hendrickson, A. R. (1996). Are you ready for virtual teams? *HRMagazine*, 41 (9), 122–7.

Voss, H. (1996). Virtual organizations: The future is now. *Strategy and Leadership*, 24 (4), 12–18.

Walters, D. (2000). Virtual organizations: New lamps for old? *Management Decision*, 38 (6), 420–36.

vocational interest inventories

Paul M. Muchinsky

Vocational interest inventories are structured paper-and-pencil assessments which measure typological profiles of occupational interests. They are used primarily to assist individuals in making choices about vocational pursuits which are consistent with their values and preferences.

Vocational interest measurement has a lengthy history. It began nearly a century ago through the pioneering efforts of Parsons (1909), with later refinements by Berdie (1944). Early vocational interest inventories consisted of many statements (several hundred would not be uncommon) that describe occupational activities.

Examples would include "building a product or object with your hands" and "dealing with complex conceptual issues which have no correct solutions." Individuals are asked to indicate their preference for engaging in such activities, usually reflecting a three-point response format of liking, disliking, or being indifferent. The individual statements are organized into homogeneous categories, or dimensions, as reflected by, for example, interest in outdoor activities, artistic expressions, and interacting with other people. The individuals' responses to the interest inventory would be evaluated to yield a score on each dimension in the inventory. The typical inventory would include 10 to 15 such dimensions. Dimensions receiving high scores would reflect activities the individual likes to engage in; low scores would reflect activities with low interests.

Norm groups have been created by assessing the vocational interests of incumbent members of hundreds of occupations (e.g., firefighters). The vocational interests of each occupational group were aggregated to yield a "typical" vocational interest profile for the members of that occupation. Any given individual's interest profile would be compared with the various norm groups to identify the most similar profile matches. Individuals would be counseled to pursue vocations based on the similarity of profiles' shape to the vocational norm groups.

More recent vocational interest inventories contain fewer items because of advances in psychometric test construction principles. The profile-matching process has also been modified. Instead of making profile matches based on specific occupational groups (e.g., secretaries), larger vocational groupings (e.g., clerical occupations) are used to guide individual decision-making. Matches are no longer expressed in "either/or" terms, but in probabilistic terms. Some interest inventories can also be completed via a computer software program. Nevertheless, the basic logic and purpose of vocational interest inventories have remained unchanged over the years.

Major concepts of salience in vocational interest measurement include "differentiation" and "indecision." Differentiation refers to the strength or clarity of an individual's vocational interests. High differentiation is marked by a profile pattern of extreme highs and lows. Indecision reflects an undifferentiated pattern of vocational interests, which retard the individual's capacity to commit to a career choice.

Vocational interest inventories have been criticized because they generally fail to make accurate assessments of abilities, which are just as important as interests in determining vocational congruence. It is also a matter of debate as to *when* vocational interests begin to manifest themselves within the lifespan of the individual, as well as their stability in midlife. These issues have obvious implications for the accuracy of vocational interest measurement. There are also concerns about the capacity of vocational interest inventories to accurately assess the vocational interests of females, which have changed markedly over the past 30 years. Despite these issues, vocational interest inventories are frequently used to aid individuals in making career choices and to provide individuals with the opportunity to crystalize their own vocational interests. For the most part, extensive validation evidence reveals that vocational interests are related to vocational satisfaction (*see* JOB SATISFACTION) and stability, but not JOB PERFORMANCE within a vocation.

Classic references which the reader would find useful in understanding vocational interest measurement include Strong (1943), Super (1957), and Holland (1985). More recent references include Weiss (1983), Dawis (1992), and Muchinsky (1994). Specific vocational interest inventories of prominence include the Strong Interest Inventory (Harmon et al., 1994) and the Self-Directed Search (Holland, 1994). The best single source of current information on vocational interest inventories can be obtained through the Division of Counseling Psychology of the American Psychological Association.

Bibliography

Berdie, R. F. (1944). Factors related to vocational interests. *Psychological Bulletin*, **41**, 137–55.

Dawis, R. V. (1992). The individual differences tradition in counseling psychology. *Journal of Counseling Psychology*, **39**, 7–19.

Harmon, L. W., Hansen, J. I., Borgen, F. H., and Hammer, A. L. (1994). *Strong Applications and Technical Guide*. Palo Alto, CA: Consulting Psychologists Press.

Holland, J. L. (1985). *Making Vocational Choices: A Theory of Vocational Personalities and Work Environments*, 2nd edn. Englewood Cliffs, NJ: Prentice-Hall.

Holland, J. L. (1994). *The Self-Directed Search*. Odessa, FL: Psychological Assessment Resources.

Muchinsky, P. M. (1994). The influence of life history experiences on vocational interests and choices. In G. S. Stokes, M. D. Mumford, and W. C. Owens (eds.), *Biodata Handbook: Theory, Research, and Use of Biographical Information in Selection and Performance Prediction*. Palo Alto, CA: Consulting Psychologists Press.

Parsons, F. (1909). *Choosing a Vocation*. Boston: Houghton-Mifflin.

Strong, E. K., Jr. (1943). *Vocational Interests of Men and Women*. Stanford, CA: Stanford University Press.

Super, D. E. (1957). *The Psychology of Careers*. New York: Harper and Row.

Weiss, D. J. (ed.) (1983). *New Horizons in Testing*. San Diego, CA: Academic Press.

wage/pay policy line

Jerry M. Newman

Typically, an organization determines the market wage rate across its jobs. The line that illustrates the relationship between the external value of a job (from salary survey information) and the internal value of jobs (from job evaluation) represents the market line. A pay policy line portrays an organization's pay policy with respect to the market line. A lead policy means an organization chooses to pay above the market rate (and, therefore, above the market line) for designated jobs. A match policy is used when the goal is to pay at the market rate. A lag policy is used when the goal is to pay less for particular jobs (below the market line) than market competitors.

wage/pay/salary structure

Jerry M. Newman

A wage structure represents a series of pay grades (*see* PAY GRADE) that order jobs on the basis of worth. As such, it reflects the entire spectrum, from low-wage jobs to high-wage jobs. Organizations with rapid PROMOTION policies, but little pay advance for any given promotion, have relatively flat structures: the wage progression from grade to grade is small. Conversely, organizations with few promotion opportunities and sizable increases for any given promotion have steep structures.

wage and salary surveys

George F. Dreher

A wage and salary survey is a systematic way to collect information about the COMPENSATION systems of other employers (Milkovich and Newman, 1993: 223). This information can be collected using a variety of means, ranging from telephone interviews to mail survey instruments. The goal of such a survey is to generate estimates of the market wage for positions that tend to be common across a variety of employers (Rynes and Milkovich, 1986). These data are used to make decisions related to the EXTERNAL EQUITY/EXTERNAL COMPETITIVENESS of a company's salary structure.

Conducting such a survey requires a sequence of decisions that can have critical consequences for the results of the survey and the interpretability of the incoming data (Rynes and Milkovich, 1986). These decisions relate to such things as (1) defining the RELEVANT LABOR MARKET; (2) choosing benchmark jobs; (3) considering how to gather and interpret information about indirect forms of compensation and other attributes about the total pay system; and (4) making regional or international adjustments based upon the cost of living and/or currency exchange rates.

Incoming survey data from multiple organizations are typically combined in such a way that estimates can be made about the midpoints and pay rate ranges associated with a key job/benchmark job. These estimates about direct pay must be interpreted in relation to other compensation-related employer costs (particularly expenditures associated with employee BENEFITS).

Bibliography

Milkovich, G. T. and Newman, J. M. (1993). *Compensation*, 4th edn. Homewood, IL: Richard D. Irwin.

Rynes, S. L. and Milkovich, G. T. (1986). Wage surveys: Dispelling some myths about the "market wage." *Personnel Psychology*, **39**, 71–90.

waiver

Kelly A. Vaverek

A waiver, or release, is "an express or implied relinquishment of a legal right" (Black's Law Dictionary, 1990: 1590). With a waiver, an employee agrees to abandon claims against a current or former employer in exchange for a benefit, such as severance pay or continued employment. Waivers generally require the voluntary consent of an employee with full knowledge of the important, relevant facts. Absent a clear showing of duress or unconscionability, waivers are generally effective at barring contract-related claims against employers.

Bibliography

Black's Law Dictionary (1990). *Black's Law Dictionary*, 6th edn. St. Paul, MN: West Publishing.

Perritt, H. H., Jr. (1992). *Employee Dismissal Law and Practice*, 3rd edn. New York: John Wiley.

Walsh-Healy Act of 1936

Charles H. Fay

Under this prevailing wage law, any employer with a federal government contract for the manufacture or provision of materials, supplies, articles, or equipment in excess of $10,000 must pay wages found to be prevailing locally (as determined by the Department of Labor). The employer must in any case pay at least minimum wages under the FAIR LABOR STANDARDS ACT OF 1938. The impact of the Walsh-Healy Act (as is the case with the Services Contract Act and the DAVIS-BACON ACT OF 1931) is that employers pay local union rates.

Bibliography

Dixon, R. B. (2002). *Federal Wage and Hour Laws*, 2nd edn. Washington, DC: SHRM Foundation.

Shilling, D. (2001). *Human Resources and the Law: The Complete Guide with Supplement*. Englewood Cliffs, NJ: Prentice-Hall.

Steingold, F. S. (2003). *The Employer's Legal Handbook*, 5th edn. Berkeley, CA: Nolo Press.

Wards Cove Packing Co. v. *Antonio*, 490 US 642 (1989)

Leonard Bierman

In *Wards Cove* several minority cannery workers claimed that the employer's hiring and promotion practices constituted adverse impact (*see* DISPARATE IMPACT). The plaintiffs relied on statistics that cannery jobs were predominantly filled by minorities, while the higher-paying, skilled noncannery positions were predominantly filled by whites. The Supreme Court, in a decision later in part reversed by Congress, held that the relevant statistical comparison was between minorities holding skilled noncannery jobs and the RELEVANT LABOR MARKET that applied for those jobs. Therefore, simply showing a statistical disparity in an employer's workforce was not enough to establish a prima facie adverse impact discrimination case.

Washington v. *Davis*, 426 US 229 (1976)

Leonard Bierman

The validation of a qualifying test administered to applicants for positions as police officers is the subject of this case. *Test 21* was designed to test verbal ability, such as vocabulary, reading, and comprehension. In considering the validity of this test, the court considered whether the test was directly related to satisfactory progress in the police training program. The court held that it is permissible for the department to use a test for the purpose of predicting ability to master a training program, even if the test does not otherwise predict ability to perform on the job.

Watson v. *Fort Worth Bank and Trust*, 487 US 977 (1988)

Leonard Bierman

In *Watson* a black employee claimed that her employer's practice of committing promotion decisions to the subjective discretion of supervisory employees was discriminatory. The court held that DISPARATE IMPACT analysis is no less applicable to subjective employment criteria than to objective or standardized tests. Even a facially neutral practice without a discriminatory intent may result in effects that are indistinguishable from intentional discriminatory practices.

weighted application blanks

Craig J. Russell

Weighted application blanks (WABs) use empirical keying procedures (*see* BIOGRAPHICAL HISTORY INVENTORIES) to predict applicants' future JOB PERFORMANCE (England, 1961). Prediction tends to be very accurate, though keys need to be redeveloped approximately every three years. A WAB key assigns points to each possible answer to application blank questions, breaking down applicant answers into the smallest possible units of information (usually individual response options to each question). For example, "How much income did you earn from your last full-time position?" might have the following five response options: 1 = $15,000 to $25,000; 2 = $25,001 to $35,000; 3 = $35,001 to $45,000; 4 = $45,001 to $55,000; 5 = $55,001 to $65,000. A WAB key is typically developed using the vertical percentage difference method of empirical keying.

In theory, WABs accurately predict job performance for the same reasons as biographical history inventories (i.e., there is some causal relationship between the prior life event reflected in answers to application blanks and subsequent behavior). Problems occur when (1) keys developed from one population are applied to different populations and (2) applicants lie or distort answers to application blank questions. Population shifts can only be addressed through frequent development of new keys to keep up with changes in applicant pool experiences and the relationship of those experiences to subsequent job performance. Kluger, Reilly, and Russell (1991) found that when applicants "fake" answers, vertical percentage difference keying prevents them from obtaining an advantage (though predictive accuracy decreases).

Bibliography

England, G. W. (1961). Development and Use of Weighted Application Blanks. Dubuque, IA: Brown.

Kluger, A. N., Reilly, R. R., and Russell, C. J. (1991). Faking biodata tests: Are option-keyed instruments more resistant? *Journal of Applied Psychology*, **76**, 889–96.

wellness

James R. Terborg

Wellness is the balance of physical, emotional, social, spiritual, and intellectual health (O'Donnell, 1989). Programs at the worksite that help employees and their families make lifestyle changes to move toward a state of wellness are called wellness programs (Terborg, 1986). An important aspect of wellness is recognition that health is not simply the absence of morbidity and mortality. Rather, a continuum exists from death to optimal wellness with lack of illness as the midpoint. Wellness programs are more comprehensive and holistic than typical worksite HEALTH PROMOTION programs. Little research exists on the CONSTRUCT VALIDITY or PREDICTIVE VALIDITY of wellness.

Bibliography

O'Donnell, M. P. (1989). Definition of health promotion. Part III: Expanding the definition. *American Journal of Health Promotion*, **3**, 5.

Terborg, J. R. (1986). Health promotion at the worksite: A research challenge for personnel and human resources management. *Research in Personnel and Human Resources Management*, **4**, 225–67.

whistleblowing

Marcia P. Miceli

Whistleblowing has been defined as "the disclosure by organization members (former or current) of illegal, immoral, or illegitimate practices under the control of their employers, to persons or organizations that may be able to effect action" (Near and Miceli, 1985: 4). Terms such as "wrongful activity" and "questionable practice" refer to omissions as well as commissions; for example, when an organization fails to warn employees of workplace hazards.

Bibliography

Near, J. P. and Miceli, M. P. (1985). Organizational dissidence: The case of whistleblowing. *Journal of Business Ethics*, **4**, 1–16.

wildcat strikes

John C. Shearer

Wildcat strikes are strikes that occur during the term of a labor agreement in violation of that agreement (*see* STRIKE). Employees who participate in wildcat strikes are subject to discharge or discipline by the employer with the union able to do little or nothing in their defense. In the US, the existence of grievance procedures (*see* GRIEVANCE PROCEDURE) culminating in binding ARBITRATION makes wildcat strikes difficult to justify. Arbitration rulings have developed a general rule that employees should generally "obey now and grieve later."

women's career issues

Lisa Mainiero

Women's career issues are defined as those issues that affect the progress of women in organizations, such as barriers to entry, sex segregation of occupational CAREER PATHING, the CAREER STAGES experienced by women, how women cope with WORK–FAMILY CONFLICT, and the factors affecting women's ability to break through the upper executive level. This discussion will focus on the organizational issues that affect the promotion of women as a group.

INITIAL STAFFING AND PROMOTION DECISIONS

Women often are hired into staff rather than line positions and subsequently find it hard to move into a line or field capacity. When women are stuck in career paths that preclude line experiences, their prospects for career advancement are limited. Researchers Karen Lyness and Donna Thompson, in a comparative study of 69 men and women executives, found that women reported greater barriers to advancement, such as lack of culture fit and exclusion from informal networks, as well as the need to develop relationships to facilitate advancement (Lyness and Thompson, 2000). According to a Catalyst, Inc. survey, female executives cite obstacles to advancement such as: lack of general management or line experience (79% agreement), stereotypes about women's roles and abilities (72% agreement), and failure of top leaders to assume accountability for women's advancement (68% agreement). Additionally, 67% agreed that "commitment to personal or family responsibilities" was the most important challenge for women advancing to the upper levels (see Wellington, Kropf, and Gerkovich, 2003). Current Bureau of Labor statistics further confirm that even in 2003, fewer than 20% of women held positions at the upper executive level in Fortune 500 corporations, although progress is being made. Although women are being promoted, their promotions do not seem to be as vital and may lead to early CAREER PLATEAU.

CAREER PROGRESS ISSUES

Among those women who have broken through the GLASS CEILING to the upper executive level, defined as the vice president level or higher, studies of their career histories show five factors that affect their ability to become fast-tracked in their early career:

1. getting assigned to a high-visibility project;
2. demonstrating critical skills for effective JOB PERFORMANCE;
3. attracting top-level support;
4. displaying entrepreneurial initiative; and
5. accurately identifying what the company values (Mainiero, 1994).

In summary, substantial groups of women have not sufficiently progressed to the upper levels to permit tracking of their career progress in a coherent manner. Most women who have made it to the upper levels, or even middle levels, have experienced a variety of career issues along the way, such as difficulties in obtaining mentors, coping with corporate politics, and work–family conflicts that may impede their career progress. Of particular concern is the number of women "opting-out" of the workforce to care for family at crucial times in their career development.

Bibliography

Catalyst, 2004. Women in corporate leadership: 2003.

Lyness, K. S. and Thompson, D. E. (2000). Climbing the corporate ladder: Do female and male executives follow the same route? *Journal of Applied Psychology*, 85 (1), 86–101.

Mainiero, L. A. (1994). Getting anointed for advancement: The case of executive women. *Academy of Management Executive*, 8, 53–67.

Powell, G. N. and Mainiero, L. A. (1993). Crosscurrents in the river of time: Conceptualizing the complexities of women's careers. *Journal of Management*, 18, 215–38.

Wellington, S., Kropf, M. B., and Gerkovich, P. R. (2003). What's holding women back? *Harvard Business Review*, 18 (6), 18–20.

work constraints

Peter Villanova

Work constraints refer to a variety of situational factors that interfere with the translation of task-relevant INDIVIDUAL DIFFERENCES into corresponding differences in JOB PERFORMANCE. Although situational factors had long been recognized as potentially important determinants of performance, research and understanding of work constraints was hampered by the absence of a formal conceptual framework to organize work in the area. Systematic efforts to study work constraints in their own right appeared only in the early 1980s (see Peters and O'Connor, 1980). Peters and O'Connor conceptualized situational constraints as factors beyond the control of the individual that are part of the immediate work environment, and that prevent people from fully utilizing their capabilities.

Peters and O'Connor (1980) used the CRITICAL INCIDENTS TECHNIQUE to develop a fairly generalizable taxonomy of work constraints, and they provided a conceptual framework with testable propositions about the constraint construct. There are three hypotheses central to the Peters and O'Connor situational constraint framework. First, situational constraints were hypothesized to have direct negative effects on job performance and work attitudes (e.g., JOB SATISFACTION). Second, situational constraints were predicted to moderate the relationship between task-relevant individual differences and performance – individual differences would be expected to product a stronger relationship with performance in low-constraint as opposed to high-constraint conditions. Finally, the observed variability in performance was expected to be greater in low-constraint as opposed to high-constraint conditions. In effect, constraints were hypothesized to impose an artificial ceiling on potential performance and thereby impede the translation of task-relevant attributes into corresponding performance differences.

RESEARCH ON WORK CONSTRAINTS

Empirical support for these three predictions is mixed and largely inconclusive. One explanation for these mixed results, as Peters, O'Connor, and Eulberg (1985) noted, may be that few work settings have very severe work constraints. They characterized these low levels of constraints as resembling "nuisances" rather than obstacles. More significantly, they offered a set of boundary conditions to explain when constraints would be expected to influence performance, including: (1) the assignment of persons to tasks that demand the use of their abilities; (2) the maintenance of sufficiently demanding performance standards; (3) raters who do not somehow compensate for the presence of constraints in their ratings; and (4) that resources vary in their availability across individuals. Each of these is considered a necessary but not sufficient condition to sustain the hypothesized constraint–performance relationship. Information about these boundary conditions seems necessary to formulate confident conclusions.

PROBLEMS AND PROSPECTS

The consistent finding of small and seemingly negligible effects of constraints on performance (e.g., Olson and Borman, 1989) has stimulated interest in alternative conceptualizations of constraints and models of the constraint–performance

MANAGEMENT (and the emphasis it places on work system factors) and the potential practical significance promised from better understanding of constraints are likely to result in additional efforts to investigate this long-overlooked performance determinant.

Bibliography

Olson, D. M. and Borman, W. C. (1989). More evidence on relationships between the work environment and job performance. *Human Performance*, 2, 113–30.

Peters, L. H. and O'Connor, E. J. (1980). Situational constraints and work outcomes: The influences of a frequently overlooked construct. *Academy of Management Review*, 5, 391–7.

Peters, L. H., O'Connor, E. J., and Eulberg, J. R. (1985). Situational constraints: Sources, consequences, and future considerations. In G. R. Ferris and K. M. Rowland (eds.), *Research in Personnel and Human Resources Management*. Greenwich, CT: JAI Press.

Schoorman, F. D. and Schneider, B. (1988). *Facilitating Work Effectiveness*. Lexington, MA: Lexington Books.

Villanova, P. and Roman, M. A. (1993). A meta-analytic review of situational constraints and work-related outcomes: Alternative approaches to conceptualization. *Human Resource Management Review*, 3, 147–75.

work–family conflict

Stephen Poelmans

Work–family conflict is the term traditionally used to refer to a specific type of interrole conflict, between expectations and demands associated with the role of worker (employee, supervisor, self-employed) and the role of family member (parent, spouse, child). In order to include broader nonwork responsibilities and nontraditional families, the term work–life conflict has been proposed as a more inclusive term.

According to the dominant theory in the field, role theory (Kahn et al., 1964), conflicting expectations associated with different roles have detrimental effects for wellbeing. The reasoning is that both work and family claim time and energy. Work is an important source of income, financial security, and status. The family functions as a nucleus, where two partners find intimacy, support, and raise children. To make a choice between work and family is very difficult. Work and family are not independent (Kanter, 1977). As a consequence, conflicts may arise.

Another influential theory is spillover theory (Piotrkowski, 1979; Staines, 1980; Zedeck and Mosier, 1990). This theory assumes that time, tasks, attitudes, emotions, strain, and behavior spill over from one domain to the other (Greenhaus and Beutell, 1985). Contrary to role theory, spillover theory claims that work and family do not necessary have to conflict. They can influence each other in positive or negative ways. A distinction was made between the work-to-family conflict (work influencing family) and the family-to-work conflict (family influencing work) (Greenhaus and Beutell, 1985; Greenhaus, 1988; Gutek, Searle, and Klepa, 1991; Frone, Russell, and Cooper, 1992) and between three types of work–family conflict:

1 strain-based work–family conflict, or the spillover of stress (e.g., being irritable, exhausted after work);
2 time-based work–family conflict, or the competition for scarce time (e.g., working extra hours, working at home, arriving late at work);
3 behavior-based work–family conflict, or the fact that behavior that is appropriate in one domain may not be appropriate in another domain (e.g., a police officer controlling and disciplining his children).

A general, integrative framework of the work–family interface was offered by Frone, Yardley, and Markel (1997). It integrates social support, time commitment, and overload, both at work and in the family, as antecedents, work–family conflict and family–work conflict as core variables, and distress, dissatisfaction, and performance as outcomes. This model gives a good overview of the most established antecedents and consequences of work–family conflict. Only a few studies proffer theories that challenge or integrate the basic pretences of role theory and spillover theory, such as conservation of resources theory (Hobfoll, 1989; Grandey and Cropanzano, 1999; Rosenbaum and Cohen, 1999), self-discrepancy theory (Higgins et al., 1986; Polasky and Holahan, 1998), social identity theory (Tajfel and Turner, 1985; Lobel,

1992), expansionist theory of gender, work, and family (Barnett and Hyde, 2001), the work/family border theory (Clark, 2000), and the decision-process theory (Poelmans, 2004). Probably one of the most important challenges of the field is to test the generalizability of the concepts suggested above in different cultural settings, a stream of research that has only recently started to develop (Poelmans, 2003).

Bibliography

Barnett, R. C. and Hyde, J. S. (2001). Women, men, work, and family: An expansionist theory. *American Psychologist*, 56 (10), 781–96.

Clark, C. S. (2000). Work/family border theory: A new theory of work/family balance. *Human Relations*, 53 (6), 747–70.

Frone, M. R., Russell, M., and Cooper, M. L. (1992). Antecedents and outcomes of work–family conflict: Testing a model of the work–family interface. *Journal of Applied Psychology*, 77 (1), 65–78.

Frone, M. R., Yardley, J., and Markel, K. S. (1997). Developing and testing an integrative model of the work–family interface. *Journal of Vocational Behavior*, 50, 145–67.

Grandey, A. A. and Cropanzano, R. (1999). The conservation of resources model applied to work–family conflict and strain. *Journal of Vocational Behavior*, 54, 350–70.

Greenhaus, J. H. (1988). The intersection of work and family roles: Individual, interpersonal, and organizational issues. *Journal of Social Behavior and Personality*, 3 (4), 23–44.

Greenhaus, J. H. and Beutell, N. (1985). Sources of conflict between work and family roles. *Academy of Management Review*, 10, 76–88.

Gutek, B. A., Searle, S., and Klepa, L. (1991). Rational versus gender role explanations for work–family conflict. *Journal of Applied Psychology*, 76 (4), 560–8.

Higgins, E. T., Bond, R. N., Klein, R., and Strauman, T. (1986). Self-discrepancies and emotional vulnerability: How magnitude, accessibility, and type of discrepancy influence affect. *Journal of Personality and Social Psychology*, 51, 5–15.

Hobfoll, S. E. (1989). Conservation of resources: A new attempt at conceptualizing stress. *American Psychologist*, 44, 513–24.

Kahn, R. L., Wolfe, D. M., Quinn, R. P., Snoek, J. D., and Rosenthal, R. A. (1964). *Organizational Stress: Studies in Role Conflict and Ambiguity*. New York: John Wiley.

Kanter, R. (1977). *Work and Family in the United States: A Critical Review and Agenda for Research and Policy*. New York: Sage.

Katz, D. and Kahn, R. L. (1978). *The Social Psychology of Organizations*, 2nd edn. New York: John Wiley.

Lobel, S. A. (1992). A value-laden approach to integrating work and family life. *Human Resource Management*, 31 (3), 249–65.

Piotrkowski, C. S. (1979). *Work and the Family System*. New York: Free Press.

Poelmans, S. A. Y. (2003). The multi-level "fit" model of work and family. *International Journal of Cross-Cultural Management*, 3, 3.

Poelmans, S. A. Y. (2004). The decision process theory of work and family. In E. E. Kossek and S. Lambert (eds.), *Managing Work–Life Integration in Organizations: Future Directions for Research and Practice*. Mahwah NJ: Erlbaum.

Polasky, L. J. and Holahan, C. K. (1998). Maternal self-discrepancies, interrole conflict, and negative affect among married professional women with children. *Journal of Family Psychology*, 12 (3), 388–401.

Rosenbaum, M. and Cohen, E. (1999). Equalitarian marriages, spousal support, resourcefulness, and psychological distress among Israeli working women. *Journal of Vocational Behavior*, 54, 102–13.

Staines, G. L. (1980). Spill-over versus compensation: A review of the literature on the relationship between work and non-work. *Human Relations*, 33, 11–129.

Tajfel, H. C. and Turner, J. C. (1985). The social identity theory of intergroup behavior. In S. Worchel and W. G. Austin (eds.), *Psychology of Intergroup Relations*, 2nd edn. Chicago: Nelson-Hall, pp. 7–24.

Zedeck, S. and Mosier, K. L. (1990). Work in the family and employing organization. *American Psychologist*, 45 (2), 240–51.

See also *work–nonwork role issues*

work–nonwork role issues

Ellen Ernst Kossek

Work–nonwork role issues involve individuals' perceptions of role conflict between family roles and work roles (*see* WORK–FAMILY CONFLICT). Theories linking work and family roles have tended to focus on the extent to which they are experienced as structurally differentiated, and whether connections are positive, negative, or nonrelated (Greenhaus, 1989). One dominant view, the segmentation perspective, suggests that work and family roles are generally independent, do not affect one another, and are distinct in that an individual can successfully function in one environment without any impact on the other (Barling, 1994). An individual's subjective reactions to objective conditions in one domain do not affect outcomes in the other.

In contrast, the spillover framework predicts that the effects of each role, both positive and negative, can carry over to the other (Zedeck and Mosier, 1990). Research on spillover can be organized along two competing perspectives. The scarcity view assumes that individuals have limited time and energy, and competing demands generally result in role overload and conflict, indicating negative spillover (Clay, 1995). The enhancement view argues that increased support, self-esteem, and skill development from participating in multiple roles outweigh the costs, and positive spillover from participating in multiple roles is generally expected (Clay, 1995).

Bibliography

Barling, J. (1994). Work and family: In search of more effective workplace interventions. In C. Cooper and D. Rousseau (eds.), *Trends in Organizational Behavior*, vol. 1. New York: John Wiley.

Clay, R. A. (1995). Working mothers: Happy or haggard? *APA Monitor*, **26** (1), 37.

Greenhaus, J. H. (1989). The intersection of work and family roles: Individual, interpersonal, and organizational issues. In E. B. Goldsmith (ed.), *Work and Family: Theory, Research, and Applications*. Newbury Park, CA: Sage.

Zedeck, S. and Mosier, K. L. (1990). Work in the family and employing organization. *American Psychologist*, **45**, 240–51.

work samples

Richard Klimoski

Work samples (or job sample tests) require an applicant to perform a selected subset of tasks derived from the job of interest (*see* JOB ANALYSIS). Procedures are standardized and scoring is usually developed with the aid of experts (Schmitt and Klimoski, 1992). Work sample tests have been used since the first quarter of the twentieth century (Asher and Sciarrino, 1974).

The logic underlying work samples reflects the belief that *if* the behaviors and performance sampled in the assessment context are as similar as possible to the behaviors and performance required by the target job, it would require minimal inferences to judge a person's ability or capacity. Work sample tests are usually defensible on content-valid bases (*see* CONTENT VALIDITY), and they look appropriate to the general public, to examinees, and to the courts (*see* FACE VALIDITY). Hence, they are an attractive option in testing (Schmitt and Klimoski, 1992).

Work samples are costly and time-consuming to develop and administer. Moreover, Arnold et al. (1982), in their study dealing with the selection of workers in the steel industry, pointed out that such tests can be potentially dangerous to applicants.

In the context of PERSONNEL SELECTION, reviews have usually found evidence of respectable CRITERION-RELATED VALIDITY (Hunter and Hunter, 1984; Schmidt et al., 1984). Furthermore, Schmidt et al. (1977) reported that such tests had less adverse impact (*see* DISPARATE IMPACT) than paper-and-pencil tests in the assessment of competence in the metalworking trades. Work sample tests have also been used successfully for identifying workers who would be suitable for training (Robertson and Downs, 1989). Finally, work sample tests have been created to serve as criterion measures for research on personnel selection systems (Borman, 1992).

Bibliography

Arnold, J. D., Rouschenberger, J. M., Souble, W. G., and Guion, R. M. (1982). Validation and utility of a strength test for selecting steelworkers. *Journal of Applied Psychology*, **67**, 588–604.

Asher, J. J. and Sciarrino, J. A. (1974). Realistic work sample tests: A review. *Personnel Psychology*, **27**, 519–33.

Borman, W. C. (1992). Job behavior, performance and effectiveness. In M. D. Dunnette and L. M. Hough (eds.), *Handbook of Industrial and Organizational Psychology*. Palo Alto, CA: Consulting Psychologists Press.

Hunter, J. E. and Hunter, R. F. (1984). Validity and utility of alternative predictors of job performance. *Psychological Bulletin*, **96**, 72–98.

Robertson, I. T. and Downs, S. (1989). Work sample tests of trainability: A meta-analysis. *Journal of Applied Psychology*, **74**, 402–10.

Schmidt, F. L., Gooding, R. Z., Noe, R. A., and Kirsch, M. P. (1984). Meta-analysis of validity studies published between 1964 and 1982 and the investigation of study characteristics. *Personnel Psychology*, 37, 407–22.

Schmidt, F. L., Greenthal, A. L., Hunter, J. E., Berner, J. G., and Seaton, F. W. (1977). Job sample vs. paper-and-pencil trades and technical tests: Adverse impact and examinee attitudes. *Personnel Psychology*, 30, 187–97.

Schmitt, N. and Klimoski, R. J. (1992). *Research Methods in Human Resource Management*. Cincinnati, OH: South-Western Publishing.

work sampling

James B. Shaw

Work sampling is a method of collecting job data in which samples of work activity are observed and recorded at predetermined time intervals. Work sample data may be collected by: (1) observing employees doing the job and recording their actions at given time intervals; (2) videotaping employees, then observing their actions at predetermined times throughout the tape; or (3) asking employees to stop work at a specific time and to write down what they are doing. Regardless of the method used, it is essential that a sufficient number of job incumbents are included in the work sample project. This will help to insure that the resultant data reliably reflect the job under study.

The output of a work sample analysis is usually a list of activities performed, accompanied by the percentage of total time spent on each activity. In general, work samples can be collected only on those aspects of a job that can be readily observed. However, if job incumbents are sufficiently trained, they may be able to accurately report on less observable, mental and communication activities. Work sampling is useful in setting time standards for the performance of job activities (*see* TIME AND MOTION STUDY) and can also help to identify situations where employees spend an inappropriate amount of time performing activities that have little connection with efficient task performance.

work values

Bruce M. Meglino

Values represent a social system's effort to encourage its members to behave in ways that foster the system's welfare. As such, values are enduring beliefs about how an individual *ought* to behave. The type of values and their specificity depend on the particular social system (e.g., society, a formal organization, one's group). The subset of values that are relevant to the workplace are called work values. This definition differs from the "value" one places on objects (Locke, 1991), although one's work values are important standards for making such evaluations.

Values found to be important in the workplace include achievement, concern for others, honesty, working hard, positive outlook, helping others, and fairness (Ravlin and Meglino, 1987), although certain organizations may endorse more specific values (e.g., customer service). Because values describe socially desirable behavior, one's choice of behavior depends on the centrality (i.e., relative importance) of his or her specific values. Values are, therefore, held in hierarchical form. Values can characterize individuals as well as social systems such as organizations (Meglino and Ravlin, 1998). An organization's system of values is said to underlie its organizational culture. Organizations impart their values on individuals through avenues that include ORGANIZATIONAL SOCIALIZATION. Value similarity among organizational members is also enhanced through a process that reflects the ATTRACTION–SELECTION–ATTRITION model.

Work values are also assessed as part of PERSONNEL SELECTION and PROMOTION processes. Work values affect one's perception and interpretation of environmental stimuli and encourage individuals to behave in accordance with their more dominant values (Ravlin and Meglino, 1987). Values also affect relationships through the process of value congruence. The more an individual's value system is similar or congruent with that of another person or work system, the more his or her interactions with that person and within that work system are likely to be positive (Meglino, Ravlin, and Adkins, 1989).

See also *work values assessment*

Bibliography

Locke, E. A. (1991). The motivation sequence, the motivation hub, and the motivation core. *Organizational Behavior and Human Decision Processes*, **50**, 288–99.
Meglino, B. M. and Ravlin, E. C. (1998). Individual values in organizations: Concepts, controversies, and research. *Journal of Management*, **24**, 351–89.
Meglino, B. M., Ravlin, E. C., and Adkins, C. L. (1989). A work values approach to corporate culture: A field test of the value congruence process and its relationship to individual outcomes. *Journal of Applied Psychology*, **74**, 424–32.
Ravlin, E. C. and Meglino, B. M. (1987). Issues in work values measurement. In W. C. Frederick (ed.), *Research in Corporate Social Performance and Policy*, vol. 9. Greenwich, CT: JAI Press.

work values assessment

Bruce M. Meglino

Because values are socially desirable constructs (*see* WORK VALUES), assessment needs to control for RATING ERRORS resulting from individuals' desires to present themselves in a favorable light (socially desirable response). This has led to the use of "ipsative" rating scales. Such scales require each person to identify the relative importance (to him or her) of those values listed on the measure. In this sense, ipsative measures require persons to identify more central versus more peripheral values, and this helps to capture the hierarchical rank ordering of values (Ravlin and Meglino, 1987). Indices of the *similarity* of these rank orderings (value congruence) have been used to assess how well an individual's values *fit* with important organizational values or with the values held by other persons (Meglino and Ravlin, 1998). The centrality of a particular value in an individual's hierarchy has also been used to predict specific behaviors.

Frequently used ipsative measures of work values include the Organizational Culture Profile (OCP; O'Reilly, Chatman, and Caldwell, 1991) and the Comparative Emphasis Scale (CES; Ravlin and Meglino, 1987). The OCP requires respondents to sort 54 value statements into nine categories based on their desirability. When used to assess individuals' fit with an organization, findings indicate that the OCP predicts JOB SATISFACTION, organizational commitment, and EMPLOYEE TURNOVER. The CES uses a forced-choice format that requires respondents to choose between 24 pairs of equally desirable statements representing four different values. When used to assess individuals' fit with their supervisor, the CES has been found to predict job satisfaction, organizational commitment, and attendance (Meglino, Ravlin, and Adkins, 1989). Also, the dominance of specific CES values (e.g., concern for others) has been found to predict value-related behaviors (e.g., helping coworkers with personal problems; McNeely and Meglino, 1994).

Bibliography

McNeely, B. L. and Meglino, B. M. (1994). The role of dispositional and situational antecedents in prosocial organizational behavior: An examination of the intended beneficiaries of prosocial behavior. *Journal of Applied Psychology*, **79**, 836–44.
Meglino, B. M. and Ravlin, E. C. (1998). Individual values in organizations: Concepts, controversies, and research. *Journal of Management*, **24**, 351–89.
Meglino, B. M., Ravlin, E. C., and Adkins, C. L. (1989). A work values approach to corporate culture: A field test of the value congruence process and its relationship to individual outcomes. *Journal of Applied Psychology*, **74**, 424–32.
O'Reilly, C. A., III, Chatman, J., and Caldwell, D. F. (1991). People and organizational culture: A profile comparison approach to assessing person–organization fit. *Academy of Management Journal*, **34**, 487–516.
Ravlin, E. C. and Meglino, B. M. (1987). Issues in work values measurement. In W. C. Frederick (ed.), *Research in Corporate Social Performance and Policy*, vol. 9. Greenwich, CT: JAI Press.

Worker Adjustment and Retraining Notification Act of 1988

Vida Scarpello

The extensive economic restructuring of industries during the late 1970s and massive worker terminations due to permanent plant closings and workforce reduction motivated unions to lobby for the passage of the Worker Adjustment and Retraining Notification Act (WARN). Nevertheless, at the time of its passage, the law affected only 2 percent of the businesses in the US and only those businesses that employ 100 or more employees. Moreover, a business is exempt from the law if the need to shut down suddenly has not been foreseen (Congressional Record – Senate, June 22, 1988: 15514).

During Senate debates on the bill, Senator Hatch and other Republicans saw dire consequences for employer welfare and US trade if the law should pass. Senator Dole, on the other hand, noted that most unions have already taken care of this problem through COLLECTIVE BARGAINING, and, therefore, the issue was simply politics, as the plant closing legislation was linked to the trade bill, which Congress was ready to pass. To Dole's charge, Senator Kennedy countered with: "if companies had begun giving notice after Congress urged them to do so in the Trade Act of 1974, we would not be here today" (Congressional Record – Senate: 11516). Kennedy also stated that advance notice: (1) is necessary to insure successful worker adjustment; (2) saves the government money (i.e., according to studies by the Office of Technology Assessment and the Economic Policy Institute, savings are estimated to be between $257 and $400 million each year); (3) makes money appropriated for adjustment efforts go further, resulting in more effective reemployment; and (4) assures fairness for American workers. In strong support of Senator Kennedy, Republican Senator Quayle stated (Congressional Record – Senate: 15519): "As a matter of fact, any CEO in this country that does not give notice and could have – and there are exceptions in this bill – ought to be fired.... That is the only common, decent thing that an employer can do." Amid these debates was the urgency to move toward the passage of legislation perceived by many senators to be more significant for the country – the trade bill. Besides, worker notification did not seem to affect trade negatively in countries with such laws: Canada, Germany, France, the UK, Sweden, Japan, and Taiwan (Congressional Record – House, July 13: 17849).

WARN mandates that employers give a 60-day written notice, to specified parties, of their intent to permanently or temporarily shut down single or multiple facilities within a single site of employment, or to permanently reduce the size of the workforce; WARN applies in situations where the shutdown results in employment loss for at least 50 full-time employees or a mass layoff of at least six months' duration that affects at least 500 employees (or at least 50 employees, if they comprise one-third of the full-time workforce). Employers are subject to this Act if they employ 100 or more employees, who in the aggregate work 4,000 or more hours per week (excluding overtime).

Section 2(a)(6) of the Act defines *employment loss* as involuntary loss of employment through no fault of the employee. *Layoff* is defined as that exceeding six months, or as more than 50 percent reduction of hours of work during any six-month period. In the case of a sale of part or all of the business, the seller becomes responsible for providing notice of plant closing or mass layoff. Finally, the Act does not consider employees to have suffered an employment loss if the employer offers a transfer within a reasonable commuting distance with no more than a six-month break in employment or if the employer offers a transfer to any site, regardless of distance, if the employee accepts the offer within 30 days of the offer, the closing, or the layoff, whichever is later.

The closing or mass layoff notifications must be given to: (1) each union representing the affected employees or each employee, if not represented by a union; (2) the dislocated worker unit of the state in which the facility exists; and (3) the chief elected official of the unit of local government within which the closing or layoff is to occur, or, in the case of multiple unit closings, the unit of local government to which the employer paid the highest taxes for the preceding year.

Exempted from this law are employees hired for a limited employment period, or if the closing or layoff constitutes a STRIKE or LOCKOUT not intended to evade the requirements of this Act.

The WARN Act is enforced through the court system. The Act, however, imposes the civil penalties that may be charged against the employer. For failure to notify employees or their representatives, the penalty is backpay for each employee for each day of the violation, up to 60 days. For failure to notify a unit of local government, the penalty is not more than $500 per day. The court, however, is instructed to eliminate the latter penalty if the employer pays the employee liability amounts within three weeks from the date of the order to shut down or lay off. The law does not assess a penalty for failure to notify the state's dislocated worker unit.

workers' compensation benefits

John F. Burton, Jr. and James R. Chelius

Workers' compensation programs provide benefits to workers who experience work-related injuries or diseases. The benefits can include medical care, rehabilitation services, and cash benefits. In some cases, the cash benefits include compensation for a portion of noneconomic losses resulting from permanent consequences of the injuries. The primary purpose of the cash benefits is to replace a portion of lost earnings. The payments are for temporary or permanent disability and for total or partial disability, plus survivors' benefits in the case of death. In the US, benefits are established by each of the states and are tax-free. US cash benefits typically are two-thirds of the worker's pre-injury wages up to a weekly benefit amount, which in 2003 ranged from $331 in Mississippi to $1,103 in Iowa.

See also *workers' compensation law*

Bibliography

US Chamber of Commerce (2003). *Analysis of Workers' Compensation Laws*. Washington, DC: US Chamber of Commerce.

US Department of Labor, Employment Standards Administration, Office of Workers' Compensation Programs (2003). *State Workers' Compensation Laws: January 2003*. Washington, DC: US Department of Labor. (Updates through www.workerscompresources.com.)

workers' compensation law

John F. Burton, Jr. and James R. Chelius

Workers' compensation programs, which exist in virtually every country, provide medical care, rehabilitation services, and cash benefits to workers who experience work-related injuries and diseases. They are the oldest and most widespread legally mandated social insurance program. In addition to providing security for injured workers, many workers' compensation programs are designed to improve workplace safety and health through financial incentives that encourage employers to invest in prevention. Benefits typically include payment of full medical care, a portion of lost earnings, and, in some instances, a portion of noneconomic losses resulting from the permanent consequences of the injury (*see* WORKERS' COMPENSATION BENEFITS).

Workers' compensation is the original no-fault system, in that it provides benefits to injured workers without regard to who was responsible for causing the injury. The compromise embodied in workers' compensation is that injured workers are provided benefits without the need to demonstrate employer negligence, while the employer's liability is limited to the benefits established by the workers' compensation statute. This exclusive remedy rule is found in some countries, such as the US, while in other countries, such as the UK, injured workers may be able to recover additional amounts through a lawsuit if employer negligence can be demonstrated.

National laws establish workers' compensation programs, except in the US, Canada, and Australia, where the states or provinces control the programs. Workers' compensation in some countries is a separate program that provides cash and medical benefits, as in the US; in some countries, workers' compensation provides the cash benefits and the medical benefits are provided through the general healthcare system, as in the UK and Canada; and in some countries, the benefits for work-related injuries and diseases are provided through the general program for disabled persons, as in the Netherlands. The benefit obligation is guaranteed through a public fund, private insurance, or self-insurance, depending on the jurisdiction. The system is typically funded by employer contributions, which are either the same percentage for all employers, the same for all employers in an industry, or are related to individual employer experience. Although employers nominally fund workers' compensation, evidence indicates that employees usually "pay" for much of this insurance coverage in the form of wages that are lower than they would be without the program.

Bibliography

Leigh, J. P. Markowitz, S., Fahs, M., and Landrigan, P. (2000). *Costs of Occupational Injuries and Illnesses.* Ann Arbor, MI: University of Michigan Press.

Thomason, T., Hyatt, D., and Burton, J. F. (1998). *New Approaches to Disability in the Workplace.* Ithaca, NY: Industrial Relations Research Association and Cornell University Press.

US Department of Health and Human Services, Social Security Administration (1999). *Social Security Programs Throughout the World, 1999.* Washington, DC: Social Security Administration. (Updates through www.ssa.gov/policy/docs/progdesc/ssptw.)

Williams, C. T., Reno, V. P., and Burton, J. F. (2003). *Workers' Compensation: Benefits, Coverage, and Costs, 2001.* Washington, DC: National Academy of Social Insurance. (Updates through www.nasi.org.)

workforce demographics

R. Roosevelt Thomas, Jr. and Catherine A. Ouellette

Demographics are statistical descriptions of populations. Workforce demographics describe a particular collection of attributes deemed to impact workplace functioning. For example, the landmark Hudson Institute report, *Workforce 2000: Work and Workers for the 21st Century* (Johnston and Packer, 1987), discusses trends of four demographic characteristics: age, gender, nationality/immigrant status, and race. Additionally, the term workforce demographics is used in conjunction with DIVERSITY, which refers to various attributes used to identify people as similar or different. Some of the more common attributes on which similarity is judged include PHYSICAL ABILITIES, SEXUAL ORIENTATION, and RELIGION.

Bibliography

Johnston, N. B. and Packer, A. E. (1987). *Workforce 2000: Work and Workers for the 21st Century.* Indianapolis, IN: Hudson Institute.

Loden, M. and Rosener, J. B. (1991). *Workforce America! Managing Employee Diversity as a Vital Resource.* Homewood, IL: Business One Irwin.

Thomas, R. R., Jr. (1991). *Beyond Race and Gender: Unleashing the Power of Your Total Workforce by Managing Diversity.* New York: AMACOM.

workforce flexibility

John D. Keiser and Gerald R. Ferris

Workforce flexibility refers to an organization's ability to adapt its human resources in a manner appropriate to increasingly changing environmental conditions. To be flexible, an organization has the ability to adapt its workforce to new organizational structures, and workers have the background and ability to learn new skills and adapt to new functions (Dalton, 1998). This means two things; first, that firms can quickly and effectively meet human resource staffing needs with qualified and capable workers; and second, that workers have multiple skills, both technical and interpersonal, with the ability to learn more as new demands require. Moreover, workforce flexibility requires that employees have the ability to adapt with relatively little management supervision, instead relying on self-managing mechanisms (*see* EMPLOYEE EMPOWERMENT; SELF-MANAGING TEAMS). Closely related to workforce flexibility are the concepts BUSINESS PROCESS REENGINEERING, CROSS-TRAINING, contingent workers (*see* CONTINGENT EMPLOYMENT), and organizational cultures. In defining workforce flexibility we first examine the transformation of organizational contexts which creates the need for workforce flexibility, and then we review some of the human resource systems that need to be put in place or modified in order to support a flexible workforce.

Transformation of Organizational Contexts

Realizing that traditional organizational structures may not be efficient for global market competition, many organizations have taken on considerable changes in size, structure, and designs of organizations and work systems.

Downsizing. A common strategy of American businesses since the 1980s has been reducing the size of an organization's workforce, more commonly known as DOWNSIZING. Two predominant reasons explain this: (1) to lower overhead costs by eliminating unnecessary positions; and (2) to increase the organization's ability to react quickly to environmental conditions. Combined, lower overhead and quicker responsiveness allow the organization better competitive positioning. Yet the actual task of reducing workforces proved to be a daunting challenge, as evidenced by the disappointing results found by many firms pursuing this strategy (Cascio, 1993). Too often the results of downsizing initiatives didn't lead to smaller organizations doing things more efficiently, but instead the downsized organizations were merely the same organizations doing things the same way, only with fewer workers ill-equipped to handle the transition.

Restructuring, redesigning, and reengineering. Organizational change can include restructuring communication channels of the organization, redesigning the hierarchical chains of command, or changing the technologies so that work itself is performed differently. Definitions of what constitutes organizational restructuring are plentiful and varied, but a helpful approach for understanding it is to ask the question, "If we were to build the organization from the ground up, how would we do it?" It requires abandoning the status quo altogether to design a way of doing things that would not be hindered by existing practices, individuals, or other sacred cows. Characteristics of redesigned companies emphasize greater HORIZONTAL MANAGEMENT with fewer organizational levels, more direct interaction between organizational members (thereby deemphasizing formal chains of command), and more boundary personnel (i.e., greater direct contact with parties outside of the organization, specifically customers and suppliers). In turn, this increased interaction will mean the organization will have a better sense of what customers want and an improved awareness of environmental conditions. Reengineering jobs go hand in hand with technological change. As improved technology changes how work is performed, so too does it change how work is organized. Different technologies allow for changes in the work sequence and who performs the work (Frenkel, 2003).

Creation of a Flexible Workforce

For organizational change to occur successfully, the workforce must change accordingly to adapt to new structures and technologies that accompany reengineering. Leaner workforces will have greater responsibility for PRODUCTIVITY, quality, and customer service. Furthermore, the organizational context changes will also bring about a need for employees to be multiskilled, to be more internally controlled and self-managed, and for work to be more team- or group-based rather than individual-based. When managed effectively, these changes can contribute to even greater levels of performance and more favorable employee reactions (McCune, 1994; Pfeffer, 1998).

Organizational Culture

Changing organizational structures and the roles of its members has a profound effect on the organization's culture. Organizational cultures are meant to provide an anchor for molding members' opinions and actions. In a rapidly changing environment, the organization is faced with a paradoxical dilemma of trying to achieve high levels of flexibility while simultaneously maintaining a stable culture. To reconcile, firms must embrace cultures that value change and innovation, and discourage complacency.

Human Resource Systems to Support Workforce Flexibility

The success or failure of organizational-context changes depends immeasurably on the efforts of a firm's workforce. As Pfeffer (1998) argues, in a rapidly changing business environment, it makes sense to invest in an organization's human capital since technical obsolescence occurs sooner and more frequently. The HUMAN RESOURCE FUNCTION must be "ahead of the curve" so that it can assist the rest of the organization through its transition. In the following sections, we identify several human resource functions, and discuss how current trends of organizational change are likely to affect the services offered by these functions.

Human resource planning. In their quests to become leaner and quicker to react, organizations have found it necessary to focus their efforts on fewer core employees. When staffing requirements go beyond the flexibility potential of core employees, companies can outsource contingent workers, or workers who do not have expectations of permanent, full-time employment. TEMPORARY WORKERS, part-time workers (*see* PART-TIME EMPLOYMENT), and INDEPENDENT CONTRACTORS make up the contingent workforce who offer their services without the added obligations of BENEFITS, and the flexibility of ending their employment once their services are no longer needed (Larson, 1996).

Although economically desirable, contingent workers create a challenge to an organization since they may not intrinsically embrace the organization's culture, or they may not share the same level of commitment. For this reason, it is imperative that organizations match their core responsibilities with core employees, and only outsource secondary obligations (*see* STRATEGIC OUTSOURCING).

Performance evaluation and promotion. Perhaps the most dramatic change to careers in the changing environment is that vertical mobility will no longer be the standard reward for job success. Flatter organizations have fewer opportunities for advancement, and downsizing initiatives have eliminated layers of middle management. However, this does not suggest a diminished need for PERFORMANCE APPRAISAL. Instead, the dizzying pace of change makes it necessary that all workers be at their required skill levels, which places greater importance on evaluations. To complicate matters, the increasing use of teams changes how work is evaluated, since distinguishing between individual and group contributions becomes unclear. As a result, flexible organizations must implement performance appraisal procedures that identify job-related skills and individuals' competence levels in them. SUPERVISORY RATINGS will be less common for two reasons: (1) managerial spans of control are broader in horizontal organizations, making individual managers less able to observe the behaviors of their workers; and (2) as mentioned earlier, jobs organized within team structures make identifying individual contributions difficult for outsiders. To compensate, performance appraisals will rely increasingly on PEER RATINGS, in which workers appraise their coworkers or team members. Additionally, the greater focus on customer service provides an opportunity for customers to rate workers (*see* 360-DEGREE APPRAISALS). Not only will this provide more accurate information regarding service, but it will also alleviate the burden put upon managers.

Promotions, although more rare, will still occur and it is important to note that firms must be cautious in their selections for advancement (*see* PROMOTION). In fact, some might argue that organizations would profit from moving away from a "fast-track" system (with respect to mobility) toward a slower evaluation and promotion system, with longer time spent in positions before eligibility for promotion is achieved. This slower movement accomplishes at least two objectives of the organization. First, with people spending a longer time period in a job, organizations can gain a more accurate and informed assessment of their performance. Second, because skill acquisition and development are objectives of moving people through different jobs, it makes sense that longer time in grade will contribute to better skill acquisition, development, and learning than is often the case in fast-track systems (Ferris and King, 1991).

Compensation. We have already established that if an organization expects to successfully turn into a flexible organization, it must rely on its human resources to carry out the transition. For this reason, there should be a premium on the caliber of employees, and their COMPENSATION should reflect this. In matters of compensation, conventional wisdom is correct when it suggests, "you get what you pay for." So companies should be willing to pay at least the market value to recruit and maintain a qualified workforce. Not only do premium wages send a positive signal of worth to the employees, from a more pragmatic perspective, they discourage other companies from recruiting that firm's workers.

As alluded to above, the nature of work in a flexible organization is vastly different from that in traditional workplaces. As a result, typical organizational pay schemes such as salaries or hourly wages may be inappropriate for flexible organizations. To reward a flexible workforce, SKILL-BASED PAY DESIGN systems may be a preferred option, since they reflect what is important to the reorganizing efforts.

Much of the focus on flexible organizations pertains to teamwork and group processes. If reorganized companies pursue this structure, their compensation administration should reflect it as well. Team-based pay motivates the team to excel (see TEAM-BASED INCENTIVES) and, when properly administered, is fair to each of the members. Moreover, proper team-based compensation plans should minimize individual interests over those of the group and discourage detrimental individual behaviors such as grandstanding or free-riding.

Lastly, organizations seek flexibility for the simple reason of being more competitive and more profitable. As a result, tying organizational performance to the salary structure is a logical means to instill the purpose of the reorganization (see PAY FOR PERFORMANCE).

Training and development. Of the responsibilities added to the human resource function, perhaps none is more prevalent than the specialty of training and development (see TRAINING). Restructuring and reengineering demand sophisticated new skills to accommodate new technologies. And because flexible workforces require higher overall skill levels of their workers, training becomes especially vital. Realistically, the human resource function will not be able to keep up with the multitude of technological advancements to provide training from within the human resource function. Instead, organizations will rely on vendors or third-party trainers to provide this service. However, it is necessary that the human resource function be actively involved with these transactions to identify training needs and monitor training effectiveness (see TRAINING EVALUATION).

Increasing employees' technical abilities is only one area of training necessary for a firm to become more flexible. An additional component of training includes the relationship skills necessary to contribute, since employee participation is a fundamental premise of flexible organizations (Ashmos et al., 2002). Skills in the areas of team building, leadership, and networking have been shown to improve the effectiveness of managers in flexible organizations (Kathuria and Partovi, 1999). Furthermore, social and political skill increasingly have become regarded as absolutely critical for managerial success (e.g., Luthans, Hodgetts, and Rosenkrantz, 1988; Ferris et al., 2004).

Beyond the basic skill requirements of new technologies and interpersonal skills, flexible workforces require additional capabilities that are less obvious. While individuals can readily learn how to perform their jobs, they will simultaneously have to learn how to continuously improve their jobs. This is the type of "second-level thinking" that will become an integral component of organizational training programs.

IMPLICATIONS AND CONCLUSION

Flexible organizations have yet to replace traditional structures in the commercial environment, but increasingly we are seeing more firms adopt the characteristics of those presented here. Unfortunately, while attempting to make an organization more flexible is generally desirable, the actual implementation is proving very difficult, as evidenced by disappointing results (Cascio, 1993). For this reason, we see the human resource function as a vital linchpin between the strategy formulation and the implementation. This will require the human resource function to change in concert with the rest of the organization (Whetten, Keiser, and Urban, 1995), and in the spirit of flexible workforces, it will have to continue adapting to accommodate the changing nature of organizations and business (see HUMAN RESOURCE STRATEGY).

Bibliography

Ashmos, D. P., Duchon, D., McDaniel, R. R., and Huonker, J. W. (2002). What a mess! Participation as a simple managerial rule to "complexify" organizations. *Journal of Management Studies*, 39, 189–206.

Capelli, P. and Rogovsky, N. (1994). New work systems and skill requirements. *International Labor Review*, 133, 205–20.

Cascio, W. F. (1993). Downsizing: What do we know? What have we learned? *Academy of Management Executive*, 7, 95–104.

Dalton, G. L. (1998). The collective stretch. *Management Review*, 87, 54–9.

Ferris, G. R. and King, T. R. (1991). Politics in human resources decisions: A walk on the dark side. *Organizational Dynamics*, 20, 59–71.

Ferris, G. R., Treadway, D. C., Kolodinsky, R. W., Hochwarter, W. A., Kacmar, C. J., Douglas, C., and Frink, D. D. (2004). Development and validation of the political skill inventory. *Journal of Management*.

Frenkel, S. J. (2003). The embedded character of workplace relations. *Work and Occupations*, 30, 135–53.

Kathuria, R. and Partovi, F. (1999). Work force management practices for manufacturing flexibility. *Journal of Operations Management*, 18, 21–39.

Larson, J. (1996). Temps are here to stay. *American Demographics*, 18, 26–31.

Luthans, F., Hodgetts, R. M., and Rosenkrantz, S. A. (1988). *Real Managers*. Cambridge, MA: Ballinger.

McCune, J. C. (1994). On the train gang: In the new flat organizations employees who want to be competitive must be versatile enough to perform a variety of tasks. *Management Review*, 83, 57–60.

Pfeffer, J. (1998). *The Human Equation*. Boston: Harvard Business School Press.

Whetten, D. A., Keiser, J. D., and Urban, T. F. (1995). Implications of organizational downsizing for the human resource management function. In G. R. Ferris, S. D. Rosen, and D. T. Barnum (eds.), *Handbook of Human Resource Management*. Oxford: Blackwell.

workplace security

Ricky W. Griffin

Workplace security is a programmatic effort by an organization to protect itself, its property (both tangible and intangible), and its members from various unlawful threats such as theft, fraud, sabotage, industrial espionage, terrorism, and WORKPLACE VIOLENCE. Theft (or stealing) is the unauthorized use and/or consumption of organizational resources by employees and/or nonemployees. Fraud refers to deceptions deliberately undertaken to secure unfair or illegal gain. Industrial espionage is unethical and/or illegal efforts to learn about another organization's confidential or proprietary plans, procedures, and practices. Terrorism is the unlawful use of force or violence to intimidate or to coerce the organization to respond or react in a certain way. Finally, workplace violence involves significant negative effects on persons or property that occur as a result of aggressive behavior.

Most workplace security programs focus on risk prevention, detection, and intervention. Risk prevention involves the initial planning, design, and implementation of various security systems. Some security systems are highly visible and represent tangible, hardware-based mechanisms. For example, some organizations require visitors to pass through metal detection devices before entering the offices of certain top managers. Traditional burglar alarm systems and video monitoring systems would also fit into this category.

Other systems are more administrative in nature. For example, most larger businesses require that all visitors sign in at a reception desk and secure an identification badge before entering other parts of the organization. Finally, other systems are more indirect in nature. For example, many work settings require that employees enter and leave the organization through one or a few doors. Among other things, this makes it more difficult for employees to steal resources.

Detection refers to mechanisms put in place to alert the organization to a security breach of some form or another. A wide array of detection mechanisms is used. In the case of a hardware-based system, for example, detection results in the activation of an alarm. Administrative control systems provide various channels for detection. For example, if all visitors are required to wear name badges, an individual seen on company premises without such a badge represents a security breach. Observation and other control devices are used to detect security problems in various other contexts.

Intervention refers to what steps, if any, the organization takes if a security problem is detected. In general, the intervention will be closely integrated with the nature and severity of the problem itself. A burglar alarm being set off in the middle of the night, for example, will likely prompt a police investigation. Alternatively, someone on company premises without a name badge might be handled simply by directing the individual back to the reception desk to secure a badge.

Bibliography

Crino, M. D. (1994). Employee sabotage: A random or preventable phenomenon? *Journal of Managerial Issues*, 6, 311–30.

Gardiner, R. A. and Grassie, R. P. (1994). A comprehensive approach to workplace security. *Security Management*, 38, 97–102.

Kandel, W. L. (1990). Employee dishonesty and workplace security: Precautions about prevention. *Employee Relations Law Journal*, 16, 217–31.

workplace violence

Ricky W. Griffin

Workplace violence involves significant negative effects on persons or property as a result of organization-motivated aggression. Workplace violence can stem from a variety of sources. In many cases, workplace violence results from the efforts of external individuals or groups attempting to steal organizational resources. The commission of violence in conjunction with an armed robbery attempt would be a common example. Workplace violence is also frequently perpetrated by current or former employees. A former employee who feels unjustly terminated and who returns to the workplace to exact revenge would be an example. Occasionally, workplace violence is committed by an individual who is a personal acquaintance of an organizational member but who himself or herself is not a member of the organization. For example, an estranged spouse might come to the workplace of his or her spouse with the possible consequence of violence. Finally, there are relatively infrequent situations in which the occurrence of workplace violence is a random event. For example, a deranged individual might enter an organization at random and enact violent behavior.

Workplace violence may be targeted in a number of different ways. In some situations, perpetrators wish to do harm to the organization itself, in an abstract manner, and the victims of that harm either are symbols of the organization (e.g., the chief executive officer) or simply happen to have been in the wrong place at the wrong time. In other situations, the target may be a specific individual. For example, an individual who was fired may attempt to do harm to the supervisor or human resource manager perceived by the aggressor to be the cause of the termination.

Workplace violence is triggered by a number of factors. In most cases, the individual who commits violence has been in a dysfunctional work setting for some time. He or she may have been passed over for promotion, may be experiencing personal difficulties, or may be overly anxious and/or under excessive stress. Specific triggers might be a termination notice, a work-related setback, a disagreement with someone else, or a similar event.

Workplace violence takes a number of forms. The most tragic and public form of violence is murder in the workplace. Assaults, fights, and other physical attacks are also clear examples of workplace violence. In addition, violence can take the form of verbal threats, invasion of personal space, SEXUAL HARASSMENT, rape, and other forms of sexual assault, and any other stimulus that results in a threatening work environment.

Organizations that seek to control or minimize the potential for workplace violence have relatively few alternatives. One step they can take is to conduct thorough background checks of new employees. Another step is to closely monitor the processes used to terminate employees and/or provide other forms of negative feedback. Developing and maintaining an adequate workplace security system is another method that can be used to decrease the incidence of violence (*see* WORKPLACE SECURITY). Finally, organizations can also develop, communicate, and enforce policies and procedures consistent with the prevention of workplace violence. For example, an organization can maintain a policy that striking someone else in the workplace is grounds for immediate dismissal, and can then strictly enforce this policy.

Bibliography

Bandura, A. (1973). *Aggression: A Social Learning Analysis*. Englewood Cliffs, NJ: Prentice-Hall.

Berkowitz, L. (1993). *Aggression: Its Causes, Consequences, and Control*. New York: McGraw-Hill.

O'Leary-Kelly, A. M., Griffin, R. W., and Glew, D. J. (1996). Organization-motivated aggression: A research framework. *Academy of Management Review*.

WorldatWork

Robert M. McCaffery

WorldatWork (formerly the American Compensation Association) is a not-for-profit association of some 26,000 members (2003) engaged in the design, implementation, and management of employee reward programs. The association was founded in 1955 and is headquartered in Scottsdale, Arizona.

WorldatWork sponsors a comprehensive educational and professional development program; administers certification programs for compensation professionals (CCP) and benefits professionals (CBP); and publishes *WorldatWork Journal* (quarterly), *WorldatWork News* (monthly), Building Block Booklets, and various other booklets and software; funds research projects; and provides informational services.

Descriptive information is available on request from: WorldatWork, 14040 N. Northsight Blvd., Scottsdale, AZ 85260. Telephone 480-951-9191. Fax 480-483-8352.

Y

yield ratio

James A. Breaugh

A yield ratio reflects the percentage of job candidates at the beginning of a step in the recruitment/selection process who move on to the next step in that process (Breaugh, 1992). Consider the following example. A company receives 20 applications for a job opening. After initial screening, the company invites eight individuals for interviews. The yield ratio for this stage of the recruitment process is 40 percent. However, not everyone who receives an interview invitation might accept it (Hawk, 1967). If, for example, only six of the eight people accepted their invitation to interview, the yield ratio for this stage of the recruitment process is 75 percent.

Bibliography

Breaugh, J. A. (1992). *Recruitment: Science and Practice*. Boston: PWS-Kent.

Hawk, R. H. (1967). *The Recruitment Function*. New York: American Management Association.

Index

Note: Headwords are in bold type

Abelson, M. 115
abilities
  individual differences 183
  mental 238
  person–job fit 282–3
  physical 285, 285–6
  psychomotor 302–3
  tests 302
  see also KSAOs
absenteeism 1–3
  and bullying 32
  and counseling 76
  and distributive justice 93
  and elder care 105
  and flextime 135
  and pay satisfaction 274
  and self-management training 338
  and union–management cooperation 401
  and urinalysis testing 98
  and work schedules 65
Academy of Management Human Resource Division 168–9
ACAS *see* Advisory, Conciliation, and Arbitration Service
accidents
  reducing human error 162–3
  see also safety and health
accountability, and performance evaluation 347–8
accuracy, rating *see* rating accuracy
achievement tests 187
action learning 3
ACTU *see* Australian Council of Trade Unions
ADA *see* Americans with Disabilities Act of 1990
Adams, Roy J. 36–7
Adarand Constructors, Inc. v. Pena 56
add-on pay 12
Addison, J. T. 400, 405–6
ADEA *see* Age Discrimination in Employment Act of 1967
Adler, N. J. 88, 147

ADR *see* alternative dispute resolution
adverse impact *see* disparate impact
advertisements, recruitment 142
Advisory, Conciliation, and Arbitration Service (ACAS; UK) 410
AFDC *see* aid to families with dependent children
affirmative action 3–4, 56
  Adarand Constructors, Inc. v. Pena 56
  availability analysis 17–18, 317
  Connecticut v. Teal 67–8
  executive orders 3, 123
  glass ceiling 146–7
  Johnson v. Transportation Agency, Santa Clara County 215, 322
  Martin v. Wilks 238
  for non-victims 4
  Office of Federal Contract Compliance Programs 263
  relevant labor markets 317
  and reverse discrimination 322
  Steelworkers v. Weber 4, 322, 354
  utilization analysis 317, 411–12
AFL-CIO (American Federation of Labor and Congress of Industrial Organizations) 4
age
  and absence 1
  benefits 349, 350
  and career plateauing 42
  Older Workers Benefit Protection Act of 1991 175
  and productivity 104
  and workforce demographics 390–1, 433
age discrimination

Age Discrimination in Employment Act of 1967 (ADEA) 5
  and bona fide occupational qualifications 30
  and executive orders 123
  and interviews 195
  and pension plans 113
  and tests 187, 390–1
  see also discrimination
agency shop 6
aggression *see* bullying; sexual harassment; workplace, violence
agricultural workers, and secondary boycotts 334
AHRI *see* Australian Human Resources Institute
aid to families with dependent children (AFDC) 349
AIDS/AIDS-related complex 6
  awareness training 6
  employee assistance programs 106–7
  see also blood-borne pathogens
airline industries, regulation 306
Ajzen, I. 207
Albemarle Paper Company v. Moody 7
alcohol *see* drugs
Alexander, R. A. 101, 336
alliances
  strategic 354–6
  virtual organizations 417–18
Alliger, George M. 84–5, 206–7
ALP *see* Australian Labor Party
alternative dispute resolution (ADR) 7
  see also arbitration; disputes; grievances; mediation; nonunion employee grievance procedures
American Compensation Association *see* WorldatWork
American Society for Training and Development (ASTD) 7

Americans with Disabilities Act
 of 1990 (ADA)   7–8, 155, 159,
 219
 and AIDS   6
 and blood-borne pathogens   328
Ameritech   136
anchoring and adjustment   250
Andrews, D. C.   34–5
Andrews, K. R.   365
Angoff method   84–5
annual hours   8
annuities, tax-deferred   377
Appelbaum, E.   402
appraisal
 feedback   8–9, 48
 see also performance appraisal and
  evaluation
aptitude tests   187
arbitration   7, 9–10
 Advisory, Conciliation, and
  Arbitration Service
  (UK)   410
 Australia   15
 Federal Mediation and
  Conciliation Service   133,
  324
 final offer arbitration   10, 133
 interest arbitration   10, 189
 mediation   238
 National Academy of
  Arbitrators   247, 324
 nonunion systems   254
 published decisions   324
 rights arbitration   323–4
ARC see AIDS/AIDS-related
 complex
Arizona Governing Committee v.
 Norris   113
Armed Services Vocational
 Aptitude Battery   302
Army Alpha intelligence test   188
Army Beta intelligence test   188
Arnold, J. D.   428
Arthur, J. B.   168
Arvey, Richard D.   285–6
ASA see
 attraction–selection–attrition
Ash, Ronald A.   139–40, 204–5,
 376–7
assessment centers   10–12, 103,
 389
assessment skills training   308
ASTD see American Society for
 Training and Development
at-risk pay   12
AT&T   136
attitude surveys   12
attitudinal structuring   13
attorney's fees, award of see award of
 attorney's fees
attraction–selection–attrition
 (ASA)   13–14

atypical employment see contingent
 employment
audiovisual training
 techniques   14
Austin, James T.   64–5, 78–9, 101,
 208–9, 233–4
Australia   14–16
 health promotion programs   158
 workers' compensation   432
Australian Council of Trade Unions
 (ACTU)   14–16
Australian Labor Party (ALP)   15
Australian Human Resources
 Institute (AHRI)   16–17
automation
 effects on producers   389
 and human error   163
autonomous work teams see self-
 managing teams
availability   250
availability analysis   17–18,
 317
award of attorney's fees   18

background checking
 (generic)   19
 reference checks   316
Bailey, C. T.   208
balanced scorecard   19–20
Baldrige Award see Malcolm
 Baldrige National Quality
 Award
Baldwin, Timothy T.   213, 263,
 324, 337–8, 340, 343, 387
Balkin, David B.   30, 30–1, 287–8,
 300, 307
Balma, J. J.   375
Balma, M. J.   129
Bamber, Greg J.   14–16, 16–17
Banks, C. G.   277, 308
Baratta, J. E.   101
Barbash, J.   372
Barber, A. E.   210, 368
bargaining
 agency shop   6
 attitudinal structuring   13
 Australia   15
 bargaining units   20
 China   51
 distributive   92–3
 executive orders about   123
 France   139
 Germany   145
 good faith   149
 integrative   186
 intra-organizational   195–6
 Italy   197
 mandatory bargaining
  issues   236
 multinational   245–6
 pattern   270
 public sector   303

 see also arbitration; collective
  bargaining; disputes;
  grievances; mediation;
  negotiation
Barnard, Chester   163
Barnes v. *Costle*   20, 342
Barnett, W. P.   114–15
Barney, J.   165
Barr, Steve H.   274–5, 322–3
Barrett, G. V.   101
BARS see behaviorally anchored
 rating scales
Bartholomew, S.   88
base rate of success   20
Bass, A. R.   380
Bass, B. M.   22
Bassi, L. J.   385
Batt, R.   402
Baxter Healthcare   181
Beatty, Richard W.   230–2
Beaumont, P. B.   255–7
Beck v. *Communication Workers*   6
Beehr, T. A.   115
behavior   20–1
 see also traits
behavior modeling   21
 and role playing   324, 387
behavioral consistency
 principle   21
behavioral observation scales
 (BOS)   21–2, 59, 149–50, 312
behaviorally anchored rating
 scales (BARS)   22–3, 60,
 149–50, 312
 and situational interviews   344
Belbin, R. M.   23–4
Belbin teams   23–4
Bell, C. H.   264
Bell Aircraft case   301
Bell Atlantic   136
Bem Sex Role Inventory   342
benchmark jobs   131, 217
benchmarking
 and competitor
  analysis   24–5
 and human resource audits   164
Bendix, R.   398
benefits   26, 64
 administration   26–7, 114
 aid to families with dependent
  children   349
 benefit programs:
  evolution   25–6
 cafeteria plans see flexible benefit
  plans
 childcare   49
 coinsurance   25
 communication   27
 and contingent workers   71
 coordination   75
 copayment   25
 and diverse workforce   95

elder care   105
Employee Benefit Research Institute   107–8
Employee Benefits Infosource   193
executives   122
Family and Medical Leave Act of 1993   49, 100, 132, 172
financial assistance plans   133–4
flexible benefit plans   25, 26, 134–5
group disability benefits   153–4
group life insurance/survivor benefits   154
International Foundation of Employee Benefit Programs   192–3
intra-organizational benefits   195–6
and job sharing   213
Mexico   241, 243–4
Older Workers Benefit Protection Act of 1991   175
paid time off   269
as percentage of compensation costs   25
retirement benefits   349
Russia   326
Social Security Act of 1935   349, 397
social security benefits   349–50
survivor benefits   154, 349
temporary workers   379
union effects   405
US   173
workers' compensation benefits   432
workers' compensation law   432–3
see also compensation; healthcare; pension plans
Bennett, Hadyn   19–20, 23–4, 87, 143, 161–2, 189–90, 222, 283, 417–18
Bennett, N.   101
Bennis, Warren   163
Bentson, C.   11
Berdie, R. F.   418
Bereman, Nancy A.   148–9, 182
Berk, R. A.   84
Bernardin, H. John   21–2, 22–3, 244–5
Berner, J. G.   343
Bernstein, I. H.   299
Berr, S. A.   264
Berry, L. L.   341
BFOQ *see* bona fide occupational qualification
bias, rating *see* rating bias

Bierman, Leonard   7, 67–8, 116–17, 120–1, 134, 153, 157, 215, 226, 227, 238, 263, 354, 378, 422–3
Big Five personality tests   27–8
biodata inventories   28–30
biographical history inventories   28–30
bisexuality *see* sexual orientation
Bjorkman, I.   51
Black, Stewart   293–5
black lung benefits   349
Blackburn, Richard S.   227–8, 352–4, 382–5
Blair, Tony   409
Blake, R. R.   366
Blake, S.   363
Blanco, R. Ivan   128–9
Blantz, F.   245
Blinet, Alfred   187–8
blood-borne pathogens   328
see also AIDS/AIDS-related complex
Bloom, Matthew C.   57, 131, 156, 205–6
Blum, T. C.   107
Bobko, P.   281, 282
Boehm, V. R.   343
bona fide occupational qualification (BFOQ)   30, 55
bona fide seniority system   30, 55
Firefighters Local 1784 v. *Stotts*   134
Lorance v. *AT&T*   226
Teamsters v. *United States*   378
bonuses   30, 182, 273
executives   122
Russia   326
see also gainsharing; profit sharing
Borman, Walter C.   208–9, 265–6, 275, 309, 374, 381
BOS *see* behavioral observation scales
Boudreau, John W.   169–70, 193–4, 333, 336, 394
Boureslan v. *Aramco*   130
Bowen, David E.   84, 265, 340–1
Boyatzis, R. E.   272
boycotts *see* secondary boycotts
Boyd, Brian K.   122–3
Bracken, David W.   381
Brannick, Michael T.   88–9, 201–2, 202–3, 204, 213–14
Breaugh, James A.   17–18, 124–5, 209–10, 313–15, 440
Breslin, J. William   366
Bretz, Robert D., Jr.   212–13, 289, 368
Brinkerhoff, R. O.   386
broadbanding   30–1

Brockner, J.   116
Brogden, H. E.   333, 335, 336, 337
Brooks, A.   402
Brooks, L.   260
Brown, D. L.   260
Buchholtz, A. K.   148
building trades, and unions   332
bulletin boards, electronic   193–4
bullying   31–3
see also sexual harassment; workplace, violence
Burack, Elmer H.   40–1, 395
burden of proof   33, 56, 90, 91, 227
Albemarle Paper Company v. *Moody*   7
Burke, Michael J.   20, 333, 335–7
Burnes, B.   47
burnout, job   203–4
Burton, John F., Jr.   432–3
business necessity   33, 56, 90
job-relatedness   210, 56, 90
business process reengineering   33–5
and human resource audits   164
information technology enablers   185–6
business processes   35
Butler, Mark C.   236–7, 240–4

cafeteria benefit plans *see* flexible benefit plans
Cafferty, T. P.   60
CAI *see* computer-assisted instruction
Caldwell, D. F.   114–15, 265, 283
Caldwell, M.   101
California Federal Savings and Loan v. *Guerra*   293
California Psychological Inventory (CPI)   284
call centers, UK   408–9
Callender, John   414
Campbell, Donald J.   229–30
Campbell, J. P.   233
Campion, M. A.   344
Canada   36–7
unions   36, 37, 256, 398
workers' compensation   432
Canadian Council of Chief Executives (CCCE)   36
Canadian Labor Congress   36
Cannella, A. A.   125
capital, human   161–2
Cardy, Robert L.   149–50, 276–7, 280–1, 307
career   37
personal development plans   283
career anchors   37–9, 40
career choice   39, 260–1
vocational interest inventories   418–20

career concepts 40
career derailing 87
career life cycles *see* career stages
career models 39–40
career pathing (CP) 40–1, 44
career patterns of scientists and engineers 41–2
career planning *see* political influences in career planning
career plateau 42–3
  and cross-training 81
career stages 39, **43**–4
career success 40, 43, **45**–6
Carlyle, J. 282
carpal tunnel syndrome (CTS) *see* repetitive motion strain injury
Carroll, S. J. 233
Cartwright, Susan 47–8, 105–6, 121, 408–11
Cascio, Wayne F. 22, 95–7, 176, 305, 336, 346, 393–4
Cascio–Ramos estimate of performance in dollars (CREPID) 333, 336
case study/discussion method 46
cash balance pension plans 276
Cattell, R. B. 23
Cattell's 16PF test 23
CCCE *see* Canadian Council of Chief Executives
CEBS program *see* Certified Employee Benefits Specialist program
central tendency effects 46, 311, 312
  avoiding 138
certification, human resource staff 166–7
Certified Employee Benefits Specialist (CEBS) program 193
CES *see* Comparative Emphasis Scale
change
  anticipation 119–20
  management 46–7
  see also organization development and change
"change-in-control" arrangements *see* golden parachutes
Chao, George T. 142–3
Chartered Institute of Personnel and Development (CIPD) 47–8
Chatman, J. 265
Chavez-Thompson, Linda 5
checklist method of performance evaluation 48–9
Chelius, James R. 432–3

chemicals *see* hazardous materials in the workplace
Cherrington, David J. 316–17
children
  aid to families with dependent children 349
  child employment 131–2
  childcare benefit 49
  Family and Medical Leave Act of 1993 49, 100, **132**, 172
  intelligence tests 188
  see also families
China 49–53
cholesterol reduction, and health promotion programs 158
Christal, R. E. 202
Church, A. H. 264
CIPD *see* Chartered Institute of Personnel and Development
CIT *see* critical incidents technique
citizenship, and employment 179
City of Los Angeles Department of Water and Power v. *Manhart* 113
Civil Rights Act of 1866 53
Civil Rights Act of 1871 53
Civil Rights Act of 1964 **54**–6, 172
  award of attorney's fees 18
  color 62
  enforcement guidelines 397
  national origin 249
  pattern or practice cases 270–1
  race 306
  religion 319
  sex 341
Civil Rights Act of 1991 56
  and court judgments on discrimination 238, 295
  and cutoff scores 84
  and seniority systems 226
  classification 56–7
  classification job evaluation method 57
Cleary, T. A. 380
Cleveland, Jeannette N. 20–1, 281, 298–9, 310, 311, 394–5
coaching 57–8
  performance coaching 277–9
  see also mentoring programs
coal miners, and benefits 349
Coats, Gwen 84–5
COBRA *see* Consolidated Omnibus Budget Reconciliation Act of 1985
CODAP *see* Comprehensive Occupational Data Analysis Programs
codes of conduct, employee 108
coefficient alpha 318

cognitive process models of performance appraisal 58–61
coinsurance benefits 25
Colella, Adrienne 159–60, 281–2
Collarelli, S. M. 115
collective bargaining 61–2
  agency shop 6
  bargaining units 20
  China 51
  contract administration 72–4
  Europe 255
  executive orders 123
  France 139
  Germany 145
  Labor Management Relations Act of 1947 133, 149, **220**–1, 372
  Labor Management Reporting and Disclosures Act of 1959 **221**–2
  multinational 245–6
  National Labor Relations Act of 1935 149, 172, **220**–1, **248**–9, 323, 334
  pattern bargaining 270
  public sector bargaining 303
  railroad and airline industries 306–7
  right to work 323
  strategic approach 361–2
  UK 410
  see also arbitration; bargaining; disputes; grievances; mediation
Collings, Lisa M. 277–9
color
  managing diversity 94–5
color discrimination 62
  Connecticut v. *Teal* 67–8
  executive orders about 123–4
  and federal contractors 123–4, 172
  Fourteenth Constitutional Amendment 53, 138, 296, 343
  Griggs v. *Duke Power* 56, **153**, 188–9
  interviews 195
  Martin v. *Wilks* 238
  testing 84, 89, 187, 188–9, 258, 379–81, 390–1
  working overseas 130
  see also Civil Rights Act of 1964; discrimination; disparate impact; disparate treatment; race discrimination
commission-based pay 62–3
compa-ratios 63
  and merit pay 239
comparable worth 63

Index

Comparative Emphasis Scale (CES) 430
compensable factors 63
  in Hay plan 156
  and point job evaluation method 287–8
compensation 63–4
  and benchmarking 25
  bonuses 30, 182, 273
  Canada 36–7
  China 50
  employee stock ownership plans (ESOPs) 113
  executive 122–3
  expatriates 128
  gainsharing 30, 141
  golden parachutes 148–9
  Improshare 181
  international 191–2
  long-term 122
  McNamara-O'Hara Service Contract Act of 1965 227
  membership-based 382
  Mexico 241, 243–4
  organizations designing programs 439
  profit sharing 300
  reward systems 322–3
  Rucker plan 325
  Russia 325, 326
  salesforce 62–3, 331–2
  Scanlon plan 333
  strategy 64
  team-based incentives 378, 436
  unemployment 397
  variable 415–16
  and workforce flexibility 435–6
  WorldatWork 439
  see also benefits; pay
compensatory remedies 227, 248–9
competency-based pay 272
competitive advantage
  and diverse workforces 362–3
  human resource-based 165–6
competitor analysis and benchmarking 24–5
composite and multiple criteria 64–5
Comprehensive Occupational Data Analysis Programs (CODAP) 377
compressed work schedules 65–6
computer-assisted instruction (CAI) 66, 385
  and programmed instruction 300
computer design 163

Computer Matching and Privacy Protection Act of 1988 66
computer use
  surveillance 374–5
concurrent validity 67, 69
conditional probability model of test fairness 380
conduct, employee codes of 108
Confederation of National Trade Unions (Canada) 36
conference method 67
Conger, J. A. 108
Connecticut v. ***Teal*** 67–8
consent elections 403
Conservative Party (UK) 409, 410
Consolidated Omnibus Budget Reconciliation Act of 1985 (COBRA) 68
constant ratio model of test fairness 380
constraints *see* work constraints
construct validity 68–9, 286
  and intelligence tests 188
consultancy
  management 230
  outplacement 267
content validity 68, 69, 286
content validity ratio (CVR) 70
contextual performance 265–6
contingency approach 70
contingent employment 71, 176, 435
  Japan 199
  see also employees, leasing; employees, subcontracting; independent contractors; interim management; part-time employment; part-time work schedules; temporary workers
continuous improvement 72
contracts
  administration 72–4
  France 139
  labor 220
  psychological 301
contractors, independent *see* independent contractors
control issues in foreign holdings 74–5
Cooke, Fang Lee 8, 76, 163–4, 285, 333
Cooke, N. J. 389
Cooke, William N. 400–2
Cooper, W. 155
Coopers and Lybrand 83
coordination of benefits 75
copayment benefits 25
Cordes, C. L. 203
corrective discipline 75

correspondence method 76
Cory Corporation case 287
counseling 76
  and wellness programs 158
countercyclical hiring 76–7
court cases, employment
  Adarand Constructors, Inc. v. *Pena* 56
  Albemarle Paper Company v. *Moody* 7
  Arizona Governing Committee v. *Norris* 113
  Barnes v. *Costle* 20, 342
  Beck v. *Communication Workers* 6
  Bell Aircraft case 301
  Boureslan v. *Aramco* 130
  California Federal Savings and Loan v. *Guerra* 293
  City of Los Angeles Department of Water and Power v. *Manhart* 113
  Connecticut v. *Teal* 67–8
  Cory Corporation case 287
  EEOC v. *AT&T* 4
  Ellison v. *Brady* 343
  Firefighters Local 1784 v. *Stotts* 134
  General Electric v. *Gilbert* 293
  Griggs v. *Duke Power* 56, 153, 188–9
  Harris v. *Forklift Systems* 342, 343
  Hazelwood School District v. *United States* 157
  Hazen Paper Co. v. *Biggins* 5
  Johnson v. *Transportation Agency, Santa Clara County* 215, 322
  Larry P. v. *Riles* 188–9
  Local 28 of the Sheet Metal Workers International Association v. *EEOC* 4
  Lorance v *AT&T* 226
  McDonnell Douglas v. *Green* 227
  MacNamara v. *Korean Airlines* 130
  Martin v. *Wilks* 238
  Meritor Savings Bank v. *Vinson* 240, 342
  Newport News Shipbuilding and Dry Dock Co. v. *EEOC* 293
  NLRB v. *Borg Warner* 236
  NLRB v. *Town and Country Electric* 332
  Price Waterhouse v. *Hopkins* 295
  Steelworkers v. *Weber* 4, 322, 354
  Sumitomo Shoji America v. *Avigliano* 130

court cases, employment (cont'd)
  Teamsters v. United States 378
  Thornhill v. Alabama 287
  Toussaint v. Blue Cross and Blue Shield of Michigan 116
  United Steelworkers of America v. American Manufacturing Company 10
  United Steelworkers of America v. Enterprise Wheel and Car Company 10
  United Steelworkers of America v. Warrior and Gulf Navigation Company 10
  Wards Cove Packing Co. v. Antonio 422
  Washington v. Davis 422
  Watson v. Fort Worth Bank and Trust 422–3
  Western Airlines v. Criswell 30
  Wygant v. Jackson Board of Education 4, 322
Cox, Annette 70, 83, 151
Cox, T. H., Jr. 363
CP see career pathing
CPI see California Psychological Inventory
Craft, James A. 176–8
craft unions 77, 185
  and labor contracts 220
Crant, J. M. 289
Cravens, David W. 331–2
CREPID see Cascio–Ramos estimate of performance in dollars
criteria see composite and multiple criteria; dynamic criteria
criterion contamination 77–8
criterion deficiency 78
criterion problem 78–9
  dynamic criteria 101
criterion relevance 80
  and criterion contamination 77
  and criterion deficiency 78
criterion-related validity 69, 80, 286
  and background checking 19, 316
  concurrent validity 67, 69
  cross-validation 81–2
  predictive validity 67, 69, 292–3
  and synthetic validity 375
  and work samples 428
critical incidents technique (CIT) 80–1
  and behavioral observation scales 21
  and situational interviews 344
  and work constraints 425
critical scores see cutoff scores
Cronbach, L. J. 68, 183, 310, 336

Cronshaw, S. F. 336
cross-training 81
  and self-managing teams 339
cross-validation 81–2
Crown, D. F. 98
CTM (Mexican union) 242
CTS (carpal tunnel syndrome) see repetitive motion strain injury
culpability 329
cultural literacy 82–3
culture, organizational see organizational culture
Cummings, T. G. 264
custom and practice 83
customers
  customer-oriented human resource management 83–4
  customer service training 84
    dealing with diverse 363
    and lean production 223
    as performance feedback sources 78–9, 435
    pleasing through quality 383–4
  service quality 340–1
Cutcher-Gershenfeld, Joel E. 362, 366
cutoff scores 84–5
  and differential validity 89
  multiple cutoff selection procedures 246
  and test fairness 380
CVR see content validity ratio

Dalton, D. 115
Dauffenbach, Robert C. 41–2
Davenport, T. H. 34–5, 185–6
David, Jennifer 193
Davidow, W. H. 417–18
Davis-Bacon Act of 1931 86
Dawis, R. V. 260, 282–3
De Cieri, Helen L. 87–8, 160–1
Deadrick, D. L. 101
Dean, J. 383
decertification elections 86
decision-making
  contingency approach 70
  employee involvement 110–11
  and occupational choice 260
  selection models 334–5
defamation waivers 86–7
defined benefit pensions 276
defined contribution pensions 276
Delaney, John T. 61–2, 168, 323, 362
Delery, John E. 171–4
DeMarr, Beverly 105
Deming, W. Edwards 352–3, 383
demographics, workforce see workforce demographics

DeNisi, Angelo S. 46, 60, 91–2, 154, 225
density, union 62, 396, 398, 407–8
derailing 87
derivation subsamples 82
design, human-centered 162–3
deskilling 87
developing globally competent executives/managers 87–8
  see also overseas working and businesses
diabetics, and discrimination 316
diaries see performance diaries
Dictionary of Occupational Work Titles (DOT) 88–9
diet, and health promotion programs 158
differences
  individual 183
  managerial value differences 234–5
differential accuracy 310
differential elevation 310
differential validity 69, 89
  and single-group validity 343–4
Ding, D. Z. 51
Dipboye, Robert L. 80, 117–18, 194–5, 344
disabled see handicapped/disabled
disabled discrimination
  Americans with Disabilities Act of 1990 7–8, 155, 159, 219
  hiring persons with disabilities 159–60
  and pension plans 113
  physical ability testing 286
  Rehabilitation Act of 1973 155, 159, 316
  see also job analysis
discipline
  and absence 2
  corrective 75
  and grievances 151
  positive 292
  progressive 300–1
disclaimers 89–90
discretion, time span of see time span of discretion
discrimination 90
  age see age discrimination
  and AIDS/ARC 6
  bona fide occupational qualification 30, 55
  bona fide seniority systems 30, 55
  burden of proof 33, 56, 90, 91
  Civil Rights Act of 1866 53
  Civil Rights Act of 1871 53
  Civil Rights Act of 1991 56
  color see color discrimination

disabled *see* disabled discrimination
discrimination when working overseas 130
and drug users 8, 155
Equal Employment Opportunity Commission 120–1
executive orders 123–4
and federal contractors 123–4, 172
Fourteenth Constitutional Amendment 53, 138, 296, 343
France 139
gender *see* gender issues in HRM
Hazelwood School District v. *United States* 157
Immigration Reform and Control Act of 1986 179–80
interviews 195
Johnson v. *Transportation Agency, Santa Clara County* 215, 322
Lorance v. *AT&T* 226
make-whole/compensatory remedies 227, 248–9
managing diversity 94–5
national origin *see* national origin discrimination
Office of Federal Contract Compliance Programs 263
pattern or practice cases 270–1
and pension plans 113
Pregnancy Discrimination Act of 1978 293
Price Waterhouse v. *Hopkins* 295
punitive damages 303
race *see* race discrimination
and rating bias 311
relevant labor markets 317
religion *see* religion discrimination
remedies for victims 56
reverse *see* reverse discrimination
sex *see* gender issues in HRM
and situational interviews 344
and subjective employment criteria 423
and tests 84, 89, 187, 188–9, 258, 379–81, 390–1
UK regulation 409–10
Uniform Guidelines on Employee Selection Procedures 380, 397
and unions 4
US 172
utilization analysis 317, 411–12

veteran status 416
working overseas 130
see also affirmative action; Civil Rights Act of 1964; disparate impact; disparate treatment; job analysis; sexual harassment
discussion lists, electronic 193–4
discussion method 46
dismissals *see* layoffs
disparate impact 54, 90–1
and age discrimination 5
Albemarle Paper Company v. *Moody* 7
burden of proof 33, 56, 90
business necessity 33, 56, 90
Civil Rights Act of 1866 53
Civil Rights Act of 1991 56
Connecticut v. *Teal* 67–8
Firefighters Local 1784 v. *Stotts* 134
Griggs v. *Duke Power* 56, 153, 188–9
job-relatedness 56, 90, 210
and physical ability testing 286
procedure justification guidelines 397
and tests 188–9
Wards Cove Packing Co. v. *Antonio* 422
Washington v. *Davis* 422
see also Civil Rights Act of 1964
disparate treatment 54, 90, 91
burden of proof 33, 56, 91, 227
Civil Rights Act of 1866 53
Civil Rights Act of 1991 56
Griggs v. *Duke Power* 56, 153, 188–9
McDonnell Douglas v. *Green* 227
mixed motives model 295
and pattern or practice cases 271
and subjective employment criteria 422–3
systemic 270–1
Teamsters v. *United States* 378
see also Civil Rights Act of 1964
disputes
alternative dispute resolution (ADR) 7
Australia 15, 16
Canada 37
France 139
interest disputes 9
lockouts 189, 225–6
mediation 133, 238
Mexico 241, 242–3
Norris-LaGuardia Anti-Injunction Act of 1932 258–9
picketing 221, 286–7, 404

railroad and airline industries 306–7
Russia 326
secondary boycotts 221, 334, 404
South Korea 351
strikes 372
strikes, right to 9–10, 61–2, 189, 221, 306–7
UK 410
wildcat strikes 424
workdays lost 220
see also arbitration; grievances
distance learning 91
distributional effects in performance appraisal 91–2
central tendency effects 46, 138
leniency effects 138, 225
distributive bargaining 92–3
distributive justice 93–4
China 51
and grievances 73
diversity 94–5
multicultural workforce 245, 390
strategic issues 362–4
and workforce demographics 433
Dobbins, Gregory H. 276–7, 280–1
Doeringer, P. 190
Dole, Senator Bob 431
Dorsey, D. W. 209
DOT *see* Dictionary of Occupational Work Titles
Dougherty, T. W. 203
Dowling, Peter J. 51, 87–8, 147, 148, 160–1
Downs, S. 389
downsizing 95–7, 176, 434
and career choice 260
Dreher, George F. 129–30, 190, 421
Drucker, P. 229, 234
drugs
drug testing 97–9
drug users and discrimination 8, 155, 316
employee assistance programs 106–7
dual-earner and dual-career couples 99–101
and antinepotism policies 252
Dulebohn, J. H. 347
Dunham, Randall B. 65–6, 135–6, 136–7
Dunlop, J. T. 184, 190, 361, 406
duty 101
Duxbury, L. E. 100
Dworkin, James B. 77, 185

Dyer, L.   177
dynamic criteria   101
dysfunctional performance appraisals   102
dyslectics, and discrimination   316

EAPs *see* employee assistance programs
early identification of management talent   10–12, 103–4
see also management; managers
early retirement buyout   104
early retirement policy   104–5, 175
Eastman Kodak   398
Ebel method   85
EBIS *see* Employee Benefits Infosource
EBRI *see* Employee Benefit Research Institute
education
  UK   409
  and veterans   416–17
EEOC *see* Equal Employment Opportunity Commission
EEOC v. *AT&T*   4
Edwards, J.   282
Edwards Personal Preference Schedule (EPPS)   284
EI *see* emotional intelligence
Einarson, Ståle   31–3
Einhorn, H. J.   380
elder care benefit   105
elevation   310
Ellison, T.   282
Ellison v. *Brady*   343
emotional abuse *see* bullying
emotional intelligence (EI)   105–6
  and stress   105, 215
empirical scoring keys   29
employability   106
employee abuse *see* bullying
employee assistance programs (EAPs)   106–7, 114
  and counseling   76
  and stress   215, 371–2
Employee Benefit Research Institute (EBRI)   107–8
Employee Benefits Infosource (EBIS)   193
employee empowerment   19, 108–10
  and diverse workforces   363
  and horizontal management   160
  and productivity   165
  and self-managing teams   339
employee handbooks   110
  disclaimers   89–90
  and grievance procedures   152

employee involvement   110–11, 168
  and gainsharing programs   141
  see also quality circles; quality of work life; total quality management
employee loyalty
  and drug testing   98
  and employability   106
  and ESOPs   113
  and grievances   73
  see also job involvement; psychological contracts
employee morale   111
  and quality of work life   305
  and union–management cooperation   402
  see also job satisfaction
employee orientation *see* new employee orientation
Employee Polygraph Protection Act of 1988   111–12, 290
Employee Retirement Income Security Act of 1974 (ERISA)   27, 68, 112–13, 183, 332, 377
employee selection and recruitment *see* personnel selection and recruitment
employee stock ownership plans (ESOPs)   113
employee turnover   114–16
  and bullying   32
  China   50
  and counseling   76
  and demographic diversity   94
  and distributive justice   93
  and elder care   105
  Hong Kong   52
  and HRM practices   168
  and organizational socialization   266
  and pay   130, 274
  and realistic job previews   312–13, 314
  and union coverage   405
  and urinalysis testing   98
employees
  assessing potential   10–12; *see also* tests
  attitude *see* attitude surveys
  behavior   20–1
  code of conduct   108
  empowerment *see* employee empowerment
  leasing   111
  subcontracting   113–14
employer associations
  Australia   16
  Canada   36
  France   139
employment-at-will   116–17

employment interview   117–18, 313
  situational interviews   117, 344
employment tribunals, UK   409–10
Environmental Protection Agency (EPA)   247, 248
environmental scanning   119–20, 235
EOC *see* Equal Opportunities Commission
EPA *see* Environmental Protection Agency
epileptics, and discrimination   316
EPPS *see* Edwards Personal Preference Schedule
equal employment *see* discrimination
Equal Employment Opportunity Commission (EEOC)   54, 120–1, 172
Equal Opportunities Commission (EOC; UK)   410
Equal Pay Act of 1963   63, 121
equal risk model of test fairness   380
equity theory   93
ergonomics   162–3
  and repetitive motion strain injury   320
ERISA *see* Employee Retirement Income Security Act of 1974
Ernst and Young   181
ESOPs *see* employee stock ownership plans
ESS *see* expatriate support system
ethics *see* professional ethics
EU *see* European Union
Eulberg, J. R.   425
European Union (EU)   121, 144
  EU Social Charter   121, 410
  unions   245, 255–6
European Trade Union Confederation   245
eustress   214
Evans, J.   383
executive compensation   122–3
executive orders   3, 123–4
  Office of Federal Contract Compliance Programs   3, 263
executive search   124–5
executive selection   125–6
executives *see* developing globally competent executives/ managers; managers
exercise, and health promotion programs   158
exit interviews   126
exit–voice theory   405

expatriate assignment 126–7, 161, 390
  see also overseas working and businesses
expatriate human resource issues 127–8
expatriate support system (ESS) 128–9
expectancy charts 129
external equity/external competitiveness 129–30
wage and salary surveys 421
extraterritorial application of employment law 130
Eyde, L. D. 205

face validity 131
  and graphic rating scales 149
factor-comparison job evaluation method 131
Fagenson-Eland, Ellen A. 99–101, 341–2
Fair Labor Standards Act of 1938 (FLSA) 131–2, 227
families
  aid to families with dependent children 349
  childcare benefit 49
  elder care benefit 105
  Family and Medical Leave Act of 1993 49, 100, 132, 172
  nepotism policies 252
  and overseas assignments 294
  see also work–family conflict; work–nonwork role issues
farm workers, and secondary boycotts 334
FASB 106 132
Fay, Charles H. 21, 25–6, 26–7, 86, 104, 121, 131–2, 133–4, 138, 157, 159, 182, 183, 227, 228–9, 276, 290, 300, 332–3, 349, 377, 422
Fayol, H. 233
Federal Election Campaign Act of 1971 288
federal government contracts
  and discrimination 123–4, 172
  Office of Federal Contract Compliance Programs (OFCCP) 3, 172, 263
  pay 86, 227, 422
  record keeping 171
  relevant labor markets 317
  utilization analysis 317, 411–12
federal government employees, privacy 296
Federal Mediation and Conciliation Service (FMCS) 133, 324

Federal Unemployment Tax Act of 1935 (FUTA) 133
Federation of Independent Trade Unions (Russia) 326
feedback
  appraisal 8–9, 48, 231
  customers 78–9
  for learning reinforcement 224
  performance coaching 276–7
  rater training 308
  and succession planning 373
  360-degree 337, 381
Feldman, Daniel C. 37, 81, 104, 115, 321–2
Feldman, Jack 58–61
Ferris, Gerald R. 346–9, 433–7
Feuille, Peter 133, 189, 303
FFM see Five Factor Model of personality
FICA taxes 349
Fielden, Sandra 46–7, 230
final offer arbitration (FOA) 10, 133
financial assistance plans 133–4
  see also benefits
Fine, S. A. 140
Finland, collective bargaining 255
Fiorito, Jack 183–5, 362, 406–8
Firefighters Local 1784 v. Stotts 134
firings see layoffs
Fishbein, M. 207
Fisher, Cynthia D. 252, 253, 266
Fisher, Roger 366
Five Factor Model (FFM) of personality 27–8
FJA see functional job analysis
Flanagan, J. C. 80
flexibility, workforce see workforce flexibility
flexible benefit plans (cafeteria benefit plans) 25, 26, 134–5
flexible working hours 135–6, 371
  Family and Medical Leave Act of 1993 49, 100, 132, 172
flexible workplace/telecommuting 136–7
  and diverse workforce 95
flextime see work schedules
FLSA see Fair Labor Standards Act of 1938
FMCS see Federal Mediation and Conciliation Service
FOA see final offer arbitration
Folger, Robert 93–4, 298
FOR training see frame-of-reference training

forced distribution method of performance evaluation 137–8
Ford 41
Ford, J. Kevin 46, 67, 76, 91, 183, 224–5, 379, 387, 388, 392, 416
foreign holdings see control issues in foreign holdings
Fossum, John A. 63
401(k) plans 138, 332
Fourteenth Constitutional Amendment 53, 138, 296, 343
Fox, Vicente 242
frame-of-reference (FOR) training 309
framing 250
France 139
Frayne, Colette A. 21, 338, 387
Freeman, R. B. 405–6
French, W. L. 264
Freudenberger, H. J. 203
Friesen, P. H. 370
fringe benefits see benefits
Frink, Dwight D. 346–9
Frito-Lay 83
Frone, M. R. 426
Fu, P. P. 50
Fukutomi, G. D. S. 125
functional job analysis (FJA) 139–40
funeral leave 269
FUTA see Federal Unemployment Tax Act of 1935

G-ZTS see Guilford-Zimmerman Temperate Survey
gainsharing 30, 141, 273
  and grievances 151
  Improshare 181
  and quality circles 304
  Rucker plan 273, 325
  Scanlon plan 273, 333
  see also incentive pay; profit sharing
Gallagher, Daniel G. 270, 399–400
gambling, compulsive, and discrimination 155
Garvin, D. A. 223, 224, 383
Gatewood, Robert D. 209–10, 315
Gattiker, U. 424
Gaugler, B. B. 11
Gaugler, Eduard 144–6
GE see General Electric
gender issues in HRM
  and absence 1
  comparable worth 63
  cutoff scores 84
  discrimination when working overseas 130

gender issues in HRM (*cont'd*)
  dual-earner and dual-career couples 99–101
  EEOC v. *AT&T* 4
  Equal Pay Act of 1963 63, 121
  executive orders about discrimination 123–4
  expatriate assignments 127
  Fair Labor Standards Act of 1938 131–2, 227
  and federal contractors 123–4, 172
  Fourteenth Constitutional Amendment 53, 138, 296, 343
  gender effects in recruiting 141–2
  gender issues in international assignments 142–3
  glass ceiling 146–7
  Johnson v. *Transportation Agency, Santa Clara County* 215, 322
  Lorance v. *AT&T* 226
  managing diversity 94–5
  occupational choice 260
  and outplacement 267
  and part-time employment 269–70
  pay 63, 121, 173
  pension plans 112–13
  physical ability testing 286
  Pregnancy Discrimination Act of 1978 55, 293
  Price Waterhouse v. *Hopkins* 295
  and reverse discrimination 322
  sex discrimination 341
  sex-role stereotypes 142, 341–2
  sexual orientation 343
  South Korea 351
  tests 84, 89, 187, 188–9, 258, 379–81, 390–1
  UK discrimination regulation 410
  women's career issues 424–5
  workforce demographics 433
  see also Civil Rights Act of 1964; discrimination; disparate impact; disparate treatment; sexual harassment; work–family conflict; work–nonwork role issues
General Electric (GE) 83
General Electric v. *Gilbert* 293
General Schedule (GS) system 57
Generation X 143
genetic screening 143–4
George, Jennifer M. 6
Gerhart, B. 195

Geringer, J. Michael 74–5
Germany 144–6
  collective bargaining 255
Ghadar, F. 147
Ghiselli, E. E. 101, 245
Ghorpade, J. 214
Giacalone, Robert A. 126
Giacobbe-Miller, J. K. 51
Gillen, D. A. 233
glass ceiling 146–7
  breaking through 424–5
  and sex-role stereotypes 341–2
  see also affirmative action; gender issues in HRM
Gleser, G. C. 336
Glick, William H. 33–5, 185–6
global human resource strategies 147–8
host-country human resource management 160–1
  see also Australia; Canada; European Union; France; Germany; Italy; Japan; Mexico; overseas working and businesses; Russia; South Korea; United Kingdom; United States
Goffman, Erving 346
golden parachutes 122, 148–9
Goleman, Daniel 105
Goldstein, H. W. 14
Goldstein, Irwin L. 385–92
Gomez-Mejia, Luis R. 64, 378
good faith bargaining 149
Gordon, Michael E. 151, 153, 399
Gottfredson, Linda S. 68–9, 187–9, 257–8
government contracts and the disabled 316
  see also federal government contracts
government employees privacy 296
  public sector bargaining 303
Graham, A. 383
Gramm, Cynthia L. 361–2
graphic rating scale method of performance evaluation 149–50
graphology 150–1
Gray, David A. 6, 20, 225–6, 149
Green, S. B. 22
Greenberg, J. 348
greenfield sites 151
Greenhaus, Jeffrey H. 260–1
Greer, Charles R. 7, 76–7, 86, 149, 320–1
Gregersen, Hal B. 127–8, 319
Greller, Martin M. 180–1
grievances 153
  definition 9
  determinants 151

Federal Mediation and Conciliation Service (FMCS) 133, 324
filing rates 73, 151
mediation 7, 238
nonunion employee grievance procedures 253–5
procedures 72–3, 152–3, 253–5
railroad and airline industries 306–7
  see also arbitration; contract administration; disputes
Griffeth, R. W. 114, 115
Griffin, Ricky W. 437–9
Griggs v. *Duke Power* 56, 153, 188–9
group disability benefits 153–4
group life insurance/survivor benefits 154
GS system *see* General Schedule system
Guilford-Zimmerman Temperate Survey (G-ZTS) 284
Guion, Robert M. 69–70, 295–6, 352, 379, 413–14

Hackman, J. R. 35, 339
Haier Group 50
Hall, A. T. 348
halo effects 60, 92, 155, 311, 312
Hambrick, D. C. 123, 125
Hammer, M. 33, 34–5
handicapped/disabled 155
  disability benefits 349, 350
  group disability benefits 153–4
  workers' compensation benefits 432
  workers' compensation law 432–3
handwriting analysis *see* graphology
Harrington, H. J. 34–5
Harris, H. 402
Harris, M. M. 275, 340
Harris v. *Forklift Systems* 342, 343
Harvey, Robert J. 101, 200–1, 206, 376
Hatch, Senator 431
Hawke, Bob 15
Hawthorne experiments 163
Hay method and other hybrid job evaluation methods 156
Hayes, R. 383
hazardous materials in the workplace 156, 262
  legislation controlling notices 329–31
reproductive health hazards 321

hazards in the
    workplace   156–7, 262
Hazelwood School District v.
    United States   157
Hazen Paper Co. v. *Biggins*   5
HCI *see* human–computer
    interaction
headhunters   124–5
health
    and absence   1
    **AIDS/AIDS-related
        complex**   6
    blood-borne pathogens   328
    conditions considered to be
        disabilities   316
    **Family and Medical Leave
        Act of 1993**   49, 100, **132**, 172
    genetic screening   143–4
    **group disability
        benefits**   153–4
    insurance   349–50
    **occupational injury/illness
        measurement**   261
    promotion   114, 157–9, 215,
        346, 371, 423
    **reproductive health
        hazards**   321
    sick pay   269
    **smoke-free work
        environment**   345–6
    smoking cessation   158, 346
    UK   411
    US illness statistics   329
    wellness   423
    **workers' compensation
        benefits**   432
    **workers' compensation
        law**   432–3
    in the workplace   157
    see also safety and health
health maintenance
    organizations (HMOs)   157
healthcare
    for the aged and disabled   349
    coordination of benefits   75
    expense   159
    extending   68
    **health maintenance
        organizations**   157
    indemnity plans   182
    managed care   25, **228–9**
    Mexico   241
    retiree benefits   68, 132
    and smokers   346
Hedge, J. W.   308
Helburn, I. B.   247
Helmreich, R. L.   342
Hendricks, W. E.   362
Heneman, Robert L.   239–40,
    273–4, 287
Henry, R.   101
hepatitis   328

Hewlett-Packard   398
HFE *see* human factors engineering
Higgins, C. A.   100
hiring
    countercyclical   76–7
    negligent   249
    **persons with
        disabilities**   159–60
    see also personnel selection and
        recruitment; staffing
Hirsch, B. T.   400, 405–6
Hirschman, A. O.   405
HIV/AIDS *see* AIDS
HMOs *see* health maintenance
    organizations
Hoel, Helge   31–3
Hofmann, D. A.   101
Hogan, J. C.   286
Hogan Personality Inventory
    (HPI)   28
Holder, G. W.   177
holdout subsamples   82
holidays *see* paid time off
Holland, J. L.   260
Holley, William H., Jr.   152–3,
    323–4
Hom, P. W.   114, 115
homosexuality *see* sexual orientation
Honda   191
honesty testing *see* integrity testing
Hong Kong   51–2
Hoopes, D. G.   165
horizontal management   160,
    434
    see also knowledge teams; self-
        managing teams
hospital insurance   349, 350
**host-country human resource
    management**   160–1
    see also overseas working and
        businesses
hostile environment model of
    discrimination   90
hot-cargo agreements   404
hours worked *see* work schedules
Howard, John   15
Howell, William C.   80, 162–3,
    389
HRCI *see* Human Resource
    Certification Institute
HRIS *see* human resource
    information systems
HRNET   194
HRPS *see* Human Resource
    Planning Society
HRS *see* human resource strategy
Hui, C.   50
Hulin, C. L.   101
human capital theory   161–2
human–computer interaction
    (HCI)   163
human error, reducing   162–3

**human factors engineering
    (HFE)**   162–3
**human relations
    approach**   163–4
human resource audits   164–5
**human resource-based
    competitive
    advantage**   165–6
**Human Resource Certification
    Institute (HRCI)**   166–7
human resource
    departments   167
    effectiveness   167–8
Human Resource Division,
    Academy of
    Management   168–9
human resource function   169
    outsourcing   173–4
**human resource information
    systems (HRIS)**   169–70
    and human resource audits   164
**human resource
    inventories**   170–1
human resource management
    customer oriented   83–4
    international *see* Australia;
        Canada; European Union;
        France; Germany; Italy; Japan;
        Mexico; overseas working and
        businesses; Russia; South
        Korea; United Kingdom
    nonunion firms   255–7
    in the US   171–4
    see also strategic human resource
        management
**human resource
    planning**   174–5
    forecasting tools   237–8
    Germany   145
    managing the process
        235–6
    strategic   174, 357–8, 358–61
**Human Resource Planning
    Society (HRPS)**   175
human resource professional
    societies
    Australia   16–17
    IPMA-HR   193
    UK   47–8
    US   166–7, 350
    worldwide   350
**human resource
    programming**   175–6
human resource staff,
    certification   166–7
**human resource strategy
    (HRS)**   176–8
    contingency approach   70
**human resources, strategic role
    of**   368–9
Hunter, J. R.   344
Hunter, John E.   234, 414

Huselid, Mark A.   164–5, 167–8, 169

IBM   255, 398
Ichniowski, C.   168
IFEBP *see* International Foundation of Employee Benefit Programs
Ilgen, D. R.   60
illness *see* health
ILMs *see* internal labor markets
immigrants
  labor, UK   411
  see also national origin discrimination
Immigration and Naturalization Service   180
Immigration Reform and Control Act of 1986 (IRCA)   179–80
impact
  disparate *see* disparate impact
  of mergers and acquisitions   180–1
Improshare   181
in-bond program *see* maquiladora
incentive pay   182
  commission-based pay   62–3
  and leniency effects   225
  and salesforce   332
  standard hour plan   352
  team-based incentives   378, 436
  see also bonuses; gainsharing; profit sharing
incidence rates   261
indemnity plans   182
independent contractors   182–3
individual differences   183
  managerial value differences   234–5
individual retirement accounts (IRAs)   183
industrial relations   183–5
  professional associations   184
  strategic   361–2
  see also arbitration; bargaining; disputes; grievances; labor relations
industrial unions   185
information systems, human resource   169–70
information technology enablers   185–6
injuries
  occupational injury/illness measurement   261
  repetitive motion strain injury   319–20
  US statistics   329
  workers' compensation benefits   432

workers' compensation law   432–3
  see also safety and health
Institute of Personnel Management (UK)   47, 48
Institute of Training and Development (UK)   47, 48
Institutional Revolutionary Party (PRI; Mexico)   242
insurance, hospital   349, 350
insurance, life *see* group life insurance/survivor benefits
insurance, unemployment   133, 349, 397
integrative bargaining   186
integrity testing   172, 186–7
  testing potential drug use   98
Intel   106
intelligence tests   187–9
  norms   257–8
interest arbitration   10, 189
  see also final offer arbitration
interim management   189–90
internal equity/internal consistency   190
internal labor markets (ILMs)   190–1
international assignments *see* overseas working and businesses
international compensation   191–2
International Foundation of Employee Benefit Programs (IFEBP)   192–3
international human resources management   147–8
  see also Australia; Canada; European Union; France; Germany; Italy; Japan; Mexico; overseas working and businesses; Russia; South Korea; United Kingdom; United States
International Public Management Association for Human Resources (IPMA-HR)   193
Internet   193–4
interviewer errors   194–5
  see also rating errors
interviews
  appraisal   280
  job analysis   202
  see also employment interview; exit interviews; situational interview
intra-organizational bargaining   195–6
inventories
  human resource   170–1
  personality   284

Strong Interest Inventory   419
task   376
vocational interest   302, 418–20
IPMA-HR *see* International Public Management Association for Human Resources
ipsative rating scales   430
IRAs *see* individual retirement accounts
IRCA *see* Immigration Reform and Control Act of 1986
Ireland, T. C.   77
ISO 9000   196
Italy   196–7

Jackofsky, Ellen F.   356
Jackson, Susan E.   94–5, 115
Jacobs, Rick   48–9, 101, 137–8, 247
Jain, Vinod K.   72, 223–4
James, Larry   89, 343–4, 379–81
Japan   198–200
  organization performance measures   126
  pay   272, 415
  production systems   216, 222–3
  quality   304, 383
  unions   256
Jaques, Elliot   382
Jarley, Paul   13, 92–3, 186, 195–6, 362, 404–5
Jarrell, Donald W.   170–1, 235–6
Jarrett, R. F.   337
Jensen, M.   148
JIT production systems *see* just-in-time production systems
job analysis   201–2
  booklets about   296
  functional   139–40
  information sources   202–3
  and interviews   117
  job element method   204–5
  and job specifications   213
  KSAOs   218–19
  managerial jobs   234
  and performance appraisal   48
  Position Analysis Questionnaires   291–2
  strategic   364
  task inventory approach   376–7
  see also validity
job-based pay   203
job behavior   20
job burnout   203–4
job descriptions   204
  classification   57
  Dictionary of Occupational Work Titles   88–9
job design   163–4
job element method of job analysis   204–5

job evaluation
    administrative issues 205
    classification method 57
    and comparable worth 63
    compensable factors 63
    external equity/external
        competitiveness 129–30
    factor-comparison
        method 131
    forced distribution
        method 137–8
    functions 190
    Hay method and other hybrid
        methods 156
    internal equity/internal
        consistency 190
    methods 205–6
    and pay grades 274
    point method 287–8, 414
    ranking method 307
    time span of discretion 382
job families 206
    and job analysis 377
job fit 13–14, 282–3
job involvement 206–7
job loss 207–8
    outplacement 266–8
    see also layoffs
job performance 208–9
    definitions 393
    and KSAOs 334
    and smoking 346
    and work constraints 425–6
    see also performance appraisal and
        evaluation; performance-based
        pay; performance coaching;
        performance diaries;
        performance management;
        performance outcome;
        performance standards
job posting 209–10
job previews see realistic job
    previews
job-relatedness 56, 90, 210
    Albemarle Paper Company v.
        Moody 7
    and situational interviews 344
job rotation 210–11
job sample tests 428–9
job satisfaction 211–12
    and absence 2
    assessing 12
    career plateauing 42–3
    and career success 45
    China 50
    and deskilling 87
    and merit pay 240
    and organizational
        socialization 266
    and performance-based pay 273
    and performance standards 282
    and person–job fit 282–3

and realistic job
    previews 312–13, 314
and union coverage 405
and union–management
    cooperation 401–2
see also employee morale; pay
    satisfaction; quality of work life
job search 212–13
    after layoff 266–8
job sharing 213
job-skills training 213
job specifications 213–14
jobs 200–1
    classification 88–9
    key/benchmark 131, 217
    occupational choice 39,
        260–1
    red circle 315
Johns, Gary 1–3
Johnson, Nancy Brown 400, 405–6
Johnson v. *Transportation Agency,
    Santa Clara County* 215,
    322
Journal of Vocational Behavior 260
Judge, Timothy A. 39–40, 45–6,
    289, 368
judgment
    and cutoff scores 84–5
    and graphic rating scales 150
    and performance
        appraisals 59–60
Juran, Joseph 383
Juravich, T. 402
jurisdictional strikes 372
jury duty 269
just-in-time (JIT) production
    systems 216
    information technology
        enablers 186
justice see distributive justice;
    procedural justice

Kahn, R. L. 426
Kaiser Aluminum and Chemical
    Corporation 354
Kamiya, Shotaro 223
Kandola, B. 409, 411
Kane, J. S. 275
Kanungo, R. N. 108
Kaplan, L. B. 65
Kaplan, R. S. 19
Katz, H. C. 361, 406
Kavanaugh, M. J. 308
Keaveny, Timothy J. 62–3, 205,
    282, 352, 382
Keck, S. L. 125
Keen, P. 35
Keiser, John D. 433–7
Kennedy, Senator Edward 431
Kerr, C. 190
Kessler, Ian 272–3
key jobs 131, 217

Kim, Peter H. 250–1
Kipnis, D. 347
Kipnis's taxonomy of political
    behavior 289
Kiser, K. 383
Klein, Katherine J. 113
kleptomania, and
    discrimination 155
Klimoski, Richard 10–12, 21,
    344–5, 428–9
Kline, P. 23
Kluger, A. N. 423
Knapp, E. 35
knowledge
    knowledge teams 217–18
    knowledge work 218, 345
    learning organization 223–4
    learning
        reinforcement 224–5
    and strategic alliances 354–5
    see also KSAOs; learning; training
knowledge, skills, and
    competencies, pay
    for 271–2
Koch, Marianne J. 351
Kochan, T. A. 184, 361, 406
Kolb, Deborah M. 238
Konz, A. M. 364
Korea see South Korea
Korman, A K. 45
Kossek, Ellen Ernst 49, 105,
    427–8
Krackhardt, D. 115
Kraiger, K. 387, 392
Kraimer, M. L. 289
Kram, Kathy E. 239
Krider, Charles E. 220–1, 221–2,
    248–9, 258–9, 306–7
Kristof, A. L. 283
Kruse, D. L. 300
KSAOs 20, 218–19
    assessing 10–12
    and career success 45
    and job analysis 364
    and job performance 334
Kuhn, T S. 114

Laabs, J. J. 346
Labig, C. E., Jr. 315
labor
    availability analysis 17–18,
        317
    certification 180
    independent
        contractors 182–3
Labor, Department of 180
labor contracts 220
labor disputes see disputes
Labor Management Relations
    Act of 1947 (Taft-Hartley
    Act) 133, 149, 220–1,
    372

Labor Management Reporting and Disclosures Act of 1959 (Landrum-Griffin Act) 221–2
labor markets
  internal 190–1
  relevant 317
labor mobility 222
  scientists and engineers 41–2
  UK 411
labor relations
  Australia 14–16
  Canada 36–7
  China 50–2
  and the EU 121
  France 139
  Hong Kong 52
  Italy 196–7
  Labor Management Relations Act of 1947 133, 149, 220–1, 372
  Mexico 240–4
  National Labor Relations Act of 1935 149, 172, 220–1, 248–9, 323, 334
  National Labor Relations Board 149, 248–9, **249**, 320–1, 403
  nonunion firms 253–7
  Railway Labor Act of 1926 306–7
  Russia 325–7
  South Korea 351
  UK 255, 409–11
  see also arbitration; bargaining; disputes; grievances; industrial relations
labor unions *see* unions
Labour Party (UK) 409, 410
lag pay policy 421
Laming, D. 150
Landrum-Griffin Act *see* Labor Management Reporting and Disclosures Act of 1959
Larry P. v. *Riles* 188–9
Larwood, L. 424
lateral management *see* horizontal management
Latham, Gary P. 21, 57–8, 210–11, 232, 281, 308, 344, 387
Lau, Chung-Ming 49–53
Law, K. S. 50
Lawler, E. E. 12, 275
Lawrence, Stephen 410
Lawshe, C. H. 70, 129
layoffs 115–16, 176, 207–8
  and affirmative action 4
  avoiding 175
  and discrimination 134, 322
  downsizing 95–7, 176, 434
  early retirement in Japan 199
  and employment-at-will 116–17
  France 139
  Mexico 241–2
  outplacement 266–8
  Russia 326
  severance pay 269
  UK 409
Worker Adjustment and Retraining Notification Act of 1988 176, **430**–2
Leach, Graeme 411
lead pay policy 421
leadership
  and bullying 32
  and emotional intelligence 105
  leadership competencies 373
  self-leaders 109
  strategic leaders 230–1
lean production 222–3
  Japan 199
  see also just-in-time production systems
Leana, Carrie R. 104–5, 115, 207–8
Leap, Terry L. 130, 236, 404
learning 387
  action 3
  American Society for Training and Development (ASTD) 7
  distance 91
  pay for 271–2
  transfer of 395
  see also knowledge; training
learning organization 223–4
learning reinforcement
  feedback 224
  practice 224–5
leave
  Family and Medical Leave Act of 1993 49, 100, **132**, 172
  see also paid time off
lecture method 225
  and rater training 308
Ledford, Gerald E., Jr. 12, 265, 271–2, 345, 415–16
Ledgerwood, Donna E. 156–7, 247–8, 261, 263, 319–20, 321, 328–31
Lee, Barbara A. 3–4, 18, 30, 33, 210, 227, 249–50, 253, 303, 322, 342–3
Lee, Thomas W. 111, 114–16
legislation, employment
  Age Discrimination in Employment Act of 1967 5
  Americans with Disabilities Act of 1990 7–8, 155, 159, 219
  Civil Rights Act of 1866 53
  Civil Rights Act of 1871 53
  Civil Rights Act of 1964 54–6
  Civil Rights Act of 1991 56
  Computer Matching and Privacy Protection Act of 1988 66
  Consolidated Omnibus Budget Reconciliation Act of 1985 68
  Davis-Bacon Act of 1931 86
  Employee Polygraph Protection Act of 1988 111–12
  Employee Retirement Income Security Act of 1974 27, 68, 112–13, 183, 332, 377
  extraterritorial application of employment law 130
  Fair Labor Standards Act of 1938 131–2, 227
  Family and Medical Leave Act of 1993 49, 100, **132**, 172
  Federal Election Campaign Act of 1971 288
  Federal Unemployment Tax Act of 1935 133
  Germany 145
  Immigration Reform and Control Act of 1986 (IRCA) 179–80
  Labor Management Relations Act of 1947 133, 149, **220**–1, 372
  Labor Management Reporting and Disclosures Act of 1959 221–2
  McNamara-O'Hara Service Contract Act of 1965 227
  Mexico 240–2
  Multiemployer Pension Amendments Act of 1980 (MPPAA) 112
  National Labor Relations Act of 1935 149, 172, 220–1, 248–9, 323, 334
  Norris-LaGuardia Anti-Injunction Act of 1932 258–9
  Occupational Safety and Health Act of 1970 172, 261–2, 328–31
  Older Workers Benefit Protection Act of 1991 175
  Portal to Portal Act of 1947 290
  Pregnancy Discrimination Act of 1978 293
  Privacy Act of 1974 296–7
  Railway Labor Act of 1926 306–7
  Rehabilitation Act of 1973 155, 159, 316

Retirement Equity Act of 1984 (REAct) 112–13
Russia 326
Social Security Act of 1935 349, 397
Tax Reform Act of 1986 377–8
UK 409–10
US overview 172
Vietnam-Era Veterans' Readjustment Assistance Act of 1972 416–17
Walsh-Healy Act of 1936 422
Worker Adjustment and Retraining Notification Act of 1988 176, 430–2
workers' compensation law 432–3
Lei, David 354–6
Lengnick-Hall, Mark L. 266–8
leniency effects 225, 311, 312
  avoiding 138
  and mixed-standard scales 245
lesbianism *see* sexual orientation
Leslie, J. B. 337
Levine, Edward L. 88–9, 201–2, 202–3, 204, 213–14
Lewin, David 72–4, 361–2
Lewis, H. G. 400
Lichtenberger, Steffen 144–6
Liden, R. C. 347
lie detector tests *see* polygraph testing
lifestyle *see* work–family conflict; work–nonwork role issues
Lipshitz, R. 278
Lissitz, R. W. 22
literacy *see* cultural literacy
Local 28 of the Sheet Metal Workers' International Association v. *EEOC* 4
Locke, E. 229, 281
lockouts 189, **225–6**
Lofquist, L. H. 260, 282–3
Lombardo, M. M. 87
London, Oliver 175, 277–9
Longenecker, Clinton O. 102
Lorance v. *AT&T* 226
Los Angeles police and riots 386
loyalty *see* employee loyalty
Lu, Y. 51
Lubatkin, M. 125
Lui, S. 52

Mabe, P. A. 340
McCabe, Douglas M. 153–5
McCaffery, Robert M. 27, 75, 107–8, 134–5, 153–4, 192–3, 269, 349–50, 397, 439
McCall, M. W. 87
McCormick, Ernest J. 291
MacCrimmon, K. R. 237

McDaniel, Michael A. 56–7, 285, 287, 301, 351–2
McDonald's 255
McDonnell Douglas v. *Green* 227
MacDuffie, J. P. 168
McGregor, Douglas 163
Macik-Frey, Marilyn 214–15
McKersie, R. B. 361, 362, 366, 406
McMahan, G. 356
McNamara-O'Hara Service Contract Act of 1965 227
MacNamara v. *Korean Airlines* 130
Macpherson Inquiry 410
McQuarrie, Fiona A. E. 141–2, 146–7
Madsen, T. L. 165
Mainiero, Lisa 424–5
make-whole/compensatory remedies 227, 248–9
Malcolm Baldrige National Quality Award (MBNQA) 196, 227–8
Malone, M. S. 417–18
managed care 25, **228–9**
  health maintenance organizations 157
management
  horizontal 160, 434
  human relations approach 163–4
  interim 189–90
  management practices standards 196
  managing voluntary turnover 115
  scientific 333
  self-management 109
  self-managing teams 109, 171, **338–40**
  strategic 96, **364–5**
  union–management cooperation 400–2
management by objectives (MBO) 173, **229–30,** 234
management consultancy 230
management development 230–2
  Australia 15
  see also early identification of management talent
management games 232
management localization 232–3
  see also overseas working and businesses
management prerogatives 233
  Europe 255
managers
  and career plateauing 43
  countercyclical hiring 76–7

developing 87–8, 356, 373
early identification of talent 10–12, **103–4**
executive compensation 122–3
executive management review sessions 373
executive search 124–5
executive selection 125–6
gender issues 147, 341–2
golden parachutes 148–9
and job satisfaction 45
manager–employee pay differentials 173
managers' attitude and grievances 151
outplacement 267–8
pay 122–3
and performance appraisals 102
performance assessment 233–4
roles 103, 233–4
succession planning 239, 372–4
training 436
value differences 234–5
managing the human resource planning process 235–6
  see also human resource planning; strategic human resource planning; strategic human resource planning processes
mandatory bargaining issues 236
Manning, Michael R. 345–6
Manz, Charles C. 108–10
maquiladora 236–7
Markel, K. S. 426
Markov analysis 237–8
Marquardt, L. D. 291
Martin, Cornelia 144–6
Martin, James E. 396
Martin v. *Wilks* 238
Martinko, M. J. 202
Maslach, C. 203
Maslow, Abraham 163
Masters, Marick F. 288
match pay policy 421
material safety data sheets (MSDs) 262
maternity leave
  Family and Medical Leave Act of 1993 49, 100, **132,** 172
  Mexico 241
Mathur-Helm, B. 142
Mathys, Nicholas J. 320, 325, 395
Maurer, T. 336
Mayo, Elton 163
Mazda 389
MBNQA *see* Malcolm Baldrige National Quality Award
MBO *see* management by objectives

mediation 7, 238
   Federal Mediation and
      Conciliation Service
      (FMCS) 133, 324
   medical leave
   Family and Medical Leave
      Act of 1993 49, 100, **132**, 172
Medicare/Medicaid 349, 350
Medoff, J. L. 405–6
Meglino, Bruce M. 12, 56, 429–30
membership-based
   compensation 382
memory, and performance
   appraisal 59
Mendenhall, Mark E. 82–3,
   126–7, 294
mental abilities 238–9
mentoring programs 239
   and managing diversity 95
   see also coaching
mergers and acquisitions
   impact 180–1
   keeping staff 148–9
   UK employee protection 410
merit pay 239–40
   see also bonuses; incentive pay;
      performance-based pay
Meritor Savings Bank v.
   Vinson 240, 342
Messick, S. 79
Mexico 240–4
   maquiladora 236–7
Miceli, Marcia P. 423–4
Miles, R. E. 370
military service, short-term 269
Milkovich, G. T. 57
Miller, D. 370
Miner Sentence Completion Scale
   (MSCS) 284
minimum wage 131–2
   Mexico 241
Mintzberg, H. 103, 233, 364, 370
Mitchell, T. R. 114
mixed-standard scales 244–5
mobbing *see* bullying
mobility *see* labor mobility
Mobley, W. H. 114
Mohrman, Susan Albers 160,
   217–18, 304–5, 338–40
monitoring employees *see*
   surveillance
Montesino, M. U. 386
Morin, Lucie 57–8, 210–11,
   232
Morris, Shad S. 165–6
Morrison, A. M. 87
Mossholder, Kevin W. 289
motivation
   and HRM practices 167
   and performance-based pay
      272
   and performance standards 282

see also incentive pay;
   performance appraisal and
   evaluation; promotion
Motorola 41, 83
Motowidlo, S. J. 265–6
Mount, Michael K. 27–8, 283–5
Mouton, J. A. 366
Muchinsky, Paul M. 77, 80,
   282–3, 418–20
multicultural workforce 245,
   390
   see also diversity
Multiemployer Pension
   Amendments Act of 1980
   (MPPAA) 112
multinational
   bargaining 245–6
multinational human resource
   strategies *see* global human
   resource strategies
multiple criteria *see* composite and
   multiple criteria
multiple cutoff selection
   procedures 246
   cutoff scores 84–5
multiple-hurdle selection
   procedures 246
Mumford, M. D. 28
Murphy, Kevin R. 301–2,
   309–12
Myers–Briggs type indicator 337

Nacamulli, Raoul C. D. 196–7
NACLC *see* North American
   Commission on Labor
   Cooperation
narcotics *see* drugs
narrative method of
   performance
   evaluation 247
Nathan, B. E. 265
National Academy of
   Arbitrators 247, 324
National Action Party (PAN;
   Mexico) 242
National Emergency Strike 372
National Institute for
   Occupational Safety and
   Health (NIOSH) 247–8,
   262, 263
National Labor Relations Act of
   1935 (NLRA; Wagner
   Act) 149, 172, 220–1, **248–9**,
   323, 334
National Labor Relations Board
   (NLRB) 149, 248–9, **249**,
   320–1, 403
National Mediation Board 306
national origin
   managing diversity 94–5
   and workforce
      demographics 433

national origin
   discrimination 180,
   249
   discrimination when working
      overseas 130
   executive orders about
      discrimination 123–4
   and federal contractors 123–4,
      172
   Fourteenth Constitutional
      Amendment 53, **138**, 296,
      343
   Immigration and Naturalization
      Service 180
   Immigration Reform and
      Control Act of 1986
      (IRCA) 179–80
   interviews 195
   and tests 84, 89, 187, 188–9,
      258, 279–81, 390–1
   see also Civil Rights Act of 1964;
      discrimination; disparate
      impact; disparate treatment
Nationwide Insurance 41
Native Americans, and
   discrimination 54
Near, J. P. 424
Neck, Christopher P. 108–10
Nedelsky method 85
negligent hiring 249
negligent retention 249–50
negligent supervision 250
negotiation
   biases 250–1
   strategic negotiations 366
   tactics 93, **251–2**
   see also bargaining
Nelson, Debra L. 214–15
NEO-PI 28
nepotism policies 252
Netherlands, workers'
   compensation 433
networking
   and headhunters 125
   overseas 126–7
   see also strategic alliances
new employee orientation
   253
   and coaching 57
   Japan 199–200
   and organizational culture 265
   see also organizational
      socialization
New Labour (UK political
   party) 409, 410
Newman, Jerry M. 57, 63, 217,
   274, 421
*Newport News Shipbuilding and Dry
   Dock Co.* v. *EEOC* 293
Ngo, H. Y. 51, 52
Nicholson, Nigel 42–3
Nike 417

Index 457

NIOSH *see* National Institute for Occupational Safety and Health
Nkomo, Stella M.   175–6, 369–70
NLRA *see* National Labor Relations Act of 1935
NLRB *see* National Labor Relations Board
NLRB v. *Borg Warner*   236
NLRB v. *Town and Country Electric*   332
Noe, Raymond A.   14, 66, 300
Nollen, Stanley   71, 111, 113–14, 182–3, 213, 270, 315–16, 379
Nonaka, I.   223–4
non-compete agreements   253
nonunion employee grievance procedures   152, **253–5**, 324
nonunion firms   255–7
Noon, S.   101
Normand, J.   336–7
norms   257–8
  race norming   56
Norris-LaGuardia Anti-Injunction Act of 1932   258–9
North American Commission on Labor Cooperation (NACLC)   242–3
Norton, D. P.   19
Nunnally, J. C.   299
Nussbaum, Karen   5
Nyaw, M. K.   52

OASDHI *see* Old Age, Survivor, Disability, and Health Insurance Program
objectives, management by *see* management by objectives
O'Brien, Christine Neylon   53
observational training   308
occupational choice   39, **260–1**
  vocational interest inventories   418–20
occupational injury/illness measurement   261
Occupational Safety and Health Act of 1970 (OSHA)   172, 261–2, 328–31
Occupational Safety and Health Administration (OSHA)   247, 262, 263, 328
Occupational Safety and Health Review Commission (OSHRC)   262
O'Connor, E. J.   22, 425
OCP *see* Organizational Culture Profile
Oddou, G. R.   294
Office of Federal Contract Compliance Programs (OFCCP)   3, 172, 263

and availability analysis   17
Ohno, Taiichi   216, 222–3
Old Age, Survivor, Disability, and Health Insurance Program (OASDHI)   349
Older Workers Benefit Protection Act of 1991   175
Oldham, G. R.   35
Oldsmobile   136
Olian, Judy D.   143–4, 368
Olson, C. A.   385
O'Malley, Colleen   99–101
omega   318
on-the-job training (OJT)   84, 253, 263
open-door policies   254
O'Reilly, C. A.   114–15, 265, 283
organization development and change   47, **264–5**
  business process reengineering   33–5
  change management   46–7
  conference method   67
  continuous improvement   72
  downsizing   95–7, 176, 434
  greenfield sites   151
  information technology enablers   185–6
  strategic leadership   230–1
  total quality management   382–5
organizational behavior
  attraction–selection–attrition   13–14
organizational culture
  and bullying   32
  and change   434
  and selection   265–6
  see also work values
Organizational Culture Profile (OCP)   430
organizational fit   13–14
  realistic job previews   212, 312–13, 368
organizational socialization   266
  and coaching   57
  Japan   199–200
  new employee orientation   253
  and organizational culture   265
organizational structures and forms
  and benchmarking   25
  and business process reengineering   34
  and career plateauing   43
  and career success   45
  and employee involvement   110–11, 168
  and flexibility   171

  horizontal management   160, 434
  lean production   222–3
  learning organizations   223–4
  replacement charts   320
  and strategic alliances   355
  and TQM   384
  virtual organizations   417–18
  see also workforce flexibility
Osburn, Hobart G.   101, 414
OSHA *see* Occupational Safety and Health Act of 1970; Occupational Safety and Health Administration
OSHRC *see* Occupational Safety and Health Review Commission
Osipow, S. H.   260
Osterman, Paul   190–1
Ouellette, Catherine A.   245, 362–4, 433
outplacement   266–8
outsourcing
  employee leasing   111
  employee subcontracting   113–14
  and grievances   153
  HRM functions   173–4
  independent contractors   182–3
  and recruitment   114, 172–3
  strategic   367–8
overconfidence   250
overseas working and businesses
  control issues in foreign holdings   74–5
  cultural literacy   82–3
  developing globally competent executives/managers   87–8
  downsizing   96
  expatriate assignment   126–7, 161, 390
  expatriate human resources issues   127–8
  expatriate support system   128–9
  extraterritorial application of employment law   130
  gender issues in international assignments   142–3
  global human resource strategies   147–8
  host-country human resource management   160–1
  international compensation   191–2
  management localization   232–3
  multicultural workforce   245, 390

overseas working and businesses (*cont'd*)
  multinational bargaining 245–6
  preparation for an international work assignment 293–5
  and realistic job previews 312–13
  repatriation 128, 129, 294, 319
  see also Australia; Canada; European Union; France; Germany; Italy; Japan; Mexico; Russia; South Korea; United Kingdom; United States
overtime pay 131–2, 241
Oviatt, Benjamin M. 364–5, 370–1
Owens, W. C. 28

Pace, L. A. 107
PACs *see* political action committees
Paetzold, Ramona L. 5, 33, 62, 68, 90–1, 112–13, 123–4, 132, 138, 155, 249, 270–1, 293, 306, 319, 341, 343, 377–8, 381, 416
paid time off 269
  Mexico 241, 242
  Russia 326
PAN *see* National Action Party
PAQs *see* Position Analysis Questionnaires
Parasaraman, A. 341
Pareto optimality 186
Parsons, F. 418
part-time employment 269–70
  contingent workers 71, 176
  job sharing 213
  piecework 287
  Family and Medical Leave Act of 1993 49, 100, 132, 172
part-time work schedules 270
passing scores *see* cutoff scores
pattern bargaining 270
pattern or practice cases 270–1
patterned interview 117
Paullay, I. M. 206–7
pay 64
  for activities preliminary to work 290
  add-on pay 12
  at-risk 12
  broadbanding 30–1
  commission-based 62–3
  compa-ratios 63
  comparable worth 63
  compensable factors 63
  Davis-Bacon Act of 1931 86
  distributive justice 93–4
  Equal Pay Act of 1963 63, 121

external equity/external competitiveness 129–30
federal government contracts 86, 227, 422
401(k) plans 138, 332
Germany 144
grades 274
incentive 62–3, 182, 225, 352
internal equity/internal consistency 190
Japan 200
job-based 203
  and job sharing 213
  for knowledge, skills, and competencies 271–2
legislation 86
manager–employee differentials 173
merit 239–40
Mexico 241, 242
minimum wage 131–2
overtime 131–2, 241
paid time off 269
pay for performance 173, 272–3, 322–3
pay for performance plans 273–4
person-based 282
piecework 182, 273, 287
Portal to Portal Act of 1947 290
potential base pay at risk 12
rate ranges 307–8
record keeping 132
red circle jobs 315
Russia 325
satisfaction 274
secrecy 274–5
skills-based 271–2, 273, 345
standard hour plan 352
time-based 273, 382
two-tiered pay structures 396
union effects on 400, 405
US 173
wage/pay policy line 421
wage/pay/salary structure 421
wage and salary surveys 421
Walsh-Healy Act of 1936 422
see also bargaining; benefits; compensation; job evaluation
PCI *see* Personal Characteristics Inventory
PDA *see* Pregnancy Discrimination Act of 1978
PDPs *see* personal development plans
Pearce, J. A., II 364
pedophilia, and discrimination 155
peer ratings 275, 311, 340

peer review systems 254
Pension Benefit Guaranty Corporation 276
pension plans 276
  Consolidated Omnibus Budget Reconciliation Act of 1985 (COBRA) 68
  401(k) plans 138, 332
  early retirement buyout 104
  early retirement policy 104–5
  Employee Retirement Income Security Act of 1974 27, 68, 112–13, 183, 332, 377
  individual retirement accounts 183
  Mexico 241
  Pension Benefit Guaranty Corporation 276
  Russia 326
  savings or thrift plans 332–3
  and survivor benefits 154
  tax-deferred annuities 377
  and taxation 377–8
performance appraisal and evaluation 276–7, 280–1
  appraisal feedback 8–9, 48, 231
  appraisal interviews 280
  balanced scorecard 19–20
  checklist method 48–9
  cognitive process models 58–61
  criterion contamination 77–8
  criterion deficiency 78
  criterion problem 78–9, 101
  criterion relevance 79
  critical incidents technique 80–1
  diaries 279–80
  distributional effects 91–2
  diverse workforce 94–5
  and duty 101
  dysfunctional appraisals 102
  expatriates 128
  expectancy charts 129
  forced distribution method 137–8
  graphic rating scale method 149–50
  host-country 161
  and identifying managers 103–4
  management by objectives (MBO) 173, 229–30, 234
  managerial 233–4
  narrative method 247
  norms 257–8
  peer ratings 275, 311, 340
performance management 280–1

and Position Analysis
    Questionnaires   291
ranking method   307
self-ratings   275, 310–11, **340**
social influence   346–9
supervisory ratings   275, 340, 374, 435
360-degree appraisals   95, 231, 381
    US   173
    and workforce flexibility   435
    see also rating accuracy; rating bias; rating errors; rating scales; tests
performance-based pay   173, 272–3, 273–4, 322–3
    see also bonuses; incentive pay; merit pay
performance coaching   277–9
    and appraisal   48
    see also coaching; mentoring programs
performance diaries   202, 279–80
performance management   280–1
    and self-managing teams   339
performance outcome   281
performance standards   281–2
person-based pay   282
person–job fit   13–14, 282–3
Personal Characteristics Inventory (PCI)   28
personal development plans (PDPs)   283
personality tests   187, 302, 283–5
    Big Five personality tests   27–8
    Cattell's 16PF test   23
    and executive selection   125
    testing potential drug use   98
personality traits *see* traits
personnel selection and recruitment   285, 351
    assessment centers   10–12, 103, 389
    background checking   19
    behavioral consistency principle   21
    biographical history inventories   28–30
    customer involvement   83
    cutoff scores   84–5
    disabled applicants   159
    executive search   124–5
    executive selection   125–6
    for expatriate assignment   127
    gender effects in recruiting   141–2
    genetic screening   143–4
    graphology   150–1
    internal   209–10

internal v. external recruitment   176
interviewer errors   194–5
interviews   117–18, 313, 344
Japan   199
job posting   209–10
KSAOs   218–19
mental abilities   238–9
multiple cutoff selection procedures   246
multiple-hurdle selection procedures   246
outsourcing   114, 172–3
and organizational culture   265–6
physical abilities   285–6
Principles for the Use of Personnel Selection Procedures   295–6
profile-matching procedures   283, **299**
realistic job previews (RJPs)   212, 312–13, 368
recruiting   313–15
recruiting sources   315
reference checks   316
Russia   326
selection models   334–5
selection utility models   335–7
strategic recruiting   368
and training   388–9
Uniform Guidelines on Employee Selection Procedures   380, 397
US   172–3
weighted application blanks   423
yield ratio   440
    see also organizational socialization; rating accuracy; rating bias; rating errors; rating scales; staffing; tests; validity
persuasion, burden of   33
pest analysis   285
Peters, Lawrence H.   92, 305, 317, 342, 411–12, 425
Peterson, Richard B.   402–3
Pfeffer, J.   435
Phillips, James S.   81–2, 131, 375
physical abilities   285
    testing   285–6
picketing   221, 286–7, 404
    secondary boycotts   221, 334, 404
piecework   182, 273, 287
    compared to standard hour plan   352
Pieper, K. F.   101
Pierce, Jon L.   65–6, 135–6, 136–7
Piore, M.   190
placement   287

planning *see* human resource planning; strategic human resource planning; succession planning
Poelmans, Stephen   426–7
point job evaluation method   287–8, 414
Polaroid   398
police
    Los Angeles police and riots   386
    qualifying tests   422
political action committees (PACs) and labor unions   288
political influences in career planning   289
polygraph testing   289–90
    Employee Polygraph Protection Act of 1988   111–12, 290
Polzer, Jeffrey T.   251–2
Popper, M.   278
Portal to Portal Act of 1947   290
Porter, M. E.   365, 370
Position Analysis Questionnaires (PAQs)   291–2
positive discipline   292
post-traumatic stress disorder, and discrimination   316
potential base pay at risk   12
practice
    and learning reinforcement   224
    and rater training   308
predictive validity   67, 69, 292–3
predictive yield, Thorndike method   85
Pregnancy Discrimination Act of 1978 (PDA)   55, 293
Prennushi, G.   168
preparation for an international work assignment   293–5
    see also overseas working and businesses
Price Waterhouse v. *Hopkins*   295
Primoff, Ernest   204–5
Principles for the Use of Personnel Selection Procedures   295–6
privacy
    Computer Matching and Privacy Protection Act of 1988   66
    Employee Polygraph Protection Act of 1988   111–12, 290
    Fourteenth Constitutional Amendment   53, 138, 296, 345
    and graphology   150
    and human resource information systems   170

privacy (cont'd)
  in organizations 297
  surveillance 374–5
Privacy Act of 1974 296–7
Privacy Protection Study
  Commission 297
procedural justice 93, **298**
  China 51
  and drug testing 98
process control,
  statistical 352–4
process innovation *see* business
  process reengineering; business
  processes
production
  lean 222–3
  statistical process control
    (SPC) 352–4
production, burden of 33
production systems *see* just-in-time
  production systems
productivity 298–9
  and age 104
  and benchmarking 25
  and bullying 32
  and compensation 333
  and distributive justice 93
  and downsizing 96, 176
  and employability 106
  and flextime 135
  Germany 145
  and HRM practices 168
  improving 141
  and job rotation 210
  and management by
    objectives 234
  and merit pay 240
  and profitability 415
  sharing gains with
    employees 181
  and skills-based pay 271
  time and motion
    study 381–2
  union effect on 405–6
  and union–management
    cooperation 401–2
  work sampling 429
  see also quality
professional ethics 299
  assessing 126
  codes of conduct 108
profile-matching selection
    procedures 283, **299**
profit sharing 273, **300**
  variations 300
  see also gainsharing; incentive pay
profitability
  and pay 415
  and productivity 415
  union effect on 406
programmed instruction 300
progressive discipline 300–1

Projects with Industry (PWI) 160
promotion 301, 351–2
  assessing potential 10–12
  gender issues 147
  performance
    standards 281–2
  and women 424
  and workforce flexibility 435
  see also personnel selection and
    recruitment; tests
proof, burden of *see* burden of
    proof
Protestant work ethic 206
Pruitt, D. B. 366
psychological contracts 96, **301**
  employability 106
psychological tests 301–2
  see also intelligence tests;
    personality tests; situational
    tests; vocational interest
    inventories
psychology
  behavior 20–1
  psychomotor abilities 302–3
  Society for Industrial and
    Organizational
    Psychology 350
  Standards for Educational and
    Psychological
    Testing 69–70, 296, 302, **352**,
    413
  traits 394–5
  see also validity
public sector bargaining 303
Puffer, Sheila M. 325–7
Pulakos, Elaine D. 308–9
Puma 417
punitive damages 303
Purcell, E. D. 387
Pursell, E. D. 308, 344
PWI *see* Projects with Industry

quality
  continuous improvement 72
  and downsizing 96
  Malcolm Baldrige National
    Quality Award 196, **227**–8
  service quality 340–1
  standards 196
  statistical process
    control 352–4
  total quality
    management 363, **382–5**
  and union–management
    cooperation 401–2
  quality circles 304–5
  quality of work life (QWL) 305
  and flexible working hours 135
  and union–management
    cooperation 400–1
Quayle, Senator 431
questionnaires

job analysis 202
pay satisfaction 274
Position Analysis
  Questionnaires 291–2
Spence and Helmreich Personal
  Attributes Questionnaire 342
Quick, James Campbell 203–4,
  214–15, 371–2
Quick, Jonathan D. 371–2

race
  managing diversity 94–5
  minorities in UK workforce 411
  and occupational choice 260
  UK race relations 408
  and workforce
    demographics 433
  race discrimination 179–80,
    306
  and bona fide occupational
    qualification 30
  Civil Rights Act of 1866 53
  discrimination when working
    overseas 130
  executive orders about
    discrimination 123–4
  and federal contractors 123–4,
    172
  Fourteenth Constitutional
    Amendment 53, **138**, 296,
    343
  interviews 195
  Local 28 of the Sheet Metal
    Workers' International
    Association v. *EEOC* 4
  race norming 56
  and tests 84, 89, 187, 188–9,
    258, 379–81, 390–1
  UK regulation 410
  Wards Cove Packing Co. v.
    Antonio 422
  Watson v. *Fort Worth Bank and*
    Trust 422–3
  Wygant v. *Jackson Board of*
    Education 4, 322
  see also Civil Rights Act of 1964;
    color discrimination;
    discrimination; disparate
    impact; disparate treatment
Railway Labor Act of
  1926 306–7
Raju, Nambury S. 336–7, 414
Ralston, David A. 234–5
Ramos, R. A. 336
ranking job evaluation
  method 307
ranking method of performance
  evaluation 307
Rapoport, R. 99
rate ranges 307–8
rater training 308–9, 311–12
rating *see* scores

rating accuracy 309–10
 and halo effects 155
 and performance diaries 279
 rater accuracy training 308–9
 and work values assessment 430
rating bias 310–11
 see also leniency effects
rating errors 311–12
 and behavioral observation
  scales 22
 central tendency effects 46,
  138, 311, 312
 controlling 307
 criterion contamination 77
 distributional effects 91–2
 halo effects 60, 92, 155, 311,
  312
 leniency effects 138, 225, 245,
  311, 312
 rater error training 309
rating scales
 behavioral observation
  scales 21–2, 59, 149–50, 312
 behaviorally anchored rating
  schemes 22–3, 60, 149–50,
  312
 graphic rating scale
  method 149–50
 ipsative 430
 mixed-standard
  scales 244–5
 for task inventories 376
rationale scoring keys 28–9
Raynaud's phenomenon 319–20
REAct see Retirement Equity Act of
 1984
realistic job previews
 (RJPs) 212, 312–13, 368
reasonable accommodation model of
 discrimination 90
recognition strikes 372
recruiting 313–15
 sources 315
 strategic 368
 see also personnel selection and
  recruitment
red circle jobs 315
redeployment 315–16
redundancies see layoffs
Ree, M. J. 347
Rees, A. 406
reference checks 316
 defamation waivers 86–7
reference groups 258
regression model of test
 fairness 380
Rehabilitation Act of 1973 155,
 159, 316
Reilly, R. R. 423
reinforcement 316–17
relaxation training and
 techniques 371

relevant labor markets 317
reliability 318–19
religion discrimination 319
 discrimination when working
  overseas 130
 executive orders about
  discrimination 123–4
 and federal contractors 123–4,
  172
 Fourteenth Constitutional
  Amendment 53, 138, 296,
  343
 managing diversity 94–5
 and tests 84, 89, 187, 188–9,
  258, 378–81, 390–1
 see also Civil Rights Act of 1964;
  discrimination; disparate
  impact; disparate treatment
Repas, B. 153
repatriation 128, 129, 294, 319
repetitive motion strain
 injury 319–20
replacement charts 320
representation elections 249,
 256, 320–1
representation procedures 403
reproductive health
 hazards 321
retention, negligent 249–50
retirement
 early retirement in Japan 199
 early retirement
  policy 104–5, 175
 healthcare benefits 68, 132
 social security benefits 349
 see also pension plans
Retirement Equity Act of 1984
 (REAct) 112–13
retraining 321–2
 Worker Adjustment and
  Retraining Notification Act
  of 1988 176, 430–2
reverse discrimination 56, 322
 Steelworkers v. Weber 4, 322,
  354
reward systems 322–3
 WorldatWork 439
 see also benefits; compensation;
  pay
right-sizing 363
right to work 220, 323
rights arbitration 323–4
Robertson, I. T. 389
Robertson, L. 277, 308
Robinson, R. B., Jr. 364
Rodgers, R. 234
Roehling, M. V. 210
Rojot, Jacques R. 139
role playing 324
role theory of work–family
 conflict 426
Roman, P. M. 107

Ronen, S. 390
Rorschach Inkblot Technique 284
Rosenthal, D. E. 11
Rosse, Joseph G. 97–9
Rothstein, Hannah R. 150–1
Rouillier, J. Z. 386
Rousseau, Denise M. 301
Rowan, Richard L. 245–6
Rubery, Jill 269–70
Rucker plan 273, 325
rule of thumb 325
Russell, Craig J. 19, 28–30, 101,
 316, 423
Russell, J. S. 387
Russia 325–7
Rynes, S. L. 195, 315, 368

Saari, L. M. 21, 344, 388
Sackett, Paul R. 186–7, 289–90
safety and health
 blood-borne pathogens 328
 Environmental Protection
  Agency 247, 248
 hazardous materials in the
  workplace 156
 hazards in the
  workplace 156–7
 material safety data sheets 262
 Mexico 241
 National Institute for
  Occupational Safety and
  Health 247–8, 262, 263
 occupational injury/illness
  measurement 261
 Occupational Safety and
  Health Act of 1970 172,
  261–2, 328–31
 Occupational Safety and
  Health
  Administration 247, 262,
  263, 328
 repetitive motion strain
  injury 319–20
 rights and
  responsibilities 328–31
 standards 261, 262, 263
 UK legislation 410
 workers' compensation
  benefits 432
 workers' compensation
  law 432–3
 in the workplace 331
 see also health
safety ratios 261
Salas, E. 392
salesforce compensation 62–3,
 331–2
salting 332
Sandver, Marcus Hart 237–8
Sashkin, M. 383
satisfaction see job satisfaction; pay
 satisfaction

SATs 188
savings or thrift plans 332–3
SBP *see* skills-based pay
Scanlon plan 273, 333
  and grievances 151
scanning,
  environmental 119–20, 235
Scarpello, Vida 66, 111–12,
  179–80, 261–2, 296–7, 416–17,
  430–2
Schaffer, R. 384
Schaubroeck, J. 275, 340
Schein, Edgar H. 37–9, 43–4, 265
Schein Descriptive Index 342
Schelling, T. C. 366
Schmidt, Frank L. 65, 335, 344,
  414–15, 428
Schmidt, S. M. 347
Schmitt, Neal 129, 246, 299,
  334–5, 392–3
Schneider, Benjamin 13–14,
  265–6, 364, 425
Schnell, J. F. 362
Schoenfeldt, Lyle F. 103–4, 125–6
Schoorman, F. D. 426
Schriesheim, Chester A. 67, 80,
  292–3, 413–14
Schuler, Randall S. 119–20, 147,
  148, 177, 358–61
Schuster, J. R. 12
scientific management 333
scores
  cutoff 84–5
  multiple cutoff selection
    procedures 246
  norms 257–8
  reliability 318–19
scoring keys
  empirical 29
  rationale 28–9
Sd_y 333, 335–6
seasonal workers 179–80
secondary boycotts 221, 334,
  404
  injunctions 258–9
secrecy, pay 274–5
security, workplace 437–8
Seibert, S. E. 289
selection *see* personnel selection and
  recruitment
selection models 334–5
selection ratio 335
selection utility models 335–7
Sd_y 333, 335–6
self-awareness training
  337–8
Self-Directed Search 419
self-efficacy
  and occupational choice 260
  training 338
self-leadership 109
self-management 109

self-management training 338,
  387
  and absence 2
self-managing teams
  (SMTs) 109, 171, 338–40
self-ratings 275, 310–11, 340
self-regulation 108–9
Senge, P. M. 223
Serapio, Manuel G., Jr. 232–3
service quality 340–1
severance pay 269
sex 341
  sex-role stereotypes 142,
    341–2
  see also gender issues in HRM
sexual harassment 55, 342–3
  Barnes v. *Costle* 20, 342
  Meritor Savings Bank v.
    Vinson 240, 342
sexual orientation 55, 155, 172,
  343
  and sexual harassment 343
shares *see* employee stock ownership
  plans
Shaw, James B. 80–1, 291–2,
  381–2, 429
Shaw, K. 168
Shearer, John C. 233, 403–4, 424
Sherman, Mark R. 75, 292, 300–1
Shewart, W. 383
Shiba, S. 383
shift work *see* work schedules
Shingo, Shigeo 216, 222
shrinkage 82
SHRM *see* Society for Human
  Resource Management;
  strategic human resource
  management
sick pay 269
signal detection theory 310
Simon, Théophile 187–8
simulations 343, 386–7
  and behavior-modeling
    training 21
  management games 232
  role playing 324
single-group validity 69, 343–4
Sinicropi, Anthony V. 9–10
SIOP *see* Society for Industrial and
  Organizational Psychology
situational constraints *see* work
  constraints
situational interviews 117, 344
situational tests 344–5
  see also simulations
skills 345
  assessment skills training 308
  job-skills training 213
skills-based pay (SBP) 271–2,
  273
skills-based pay design 345
slavery, outlawing of 381

Civil Rights Act of 1866 53
Smith, C. S. 80
Smith, D. Brent 13–14, 265–6,
  364
Smith, Patricia Cain 78, 79
Smits, S. J. 107
smoking
  smoke-free work
    environment 345–6
  smoking cessation 158, 346
SMTs *see* self-managing teams
Sneiderman, Marilyn 5
Snell, Scott A. 165–6
Snow, C. C. 123, 370
Snow, R. E. 183
Snyder, David J. 56–7, 285, 287,
  301, 351–2
social contracts 366
social influence in the
  performance evaluation
  process 346–9
social relations, and stress 371
Social Security Act of 1935 349,
  397
social security benefits 349–50
Society for Human Resource
  Management (SHRM) 350
Society for Industrial and
  Organizational Psychology
  (SIOP) 295–6, 350
software, task inventory
  analysis 377
South Korea 351
Southwest Airlines 83
SPC *see* statistical process control
Spector, Paul E. 22, 218–19,
  238–9, 285, 302–3, 345
Spence and Helmreich Personal
  Attributes Questionnaire 342
spillover theory of work–family
  conflict 426, 428
staffing 351–2
  and benchmarking 25
  career pathing 40–1
  countercyclical hiring 76–7
  forecasting requirements 325,
    360, 395
  and job analysis 201
  strategic 369–70
  see also personnel selection and
    recruitment; promotion
staffing tables 325
Stalick, S. K. 34–5
standard hour plan 352
standardization samples 258
standards
  management practices 196
  performance 281–2
  safety and health 261, 262,
    263
*Standards for Educational and
  Psychological*

Index

Testing 69–70, 296, 302, **352**, 413
Stanton, S. A. 33
statistical packages, task inventory analysis 377
statistical process control (SPC) 352–4
Stedham, Yvonne 77, 191–2
Steele-Johnson, D. 101
Steers, Richard M. 351
stereotype accuracy 310
stocks *see* inventories
Stokes, G. S. 28
Stone, Dianna L. 110–11, 297
Stone, Thomas H. 63, 87, 203, 307–8, 315
Stone-Romero, Eugene F. 206–7, 211–12, 297
Storey, John 367–8
Strack, F. 60
strategic alliances 354–6
strategic development 356
strategic human resource management (SHRM) 356–7
  and competency identification 171
  and executive compensation 123
  see also human resource management
strategic human resource planning 174, 357–8
  processes 358–61
  see also human resource planning
strategic industrial relations 361–2
  see also industrial relations
strategic issues in diversity 362–4
  see also diversity
strategic job analysis 364
  see also job analysis
strategic leadership 230–1
strategic management 364–5
  and downsizing 96
  see also management
strategic negotiations 366
  see also bargaining; negotiation
strategic outsourcing 367–8
  see also outsourcing
strategic recruiting 368
  see also personnel selection and recruitment; recruiting
strategic role of human resources 368–9
strategic staffing 369–70
  see also staffing
strategy 370–1
  compensation strategy 64
  and executive selection 125

human resource strategy 70, 176–8
stress 214–15
  and bullying 32
  and downsizing 97
  and emotional intelligence 105, 215
  gender differences 100
  job burnout 203–4
  and organizational socialization 266
  post-traumatic stress disorder 316
  UK 410, 411
  see also work–family conflict
stress management programs 215, 371–2
  job burnout 203–4
strikes 372
  Australia 15, 16
  Canada 37
  France 139
  injunctions 258–9
  jurisdictional strikes 372
  Mexico 241
  National Emergency Strike 372
  picketing 221, 286–7, 404
  recognition strikes 372
  right to 9–10, 61–2, 189, 221, 306–7
  Russia 326
  secondary boycotts 221, 334, 404
  UK 410
  wildcat strikes 372, 424
  workdays lost statistics 220
  see also disputes
Strong Interest Inventory 419
Stumpf, Stephen A. 39
Stybel, L. J. 268
subsamples
  derivation 82
  holdout 82
success
  career success 40, 43, 45–6
  criteria 78
succession planning 239, 372–4
Sulsky, Lorne 77–8, 80
Sumitomo Shoji America v. Avigliano 130
Summer, C. E. 364
Super, D. E. 260
supervision, negligent 250
supervisory ratings 275, 340, 374, 435
Supplemental Security Income 349
surveillance 374–5
  see also privacy
survivor benefits 154, 349
Sweden, employment 390
Sweeney, John J. 5

SWOT analysis 357
synthetic validity 375

Taft-Hartley Act *see* Labor Management Relations Act of 1947
Taira, Koji 198–200
takeovers, and golden parachutes 148
Tannenbaum, Scott I. 7, 387
task inventory approach to job analysis 376–7
task statements 140, 376
tasks 376
  and functional job analysis 139–40
TAT *see* Thematic Apperception Test
Tata, J. 50
tax-deferred annuities 377
Tax Reform Act of 1986 (TRAC) 377–8
taxation
  FICA taxes 349
  and international compensation 192
  and pension plans 332
  and profit sharing 300
Taylor, Frederick Winslow 333
Taylor, M. Susan 8–9, 168–9
Taylorism 333
Taynor, J. 342
Teagarden, Mary B. 240–4
teams
  Belbin teams 23–4
  knowledge teams 217–18
  and lean production 223
  self-managing 109, 171, 338–40
  team-based incentives 378, 436
  team-building training 378
  US use 173
  virtual teamworking 418
Teamsters v. United States 378
technology
  effects on producers 389
  information technology enablers 185–6
telecommuting 136–7
teleconferencing method 379
temporary workers 379
  UK 411
Terborg, James R. 157–9, 342, 346, 423
test–retest reliability 318
tests and testing
  achievement tests 187
  aptitude tests 187
  Big Five personality tests 27–8
  Cattell's 16PF test 23

tests and testing (*cont'd*)
  cutoff scores 84–5
  and disabled candidates 159
  drug testing 95–7
  for emotional intelligence 105
  group tests 302
  integrity testing 172, **186–7**
  intelligence tests **187–9**, 257–8
  job sample tests 428–9
  personality tests 185, 302, **283–5**
  physical ability testing 285–6
  police officers 422
  polygraph testing 111–12, **289–90**
  psychological tests 301–2
  race norming 56
  retraining 430–2
  reviews and guides 302
  situational tests 344–5
  Standards for Educational and Psychological Testing 69–70, 296, 302, **352**, 413
  test fairness 379–81
  trainability testing 389
  work samples 428–9
  see also rate ranges; rating accuracy; rating bias; rating errors; rating scales; scores; validity
Thacker, Rebecca A. 166–7, 350
Tharenou, P. 289
Thatcher, Margaret 409
Thematic Apperception Test (TAT) 284
Thibaut, J. 298
Thirteenth Constitutional Amendment 53, **381**
Thomas, R. Roosevelt, Jr. 245, 362–4, 433
Thomas, Stephen L. 26, 63–4
Thompson, H. 384
Thorndike, R. L. 380
Thorndike method of predictive yield 85
Thornhill v. *Alabama* 287
Thornton, G. C. 11
Three Mile Island accident 392
360-degree appraisals 95, 231, 337, 381
thrift plans 332–3
time and motion study 381–2
  work sampling 429
time-based pay 273, **382**
time span of discretion 382
total quality management (TQM) 363, 382–5
total time off (TTO) 269

Toussaint v. *Blue Cross and Blue Shield of Michigan* 116
Toyota Motor Company 216, 222–3
TQM *see* total quality management
TRAC *see* Tax Reform Act of 1986
Trade Union Congress (TUC; UK) 410–11
trainability testing 389
training 385–92
  action learning 3
  AIDS awareness training 6
  American Society for Training and Development (ASTD) 7
  assessment centers 10–12, 103, 389
  assessment skills training 308
  audiovisual training techniques 14
  behavior-modeling training 21, 387
  and benchmarking 25
  capabilities 395
  case study/discussion method 46
  coaching 57–8, 277–9
  computer-assisted instruction 66, 385
  conference method 67
  correspondence method 76
  cross-training 81
  customer involvement and orientation 83
  customer service training 84
  determining employee needs 81
  developing globally competent executives/managers 87–8
  distance learning 91
  for emotional intelligence 105
  in employee benefits 193
  environment 386–7
  evaluation 387–8, **392–3**
  for expatriate assignment 127, 128, 160–1, 293–4
  frame-of-reference training 309
  individual differences 183
  Japan 200
  job rotation training 210–11
  job-skills training 213
  lecture method 225
  management games 232
  for managers 436
  and managing diversity 94–5, 363
  mentoring programs 239
  Mexico 242, 243–4
  needs assessment 386, 428
  new employee orientation 253
  observational training 308

on-the-job training 84, 253, 263
performance coaching 277–9
performance standards 281–2
  and person–job fit 282
programmed instruction 300
rater training 308–9, 311–12
relaxation training 371
retraining 176, 321–2, 430–2
role playing 324
self-awareness training 337–8
self-efficacy training 338
self-management training 338, 387
simulations 343, 386–7
team-building training 378
teleconferencing method 379
transfer of 395
  US 173
vestibule method 416
and veterans 417
for virtual teamworking 418
for workforce flexibility 436
training utility 393–4
  Sd_y 333
traits 394–5
  and advancement 289
  and construct validity 68–9
  personality tests 283–5
  see also behavior
transfer of learning 395
Treadway, Darren C. 346–9
trend extrapolation 395
trends in unionism 395–6
Treviño, Linda Klebe 108, 299
Trompenaars, F. 47, 272
Troy, Leo 395–6
Trumpka, Richard L. 5
TTO *see* total time off
tuberculosis 328
TUC *see* Trade Union Congress
Tudor, W. 115
turnover, employee *see* employee turnover
Tushman, M. L. 125
Twomey, David P. 54–6
two-tiered pay structures 396

UGESP *see* Uniform Guidelines on Employee Selection Procedures
Ulrich, Dave 24–5, 83–4
unemployment compensation 133, 349, 397
unfair labor practices, union 404

Index   465

Uniform Guidelines on Employee Selection Procedures (UGESP)   380, 397
union shops   403–4
union voice   404–5
unionization
  determinants   406–8
unions
  AFL-CIO   4
  agency shop   6
  Australia   14–16
  avoidance   397–9
  Canada   36, 37, 256, 398
  China   50–1
  commitment to   399–400
  craft   77, 185
  decertification elections   86
  density   62, 396, 398, 407–8
  and discrimination   4
  effects   405–6
  effects on pay   62, **400**, 405
  effects on safety and health   328
  Europe   245, 255–6
  European Trade Union Confederation   245
  France   139
  Germany   145
  and grievance procedures   152
  industrial   185
  international trade secretariats   245
  Italy   197
  Japan   256
  and labor contracts   220
  Labor Management Relations Act of 1947   133, 149, 220–1, 372
  Labor Management Reporting and Disclosures Act of 1959   221–2
  legislative control   221–2, 248–9, 258–9
  Mexico   240, 241, 242
  and multinational bargaining   245, 246
  organizational structure   362
  organizing   402–3
  and political action committees   288
  public sector   303
  Railway Labor Act of 1926   306–7
  recognition strikes   372
  representation elections   249, 256, 320–1
  representation procedures   403
  right to work   323
  Russia   326
  salting   332
  South Korea   351
  trends in unionism   395–6
  UK   256, 257, 410–11
  unfair labor practices   404
  union–management cooperation   400–2
  US   62, 255–7, 303, 398, 407–8
  see also bargaining; collective bargaining; disputes; grievances; industrial relations; labor relations; negotiations
United Kingdom   408–11
  Chartered Institute of Personnel and Development   47–8
  labor relations   255
  performance-based pay   272
  unions   256, 257, 410–11
  workers' compensation   432
United States
  declining workforce   390
  health promotion programs   158
  human resource management   171–4
  illness and injury statistics   329
  performance-based pay   272, 273
  quality circles   304
  strikes   372
  trade with Germany   144
  unions   62, 255–7, 303, 398, 407–8
  use of self-managing teams   339
  workers' compensation   432
United Steelworkers v. Weber   4, 322, 354
United Steelworkers of America v. American Manufacturing Company   10
United Steelworkers of America v. Enterprise Wheel and Car Company   10
United Steelworkers of America v. Warrior and Gulf Navigation Company   10
urinalysis testing   98
Ury, William   366
US General Services Administration   136
utility
  selection   335–7
  training   393–4
utilization analysis   317, 411–12
  relevant labor markets   317

vacations see paid time off
validity   79, 413–14
  and assessment centers   11
  and background checking   19
  and biographical history inventories   29
  booklets about   296
  concurrent   67, 69
  construct   68–9, 286
  content   68, 69, 286
  criterion-related   69, 80, 286
  cross-validation   81–2
  differential   69, 89
  drug testing   98
  face   131
  generalization   101, 296, 414–15
  and genetic screening   143
  and graphic rating scales   149
  and intelligence tests   188
  and interviews   117
  and multiple-hurdle selection procedures   246
  predictive   67, 69, 292–3
  personality tests   284
  and reference checks   316
  single-group   69, 343–4
  synthetic   375
  test fairness   379–81
  and training   392–3
  and work samples   428
value chains   83
values, work see work values
Van Buren, M. E.   385
Van Scotter, J. R.   265
Van Velsor, E.   337
variable compensation   415–16
  bonuses   30, 182, 273
  see also commission-based pay; employee stock ownership plans; gainsharing; incentive pay; profit sharing
variance
  random error   318
  true score   318
Vaverek, Kelly A.   20, 86–7, 89–90, 240, 295, 422
Verma, Anil   397–9
vestibule training method   416
veteran status   416
videodiscs, interactive   387
Vietnam-Era Veterans' Readjustment Assistance Act of 1972   416–17
Villanova, Peter   78–9, 208–9, 282–3, 426
Vincennes incident   163
violence, workplace   438–9
  see also sexual harassment
virtual organizations   417–18
Vobejda, B.   389
vocational interest inventories   302, 418–20
voice stress analyzers   290
Von Glinow, Mary Ann   147–8
Vroom, V. H.   237

WABs see weighted application blanks
Waclawski, J.   264

wages
   wage/pay policy line 421
   wage/pay/salary
      structure 421
   wage and salary surveys 421
   see also pay
Wagner Act *see* National Labor
   Relations Act of 1935
WAIS-III *see* Wechsler Adult
   Intelligence Scale-III
waivers 422
   defamation 86–7
Walden, D. 383
Walker, G. 165
Walker, James W. 174–5, 177,
   357–8
Walker, L. 298
Walsh-Healy Act of 1936 422
Walters, D. 418
Walton, R. E. 305, 362, 366
Wanous, John P. 312–13
Wards Cove Packing Co. v.
   Antonio 422
WARN *see* Worker Adjustment and
   Retraining Notification Act of
   1988
Warner, M. 50, 51
Washington v. *Davis* 422
Wasson, Deidre 46, 67, 76, 91,
   183, 224–5, 379, 395, 416
Watson v. *Fort Worth Bank and
   Trust* 422–3
Wayne, S. J. 347
Webb, B. 410
Webb, S. 410
Wechsler Adult Intelligence Scale-
   III (WAIS-III) 188, 302
Wechsler Intelligence Scale for
   Children (WISC-IV) 188
Wegman, R. 268
Wei, Liqun 49–53
Weick, K. 344
weighted application blanks
   (WABs) 423
Weissmuller, J. J. 202
Welbourne, Theresa M. 141, 181,
   325, 333
Welfare Workers Association
   (WWA; UK) 48
wellness 423
   programs 114, 157–9, 215, 346,
      371, 423
   see also health
West, S. J. 340
Western Airlines v. *Criswell* 30
Western Electric 383
Wexley, K. N. 57, 308
WFPMA *see* World Federation of
   Personnel Management
   Associations
Wheeler, Hoyt N. 286–7, 334, 372
whistle-blowing 423–4

White, L. A. 209
wildcat strikes 372, **424**
   injunctions 258–9
   see also strikes
Wilkinson, I. 347
Williams, Charles R. 315, 395
Williams, Kevin J. 60, 279–80
Williams, Larry J. 318–19
WISC-IV *see* Wechsler Intelligence
   Scale for Children
Womack, James P. 216, 222–3
women
   and absence 1
   career issues **424–5**
   comparable worth 63
   discrimination when working
      overseas 130
   dual-earner and dual-career
      couples **99–101**
   EEOC v. *AT&T* 4
   Equal Pay Act of 1963 63, 121
   executive orders about
      discrimination 123–4
   and expatriate assignments 127
   Fair Labor Standards Act of
      1938 131–2, 227
   and federal contractors 123–4,
      172
   Fourteenth Constitutional
      Amendment 53, 138, 296,
      343
   gender effects in
      recruiting 141–2
   gender issues in international
      assignments 142–3
   glass ceiling 146–7
   Johnson v. *Transportation
      Agency, Santa Clara
      County* 215, 322
   Lorance v. *AT&T* 226
   interview discrimination 195
   managing diversity 94–5
   occupational choice 260
   and outplacement 267
   and part-time
      employment 269–70
   and pay 173
   and pensions 112–13
   and physical ability testing 286
   Pregnancy Discrimination
      Act of 1978 55, **293**
   Price Waterhouse v.
      Hopkins 295
   and reverse discrimination 322
   sex discrimination 341
   sex-role stereotypes 142,
      341–2
   in South Korean workforce 351
   and tests 84, 89, 187, 188–9,
      258, 379–81, 390–1
   UK discrimination
      regulation 410

   in UK workforce 409, 411
   and unions 5
   workforce demographics 433
   see also Civil Rights Act of 1964;
      discrimination; disparate
      impact; disparate treatment;
      sexual harassment;
      work–family conflict;
      work–nonwork role issues
Women as Managers Scale 342
Wonderlic Personnel Test 188,
   302
Wong, C. S. 50, 51
Wong, Y. T. 50, 51
Woodman, Richard W. 264–5,
   378
Wooliams, P. 47
work constraints **425–6**
work–family conflict 49, **426–7**
   and dual-earner and dual-career
      couples 99–101, 252
work hours *see* work schedules
work–nonwork role
   issues **427–8**
work planning and review
   (WP&R) 234
work samples **428–9**
work sampling 429
work schedules
   annual hours 8
   compressed 65–6
   flexible working hours 8,
      135–6, 371
   Mexico 242
   part-time 269–70, **270**
   record keeping 132
   Russia 326
   UK 410, 411
work values **429–30**
   assessment 430
   managerial 234–5
Worker Adjustment and
   Retraining Notification Act
   of 1988 (WARN) 176, **430–2**
workers' compensation
   benefits 432
workers' compensation
   law 432–3
workforce
   demographics 390–1, 433
   UK 409
workforce flexibility 71, **433–7**
   and cross-training 81
   and deskilling 87
   Japan 199
   and organizational
      structures 171
   UK 411
   see also business process
      reengineering; contingent
      employment; employees,
      leasing; employees,

subcontracting; independent contractors; interim management; part-time employment; part-time work schedules; temporary workers
workplace
   flexible 136–7, 171
   greenfield sites 151
   hazardous materials 156, 262
   hazards 156–7, 262
   health 157
   security 437–8
   violence 438–9
   see also health; safety and health
works councils
   France 139
   Germany 145
   UK 410
World Federation of Personnel Management Associations (WFPMA) 350
WorldatWork 439
worldwide web 194
Worley, C. G. 264
WP&R *see* work planning and review
Wright, Patrick W. 356–7, 368–9
Wright, Thomas A. 203–4
Wu, R. 50
WWA *see* Welfare Workers Association
Wygant v. *Jackson Board of Education* 4, 322

Yang, Jixia 289
Yardley, J. 425
yellow dog contracts 259
Yeung, Arthur K. 106, 372–4
yield ratio 440
Youngblood, Stuart A. 4–5, 7–8, 106–7, 110, 316, 317, 332, 350, 374–5, 397, 411–12
Youngdahl, William E. 196
Yukl, G. 387

Zeithaml, V. A. 341
Zhu, C. J. 51
Zielinski, C. 321
Zingheim, P. K. 12